Workbook and Study Guide

Economics

N. Gregory Mankiw and Mark P. Taylor

Prepared by

David Hakes, Barry Harrison and Yulia Vymyatnina

THOMSON

Australia • Canada • Mexico • Singapore • Spain • United Kingdom • United States

Workbook and Study Guide to Economics

N. Gregory Mankiw and Mark P. Taylor

Prepared by

David R. Hakes, Barry Harrison and Yulia Vymyatnina

Publishing Director
John Yates

Production Editor
Sonia Pati

Typesetter
Newgen

Cover Design
Adam Renvoize

Publisher
Patrick Bond

Manufacturing Manager
Helen Mason

Production Controller
Maeve Healy

Development Editor
Anna Carter

Editorial Assistant
Thomas Rennie

Marketing Manager
Katie Thorn

Printer
Zrinski d. d., Croatia

British Library Cataloguing-in-Publication Data
A catalogue record for this book is available from the British Library

Contents

One must learn by doing the thing;
For though you think you know it
You have no certainty, until you try.

Sophocles, c. 496–406 B.C.
Greek playwright
Trachiniae

Preface

This *Workbook and Study Guide* accompanies N. Gregory Mankiw and Mark P. Taylor's *Economics*. It was written with only one audience in mind—you, the student.

Your time is scarce. To help you use it efficiently, this *Workbook and Study Guide* focuses strictly on the material presented in Mankiw and Taylor's *Economics*. It does not introduce extraneous material.

Objectives of the Workbook and Study Guide

There are three broad objectives to the *Workbook and Study Guide*. First, the *Workbook and Study Guide* reinforces the text and improves your understanding of the material presented in the text. Second, it provides you with experience in using economic theories and tools to solve actual economic problems. That is, this *Workbook and Study Guide* bridges the gap between economic concepts and economic problem solving. This may be the most important objective of the *Workbook and Study Guide* because those students who find economics inherently logical often think that they are prepared for exams just by reading the text or attending lectures. However, it is one thing to watch an economist solve a problem in class and another thing altogether to solve a problem alone. There is simply no substitute for hands-on experience. Third, the *Workbook and Study Guide* includes a self-test to validate areas of successful learning and to highlight areas needing improvement.

It is unlikely that you will truly enjoy any area of study if you fail to understand the material or if you lack confidence when taking tests over the material. It is our hope that this *Workbook and Study Guide* improves your understanding of economics and improves your test performance so that you are able to enjoy economics as much as we do.

Organization of the Workbook Study Guide

Each chapter in the *Workbook and Study Guide* corresponds to a chapter in Mankiw and Taylor's *Economics*. Each chapter is divided into the following sections:

- The Chapter Overview begins with a description of the purpose of the chapter and how it fits into the larger framework of the text. Following this context and purpose section are learning objectives, a section-by-section Chapter Review, and some helpful hints for understanding the material. The Chapter Overview ends with terms and definitions. This part is particularly important because it is impossible for the text to communicate information to you or for you to communicate information to your instructor on your exams without the use of a common economic vocabulary.

- Problems and Short-Answer Questions provide hands-on experience with problems based on the material presented in the text. The practice problems are generally multiple-step problems while the short-answer questions are generally based on a single issue.

- The Self-Test is composed of True/False questions followed by Multiple-Choice questions.

- The Advanced Critical Thinking section is a real-world problem that employs the economic reasoning and tools developed in the chapter. It is an applied story problem.

- Solutions are provided for all questions in the *Workbook and Study Guide*. Explanations are also provided for false responses to True/False questions in the Self-Test.

Use of the Workbook and Study Guide

We hesitate to suggest a method for using this *Workbook and Study Guide* because how one best uses a study guide is largely a personal matter. It depends on your preferences and talents and on your instructor's approach to the material. We will, however, discuss a few possible approaches, and trial and error may help you sort out an approach that best suits you.

Some students prefer to read an entire chapter in the text prior to reading the *Workbook and Study Guide*. Others prefer to read a section in the text and then read the corresponding section in the Chapter Overview portion of the *Workbook and Study Guide*. This second method may help you focus your attention on the most important aspects of each section in the text. Some students who feel particularly confident after reading the text may choose to take the Self-Test immediately. We do not generally support this approach. We suggest that you complete all of the Practice Problems and Short-Answer Questions before you attempt the Self-Test. You will receive more accurate feedback from the Self-Test if you are well prepared prior to taking it.

A study guide is not a substitute for a text, and it is always a mistake to think there is a short cut to learning! We therefore strongly recommend that you use this *Workbook and Study Guide* in conjunction with Mankiw and Taylor's *Economics*, not in place of it.

Final Thoughts

All of the problems and questions in this *Workbook and Study Guide* have been checked by a number of accuracy reviewers. However, if you find a mistake, or if you have comments or suggestions for future editions, please feel free to contact us via e-mail at barry.harrison@ntu.ac.uk or yv@eu.spb.ru

Acknowledgements

We would like to thank Greg Mankiw and Mark Taylor for having written such a well thought-out text that it made writing the *Workbook and Study Guide* a truly enjoyable task. We thank Pat Bond, Publisher at Thomson Learning, for keeping in close contact with us throughout the project and for his patience when we strained to meet deadlines. Tom Rennie, Editorial Assistant at Thomson Learning, quickly dealt with our requests for assistance and helped ensure that the whole task ran smoothly. We also thank our colleagues at Nottingham Trent University, the European University at St Petersburg and the University of Northern Iowa for helpful comments on various parts of our work as it took shape. The usual disclaimer applies and we take full responsibility for any errors that remain.

Finally, we thank our families for their support during the time we spent working on this *Workbook and Study Guide*.

David R. Hakes
Northern Iowa

Barry Harrison
Nottingham, England

Yulia Vymyatnina
St Petersburg, Russia

January 2006

TEN PRINCIPLES OF ECONOMICS

CHAPTER OVERVIEW

Context and Purpose

Chapter 1 is the first chapter in a three-chapter section that serves as the introduction to the text. Chapter 1 introduces ten fundamental principles on which the study of economics is based. In a broad sense, the rest of the text is an elaboration on these ten principles. Chapter 2 will develop ideas about how economists approach problems while Chapter 3 will explain how individuals and countries gain from trade.

The purpose of Chapter 1 is to lay out ten economic principles that will serve as building blocks for the rest of the text. The ten principles can be grouped into three categories: how people make decisions, how people interact, and how the economy works as a whole. Throughout the text, reference will be made repeatedly to these ten principles.

CHAPTER REVIEW

Introduction

Households and society face decisions about how to allocate **scarce** resources to the production of the goods and services we consume. Resources are **scarce** in that we have fewer resources than we wish. This is the heart of economics! We have fewer resources than we wish because our desire to consume goods and services outstrips our ability to produce them. It doesn't seem to matter how much output increases, we always seem to want more. As long as this continues, resources will always be scarce.

Economics is the study of how society manages its scarce resources. Economists study how people make decisions about buying and selling, and saving and investing. We study how people interact with one another in markets where prices are determined and quantities are exchanged. We also study the economy as a whole when we concern ourselves with total income, unemployment, and inflation.

This chapter addresses ten principles of economics. The text will refer to these principles throughout. The ten principles are grouped into three categories: how people make decisions, how people interact, and how the economy works as a whole.

How People Make Decisions

People face tradeoffs. Economists often say, 'There is no such thing as a free lunch'. This means that there are always tradeoffs—to get more of something we like, we have to give up something else that we like. For example, if you spend money on dinner and a movie, you won't be able to spend it on new clothes. Socially, we face tradeoffs as a group. For example, there is the classic tradeoff between 'guns and butter'. That is, if we decide to spend more on national defence (guns), then we will have less to spend on social programmes (butter). There is also a social tradeoff between efficiency (getting the most from our scarce resources) and equity (benefits being distributed fairly across society). Policies such as taxes and welfare make incomes more equal, but these policies reduce returns to hard work and thus the economy doesn't produce as much as it otherwise might. As a result, when the government tries to cut the pie into more equal pieces, the pie gets smaller.

The cost of something is what you give up to get it. The opportunity cost of an item is what you give up to get that item. It is the true cost of the item. The opportunity cost of going to college obviously includes your tuition payment. It also includes the value of the time that you could have spent working, valued at your potential wage. It would exclude your room and board payment because you have to eat and sleep whether you are in school or not.

Rational people think at the margin. Marginal changes are incremental changes to an existing plan. Rational decision-makers only proceed with an action if the *marginal benefit* exceeds the *marginal cost*. For example, you should only go to another year of school if the benefits from that year of schooling exceed the cost of attending that year. A farmer should produce another bushel of corn only if the benefit (price received) exceeds the cost of producing it.

People respond to incentives. Since rational people weigh marginal costs and marginal benefits of activities, they will respond when these costs or benefits change. For example, when the price of cars rises, buyers have an incentive to buy fewer cars while car producers have an incentive to hire more workers and produce more cars. Public policy can alter the costs or benefits of activities. For example, a luxury tax on expensive boats raises the price and discourages purchases.

How People Interact

Trade can make everyone better off. Trade is not a contest where one wins and one loses. Trade can make each trader better off. Trade allows each trader to specialize in what they do best, whether it be farming, building, or manufacturing, and trade their output for the output of other producers. This is as true for countries as it is for individuals.

Markets are usually a good way to organize economic activity. In a market economy, the decisions about what goods and services to produce, how much to produce, and who gets to consume them, are made by millions of firms and households. Firms and households, guided by self-interest, interact in the marketplace where prices and quantities are determined. While this may appear like chaos, Adam Smith made the famous observation in the Wealth of Nations in 1776 that self-interested households and firms interact in markets and generate desirable social outcomes as if guided by an 'invisible hand'. These optimal social outcomes were not their original intent. The prices generated by their competitive activity signal the value of costs and benefits to producers and consumers, whose activities unknowingly maximize the welfare of society. Alternatively, the prices dictated by central planners contain no information on costs and benefits and therefore, these prices fail to efficiently guide economic activity. Prices also fail to efficiently guide economic activity when governments distort prices with taxes or restrict price movements with price controls.

Governments can sometimes improve market outcomes. Government must first protect property rights in order for markets to work. In addition, government can sometimes intervene in the market to improve efficiency or equity. When markets fail to allocate resources efficiently there has been *market failure*. There are many different sources of market failure. *An externality* is when the actions of one person or organization affect the well-being of at least one other person. Pollution is a standard example. *Market power* is when a single person or group can influence market price. On the supply side, greatest market power exists when supply is controlled by a single supplier, that is, a monopolist. In these cases, the government may be able to intervene and improve economic efficiency. The government may also intervene to improve equity with income taxes and social security payments. Sometimes, well-intentioned policy intervention has unintended consequences.

How the Economy as a Whole Works

A country's standard of living depends on its ability to produce goods and services. There is great variation in average incomes across countries at a point in time and within the same country over time. These differences in incomes and standards of living are largely attributable to differences in productivity. **Productivity** is the amount of goods and services produced by each hour of a worker's time. As a result, public policy intended to improve standards of living should improve education, generate more and better tools, and improve access to current technology.

Prices rise when the government prints too much money. Inflation is an increase in the overall level of prices in the economy. High inflation is costly to the economy. Large and persistent inflation is caused by rapid growth in the quantity of money. Policy-makers wishing to keep inflation low should maintain slow growth in the quantity of money.

Society faces a short-run tradeoff between inflation and unemployment. An increase in inflation tends to reduce unemployment. The short-run tradeoff between inflation and unemployment is known as the Phillips curve. The tradeoff is temporary, but can last for several years. Understanding this tradeoff is important for understanding the fluctuations in economic activity known as the business cycle. In the short run, policy-makers may be able to affect the mix of inflation and unemployment by changing government spending, taxes, and the quantity of money.

HELPFUL HINTS

1. Place yourself in the story. Throughout the text, most economic situations will be composed of economic agents—buyers and sellers, borrowers and lenders, firms and workers, and so on. When you are asked to address how any economic agent would respond to economic incentives, place yourself in the story as the buyer or the seller, the borrower or the lender, the producer or the consumer. Don't think of yourself always as the buyer (a natural tendency) or

always as the seller. You will find that your role-playing will usually produce the right response once you learn to think like an economist—which is the topic of the next chapter.

2. Trade is not a zero-sum game. Some people see an exchange in terms of winners and losers. Their reaction to trade is that, after the sale, if the seller is happy the buyer must be unhappy because the seller must have taken something from the buyer. That is, they view trade as a **zero-sum game** where what one gains, the other must have lost. They fail to see that both parties to a voluntary transaction gain because each party is allowed to specialize in what it can produce most efficiently, and then trade for items that are produced more efficiently by others. Nobody loses, because trade is voluntary. Therefore, a government policy that limits trade reduces the potential gains from trade.

3. An externality can be positive. Because the classic example of an externality is pollution, it is easy to think of an externality as a cost that lands on a bystander. However, an externality can be positive in that it can be a benefit that lands on a bystander. For example, education is often cited as a product that emits a positive externality because when your neighbour educates herself, she is likely to be more reasonable, responsible, productive, and politically astute. In short, she is a better neighbour. Positive externalities, just as much as negative externalities, may be a reason for the government to intervene to promote efficiency.

TERMS AND DEFINITIONS

Choose a definition for each key term.

Key terms:

_____ Scarcity

_____ Economics

_____ Efficiency

_____ Opportunity cost

_____ Marginal changes

_____ Market economy

_____ Invisible hand

_____ Market failure

_____ Externality

_____ Market power

_____ Monopoly

_____ Productivity

_____ Inflation

_____ Phillips curve

_____ Business cycle

Definitions:

1. A situation in which the market fails to allocate resources efficiently

2. Limited resources and unlimited wants

3. The amount of goods and services produced per hour by a worker

4. The case in which there is only one seller in the market

5. The principle that self-interested market participants may unknowingly maximize the welfare of society as a whole

6. The property of society getting the most from its scarce resources

7. An economic system where interaction of households and firms in markets determine the allocation of resources

8. Fluctuations in economic activity

9. When the actions of one person or firm impacts on at least one other person

10. An increase in the overall level of prices

11. Incremental adjustments to an existing plan

12. Study of how society manages its scarce resources

13. Whatever is given up to get something else

14. The ability of an individual or group to substantially influence market prices

15. The short-run tradeoff between inflation and unemployment

PROBLEMS AND SHORT-ANSWER QUESTIONS

Practice Problems

1. People respond to incentives. Governments can alter incentives and hence behaviour with public policy. However, sometimes public policy generates unintended consequences by producing results that were not anticipated. Try to find an unintended consequence of each of the following public policies.
   a. To help the 'working poor', the government raises the minimum wage to €25 per hour.
   b. To help the homeless, the government places rent controls on apartments restricting rent to €30 per month.
   c. To reduce the central government budget deficit and limit consumption of petrol, the government raises the tax on petrol by €2.00 per gallon.
   d. To raise the population of wolves, the government prohibits the killing of wolves.

2. Opportunity cost is what you give up to get an item. Since there is no such thing as a free lunch, what would likely be given up to obtain each of the items listed below?
   a. Susan can work full time or go to college. She chooses college.
   b. Farmer Jones has 100 acres of land. He can plant corn, which yields 100 bushels per acre, or he can plant beans, which yield 40 bushels per acre. He chooses to plant corn.

Short-Answer Questions

1. Is air scarce? Is clean air scarce?

2. What is the opportunity cost of saving some of your salary?

3. Why is there a tradeoff between equity and efficiency?

4. Water is necessary for life. Diamonds are not. Is the marginal benefit of an additional glass of water greater or less than an additional one carat diamond? Why or why not?

5. Your car needs to be repaired. You have already paid €500 to have the transmission fixed, but it still doesn't work properly. You can sell your car 'as is' for €2,000. If your car were fixed, you could sell it for €2,500. Your car can be fixed with a guarantee for another €300. Should you repair your car? Why or why not?

6. In the *Wealth of Nations* Adam Smith said, 'It is not from the benevolence of the butcher, the brewer, or the baker that we expect our dinner, but from their regard to their own interest.' What do you think he meant?

7. If we save more and use it to build more physical capital, productivity will rise and we will have rising standards of living in the future. What is the opportunity cost of future growth?

8. If the government printed twice as much money, what do you think would happen to prices and output if the economy were already producing at maximum capacity?

SELF-TEST

True/False Questions

_____ 1. When the government redistributes income with taxes and welfare, the economy becomes more efficient.

_____ 2. Rational people act only when the marginal benefit of the action exceeds the marginal cost.

_____ 3. When a jet flies overhead, the noise it generates is an externality.

_____ 4. In the short run, a reduction in inflation tends to cause a reduction in unemployment.

_____ 5. An unintended consequence of public support for higher education is that low tuition provides an incentive for many people to attend state universities even if they have no desire to learn anything.

_____ 6. To a student, the opportunity cost of going to a basketball game is the price of the ticket.

_____ 7. Workers in Europe have a relatively high standard of living because Europe has a relatively high minimum wage.

_____ 8. Sue is better at cleaning and Bob is better at cooking. It will take fewer hours to eat and clean if Bob specializes in cooking and Sue specializes in cleaning than if they share the household duties evenly.

_____ 9. High and persistent inflation is caused by excessive growth in the quantity of money in the economy.

Multiple-Choice Questions

1. Which of the following involve a tradeoff?
    a. buying a new car.
    b. going to college.
    c. watching a football game on Saturday afternoon.
    d. taking a nap.
    e. all of the above involve tradeoffs.

2. Tradeoffs are required because wants are unlimited and resources are
    a. efficient.
    b. economical.
    c. limited.
    d. unlimited.
    e. marginal.

3. A rational person does not act unless
    a. the action makes money for the person.
    b. the action is ethical.
    c. the action produces marginal costs that exceed marginal benefits.
    d. the action produces marginal benefits that exceed marginal costs.

4. Suppose you find €20. If you choose to use the €20 to go to the football game, your opportunity cost of going to the game is

a. nothing, because you found the money.

b. €20 (because you could have used the €20 to buy other things).

c. €20 (because you could have used the €20 to buy other things) plus the value of your time spent at the game.

d. €20 (because you could have used the €20 to buy other things) plus the value of your time spent at the game, plus the cost of the dinner you purchased at the game.

5. Since people respond to incentives, we would expect that if the average salary of accountants increases by 50% while the average salary of teachers increases by 20%,

a. students will shift majors from education to accounting.

b. students will shift majors from accounting to education.

c. fewer students will attend college.

d. none of the above.

6. The problem of scarcity could be solved by

a. giving everyone more money.

b. a reduction in population.

c. increasing production.

d. economising on the use of resources.

e. none of the above.

7. The Phillips curve shows that

a. an increase in inflation temporarily increases unemployment.

b. a decrease in inflation temporarily increases unemployment.

c. inflation and unemployment are unrelated in the short run.

d. the business cycle has been eliminated.

8. An increase in the price of beef provides information which

a. tells consumers to buy more beef.

b. tells consumers to buy less pork.

c. tells producers to produce more beef.

d. provides no information because prices in a market system are managed by planning boards.

9. Which of the following is *not* part of the opportunity cost of going on vacation?

a. the money you could have made if you had stayed home and worked.

b. the money you spent on food.

c. the money you spent on aeroplane tickets.

d. the money you spent on presents for friends and relatives.

ADVANCED CRITICAL THINKING

Suppose your university decides to lower the cost of parking on campus by reducing the price of a parking permit from €200 per semester to €5 per semester.

1. What do you think would happen to the number of students desiring to park their cars on campus?

2. What do you think would happen to the amount of time it would take to find a parking place?

3. Thinking in terms of opportunity cost, would the lower price of a parking permit necessarily lower the true cost of parking?

4. Would the opportunity cost of parking be the same for students with no outside employment and students with jobs earning €15 per hour?

SOLUTIONS

Terms and Definitions

1	Market failure	9	Externality
2	Scarcity	10	Inflation
3	Productivity	11	Marginal changes
4	Monopoly	12	Economics
5	Invisible hand	13	Opportunity cost
6	Efficiency	14	Market power
7	Market economy	15	Phillips curve
8	Business cycle		

Practice Problems

1. a. Many would want to work at €25/hour, but few firms would want to hire low productivity workers at this wage; therefore it would simply create unemployment.
   b. Many tenants would want to rent an apartment at €30/month, but few landlords would be prepared to rent out an apartment at this price; therefore this rent control would create more homelessness.
   c. Higher petrol prices would reduce the miles driven. This would lower car accidents, put less wear and tear on roads and cars, and reduce the demand for cars and road repairs. The result might also be a fall in tax receipts and an increase in the budget deficit!
   d. Restrictions on killing wolves reduces the population of animals upon which wolves may feed (rabbits, deer, etc).

2. a. She gives up income from work (and must pay tuition).
   b. He gives up 4,000 bushels of beans.

Short-Answer Questions

1. No, you don't have to give up anything to get it. Yes, you can't have as much as you want without giving up something to get it (fitting pollution equipment on cars, etc.).

2. The items you could have enjoyed had you spent it (current consumption).

3. Taxes and welfare make us more equal, but reduce incentives for hard work thus lowering total output.

4. The marginal benefit of another glass of water is generally lower because we have so much water that one more glass is of little value. The opposite is true for diamonds.

5. Yes, because the marginal benefit of fixing the car is €2,500 − €2,000 = €500 and the marginal cost is €300. The original repair payment is not relevant.

6. The butcher, brewer, and baker produce the best food possible not out of kindness, but because it is in their best interest to do so. Self-interest can maximize social welfare.

7. We must give up consumption today.

8. Spending would double but since the quantity of output would remain the same, prices would double.

True/False Questions

1. F; the economy becomes less efficient because it decreases the incentive to work hard.

2. T

3. T

4. F; it increases unemployment because profits from production fall.

5. T

6. F; it is the price of the ticket plus the time that could have been spent doing something else. Studying for example!

7. F; workers in Europe have a relatively high standard of living because they are relatively productive.

8. T

9. T

Multiple-Choice Questions

1.	e	6.	e
2.	c	7.	b
3.	d	8.	c
4.	c	9.	b
5.	a		

Advanced Critical Thinking

1. More students would wish to park on campus.

2. It would take much longer to find a parking place.

3. No, because we would have to factor in the value of our time spent looking for a parking place.

4. No. Students that could be earning money working are giving up time that could be spent working while looking for a parking place. Therefore, their opportunity cost is higher.

THINKING LIKE AN ECONOMIST

CHAPTER OVERVIEW

Context and Purpose

Chapter 2 is the second chapter in a three-chapter section that serves as the introduction of the text. Chapter 1 introduced ten principles of economics that will be revisited throughout the text. Chapter 2 develops ideas about how economists approach problems, while Chapter 3 will explain how individuals and countries gain from trade.

The purpose of Chapter 2 is to familiarize you with the way in which economists approach economic problems. With practice, you will learn how to approach similar problems in this dispassionate systematic way. You will see how economists employ the scientific method, the role of assumptions in model building, and the application of two specific economic models. You will also learn the important distinction between two roles economists can play: as scientists when we try to explain the economic world and as policy-makers when we try to improve it.

CHAPTER REVIEW

Introduction

Like other fields of study, economics has its own jargon and way of thinking. It is necessary to learn the special language of economics because knowledge of the economist's vocabulary will help you communicate with precision to others about economic issues. This chapter will also provide an overview of how economists look at the world.

The Economist as Scientist

While economists don't use test tubes or telescopes, they are scientists because they employ the *scientific method*—the dispassionate and objective development and testing of theories.

The scientific method: observation, theory, and more observation. Just as in other sciences, an economist observes an event, develops a theory, and collects data to test the theory. An economist observes inflation, creates a theory that excessive growth in money causes inflation and then collects data on money growth and inflation to see if there is a relationship. However, collecting data to test economic theories is difficult because economists usually cannot create data from experiments. That is, economists cannot manipulate the economy just to test a theory. Therefore, economists often use data gathered from historical economic events.

The role of assumptions. Assumptions are made to make the world easier to understand. A physicist assumes an object is falling in a vacuum when measuring acceleration due to gravity. This assumption is reasonably accurate for a marble, but not for a beach ball. An economist may assume that prices are fixed (can't be changed) or may assume that prices are flexible (can move up or down in response to market pressures). Since prices often cannot be changed quickly (the menu in a restaurant is relatively expensive to change) but can be changed easily over time, it is reasonable for economists to assume that prices are fixed in the short run but flexible in the long run. The art of scientific thinking is deciding which assumptions to make.

Economic models. Biology teachers employ plastic models of the human body. They are simpler than the actual human body, but that is what makes them useful. Economists use economic models that are composed of diagrams and equations. Economic models are based on assumptions and are simplifications of economic reality.

Our first model: the circular-flow diagram. The circular-flow diagram shows the flow of goods and services, factors of production, and monetary payments between households and firms. Households sell the factors of production, such as land, labour, and capital to firms, in the market for factors of production. In exchange, the households receive wages, rent, and profit. Households use these earnings to buy goods and services from firms in the market for goods and services. The firms use this revenue to pay for the factors of production, and so on. This is a simplified model of the entire economy. This version of the circular flow diagram has been simplified because it excludes international trade and the government.

Our second model: the production possibilities frontier. A production possibilities frontier is a graph that shows the combinations of output the economy can possibly produce given the available factors of production and the available production technology. It is drawn assuming the economy produces only two goods. This model demonstrates the following economic principles:

- If the economy is operating on the production possibilities frontier, it is operating *efficiently* because it is producing a mix of output that is the maximum possible from the resources available.

- Points inside the curve are therefore *inefficient*. Points outside the curve are currently unattainable.

- If the economy is operating on the production possibilities frontier, we can see the *trade offs* society faces. To produce more of one good, it must produce less of another good. The amount of one good given up when producing more of another good is the *opportunity cost* of the additional production.

- The production possibilities frontier is bowed outward because the opportunity cost of producing more of a good increases as we near maximum production of that good. This is because we use resources better suited toward production of the other good in order to continue to expand production of the first good.

- A technological advance in production shifts the production possibilities frontier outward. This is a demonstration of *economic growth*.

Microeconomics and macroeconomics. Economics is studied on various levels. **Microeconomics** is the study of how individuals and firms make decisions and how they interact in specific markets. **Macroeconomics** is the study of economy-wide phenomena such as the central government budget deficit, the rate of unemployment, and policies to improve our standard of living. Microeconomics and macroeconomics are related because changes in the overall economy arise from decisions of millions of individuals. Although related, the methods employed in microeconomics and macroeconomics differ enough for them to be often taught in separate courses.

The Economist as Policy Advisor

When economists attempt to explain the world as it is, they act as scientists. When economists attempt to improve the world, they act as policy advisors. Correspondingly, **positive statements** can be checked by reference to the facts, while **normative statements** prescribe how the world *ought to be* according to a particular person's opinion. Positive statements can be confirmed or refuted with evidence. Normative statements involve values (ethics, religion, political philosophy) as well as facts.

For example, 'Money growth causes inflation' is a positive statement (of a scientist). 'The government ought to reduce inflation' is a normative statement (of a policy advisor). The two statements are related because evidence about whether money causes inflation might help us decide what tool the government should use if it chooses to reduce inflation.

Economists act as policy advisors to the government in many different areas including the Treasury and the Departments of Employment, Environment, Transport, and so on.

Why Economists Disagree

There are two reasons why economists have a reputation for giving conflicting advice to policy-makers.

- Economists may have different scientific judgments. That is, economists may disagree about the validity of alternative positive theories about how the world works. For example, economists differ in their views of the sensitivity of household saving to changes in the after-tax return to saving.

- Economists may have different values. That is, economists may have different normative views about what policy should try to accomplish. For example, economists differ in their views of whether taxes should be used to redistribute income.

In reality, although there are legitimate disagreements among economists on many issues, there is tremendous agreement on many basic principles of economics.

Let's Get Going

In the next chapter, we will begin to apply the ideas and methods of economics. As you begin to think like an economist, you will use a variety of skills—mathematics, history, politics, philosophy—with the objectivity of a scientist.

HELPFUL HINTS

1. Opportunity costs are usually not constant along a production possibilities frontier. Notice that the production possibilities frontier shown in Exhibit 1 is bowed outwards. It shows the production trade offs for an economy that produces only paper and pencils.

EXHIBIT 1

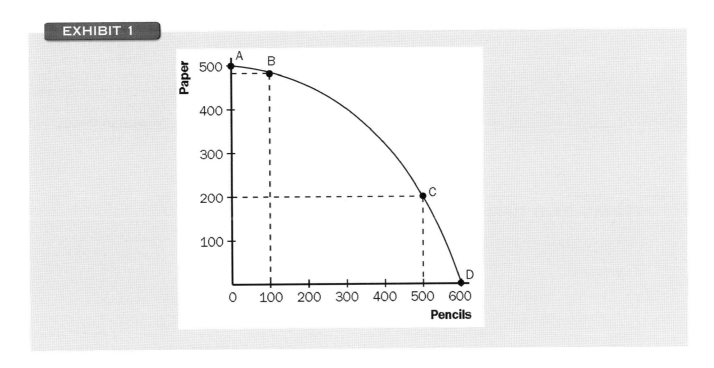

If we start at the point where the economy is using all of its resources to produce paper, producing 100 units of pencils only requires a trade off or an opportunity cost of 25 units of paper (point A to point B). This is because when we move resources from paper to pencil production, we first move those resources best suited for pencil production and poorly suited for paper production.

Therefore, pencil production increases with very little decrease in paper production. However, if the economy were operating at point C, the opportunity cost of an additional 100 pencils (point C to D) is 200 units of paper. This is because we now move resources towards pencil production that were extremely well suited for paper production and are poorly suited for pencil production. Therefore, as we produce more and more of any particular good, the opportunity cost per unit tends to rise because resources are specialized. That is, resources are not equally well suited for producing each output.

The argument above applies when moving either direction on the production possibilities frontier. For example, if we start at point D (maximum production of pencils) a small reduction in pencil production (100 units) releases enough resources to increase production of paper by a large amount (200 units). However, moving from point B to point A only increases paper production by 25 units.

2. A production possibilities frontier only shows the choices available—not which point of production is best. A common mistake made by students when using production possibilities frontiers is to look at a production possibilities frontier and suggest that a point somewhere near the middle 'looks best'. Students make this subjective judgement because the middle point appears to provide the biggest total number of units of production of the two goods. However, ask yourself the following question. Using the production possibilities frontier in Exhibit 1, what production point would be best if paper were worth €10 per sheet and pencils were worth 1 cent per dozen? We would move our resources toward paper production. What if paper was worth 1 cent per sheet and pencils were worth €50 each? We would move our resources towards pencil production. Clearly, what we actually choose to produce depends on the price of each good. Therefore, a production possibilities frontier only provides the choices available; it alone cannot determine which choice is best.

3. Economic disagreement is interesting, but economic consensus is more important. Economists have a reputation for disagreeing with one another because we tend to highlight our differences. While our disagreements are interesting to us, the matters on which we agree are more important to you. There are a great number of economic principles for which there is near unanimous support within the economics profession. The aim of this text is to concentrate on the areas of agreement within the profession as opposed to the areas of disagreement.

TERMS AND DEFINITIONS

Choose a definition for each key term.

Key terms:

_____ Scientific method

_____ Economic models

_____ Circular-flow diagram

_____ Factors of production

_____ Production possibilities frontier

_____ Opportunity cost

_____ Efficiency

_____ Microeconomics

_____ Macroeconomics

_____ Positive statements

_____ Normative statements

Definitions:

1. Inputs such as land, labour, and capital

2. The study of economy-wide phenomena

3. Objective development and testing of theories

4. Whatever is given up to get something else

5. Prescription for how the world ought to be

6. Getting maximum output from the resources available

7. Descriptions of the world that can be verified by factual evidence

8. Simplifications of economic reality based on assumptions

9. A graph that shows the combinations of output the economy can possibly produce given the available factors of production and the available production technology

10. The study of how individuals and firms make decisions and how they interact in markets

11. A diagram of the economy that shows the flow of goods and services, factors of production, and monetary payments between households and firms

PROBLEMS AND SHORT-ANSWER QUESTIONS

Practice Problems

1. Identify the parts of the circular-flow diagram immediately involved in the following transactions.
   a. Mary lives in Germany and buys a car from BMW for €30,000.
   b. BMW pays Karl €5,000/month for work on the assembly line.
   c. Karl gets a €15 hair cut.
   d. Mary receives €10,000 of dividends on her BMW stock.

2. The following table provides information about the production possibilities frontier of Athletic Country.

Bats	Rackets
0	420
100	400
200	360
300	300
400	200
500	0

a. In Exhibit 2, plot and connect these points to create Athletic Country's production possibilities frontier.

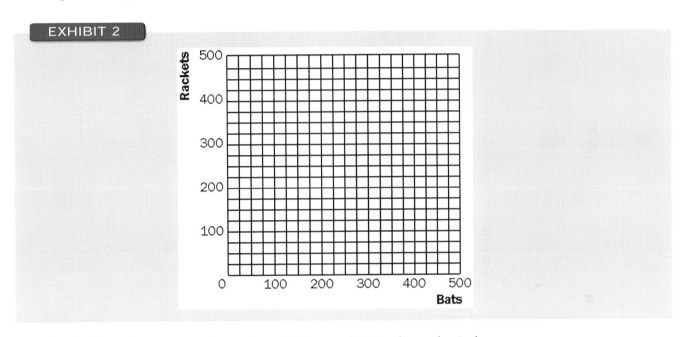

EXHIBIT 2

b. If Athletic Country currently produces 100 bats and 400 rackets, what is the opportunity cost of an additional 100 bats?

c. If Athletic Country currently produces 300 bats and 300 rackets, what is the opportunity cost of an additional 100 bats?

d. Why does the additional production of 100 bats in part (c) cause a greater trade off than the additional production of 100 bats in part (b)?

e. Suppose Athletic Country is currently producing 200 bats and 200 rackets. How many additional bats could they produce without giving up any rackets? How many additional rackets could they produce without giving up any bats?

f. Is the production of 200 bats and 200 rackets efficient? Explain.

3. The production possibilities frontier in Exhibit 3 shows the available trade offs between consumption goods and capital goods. Suppose two countries face this identical production possibilities frontier.

a. Suppose Party Country chooses to produce at point A while Parsimonious Country chooses to produce at point B. Which country will experience more growth in the future? Why?

b. In this model, what is the opportunity cost of future growth?

c. Demonstrate in Exhibit 4 the impact of growth on a production possibilities frontier such as the one shown above. Would the production possibilities frontier for Parsimonious Country shift more or less than that for Party Country? Why?

EXHIBIT 3

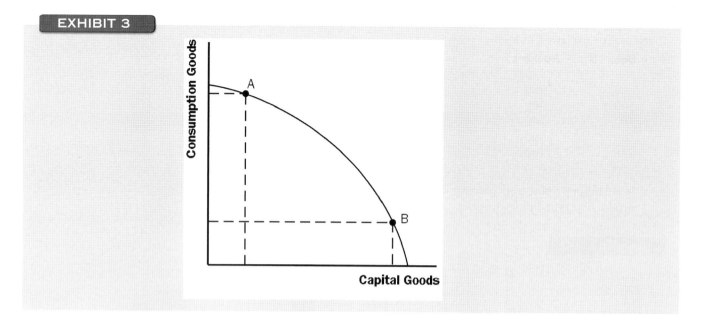

EXHIBIT 4

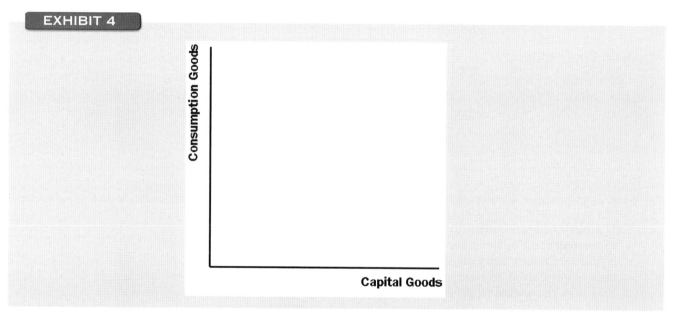

Short-Answer Questions

1. What is the role of assumptions in any science?

2. Is a more realistic model always better?

3. Why does a production possibilities frontier have a negative slope (slope down from left to right)?

4. Why is the production possibilities frontier bowed outward?

5. Which statements are testable: positive statements or normative statements? Why?

6. Name two reasons why economists disagree.

7. How does macroeconomics differ from microeconomics?

8. Which flows are included in the circular flow diagram?

SELF-TEST

True/False Questions

_____ 1. Economic models must mirror reality or they are of no value.

_____ 2. When people act as scientists, they must try to be objective.

_____ 3. If an economy is operating on its production possibilities frontier, it must produce less of one good if it produces more of another.

_____ 4. By importing more from abroad, countries can sometimes locate on a position outside of the production possibilities frontier.

_____ 5. If an economy were experiencing substantial unemployment, the economy is producing inside the production possibilities frontier.

_____ 6. An advance in production technology would cause the production possibilities curve to shift outward.

_____ 7. The statement, 'An increase in inflation tends to cause unemployment to fall in the short run', is normative.

_____ 8. The circular flow diagram shows how the economy operates when resources are fully employed.

Multiple-Choice Questions

1. Which of the following will not shift a country's production possibilities frontier outward?
   a. an increase in the capital stock.
   b. an advance in technology.
   c. a reduction in unemployment.
   d. an increase in the labour force.

Use Exhibit 5 to answer questions 2–5.

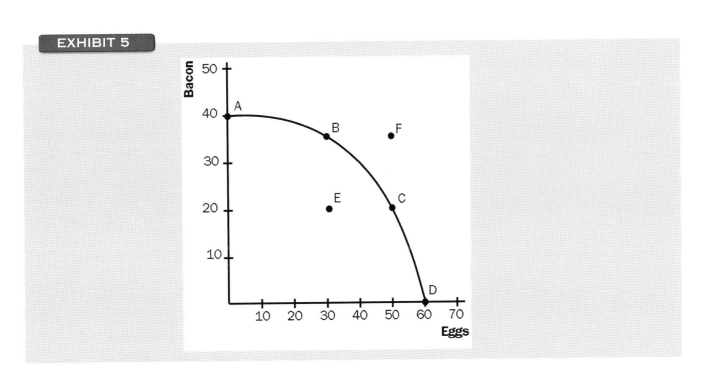

EXHIBIT 5

2. If the economy is operating at point C, the opportunity cost of producing an additional 15 units of bacon is
    a. 10 units of eggs.
    b. 20 units of eggs.
    c. 30 units of eggs.
    d. 40 units of eggs.
    e. 50 units of eggs.

3. If the economy were operating at point E,
    a. the opportunity cost of 20 additional units of eggs is 10 units of bacon.
    b. the opportunity cost of 20 additional units of eggs is 20 units of bacon.
    c. the opportunity cost of 20 additional units of eggs is 30 units of bacon.
    d. 20 additional units of eggs can be produced with no impact on bacon production.

4. Point F represents
    a. a combination of production that can be reached if we reduce the production of eggs by 20 units.
    b. a combination of production that is inefficient because there are unemployed resources.
    c. a combination of production that can be reached if there is a sufficient advance in technology.
    d. none of the above.

5. As we move from point A to point D,
    a. the opportunity cost of eggs in terms of bacon is constant.
    b. the opportunity cost of eggs in terms of bacon falls.
    c. the opportunity cost of eggs in terms of bacon rises.
    d. the economy becomes more efficient.
    e. the economy becomes less efficient.

6. Which of the following issues is related to microeconomics?
    a. the impact of money on inflation.
    b. the impact of technology on economic growth.
    c. the impact of the deficit on saving.
    d. the impact of oil prices on car production.

7. Which of the following statements is normative?
    a. Printing too much money causes inflation.
    b. The unemployment rate should be lower.
    c. People work harder if the wage is higher.
    d. Large government deficits cause an economy to grow more slowly.

8. Suppose two economists are arguing about policies that deal with unemployment. One economist says, 'The government could lower unemployment by one percentage point if it would just increase government spending by 50 billion euros.' The other economist responds, 'That's not true! If the government spent an additional 50 billion euros, it would reduce unemployment by only one-tenth of 1 per cent, and that effect would only be temporary!' These economists
    a. disagree because they have different scientific judgements.
    b. disagree because they have different values.
    c. really don't disagree at all. It just looks that way.
    d. none of the above.

ADVANCED CRITICAL THINKING

You are watching a documentary on public television. The first focus segment is a discussion of the pros and cons of free trade (lack of obstructions to international trade). For balance, there are two economists present—one in support of free trade and one opposed. Your roommate says, 'Those economists have no idea what's going on. They can't agree on anything. One says free trade makes us rich. The other says it will drive us into poverty. If the experts don't know, how is the average person ever going to know whether free trade is best?'

1. Can you give your roommate any insight into why economists might disagree on this issue?

2. Suppose you discover that 93 per cent of economists believe that free trade is generally best. Could you now give a more precise answer as to why economists might disagree on this issue?

3. What if you later discovered that the economist opposed to free trade worked for a trade union. Would that help you explain why there appears to be a difference of opinion on this issue?

SOLUTIONS

Terms and Definitions

_1_	Factors of production	_7_	Positive statements
_2_	Macroeconomics	_8_	Economic models
_3_	Scientific method	_9_	Production possibilities frontier
_4_	Opportunity cost	_10_	Microeconomics
_5_	Normative statements	_11_	Circular flow diagram
_6_	Efficiency		

Practice Problems

1. a. €30,000 of spending from households to market for goods and services. Car moves from market for goods and services to household. €30,000 of revenue from market for goods and services to firms while car moves from firm to market for goods and services.
   b. €5,000 of wages from firms to market for factors of production. Inputs move from market for factors of production to firms. Labour moves from households to market for factors of production while €5,000 income moves from market for factors to households.
   c. €15 of spending from households to market for goods and services. Service moves from market for goods and services to household. Service moves from firms to market for goods and services in return for €15 revenue.
   d. €10,000 of profit from firms to market for factors of production. Inputs move from market for factors of production to firms. Capital services move from households to market for factors of production in return for €10,000 income.

2. a. See Exhibit 6.
   b. 40 rackets.
   c. 100 rackets.
   d. Because as we produce more bats, the resources best suited for making bats are already being used. Therefore it takes even more resources to produce 100 bats and greater reductions in racket production.
   e. 200 bats; 160 rackets.
   f. No. Resources were not used efficiently if production can be increased with no opportunity cost.

EXHIBIT 6

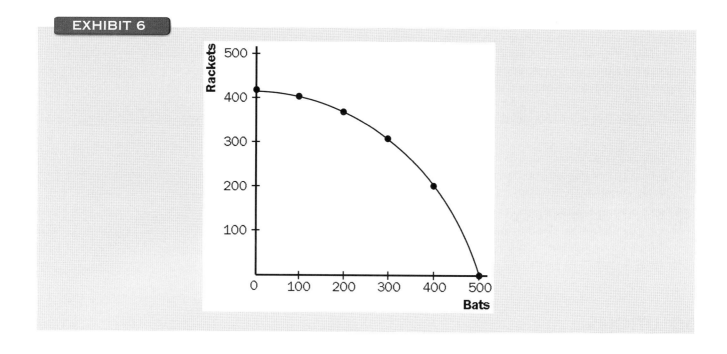

3. a. Parsimonious Country. Capital (plant and equipment) is a factor of production and producing more of it now will increase future production.
   b. Fewer consumption goods are produced now.
   c. See Exhibit 7. The production possibilities curve will shift more for Parsimonious Country because they have experienced a greater increase in factors of production (capital).

Short-Answer Questions

1. To simplify reality so that we can focus our thinking on what is actually important.

2. Not necessarily. Realistic models are more complex. They may be confusing and they may fail to focus on the relationships being investigated.

EXHIBIT 7

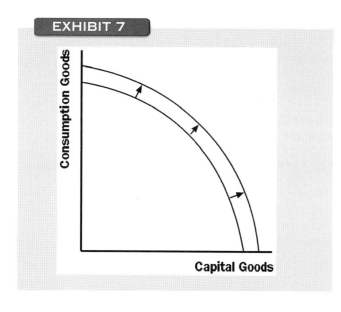

3. Because if an economy is operating efficiently, production choices have opportunity costs. If we want more of one thing, we must have less of another.

4. Because resources are specialized and thus, are not equally well-suited for producing different outputs.

5. Positive statements are statements of fact and are refutable by examining evidence.

6. Economists may have different scientific judgements. Economists may have different values.

7. Macroeconomics studies economy-wide phenomena resulting from interaction between all economic agents in all markets. Microeconomics studies the interaction of decisions by individual economic agents in individual markets.

8. Flows of expenditure, flows of payments to the factors of production and flows of production.

True/False Questions

1. F; economic models are simplifications of reality.

2. T

3. T

4. F; a production possibilities frontier shows only what a country can produce using its available resources.

5. T

6. T

7. F; normative statements cannot be refuted.

8. F; the circular flow diagram shows output produced, income received and spending on output.

Multiple-Choice Questions

1.	c	5.	c
2.	b	6.	d
3.	d	7.	b
4.	c	8.	a

Advanced Critical Thinking

1. Economists may have different scientific judgements. Economists may have different values. There may not really be any real disagreement because the majority of economists may actually agree.

2. Those opposed to free trade are likely to have different values than the majority of economists. There is not much disagreement on this issue among the mainstream economics profession.

3. Yes. It suggests that impediments to international trade may benefit some groups (organised labour) but these impediments are unlikely to benefit the public in general. Supporters of these policies are promoting their own interests.

APPENDIX

Practice Problems

1. The following ordered pairs of price and quantity demanded describe Simon's demand for cups of gourmet coffee.

Price per Cup of Coffee (€)	Quantity of Coffee Demanded
5	2 cups
4	4 cups
3	6 cups
2	8 cups
1	10 cups

   a. Plot and connect the ordered pairs on the graph in Exhibit 8.
   b. What is the slope of Simon's demand curve for coffee in the price range of €5 and €4?
   c. What is the slope of Simon's demand curve for coffee in the price range of €2 and €1?
   d. Are the price of coffee and Simon's quantity demanded of coffee positively correlated or negatively correlated? How can you tell?
   e. If the price of coffee moves from €2 per cup to €4 per cup, what happens to the quantity demanded? Is this a movement along a curve or a shift in the curve?

EXHIBIT 8

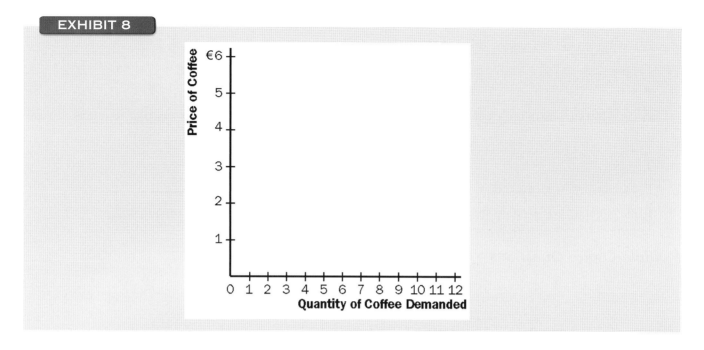

f. Suppose Simon's income doubles from €20,000 per year to €40,000 per year. Now the following ordered pairs describe Simon's demand for gourmet coffee. Plot these ordered pairs on the graph provided in part (a) above.

Price per Cup of Coffee (€)	Quantity of Coffee Demanded
5	4 cups
4	6 cups
3	8 cups
2	10 cups
1	12 cups

g. Did the doubling of Joe's income cause a movement along his demand curve or a shift in his demand curve? Why?

2. An alien lands on earth and observes the following: on mornings when people carry umbrellas, it tends to rain later in the day. The alien concludes that umbrellas cause rain.
   a. What error has the alien committed?
   b. What role did *expectations* play in the alien's error?
   c. If rain is truly caused by humidity, temperature, wind currents, and so on, what additional type of error has the alien committed when it decided that umbrellas cause rain?

True/False Questions

_____ 1. When graphing in the coordinate system, the x-coordinate tells us the horizontal location while the y-coordinate tells us the vertical location of the point.

_____ 2. When a line slopes upward in the x, y coordinate system, the two variables measured on each axis are positively correlated.

_____ 3. Price and quantity demanded for most goods are positively related.

_____ 4. If three variables are related, one of them must be held constant when graphing the other two in the x, y coordinate system.

_____ 5. If three variables are related, a change in the variable not represented on the x, y coordinate system will cause a movement along the line drawn in the x, y coordinate system.

_____ 6. The slope of a line is equal to the change in y divided by the change in x along the line.

_____ 7.   When a line has negative slope, the two variables measured on each axis are positively correlated.

_____ 8.   Reverse causality means that while we think A causes B, B may actually cause A.

SOLUTIONS FOR APPENDIX

Practice Problems

1.   a. See Exhibit 9.
     b. −1/2.
     c. −1/2.
     d. Negatively correlated, because an increase in price is associated with a decrease in quantity demanded. That is, the demand curve slopes negatively.
     e. Decrease by 4 cups. Movement along curve.
     f. See Exhibit 10.
     g. Shift in curve because a variable changed (income) which is not measured on either axis.

2.   a. Reverse causality.
     b. Since rain can be predicted, people's expectation of rain causes them to carry umbrellas *before* it rains, making it appear as if umbrellas cause rain.
     c. Omitted variables.

True/False Questions

1.   T

2.   T

3.   F; they are negatively correlated.

4.   T

5.   F; a change in a variable not represented on the graph will cause a shift in the curve.

6.   T

7.   F; negative slope implies negative correlation.

8.   T

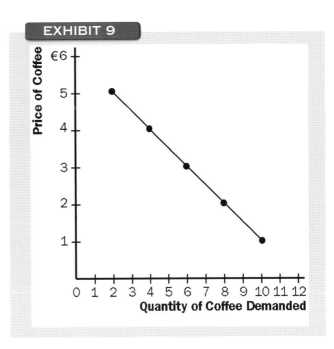

EXHIBIT 9

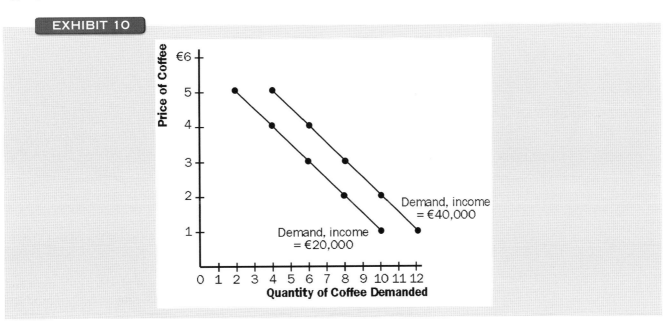

EXHIBIT 10

GOALS

In this chapter you will

Consider how everyone can benefit when people trade with one another

Learn the meaning of absolute advantage and comparative advantage

See how comparative advantage explains the gains from trade

Apply the theory of comparative advantage to everyday life and national policy

OUTCOMES

You should be able to

Show how total production rises when individuals specialize in the production of goods for which they have a comparative advantage

Explain why all people have a comparative advantage even if they have no absolute advantage

Demonstrate the link between comparative advantage and opportunity cost

Explain why people who are good at everything still tend to specialize

INTERDEPENDENCE AND THE GAINS FROM TRADE

CHAPTER OVERVIEW

Context and Purpose

Chapter 3 is the third chapter in the three-chapter section that serves as the introduction of the text. The first chapter introduced ten fundamental principles of economics. The second chapter developed how economists approach problems. This chapter shows how people and countries gain from trade (which is one of the ten principles discussed in Chapter 1).

The purpose of Chapter 3 is to demonstrate how everyone can gain from trade. Trade allows people to specialize in the production of goods for which they have a comparative advantage and then trade for goods other people produce. Because of specialization, total output rises and through trade we are all able to share in the bounty. This is as true for countries as it is for individuals. Since everyone can gain from trade, restrictions on trade tend to reduce welfare.

CHAPTER REVIEW

Introduction

Each of us consumes products every day that are produced in a number of different countries. Complex products contain components that are produced in many different countries so these products have no single country of origin. Those who produce are neither generous nor ordered by government to produce. People produce because they wish to trade and get something in return. Hence, trade makes us interdependent.

A Parable for the Modern Economy

Imagine a simple economy. There are two people—a cattle farmer and a potato farmer. There are two goods—meat and potatoes.

- If each can produce only one product (the cattle farmer can produce only meat and the potato farmer potatoes) they will trade just to increase the variety of products they consume. Each benefits because of increased variety.

- If each can produce both goods, but each is more efficient than the other at producing one good, then each will specialize in what he or she does best (again the cattle farmer produces meat and the potato farmer produces potatoes), total output will rise, and they will trade. Trade allows each to benefit because trade allows for specialization, and specialization increases the total production available to share.

- If one producer is better than the other at producing *both* meat and potatoes, there are the same advantages to trade, but it is more difficult to see. Again, trade allows each to benefit because trade allows for specialization, and specialization increases the total production available to share. To understand the source of the gains from trade when one producer is better at producing both products, we must understand the concept of comparative advantage.

The Principle of Comparative Advantage

To understand **comparative advantage**, we begin with the concept of **absolute advantage**. Absolute advantage compares the quantity of inputs required to produce a good. The producer that requires fewer resources (say fewer hours worked) to produce a good is said to have an absolute advantage in the production of that good. That is, the most efficient producer (the one with the highest productivity) has an absolute advantage.

While absolute advantage compares the actual cost of production for each producer, *comparative advantage* compares **opportunity costs** of production for each producer. The producer with the lower opportunity cost of production is said to have a comparative advantage. Regardless of absolute advantage, if producers have *different opportunity costs* of production for each good, each should specialize in the production of the good for which their opportunity cost of production is lower. That is, each producer should produce the item for which they have a comparative advantage. They can then trade some of their output for the other good. Trade makes both producers better off because trade allows for specialization, and specialization increases the total production available to be shared.

The decision to specialize and the resulting gains from trade are based on comparative advantage, not absolute advantage. Although a single producer can have an absolute advantage in the production of both goods, he/she cannot have a comparative advantage in the production of both goods because a low opportunity cost of producing one good implies a high opportunity cost of producing the other good.

In summary, trade allows producers to exploit the differences in their opportunity costs of production. Each specializes in the production of the good for which they have the lower opportunity cost of production and thus, a comparative advantage. This increases total production and makes the economic pie larger. Everyone can benefit. The additional production generated by specialization is the gain from trade.

Adam Smith, in his 1776 book, *An Inquiry into the Nature and Causes of the Wealth of Nations* and David Ricardo, in his 1817 book *Principles of Political Economy and Taxation*, both recognized the gains from trade through specialization and the principle of comparative advantage. Current arguments for free trade are still based on their work.

Applications of Comparative Advantage

The principle of comparative advantage applies to individuals as well as countries.

Recall, absolute advantage does not determine specialization in production. For example, David Beckham may have an absolute advantage in both football and lawn mowing. However, because he can earn €5,000/hour playing football, he is better off paying someone to mow his lawn (even if they do it more slowly than he) as long as he can get someone to do it for less than €5,000/hour. This is because the opportunity cost of an hour of mowing for David Beckham is €5,000. David Beckham will likely specialize in football and trade for other services. He does this because he has a comparative advantage in football and a comparative disadvantage in lawn mowing even though he has an absolute advantage in both.

Trade between countries is subject to the same principle of comparative advantage. Goods produced abroad and sold domestically are called **imports**. Goods produced domestically and sold abroad are called **exports**. Even if Europe has an absolute advantage in the production of both cars and food, it should specialize in the production of the item for which it has a comparative advantage. Since the opportunity cost of food is low in Europe (better land) and high in Japan, Europe should produce more food and export it to Japan in exchange for imports of cars from Japan. While Europe gains from trade, the impact of trade on European car workers is different from the impact of trade on European farmers.

A reduction in barriers to free trade improves the welfare of the importing country *as a whole*, but it does not improve the welfare of the domestic producers in the importing country. For this reason, domestic producers lobby their governments to maintain (or increase) barriers to free trade. For example, the European textile industry has been able to maintain barriers to the importing of clothes from China to the detriment of European consumers.

HELPFUL HINTS

1. A step by step example of comparative advantage will demonstrate most of the concepts discussed in Chapter 3. It will give you a pattern to follow when answering questions at the end of the chapter in your text and for the problems that follow in this Study Guide.

    Suppose we have the following information about the productivity of industry in Japan and Korea. The data are the units of output per hour of work.

	Steel	Televisions
Japan	6	3
Korea	8	2

    A Japanese worker can produce 6 units of steel or 3 TVs per hour. A Korean worker can produce 8 units of steel or 2 TVs per hour.

    We can plot the production possibilities frontier for each country assuming each country has only one worker and the worker works only one hour. To plot

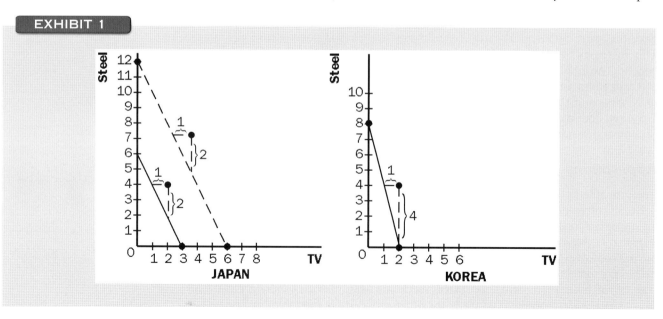

EXHIBIT 1

the frontier, plot the end points and connect them with a line. For example, Japan can produce 6 units of steel with its worker or 3 TVs. It can also allocate one half hour to the production of each and get 3 units steel and 1 1/2 TVs. Any other proportion of the hour can be allocated to the two productive activities. The production possibilities frontier is linear in these cases because the labour resource can be moved from the production of one good to the other at a constant rate. We can do the same for Korea. Without trade, the production possibilities frontier is the consumption possibilities frontier, too.

Comparative advantage determines specialization and trade. The opportunity cost of a TV in Japan is 2 units of steel, which is shown by the slope of the production possibilities frontier in Exhibit 1. Alternatively, the opportunity cost of one unit of steel in Japan is 1/2 of a TV. In Korea, the opportunity cost of a TV is 4 units of steel and the cost of a unit of steel is 1/4 of a TV. Since the opportunity cost of a TV is lower in Japan, Japan has a comparative advantage in TV production and should specialize in TVs. Since the opportunity cost of steel is lower in Korea, Korea has a comparative advantage in steel production and should specialize in steel.

What is the range of prices at which each country would be willing to exchange? If Japan specializes in TV production and produces 3 televisions, it would be willing to trade TVs for steel as long as the price of steel is below 1/2 TV per unit of steel because that was the Japanese price for a unit of steel prior to trade. Korea would be willing to specialize in steel production and trade for TVs as long as the price of a TV is less than 4 units of steel because that was the Korean price of a TV prior to trade. In short, the final price must be between the original tradeoffs each faced in the absence of trade. One TV will cost between 2 and 4 units of steel. One unit of steel will cost between 1/2 and 1/4 of a TV.

2. Trade allows countries to consume outside their original production possibilities frontier. Suppose that Japan and Korea settle on a trading price of 3 units of steel for 1 TV (or 1/3 of a TV for 1 unit of steel). (I am giving you this price. There is nothing in the problem that would let you calculate the actual final trading price. You can only calculate the range in which it must lie.) This range lies between 4 units of steel for 1 TV to 2 units of steel for 1 TV.

If Japan specializes in TV production, produces 3 televisions, and exports 1 TV for 3 units of steel, Japan will be able to consume 2 TVs and 3 units of steel. If we plot this point (2 TVs and 3 steel) on Japan's graph, we see that it lies outside its production possibilities frontier. If Korea specializes in steel, produces 8 units of steel, and exports 3 units for 1 TV, Korea will be able to consume 5 units of steel and 1 TV. If we plot this point (5 steel and 1 TV) on Korea's graph, we see that it also lies outside its production possibilities frontier.

This is the gain from trade. Trade allows countries (and people) to specialize. Specialization increases world output. After trading, countries consume outside their individual production possibilities frontiers. In this way, trade is like an improvement in technology. It allows countries to move beyond their current production possibilities frontiers.

3. Only comparative advantage matters—absolute advantage is irrelevant. In the previous example, Japan had an absolute advantage in the production of TVs because it could produce 3 per hour while Korea could only produce 2. Korea had an absolute advantage in the production of steel because it could produce 8 units per hour compared to 6 for Japan.

To demonstrate that comparative advantage, not absolute advantage, determines specialization and trade, we alter the previous example so that Japan has an absolute advantage in the production of both goods. To this end, suppose Japan becomes twice as productive as in the previous table. That is, a worker can now produce 12 units of steel or 6 TVs per hour.

	Steel	Televisions
Japan	12	6
Korea	8	2

Now Japan has an absolute advantage in the production of both goods. Japan's new production possibilities frontier is the dashed line in Exhibit 1. Will this change the analysis? Not at all. The opportunity cost of each good within Japan is the same—2 units of steel per TV or 1/2 TV per unit of steel (and Korea is unaffected). For this reason, Japan still has the identical comparative advantage as before and it will specialize in TV production while Korea will specialize in steel. However, since productivity has doubled in Japan, its entire set of choices has improved and thus, its material welfare has improved.

TERMS AND DEFINITIONS

Choose a definition for each key term.

Key terms:

_____ Absolute advantage

_____ Comparative advantage

_____ Gains from trade

_____ Imports

_____ Exports

Definitions:

1. The comparison among producers of a good based on their opportunity cost

2. Goods produced domestically and sold abroad

3. Goods produced abroad and sold domestically

4. The comparison among producers of goods based on their productivity

5. The increase in total production due to specialization allowed by trade

PROBLEMS AND SHORT-ANSWER QUESTIONS

Practice Problems

1. Suppose a worker in Germany can produce 15 computers or 5 tons of grain per month. Suppose a worker in Poland can produce 4 computers or 4 tons of grain per month. For simplicity, assume that each country has only one worker.
   a. Fill out the following table showing the maximum amount of each product that each country can produce if each worker fully specializes in the production of only one good:

	Computers	Grain
Germany	—	—
Poland	—	—

   b. Graph the production possibilities frontier for each country in Exhibit 2.
   c. What is the opportunity cost of a computer in Germany? What is the opportunity cost of a ton of grain in Germany?
   d. What is the opportunity cost of a computer in Poland? What is the opportunity cost of a ton of grain in Poland?
   e. Which country has the absolute advantage in producing computers? Grain?
   f. Which country has the comparative advantage in producing computers? Grain?
   g. Each country should tend towards specialization in the production of which good? Why?

EXHIBIT 2

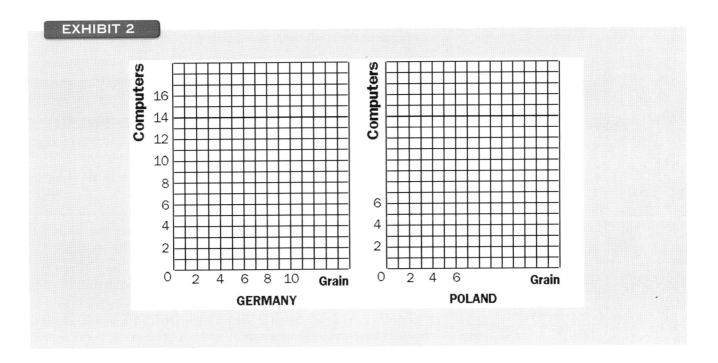

h. What is the range of prices for computers and grain for which both countries would benefit?

i. Suppose Germany and Poland settle on a price of 2 computers for 1 ton of grain or 1/2 ton of grain for a computer. Suppose each country specializes in production and they trade 4 computers for 2 tons of grain. Plot the final consumption points on the graphs you made in part (b) above. Are these countries consuming inside or outside of their production possibilities frontier?

j. Suppose the productivity of a worker in Poland doubles so that a worker can produce 8 computers or 8 tons of grain per month. Which country has the absolute advantage in producing computers? Grain?

k. After the doubling of productivity in Poland, which country has a comparative advantage in producing computers? Grain? Has the comparative advantage changed? Has the material welfare of either country changed?

l. How would your analysis change if you assumed, more realistically, that each country had 10 million workers?

Short-Answer Questions

1. Why is comparative advantage important in determining trade instead of absolute advantage?

2. What are the gains from trade?

3. Why is a restriction of trade likely to reduce material welfare?

4. Suppose a lawyer who earns €200 per hour can also type at 200 words per minute. Explain whether the lawyer should hire a secretary who can type only 50 words per minute?

SELF-TEST

True/False Questions

_____ 1. If Japan has an absolute advantage in the production of an item, it must also have a comparative advantage in the production of that item.

_____ 2. Talented people that are the best at everything have a comparative advantage in the production of everything.

_____ 3. Comparative advantage is a comparison based on opportunity cost.

_____ 4. If a producer is self-sufficient, the production possibilities frontier is also the consumption possibilities frontier.

_____ 5. If trade benefits one country, its trading partner must be worse off due to trade.

_____ 6. Absolute advantage is a comparison based on productivity.

_____ 7. The gains from trade can be measured by the increase in total production that comes from specialization.

_____ 8. If Germany's productivity doubles for everything it produces, this will not alter its prior pattern of specialization because it has not altered its comparative advantage.

_____ 9. If an advanced country has an absolute advantage in the production of everything, it will benefit if it eliminates trade with less developed countries and becomes completely self-sufficient.

_____ 10. If gains from trade are based solely on comparative advantage, and if all countries have the same opportunity costs of production, then countries will still gain from specialization.

Multiple-Choice Questions

1. If a nation has an absolute advantage in the production of a good,
   a. it can produce that good at a lower opportunity cost than its trading partner.
   b. it can produce that good using fewer resources than its trading partner.
   c. it can benefit by restricting imports of that good.
   d. it will specialize in the production of that good and export it.

2. If a nation has a comparative advantage in the production of a good,
   a. it can produce that good at a lower opportunity cost than its trading partner.
   b. it can produce that good using fewer resources than its trading partner.
   c. it can benefit by restricting imports of that good.
   d. it must be the only country with the ability to produce that good.

3. Suppose a country's workers can produce 4 watches per hour or 12 rings per hour. If there is no trade,
   a. the opportunity cost of 1 watch is 3 rings.
   b. the opportunity cost of 1 watch is 1/3 of a ring.
   c. the opportunity cost of 1 watch is 4 rings.
   d. the opportunity cost of 1 watch is 1/4 of a ring.
   e. the opportunity cost of 1 watch is 12 rings.

4. The table below shows five combinations of goods (X and Y) which could be produced in two countries (M and N) if each country were allowed to allocate half of its resources to the production of each good.

	Country M		Country N	
	Good X	Good Y	Good X	Good Y
A	1	3	2	9
B	2	3	6	9
C	3	3	4	6
D	1	4	2	6
E	3	1	1	3

The only situation when the total output of both goods could not be increased if both countries specialized where they each have a comparative advantage is
a. A.
b. B.
c. C.
d. D.
e. E.

5. Suppose the UK and France produce two goods (X and Y) and that the domestic prices of these in both areas are

Price in the UK (£)		Price in France (€)	
Good X	Good Y	Good X	Good Y
10.00	14.00	15.00	18.00

If producers require the same revenue from selling abroad that they receive by selling in the domestic market and transport costs are negligible, which one of the following exchange rates will allow both countries to specialize where they have a comparative advantage?
a. £1 = €1.2.
b. £1 = €1.4.
c. £1 = €1.5.
d. £1 = €1.6.
e. £1 = €1.8.

Use the production possibilities frontiers in Exhibit 3 to answer questions 6–8. Assume each country has the same number of workers, say 20 million, and that each axis is measured in metric tonnes per month.

6. Argentina has a comparative advantage in the production of
a. both fruit and beef.
b. fruit.
c. beef.
d. neither fruit nor beef.

EXHIBIT 3

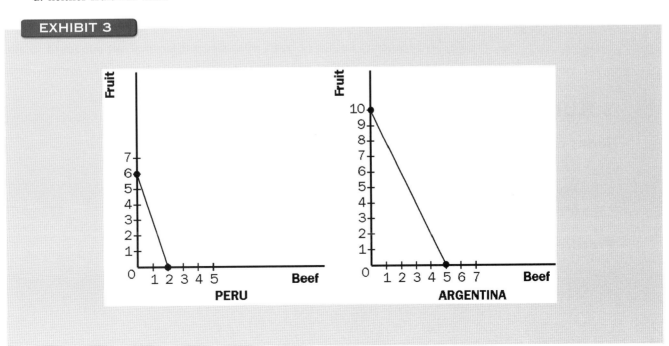

7. Peru will export
    a. both fruit and beef.
    b. fruit.
    c. beef.
    d. neither fruit nor beef.

8. The opportunity cost of producing a metric ton of beef in Peru is
    a. 1/3 ton of fruit.
    b. 1 ton of fruit.
    c. 2 tons of fruit.
    d. 3 tons of fruit.
    e. 6 tons of fruit.

9. The data below show the resources required to produce tractors and wheat in two countries (A and B).

	Units of Resources Required	
	Country A	Country B
To produce one tractor	10	8
To produce 1 tonne of wheat	8	4

Which one of the following statements is correct?

a. Country A has a comparative advantage in the production of wheat.
b. Country B has a comparative advantage in the production of wheat.
c. Country A has an absolute and comparative advantage in the production of tractors.
d. Country B has an absolute and comparative advantage in the production of tractors.

ADVANCED CRITICAL THINKING

You are watching an election debate on television. A candidate says, 'We need to stop the flow of Japanese cars into Europe. If we limit the importation of Japanese cars, our domestic car production will rise and Europe will be better off.'

1. Is it likely that *Europe* will be better off if we limit Japanese car imports? Explain.

2. Will anyone in Europe be better off if we limit Japanese car imports? Explain.

3. In the real world, does every person in the country gain when restrictions on imports are reduced? Explain.

SOLUTIONS

Terms and Definitions

_1_ Comparative advantage   _4_ Absolute advantage

_2_ Exports   _5_ Gains from trade

_3_ Imports

Practice Problems

1. a.

	Computers	Grain
Germany	15	5
Poland	4	4

b. See Exhibit 4.

c. 1/3 ton grain. 3 computers.

d. 1 ton grain. 1 computer.

e. Germany because one worker can produce 15 computers compared to 4. Germany because one worker can produce 5 tons of grain compared to 4.

f. Germany because a computer has the opportunity cost of only 1/3 ton of grain compared to 1 ton of grain in Poland. Poland because a ton of grain has the opportunity cost of only 1 computer compared to 3 computers in Germany.

g. Germany should produce computers while Poland should produce grain because the opportunity cost of computers is lower in Germany and the opportunity cost of grain is lower in Poland. That is, each has a comparative advantage in those goods.

EXHIBIT 4

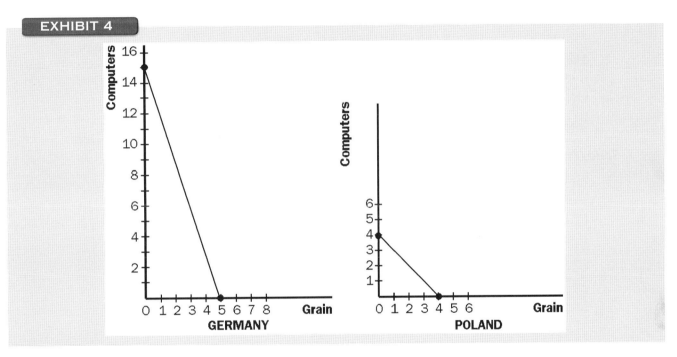

EXHIBIT 5

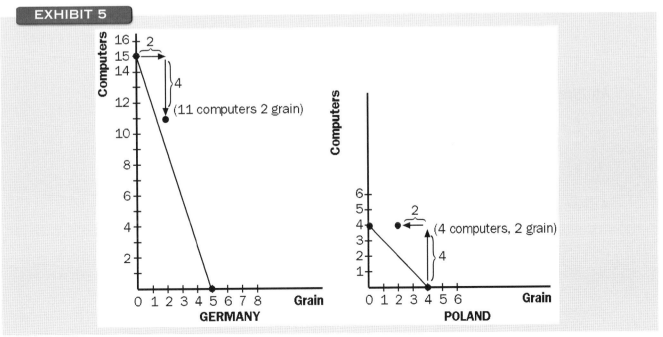

h. Grain must cost less than 3 computers to Germany. Computers must cost less than 1 ton of grain to Poland.

i. See Exhibit 5 They are consuming outside their production possibilities frontier.

j. Germany because one worker can produce 15 compared to 8. Poland because one worker can produce 8 compared to 5.

k. Germany has comparative advantage in computers. Poland has comparative advantage in grain. No change in comparative advantage. Poland is better off, however, because it now has a larger set of choices.

l. It would not change absolute advantage or comparative advantage. It would change the scale in the previous two graphs by a factor of 10 million.

Short-Answer Questions

1. What is important in trade is how a country's costs without trade differ from each other. This is determined by the relative opportunity costs across countries.

2. The additional output that comes from countries with different opportunity costs of production specializing in the production of the item for which they have the lower domestic opportunity cost.

3. Because it forces people to produce at a higher cost than they pay when they trade.

4. Yes, as long as the secretary earns less than €50/hour, the lawyer is ahead.

True/False Questions

1. F; absolute advantage compares the quantities of inputs used in production while comparative advantage compares the opportunity costs.

2. F; a low opportunity cost of producing one good implies a high opportunity cost of producing the other good.

3. T

4. T

5. F; voluntary trade benefits both traders.

6. T

7. T

8. T

9. F; voluntary trade benefits both traders.

10. F; if countries have identical opportunity cost ratios, comparative advantage cannot exist.

Multiple-Choice Questions

1. b   4. b   7. b
2. a   5. e   8. d
3. a   6. c   9. b

Advanced Critical Thinking

1. No. If we import cars, it is because the opportunity cost of producing them elsewhere is lower than in Europe.

2. Yes. Those associated with the domestic car industry—stockholders of domestic car producers and car workers.

3. No. When we reduce restrictions on imports, the country gains from the increased trade, but individuals in the affected domestic industry may lose.

⌐In this chapter you will

Learn what a competitive market is

Examine what determines
the demand for a good in a
competitive market

Examine what determines the
supply of a good in a competitive
market

See how supply and demand
together set the price of a good
and the quantity sold

Consider the key role of prices
in allocating scarce resources in
market economies

⌐You should be able to

List the two characteristics of a
competitive market

List the factors that affect the
amount that consumers wish to
buy in a market

List the factors that affect the
amount that producers wish to sell
in a market

Draw a graph of supply and
demand in a market and find the
equilibrium price and quantity

Shift supply and demand in
response to an economic event and
find the new equilibrium price
and quantity

THE MARKET FORCES OF SUPPLY AND DEMAND

CHAPTER OVERVIEW

Context and Purpose

Chapter 4 is the first chapter in a three-chapter sequence that deals with supply and demand and how markets work. Chapter 4 shows how supply and demand for a good determines both the quantity produced and the price at which the good sells. Chapter 5 will add precision to our discussion of supply and demand by addressing the concept of elasticity—the sensitivity of the quantity supplied and quantity demanded to changes in economic variables. Chapter 6 will address the impact of government policies on prices and quantities in markets.

The purpose of Chapter 4 is to establish the model of supply and demand. The model of supply and demand is the foundation for our discussion for the remainder of this text. For this reason, time spent studying the concepts in this chapter will return benefits to you throughout your study of economics. Many instructors would argue that this chapter is the most important chapter in the text.

CHAPTER REVIEW

Introduction

In a market economy, supply and demand determine both the quantity of each good produced and the price at which each good is sold. In this chapter, we develop the determinants of supply and demand. We also address how changes in supply and demand alter prices and change the allocation of the economy's resources.

Markets and Competition

A **market** is a group of buyers and sellers of a particular good or service. It can be highly organized like a stock market or less organized like the market for ice cream. A **competitive market** is a market in which there are many buyers and sellers so that each has a negligible impact on the market price.

A **perfectly competitive** market has two main characteristics:

- The goods offered for sale are all the same.
- The buyers and sellers are so numerous that no one buyer or seller can influence the price.

If a market is perfectly competitive, both buyers and sellers are said to be *price takers* because they cannot influence the price. The assumption of perfect competition applies well to agricultural markets because the product is similar and no individual buyer or seller can influence the price.

There are other types of markets. If a market has only one seller, the market is known as a *monopoly*. If there are only a few sellers, the market is known as an *oligopoly*. If there are many sellers but each product is slightly different so that each seller has some ability to set its own price, the market is called *monopolistically competitive*.

Demand

The behaviour of buyers is captured by the concept of demand. The **quantity demanded** is the amount of a good that buyers are willing and able to purchase. While many things determine the quantity demanded of a good, the *price* of the good plays a central role. Other things equal, an increase in the price of a good reduces the quantity demanded. This negative relationship between the price of a good and the quantity demanded of a good is known as the **law of demand**.

The **demand schedule** is a table that shows the relationship between the price of a good and the quantity demanded. The **demand curve** is a graph of this relationship with the price on the vertical axis and the quantity demanded on the horizontal axis. The demand curve is downwards sloping due to the law of demand.

Market demand is the sum of the quantities demanded for each individual buyer at each price. That is, the market demand curve is the horizontal sum of the individual demand curves. The market demand curve shows the total quantity demanded of a good at each price, while all other factors that affect how much buyers wish to buy are held constant.

Shifts in the demand curve. When people change how much they wish to buy at each price, the demand curve shifts. If buyers increase the quantity demanded at each price, the demand curve shifts right which is called an *increase in demand*. Alternatively, if buyers decrease the quantity demanded at each price, the demand curve shifts left which is called a *decrease in demand*. The most important factors that shift demand curves are:

- *Income*: A **normal good** is a good for which an increase in income leads to an increase in demand. An **inferior good** is a good for which an increase in income leads to a decrease in demand.

- *Prices of Related Goods*: If two goods can be used in place of one another, they are known as **substitutes**. When two goods are substitutes, an increase in the price of one good leads to an increase in the demand for the other good. If two goods are used together, they are known as **complements**. When two goods are complements, an increase in the price of one good leads to a decrease in the demand for the other good.

- *Tastes*: If your preferences shift towards a good, it will lead to an increase in the demand for that good.

- *Expectations*: Expectations about future income or prices will affect the demand for a good today.

- *Number of Buyers*: An increase in the number of buyers will lead to an increase in the market demand for a good because there are more individual demand curves to horizontally sum.

A demand curve is drawn with price on the vertical axis and quantity demanded on the horizontal axis while holding other things equal. Therefore, a change in the price of a good represents a movement along the demand curve while a change in income, prices of related goods, tastes, expectations, and the number of buyers causes a shift in the demand curve.

Supply

The behaviour of sellers is captured by the concept of supply. The **quantity supplied** is the amount of a good that sellers are willing and able to sell. While many things determine the quantity supplied of a good, the *price* of the good is central. Other things equal, an increase in the price makes production more profitable and increases the quantity supplied. This positive relationship between the price of a good and the quantity supplied is known as the **law of supply**.

The **supply schedule** is a table that shows the relationship between the price of a good and the quantity supplied. The **supply curve** is a graph of this relationship with the price on the vertical axis and the quantity supplied on the horizontal axis. The supply curve is upwards sloping due to the law of supply.

Market supply is the sum of the quantity supplied for each individual seller at each price. That is, the market supply curve is the horizontal sum of the individual supply curves. The market supply curve shows the total quantity supplied of a good at each price, while all other factors that affect how much producers wish to sell are held constant.

Shifts in the supply curve. When producers change how much they wish to sell at each price, the supply curve shifts. If producers increase the quantity supplied at each price, the supply curve shifts right, which is called an *increase in supply*. Alternatively, if producers decrease the quantity supplied at each price, the supply curve shifts left, which is called a *decrease in supply*. The most important factors that shift supply curves are:

- *Input Prices*: A decrease in the price of an input makes production more profitable and increases supply.
- *Technology*: An improvement in technology reduces costs, makes production more profitable, and increases supply.
- *Expectations*: Expectations about the future will affect the supply of a good today.
- *Number of Sellers*: An increase in the number of sellers will lead to an increase in the market supply for a good because there are more individual supply curves to horizontally sum.

A supply curve is drawn with price on the vertical axis and quantity supplied on the horizontal axis while holding other things equal. Therefore, a change in the price of a good represents a movement along the supply curve while a change in input prices, technology, expectations, and the number of sellers causes a shift in the supply curve.

Supply and Demand Together

When placed on the same graph, the intersection of supply and demand is called the market's **equilibrium**. Equilibrium is a situation in which the price has reached the level where quantity supplied equals quantity demanded. The **equilibrium price**, or the market-clearing price, is the price that balances the quantity demanded and the quantity supplied. When the quantity supplied equals the quantity demanded at the equilibrium price, we have determined the **equilibrium quantity**.

The market naturally moves towards its equilibrium. If the price is above the equilibrium price, the quantity supplied exceeds the quantity demanded and there is a **surplus**, or an excess supply of the good. A surplus causes the price to fall until it reaches equilibrium. If the price is below the equilibrium price, the quantity demanded exceeds the quantity supplied and there is a **shortage**, or an excess demand for the good. A shortage causes the price to rise until it reaches equilibrium. This natural adjustment of the price to bring the quantity supplied and the quantity demanded into balance is known as the **law of supply and demand**.

When an economic event shifts the supply or the demand curve, the equilibrium in the market changes. The analysis of this change is known as *comparative statics* because we are comparing the initial equilibrium to the new equilibrium. When analysing the impact of some event on the market equilibrium, employ the following three steps:

- Decide whether the event shifts the supply curve or the demand curve or both.

- Decide which direction the curve shifts.

- Use the supply and demand diagram to see how the shift changes the equilibrium price and quantity.

A shift in the demand curve is called a 'change in demand'. It is caused by a change in a variable that affects the amount people wish to purchase of a good *other than the price of the good*. A change in the price of a good causes a movement along a given demand curve and is called a 'change in the quantity demanded'. Likewise, a shift in the supply curve is called a 'change in supply'. It is caused by a change in a variable that affects the amount producers wish to supply of a good *other than the price of the good*. A change in the price of a good causes a movement along a supply curve and is called a 'change in the quantity supplied'.

For example, a drought that destroys much of the potato crop causes a decrease in the supply of potatoes (supply of potatoes shifts to the left). This increases the price of potatoes and decreases the quantity demanded of potatoes. In other words, a decrease in the supply of potatoes increases the price of potatoes and decreases the quantity of potatoes purchased.

If both supply and demand shift at the same time, there may be more than one possible outcome for the changes in the equilibrium price and quantity. For example, if demand were to increase (shift right) while supply were to decrease (shift left), the price will certainly rise, but the impact on the equilibrium quantity is ambiguous. In this case, the change in the equilibrium quantity depends on the magnitudes of the shifts in supply and demand.

Conclusion: How Prices Allocate Resources

Markets generate equilibrium prices. These prices are the signals that guide the allocation of scarce resources. Prices of products rise to the level necessary to allocate the products to those who are willing and able to pay for them. Prices of inputs (say labour) rise to the level necessary to induce people to do the jobs that need to get done. In this way, no jobs go undone and there is no shortage of goods and services for those willing and able to pay for them.

HELPFUL HINTS

1. Equilibrium in a market is a static state. That is, once a market is in equilibrium, there are no further forces for change. That is why economists use the term *comparative statics* to describe the analysis of comparing an initial static equilibrium to a new static equilibrium.

2. By far, the greatest difficulty students have when studying supply and demand is distinguishing between a 'change in demand' and a 'change in the quantity demanded' and between a 'change in supply' and a 'change in the quantity supplied'. It helps to remember that 'demand' is the entire relationship between price and quantity demanded. That is, demand is the entire demand curve, not

a point on a demand curve. Therefore, a change in demand is a shift in the entire demand curve, which can only be caused by a change in a determinant of demand other than the price of the good. A change in the quantity demanded is a movement along the demand curve and is caused by a change in the price of the good. Likewise, 'supply' refers to the entire supply curve, not a point on the supply curve. Therefore, a change in supply is a shift in the entire supply curve, which can only be caused by a change in a determinant of supply other than the price of the good. A change in the quantity supplied is a movement along the supply curve and is caused by a change in the price of the good.

3. If both supply and demand shift at the same time and we do not know the magnitude of each shift, then the change in either the price or the quantity must be ambiguous. For example, if there is an increase in supply (supply shifts right) and an increase in demand (demand shifts right), the equilibrium quantity must certainly rise, but the change in the equilibrium price is ambiguous. Do this for all four possible combinations of changes in supply and demand. You will find that if you know the impact on the equilibrium price with certainty, then the impact on the equilibrium quantity must be ambiguous. If you know the impact on the equilibrium quantity with certainty, then the impact on the equilibrium price must be ambiguous.

TERMS AND DEFINITIONS

Choose a definition for each key term.

Key terms:

_____ Market

_____ Competitive market

_____ Monopoly

_____ Oligopoly

_____ Monopolistically competitive

_____ Law of demand

_____ Demand schedule

_____ Normal good

_____ Inferior good

_____ Substitutes

_____ Complements

_____ Quantity supplied

_____ Law of supply

_____ Equilibrium

_____ Equilibrium price

_____ Market surplus

Definitions:

1. A table that shows the relationship between the price of a good and the quantity demanded

2. Market with sellers offering slightly different products

3. A group of buyers and sellers of a particular good or service

4. Market with only one seller

5. A good for which, other things equal, an increase in income leads to a decrease in demand

6. A situation in which quantity supplied is greater than quantity demanded

7. A situation in which the price has reached the level where quantity supplied equals quantity demanded

8. A market in which there are many buyers and sellers so that each has a negligible impact on the market price

9. The claim that, other things equal, the quantity demanded of a good falls when the price of the good rises

10. Market with only a few sellers

11. The price that balances quantity supplied and quantity demanded

12. The amount of a good that sellers are willing and able to sell

13. The claim that, other things equal, the quantity supplied of a good rises when the price of the good rises

14. Two goods for which an increase in the price of one leads to a decrease in the demand for the other

15. A good for which, other things equal, an increase in income leads to an increase in demand

16. Two goods for which an increase in the price of one leads to an increase in the demand for the other

PROBLEMS AND SHORT-ANSWER QUESTIONS

Practice Problems

1. Suppose we have the following market supply and demand schedules for bicycles:
    a. Plot the supply curve and the demand curve for bicycles in Exhibit 1.

Price (€)	Quantity Demanded	Quantity Supplied
100	70	30
200	60	40
300	50	50
400	40	60
500	30	70
600	20	80

EXHIBIT 1

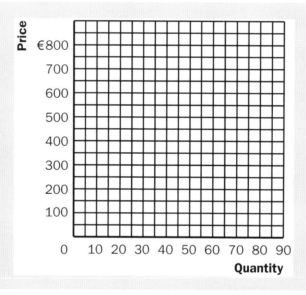

EXHIBIT 2

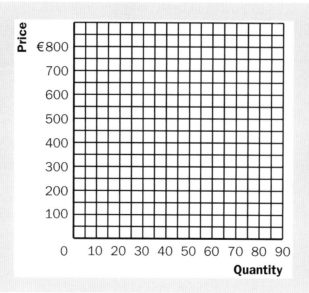

b. What is the equilibrium price of bicycles?

c. What is the equilibrium quantity of bicycles?

d. If the price of bicycles were €100, is there a surplus or a shortage? How many units of surplus or shortage are there? Will this cause the price to rise or fall?

e. If the price of bicycles were €400, is there a surplus or a shortage? How many units of surplus or shortage are there? Will this cause the price to rise or fall?

f. Suppose that the wages of bicycle workers increase and as a result the costs of producing bicycles rise. This makes bicycle manufacturing less profitable, and reduces the quantity supplied of bicycles by 20 units at each price. Plot the new supply curve and the original supply and demand curves in Exhibit 2. What is the new equilibrium price and quantity in the market for bicycles?

2. Each of the events listed below has an impact on the market for bicycles. For each event, which curve is affected (supply or demand for bicycles), what direction is it shifted, and what is the resulting impact on the equilibrium price and quantity of bicycles?

a. The price of cars increases.

b. Consumers' incomes decrease. (Assume that bicycles are a normal good.)

c. The price of steel used to make bicycle frames increases.

d. An environmental movement shifts tastes towards cycling.

e. Consumers expect the price of bicycles to fall in the future.

f. A technological advance in the manufacture of bicycles occurs.

g. The price of bicycle helmets and shoes is reduced.

3. The following questions address a market when both supply and demand shift.

a. What would happen to the equilibrium price and quantity in the bicycle market if there is an increase in both the supply and the demand for bicycles?

b. What would happen to the equilibrium price and quantity in the bicycle market if the demand for bicycles increases more than the increase in the supply of bicycles?

Short-Answer Questions

1. Outline the law of demand.

2. What are the variables that affect the amount of a good that consumers wish to buy, other than its price?

3. What is the difference between a normal good and an inferior good?

4. Outline the law of supply.

5. What are the variables that affect the amount of a good that producers wish to sell, other than its price?

6. Suppose *suppliers* of oil expect the price of oil to rise in the future. How would this affect the supply and demand for oil and the equilibrium price and quantity of oil?

7. If there is a surplus of a good, is the price above or below the equilibrium price for that good?

8. Throughout Europe, more cars were sold in 2005 than in 1995, and yet the price of an average car was higher in 2005 that in 1995. Does this invalidate the law of demand?

9. Is a market always in equilibrium when supply equals demand?

10. If consumers expect an increase in the price of a good or a service next month, will this lead to an increase in demand for the good or service this month?

SELF-TEST

True/False Questions

_____ 1. A perfectly competitive market consists of products that are all slightly different from one another.

_____ 2. An oligopolistic market has only a few sellers.

_____ 3. The law of demand states that an increase in the price of a good decreases the demand for that good.

_____ 4. If apples and oranges are substitutes, an increase in the price of apples will decrease the demand for oranges.

_____ 5. If golf clubs and golf balls are complements, an increase in the price of golf clubs will decrease the demand for golf balls.

_____ 6. The law of supply states that an increase in the price of a good increases the quantity supplied of that good.

_____ 7. When the price of a good is below the equilibrium price, it causes a surplus.

_____ 8. The market supply curve is the horizontal summation of the individual supply curves.

_____ 9. If there is a shortage of a good, then the price of that good tends to fall.

_____10. If pencils and paper are complements, an increase in the price of pencils causes the demand for paper to decrease or shift to the left.

_____11. If Coke and Pepsi are substitutes, an increase in the price of Coke will cause an increase in the equilibrium price and quantity in the market for Pepsi.

_____12. An advance in the technology employed to manufacture roller blades will result in a decrease in the equilibrium price and an increase in the equilibrium quantity in the market for roller blades.

_____13. If there is an increase in supply accompanied by a decrease in demand for coffee, then there will be an increase in both the equilibrium price and quantity in the market for coffee.

_____14. An increase in population lowers the price of food.

Multiple-Choice Questions

1. A perfectly competitive market has
    a. differentiated products on sale.
    b. at least a few sellers.
    c. many buyers and sellers.
    d. firms that set their own prices.
    e. none of the above.

2. If an increase in the price of motor cars leads to an increase in the demand for public transport, then motor cars and public transport are
    a. substitutes.
    b. complements.
    c. normal goods.
    d. inferior goods.
    e. none of the above.

3. If an increase in consumer incomes leads to a decrease in the demand for camping equipment, then camping equipment is
    a. a complementary good.

    b. a substitute good.
    c. a normal good.
    d. an inferior good.
    e. none of the above.

4. Which of the following shifts the demand for watches to the right?
    a. a decrease in the price of watches.
    b. a decrease in consumer incomes if watches are a normal good.
    c. a decrease in the price of watch batteries if watch batteries and watches are complements.
    d. an increase in the price of watches.
    e. none of the above.

5. If the price of a good is above the equilibrium price,
    a. there is a surplus and the price will rise.
    b. there is a surplus and the price will fall.
    c. there is a shortage and the price will rise.
    d. there is a shortage and the price will fall.
    e. the quantity demanded is equal to the quantity supplied and the price remains unchanged.

6. An increase (rightward shift) in the demand for a good will tend to cause
    a. an increase in the equilibrium price and quantity.
    b. a decrease in the equilibrium price and quantity.
    c. an increase in the equilibrium price and a decrease in the equilibrium quantity.
    d. a decrease in the equilibrium price and an increase in the equilibrium quantity.
    e. none of the above.

7. A decrease (leftward shift) in the supply for a good will tend to cause
    a. an increase in the equilibrium price and quantity.
    b. a decrease in the equilibrium price and quantity.
    c. an increase in the equilibrium price and a decrease in the equilibrium quantity.
    d. a decrease in the equilibrium price and an increase in the equilibrium quantity.
    e. none of the above.

8. Suppose a pest destroys much of the olive oil crop in Europe and North Africa. At the same time, suppose consumer tastes shift towards olive oil. What would we expect to happen to the equilibrium price and quantity in the market for olive oil?
    a. Price will increase; quantity is ambiguous.
    b. Price will increase; quantity will increase.
    c. Price will increase; quantity will decrease.
    d. Price will decrease; quantity is ambiguous.
    e. The impact on both price and quantity is ambiguous.

9. A normal supply curve slopes upwards to the right (varies positively with price) because
    a. producers have to limit demand at higher prices.
    b. producers take advantage of higher demand to increase profit.
    c. producers experience increasing costs as output increases.
    d. producers expect incomes to rise in the future.
    e. producers use higher prices to ration supply.

10. Suppose a technological improvement occurred in the production of potatoes. How will this impact on the market for crisps?
    a. There will be an increase in the equilibrium price and quantity of crisps.
    b. There will be a decrease in the equilibrium price and quantity of crisps.
    c. There will be a decrease in the equilibrium quantity and an increase in equilibrium price of crisps.
    d. There will be an increase in the equilibrium quantity and a decrease in equilibrium price of crisps.

ADVANCED CRITICAL THINKING

Imagine that you are watching a national news broadcast. It is reported that gale force winds are expected to sweep across the south of England destroying much of the apple crop. Your roommate says, 'If there is going to be fewer apples available, I'll bet apple prices will rise. We should buy enormous quantities of apples now and put them in storage. Later we'll be able to sell them at a big profit.'

1. If this information about the storm is publicly available so that all buyers and sellers in the apple market expect the price of apples to rise in the future, what will happen immediately to the supply and demand for apples and the equilibrium price and quantity of apples?

2. Can you 'beat the market' with public information? That is, can you use publicly available information to help you buy something cheap and quickly and sell it later at a higher price? Why or why not?

3. Suppose a friend of yours works for the Meteorological Office. She calls you and provides you with inside information about the approaching storm-information not available to the general public. Can you 'beat the market' with inside information? Why or why not?

SOLUTIONS

Terms and Definitions

_1_ Demand schedule

_2_ Monopolistically competitive

_3_ Market

_4_ Monopoly

_5_ Inferior good

_6_ Market surplus

_7_ Equilibrium

_8_ Competitive market

_9_ Law of demand

_10_ Oligopoly

_11_ Equilibrium price

_12_ Quantity supplied

_13_ Law of supply

_14_ Complements

_15_ Normal good

_16_ Substitutes

Practice Problems

1. a. See Exhibit 3.
    b. €300.
    c. 50 bicycles.
    d. Shortage, 70 − 30 = 40 units, the price will rise.
    e. Surplus, 60 − 40 = 20 units, the price will fall.
    f. See Exhibit 4. Equilibrium price = €400, equilibrium quantity = 40 bicycles.

2. a. demand, shifts right, equilibrium price and quantity rise.
    b. demand, shifts left, equilibrium price and quantity fall.
    c. supply, shifts left, equilibrium price rises, equilibrium quantity falls.
    d. demand, shifts right, equilibrium price and quantity rise.
    e. demand, shifts left, equilibrium price and quantity fall.
    f. supply, shifts right, equilibrium price falls, equilibrium quantity rise.
    g. demand, shifts right, equilibrium price and quantity rise.

3. a. equilibrium quantity will rise, equilibrium price is ambiguous.
    b. equilibrium price and quantity will rise.

EXHIBIT 3

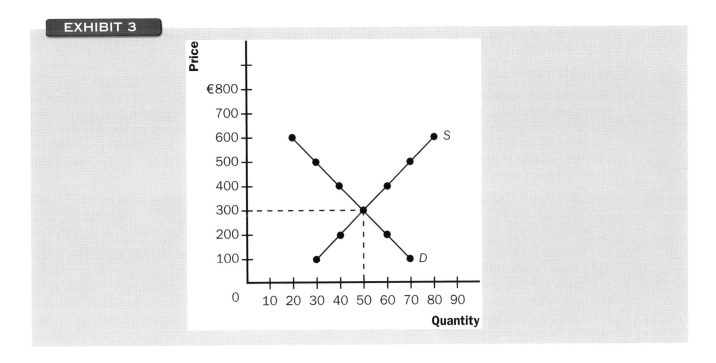

EXHIBIT 4

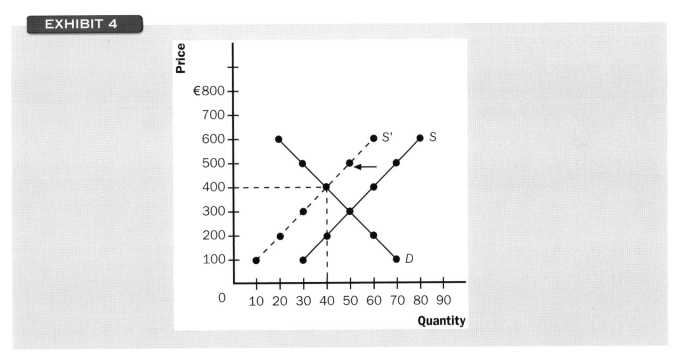

Short-Answer Questions

1. Other things equal, price and quantity demanded of a good are negatively related.

2. Income, prices of related goods, tastes, expectations, and number of buyers in the market.

3. When income rises, demand for a normal good increases or shifts right. When income rises, demand for an inferior good decreases or shifts left.

4. Other things equal, price and quantity supplied of a good are positively related.

5. The variables are input prices, technology, expectations, and number of sellers in the market.

6. The supply of oil in today's market would decrease (shift left) as sellers hold back their offerings in anticipation of greater profits if the price rises in the future. If only suppliers expect higher prices, demand would be unaffected. The equilibrium price would rise and the equilibrium quantity would fall.

7. The price must be above the equilibrium price.

8. Demand curves slope downwards with respect to price so that a rise in price will never cause an increase in quantity demanded. However, over the ten years between 1995 and 2005, incomes in Europe have risen and, as a consequence, there has been an increase in demand for cars. In other words, the demand curve for cars has moved outwards to the right and this has caused a rise in the average price of cars. Correspondingly there has been a movement along the supply curve for cars and so the equilibrium quantity traded has increased.

9. Not necessarily! The amount supplied might be brought into equality with the amount bought because output is rationed or through the operation of price controls. If there is excess demand in a market, then, by definition, the amount supplied will equal the amount bought, but the market is hardly in equilibrium!

10. Not necessarily! It is usually very difficult to bring the purchase of personal services forward. This is true of hair cuts, visits to the dentist because of toothache, and so on. However, it is also true of many other purchases. It is impossible to buy extra electricity now for consumption in the future, and social activities such as trips to the cinema or dinner with your friend run to the calendar rather than expectations of price. On the other hand, the purchase of most manufactured products can be brought forward if income or borrowing capability permit!

True/False Questions

1. F; a perfectly competitive market consists of goods offered for sale that are all the same.

2. T

3. F; the law of demand states that an increase in the price of a good decreases the *quantity demanded* of that good (a movement along the demand curve).

4. F; it will increase the demand for oranges.

5. T

6. T

7. F; it causes excess demand, that is, a shortage.

8. T

9. F; an excess demand causes the price to rise.

10. T

11. T

12. T

13. F; there will be a decrease in the equilibrium price, but the impact on the equilibrium quantity is ambiguous.

14. F; an increase in population will lead to an increase in demand for food and this shifts the demand curve for food to the right. This will lead to an increase in the equilibrium price of food.

Multiple-Choice Questions

1. c   6. a
2. a   7. c
3. d   8. a
4. c   9. c
5. b   10. d

Advanced Critical Thinking

1. Sellers reduce supply (supply shifts left) in the hope of selling apples later at a higher price and buyers increase demand (demand shifts right) in the hope of buying apples now before the price goes up. The price will immediately rise and the quantity exchanged is ambiguous.

2. No. Usually the market immediately adjusts so that the price has already moved to its new equilibrium value before the amateur speculator can make his or her purchase.

3. Yes. In this case, you can make your purchase before the market responds to the information about the storm.

ELASTICITY AND ITS APPLICATION

CHAPTER OVERVIEW

Context and Purpose

Chapter 5 is the second chapter of a three-chapter sequence that deals with supply and demand and how markets work. Chapter 4 introduced supply and demand. Chapter 5 shows how much buyers and sellers respond to changes in market conditions. Chapter 6 will address the impact of government policies on competitive markets.

The purpose of Chapter 5 is to add precision to our supply and demand model. We introduce the concept of elasticity, which measures the responsiveness of buyers and sellers to changes in economic variables such as prices and income. The concept of elasticity allows us to make quantitative observations about the impact of changes in supply and demand on equilibrium prices and quantities.

CHAPTER REVIEW

Introduction

In Chapter 4, we learned that an increase in price reduces the quantity demanded and increases the quantity supplied in a market. In this chapter, we will develop the concept of elasticity so that we can address how much the quantity demanded and the quantity supplied responds to changes in market conditions such as price.

The Elasticity of Demand

To measure the response of demand to its determinants, we use the concept of **elasticity. Price elasticity of demand** measures how much the quantity demanded responds to a change in the price of that good, computed as the percentage change in quantity demanded divided by the percentage change in price.

If the quantity demanded changes more than proportionately from a change in price, demand is *elastic*. If the quantity demanded changes less than proportionately from a change in price, demand is *inelastic*. The degree of elasticity of demand for a product is determined by the following:

- *Availability of close substitutes*: The demand for goods with close substitutes is more sensitive to changes in price and, thus, is more price elastic.

- *Necessities versus luxuries*: The demand for necessities is inelastic while the demand for luxuries tends to be more elastic. Since one cannot do without a necessity, an increase in the price has little impact on the quantity demanded. However, an increase in price will have a greater impact on the quantity demanded of a luxury.

- *Definition of the market*: The more narrowly we define the market, the more likely there are to be close substitutes and the more price elastic demand for the product.

- *Time horizon*: The longer the time period considered, the greater the availability of close substitutes and the more price elastic demand for the product.

The formula for computing the price elasticity of demand is:

$$\text{Price elasticity of demand} = \frac{\text{Percentage change in quantity demanded}}{\text{Percentage change in price}}$$

Since price elasticity of demand is always negative, it is customary to drop the negative sign.

When we compute price elasticity between any two points on a normal demand curve, we get a different answer depending on which point we choose to start and which point we choose to finish if we take the change in price and quantity as a per cent of the starting value for each. To avoid this problem, economists often employ the *midpoint method* to calculate elasticities. With this method, the percentage changes in quantity and price are calculated by dividing the change in the variable by the *average* or midpoint value of the two points on the curve, not the starting point on the curve. Thus, the formula for the price elasticity of demand using the midpoint method is:

$$\text{Price elasticity of demand} = \frac{(Q_2 - Q_1)/[(Q_2 + Q_1)/2]}{(P_2 - P_1)/[(P_2 + P_1)/2]}$$

If price elasticity of demand is greater than one, demand is elastic. If elasticity is less than one, demand is inelastic. If elasticity is equal to one, demand is said to have unit elasticity. If elasticity is zero, demand is perfectly inelastic (vertical). If elasticity is infinite, demand is perfectly elastic (horizontal).

Total revenue is the amount paid by buyers and received by sellers, computed simply as price times quantity. The elasticity of demand determines the impact of a change in price on total revenue:

- If demand is price inelastic (less than 1) an increase in price increases total revenue because the price increase is proportionately larger than the reduction in quantity demanded.

- If demand is price elastic (greater than 1) an increase in price decreases total revenue because the decrease in the quantity demanded is proportionately larger than the increase in price.

- If demand is unit price elastic (exactly equal to 1) a change in price has no impact on total revenue because the increase in price is proportionately equal to the decrease in quantity.

Along a linear demand curve, price elasticity is not constant. At higher prices and lower quantities, price elasticity is higher because a change in price causes a larger *percentage* change in quantity. When price is lower and quantity is higher, price elasticity is smaller because a change in price causes a smaller *percentage* change in quantity.

There are additional demand elasticities. The income elasticity of demand is a measure of how much the quantity demanded responds to a change in consumers' income, computed as the percentage change in quantity demanded divided by the percentage change in income or:

$$\text{Income elasticity of demand} = \frac{\text{Percentage change in quantity demanded}}{\text{Percentage change in income}}$$

For normal goods, income elasticity is positive. For *inferior goods*, income elasticity is negative. Within the group of normal goods, necessities like food have small income elasticities because the quantity demanded changes little when income changes. Luxuries have larger income elasticities.

The **cross-price elasticity of demand** is a measure of the response of the quantity demanded of one good to a change in the price of another good, computed as the percentage change in the quantity demanded of one good divided by the percentage change in the price of another good or:

$$\text{Cross-price elasticity of demand}$$
$$= \frac{\text{Percentage change in quantity demanded of good 1}}{\text{Percentage change in the price of good 2}}$$

The cross-price elasticity of demand is positive for *substitutes* and *negative* for *complements*.

The Elasticity of Supply

Price elasticity of supply measures the responsiveness of quantity supplied of a good to a change in the price of that good, computed as the percentage change in quantity supplied divided by the percentage change in price.

If the quantity supplied changes more than proportionately to a change in price, supply is *elastic*. If the quantity supplied changes less than proportionately to a change in price, supply is *inelastic*. Supply is more elastic when the sellers have greater flexibility to change the amount of a good they produce in response to a change in price. Generally, the shorter the time period considered, the less flexibility the seller has in choosing how much to produce, and the more inelastic the supply curve. Elasticity of supply is also influenced by whether products can be stored or whether they are perishable. Time is also a major determinant of elasticity of supply and over time existing producers can expand supply to a greater extent in response to a rise in price while additional firms will be encouraged to undertake production at higher prices.

The formula for computing the price elasticity of supply is:

$$\text{Price elasticity of supply} = \frac{\text{Percentage change in quantity supplied}}{\text{Percentage change in price}}$$

If price elasticity of supply is greater than one, supply is elastic. If elasticity is less than one, supply is inelastic. If elasticity is equal to one, supply is said to have unit elasticity. If elasticity is zero, supply is perfectly inelastic (vertical). If elasticity is infinite, supply is perfectly elastic (horizontal).

Price elasticity of supply may not be constant along a given supply curve. At lower quantities, a relatively small increase in price may stimulate a relatively large increase in quantity supplied because there is excess capacity in the production facility. Therefore, price elasticity will tend to be relatively large. At higher quantities, a relatively large increase in price may cause only a relatively small increase in quantity supplied because the production facility is at full capacity. Therefore, price elasticity is relatively small.

Three Applications of Supply, Demand, and Elasticity

- *The market for agricultural products*: Advances in technology have shifted the supply curve for agricultural products to the right. However, the demand for food is generally inelastic because food is inexpensive and a necessity. As a result, the rightward shift in supply has caused a reduction in the equilibrium price, but only a small increase in the equilibrium quantity. Thus, ironically, technological advances in agriculture reduce total revenue paid to farmers as a group.

- *The market for oil*: In the 1970s, the Organization of Petroleum Exporting Countries (OPEC) reduced the supply of oil in order to raise its price. In the short run, the demand for oil tends to be relatively inelastic because consumers cannot easily find substitutes. Thus, the decrease in supply raised the price more than proportionately and increased total revenue to the producers. However, in the long run consumers found substitutes and drove more fuel efficient cars causing the demand for oil to become more elastic. Producers also searched for more oil (because of the higher market price) increasing the quantity supplied and causing supply to become more elastic. As a result, while the price of oil rose a great deal in the short run, the long run effect was less significant.

- *The market for illegal drugs*: In the short run, the demand for illegal addictive drugs is relatively inelastic. As a result, drug interdiction policies that reduce the supply of drugs tend to greatly increase the price of drugs while reducing the quantity consumed very little. As a consequence, total expenditure of drug users (total revenue of drug dealers) increases. This need for additional funds by drug users may cause drug-related crimes to rise. This increase in total revenue and in crime is likely to be smaller in the long run because the demand for illegal drugs becomes more elastic as time passes. Alternatively, policies aimed at reducing the demand for drugs reduce total revenue in the drugs market and reduce drug-related crime.

Conclusion

The tools of supply and demand allow you to analyse the most important events and policies that shape the economy.

HELPFUL HINTS

1. An easy way to remember the difference between the terms elastic and inelastic is to substitute the word *sensitivity* for elasticity. For example, price elasticity of demand becomes price *sensitivity* of demand. If the quantity demanded is sensitive to a change in price, demand is elastic. If the quantity demanded is insensitive to a change in price, demand is inelastic. The same is true for the price elasticity of supply. If the quantity supplied is sensitive to a change in price, supply is elastic. If the quantity supplied is insensitive to a change in price, supply is inelastic.

2. While elasticity and slope are similar, they are not the same. Along a straight line, slope is constant. Slope is the same anywhere on the line and is measured as the change in the dependent variable divided by the change in the independent variable. However, elasticity is measured as the *percentage* change in the dependent variable divided by the *percentage* change in the independent variable. This value changes as we move along a line because a one-unit change in a variable is a larger percentage change when the initial values are small as opposed to when they are large. Slope and elasticity are therefore NOT the same.

3. The term 'elasticity' is used to describe how much the quantity stretches (or changes) in response to some economic event such as a change in price or income. This mental picture should also help you to remember how to calculate an elasticity value—in the numerator you will always find the per cent change in quantity and in the denominator you will always find the per cent change in the variable that is the source of the change in quantity.

TERMS AND DEFINITIONS

Choose a definition for each key term.

Key terms:

_____ Price elasticity of demand

_____ Total revenue

_____ Income elasticity of demand

_____ Cross-price elasticity of demand

_____ Price elasticity of supply

_____ Normal good

_____ Inferior good

Definitions:

1. A measure of how much the quantity demanded of a good responds to a change in consumers' income

2. A good characterized by a negative income elasticity

3. A measure of how much the quantity demanded of one good responds to a change in the price of another good

4. A measure of how much the quantity supplied of a good responds to a change in the price of that good

5. The amount paid by buyers and received by sellers of a good computed as $P \times Q$

6. A measure of how much the quantity demanded of a good responds to a change in the price of that good

7. A good characterized by a positive income elasticity

PROBLEMS AND SHORT-ANSWER QUESTIONS

Practice Problems

1. For each pair of goods listed below, which good would you expect to have the more elastic demand? Why?
   a. cigarettes; a trip to London over the spring break.
   b. an AIDS vaccine over the next month; an AIDS vaccine over the next five years.
   c. beer; Stella Artois.
   d. insulin; aspirin.

2. Suppose the _Daily Newspaper_ estimates that if it raises the price of its newspaper from €1.00 to €1.50 then the number of subscribers will fall from 50,000 to 40,000.
   a. What is the price elasticity of demand for the _Daily Newspaper_ when elasticity is calculated using the midpoint method?
   b. What is the advantage of using the midpoint method?
   c. If the _Daily Newspaper_'s only concern is to maximize total revenue, should it raise the price of a newspaper from €1.00 to €1.50? Why or why not?

3. The table below provides the demand schedule for hotel rooms at Small Town Hotel. Use the information provided to complete the table. Answer the following questions based on your responses in the table. Use the midpoint method to calculate the percentage changes used to generate the elasticities.

Price (€)	Quantity Demanded	Total Revenue	% Change in Price	% Change in Quantity	Elasticity
20	24	_____			
40	20	_____			
60	16	_____	_____	_____	_____
80	12	_____	_____	_____	_____
100	8	_____	_____	_____	_____
120	4	_____			

   a. Over what range of prices is the demand for hotel rooms elastic? To maximize total revenue, should Small Town Hotel raise or lower the price within this range?
   b. Over what range of prices is the demand for hotel rooms inelastic? To maximize total revenue, should Small Town Hotel raise or lower the price within this range?
   c. Over what range of prices is the demand for hotel rooms unit elastic? To maximize total revenue, should Small Town Hotel raise or lower the price within this range?

4. The demand schedule from question 3 above is reproduced below along with another demand schedule when consumer incomes have risen to €60,000 from €50,000. Use this information to answer the following questions. Use the midpoint method to calculate the percentage changes used to generate the elasticities.

Price (€)	Quantity Demanded When Income is €50,000	Quantity Demanded When Income is €60,000
20	24	34
40	20	30
60	16	26
80	12	22
100	8	18
120	4	14

   a. What is the income elasticity of demand when hotel rooms rent for €40?
   b. What is the income elasticity of demand when hotel rooms rent for €100?
   c. Why might some hotels be inferior goods while others are normal goods?

Short-Answer Questions

1. If demand is inelastic, will an increase in price raise or lower total revenue? Why?

2. If the price of a soft drink doubles from €1.00 per can to €2.00 per can and you buy the same amount, what is your price elasticity of demand for the soft drink and is it considered elastic or inelastic?

3. If the price of Pepsi increases by 1 cent and this induces you to stop buying Pepsi altogether and to switch to Coke, what is your price elasticity of demand for Pepsi and is it considered elastic or inelastic?

4. Suppose your income rises by 20 per cent and your demand for eggs falls by 10 per cent. What is the value of your income elasticity of demand for eggs? Are eggs normal or inferior goods to you?

5. Suppose a firm is operating at half capacity. Is its supply curve for output likely to be relatively elastic or relatively inelastic? Why?

6. Is the price elasticity of supply for fresh fish likely to be elastic or inelastic when measured over the time period of one day? Why?

7. Which part of a normal demand curve tends to be elastic and which part tends to be inelastic? Why?

8. Suppose that at a price of €2.00 per bushel, the quantity supplied of corn is 25 million metric tons. At a price of €3.00 per bushel, the quantity supplied is 30 million metric tons. What is the elasticity of supply for corn? Is supply elastic or inelastic?

9. Suppose that when the price of apples rises by 20 per cent, the quantity of oranges demanded rises by 6 per cent. What is the cross-price elasticity of

demand between apples and oranges? Are these two goods substitutes or complements?

10. Why is it useful for a firm to have some knowledge of the elasticities of demand for the variables over which it has some control?

11. Why is it useful for a firm to have some knowledge of the elasticities of demand for the variables over which the firm has no control?

SELF-TEST

True/False Questions

_____ 1. Any supply curve drawn through the origin has unit elasticity of supply.

_____ 2. Using the midpoint method to calculate elasticity, if an increase in the price of pencils from 10 cents to 20 cents reduces the quantity demanded from 1,000 pencils to 500 pencils, then the demand for pencils is unit price elastic.

_____ 3. The demand for tyres should be more inelastic than the demand for Goodyear brand tyres.

_____ 4. If the cross-price elasticity of demand between two goods is positive, the goods are likely to be complements.

_____ 5. If the demand for a good is price inelastic, an increase in its price will increase total revenue in that market.

_____ 6. The demand for a necessity such as insulin tends to be elastic.

_____ 7. If a demand curve is linear, the price elasticity of demand is always constant along it.

_____ 8. If the income elasticity of demand for a bus ride is negative, then a bus ride is an inferior good.

_____ 9. The supply of cars for this week is likely to be more price inelastic than the supply of cars for this year.

_____10. If the price elasticity of supply for blue jeans is 1.3, an increase in the price of blue jeans of 10 per cent would increase the quantity supplied of blue jeans by 13 per cent.

_____11. The price elasticity of supply tends to be more inelastic as the firm's production facility reaches maximum capacity.

_____12. An advance in technology that shifts the market supply curve to the right always increases total revenue received by producers.

_____13. If demand for a product increases, at any given point, price elasticity of demand for the product will increase.

Multiple-Choice Questions

1. The price elasticity of demand is defined as
   a. the percentage change in price of a good divided by the percentage change in the quantity demanded of that good.
   b. the percentage change in income divided by the percentage change in the quantity demanded.
   c. the percentage change in the quantity demanded of a good divided by the percentage change in the price of that good.
   d. the percentage change in the quantity demanded divided by the percentage change in income.

2. The demand for which of the following is likely to be the most price inelastic?
   a. airline tickets.
   b. bus tickets.
   c. taxi rides.
   d. transportation.

3. If the cross-price elasticity between two goods is negative, the two goods are likely to be
   a. luxuries.
   b. necessities.
   c. complements.
   d. substitutes.

4. If a fisherman must sell all of his daily catch before it spoils for whatever price he is offered, once the fish are caught the fisherman's price elasticity of supply for fresh fish is
   a. zero.
   b. one.
   c. infinite.
   d. unable to be determined from this information.

5. A decrease in supply (shift to the left) will increase total revenue in that market if
   a. supply is price elastic.
   b. supply is price inelastic.
   c. demand is price elastic.
   d. demand is price inelastic.

6. If an increase in the price of a good has no impact on the total revenue in that market, demand must be
   a. price inelastic.
   b. price elastic.
   c. unit price elastic.
   d. all of the above.

7. If consumers always spend 15 per cent of their income on food, then the income elasticity of demand for food is
   a. 0.15.
   b. 1.00.
   c. 1.15.
   d. 1.50.

8. Technological improvements in agriculture that shift the supply of agricultural commodities to the right tend to
   a. reduce total revenue to farmers as a whole because the demand for food is inelastic.
   b. reduce total revenue to farmers as a whole because the demand for food is elastic.
   c. increase total revenue to farmers as a whole because the demand for food is inelastic.
   d. increase total revenue to farmers as a whole because the demand for food is elastic.

9. If all other things are equal, which one of the following elasticity combinations is likely to be associated with greatest fluctuations in price?

Elasticity of demand	Elasticity of supply
a. elastic	inelastic
b. elastic	elastic
c. inelastic	elastic
d. inelastic	inelastic

ADVANCED CRITICAL THINKING

In order to reduce underage smoking, the government places an additional tax of €2 per pack on cigarettes. After one month, while the price to the consumer has increased by a relatively large amount, the quantity demanded of cigarettes has been reduced only slightly.

1. Is the demand for cigarettes over the period of one month elastic or inelastic?

2. Suppose you are in charge of pricing for a tobacco firm. The chief executive officer (CEO) of your firm suggests that the evidence received over the last month demonstrates that the cigarette industry should get together and raise the price of cigarettes further because total revenue to the tobacco industry will certainly rise. Is the CEO of your firm correct? Why?

3. As an alternative, suppose the CEO of your tobacco firm suggests that your firm should raise the price of your cigarettes independent of the other tobacco firms because the evidence clearly shows that smokers are insensitive to changes in the price of cigarettes. Is the CEO of your firm correct if it is his/her desire to maximize total revenue? Why?

SOLUTIONS

Terms and Definitions

_1_   Income elasticity of demand

_2_   Inferior good

_3_   Cross price elasticity of demand

_4_   Price elasticity of supply

_5_   Total revenue

_6_   Price elasticity of demand

_7_   Normal good

Practice Problems

1. a. a trip to London because it is a luxury while cigarettes are a necessity (to smokers).
    b. an AIDS vaccine over the next five years because there are likely to be more substitutes (alternative medications) developed over this time period and consumers' behaviour may be modified over longer time periods.
    c. Stella Artois because it is a more narrowly defined market than beer so there are more substitutes for Stella Artois than for beer.
    d. aspirin because there are many substitutes for aspirin, but few substitutes for insulin.

2. a. (10,000/45,000)/(€.50/€1.25) = 0.56.
    b. With the midpoint method, the value of the elasticity is the same whether you begin at a price of €1.00 and raise it to €1.50 or begin at a price of €1.50 and reduce it to €1.00.
    c. Yes. Since the price elasticity of demand is less than one (inelastic), an increase in price will increase total revenue. Notice that this action will also increase profit from sales of the newspaper because fewer sales implies a lower total cost of production.

3. a. €80 to €120; lower its prices.
    b. €20 to €60; raise its prices.
    c. €60 to €80; it doesn't matter. For these prices, a change in price proportionately changes the quantity demanded so total revenue is unchanged.

3.

Price (€)	Quantity Demanded	Total Revenue	% Change in Price	% Change in Quantity	Elasticity
20	24	480			
			0.67	0.18	0.27
40	20	800			
			0.40	0.22	0.55
60	16	960			
			0.29	0.29	1.00
80	12	960			
			0.22	0.40	1.82
100	8	800			
			0.18	0.67	3.72
120	4	480			

4. a. $(10/25)/(€10,000/€55,000) = 2.2$.
    b. $(10/13)/(€10,000/€55,000) = 4.2$.
    c. Most people prefer better quality accommodation and when income rises, people will substitute better quality hotels for cheaper inferior quality hotels.

Short-Answer Questions

1. It will increase total revenue because an increase in price will be accompanied by a proportionately smaller reduction in the quantity demanded when demand is inelastic.

2. Zero, therefore it is considered perfectly inelastic.

3. Infinite, therefore it is considered perfectly elastic.

4. $-0.10/0.20 = -1/2$. Eggs are inferior goods.

5. Relatively elastic because, other things equal, the firm will be able to increase production in response to even a relatively small change in price.

6. Inelastic because once the fish are caught, the quantity offered for sale is fixed and must be sold before it spoils regardless of the price.

7. The upper part tends to be elastic while the lower part tends to be inelastic. This is because on the upper part, for example, a one unit change in the price is a small percentage change while a one unit change in quantity is a large percentage change. This effect is reversed on the lower part of the demand curve.

8. Price elasticity of supply $= \dfrac{(30 - 25)/ [(25 + 30)/2]}{(3 - 2)/[(2 + 3)/2]} = 0.45$, inelastic

9. $0.06/0.20 = 0.30$, apples and oranges are substitutes because the cross-price elasticity is positive (an increase in the price of apples increases the quantity of oranges demanded).

10. By changing its output, a firm might be able to influence market price. Knowledge of elasticity of demand is very useful in these circumstances since a firm will be able to change the output and price combination so as to influence its level of profit.

11. Knowledge of income and cross price elasticities of demand might enable the firm to adjust the variables under its control so as to offset any negative consequences of changes in the variables over which it has no control. For example, knowledge of income elasticity of demand will enable the firm to make plans about future production, investment, recruitment and training in response to forecasts of income growth. Knowledge of cross price elasticity of demand will enable firms to identify the extent to which their product competes with substitutes. This will influence their marketing policies and so on.

True/False Questions

1. T; the percentage change in quantity supplied is always equal to the percentage change in price when the supply curve is drawn through the origin.

2. T

3. T

4. F; the two goods are likely to be substitutes.

5. T

6. F; the demand for necessities tends to be inelastic.

7. F; except in the limiting case ($Ed = \infty$ and 0) demand will be price elastic in its upper portion and price inelastic in its lower portion.

8. T

9. T

10. T

11. T

12. F; it will increase total revenue only if demand is price elastic.

13. F; it will result in a fall in elasticity of demand because a given change in price will lead to a smaller *percentage* change in quantity demanded.

Multiple-Choice Questions

1. c		6. c	
2. d		7. b	
3. c		8. a	
4. a		9. d	
5. d			

Advanced Critical Thinking

1. Inelastic.

2. Not necessarily. Demand tends to be more elastic over longer periods. In the case of cigarettes, some consumers will substitute toward cigars and pipes. Others may quit or never start to smoke.

3. No. While the demand for cigarettes (the market broadly defined) may be inelastic, the demand for any one brand (market narrowly defined) is likely to be much more elastic because consumers can substitute towards other lower priced brands.

⌐In this chapter you will

Examine the effects of government policies that place a ceiling on prices

Examine the effects of government policies that put a floor under prices

Consider how a tax on a good affects the price of the good and the quantity sold

Learn that taxes levied on buyers and taxes levied on sellers are equivalent

See how the burden of a tax is split between buyers and sellers

OUTCOMES

⌐You should be able to

Describe the conditions necessary for a price ceiling to be a binding constraint

Explain why a binding price floor creates a surplus

Demonstrate why a tax placed on a good generally reduces the quantity of the good sold

Demonstrate why the results are the same when a tax is placed on the buyers or sellers of a good

Show whether the buyers or sellers of a good bear the burden of the tax when demand is inelastic and supply is elastic

SUPPLY, DEMAND, AND GOVERNMENT POLICIES

CHAPTER OVERVIEW

Context and Purpose

Chapter 6 is the third chapter in a three-chapter sequence that deals with supply and demand and how markets work. Chapter 4 developed the model of supply and demand. Chapter 5 added precision to the model of supply and demand by developing the concept of elasticity—the sensitivity of the quantity supplied and quantity demanded to changes in economic conditions. Chapter 6 addresses the impact of government policies on competitive markets using the tools of supply and demand that you learned in Chapters 4 and 5.

The purpose of Chapter 6 is to consider two types of government policies—price controls and taxes. Price controls set the maximum or minimum price at which a good can be sold, while a tax creates a wedge between what the buyer pays and the seller receives. These policies can be analysed within the model of supply and demand. We will find that government policies sometimes produce unintended consequences.

CHAPTER REVIEW

Introduction

In Chapters 4 and 5, we acted as scientists because we built the model of supply and demand to describe the world as it is. In Chapter 6, we act as policy advisors because we address how government policies are used to try to improve the world. We address two policies—price controls and taxes. Sometimes these policies produce unintended consequences.

Controls on Prices

There are two types of controls on prices: price ceilings and price floors. A **price ceiling** sets a legal maximum on the price at which a good can be sold. A **price floor** sets a legal minimum on the price at which a good can be sold.

Price ceilings. Suppose the government is persuaded by buyers to set a price ceiling. If the price ceiling is set above the equilibrium price, it is *not binding*. That is, it has no impact on the market because the price can move to equilibrium without restriction. If the price ceiling is set below the equilibrium price, it is a *binding constraint* because it does not allow the market to reach equilibrium. A binding price ceiling causes the quantity demanded to exceed the quantity supplied, that is, a shortage. Since there is a shortage, methods develop to ration the small quantity supplied across a larger number of buyers. Buyers willing to wait in long lines might get the good, or sellers could discriminate selling only to their friends or family, for example. Lines are inefficient and discrimination is both inefficient and unfair. Free markets are impersonal and ration goods through prices.

Price ceilings are commonly found in the markets for oil and some financial securities. When OPEC restricted the quantity of oil in 1973, the supply of oil was reduced and the equilibrium price rose above the price ceiling so that the price ceiling became binding. This caused a shortage of oil and long lines at the petrol pumps. In response, the price ceilings were later repealed. More recently OPEC has set limits on supply and allowed demand to determine the price of a barrel of oil.

Price floors. Suppose the government is persuaded by sellers to set a price floor. If the price floor is set below the equilibrium price, it is *not binding*. That is, it has no impact on the market because the price can move to equilibrium without restriction. If the price floor is set above the equilibrium price, it is a *binding constraint* because it does not allow the market to reach equilibrium. A binding price floor causes the quantity supplied to exceed the quantity demanded, or a surplus. In order to eliminate the surplus, sellers may appeal to the biases of the buyers and sell to same-race buyers or some other defined group. Free markets are impersonal and ration goods with prices.

An important example of a price floor is the minimum wage. The minimum wage is a binding constraint in the market for young and unskilled workers. When the wage is set above the market equilibrium wage, the quantity supplied of labour exceeds the quantity demanded. The result is unemployment. Some studies suggest that an increase in the minimum wage depresses teenage employment since it increases employers' costs.

Price controls often hurt those they are trying to help—usually the poor. The minimum wage may help those who find work at the minimum wage, but harm those who become unemployed as a result of the minimum wage.

Taxes

Governments use taxes to raise revenue. A tax on a good will affect the quantity sold and both the price paid by buyers and the amount received by sellers. If the tax is collected from the buyers, demand shifts downwards by the size of the tax per unit. As a result of the decrease in demand, the quantity sold decreases, the price paid by the buyer increases, and the price received by the seller decreases. If the tax is collected from the sellers, supply shifts upwards by the size of the tax per unit. As a result of the decrease in supply, the quantity sold decreases, the price paid by the buyer increases, and the price received by the seller decreases. Therefore, a tax collected from buyers has the same effect as a tax collected from sellers. After a tax has been placed on a good, the difference between what the buyer pays and the seller receives is the tax per unit and is known as the *tax wedge*. In summary:

- A tax discourages market activity. That is, the quantity sold is reduced.

- Buyers and sellers share the burden of a tax (though not necessarily equally) because the price paid by the buyers increases while the price received by the sellers decreases.

- The effect of a tax collected from buyers is equivalent to a tax collected from sellers.

- The government cannot legislate the relative burden of the tax between buyers and sellers. The relative burden of a tax is determined by the elasticities of supply and demand in that market.

Tax incidence is the manner in which the burden of a tax is shared among participants in a market. When a tax wedge is placed between buyers and sellers, the tax burden falls more heavily on the side of the market that is less elastic. That is, the tax burden falls more heavily on the side of the market that is less willing to leave the market when price movements are unfavourable to them. For example, in the market for cigarettes which are addictive, demand is likely to be less elastic than supply. Therefore, a tax on cigarettes tends to raise the price paid by buyers more than it reduces the amount received by sellers and, as a result, the burden of a cigarette tax falls more heavily on the buyers of cigarettes. With regard to the payroll tax (National Insurance contributions), since supply of labour is less elastic than the demand for labour, most of the tax burden is born by the workers.

Conclusion

Supply and demand are useful in analysing the impact of government policies such as price controls and taxes.

HELPFUL HINTS

1. Price ceilings and price floors only matter if they impose binding constraints. Price ceilings do not automatically cause a shortage. A price ceiling only causes a shortage if the price ceiling is set below the equilibrium price. In a similar manner, a price floor only causes a surplus if the price floor is set above the equilibrium price.

2. It is useful to think of taxes as causing vertical shifts in demand and supply. Since demand reflects the maximum buyers are willing to pay for each quantity, a tax imposed on the buyers in a market reduces or shifts the demand *faced by sellers* downwards by precisely the size of the tax per unit. That is, the buyers now offer the sellers an amount that has been reduced by precisely the size of the tax per unit. Alternatively since supply reflects the minimum sellers are willing to accept for each quantity, a tax imposed on the sellers in a market reduces or shifts upwards the supply *faced by buyers* by precisely the size of the tax per unit. This is because the sellers now require an additional amount from the buyers that is precisely the size of the tax per unit.

TERMS AND DEFINITIONS

Choose a definition for each key term.

Key terms:

_____ Price ceiling

_____ Price floor

_____ Tax incidence

_____ Tax wedge

Definitions:

1. The manner in which the burden of a tax is shared among participants in a market

2. A legal maximum on the price at which a good can be sold

3. The difference between what the buyer pays and the seller receives after a tax has been imposed

4. A legal minimum on the price at which a good can be sold

PROBLEMS AND SHORT-ANSWER QUESTIONS

Practice Problems

1. Use the following supply and demand schedules for bicycles to answer the questions below.

Price (€)	Quantity demanded	Quantity supplied
300	60	30
400	55	40
500	50	50
600	45	60
700	40	70
800	35	80

a. In response to lobbying by the Green Party, the government sets a price ceiling of €700 on bicycles. What effect will this have on the market for bicycles? Why?

b. In response to lobbying by the Green Party, the government places a price ceiling of €400 on bicycles. Use the information provided above to plot the supply and demand curves for bicycles in Exhibit 1. Impose the price ceiling. What is the result of a price ceiling of €400 on bicycles?

c. Does a price ceiling of €400 on bicycles make all bicycle buyers better off? Why or why not?

d. Suppose instead, in response to lobbying by the Bicycle Manufactures Association, Congress imposes a price floor on bicycles of €700. Use the information provided above to plot the supply and demand curves for bicycles in Exhibit 2. Impose the €700 price floor. What is the result of the €700 price floor?

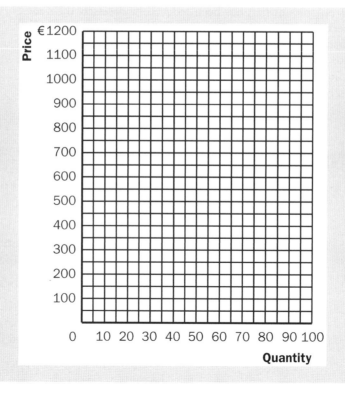

EXHIBIT 1

2. Use the following supply and demand schedules for bicycles to answer the questions below.

Price (€)	Quantity demanded	Quantity supplied
300	60	30
400	55	40
500	50	50
600	45	60
700	40	70
800	35	80

a. Plot the supply and demand curves for bicycles in Exhibit 3. On the graph, impose a tax of €300 per bicycle to be collected from the sellers. After the tax, what has happened to the price paid by the buyers, the price received by the sellers, and the quantity sold when compared to the free market equilibrium?

b. Again, plot the supply and demand curves for bicycles in Exhibit 4. On the graph, impose a tax of €300 per bicycle to be collected from the buyers. After the tax, what has happened to the price paid by the buyers, the price received by the sellers, and the quantity sold when compared to the free market equilibrium?

EXHIBIT 2

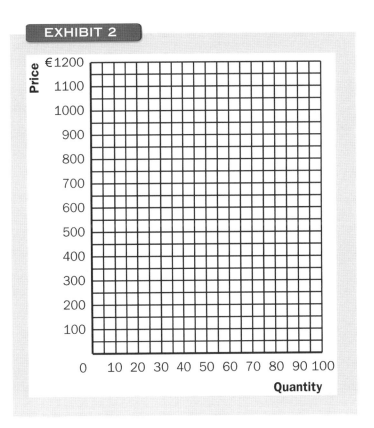

EXHIBIT 3

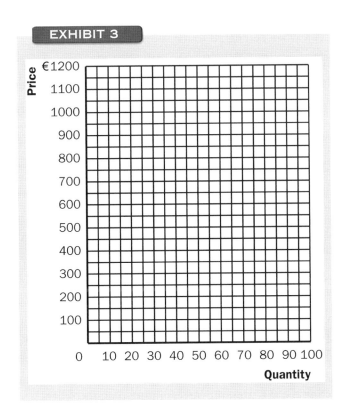

EXHIBIT 4

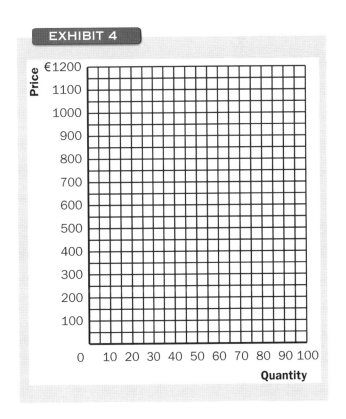

c. Compare your answers to questions (a) and (b) above. What conclusion do you draw from this comparison?

d. Who bears the greater burden of this tax, the buyers or the sellers? Why?

Short-Answer Questions

1. What are some of the problems created by a binding price ceiling?

2. Is the impact of a binding price ceiling greater in the short run or the long run? Why?

3. What is the impact on the price and quantity in a market if a price floor is set above the equilibrium price?

4. When we use the model of supply and demand to analyse a tax that is collected from the buyers, which way do we shift the demand curve? Why?

5. When we use the model of supply and demand to analyse a tax that is collected from the sellers, which way do we shift the supply curve? Why?

6. Why is a tax collected from the buyers equivalent to a tax collected from the sellers?

7. Suppose an additional tax is placed on luxury cars that are fuel inefficient according to some defined scale. Who will likely bear the greater burden of the tax, the buyers of such cars or the sellers. Why?

SELF-TEST

True/False Questions

_____ 1. A price ceiling set below the equilibrium price causes a surplus.

_____ 2. A shortage of housing caused by a binding rent control is likely to be more severe in the long run when compared to the short run.

_____ 3. The minimum wage helps all teenagers because they receive higher wages than they would otherwise.

_____ 4. A price ceiling that is not a binding constraint today could cause a shortage in the future if demand were to increase and raise the equilibrium price above the fixed price ceiling.

_____ 5. A price floor in a market always creates a surplus in that market.

_____ 6. The ultimate burden of a tax lands most heavily on the side of the market that is more elastic.

_____ 7. If medicine is a necessity, the burden of a tax on medicine will likely land more heavily on the buyers of medicine.

_____ 8. A tax collected from buyers has an equivalent impact to a same size tax collected from sellers.

_____ 9. A tax creates a tax wedge between a buyer and a seller. This causes the price paid by the buyer to rise, the price received by the seller to fall, and the quantity sold to fall.

_____10. The government can choose to place the burden of a tax on the buyers in a market by collecting the tax from the buyers rather than the sellers.

Multiple-Choice Questions

1. For a price ceiling to be a binding constraint on the market, the government must set it
    a. above the equilibrium price.
    b. below the equilibrium price.
    c. precisely at the equilibrium price.
    d. at any price because all price ceilings are binding constraints.

2. Suppose the equilibrium price for apartments is €500 per month and the government imposes rent controls of €250. Which of the following is *unlikely* to occur as a result of the rent controls?
    a. There will be a shortage of housing.
    b. Landlords may discriminate among apartment renters.
    c. Landlords may be offered bribes to rent apartments.
    d. The quality of apartments will improve.
    e. There may be long lines of buyers waiting for apartments.

3. A price floor
    a. sets a legal maximum on the price at which a good can be sold.
    b. sets a legal minimum on the price at which a good can be sold.
    c. always determines the price at which a good must be sold.
    d. is not a binding constraint if it is set above the equilibrium price.

4. Which of the following statements about a binding price ceiling is true?
    a. The surplus created by the price ceiling is greater in the short run than in the long run.
    b. The surplus created by the price ceiling is greater in the long run than in the short run.
    c. The shortage created by the price ceiling is greater in the short run than in the long run.
    d. The shortage created by the price ceiling is greater in the long run than in the short run.

5. The surplus caused by a binding price floor will be greatest if
    a. both supply and demand are elastic.
    b. both supply and demand are inelastic.
    c. supply is inelastic and demand is elastic.
    d. demand is inelastic and supply is elastic.

6. Within the supply and demand model, a tax collected from the buyers of a good shifts the
    a. demand curve upwards by the size of the tax per unit.
    b. demand curve downwards by the size of the tax per unit.
    c. supply curve upwards by the size of the tax per unit.
    d. supply curve downwards by the size of the tax per unit.

7. Within the supply and demand model, a tax collected from the sellers of a good shifts the
    a. demand curve upwards by the size of the tax per unit.
    b. demand curve downwards by the size of the tax per unit.
    c. supply curve upwards by the size of the tax per unit.
    d. supply curve downwards by the size of the tax per unit.

8. When a tax is collected from the buyers in a market,
    a. the buyers bear the burden of the tax.
    b. the sellers bear the burden of the tax.
    c. the tax burden on the buyers and sellers is the same as an equivalent tax collected from the sellers.
    d. the tax burden falls most heavily on the buyers.

9. The burden of a tax falls more heavily on the buyers in a market when
   a. demand is inelastic and supply is elastic.
   b. demand is elastic and supply is inelastic.
   c. both supply and demand are elastic.
   d. both supply and demand are inelastic.

10. Which of the following statements about the burden of a tax is correct?
    a. The tax burden generated from a tax placed on a good consumers perceive to be a necessity will fall most heavily on the sellers of the good.
    b. The tax burden falls most heavily on the side of the market (buyers or sellers) that is most willing to leave the market when price movements are unfavourable to them.
    c. The burden of a tax lands on the side of the market (buyers or sellers) from which it is collected.
    d. The distribution of the burden of a tax is determined by the relative elasticities of supply and demand and is not determined by legislation.

11. For which of the following products would the burden of a tax likely fall more heavily on the sellers?
    a. food.
    b. entertainment.
    c. clothing
    d. housing.

12. For which of the following products would the burden of a tax likely fall more heavily on the buyers?
    a. leisure travel.
    b. restaurant meals.
    c. fresh flowers.
    d. petrol.

ADVANCED CRITICAL THINKING

Suppose that the government needs to raise tax revenue. A politician suggests that the government place a tax on food because everyone must eat and, thus, a food tax would surely raise a great deal of tax revenue. However, since the poor spend a large proportion of their income on food, the tax should be collected only from the sellers of food (grocery stores) and not from the buyers of food. The politician argues that this type of tax would place the burden of the tax on corporate grocery store chains and not on poor consumers.

1. Can the government legislate that the burden of a food tax will fall only on the sellers of food? Why or why not?

2. Do you think the burden of a food tax will tend to fall on the sellers of food or the buyers of food? Why?

SOLUTIONS

Terms and Definitions

 1 Tax incidence

 2 Price ceiling

 3 Tax wedge

 4 Price floor

Practice Problems

1. a. It will have no effect. The price ceiling is not binding because the equilibrium price is €500 and the price ceiling is set at €700.
    b. See Exhibit 5. The quantity demanded rises to 55 units, the quantity supplied falls to 40 units, and there is a shortage of 15 units.
    c. No. It may make those bicycle buyers better off that actually get a bicycle. However, some buyers are unable to get a bike, must wait in line, pay a bribe, or accept a lower quality bicycle.
    d. See Exhibit 6. The quantity supplied rises to 70 units, the quantity demanded falls to 40 units, and there is a surplus of 30 units.

2. a. See Exhibit 7. The price buyers pay rises to €700, the price sellers receive falls to €400, and the quantity sold falls to 40 units.
    b. See Exhibit 8. The price buyers pay rises to €700, the price sellers receive falls to €400, and the quantity sold falls to 40 units.
    c. The impact of a tax collected from sellers is equivalent to the impact of a tax collected from buyers.
    d. The greater burden of the tax has fallen on the buyers. The free market equilibrium price was €500. After the tax, the price the buyers pay has risen €200 while the price the sellers receive has fallen €100. This is because demand is less elastic than supply.

Short-Answer Questions

1. There will be a shortage, buyers may wait in lines, sellers may be able to discriminate among buyers, the quality of the product may be reduced, and bribes may be paid to sellers.

2. The impact is greater in the long run because both supply and demand tend to be more elastic in the long run. As a result, the shortage becomes more severe in the long run.

3. There is no impact because the price can move to equilibrium without restriction. That is, the price floor is not a binding constraint.

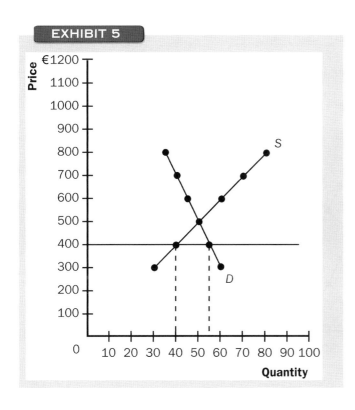

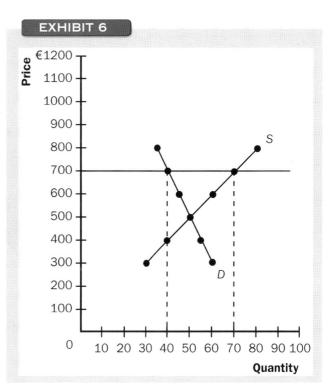

4. The demand curve is shifted downwards by the size of the tax because the amount the buyer is willing to offer the seller has been reduced precisely by the size of the tax.

5. The supply curve is shifted upwards by the size of the tax because the amount the seller requires from the buyer has been increased by precisely the size of the tax.

EXHIBIT 7

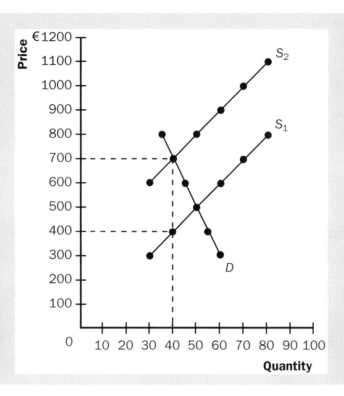

EXHIBIT 8

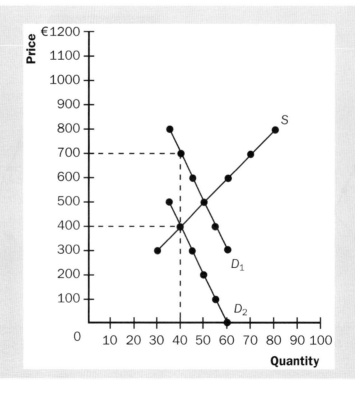

6. A tax places a wedge between what the buyer pays and the seller receives. Whether the buyer or the seller actually hands the tax to the government makes no difference whatsoever.

7. The sellers will bear the greater burden because the demand for luxuries tends to be highly elastic. That is, when the price buyers pay rises due to the tax, wealthy buyers can easily shift their purchases towards alternative items while producers cannot quickly reduce production when the price they receive falls. The burden falls on side of the market that is less elastic.

True/False Questions

1. F; it causes a shortage.

2. T

3. F; some may be helped but others become unemployed and still others quit school to earn what appears to a teenager to be a good wage.

4. T

5. F; it creates a surplus only if the floor is set above the equilibrium price.

6. F; the ultimate burden of the tax falls most heavily on the relatively less elastic side of the market.

7. T

8. T

9. T

10. F; the burden of a tax is determined by the relative elasticities of supply and demand.

Multiple-Choice Questions

1. b	5. a	9. a
2. d	6. b	10. d
3. b	7. c	11. b
4. d	8. c	12. d

Advanced Critical Thinking

1. No. The tax burden is determined by the elasticity of supply and demand. The burden of a tax falls most heavily on the side of the market that is less elastic. That is, the burden is on the side of the market least willing to leave the market when the price moves unfavourably.

2. The burden will fall most heavily on the buyers of food regardless of whether the tax is collected from the buyers or the sellers. Food is a necessity and therefore the demand for food is relatively inelastic. When the price rises due to the tax, people still must eat. Grocery chains can sell another product line when the price they receive for food falls due to the tax.

CONSUMERS, PRODUCERS, AND THE EFFICIENCY OF MARKETS

CHAPTER OVERVIEW

Context and Purpose

Chapter 7 is the first chapter in a three-chapter sequence on welfare economics and market efficiency. Chapter 7 employs the supply and demand model to develop consumer surplus and producer surplus as a measure of welfare and market efficiency. These concepts are then utilized in Chapters 8 and 9 to determine the winners and losers from taxation and restrictions on international trade.

The purpose of Chapter 7 is to develop *welfare economics*—the study of how the allocation of resources affects economic welfare. Chapters 4 through 6 employed supply and demand in a positive framework when we asked the question, 'What is the equilibrium price and quantity in a market?' We now address the normative question, 'Is the equilibrium price and quantity in a market the best possible solution to the resource allocation problem, or is it simply the price and quantity that balance supply and demand?' We will discover that under most circumstances the equilibrium price and quantity is also the one that maximizes welfare.

CHAPTER REVIEW

Introduction

In this chapter we address **welfare economics**—the study of how the allocation of resources affects economic welfare. We measure the benefits that buyers and sellers receive from taking part in a market and we discover that the equilibrium price and quantity in a market maximizes the total benefits received by buyers and sellers.

Consumer Surplus

Consumer surplus measures the benefits received by buyers from participating in a market. Each potential buyer in a market has some **willingness to pay** for a good. This willingness to pay is the maximum amount that a buyer will pay for the good. If we plot the value of the greatest willingness to pay for the first unit followed by the next greatest willingness to pay for the second unit and so on (on a price and quantity graph) we have plotted the market demand curve for the good. That is, the height of the demand curve is the marginal buyers' willingness to pay. Since some buyers value a good more than other buyers, the demand curve is downwards sloping.

Consumer surplus is a buyer's willingness to pay minus the amount the buyer actually pays. For example, if you are willing to pay €20 for a new CD by your favourite music artist and you are able to purchase it for €15, you receive consumer surplus on that CD of €5. In general, since the height of the demand curve measures the value buyers place on a good measured by the buyer's willingness to pay, *consumer surplus is the area below the demand curve and above the price.*

When the price of a good falls, consumer surplus increases for two reasons. First, existing buyers receive greater surplus because they are allowed to pay less for the quantities they were already going to purchase and second, new buyers are brought into the market because the price is now lower than their willingness to pay.

Note that since the height of the demand curve is the value buyers place on a good measured by their willingness to pay, consumer surplus measures the benefits received by buyers *as the buyers themselves perceive it.* Therefore, consumer surplus is an appropriate measure of buyers' benefits if policy-makers respect the preferences of buyers. Economists generally believe that buyers are rational and that buyer preferences should be respected except possibly in cases of drug addiction, and so on.

Producer Surplus

Producer surplus measures the benefits received by sellers from participating in a market. Each potential seller in a market has some *cost* of production. This **cost** is the value of everything a seller must give up to produce a good and it should be interpreted as the producers' opportunity cost of production—actual out-of-pocket expenses plus the value of the producers' time. The cost of production is the minimum amount a seller is willing to accept in order to produce the good. If we plot the cost of the least cost producer of the first unit, then the next least cost producer of the second unit, and so on (on a price and quantity graph), we have plotted the market supply curve for the good. That is, the height of the supply curve is the marginal sellers' cost of production. Since some sellers have a lower cost than other sellers, the supply curve is upwards sloping.

Producer surplus is the amount a seller is paid for a good minus the seller's cost. For example, if a musician can produce a CD for a cost of €10 and sell it for €15, the musician receives a producer surplus of €5 on that CD. In general, since the height of the supply curve measures the sellers' costs, *producer surplus is the area below the price and above the supply curve.*

When the price of a good rises, producer surplus increases for two reasons. First, existing sellers receive greater surplus because they receive more for the quantities they were already going to sell and second, new sellers are brought into the market because the price is now higher than their cost.

Market Efficiency

We measure economic welfare with *total surplus*—the sum of consumer and producer surplus.

$$\text{Total surplus} = (\text{value to buyers} - \text{amount paid by buyers})$$
$$+ (\text{amount received by sellers} - \text{cost to sellers})$$

$$\text{Total surplus} = \text{value to buyers} - \text{cost to sellers}.$$

Graphically, total surplus is the area below the demand curve and above the supply curve. Resource allocation is said to exhibit **efficiency** if it maximizes the total surplus received by all members of society. Free market equilibrium is efficient because it maximizes total surplus. This efficiency is demonstrated by the following observations:

- Free markets allocate output to the buyers who value it the most—those with a willingness to pay greater than or equal to the equilibrium price. Therefore consumer surplus cannot be increased by moving consumption from a current buyer to any other non-buyer.

- Free markets allocate buyers for goods to the sellers who can produce at least cost—those with a cost of production less than or equal to the equilibrium price. Therefore producer surplus cannot be increased by moving production from a current seller to any other non-seller.

- Free markets produce the quantity of goods that maximize the sum of consumer and producer surplus or total surplus. If we produce less than the equilibrium quantity, we fail to produce units where the value to buyers exceeds the cost to producers. If we produce more than the equilibrium quantity, we produce units where the cost to producers exceeds the value to buyers.

Economists generally advocate free markets because they are efficient. Since markets are efficient, many believe that government policy should be *laissez-faire* which loosely translates into 'allow them to do'. The result is that Adam Smith's 'invisible hand' of the marketplace guides buyers and sellers to an allocation of resources that maximizes total surplus. Many economists argue that free markets for human organs for transplant maximize total surplus.

In addition to efficiency, policy-makers may also be concerned with **equity**—the fairness of the distribution of welfare among the members of society. The issue of equity involves normative judgements that go beyond the realm of economics.

Conclusion: Market Efficiency and Market Failure

There are two main reasons a free market may not be efficient:

- A market may not be perfectly competitive. If individual buyers or sellers (or small groups of them) can influence the price, they have *market power* and they may use this to drive up price and reduce quantity to levels that do not maximize surplus.

- A market may generate side effects, or *externalities*, which affect people who are not participants in the market at all. These side effects, such as pollution, are not taken into account by buyers and sellers in a market so the market equilibrium may not be efficient for society as a whole.

Market power and externalities are the two main types of *market failure*—the inability of some unregulated markets to allocate resources efficiently.

HELPFUL HINTS

1. To better understand 'willingness to pay' for the buyer and 'cost' to seller, read both demand and supply backwards. That is, read both demand and supply from the quantity axis to the price or euro axis. When we read demand from quantity to price, we find that the potential buyer for the first unit has a very high willingness to pay because that buyer places a great value on the good. As we move farther out along the quantity axis, the buyers for those quantities have a somewhat lower willingness to pay and thus, the demand curve slopes negatively. When we read supply from quantity to price, we find that the

potential seller for the first unit is extremely efficient and accordingly, has a very low cost of production. As we move farther out along the quantity axis, the sellers for those quantities have somewhat higher costs and thus, the supply curve slopes upwards. At equilibrium between supply and demand, only those units are produced which generate a value to buyers that exceeds the cost to the sellers.

2. Consumer surplus exists, in part, because in a competitive market there is one price and all participants are price takers. With a single market price determined by the interactions of many buyers and sellers, individual buyers may have a willingness to pay that exceeds the price and, as a result, some buyers receive consumer surplus. However, if sellers are aware of the buyers' willingness to pay and the sellers engage in price discrimination, that is, charge each buyer their willingness to pay, there would be no consumer surplus. Each buyer would be forced to pay their individual willingness to pay. This issue will be addressed in later chapters.

TERMS AND DEFINITIONS

Choose a definition for each key term.

Key terms:

_____ Welfare economics

_____ Willingness to pay

_____ Consumer surplus

_____ Cost

_____ Producer surplus

_____ Efficiency

_____ Equity

_____ Market failure

Definitions:

1. A buyer's willingness to pay minus the amount the buyer actually pays

2. The property of a resource allocation of maximizing the total surplus received by all members of society

3. The study of how the allocation of resources affects economic welfare

4. The inability of some unregulated markets to allocate resources efficiently

5. The fairness of the distribution of welfare among the members of society

6. The amount a seller is paid for a good minus the seller's cost

7. The maximum amount that a buyer will pay for a good

8. The value of everything a seller must give up to produce a good

PROBLEMS AND SHORT-ANSWER QUESTIONS

Practice Problems

1. The following information describes the value a property owner places on having her five apartments (flats) repainted. She values the repainting of

EXHIBIT 1

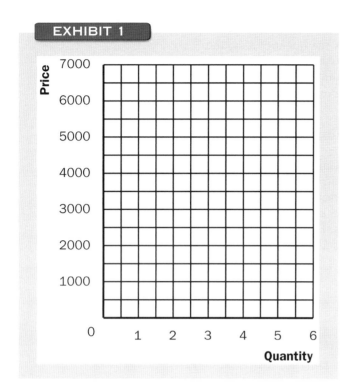

each apartment at a different amount depending on how badly it needs repainting.

Value of new paint on first apartment	€5,000
Value of new paint on second apartment	€4,000
Value of new paint on third apartment	€3,000
Value of new paint on fourth apartment	€2,000
Value of new paint on fifth apartment	€1,000

a. Plot the property owner's willingness to pay in Exhibit 1.
b. If the price to repaint her apartments is €5,000 each, how many will she repaint? What is the value of her consumer surplus?
c. Suppose the price to repaint her apartments falls to €2,000 each. How many apartments will the property owner choose to have repainted? What is the value of her consumer surplus?
d. What happened to the property owner's consumer surplus when the price of having her apartments repainted fell? Why?

2. The following information shows the costs incurred by a painter when he paints apartments. Because painting is backbreaking work, the more he paints, the higher the costs he incurs in both pain and chiropractic bills.

Cost of painting first apartment	€1,000
Cost of painting second apartment	€2,000
Cost of painting third apartment	€3,000
Cost of painting fourth apartment	€4,000
Cost of painting fifth apartment	€5,000

EXHIBIT 2

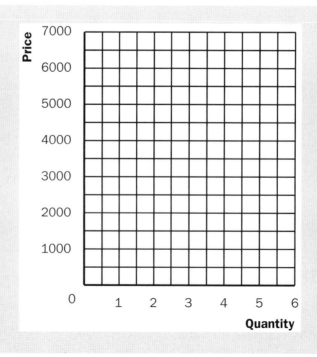

   a. Plot the painter's cost in Exhibit 2.

   b. If the price of painting apartments is €2,000 each, how many will he paint? What is the value of his producer surplus?

   c. Suppose the price to paint apartments rises to €4,000 each. How many apartments will the painter choose to repaint? What is the value of his producer surplus?

   d. What happened to the painter's producer surplus when the price to paint apartments rose? Why?

3. Use the information about willingness to pay and cost from (1) and (2) above to answer the following questions.

   a. If a benevolent social planner sets the price for painting apartments at €5,000, what is the value of consumer surplus? Producer surplus? Total surplus?

   b. If a benevolent social planner sets the price for painting apartments at €1,000, what is the value of consumer surplus? Producer surplus? Total surplus?

   c. If the price for painting apartments is allowed to move to its free market equilibrium price of €3,000, what is the value of consumer surplus, producer surplus, and total surplus in the market? How does total surplus in the free market compare to the total surplus generated by the social planner?

EXHIBIT 3

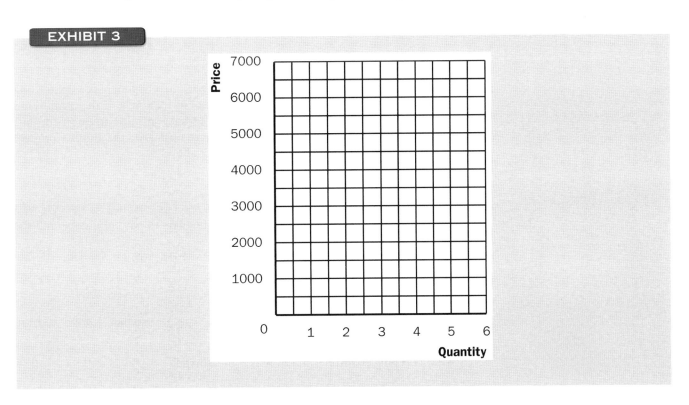

4. In Exhibit 3, plot the linear supply and demand curves for painting apartments implied by the information in questions (1) and (2) above (draw them so that they intersect the vertical axis). Show consumer and producer surplus for the free market equilibrium price and quantity. Is this allocation of resources efficient? Why?

5. Suppose the property owner in question 1 above has difficulty renting her dilapidated apartments so she increases her willingness to pay for painting by

EXHIBIT 4

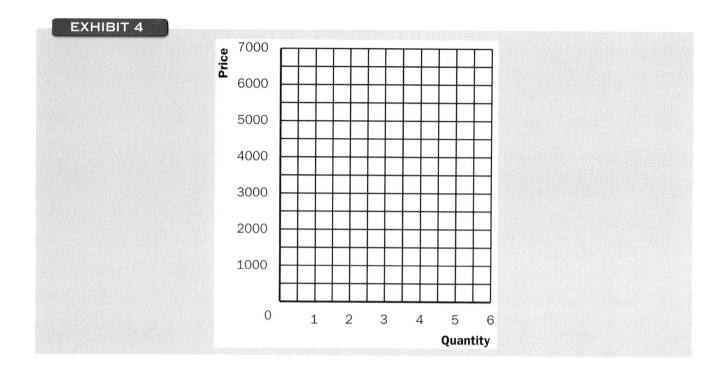

€2,000 per apartment. Plot the property owner's new willingness to pay along with the painter's cost (from question 2 above) in Exhibit 4. If the equilibrium price rises to €4,000, what is the value of consumer surplus, producer surplus, and total surplus? Show consumer and producer surplus on the graph. Compare your answer to the answer you found in 3 (c) above.

Short-Answer Questions

1. What is the relationship between buyers' willingness to pay for a good and the demand curve for that good?

2. What is consumer surplus and how is it measured?

3. What is the value of consumer surplus for the marginal buyer? Why?

4. What is the relationship between the sellers' cost to produce a good and the supply curve for that good?

5. What is producer surplus and how is it measured?

6. When the price of a good rises, what happens to producer surplus? Why?

7. Can a benevolent social planner choose a quantity that provides greater economic welfare than the equilibrium quantity generated in a competitive market? Why?

8. What does an economist mean by 'efficiency'?

9. Is a competitive market efficient? Why?

10. How does a competitive market choose which producers will produce and sell a product?

SELF-TEST

True/False Questions

_____ 1. If the demand curve in a market is stationary, consumer surplus decreases when the price in that market increases.

_____ 2. Producer surplus can be measured by the unsold inventories of suppliers in a market.

_____ 3. Cost to the seller includes the opportunity cost of the seller's time.

_____ 4. Total surplus is the seller's cost minus the buyer's willingness to pay.

_____ 5. Free markets are efficient because they allocate output to buyers who have a willingness to pay that is below the price.

_____ 6. Producer surplus is equal to the total amount producers sell multiplied by the price per unit at which it sells.

_____ 7. The major advantage of allowing free markets to allocate resources is that the outcome of the allocation is generally efficient.

_____ 8. Equilibrium in a competitive market maximizes total surplus.

_____ 9. Externalities are side effects, such as pollution, that are not taken into account by the buyers and sellers in a free market.

_____ 10. Producing more of a product always adds to total surplus.

Multiple-Choice Questions

1. If a buyer's willingness to pay for a new BMW is €40,000 and she is able to actually buy it for €38,000, her consumer surplus is
   a. €0.
   b. €2,000.
   c. €38,000.
   d. €40,000.
   e. €78,000.

2. An increase in the price of a good along a stationary demand curve
   a. increases consumer surplus.
   b. decreases consumer surplus.
   c. improves the material welfare of the buyers.
   d. improves market efficiency.

3. Suppose there are three identical vases available to be purchased. Buyer 1 is willing to pay €30 for one, buyer 2 is willing to pay €25 for one, and buyer 3 is willing to pay €20 for one. If the price is €25, how many vases will be sold and what is the value of consumer surplus in this market?
   a. One vase will be sold and consumer surplus is €30.
   b. One vase will be sold and consumer surplus is €5.
   c. Two vases will be sold and consumer surplus is €5.
   d. Three vases will be sold and consumer surplus is €0.
   e. Three vases will be sold and consumer surplus is €80.

4. Producer surplus is the area
   a. above the supply curve and below the price.
   b. below the supply curve and above the price.
   c. above the demand curve and below the price.
   d. below the demand curve and above the price.
   e. below the demand curve and above the supply curve.

5. If a benevolent social planner chooses to produce more than the equilibrium quantity of a good, then
   a. producer surplus is maximized.
   b. consumer surplus is maximized.
   c. total surplus is maximized.
   d. the value placed on the last unit of production by buyers exceeds the cost of production.
   e. the cost of production on the last unit produced exceeds the value placed on it by buyers.

6. The seller's cost of production is
   a. the seller's consumer surplus.
   b. the seller's producer surplus.
   c. the maximum amount the seller is willing to accept for a good.
   d. the minimum amount the seller is willing to accept for a good.

7. Total surplus is the area
   a. above the supply curve and below the price.
   b. below the supply curve and above the price.
   c. above the demand curve and below the price.
   d. below the demand curve and above the price.
   e. below the demand curve and above the supply curve.

8. Adam Smith's 'invisible hand' concept suggests that a competitive market outcome
   a. minimizes total externalities.
   b. maximizes total surplus.
   c. generates equality among the members of society.
   d. ensures that markets are always in equilibrium.

9. In general, if a benevolent social planner wanted to maximize the total benefits received by buyers and sellers in a market, the planner should
   a. choose a price above the market equilibrium price.
   b. choose a price below the market equilibrium price.
   c. allow the market to seek equilibrium on its own.
   d. choose any price the planner wants because the losses to the sellers (buyers) from any change in price are exactly offset by the gains to the buyers (sellers).

10. If buyers are rational and there is no market failure,
    a. free market solutions are efficient.
    b. free market solutions are equitable.
    c. free market solutions maximize revenue for producers.
    d. free market solutions ensure that producer surplus equals consumer surplus.

11. If a producer has market power (can influence the price of the product in the market) then free market solutions
    a. are equitable.
    b. are efficient.
    c. are inefficient.
    d. maximize consumer surplus.

12. If a market is efficient, then
    a. the market allocates output to the buyers that value it the most.
    b. the market allocates buyers to the sellers who can produce the good at least cost.

   c. the quantity produced in the market maximizes the sum of consumer and
      producer surplus.
   d. all of the above.

13. If a market generates a side effect or externality, then free market solutions
    a. are equitable.
    b. are efficient.
    c. are inefficient.
    d. maximize producer surplus.

14. Medical care clearly enhances peoples lives. Therefore, we should consume
    medical care until
    a. the benefit buyers place on medical care is equal to the cost of producing it.
    b. everyone has as much as they would like.
    c. buyers receive no benefit from another unit of medical care.
    d. we must cut back on the consumption of other goods.

15. Resources are allocated efficiently when
    a. the cost of producing any given level of output is minimized.
    b. it is impossible to increase the surplus of one person without reducing the
       surplus of another person by at least an equivalent amount.
    c. producer surplus is equal to consumer surplus.
    d. when income is distributed equally so that total consumer surplus can be
       maximized.

ADVANCED CRITICAL THINKING

Suppose you are having an argument with your flat mate about whether the central
government should subsidize the production of food. Your flat mate argues that
since food is something that is unambiguously good, we simply cannot have too much
of it. That is, since food is clearly good, having more of it must always improve our
economic welfare.

1. Is it true that you cannot have too much of a good thing? Conversely, is it
   possible to overproduce unambiguously good things such as food, clothing, and
   shelter? Why?

2. Using a supply and demand diagram for food, demonstrate your answer to
   question (1) above by showing the impact on economic welfare of producing
   quantities in excess of the equilibrium quantity.

SOLUTIONS

Terms and Definitions

  1   Consumer surplus

  2   Efficiency

  3   Welfare economics

  4   Market failure

  5   Equity

  6   Producer surplus

  7   Willingness to pay

  8   Cost

EXHIBIT 5

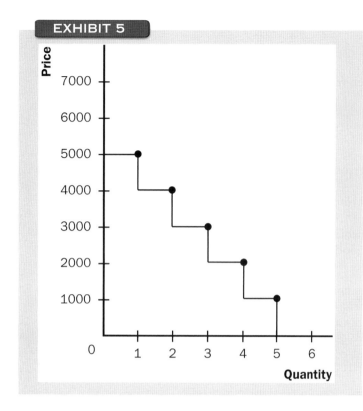

Practice Problems

1. a. See Exhibit 5.
    b. One apartment painted. €5,000 − €5,000 = 0, therefore she has no consumer surplus.
    c. Four apartments painted. (€5,000 − €2,000) + (€4,000 − €2,000) + (€3,000 − €2,000) + (€2,000 − €2,000) = €6,000 of consumer surplus.
    d. Her consumer surplus rose because she gains surplus on the unit she would have already purchased at the old price plus she gains surplus on the new units she now purchases due to the lower price.

2. a. See Exhibit 6.
    b. Two. (€2,000 − €1,000) + (€2,000 − €2,000) = €1,000 of producer surplus.
    c. Four apartments. (€4,000 − €1,000) + (€4,000 − €2,000) + (€4,000 − €3,000) + (€4,000 − €4,000) = €6,000 of producer surplus.
    d. He received greater producer surplus on the unit he would have produced anyway plus additional surplus on the units he now chooses to produce due to the increase in price.

3. a. Only one apartment will be painted so consumer surplus = (€5,000 − €5,000) = €0, producer surplus = (€5,000 − €1,000) = €4,000, and total surplus = €0 + €4,000 = €4,000.
    b. Only one apartment will be painted so consumer surplus = (€5,000 − €1,000) = €4,000, producer surplus = (€1,000 − €1,000) = €0, and total surplus = €4,000 + €0 = €4,000.
    c. Consumer surplus = (€5,000 − €3,000) + (€4,000 − €3,000) + (€3,000 − €3,000) = €3,000. Producer surplus = (€3,000 − €1,000) + (€3,000 − €2,000) + (€3,000 − €3,000) = €3,000. Total surplus = €3,000 + €3,000 = €6,000. Free market total surplus is greater than social planner total surplus.

4. See Exhibit 7. Yes, it is efficient because at a quantity that is less than the equilibrium quantity we fail to produce units that buyers value more than their cost. At a quantity above the equilibrium quantity, we produce units that cost more than the buyers value them. At equilibrium we produce all possible units that are valued in excess of what they cost, which maximizes total surplus.

5. See Exhibit 8. Consumer surplus = €3,000 + €2,000 + €1,000 + €0 = €6,000. Producer surplus = €3,000 + €2,000 + €1,000 + €0 = €6,000.

EXHIBIT 6

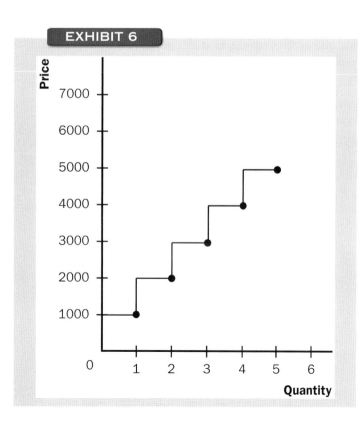

Total surplus = €6,000 + €6,000 = €12,000.

Consumer surplus, producer surplus, and total surplus have all increased.

Short-Answer Questions

1. The height of the demand curve at any quantity is the marginal buyer's willingness to pay. Therefore, a plot of buyers' willingness to pay for each quantity is a plot of the demand curve.

2. Consumer surplus is a buyer's willingness to pay minus the amount the buyer actually pays. It is measured as the area below the demand curve and above the price.

3. Zero, because the marginal buyer is the buyer who would leave the market if the price were any higher. Therefore, they are paying their willingness to pay and are receiving no surplus.

4. The height of the supply curve at any quantity is the marginal seller's cost. Therefore, a plot of the sellers' cost for each quantity is a plot of the supply curve.

5. Producer surplus is the amount a seller is paid for a good minus the seller's cost. It is measured as the area below the price and above the supply curve.

6. Producer surplus increases because existing sellers receive a greater surplus on the units they were already going to sell and new sellers enter the market because the price is now above their cost.

7. Generally, no. At any quantity below the equilibrium quantity, the market fails to produce units where the value to the buyers exceeds the cost. At any quantity above the equilibrium quantity, the market produces units where the cost exceeds the value to the buyers. However, there are exceptions. For example, when the benevolent social planner is able to account for externalities.

8. It is a resource allocation that maximizes the total surplus received by all members of society.

9. In general, yes because it maximizes the area below the demand curve and above the supply curve, or total surplus.

10. Only those producers who have costs at or below the market price will be able to produce and sell that good.

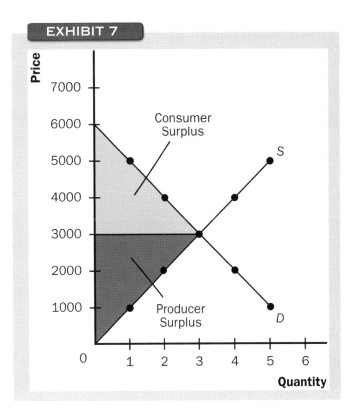

EXHIBIT 7

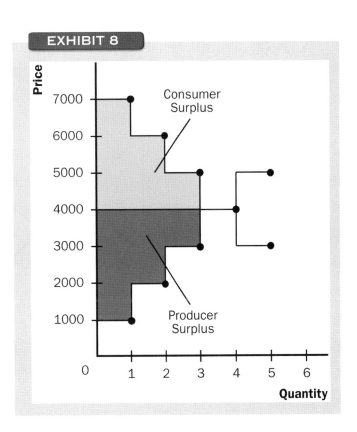

EXHIBIT 8

True/False Questions

1. T
2. F; it is a measure of the benefits of market participation to the sellers in a market.
3. T
4. F; total surplus is the buyer's willingness to pay minus the seller's cost.
5. F; free markets allocate output to buyers who have a willingness to pay that is equal to or above the price.
6. F; producer surplus is equal to the area above the supply curve and below the equilibrium price.
7. T
8. T
9. T
10. F; producing above the equilibrium quantity reduces total surplus because units are produced for which cost exceeds the value to buyers.

Multiple-Choice Questions

1. b   5. e   9. c   13. c
2. b   6. d   10. a   14. a
3. c   7. e   11. c   15. b
4. a   8. b   12. d

Advanced Critical Thinking

1. You can have too much of a good thing. Yes, any good with a positive cost and a declining willingness to pay from the consumer can be overproduced. This is because at some point of production, the cost per unit will exceed the value to the buyer and there will be a loss to total surplus associated with additional production.

2. See Exhibit 9.

EXHIBIT 9

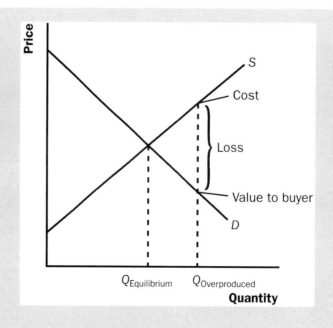

8

Examine how taxes reduce consumer and producer surplus

Learn the meaning and causes of the deadweight loss of a tax

Consider why some taxes have larger deadweight losses than others

Examine how tax revenue and deadweight loss vary with the size of a tax

Place a tax wedge in a supply and demand graph and determine the tax revenue and the levels of consumer and producer surplus

Place a tax wedge in a supply and demand graph and determine the value of the deadweight loss

Show why a given tax will generate a greater deadweight loss if supply and demand are elastic than if they are inelastic

Demonstrate why some very large taxes generate little tax revenue but a great deal of deadweight loss

APPLICATION: THE COSTS OF TAXATION

CHAPTER OVERVIEW

Context and Purpose

Chapter 8 is the second chapter in a three-chapter sequence dealing with welfare economics. In the previous section on supply and demand, Chapter 6 introduced taxes and demonstrated how a tax affects the price and quantity sold in a market. Chapter 6 also described the factors that determine how the burden of the tax is divided between the buyers and sellers in a market. Chapter 7 developed welfare economics—the study of how the allocation of resources affects economic well-being. Chapter 8 combines the lessons learned in Chapters 6 and 7 and addresses the effects of taxation on welfare. Chapter 9 will address the effects of trade restrictions on welfare.

The purpose of Chapter 8 is to apply the lessons learned about welfare economics in Chapter 7 to the issue of taxation which we addressed in Chapter 6. We will learn that the cost of a tax to buyers and sellers in a market exceeds the revenue collected by the government. We will also learn about the factors that determine the degree by which the cost of a tax exceeds the revenue collected by the government.

CHAPTER REVIEW

Introduction

Taxes raise the price buyers pay, reduce the price sellers receive, and reduce the quantity exchanged. Clearly, the welfare of the buyers and sellers is reduced and the welfare of the government is increased. However, overall welfare is reduced because the cost of a tax to buyers and sellers exceeds the revenue raised by the government.

The Deadweight Loss of Taxation

Recall from Chapter 6 that a tax places a wedge between what a buyer pays and a seller receives and reduces the quantity sold regardless of whether the tax is collected from the buyer or the seller. With regard to welfare, recall from Chapter 7 that

EXHIBIT 1

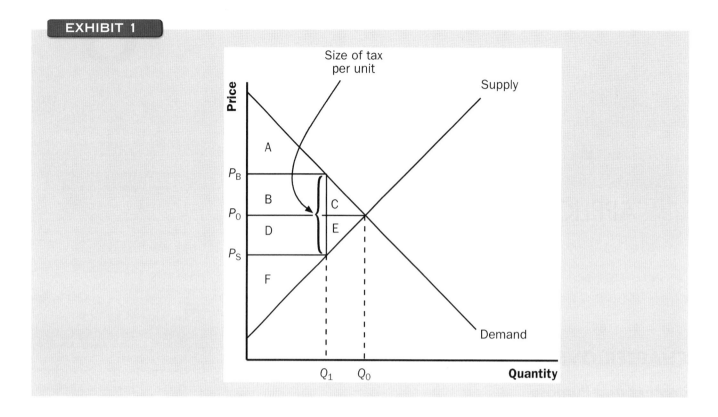

consumer surplus is the amount buyers are willing to pay minus the price they actually pay, while producer surplus is the price sellers actually receive minus their costs. The welfare or benefit to the government from a tax is the revenue it collects from the tax, which is the quantity of the good sold *after the tax is placed on the good* multiplied by the tax per unit. This benefit actually accrues to those on whom the tax revenue is spent.

Referring to Exhibit 1, without a tax the price is P_0 and the quantity is Q_0. Thus, consumer surplus is the area A + B + C and producer surplus is D + E + F. Tax revenue is zero. Total surplus is A + B + C + D + E + F.

With a tax, the price to buyers rises to P_B, the price to sellers falls to P_S, and the quantity falls to Q_1. Consumer surplus is now A, producer surplus is now F, and tax revenue is B + D. Total surplus is now A + B + D + F. Consumer surplus and producer surplus have both been reduced and tax revenue has been increased. However, consumer and producer surplus have been reduced by B + C + D + E and government revenue has been increased by only B + D. Therefore, losses to buyers and sellers from a tax exceed the revenue raised by the government. The reduction in total surplus that results from a tax is known as **deadweight loss** and is equal to C + E.

Taxes cause deadweight losses because taxes prevent buyers and sellers from realizing some of the gains from trade. That is, taxes distort incentives because taxes raise the price paid by buyers, which reduces the quantity demanded, and lowers the price received by sellers, which reduces the quantity supplied. The size of the market is reduced below its optimum and sellers fail to produce and sell goods for which the benefits to buyers exceed the costs of the producers. Deadweight loss is a loss of potential gains from trade.

The Determinants of the Deadweight Loss

The size of the deadweight loss from a tax depends on the elasticities of supply and demand. Deadweight loss from a tax is caused by the distortion in the price faced by buyers and sellers. The more sensitive buyers are to an increase in the price of the good (more elastic demand), the more they reduce their quantity demanded when a tax is placed on a good. The more sensitive sellers are to a decrease in the price of a good (more elastic supply), the more they reduce their quantity supplied when a tax is placed on a good. A greater reduction in the quantity exchanged in the market causes a greater deadweight loss. As a result, *the greater the elasticities of supply and demand, the greater the deadweight loss of a tax.*

The most important tax in Europe is the tax on labour—income taxes and social security taxes. Taxes on labour encourage workers to work fewer hours, second earners to stay home, the elderly to retire early, and the unscrupulous to enter the underground economy. The more elastic the supply of labour, the greater the deadweight loss of taxation and thus, the greater the cost of any government programme that relies on income tax revenue for funding. Economists and politicians argue about how elastic the supply of labour is and thus, how large these effects are.

Henry George, a 19th-century economist, suggested that there should be a single tax on land because the supply of land is inelastic. Therefore, the burden of the tax would be entirely on the owners of land and the tax would have no deadweight loss. Few modern economists support a single tax on land because it would not raise enough revenue and because it would need to be a tax on unimproved land (which would be difficult to implement). A tax on improved land would cause landowners to devote fewer resources towards improving their land and would create a deadweight loss.

Deadweight Loss and Tax Revenue as Taxes Vary

Deadweight loss increases as a tax increases. Indeed, deadweight loss increases at an increasing rate as a tax increases. It increases as the square of the factor of increase in the tax. For example, if a tax is doubled, the deadweight loss rises by a factor of 4. If a tax is tripled, the deadweight loss rises by a factor of 9, and so on.

Tax revenue first increases and then decreases as a tax increases. This is because, at first, an increase in a tax increases the taxes collected per unit more than it reduces the units sold. At some point, however, an ever increasing tax reduces the size of the market (the quantity sold and taxed) to such a degree that the government begins to collect a large tax on such a small quantity that tax revenue begins to fall.

The idea that a high tax rate could so shrink the market that it reduces tax revenue was expressed by Arthur Laffer in 1974. The *Laffer curve* is a diagram that shows that as the size of a tax on a good is increased, revenue first rises and then falls. The implication is that if tax rates are already extremely high, a reduction in tax rates could increase tax revenue. This is a part of what has come to be called supply-side economics. Evidence has shown that this may be true for individuals who are taxed at extremely high rates, but it is unlikely to be true for an entire economy. A possible exception is Sweden in the 1980s because its tax rates were about 80 per cent for the typical worker!

Conclusion

Taxes place a cost on market participants in two ways:

- Resources are diverted from buyers and sellers to the government.
- Taxes distort incentives so fewer goods are produced and sold than otherwise. That is, taxes cause society to lose some of the benefits of efficient markets.

HELPFUL HINTS

1. As a tax increases, it reduces the size of the market more and more. At some point, the tax is so high that it is greater than or equal to the potential surplus

even from the first unit. At that point, the tax has become a *prohibitive tax* because it eliminates the market altogether. Note that when a tax is prohibitive, the government collects no revenue at all from the tax because no units are sold. The market has reached the far side of the Laffer curve.

2. As a tax increases, the deadweight loss increases *at an increasing rate* because there are two sources to the deadweight loss and both sources are generating an increase in deadweight loss as a tax increases. First, an increase in a tax reduces the quantity exchanged and that increases deadweight loss. Second, as quantity exchanged decreases due to the tax, each successive unit that is not produced and sold *has a higher total surplus associated with it*. This further increases the deadweight loss from a tax.

TERMS AND DEFINITIONS

Choose a definition for each key term.

Key terms:

_____ Prohibitive tax

_____ Tax wedge

_____ Deadweight loss

_____ Laffer curve

Definitions:

1. The reduction in total surplus that results from a tax

2. A graph showing the relationship between the size of a tax and the tax revenue collected

3. A tax that eliminates a market for a good

4. The difference between what the buyer pays and the seller receives when a tax is placed in a market

PROBLEMS AND SHORT-ANSWER QUESTIONS

Practice Problems

1. Exhibit 2 shows the market for tyres. Suppose that a €12 road-use tax is placed on each tyre sold.
   a. In Exhibit 2, locate consumer surplus, producer surplus, tax revenue, and the deadweight loss.
   b. Why is there a deadweight loss in the market for tyres after the tax is imposed?
   c. What is the value of the tax revenue collected by the government? Why wasn't the government able to collect €12 per tyre on 60 tyres sold (the original equilibrium quantity)?
   d. What is the value of the tax revenue collected from the buyers? What is the value of the tax revenue collected from the sellers? Did the burden of the tax fall more heavily on the buyers or the sellers? Why?
   e. Suppose over time, buyers of tyres are able to substitute away from car tyres (they walk and ride bicycles). Because of this, their demand for tyres becomes more elastic. What will happen to the size of the deadweight loss in the market for tyres? Why?

2. Use Exhibit 3, which shows the market for music CDs, to answer the following questions.
   a. Complete the table on page 88. (Note: to calculate deadweight loss, the area of a triangle is 1/2 base height.)

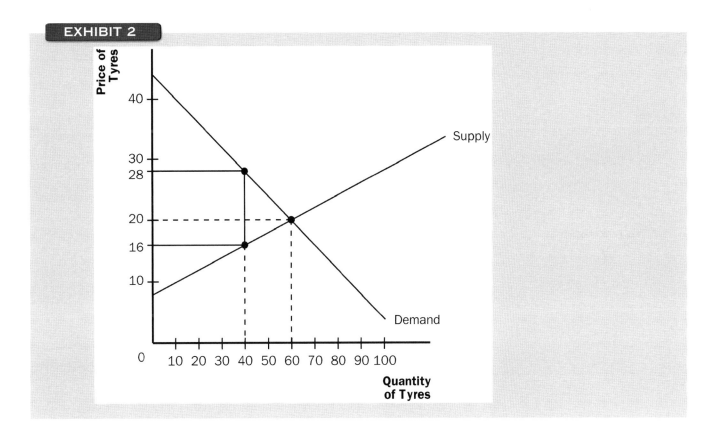

EXHIBIT 2

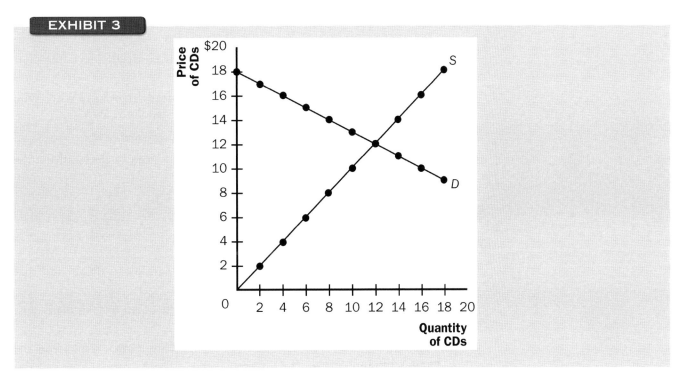

EXHIBIT 3

Tax per unit (€)	Tax revenue collected	Deadweight loss
0	_____	_____
3	_____	_____
6	_____	_____
9	_____	_____
12	_____	_____
15	_____	_____
18	_____	_____

b. As the tax is increased, what happens to the amount of tax revenue collected? Why?

c. At a tax of €18 per CD, how much tax revenue is collected? Why?

d. If the government wanted to maximize tax revenue, what tax per unit should it impose?

e. If the government wanted to maximize efficiency (total surplus) what tax per unit should it impose?

f. What happens to the deadweight loss due to the tax as the tax is increased? Why?

Short-Answer Questions

1. Why does a tax reduce consumer surplus?

2. Why does a tax reduce producer surplus?

3. Why does a tax generally produce a deadweight loss?

4. Under what conditions would a tax fail to produce a deadweight loss?

5. When a tax is placed on a good, does the government collect revenue equal to the loss in total surplus due to the tax? Why?

6. Suppose Kathryn values having her house painted at €1,000. The cost for Paul to paint her house is €700. What is the value of the total surplus or the gains from trade on this transaction? What is the size of the tax that would eliminate this trade? What is the deadweight loss from this tax? What generalization can you make from this exercise?

7. Would you expect a tax on petrol to have a greater deadweight loss in the short run or the long run? Why?

8. Would a tax on unimproved land generate a large deadweight loss? Why? Who would bear the burden of the tax, the renter or the landlord? Why?

9. As a tax on a good increases, what happens to tax revenue? Why?

10. As a tax on a good increases, what happens to the deadweight loss from the tax? Why?

SELF-TEST

True/False Questions

_____ 1. In general, a tax raises the price that buyers pay, lowers the revenue that sellers receive, and reduces the quantity sold.

_____ 2. If a tax is placed on a good and it reduces the quantity sold, there must be a deadweight loss from the tax.

_____ 3. Deadweight loss is the reduction in consumer surplus that results from the imposition of a tax.

_____ 4. When a tax is placed on a good, the revenue the government collects is exactly equal to the loss of consumer and producer surplus from the tax.

_____ 5. If Matt values having his hair cut at €20 and Elaine's cost of providing the hair cut is €10, any tax on hair cuts larger than €10 will eliminate the gains from trade and cause a €20 loss of total surplus.

_____ 6. If a tax is placed on a good in a market where supply is perfectly inelastic, there is no deadweight loss and the sellers bear the entire burden of the tax.

_____ 7. A tax on cigarettes would likely generate a larger deadweight loss than a tax on luxury boats.

_____ 8. A tax will generate a greater deadweight loss if supply and demand are inelastic.

_____ 9. A tax causes a deadweight loss because it eliminates some of the potential gains from trade.

_____10. A tax collected from buyers generates a smaller deadweight loss than a tax collected from sellers.

Multiple-Choice Questions

Use Exhibit 4 for questions 1 through10.

1. If there is no tax placed on the product in this market, consumer surplus is the area
   a. A + B + C.
   b. D + C + B.
   c. A + B + E.
   d. C + D + F.
   e. A.

2. If there is no tax placed on the product in this market, producer surplus is the area
   a. A + B + C + D.
   b. C + D + F.
   c. D.
   d. C + F.
   e. A + B + E.

3. If a tax is placed on the product in this market, consumer surplus is the area
   a. A.
   b. A + B.
   c. A + B + E.
   d. A + B + C + D.
   e. D.

4. If a tax is placed on the product in this market, producer surplus is the area
   a. A.
   b. A + B + E.
   c. C + D + F.
   d. D.
   e. A + B + C + D.

5. If a tax is placed on the product in this market, tax revenue paid by the buyers is the area
   a. A.
   b. B.

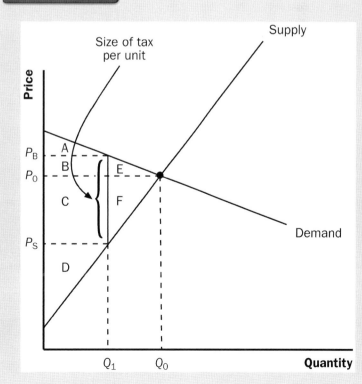

EXHIBIT 4

    c. C.
    d. B + C.
    e. B + C + E + F.

6. If a tax is placed on the product in this market, tax revenue paid by the sellers is the area
    a. A.
    b. B.
    c. C.
    d. C + F.
    e. B + C + E + F.

7. If there is no tax placed on the product in this market, total surplus is the area
    a. A + B + C + D.
    b. A + B + C + D + E + F.
    c. B + C + E + F.
    d. E + F.
    e. A + D + E + F.

8. If a tax is placed on the product in this market, total surplus is the area
    a. A + B + C + D.
    b. A + B + C + D + E + F.
    c. B + C + E + F.
    d. E + F.
    e. A + D.

9. If a tax is placed on the product in this market, deadweight loss is the area
    a. B + C.
    b. B + C + E + F.
    c. A + B + C + D.
    d. E + F.
    e. A + D.

10. Which of the following is true with regard to the burden of the tax in Exhibit 4?
    a. The buyers pay a larger portion of the tax because demand is more inelastic than supply.
    b. The buyers pay a larger portion of the tax because demand is more elastic than supply.
    c. The sellers pay a larger portion of the tax because supply is more inelastic than demand.
    d. The sellers pay a larger portion of the tax because supply is more elastic than demand.

11. Since the supply of unimproved land is relatively inelastic, a tax on unimproved land would generate
    a. a large deadweight loss and the burden of the tax would fall on the renter.
    b. a small deadweight loss and the burden of the tax would fall on the renter.
    c. a small deadweight loss and the burden of the tax would fall on the landlord.
    d. a large deadweight loss and the burden of the tax would fall on the landlord.

12. When a tax distorts incentives to buyers and sellers so that fewer goods are produced and sold than otherwise, the tax has
    a. increased efficiency.
    b. decreased equity.
    c. generated no tax revenue.
    d. caused a deadweight loss.

13. A tax on petrol is likely to
    a. cause a greater deadweight loss in the long run when compared to the short run.
    b. cause a greater deadweight loss in the short run when compared to the long run.
    c. generate a deadweight loss that is unaffected by the time period over which it is measured.
    d. none of the above.

14. Deadweight loss is greatest when
    a. both supply and demand are relatively inelastic.
    b. both supply and demand are relatively elastic.
    c. supply is elastic and demand is perfectly inelastic.
    d. demand is elastic and supply is perfectly inelastic.

ADVANCED CRITICAL THINKING

You are watching the local news report on television with your flat mate. The news reports that the central government budget has a deficit of €100 million. Since the central government currently collects exactly €100 million from its 5 per cent sales tax, your flat mate says, 'I can tell them how to fix their deficit. They should simply double the sales tax to 10 per cent. That will double their tax revenue from €100 million to €200 million and provide the needed €100 million.'

1. Is it true that doubling a tax will always double tax revenue? Why?

2. Will doubling the sales tax affect the tax revenue and the deadweight loss in all markets to the same degree? Explain.

SOLUTIONS

Terms and Definitions

__1__ Deadweight loss

__2__ Laffer Curve

__3__ Prohibitive tax

__4__ Tax wedge

Practice Problems

1. a. See Exhibit 5.
   b. The tax raises the price paid by buyers and lowers the price received by sellers causing them to reduce their quantities demanded and supplied. Therefore, they fail to produce and exchange units where the value to buyers exceeds the cost to sellers.
   c. €12 × 40 = €480. The tax distorted prices to the

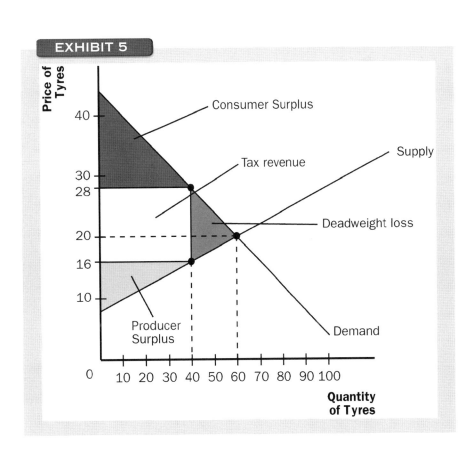

EXHIBIT 5

buyers and sellers so that the quantity supplied and demanded with the tax is reduced to 40 units from 60 units.

   d. €8 × 40 = €320 from buyers. €4 × 40 = €160 from sellers. The burden fell more heavily on the buyers because the demand for tyres was less elastic than the supply of tyres.

   e. Deadweight loss will increase because when buyers are more sensitive to an increase in price (due to the tax) they will reduce their quantity demanded even more and shrink the market more. Thus, even fewer units that are valued by buyers in excess of their cost will be sold.

2. a.

Tax per unit (€)	Tax revenue collected (€)	Deadweight loss
0	0	€0
3	30	(€3 × 2)/2 = €3
6	48	(€6 × 4)/2 = €12
9	54	(€9 × 6)/2 = €27
12	48	(€12 × 8)/2 = €48
15	30	(€15 × 10)/2 = €75
18	0	(€18 × 12)/2 = €108

   b. It first rises, then falls. At first, as the tax is increased, tax revenue rises. At some point, the tax reduces the size of the market to such a degree that the government is collecting a large tax on such a small quantity that tax revenue begins to fall.

   c. No tax revenue is collected because the tax is as large as the total surplus on the first unit. Therefore, there is no incentive to produce and consume even one unit and the entire market is eliminated.

   d. €9 per unit.

   e. €0 per unit which causes the market to return to its free market equilibrium.

   f. It increases. Indeed, it increases at an increasing rate. This is because as the tax increases it causes the quantity exchanged to be reduced on units that have an ever larger potential surplus attached to them.

Short-Answer Questions

1. Consumer surplus is what the buyer is willing to pay for a good minus what the buyer actually pays and a tax raises the price the buyer actually pays.

2. Producer surplus is the amount the seller receives for a good minus the seller's cost and a tax reduces what the seller receives for a good.

3. A tax raises the price buyers pay and lowers the price sellers receive. This price distortion reduces the quantity demanded and supplied so we fail to produce and consume units where the benefits to the buyers exceeds the cost to the sellers.

4. If either supply or demand were perfectly inelastic (insensitive to a change in price), then a tax would fail to reduce the quantity exchanged and the market would not shrink.

5. No. The tax distorts prices to buyers and sellers and causes them to reduce their quantities demanded and supplied. Taxes are collected only on the units sold after the tax is imposed. Those units that are no longer produced and sold generate no tax revenue, but those units would have added to total surplus because they were valued by buyers in excess of their cost to sellers. The reduction in total surplus is the deadweight loss.

6. Total surplus = €300. Any tax larger than €300. Deadweight loss would be €300. A tax that is greater than the potential gains from trade will eliminate trade and create a deadweight loss equal to the lost gains from trade.

7. There would be a greater deadweight loss in the long run. This is because both demand and supply tend to be more elastic in the long run as consumers and producers are able to substitute away from this market when prices move in an adverse direction. The more a market shrinks as a consequence of imposing or increasing a tax, the greater the deadweight loss.

8. No, because the supply of unimproved land is highly inelastic so the quantity supplied is not responsive to a decrease in the price received by the seller. The landlord would bear the burden of the tax for the same reason—supply of unimproved land is highly inelastic.

9. First tax revenue increases. At some point tax revenue decreases as the distortion in prices to buyers and sellers causes the market to shrink and large taxes are collected on a small number of units exchanged.

10. Deadweight loss increases continuously because as a tax increases, the distortion in prices caused by the tax causes the market to shrink continuously. Thus, we fail to produce more and more units where the benefits to buyers exceeded the costs to sellers.

True/False Questions

1. T

2. T

3. F; deadweight loss is the reduction in *total surplus* that results from a tax.

4. F; the loss of producer and consumer surplus exceeds the revenue from the tax. The difference is deadweight loss.

5. F; the loss in total surplus is the buyer's value minus the seller's cost or €20 − €10 = €10.

6. T

7. F; the more elastic the demand curve the greater the deadweight loss and the demand for cigarettes (a necessity) should be more inelastic than the demand for luxury boats (a luxury).

8. F; a tax generates a greater deadweight loss when supply and demand are more elastic.

9. T

10. F; taxes collected from the either the buyers or the sellers are equivalent. That is why economists simply use a tax wedge when analysing a tax and avoid the issue altogether.

Multiple-Choice Questions

1. c	5. b	9. d	13. a
2. b	6. c	10. c	14. b
3. a	7. b	11. c	
4. d	8. a	12. d	

Advanced Critical Thinking

1. No. Usually an increase in a tax will reduce the size of the market because the tax will increase the price to buyers causing them to reduce their quantity demanded and decrease the price to sellers causing them to reduce their quantity supplied. Therefore, when taxes double, the government collects twice as much per unit on many fewer units, so tax revenue will increase by less than double and tax revenue could, in some extreme cases, even go down.

2. No. Some markets may have extremely elastic supply and demand curves. In these markets, an increase in a tax causes market participants to leave the market and little revenue is generated from the tax increase, but deadweight loss increases a great deal. Other markets may have inelastic supply and demand curves. In these markets, an increase in a tax fails to cause market participants to leave the market and a great deal of additional tax revenue is generated with little increase in deadweight loss.

⌐In this chapter you will

Consider what determines whether a country imports or exports a good

Examine who wins and who loses from international trade

Learn that the gains to winners from international trade exceed the losses to losers

Analyse the welfare effects of tariffs and import quotas

Examine the arguments people use to advocate trade restrictions

OUTCOMES

⌐You should be able to

Determine whether a country imports or exports a good if the world price is grater than the before-trade domestic price

Show that the consumer wins and the producer loses when a country imports a good

Use consumer and producer surplus to show that the gains to the consumer exceed the losses to the producer when a country imports a good

Show the deadweight loss associated with a tariff or a quota

Defeat the arguments made in support of trade restrictions

APPLICATION: INTERNATIONAL TRADE

CHAPTER OVERVIEW

Context and Purpose

Chapter 9 is the third chapter in a three-chapter sequence dealing with welfare economics. Chapter 7 introduced welfare economics—the study of how the allocation of resources affects economic welfare. Chapter 8 applied the lessons of welfare economics to taxation. Chapter 9 applies the tools of welfare economics from Chapter 7 to the study of international trade, a topic that was first introduced in Chapter 3.

The purpose of Chapter 9 is to use our knowledge of welfare economics to address the gains from trade more precisely than we did in Chapter 3 when we studied comparative advantage and the gains from trade. We will develop the conditions that determine whether a country imports or exports a good and discover who wins and who loses when a country imports or exports a good. We will find that when free trade is allowed, the gains of the winners exceed the losses of the losers. Since there are gains from trade, we will see that restrictions on free trade reduce the gains from trade and cause deadweight losses similar to those generated by a tax.

CHAPTER REVIEW

Introduction

This chapter employs welfare economics to address the following questions:

- How does international trade affect economic welfare?

- Who gains and who loses from free international trade?

- How do the gains from trade compare to the losses from trade?

The Determinants of Trade

In the absence of international trade, a market generates a domestic price that equates the domestic quantity supplied and domestic quantity demanded in that market. The **world price** is the price of the good that prevails in the world market for that good. Prices represent opportunity costs. Therefore, comparing the world price and the domestic price of a good before trade indicates whether a country has the lower opportunity cost of production and thus, a comparative advantage in the production of a good, or if other countries have a comparative advantage in the production of the good.

- If the world price is above the domestic price for a good, the country has a comparative advantage in the production of that good and that good should be exported if trade is allowed.

- If the world price is below the domestic price for a good, foreign countries have a comparative advantage in the production of that good and that good should be imported if trade is allowed.

The Winners and Losers from Trade

Assume that the country being analysed is a small country and is therefore a *price taker* on world markets. This means that the country takes the world price as given and cannot influence the world price.

Exhibit 1 depicts a situation where the world price is higher than the before-trade domestic price. This country has a comparative advantage in the production of this good. If free trade is allowed, the domestic price will rise to the world price and it will export the difference between the domestic quantity supplied and the domestic quantity demanded.

With regard to gains and losses to an exporting country from trade, before-trade consumer surplus was A + B and producer surplus was C so total surplus was A + B + C. After trade, consumer surplus is A and producer surplus is B + C + D (the area below the price and above the supply curve). Total surplus is now A + B + C + D for a gain of area D. This analysis generates two conclusions:

- When a country allows trade and becomes an exporter of a good, domestic producers are better off and domestic consumers are worse off.

- Trade increases the economic welfare of a nation because the gains of the winners exceed the losses of the losers.

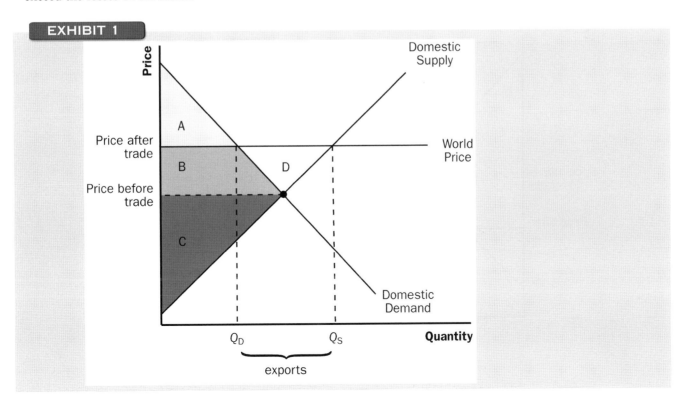

EXHIBIT 1

Exhibit 2 depicts a situation where the world price is lower than the before-trade domestic price. Other countries have a comparative advantage in the production of this good. If free trade is allowed, the domestic price will fall to the world price and it will import the difference between the domestic quantity supplied and the domestic quantity demanded.

With regard to gains and losses to an importing country from trade, before-trade consumer surplus was A and producer surplus was B + C, so total surplus was A + B + C. After trade, consumer surplus is A + B + D (the area below the demand curve and above the price) and producer surplus is C. Total surplus is now A + B + C + D for a gain of area D. This analysis generates two conclusions:

• When a country allows trade and becomes an importer of a good, domestic consumers are better off and domestic producers are worse off.

• Trade increases the economic welfare of a nation because the gains of the winners exceed the losses of the losers.

Trade can make everyone better off if the winners compensate the losers. Compensation is rarely paid so the losers lobby for trade restrictions, such as tariffs and import quotas.

Tariffs and import quotas restrict international trade. A **tariff** is a tax on goods produced abroad and sold domestically. Therefore, a tariff is placed on a good only if the country is an importer of that good. A tariff raises the price of the good, reduces the domestic quantity demanded, increases the domestic quantity supplied and thus, reduces the quantity of imports. A tariff moves the market closer to the no-trade equilibrium.

A tariff increases producer surplus, increases government revenue, but reduces consumer surplus by a greater amount than the increase in producer surplus and government revenue. Therefore, a tariff creates a deadweight loss because total surplus is reduced. The deadweight loss comes from two sources. The increase in the price due to the tariff causes the production of units that cost more to produce than the world price (overproduction) and causes consumers to fail to consume units where the value to the consumer is greater than world price (under consumption).

EXHIBIT 2

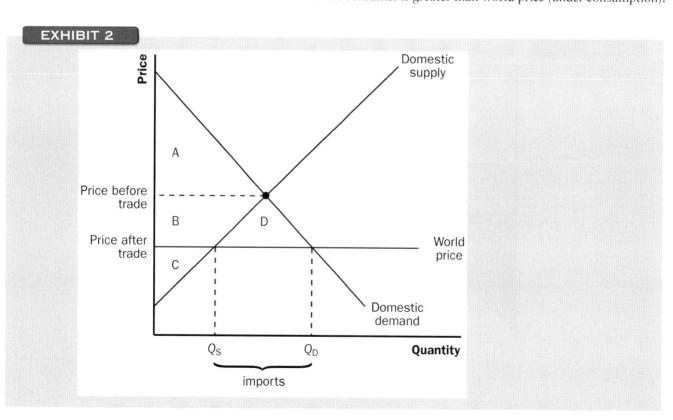

An **import quota** sets a limit on the quantity of a good that can be produced abroad and sold domestically. To accomplish this, a government can distribute a limited number of import licenses. An import quota shifts the portion of the domestic supply curve above the world price to the right by the size of the quota. An import quota raises the price of the good, reduces the domestic quantity demanded, increases the domestic quantity supplied, and thus reduces the quantity of imports. It moves the market closer to the no-trade equilibrium.

An import quota increases producer surplus, increases license holder surplus, but reduces consumer surplus by a greater amount than the increase in producer and license holder surplus. Therefore, an import quota also creates a deadweight loss in a manner similar to a tariff.

Note that the results of a tariff and an import quota are nearly the same. If the government sells the import licenses, it will collect revenue equal to the tariff revenue and a tariff and a quota become identical. If quotas are 'voluntary' in the sense that they are imposed by the exporting country, the revenue from the quota accrues to the foreign firms or governments.

Tariffs and import quotas cause deadweight losses. Therefore, if economic efficiency is a policy goal, countries should allow free trade and avoid using tariffs and import quotas.

Free trade offers benefits beyond efficiency. Free trade increases variety for consumers, allows firms to take advantage of economies of scale, makes markets more competitive, and facilitates the spread of technology.

The Arguments for Restricting Trade

Opponents of free trade (often producers hurt by free trade) offer the following arguments in support of trade restrictions:

The jobs argument. Opponents of free trade argue that trade destroys domestic jobs. However, while free trade does destroy inefficient jobs in the importing sector, it creates more efficient jobs in the export sector – industries where the country has a comparative advantage. This is always true because each country has a comparative advantage in the production of something.

The national-security argument. Some industries argue that their product is vital for national security so it should be protected from international competition. This is really a political argument and one on which economists have no professional opinion.

The infant industry argument. New industries argue that they need temporary protection from international competition until they become mature enough to compete. However, there is a problem choosing which new industries to protect and, once protected, temporary protection often becomes permanent. In addition, industries truly expected to be competitive in the future don't need protection because the owners will accept short-term losses.

The unfair competition argument. Opponents of free trade argue that other countries provide their industries with unfair advantages such as subsidies, tax breaks, and lower environmental restrictions. However, the gains to consumers in the importing country will exceed the losses to the producers in that country, and the country will gain when importing subsidized production.

The protection as a bargaining chip argument. Opponents of free trade argue that the threat of trade restrictions may result in other countries lowering their trade restrictions. Here again this is a political argument, but it is worth noting that if it does not work the country must either back down or reduce trade—neither of which is desirable.

When countries choose to reduce trade restrictions, they can take a *unilateral* approach and remove trade restrictions on their own. Alternatively, they can take a *multilateral* approach and reduce trade restrictions along with other countries. Examples of the multilateral approach are NAFTA and GATT. The rules of GATT are enforced by the WTO. The multilateral approach has advantages in that it provides freer overall trade because many countries do it together and thus it is sometimes more easily accomplished politically. However, it may fail if negotiations between countries break down. Many economists suggest a unilateral approach because there will be gains to the domestic economy and this will cause other countries to emulate it.

Globalization is blamed by the uninformed for low wages and poor working conditions in less-developed countries. However, economists argue that low wages in poor countries are due to such things as low productivity. Attempts to increase wages in poor countries by restricting trade causes workers in poor countries to lose their jobs and this makes the poor even poorer.

Conclusion

Economists overwhelmingly support free trade. Free trade between nation-states within the EU improves welfare by allowing each country to specialize in the production of goods for which they have a comparative advantage.

HELPFUL HINTS

1. Countries that restrict trade usually restrict imports rather than exports. This is because producers lose from imports and gain from exports and producers are better organized to lobby the government to protect their interests. For example, when a country imports a product, consumers win and producers lose. Consumers are less likely to be able to organize and lobby the government than the affected producers so imports may be restricted. When a country exports a product, producers win and consumers lose. But again, consumers are less likely to organize and lobby the government to restrict exports, so exports are rarely restricted.

2. The overwhelming majority of economists find no sound *economic* arguments against free trade. The only argument against free trade that may not be defeated on economic grounds is the 'national-security argument'. This is because it is the only argument against free trade that is not based on economics, but rather is based on other strategic objectives.

3. A *prohibitive* tariff or import quota is one that is so restrictive that it returns the market to its original no-trade equilibrium. This occurs if the tariff is greater than or equal to the difference between the world price and the no-trade domestic price, or if the import quota is set at zero.

TERMS AND DEFINITIONS

Choose a definition for each key term.

Key terms:

_____ World price

_____ Price takers

_____ Tariff

_____ Import quota

Definitions:

1. A limit on the quantity of a good that can be produced abroad and sold domestically

2. Market participants that cannot influence the price so they view the price as given

3. The price of a good that prevails in the world market for that good

4. A tax on goods produced abroad and sold domestically

PROBLEMS AND SHORT-ANSWER QUESTIONS

Practice Problems

1. Use Exhibit 3 to answer the following questions.
   a. If trade is not allowed, what is the equilibrium price and quantity in this market?
   b. If trade is allowed, will this country import or export this commodity? Why?
   c. If trade is allowed, what is the price at which the good is sold, the domestic quantity supplied and demanded, and the quantity imported or exported?
   d. What area corresponds to consumer surplus if no trade is allowed?
   e. What area corresponds to consumer surplus if trade is allowed?
   f. What area corresponds to producer surplus if no trade is allowed?
   g. What area corresponds to producer surplus if trade is allowed?
   h. If free trade is allowed, who gains and who loses, the consumers or the producers, and what area corresponds to their gain or loss?
   i. What area corresponds to the gains from trade?

2. Use Exhibit 4 to answer the following questions.
   a. If trade is not allowed, what is the equilibrium price and quantity in this market?
   b. If trade is allowed, will this country import or export this commodity? Why?
   c. If trade is allowed, what is the price at which the good is sold, the domestic quantity supplied and demanded, and the quantity imported or exported?
   d. What area corresponds to consumer surplus if no trade is allowed?
   e. What area corresponds to consumer surplus if trade is allowed?
   f. What area corresponds to producer surplus if no trade is allowed?
   g. What area corresponds to producer surplus if trade is allowed?
   h. If free trade is allowed, who gains and who loses, the consumers or the producers, and what area corresponds to their gain or loss?
   i. What area corresponds to the gains from trade?

3. Use Exhibit 5 to answer the following questions.
   a. If free trade is allowed, what is the domestic quantity supplied, domestic quantity demanded, and the quantity imported?

EXHIBIT 3

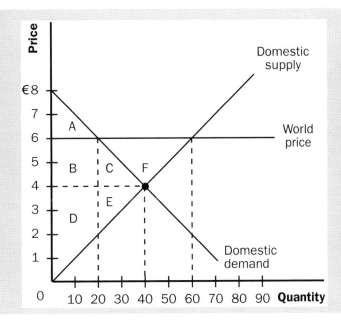

b. If a €1 tariff is placed on this good, what is the domestic quantity supplied, domestic quantity demanded, and the quantity imported?

c. What area corresponds to consumer and producer surplus before the tariff is applied?

d. What area corresponds to consumer surplus, producer surplus, and government revenue after the tariff is applied?

e. What area corresponds to the deadweight loss associated with the tariff?

f. Describe in words the sources of the deadweight loss from a tariff.

g. What is the size of the import quota that would generate results most similar to this €1 tariff?

h. What is the size of the tariff that would eliminate trade altogether (i.e. that would return the market to its no-trade domestic solution)?

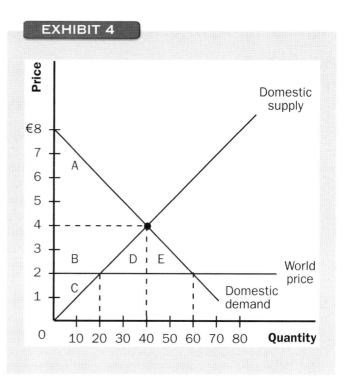

EXHIBIT 4

Short-Answer Questions

1. If the world price for a good is above a country's before-trade domestic price, will this country import or export this good? Why?

2. If residents of a country are allowed to import a good the price of which is lower on the world market, who gains and who loses when compared to the before-trade equilibrium, the producers or the consumers? Why?

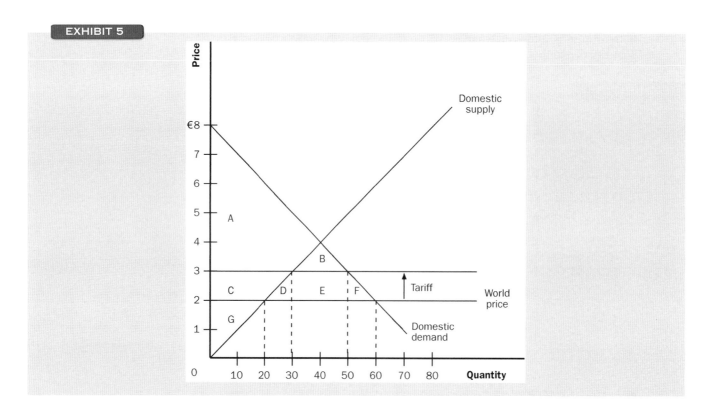

EXHIBIT 5

3. Describe in words the source of the gains from trade (the additional total surplus) received by an exporting country.

4. Describe in words the source of the gains from trade (the additional total surplus) received by an importing country.

5. Describe in words the source of the deadweight loss from restricting trade.

6. For every tariff there is an import quota that will generate a similar result. What are the short-comings of using an import quota to restrict trade versus using a tariff?

7. What arguments are made to support trade restrictions?

8. If tariffs and quotas reduce total surplus and therefore total economic welfare, why do governments impose them?

9. Give arguments in favour of unilateral and multilateral approaches to the removal of trade restrictions.

SELF-TEST

True/False Questions

_____ 1. If the world price for a good exceeds a country's before-trade domestic price for that good, the country should import that good.

_____ 2. If free trade is allowed and a country imports wheat, domestic buyers of bread are better off and domestic farmers are worse off when compared to the before-trade domestic equilibrium.

_____ 3. If free trade is allowed and a country exports a good, domestic producers of the good are worse off and domestic consumers of the good are better off when compared to the before-trade domestic equilibrium.

_____ 4. If free trade is allowed and a country exports a good, the gains of domestic producers exceed the losses of domestic consumers and total surplus rises.

_____ 5. Trade makes everyone better off.

_____ 6. Tariffs tend to benefit consumers.

_____ 7. A tariff raises the price of a good, reduces the domestic quantity demanded, increases the domestic quantity supplied, and increases the quantity imported.

_____ 8. An import quota that restricts imports to the same degree as a tariff raises more government revenue than the equivalent tariff.

_____ 9. If a foreign country subsidizes its export industries, its tax payers are paying to improve the welfare of consumers in the importing countries.

_____10. Tariffs and quotas cause deadweight losses because they raise the price of the imported good and cause overproduction and under consumption of the good in the importing country.

Multiple-Choice Questions

1. If the world price for a good exceeds the before-trade domestic price for a good, then that country must have
   a. an absolute advantage in the production of the good.

b. an absolute disadvantage in the production of the good.

c. a comparative advantage in the production of the good.

d. a comparative disadvantage in the production of the good.

2. When a country allows trade and exports a good,

a. domestic consumers are better off, domestic producers are worse off, and the nation is worse off because the losses of the losers exceed the gains of the winners.

b. domestic consumers are better off, domestic producers are worse off, and the nation is better off because the gains of the winners exceed the losses of the losers.

c. domestic producers are better off, domestic consumers are worse off, and the nation is worse off because the losses of the losers exceed the gains of the winners.

d. domestic producers are better off, domestic consumers are worse off, and the nation is better off because the gains of the winners exceed the losses of the losers.

Use Exhibit 6 to answer questions 3 through 8.

3. If free trade is allowed, consumer surplus is the area

a. A.

b. A + B.

c. A + B + C.

d. A + B + C + D + E + F.

e. A + B + C + D + E + F + G.

EXHIBIT 6

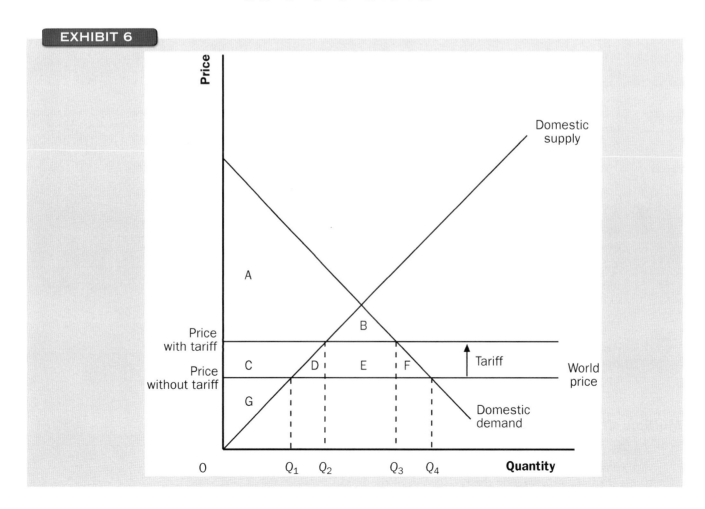

4. If a tariff is placed on this good, consumer surplus is the area
   a. A.
   b. A + B.
   c. A + B + C.
   d. A + B + C + D + E + F.
   e. A + B + C + D + E + F + G.

5. Government revenue from the tariff is the area
   a. C + D + E + F.
   b. D + E + F.
   c. D + F.
   d. G.
   e. E.

6. If a tariff is placed on this good, producer surplus is the area
   a. G.
   b. G + C.
   c. G + C + D + E + F.
   d. G + C + D + E + F + B.
   e. G + C + E.

7. The deadweight loss from the tariff is the area
   a. B + D + E + F.
   b. B.
   c. D + E + F.
   d. D + F.
   e. E.

8. What is the size of the import quota that would have the same impact on trade as the tariff?
   a. Q_2-Q_1.
   b. Q_3-Q_2.
   c. Q_4-Q_3.
   d. Q_4-Q_1.
   e. none of the above.

9. Which of the following statements about a tariff is true?
   a. A tariff increases producer surplus, decreases consumer surplus, increases revenue to the government, and reduces total surplus.
   b. A tariff increases consumer surplus, decreases producer surplus, increases revenue to the government, and reduces total surplus.
   c. A tariff increases producer surplus, decreases consumer surplus, increases revenue to the government, and increases total surplus.
   d. A tariff increases consumer surplus, decreases producer surplus, increases revenue to the government, and increases total surplus.

10. Which of the following statements about import quotas is true?
    a. Import quotas are preferred to tariffs because they raise more revenue for the imposing government.
    b. Voluntary quotas established by the exporting country reduce the importing country's deadweight loss from the trade restriction.
    c. For every tariff, there is an import quota that could have generated a similar result.
    d. An import quota reduces the price to the domestic consumers.

11. Which of the following arguments against free trade cannot be defeated on economic grounds?
    a. Protecting an infant industry.
    b. Destruction of domestic jobs.

c. Unfair competition from subsidized foreign producers.
d. Countering a threat to national security.

12. Which one of the following is likely to result from the imposition of a tariff?
a. A reduction in total surplus.
b. An increase in consumer surplus.
c. An increase in total economic welfare.
d. A reduction in deadweight loss.

ADVANCED CRITICAL THINKING

You are watching the nightly news. A political candidate being interviewed says, 'I'm for free trade, but it must be fair trade. If our foreign competitors will not raise their environmental regulations, reduce subsidies to their export industries, and lower tariffs on their imports of our goods, we should retaliate with tariffs and import quotas on their goods to show them that we won't be played for fools!'

1. If a foreign country artificially lowers the cost of production for its producers with lax environmental regulations and direct subsidies and then exports the products to us, who gains and who loses in our country, producers or consumers?

2. Continuing from question 1 above, does our country gain or lose overall? Why?

3. If a foreign country subsidizes the production of a good exported to Europe, who bears the burden of this policy action?

4. What happens to our overall economic welfare if we restrict trade with a country that subsidizes its export industries? Explain.

5. Is there any difference in the analysis of imports sold at the cost of production or sold at a subsidized price? Why?

6. Is it a good policy to threaten trade restrictions in the hope that foreign governments will reduce their trade restrictions? Explain.

SOLUTIONS

Terms and Definitions

  1   Import quota   3   World price
  2   Price takers   4   Tariff

Practice Problems

1. a. Price = €4, quantity = 40 units.
b. Export because the world price is above the domestic price which implies that this country has a comparative advantage in the production of this good.
c. Price = €6, quantity supplied = 60 units, quantity demanded = 20 units, quantity exported = 40 units.
d. A + B + C.
e. A.
f. D + E.
g. B + C + D + E + F.
h. Consumers lose B + C, producers gain B + C + F.
i. F.

2. a. Price = €4, quantity = 40 units.
   b. Import because the world price is below the domestic price, which implies that other countries have a comparative advantage in the production of this good.
   c. Price = €2, quantity supplied = 20 units, quantity demanded = 60 units, quantity imported = 40 units.
   d. A.
   e. A + B + D + E.
   f. B + C.
   g. C.
   h. Consumers gain B + D + E, producers lose B.
   i. D + E.

3. a. Quantity supplied = 20 units, quantity demanded = 60 units, quantity imported = 40 units.
   b. Quantity supplied = 30 units, quantity demanded = 50 units, quantity imported = 20 units.
   c. Consumer surplus = A + B + C + D + E + F, producer surplus = G.
   d. Consumer surplus = A + B, producer surplus = C + G, government revenue = E.
   e. D + F.
   f. First, the rise in the price due to the tariff causes *overproduction* because units are produced that cost more than the world price. Second, the rise in price causes *under consumption* because consumers fail to consume units where the value to consumers is greater than the world price.
   g. Import quota of 20 units—the same number of units imported with the €1 tariff.
   h. A €2 tariff would raise the price to €4 (the no-trade domestic price) and eliminate trade.

Short-Answer Questions

1. Export, because the domestic opportunity cost of production is lower than the opportunity cost of production in other countries.

2. Consumers gain and producers lose because, if trade is allowed, the domestic price falls to the world price.

3. The gains are the additional value placed on the exported units by buyers in the rest of the world in excess of the domestic cost of production.

4. The gains are the additional value placed by domestic buyers on the imported units in excess of their cost of production in the rest of the world.

5. The rise in price from restricting trade causes overproduction of the good (production of units that cost more than the world price) and under consumption of the good (failure to consume units valued more than the world price).

6. The revenue from an import quota will accrue to the license holders or foreign firms and governments unless the domestic government sells the import licenses for the maximum possible amount. In addition, expenditures incurred while lobbying the government to obtain import licenses add to the deadweight loss from the import quota.

7. Free trade will destroy domestic jobs, reduce national security, harm infant industries, force domestic producers to compete with foreign companies that have unfair advantages, and allow other countries to have trade restrictions while our country does not.

8. Tariffs and quotas harm domestic consumers while helping domestic producers. Producers are better able to organize than are consumers and thus, they are better able to lobby the government on their behalf.

9. Multilateral approach has an advantage in that it offers free overall trade for many countries, and this might be easier to accomplish politically. Unilateral approach brings gains for the domestic country, causing other countries to emulate it.

True/False Questions

1. F; the country should export that good.

2. T

3. F; producers gain, consumers lose.

4. T

5. F; some gain and some lose, but the gains of the winners outweigh the losses of the losers.

6. F; tariffs benefit producers.

7. F; tariffs decrease imports.

8. F; at most, a quota can raise the same revenue if the government sells the import licenses for the maximum amount possible.

9. T

10. T

Multiple-Choice Questions

1.	c	7.	d
2.	d	8.	b
3.	d	9.	a
4.	b	10.	c
5.	e	11.	d
6.	b	12.	a

Advanced Critical Thinking

1. Consumers gain, producers lose.

2. Our country gains because the gains of the consumers exceed the losses of the producers.

3. The taxpayers of the foreign country.

4. Producers gain, consumers lose, but consumers lose more than producers gain so total surplus is reduced and there is a deadweight loss. The result is no different than restricting trade when the foreign producer has no unfair advantage.

5. No. In either case, the world price is lower than the before-trade domestic price, causing consumers to gain and producers to lose from trade. Also, restrictions on trade cause consumers to lose more than producers gain whether the production of the good was subsidized or not.

6. Usually not. If the other country fails to give in to the threat, the threatening country has to choose between backing down and reducing trade—neither of which is desirable.

⌐In this chapter you will
Learn what an externality is

See why externalities can make
market outcomes inefficient

Examine how people can
sometimes solve the problem of
externalities on their own

Consider why private solutions
to externalities sometimes do
not work

Examine the various government
policies aimed at solving the
problem of externalities

⌐You should be able to
Distinguish between a positive and
a negative externality

Demonstrate why the optimal
quantity and the market quantity
differ in the presence of an
externality

Define the Coase theorem

Explain how transaction costs may
impede a private solution to an
externality

Demonstrate the potential equality
of a Pigovian tax and pollution
permits

EXTERNALITIES

CHAPTER OVERVIEW

Context and Purpose

Chapter 10 is the first chapter in the microeconomic section of the text. It is the first
chapter in a three-chapter sequence on the economics of the public sector. Chapter 10
addresses externalities—the uncompensated impact of one person's actions on the
welfare of a third party. Chapter 11 will address public goods and common resources
(goods that will be defined in Chapter 11) and Chapter 12 will address the tax system.

In Chapter 10, we address different sources of externalities and a variety of potential cures for externalities. Markets maximize total surplus to buyers and sellers in a
market. However, if a market generates an externality (a cost or benefit to someone
external to the market) the market equilibrium may not maximize the total benefit to
society. Thus, in Chapter 10 we will see that while markets are usually a good way
to organize economic activity, governments can sometimes improve market outcomes.

CHAPTER REVIEW

Introduction

An **externality** is the uncompensated impact of a consumption or production decision
on the well-being of a third party. If the effect is beneficial, it is called a *positive externality*. If the effect is adverse, it is called a *negative externality*. Markets maximize
total surplus to buyers and sellers in a market and this is usually efficient. However,
if a market generates an externality, the market equilibrium may not maximize
the total benefit to society as a whole and in these circumstances, the market is
inefficient. Because of this, government policy might be needed to improve efficiency.

Examples of negative externalities are pollution from exhaust and noise. Examples
of positive externalities are historic building restorations and research into new
technologies.

Externalities and Market Inefficiency

The height of the demand curve measures the value of the good to the marginal
consumer. The height of the supply curve measures the cost to the marginal producer.

If there is no government intervention, the price adjusts to balance supply and demand. The quantity produced maximizes consumer and producer surplus. If there is no externality, the market solution is efficient because it maximizes the welfare of buyers and sellers in the market and their welfare is all that matters. However, if there is an externality and third parties are affected by this market, the market does not maximize the total benefit to society as a whole because others beyond just the buyers and sellers in the market are affected.

There are two types of externalities:

- *Negative externality.* These arise when society is adversely affected by a production or consumption decision. For example, when the production of a good generates pollution, costs accrue to society beyond those that accrue to the producing firm. Thus, the social cost exceeds the private cost of production and, graphically, the social cost curve is above the supply curve (private cost curve). Total surplus is the value to the consumers minus the true social cost of production. Therefore, the optimal quantity that maximizes total surplus is less than the equilibrium quantity generated by the market.

- *Positive externality.* These arise when society is positively affected by a production or consumption decision. For example, a good such as education generates benefits to people beyond just the buyers of education. As a result, the social value of education exceeds the private value. Graphically, the social value curve is above the demand curve (private value curve). Total surplus is the true social value minus the cost to producers. Therefore, the optimal quantity that maximizes total surplus is greater than the equilibrium quantity generated by the market.

Internalizing an externality is the altering of incentives so that people take account of the external effects of their actions. To internalize externalities, the government can create taxes and subsidies to shift the supply and demand curves until they are the same as the true social cost and social value curves. This will make the equilibrium quantity and the optimal quantity the same and the market becomes efficient. Negative externalities can be internalized with taxes while positive externalities can be internalized with subsidies.

High-technology production (robotics, etc.) generates a positive externality for other producers known as a *technology spillover*. Some economists consider this spillover effect to be so pervasive that they believe that the government should have a *technology policy*—government intervention to promote technology-enhancing industries. Other economists are sceptical. At present, the government provides a *property right* for new ideas in the form of patent protection.

Private Solutions to Externalities

Government action is not always needed to solve the externality problem. Some private solutions to the externality problem are:

- *Moral codes and social sanctions.* People 'do the right thing' and do not litter.

- *Charities.* People give money to environmental groups and private colleges and universities.

- *Private markets that harness self-interest and cause efficient mergers.* The bee keeper merges with the owner of the apple orchard and the resulting firm produces more apples and more honey.

- *Private markets that harness self-interest and create contracts among affected parties.* The apple orchard owner and the bee keeper can agree to produce the optimal combined quantity of apples and honey.

The **Coase theorem** is the proposition that if private parties can bargain without cost over the allocation of resources, they can solve the problem of externalities on their own. In other words, regardless of the initial distribution of rights, the interested parties can always reach a bargain in which everyone is better off and the outcome is efficient. For example, if the value of peace and quiet exceeds the value of owning a barking dog, the party desiring quiet will buy the right to quiet from the dog owner and remove the dog or the dog owner will fail to buy the right to own a barking dog from the owner of quiet space. Regardless of whether one has the property right to peace and quiet or the other has the right to make noise, there is no barking dog, which, in this case, is efficient. The result is the opposite and is also efficient if the value of owning a dog exceeds the value of peace and quiet.

However, private parties often fail to reach efficient agreements due to **transaction costs**. Transaction costs are the costs that parties incur in the process of agreeing and following through on a bargain. If transaction costs exceed the potential gains from the agreement, no private solution will occur. Some sources of high transaction costs are as follows:

- lawyers' fees to write the agreement.

- costs of enforcing the agreement.

- a breakdown in bargaining when there is a range of prices that would create efficiency.

- a large number of interested parties.

Public Policies towards Externalities

When private bargaining does not work, the government can sometimes improve the outcome by responding in one of two ways: *command-and-control* policies or *market-based* policies.

- Command-and-control policies are regulations that require or prohibit (or limit) certain behaviours. The problem here is that the regulator must know all of the details of an industry and alternative technologies in order to create the efficient rules. Prohibiting a behaviour altogether can be best if the cost of a particular type of pollution is enormous.

- Market-based policies align private incentives with social efficiency. Taxes and subsidies can be used by the government to internalize externalities.

A tax enacted to correct the effects of a negative externality is known as a **Pigovian tax**. Pigovian taxes can reduce negative externalities at a lower cost than regulations because the tax essentially places a price on a negative externality say pollution. Those firms that can reduce their pollution at least cost, reduce their pollution, by more than other firms that have higher costs of reducing their pollution. The same amount of total reduction in pollution can be achieved with the tax as with regulation but at lower cost. In addition, the tax gives firms an incentive to develop cleaner technologies and reduce pollution even further than the regulation would have required. Unlike other taxes, Pigovian taxes enhance efficiency rather than reduce efficiency. For example, the tax on petrol is a Pigovian tax because, rather than causing a deadweight loss, it causes there to be less traffic congestion, safer roads, and a cleaner environment.

Tradable pollution permits allow the holder of the permit to pollute a certain amount. Those firms that have a relatively high cost of reducing their pollution will be willing to pay for the permits and those firms that can reduce pollution at a lower cost will sell their permits and reduce their pollution. The initial allocation of the permits among industries does not affect the efficient outcome. This method is similar to a Pigovian tax. While a Pigovian tax sets the price of pollution (the tax), tradable pollution permits set the quantity of pollution permitted. In the market for pollution, either method can reach the efficient solution. Tradable pollution permits may be superior because the regulator does not need to know the demand to pollute in order to restrict pollution to a particular quantity. The European Union's Emissions Trading Scheme is increasingly using pollution permits to reduce pollution.

Some people object to an economic analysis of pollution. They feel that any pollution is too much and that putting a price on pollution is immoral. Since all economic activity creates pollution to some degree and all activities involve tradeoffs, economists have little sympathy for this argument. Rich productive countries demand a cleaner environment, and market-based policies reduce pollution at a lower cost than alternatives further increasing the demand for a clean environment.

Conclusion

Markets maximize total surplus to buyers and sellers in a market and this is usually efficient. However, if a market generates an externality, the market equilibrium may not maximize the total benefit to society as a whole and thus the market is inefficient. The Coase theorem says that people can bargain among themselves and reach an efficient solution. However, if transaction costs are relatively high, government policy might be needed to improve efficiency. Pigovian taxes and pollution permits are preferred to command-and-control polices because they reduce pollution at a lower cost, and therefore increase the quantity demanded of a clean environment.

HELPFUL HINTS

1. Why do we use the word 'externality' to refer to the uncompensated impact of one person's actions on the welfare of a third party? An easy way to remember is to know that the word externality refers to the 'external effects' of a market transaction or to costs and benefits that land on a third party who is 'external to the market'.

2. Negative externalities cause the socially optimal quantity of a good to be less than the quantity produced by the market. Positive externalities cause the socially optimal quantity of a good to be greater than the quantity produced by the market. To remedy the problem, the government can tax goods that have negative externalities and subsidize goods that have positive externalities.

TERMS AND DEFINITIONS

Choose a definition for each key term.

Key terms:

—— Externality

____ Positive externality

____ Negative externality

____ Social cost

____ Internalizing an externality

____ Coase theorem

____ Transaction costs

____ Pigovian tax

Definitions:

1. The proposition that if private parties can bargain without cost over the allocation of resources, they can solve the problem of externalities on their own

2. The costs that parties incur in the process of agreeing and following through on a bargain

3. A situation when a person's actions have an adverse impact on a third party

4. A tax enacted to correct the effects of a negative externality

5. The uncompensated impact of one person's actions on the welfare of a third party

6. Altering incentives so that people take account of the external effects of their actions

7. The sum of private costs and external costs

8. A situation when a person's actions have a beneficial impact on a third party

PROBLEMS AND SHORT-ANSWER QUESTIONS

Practice Problems

1. The information below provides the prices and quantities in a hypothetical market for car antifreeze.
   a. Plot the supply and demand curves for antifreeze in Exhibit 1.

Price per Gallon (€)	Quantity Demanded	Quantity Supplied
1	700	300
2	600	400
3	500	500
4	400	600
5	300	700
6	200	800
7	100	900
8	0	1,000

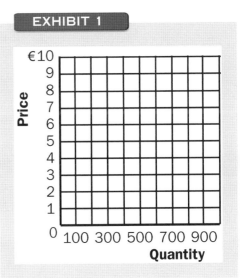

EXHIBIT 1

   b. What is the equilibrium price and quantity generated by buyers and sellers in the market?
   c. Suppose that the production of antifreeze generates pollution in the form of chemical runoff and that the pollution imposes a €2 cost on society for each gallon of antifreeze produced. Plot the social cost curve in Exhibit 1.
   d. What is the optimal quantity of antifreeze production? Does the market overproduce or underproduce antifreeze?
   e. If the government were to intervene to make this market efficient, should it impose a Pigovian tax or a subsidy? What is the value of the appropriate tax or subsidy?

2. Suppose citizens living around Metropolitan Airport value peace and quiet at a value of €3 billion.
   a. If it costs the airlines €4 billion to make their planes quieter (the airlines value noise at €4 billion), is it efficient for the government to require that the planes be muffled? Why?
   b. If it costs the airlines €2 billion to make their planes quieter, is it efficient for the government to require that the planes be muffled? Why?
   c. Suppose there are no transaction costs and suppose that *people have the right to peace and quiet*. If it costs the airlines €2 billion to make their planes quieter, what is the private solution to the problem?
   d. Suppose there are no transaction costs and suppose that *airlines have the right to make as much noise as they please*. If it costs the airlines €2 billion to make their planes quieter, what is the private solution to the problem?
   e. Compare your answers to (c) and (d) above. What are the similarities and what are the differences? What general rule can you make from the comparison?
   f. Suppose it costs the airlines €2 billion to make their planes quieter. If a private solution to the noise problem requires an additional €2 billion of transaction costs (due to legal fees, the large number of affected parties, and enforcement costs) can there be a private solution to the problem? Why?

3. Suppose there are four firms that each wish to dump one barrel of chemical waste into a river. Firm 1 produces a product that is so valued by society and sells for such a high price that it is willing to pay €8 million to dump a barrel. Firm 2 produces a somewhat less valuable product and is only willing to pay €6 million to dump a barrel. In similar fashion, suppose firm 3 is willing to pay €4 million to dump a barrel and firm 4 will pay €2 million.

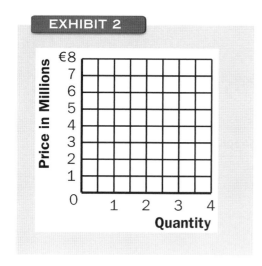

EXHIBIT 2

a. Draw the demand for the right to pollute in Exhibit 2.
b. Suppose it is estimated that the safe level of pollutants in the river is 3 barrels. At what value should they set a Pigovian tax?
c. Suppose it is estimated that the safe level of pollutants in the river is 3 barrels. How many tradable pollution permits should be allocated? At what price will the permits trade?
d. Compare part (b) and (c) above. How many barrels are dumped in each case? What is the price paid to pollute in each case? Is there an advantage to one method of internalizing the externality compared to the other?

SHORT-ANSWER QUESTIONS

Use the following information for questions 1 through 3.

Suppose that a commercial apple orchard uses pesticides in the production of apples. In the process, dangerous fumes drift across a nearby neighbourhood.

1. Is this an example of a positive or a negative externality? Explain.

2. If this externality is not internalized, does the market overproduce or underproduce apples? What does it mean to overproduce or underproduce a product?

3. To internalize this externality, should the government tax or subsidize apples? Why?

4. Suppose an individual enjoys lawn care and gardening a great deal. He uses pesticides to control insects and the harmful residue drifts across the neighbourhood. He values the use of the pesticides at €10,000 and the neighbourhood values clean air at €15,000. What does the Coase theorem suggest will take place?

5. In question 4 above, how large would the transactions costs need to be in order to ensure that no private solution to the problem can be found?

6. Does exercising market power by a firm impose an externality?

7. What are some types of private solutions to externalities?

8. What are the two types of public policies toward externalities? Describe them. Which one do economists prefer? Why?

9. Does a Pigovian tax reduce or increase efficiency? Why?

10. Why are tradable pollution permits considered superior to Pigovian taxes at reducing pollution?

SELF-TEST

True/False Questions

_____ 1. A positive externality is an external benefit that accrues to the buyers in a market while a negative externality is an external cost that accrues to the sellers in a market.

_____ 2. A market that generates a negative externality that has not been internalized generates an equilibrium quantity that is less than the optimal quantity.

_____ 3. If a market generates a negative externality, a Pigovian tax will move the market towards a more efficient outcome.

_____ 4. According to the Coase theorem, an externality always requires government intervention in order to internalize the externality.

_____ 5. To reduce pollution by some targeted amount, it is most efficient if each firm that pollutes reduces its pollution by an equal amount.

_____ 6. A tax always makes a market less efficient.

_____ 7. If Kalev values smoking in a restaurant at €10 and Michelle values clean air while she eats at €15, according to the Coase theorem, Kalev will not smoke in the restaurant only if Michelle owns the right to clean air.

_____ 8. If transactions costs exceed the potential gains from an agreement between affected parties to an externality, there will be no private solution to the externality.

_____ 9. A disadvantage of using tradable pollution permits to reduce pollution is that the regulator requires knowledge of the demand for pollution rights.

_____10. For any given demand curve for pollution, a regulator can achieve the same level of pollution with either a Pigovian tax or by allocating tradable pollution permits.

Multiple-Choice Questions

1. A negative externality (that has not been internalized) causes the
   a. equilibrium quantity to exceed the optimal quantity.
   b. optimal quantity to exceed the equilibrium quantity.
   c. equilibrium quantity to equal the optimal quantity.
   d. equilibrium quantity to be either above or below the optimal quantity.

2. To internalize a negative externality, an appropriate public policy response would be to
   a. ban the production of all goods creating negative externalities.
   b. have the government take over the production of the good causing the externality.
   c. subsidize the good.
   d. tax the good.

3. The government engages in a _technology policy_
   a. to internalize the negative externality associated with industrial pollution.
   b. to internalize the positive externality associated with technology-enhancing industries.
   c. to help stimulate private solutions to the technology externality.
   d. by allocating tradable technology permits to high technology industry.

4. When an individual buys a car in a congested urban area, this generates
   a. an efficient market outcome.
   b. a technology spillover.
   c. a positive externality.
   d. a negative externality.

5. The most efficient pollution control system would ensure that
   a. each polluter reduce its pollution by an equal amount.
   b. the polluters with the lowest cost of reducing pollution reduce their pollution by the greatest amount.
   c. no pollution of the environment is tolerated.
   d. the regulators decide how much each polluter should reduce its pollution.

6. According to the Coase theorem, private parties can solve the problem of externalities if
   a. each affected party has equal power in the negotiations.
   b. the party affected by the externality has the initial property right to be left alone.

    c. there are no transaction costs.

    d. the government requires them to negotiate with each other.

    e. there are a large number of affected parties.

7. To internalize a positive externality, an appropriate public policy response would be to

    a. ban the good creating the externality.

    b. have the government produce the good until the value of an additional unit is zero.

    c. subsidize the good.

    d. tax the good.

8. Which of the following is *not* considered a transaction cost incurred by parties in the process of contracting to eliminate a pollution externality?

    a. costs incurred to reduce the pollution.

    b. costs incurred due to lawyers fees.

    c. costs incurred to enforce the agreement.

    d. costs incurred due to a large number of parties affected by the externality.

9. Paul and Matt live in a university hall of residence. Paul values playing loud music at a value of €100. Matt values peace and quiet at a value of €150. Which of the following statements is true about an efficient solution to this externality problem if Paul has the right to play loud music and if there are no transaction costs?

    a. Paul will pay Matt €100 and Paul will stop playing loud music.

    b. Paul will pay Matt €150 and Paul will continue to play loud music.

    c. Matt will pay Paul between €100 and €150 and Paul will continue to play loud music.

    d. Matt will pay Paul between €100 and €150 and Paul will stop playing loud music.

10. Which of the following is true regarding tradable pollution permits and Pigovian taxes?

    a. Pigovian taxes are more likely to reduce pollution to a targeted amount than tradable pollution permits.

    b. Tradable pollution and Pigvian taxes both reduce pollution at no cost to society.

    c. To set the quantity of pollution with tradable pollution permits, the regulator must know everything about the demand for pollution rights.

    d. Pigovian taxes and tradable pollution permits create an efficient market for pollution.

    e. All of the above are true.

11. A Pigovian tax on pollution

    a. sets the price of pollution.

    b. sets the quantity of pollution.

    c. determines the demand for pollution rights.

    d. reduces the incentive for technological innovations to further reduce pollution.

12. Tradable pollution permits

    a. set the price of pollution.

    b. set the quantity of pollution.

    c. determine the demand for pollution rights.

    d. reduce the incentive for technological innovations to further reduce pollution.

13. How does Coase's theorem suggest that the EU solve the problem protecting future fish stocks by preventing over-fishing?

    a. Levy a tax on fishing.

    b. Issue tradable fishing quotas.

c. Sell fishing areas to private owners.

d. Set limits on fish catches.

14. Which one of the following is an example of an externality?

    a. The reduction in the possibility of an epidemic by one person being vaccinated against a contagious disease.

    b. The increased health care costs associated with treating those exposed to chemical irritants.

    c. The loss of income to farmers as a result of adverse weather conditions.

    d. The higher prices consumers pay for petrol when OPEC raises the price of oil.

ADVANCED CRITICAL THINKING

You are home for semester break. Your father opens the mail. One of the letters is your parents' property tax bill. On the property tax bill, there is a deduction if the property owner has done anything to improve his/her property. The property owner can deduct 50 per cent of any expenditure on things such as landscaping from his/her property taxes. For example, if your parents spent €2,000 on landscaping, they can reduce their tax bill by 0.50 × €2,000 = €1,000 so that the true cost of the landscaping would only be €1,000. Your father announces, 'This an outrage. If someone wants to improve their house, it is no one's business but their own. I remember some of my college economics and I know that taxes and subsidies are *always* inefficient.'

1. What is the city council trying to subsidize with this tax break?

2. What is the externality that this subsidy is trying to internalize?

3. While taxes and subsidies usually create inefficiencies, are taxes and subsidies always inefficient? Why?

SOLUTIONS

Terms and Definitions

_1_	Coase theorem	_5_	Externality
_2_	Transactions costs	_6_	Internalizing an externality
_3_	Negative externality	_7_	Social cost
_4_	Pigovian tax	_8_	Positive externality

Practice Problems

1. a. See Exhibit 3.

   b. Price = €3, quantity = 500 units.

   c. See Exhibit 4.

   d. 400 units. The market overproduces because the market quantity is 500 while the optimal quantity is 400 units.

   e. The government should impose a Pigovian tax of €2 per unit.

2. a. No, because the cost of correcting the externality exceeds the value placed on it by the affected parties.

   b. Yes, because the value placed on peace and quiet exceeds the cost of muffling the planes.

   c. The airlines could spend €2 billion and make their planes quieter or buy the right to make noise for €3 billion, so they will choose to make the planes quieter for €2 billion.

   d. The affected citizens must pay at least €2 billion and are willing to pay up to €3 billion to the airlines to have the planes made quieter.

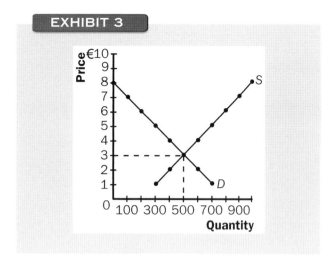

EXHIBIT 3

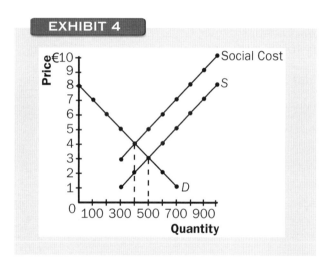

EXHIBIT 4

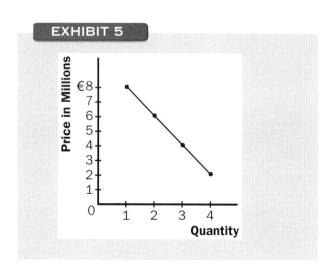

EXHIBIT 5

e. Similarities: the planes will be made quieter regardless of the original property rights because it is efficient. Differences: if the citizens have the right to quiet, citizens gain and airlines lose. If the airlines have the right to make noise, airlines gain and citizens lose. The general case is that the party possessing the property right gains and the other party loses.

f. No, because the transaction costs exceed the potential gains from trade. (The potential gains are the €3 billion value of quiet minus the €2 billion cost to muffle the planes, that is, €1 billion.)

3. a. See Exhibit 5.
   b. €4 million per barrel.
   c. 3 permits should be sold. They will trade at a price of €4 million per permit.
   d. 3 barrels. €4 million per barrel. Yes, with the tradable pollution permits the regulator does not need to know anything about the demand for pollution in this market in order to target pollution at 3 barrels and the initial allocation of pollution permits will not have an impact on the efficient solution.

Short-Answer Questions

1. Negative externality because the social cost of producing apples exceeds the private cost of producing apples.

2. Overproduce. To overproduce is to produce units where the true cost exceeds the true value. To underproduce is to fail to produce units where the true value exceeds the true cost.

3. Tax apples because to internalize this externality, it requires that the supply curve for apples be shifted upward until it equals the true social cost curve.

4. No pesticides will be used and the air will be clean, regardless of whether the individual owns the right to use pesticides or the neighbourhood residents own the right to clean air. Either the individual will fail to buy the right to pollute or the neighbourhood residents will pay the individual not to pollute.

5. There are €15,000 − €10,000 = €5,000 of potential benefits. If transaction costs exceed this amount, there will be no private solution.

6. Yes! When firms exercise market power they reduce supply and force up the price of their product. This will impose a deadweight loss on society.

7. Moral codes and social sanctions, charities, mergers between affected firms, contracts between affected firms.

8. Command-and-control policies are regulations that prohibit certain behaviours. Market-based policies align private incentives with social efficiency. Economists prefer market-based policies because they

are more efficient and they provide incentives for even further reduction in, say, pollution through advances in technology.

9. It increases efficiency by shifting the supply or demand curve towards the true social cost or value curve, thereby making the market solution equal to the optimal or efficient solution.

10. The regulator doesn't need to know anything about the demand to pollute in order to arrive at the targeted amount of pollution.

True/False Questions

1. F; a positive externality is a benefit that accrues to a *third party* and a negative externality is a cost that accrues to a *third party*.

2. F; the equilibrium quantity is greater than the optimal quantity.

3. T

4. F; the Coase theorem suggests that private parties can solve the problem of an externality on their own if there are no transaction costs.

5. F; firms that can reduce pollution at a lower cost should reduce their pollution more than firms that can reduce pollution at a greater cost.

6. F; Pigovian taxes can make a market more efficient.

7. F; the original distribution of property rights to the clean air will not affect the efficient solution.

8. T

9. F; using tradable permits, the regulator does not need to know the demand for pollution rights.

10. T

Multiple-Choice Questions

1.	a	5.	b	9.	d	13.	c
2.	d	6.	c	10.	d	14.	a
3.	b	7.	c	11.	a		
4.	d	8.	a	12.	b		

Advanced Critical Thinking

1. Expenditures on home improvement.

2. When a house is well maintained, it raises the value (or fails to reduce the value) of the nearby property. Individual buyers and sellers in the market for home repair do not take this into account when choosing the quantity of home repair and thus, the optimal quantity exceeds the equilibrium quantity.

3. No. Appropriate Pigovian taxes and subsidies move a market closer to efficiency because the market equilibrium is inefficient to begin with.

11

PUBLIC GOODS AND COMMON RESOURCES

CHAPTER OVERVIEW

Context and Purpose

Chapter 11 is the second chapter in a three-chapter sequence on the economics of the public sector. Chapter 10 addressed externalities. Chapter 11 addresses public goods and common resources—goods for which it is difficult to charge prices to users. Chapter 12 will address the tax system.

The purpose of Chapter 11 is to address a group of goods that are free to the consumer. When goods are free, market forces that normally allocate resources are absent. Therefore, free goods, such as playgrounds and public parks, may not be produced and consumed in the proper amounts. Government can potentially remedy this market failure and improve economic welfare.

CHAPTER REVIEW

Introduction

Some goods are free to the consumer—beaches, lakes, playgrounds, and so on. When goods are free, market forces that normally allocate resources are absent. Therefore, free goods, such as playgrounds and public parks, may not be produced and consumed at levels that maximize welfare. Government can potentially remedy this market failure and improve society's overall level of welfare.

The Different Kinds of Goods

There are two characteristics of goods that are useful when defining types of goods:

- **Excludability** the property of a good whereby a person can be prevented from consuming or using it. A good is excludable if a seller can exclude non-payers from consuming it (e.g. food in the grocery store, or entry into a football game) and not excludable if a seller cannot exclude non-payers from using it (e.g. broadcast television or a radio signal).

- **Rivalness** the property of a good whereby one person's use of a good diminishes other people's use. A good is rival if only one person can consume the good (e.g. food) and not rival if the good can be consumed by more than one person at the same time (e.g. a streetlight).

With these characteristics, goods can be divided into four categories:

1. **Private goods:** Goods that are both excludable and rival. Most goods like bread and blue jeans are private goods and are allocated efficiently by supply and demand mechanisms in markets.

2. **Public goods:** Goods that are neither excludable nor rival, such as national defence and street lighting.

3. **Common resources:** Goods that are rival but not excludable, such as fish in the ocean.

4. **Goods produced by a *natural monopoly*:** Goods that are excludable but not rival, such as fire protection and cable TV. Natural monopolies will be addressed in Chapter 15.

This chapter examines the two types of goods that are not excludable and, thus, are free: public goods and common resources.

Public Goods

Public goods are difficult for a private market to provide because of the *free-rider problem*. A **free rider** is a person who receives the benefit of a good, but avoids paying for it. Since public goods are not excludable, firms cannot prevent non-payers from consuming the good and thus, there is no incentive for a firm to produce a public good.

For example, a streetlight may be valued by each of ten homeowners in a neighbourhood at €1,000. If the cost is €5,000, no individual will buy a streetlight because no one can sell the right to use the light to their neighbours for €1,000 each. This is because after the streetlight is in place, their neighbours can consume the light whether they pay or not. Even though the neighbourhood values the streetlight at a total value of €10,000 and the cost of a streetlight is only €5,000, the private market will not be able to provide it. Public goods are related to positive externalities in that each neighbour ignores the external benefit provided to others when deciding whether to buy a streetlight. Often government steps in and provides goods, such as streetlights, where benefits exceed the costs and pays for them with tax revenue. In this case, the government could provide the streetlight and tax each resident €500 and everyone would be better off.

Some important public goods are national defence, basic research and possibly programmes to fight poverty.

Some goods can switch between being public goods and private goods depending on the circumstances. A lighthouse is a public good if the owner cannot charge each ship as it passes the light. A lighthouse becomes a private good if the owner can charge the port where the ships berth.

When a private market cannot produce a public good, governments must decide whether to produce the good. Their decision tool is often **cost-benefit analysis:** a study that compares the costs and benefits to society of providing a public good. There are two problems with cost-benefit analysis:

*   quantifying benefits is difficult using the results of a questionnaire

*   respondents have little incentive to tell the truth.

Some idea of the issues can be gleaned by considering whether a government should spend money on additional safety measures such as traffic lights at busy road junctions. In reaching a decision they must consider the value of a human life because the benefit of such an expenditure is the probability of saving a life times the value of a life. Try to think what value you would place on a human life—especially your own!

Common Resources

Common resources are not excludable, but are rival (fish in the ocean). Common resources are free but when one person uses it, it diminishes other people's enjoyment of it. This is similar to a negative externality because consumers of a good do not take into account the negative impact on others from their consumption. The result is that common resources are over consumed in relation to the optimal level of consumption.

The **Tragedy of the Commons** is a parable that illustrates why common resources get used more than is desirable from the perspective of society as a whole. The town common (open land to be grazed) will be overgrazed to the point where it becomes barren because, since it is free, private incentives suggest that each individual should graze as many sheep as possible. However, from a social perspective, this is over-grazing. Possible solutions are to regulate the number of sheep grazed, tax sheep, auction off sheep-grazing permits, or divide the land and sell it to individual sheep herders making grazing land a private good.

Some important common resources are clean air and water, congested non-toll roads, fish, whales, and other wildlife. Private decision-makers over consume a common resource in relation to the optimal level. Because of this, governments sometimes regulate behaviour or impose fees to reduce the problem of over consumption.

Conclusion: The Importance of Property Rights

In the case of public goods and common resources, markets fail to allocate resources efficiently because property rights are not clearly established. With private markets, no one owns the clean air so no one can charge people when they pollute. The result is that people pollute too much or use too much clean air (common resource example). Further, no one can charge those who are protected by national defence for the benefit they receive, so people produce too little national defence (public good example).

The government can potentially solve these problems by selling pollution permits, regulating private behaviour, or providing the public good.

HELPFUL HINTS

1. In general, public goods are underproduced and common resources are over-consumed in relation to the socially optimal level. This is because they are free. Since public goods are free, it is not profitable to produce them (streetlights and national defence). Since common resources are free, people overconsume them (clean air and fish in the ocean).

2. Public goods are defined by their characteristics, not by who provides them. A streetlight is a public good because it is non-excludable and non-rival. This is true even if, as an individual, I choose to buy one and put it in my front yard. Once provided, no one can be prevented from using it and when it is 'consumed' this does not diminish the ability of others to 'consume' it. A streetlight is therefore a public good. Note that if the city council sets up a food stand and sells hot dogs, the hot dogs are private goods even though they are provided by the council because the hot dogs are both excludable and rival.

3. When governments use cost-benefit analysis as a tool to help them decide whether to produce a public good, we noted that it is difficult to collect data on the true benefits that people would receive from a public good. This is because

they have an incentive to exaggerate their benefit if they would use the public good and under report their benefit if they don't plan to use the public good very much. This is sometimes called the *liars problem*.

TERMS AND DEFINITIONS

Choose a definition for each key term.

Key terms:

_____ Excludability

_____ Rivalry

_____ Private goods

_____ Public goods

_____ Common resources

_____ Natural monopoly

_____ Free rider

_____ Cost-benefit analysis

_____ Tragedy of the Commons

Definitions:

1. Goods that are both excludable and rival

2. The property of a good whereby one person's use diminishes other people's use

3. A person who receives the benefit of a good but avoids paying for it

4. A study that compares the costs and benefits to society of providing a public good

5. Goods that are rival but not excludable

6. The property of a good whereby a person can be prevented from using it

7. A parable that illustrates why common resources get used more than is desirable from the standpoint of society as a whole

8. Goods that are neither excludable nor rival

9. Firm that produces goods that are excludable but not rival

PROBLEMS AND SHORT-ANSWER QUESTIONS

Practice Problems

1. Consider the rivalry and excludability of each of the following goods. Use this information to determine whether the goods are public goods, private goods, common resources, or produced by a natural monopoly. Explain your reasons in each case.
   a. Fish in a private pond.
   b. Fish in the ocean.
   c. Broadcast television signals.
   d. Cable television signals.
   e. Basic research on lifestyle and cholesterol levels.
   f. Specific research on a cholesterol lowering drug for which a patent can be obtained.
   g. An uncongested road (no tolls).
   h. A congested road (no tolls).
   i. An uncongested toll road.
   j. A hot dog served at a private party.
   k. A hot dog sold at a stand owned by the city government.

2. Suppose a city council is debating whether to build a new road from its airport to the city centre. The city surveys its citizens and finds that, on average, each of the one million residents places a value on the new road of €50. The road costs €40 million to construct.

a. Assuming the survey was accurate, is building a new road efficient? Why?
b. Under what conditions would private industry build the road?
c. Is it likely that private industry will build the road? Why?
d. Should the city council pay to have the road built? On average, how much should it increase each resident's tax bill to pay for the road?
e. Is it certain that building the road is efficient? That is, what are the problems associated with using cost-benefit analysis as a tool for deciding whether to provide a public good?

Short-Answer Questions

1. If a cost benefit analysis into the feasibility of a project reveals an excess of costs over benefits, does this imply that the project should be undertaken?

2. Why is it difficult for private industry to provide public goods?

3. How is a streetlight (a public good) related to a positive externality?

4. Suppose for purposes of cost benefit analysis, a human life is valued at €10 million. Suppose the use of airbags in cars reduces the probability of dying in a car accident over one's lifetime from 0.2 per cent to 0.1 per cent. Further, suppose that a lifetime supply of airbags will cost the average consumer €12,000. If these numbers were accurate, would it be efficient for the government to require airbags in cars? Why?

5. What type of problem are hunting and fishing licenses intended to relieve? Explain.

6. How are fish in the ocean (a common resource) related to a negative externality?

7. How can the establishment of individual property rights eliminate the problems associated with a common resource?

8. Food is more important than roads to the public, yet the government provides roads for the public but rarely provides food. Why?

9. Why did the dodo become extinct while turkeys (a similar animal) are unlikely ever to become extinct?

10. Were the hunters that made the dodo extinct behaving irrationally? Explain.

SELF-TEST

True/False Questions

_____ 1. A common resource is neither rival nor excludable.

_____ 2. The free rider problem exists because of an absence of clearly defined property rights.

_____ 3. Goods produced by a natural monopoly are free to the consumer of the good.

_____ 4. In general, private markets do not provide public goods due to the free-rider problem.

_____ 5. If the local council provides free transport services, transport is a public good.

_____ 6. Public goods are related to positive externalities because the potential buyers of public goods ignore the external benefits those goods provide to other consumers when they make their decision about whether to purchase public goods.

_____ 7. Common resources are overused because common resources are free to the consumer.

_____ 8. The socially optimal price for a fishing license is zero.

_____ 9. Common resources are related to negative externalities because consumers of common resources ignore the negative impact of their consumption on other consumers of the common resource.

_____ 10. National defence is a classic example of a common resource.

Multiple-Choice Questions

1. If one person's consumption of a good diminishes other people's use of the good, the good is said to be
   a. a common resource.
   b. a good produced by a natural monopoly.
   c. rival.
   d. excludable.

2. A public good is
   a. both rival and excludable.
   b. neither rival nor excludable.
   c. rival but not excludable.
   d. excludable but not rival.

3. A common resource is
   a. both rival and excludable.
   b. neither rival nor excludable.
   c. excludable but not rival.
   d. rival but not excludable.

4. Suppose each of 20 neighbours on a street values street repairs at €3,000. The cost of the street repair is €40,000. Which of the following statements is true?
   a. It is not efficient to have the street repaired.
   b. It is efficient for each neighbour to pay €3,000 to repair the section of street in front of his/her home.
   c. It is efficient for the government to tax the residents €2,000 each and repair the road.
   d. It is not efficient to have the road repaired at prices greater than €1,000 per house.

5. A positive externality affects market efficiency in a manner similar to a
   a. private good.
   b. public good.
   c. common resource.
   d. rival good.

6. Which one of the following provides the best example of an externality?
   a. Someone selling a second-hand car knows more about it than the prospective buyer of the car.
   b. People are often able to use a country park without paying for it.
   c. High risk groups pay more for health insurance than low risk groups.
   d. Consumers are not consulted over a firm's plans to change the nature of the product it produces.
   e. A property developer buys a dilapidated house in a street and improves it for sale.

7. When governments employ cost-benefit analysis to help decide whether to provide a public good, measuring benefits is difficult because
   a. one can never place a value on human life or the environment.

b. respondents to questionnaires have little incentive to tell the truth.

c. there are no benefits to the public since a public good is not excludable.

d. the benefits are infinite because a public good is not rival and an infinite amount of people can consume it at the same time.

8. Which of the following is an example of a common resource?
   a. a national park.
   b. a fireworks display.
   c. national defence.
   d. iron ore.

9. When markets fail to allocate resources efficiently, the ultimate source of the problem is usually
   a. that prices are not high enough so people overconsume.
   b. that prices are not low enough so firms overproduce.
   c. that governments impose regulations.
   d. that property rights have not been well established.

10. Which one of the following provides the best example of a pure public good?
    a. A lighthouse.
    b. A road.
    c. A school.
    d. A hospital.

ADVANCED CRITICAL THINKING

Broadcast television and broadcast radio send out signals that can be received by an infinite number of receivers without reducing the quality of the reception of other consumers of the signal and it is not possible to charge any of the consumers of the signal.

1. What type of good (private, public, common resource, produced by a natural monopoly) is a broadcast television or broadcast radio signal? Explain.

2. Is this type of good normally provided by private industry? Why?

3. Private companies have been providing broadcast radio television and radio since the invention of the medium. How do they make it profitable if they cannot charge the recipient of the signal?

4. What are the 'recent' alternatives to traditional commercial television and commercial radio?

5. What type of good (private, public, common resource, produced by a natural monopoly) is this newer type of television and music provision?

SOLUTIONS

Terms and Definitions

_1_ Private goods

_2_ Rivalry

_3_ Free rider

_4_ Cost-benefit analysis

_5_ Common resources

_6_ Excludability

_7_ Tragedy of the commons

_8_ Public goods

_9_ Natural monopoly

Practice Problems

1. a. Rival and excludable, private good. Only one person can eat a fish. Since it is private, non-payers can be excluded from fishing.
   b. Rival but not excludable, common resource. Only one person can eat a fish but the ocean is not privately owned so non-payers cannot be excluded.
   c. Not rival and not excludable, public good. Additional viewers can turn on their TV without reducing the benefits to other consumers and non-payers cannot be excluded.
   d. Not rival but excludable, produced by a natural monopoly. More houses can be wired without reducing the benefit to other consumers and the cable company can exclude non-payers.
   e. Not rival and not excludable, public good. Once discovered, additional people can benefit from the knowledge without reducing the benefit to other consumers of the knowledge and once in the public domain, non-payers cannot be excluded.
   f. Not rival but excludable, produced by a natural monopoly. Additional users of the knowledge could use it without reducing the benefit to other consumers therefore it is not rival. If a patent can be obtained, no one else can produce the anti-cholesterol pill so it is excludable.
   g. Not rival and not excludable, public good. Additional cars can travel the road without reducing the benefit to other consumers and the additional cars cannot be forced to pay for the road.
   h. Rival but not excludable, common resource. Additional cars reduce the benefits of current users but they cannot be forced to pay for the use of the road.
   i. Not rival but excludable, produced by a natural monopoly. Additional cars do not reduce the benefits to current users but they can be excluded if they don't pay the toll.
   j. Rival but not excludable, common resource. If one person eats the hot dog, another person cannot. However, once provided, party-goers cannot be charged for eating the hot dogs.
   k. Rival and excludable, private good. If one person eats the hot dog, another person cannot. Even though it is supplied by the government, it is being sold so non-payers can be excluded.

2. a. Yes, because the total benefit is €50 × 1,000,000 = €50 million while the cost is €40 million.
   b. If the road could be built as a toll road, then private industry could make the road excludable and the project could be profitable.
   c. No. Toll roads are usually in rural areas where they can be made as limited-access roads and therefore excludable. It would be very difficult to make a downtown urban road limited-access or excludable.
   d. Yes. €40.
   e. No. Quantifying benefits is difficult using the results from a questionnaire and respondents have little incentive to tell the truth. Therefore, those who would use the road exaggerate their benefit and those that would rarely use it understate their benefit.

Short-Answer Questions

1. Not necessarily! It implies that it would be efficient to undertake the project, but it does not reveal whether other projects that might be undertaken as an alternative would confer an even greater excess of benefits over costs.

2. Because public goods are not excludable, the free-rider problem makes it unprofitable for private industry to produce public goods.

3. When people consider buying a street light, they fail to consider the external benefit it would provide to others and only consider their personal benefit. Thus, there is an underproduction and consumption of both public goods and goods that generate positive externalities.

4. No, because the expected benefit from airbags is (0.2 − 0.1) × €10,000,000 = €10,000 while the cost is €12,000.

5. The overconsumption of common resources. Since common resources are free, people use them excessively. Selling a limited number of hunting or fishing licenses restricts the number of users.

6. A common resource is free so it is overconsumed. Each consumer of fish fails to take into account the negative impact on others of their consumption causing overuse of the resource from a social perspective.

7. People overuse common resources because their benefit is positive and their cost is zero. If ownership over the resource exists, the cost of using the resource is realized and a socially optimal price is generated.

8. Food is both rival and excludable so it can be efficiently provided by the private market. Roads are often neither rival nor excludable so they will not be provided by private markets and may be most efficiently provided by government.

9. Dodo were a common resource and overconsumed. Turkeys are private goods and are produced and sold at the socially efficient price and quantity.

10. No. Because the dodo were a common property resource, the dodo were free. Each hunter pursued his own best interest but failed to take into account the impact of his actions on other people.

True/False Questions

1. F; it is rival but not excludable.

2. F; property rights might be clearly defined, but there will still be free riders if they are not enforceable.

3. F; they are excludable so a price must be paid to receive them, but they are not rival so they can be enjoyed by many at the same time.

4. T

5. F; goods are categorized as public or private based on their characteristics, not who provides them. Transport might be provided freely at the point of consumption, but it is not a public good.

6. T

7. T

8. F; a positive price is optimal so that the price reduces the quantity demanded of fish to the socially optimal level.

9. T

10. F; national defence is an example of a public good.

Multiple-Choice Questions

1. c	5. b	9. d
2. b	6. e	10. a
3. d	7. b	
4. c	8. a	

Advanced Critical Thinking

1. Public good. A broadcast signal is not rival and not excludable.

2. No, because it is not profitable to produce a good for which non-payers cannot be excluded from consuming it.

3. Broadcasters charge advertisers for the commercials they show during the broadcasters' programming. That is why it is called commercial television or commercial radio.

4. Cable television, pay-per-view television, and cable music included with cable television.

5. Produced by a natural monopoly because it is not rival, but it is excludable.

⌐In this chapter you will

Get an overview of how the UK government raises and spends money

Examine the efficiency costs of taxes

Learn alternative ways to judge the equity of a tax system

See why studying tax incidence is crucial for evaluating tax equity

Consider the tradeoff between efficiency and equity in the design of a tax system

OUTCOMES

⌐You should be able to

List the four largest sources of tax revenue to the UK government from the largest to the smallest source

Describe the administrative burdens of a tax

Compare the benefits principle to the ability to pay principle of allocating a tax burden

Explain why the burden of a tax often lands on someone other than the person from whom the tax is collected

Discuss the efficiency and equity of a flat tax

THE DESIGN OF THE TAX SYSTEM

CHAPTER OVERVIEW

Context and Purpose

Chapter 12 is the third chapter in a three-chapter sequence on the economics of the public sector. Chapter 10 addressed externalities. Chapter 11 addressed public goods and common resources. Chapter 12 addresses the tax system. Taxes are inevitable because when the government remedies an externality, provides a public good, or regulates the use of a common resource, it needs tax revenue to perform these functions.

The purpose of Chapter 12 is to build on the lessons learned about taxes in previous chapters. We have seen that a tax reduces the quantity sold in a market, that the distribution of the burden of a tax depends on the relative elasticities of supply and demand, and that taxes cause deadweight losses. We expand our study of taxes in Chapter 12 by addressing how the UK government raises and spends money. We then address the difficulty of making a tax system both efficient and equitable.

CHAPTER REVIEW

Introduction

Taxes are inevitable because when the government remedies an externality, provides a public good, or regulates the use of a common resource, it needs tax revenue to perform these functions. In previous chapters that dealt with taxation, we learned that a tax reduces the quantity sold in a market, that the distribution of the burden of a tax depends on the relative elasticities of supply and demand, and that taxes cause deadweight losses. We now address how the UK government raises and spends money and how difficult it is to make a tax system both efficient and equitable.

A Financial Overview of the UK Government

The government is composed of national and local governments. Over time, the government has taken a larger share of GDP in taxes—from about 8 per cent in

127

1900 to over 40 per cent in 2005. The tax burden in the UK as measured by the central government's tax revenue as a per cent of GDP is higher than in the US and Japan but lower than every other one of the G7 countries (Canada, France, Germany, and Italy). In general, wealthier countries tend to have higher tax burdens and less developed countries tend to have lower tax burdens.

The largest source of tax revenue for the central government is individual income taxes (28 per cent), followed by national insurance contributions (17 per cent), VAT (16 per cent), and all other taxes (39 per cent). Note that VAT is a sales tax and thus differs from excise taxes which are levied on production.

In 2004–2005, the central government's greatest spending was on Social Security (28.5 per cent) followed by the National Health Service (16 per cent), education (13 per cent), defence (6.2 per cent), public order and safety (6.1 per cent), transport (3.5 per cent), and other expenditures (26.6 per cent). Note that Social Security is a *transfer payments*—payments for which the government does not receive a good or service in return.

Taxes and Efficiency

A tax system should be both *efficient* and *equitable*. Here we address efficiency. A tax is more efficient than another if it raises the same amount of revenue at a smaller cost to taxpayers. The cost of a tax includes the actual tax payment itself plus

- the deadweight loss that results when taxes distort private decisions,

- the administrative burden taxpayers bear when they comply tax legislation.

Recall from Chapter 8 that the deadweight loss from a tax is the reduction in economic well-being of taxpayers in excess of the amount of revenue raised by the government. The loss is generated when buyers and sellers allocate resources according to the prices they face after the tax, rather than the true costs and benefits of the goods. As a result of a tax, we fail to produce and consume goods on which the benefits exceed the cost of production.

Income taxes place a tax on interest income and therefore discourage saving. A consumption tax would not distort people's saving decisions.

The administrative burden of a tax includes the time spent filling out tax forms, the time spent throughout the year keeping records for tax purposes, and the resources the government uses to enforce the tax laws.

The **average tax rate** is total taxes paid divided by total income. The **marginal tax rate** is the extra taxes paid on an additional euro of income. The average tax rate is most appropriate for gauging the sacrifice made by a taxpayer. However, the marginal tax rate is most appropriate for gauging how much the tax system distorts incentives and thus, how inefficient the tax is. Since people think at the margin, a high marginal tax rate discourages hard work and causes a large deadweight loss.

Rational people think at the margin and respond to incentives. In Iceland, when the government moved from collecting taxes based on the previous year's income to collecting taxes on the current year's income, a year of income had a zero marginal tax rate. As expected, hours worked and production rose during the year with the zero marginal tax rate.

A **lump-sum tax** is a tax that is the same amount for every person, regardless of income. A lump-sum tax is the most efficient tax because a lump-sum tax:

- generates a marginal tax rate of zero so it does not distort decision making and thus creates no deadweight loss,

- imposes the minimum administrative burden.

However, we rarely see lump-sum taxes because many perceive them as unfair or not equitable since rich and poor pay the same amount.

Taxes and Equity

There are different principles on which taxes can be based to generate fairness or equity. The **benefits principle** states that people should pay taxes based on the benefits they receive from government services. This principle can be used to justify petrol taxes to pay for roads, to justify that the rich should pay more taxes than the poor because the rich benefit more from fire and police protection, national defence, and the court system.

The **ability to pay principle** states that taxes should be levied on a person according to how well that person can shoulder the burden. This principle suggests that all taxpayers should make an 'equal sacrifice' to support the government. The concept of equality of sacrifice leads to two notions of equity: vertical equity and horizontal equity. **Vertical equity** states that taxpayers with a greater ability to pay taxes should pay larger amounts and **horizontal equity** states that taxpayers with similar abilities to pay taxes should pay the same amount.

A **proportional tax** is a tax for which high income and low income taxpayers pay the same fraction of income. A **regressive tax** is a tax for which high income taxpayers pay a smaller fraction of their income than do low income taxpayers. A **progressive tax** is a tax for which high income taxpayers pay a larger fraction of their income than do low income taxpayers. If taxes are based on the ability to pay principle, then vertical equity requires that the rich pay more taxes than the poor and thus, taxes should be progressive. The UK tax system is progressive because the highest income earners (those with an annual income of €100,000 or more paid an average percentage rate of tax of 33.6 per cent, while those with the lowest incomes (between €4,745 and €4,999) paid an average rate of tax of 0.2 per cent.

Horizontal equity is difficult to accomplish because it is difficult to determine when two families truly have similar abilities to pay.

It is necessary to address tax incidence in order to evaluate tax equity. This is because the person from whom the tax is collected often is not the person that bears the burden of the tax. The *flypaper theory* of tax incidence ignores the true burden of the tax and mistakenly assumes that the person from whom the tax is collected is also the one that bears the burden of the tax. For example, VAT is collected from traders, but, as we saw in Chapter 8, part of the burden of this tax is passed on to consumers.

HELPFUL HINTS

1. The benefits principle of taxation suggests that people should pay taxes based on the benefits they receive from government services. This is similar to having the government utilize a *user fee* (a price charged by the government for using a public good) when it supplies a public good. For example, the government can charge people a direct user fee when they use a publicly owned toll road. Alternatively, the government can utilize a petrol tax as an indirect user fee to pay for the entire road system. Either way, the people who benefit from the road pay for the road.

2. Remember, only people pay taxes. When we tax a business such as a corporation, the corporation is a tax collector, not a taxpayer. The burden of the tax will be shifted to the owners, customers, and workers of the corporation based on the elasticities of supply and demand in the relevant markets for the corporation's labour, capital, and products.

TERMS AND DEFINITIONS

Choose a definition for each key term.

Key terms:

_____ Budget deficit

_____ Budget surplus

_____ Average tax rate

_____ Marginal tax rate

_____ Lump-sum tax

_____ Benefits principle

_____ Ability to pay principle

_____ Vertical equity

_____ Horizontal equity

_____ Proportional tax

_____ Regressive tax

_____ Progressive tax

Definitions:

1. A tax for which high income and low income taxpayers pay the same fraction of income

2. The idea that taxes should be levied on a person according to how well that person can shoulder the burden

3. The extra taxes paid on an additional euro of income

4. A tax that is the same amount for every person

5. An excess of government receipts over government spending

6. The idea that taxpayers with a greater ability to pay taxes should pay larger amounts

7. A tax for which high income taxpayers pay a larger fraction of their income than low income taxpayers

8. An excess of government spending over government receipts

9. The idea that taxpayers with similar abilities to pay taxes should pay the same amount

10. The idea that people should pay taxes based on the benefits they receive from government services

11. Total taxes paid divided by total income

12. A tax for which high income taxpayers pay a smaller fraction of their income than low income taxpayers

PROBLEMS AND SHORT-ANSWER QUESTIONS

Practice Problems

1. a. Fill out the table below assuming that the government taxes 20 per cent of the first €30,000 of income and 50 per cent of all income above €30,000.

Income (€)	Taxes Paid (€)	Average Tax Rate	Marginal Tax Rate
10,000	_____	_____	_____
20,000	_____	_____	_____
30,000	_____	_____	_____
40,000	_____	_____	_____
50,000	_____	_____	_____

   b. Compare the taxes for someone making €10,000 to those of someone making €50,000 in part (a) above. Is this tax system progressive, regressive, or proportional? Explain.

2. a. Fill out the table below assuming that the government imposes a lump-sum tax of €6,000 on all individuals.

Income (€)	Taxes Paid (€)	Average Tax Rate	Marginal Tax Rate
10,000	_____	_____	_____
20,000	_____	_____	_____
30,000	_____	_____	_____
40,000	_____	_____	_____
50,000	_____	_____	_____

   b. Compare the taxes for someone making €10,000 to those of someone making €50,000 in part (a) above. Is this tax system progressive, regressive, or proportional? Explain.

3. a. Fill out the table below assuming that the government taxes 20 per cent of all income.

Income (€)	Taxes Paid (€)	Average Tax Rate	Marginal Tax Rate
10,000	_____	_____	_____
20,000	_____	_____	_____
30,000	_____	_____	_____
40,000	_____	_____	_____
50,000	_____	_____	_____

   b. Compare the taxes for someone making €10,000 to those of someone making €50,000 in part (a) above. Is this tax system progressive, regressive, or proportional? Explain.

4. a. Fill out the table below assuming that the government taxes 40 per cent of the first €10,000 of income and 10 per cent of all income above €10,000.

Income (€)	Taxes Paid (€)	Average Tax Rate	Marginal Tax Rate
10,000	_____	_____	_____
20,000	_____	_____	_____
30,000	_____	_____	_____
40,000	_____	_____	_____
50,000	_____	_____	_____

   b. Compare the taxes for someone making €10,000 to those of someone making €50,000 in part (a) above. Is this tax system progressive, regressive, or proportional? Explain.

5. a. Suppose the only objective of the tax system is to collect €6,000 from people who make €30,000. Which of the tax systems described in questions 1 through 4 is best? Why?
   b. Suppose the only objective of the tax system is to be efficient. Which of the tax systems described in questions 1 through 4 is best? Why?
   c. Suppose the only objective of the tax system is to be vertically equitable based on the ability to pay principle. Which of the tax systems described in questions 1 through 4 is best? Why?

Short-Answer Questions

1. What does it mean to say that a tax is *efficient*? What makes a tax efficient?

2. Is a consumption tax efficient? Explain.

3. Is a lump-sum tax efficient? Explain. Why do we rarely see lump-sum taxes in the real world?

4. Explain the difference between the benefits principle and the ability to pay principle of taxation. Which principle of taxation stresses vertical equity? Explain.

5. Are corporate income taxes truly paid by the corporation? That is, is the burden of the tax on the corporation? Explain.

6. Which is more difficult to achieve: vertical equity or horizontal equity?

7. What does the cost of a tax include?

8. How does government spending on transfer payments differ from government spending on public goods?

SELF-TEST

True/False Questions

_____ 1. VAT is more likely to achieve vertical equity than a progressive income tax.

_____ 2. Expenditures on national defence are an example of a government transfer payment.

_____ 3. To judge the vertical equity of a tax system, one should look at the average tax rate of taxpayers of differing income levels.

_____ 4. The marginal tax rate is the appropriate tax rate to judge how much a particular tax system distorts economic decision making.

_____ 5. If a tax is efficient it must also be equitable.

_____ 6. Lump-sum taxes are equitable but not efficient.

_____ 7. An efficient tax is one that generates minimal deadweight losses and minimal administrative burdens.

_____ 8. A tax system with a low marginal tax rate generates less deadweight loss and is more efficient than a similar tax system with a higher marginal tax rate.

_____ 9. If the government runs a budget deficit, it means that there is an excess of government spending over government receipts.

_____ 10. The marginal tax rate is total taxes paid divided by total income.

Multiple-Choice Questions

1. If the central government runs a budget surplus, there is a(n)
   a. excess of government spending over government receipts.
   b. excess of government receipts over government spending.
   c. equality of government spending and receipts.
   d. surplus of government workers.

2. Lea values a pair of blue jeans at €40. If the price is €35, Lea buys the jeans and generates consumer surplus of €5. Suppose a tax is placed on blue jeans that causes the price of blue jeans to rise to €45. Now Lea fails to buy a pair of jeans. This example has demonstrated
   a. the administrative burden of a tax.
   b. horizontal equity.
   c. the ability to pay principle.
   d. the benefits principle.
   e. the deadweight loss from a tax.

3. A tax for which high income taxpayers pay a smaller fraction of their income than do low income taxpayers is known as a(n)
   a. proportional tax.
   b. progressive tax.
   c. regressive tax.
   d. equitable tax.

4. An efficient tax
   a. raises revenue at the smallest possible cost to taxpayers.
   b. minimizes the deadweight loss from the tax.
   c. minimizes the administrative burden from the tax.
   d. does all of the above.

5. The marginal tax rate is
   a. total taxes paid divided by total income.
   b. the taxes paid by the average worker.
   c. the extra taxes paid on an additional euro of income.
   d. total income divided by total taxes paid.

6. The appropriate tax rate to employ to judge the vertical equity of a tax system is the
   a. marginal tax rate.
   b. average tax rate.
   c. proportional tax rate.
   d. horizontal tax rate.

7. The average tax rate is
   a. total taxes paid divided by total income.
   b. the taxes paid by the marginal worker.
   c. the extra taxes paid on an additional euro of income.
   d. total income divided by total taxes paid.

8. Which of the following taxes is the most efficient tax?
   a. a proportional income tax.
   b. a progressive income tax.
   c. a consumption tax.
   d. a lump-sum tax.

9. A progressive tax system is one where
   a. marginal tax rates are low.
   b. marginal tax rates are high.
   c. higher income taxpayers pay more taxes than do lower income taxpayers.
   d. higher income taxpayers pay a greater percentage of their income in taxes than do lower income taxpayers.

Use the following information about a tax system to answer questions 10 through 12.

Income (€)	Amount of Tax (€)
10,000	1,000
20,000	2,000
30,000	5,000
40,000	15,000

10. The average tax rate for a taxpayer earning €20,000 is
    a. 0 per cent.
    b. 5 per cent.
    c. 10 per cent.
    d. 20 per cent.
    e. none of the above.

11. This tax system is
   a. progressive
   b. lump-sum.
   c. regressive.
   d. proportional.

12. The marginal tax rate for a taxpayer whose earnings rises from €30,000 to €40,000 is
   a. 0 per cent.
   b. 16.7 per cent.
   c. 37.5 per cent.
   d. 100 per cent.
   e. none of the above.

ADVANCED CRITICAL THINKING

You are having a political debate with a friend. The discussion centres on taxation. You show your friend some data from your economics textbook that suggests that on average each person in the country paid about €7,000 in income tax in 2001. Your friend says, 'If €7,000 per person is what it takes to run this country, then I think that it would be much simpler if we just billed each person in the country €7,000 and eliminated the complex tax code.'

1. What type of tax is your friend suggesting? What is its appeal?

2. Is this type of tax supported by the 'benefits principle' of tax equity? Explain.

3. Is this type of tax supported by the 'ability to pay' principle of tax equity? Is it vertically equitable? Is it horizontally equitable?

4. Since your friend agrees that the tax she suggested is not equitable, she now suggests that we simply tax rich corporations since they can clearly afford it and then people wouldn't have to pay any taxes. Is she correct? Who would actually pay the taxes? Explain how she mistakenly employed the *flypaper theory* of taxation.

SOLUTIONS

Terms and Definitions

 1 Proportional tax

 2 Ability to pay principle

 3 Marginal tax rate

 4 Lump sum tax

 5 Budget surplus

 6 Vertical equity

 7 Progressive tax

 8 Budget deficit

 9 Horizontal equity

 10 Benefits principle

 11 Average tax rate

 12 Regressive tax

Practice Problems

1. a.

Income (€)	Taxes Paid (€)	Average Tax Rate (%)	Marginal Tax Rate (%)
10,000	2,000	20	20
20,000	4,000	20	20
30,000	6,000	20	20
40,000	11,000	27.5	50
50,000	16,000	32	50

b. Progressive because the average tax rate for a person making €50,000 exceeds the average tax rate for a person making €10,000. That is, the rich pay a larger fraction of their income than do poor people.

2. a.

Income (€)	Taxes Paid (€)	Average Tax Rate (%)	Marginal Tax Rate (%)
10,000	6,000	60	0
20,000	6,000	30	0
30,000	6,000	20	0
40,000	6,000	15	0
50,000	6,000	12	0

b. Regressive because the average tax rate for a person making €10,000 exceeds the average tax rate for a person making €50,000. That is, the poor pay a larger fraction of their income than do rich people.

3. a.

Income (€)	Taxes Paid (€)	Average Tax Rate (%)	Marginal Tax Rate (%)
10,000	2,000	20	20
20,000	4,000	20	20
30,000	6,000	20	20
40,000	8,000	20	20
50,000	10,000	20	20

b. Proportional because the average tax rate for a person making €10,000 is equal to that of a person making €50,000.

4. a.

Income (€)	Taxes Paid (€)	Average Tax Rate (%)	Marginal Tax Rate (%)
10,000	4,000	40	10
20,000	5,000	25	10
30,000	6,000	20	10
40,000	7,000	17.5	10
50,000	8,000	16	10

b. Regressive because the average tax rate for a person making €10,000 is greater than that of a person making €50,000.

5. a. They are all equally suitable because each system generates €6,000 tax revenue from people making €30,000.
   b. Taxes are more efficient if they generate smaller deadweight losses and smaller administrative burdens. The lump-sum tax in question 2 has a zero marginal rate so it does not distort economic decision making (no deadweight loss) and it is simple (small administrative burden), therefore it is most efficient. However, it is regressive.
   c. The tax system in question 1 because it is the only one that is progressive.

Short-Answer Questions

1. A tax is efficient if it raises the same amount of revenue at a smaller cost to taxpayers. It should generate a relatively small deadweight loss and have a relatively small administrative burden.

2. Yes. It is more efficient than an income tax because a consumption tax does not tax saving and thus, it does not distort the saving decision. An income tax does tax saving so it does distort the saving decision and causes a deadweight loss.

3. Yes. The marginal tax rate associated with a lump-sum tax is zero so a lump-sum tax does not distort decision making at the margin and thus, it generates no deadweight loss. It is rarely used because it is regressive.

4. The benefits principle argues that people should pay taxes based on the benefits they receive while the ability to pay principle argues that taxes should be based on how well a person can shoulder the burden.

The ability to pay principle stresses vertical equity because vertical equity requires that taxpayers with a greater ability to pay should pay larger taxes.

5. No. Corporate income taxes are collected from the corporation but only people pay taxes. The tax burden is actually divided between the shareholders, the workers, and the customers of the corporation.

6. Horizontal equity is more difficult to accomplish since it is difficult to determine whether two persons truly have equal ability to pay.

7. The cost of a tax includes the actual tax paid, the deadweight loss resulting from the distortion of private decisions and the administrative burden of a tax.

8. Transfer payments are simply a redistribution of income since they are payments made by the government which are not made in respect of some output. Government spending on public goods is clearly expenditure associated with the production of some output.

True/False Questions

1. F; VAT is a proportional tax and is levied at the same rate on all tax payers.

2. F; a transfer payment is an expenditure for which no good or service is received in return.

3. T

4. T

5. F; a tax is efficient if it causes little or no deadweight loss and is cheap to collect. It is equitable if it is levied according to ability to pay.

6. F; lump sum taxes are efficient but not equitable.

7. T

8. T

9. T

10. F; the marginal tax rate is the extra taxes paid on an additional euro of income.

Multiple-Choice Questions

1. b	5. c	9. d
2. e	6. b	10. c
3. c	7. a	11. a
4. d	8. d	12. d

Advanced Critical Thinking

1. Lump-sum tax. It is the most efficient tax—its marginal rate is zero so it does not distort incentives, and it imposes the minimum administrative burden.

2. No, if wealthy people benefit more from public services such as police and national defence, they should pay more in taxes.

3. No, wealthy people have a greater ability to pay. Therefore, it is not vertically equitable. However, to some extent, it is horizontally equitable in that people with the same ability to pay are paying the same amount because all pay the same amount.

4. No, only people pay taxes—corporations collect taxes. The taxes are paid by the owners, workers, and customers of the corporations. The flypaper theory of taxation mistakenly says that burden of a tax is on the person or company from whom the taxes are collected.

GOALS

⌐In this chapter you will

Examine what items are included
in a firm's costs of production

Analyse the link between a firm's
production process and its total
costs

Learn the meaning of average total
cost and marginal cost and how
they are related

Consider the shape of a typical
firm's cost curves

Examine the relationship between
short run and long run costs

OUTCOMES

⌐You should be able to

Explain the difference between
economic profit and accounting
profit

Utilize a production function to
derive a total-cost curve

Explain why the marginal-cost
curve must intersect the average
total-cost curve at the minimum
point of the average total-cost
curve

Explain why a production function
might exhibit increasing marginal
product at lower levels of output
and decreasing marginal product at
higher levels of output

Explain why, as a firm expands its
scale of operation, it tends to first
exhibit economies of scale,
then constant returns to scale, then
diseconomies of scale

THE COSTS OF PRODUCTION

CHAPTER OVERVIEW

Context and Purpose

Chapter 13 is the first chapter in a five-chapter sequence dealing with firm behaviour and the organization of industry. It is important that you become comfortable with the material in Chapter 13 because chapters 14 through 17 are based on the concepts developed in Chapter 13. To be more specific, Chapter 13 develops the cost curves on which firm behaviour is based. The remaining chapters in this section (Chapters 14 through 17) utilize these cost curves to develop the behaviour of firms in a variety of different market structures—competitive, monopolistic, oligopolistic, and monopolistically competitive.

The purpose of Chapter 13 is to address the costs of production and develop the firm's cost curves. These cost curves underlie the firm's supply curve. In previous chapters, we summarized the firm's production decisions by starting with the supply curve. While this is suitable for answering many questions, it is now necessary to address the costs that underlie the supply curve in order to address the part of economics known as *industrial organization*—the study of how firms' decisions about prices and quantities depend on the market conditions they face.

CHAPTER REVIEW

Introduction

In previous chapters, we analysed the firm's production decisions by focusing on the supply curve. Here we look behind the supply curve so as to consider these production decisions in more detail.

What Are Costs?

Economists generally assume that the goal of a firm is to maximize **profits**.

$$\text{Profit} = \text{total revenue} - \text{total cost}.$$

Total revenue is the level of output the firm produces times the price at which it sells the output. **Total cost** is more complex. An economist considers the firm's cost of production to include all of the *opportunity costs* of producing its output. The total opportunity cost of production is the sum of the *explicit* and *implicit* costs of production. **Explicit costs** are input costs that require an outlay of money by the firm, such as when money flows out of a firm to pay for raw materials, workers' wages, rent, and so on. **Implicit costs** are input costs that do not require an outlay of money by the firm. Implicit costs include the value of the income forgone by the owner of the firm had the owner worked for someone else, plus the forgone interest on the financial capital that the owner invested in the firm.

Accountants are only concerned with the firm's flow of money so they record only explicit costs. Economists are concerned with the firm's decision making so they are concerned with total opportunity costs, which are the sum of explicit costs and implicit costs. Since accountants and economists view costs differently, they view profits differently:

- **Economic profit** = total revenue − (explicit costs + implicit costs),

- **Accounting profit** = total revenue − explicit costs.

Because an accountant ignores implicit costs, accounting profit is greater than economic profit. The big business scandals of 2001 and 2002 begin with the fraudulent measurement of revenue, costs, and profit. The result was inflated stock prices and inflated values of stock options owned by corporate executives.

Production and Costs

For the following discussion, we assume that the size of the production facility (factory) is fixed in the short run. Therefore, this analysis describes production decisions in the short run.

A firm's costs reflect its production process. A **production function** shows the relationship between the quantity of inputs used to make a good and the level of output of that good. The **marginal product** of any input is the increase in output that arises from an additional unit of that input. The marginal product of an input can be measured as the slope of the production function. Production functions exhibit **diminishing marginal product**—the property whereby the marginal product of an input declines as the quantity of the input increases. Hence, the slope of a production function becomes flatter as more and more inputs are added to the production process.

The *total-cost curve* shows the relationship between the level of output produced and the total cost of production. Since the production process exhibits diminishing marginal product, the quantity of inputs necessary to produce equal increments of output rises as we produce more output and thus, the total-cost curve rises at an increasing rate or gets steeper as the amount produced increases.

The Various Measures of Cost

Several measures of cost can be derived from data on the firm's total cost. Costs can be divided into fixed costs and variable costs. **Fixed costs** are costs that do not vary with the level of output produced—for example, rent on factory premises. **Variable costs** are costs that do vary with the level of output produced—for example, expenditures on raw materials and temporary workers. The sum of fixed and variable cost equals total costs.

In order to choose the optimal level of output to produce, the producer needs to know the cost of the typical unit of output and the cost of producing one additional unit. The cost of the typical unit of output is measured by **average total cost** which is total cost divided by the level of output. Average total cost is the sum of **average fixed cost** (fixed costs divided by the level of output) and **average variable cost** (variable costs divided by the level of output). **Marginal cost** is the cost of producing one additional unit. It is measured as the increase in total costs that arises from an extra unit of production. In symbols, if Q = quantity, TC = total cost, ATC = average total cost, FC = fixed costs, AFC = average fixed costs, VC = variable costs, AVC = average variable costs, and MC = marginal cost, then:

$$ATC = TC/Q,$$
$$AVC = VC/Q,$$
$$AFC = FC/Q,$$
$$MC = \Delta TC/\Delta Q.$$

When these cost curves are plotted on a graph with cost on the vertical axis and quantity produced on the horizontal axis, these cost curves will have predictable shapes. At relatively low levels of production, the marginal product of an extra worker is relatively large so the marginal cost of another unit of output is relatively small. At high levels of production, the marginal product of a worker is relatively small so the marginal cost of another unit is relatively large. Therefore, because of diminishing marginal product (usually referred to simply as diminishing returns) the marginal-cost curve is increasing or upward sloping. The average total-cost curve is U-shaped because at relatively low levels of output, average costs are relatively high because fixed costs are averaged over a relatively low level of output. As output increases, average costs fall because fixed costs are spread across additional units of output. However, at some point, diminishing returns begin to increase average costs again. The **efficient scale** of the firm is the level of output that minimizes average total cost. Whenever marginal cost is less than average total cost, average total cost is falling because the additional unit produced adds less to the total cost than the existing average cost. Whenever marginal cost is greater than average total cost, average total cost is rising because the additional unit produced adds more to the total cost than the existing average cost. Therefore, the marginal-cost curve crosses the average total-cost curve at the efficient scale.

Up to this point, we have assumed that the production function exhibits diminishing marginal product at all levels of output and therefore, there are rising marginal costs at all levels of output. However, production often first exhibits increasing marginal product and decreasing marginal costs at very low levels of output as the addition of workers allows for specialization of skills. At higher levels of output, diminishing returns eventually set in and marginal costs begin to rise, causing all cost-curve relationships previously described to continue to hold. In particular:

- Marginal cost eventually rises with the level of output.

- The average total-cost curve is U-shaped.

- The marginal-cost curve crosses the average total-cost curve at the minimum of average total cost.

Costs in the Short Run and in the Long Run

The division of costs between fixed and variable depends on the time horizon. In the short run, the size of the factory is fixed and, for many firms, the only way to vary output is hiring or firing workers. In the long run, the firm can change the size of the factory and all costs are variable. The long run average total-cost curve, although flatter than the short run average total-cost curves, is still U-shaped. For each particular factory size, there is a short run average total-cost curve that lies on or above the long run average total-cost curve. In the long run, the firm is able to choose on which short run curve it wants to operate. In the short run, it must operate on the short run curve it chose in the past. Some firms reach the long run faster than do others because some firms can change the size of their factory relatively easily.

At low levels of output, firms tend to have **economies of scale**—the property whereby long run average total cost falls as the level of output increases. At relatively high levels of output, firms tend to experience **diseconomies of scale**—the property whereby long run average total cost rises as the level of output increases. At intermediate levels of output, firms tend to experience **constant returns to scale**—the property whereby long run average total cost stays the same as the level of output changes. Economies of scale may be caused by increased *specialization* among workers as the factory becomes larger, while diseconomies of scale may be caused by coordination problems inherent in extremely large organizations. Two hundred years ago, Adam Smith recognized the efficiencies experienced by larger factories that allowed workers to specialize in particular jobs.

Conclusion

This chapter developed a typical firm's cost curves. These cost curves will be used in the following chapters to see how firms make production and pricing decisions.

HELPFUL HINTS

1. Since accountants and economists view costs, and therefore profits differently, it is possible for a firm that appears profitable according to an accountant, to be unprofitable according to an economist. For example, suppose a firm incurs €20,000 in explicit costs to produce output that is sold for total revenue of €30,000. According to the accountant, the firm's profit is €10,000. However, suppose that the owner/manager of the firm could have worked for another firm and earned €15,000 during this period. While the accountant would still record the firm's profits at €30,000 − €20,000 = €10,000, the economist would argue that the firm is not profitable because the total explicit and implicit costs are €20,000 + €15,000 = €35,000 which exceeds the €30,000 of total revenue.

2. In the case of discrete numerical examples, marginal values are determined over a range of a variable rather than at a point. Therefore, when we plot a marginal value, we plot it halfway between the two end points of the range of the variable of concern. For example, if we are plotting the marginal cost of production as we move from the fifth unit to the sixth unit of production, we calculate the change in cost as we move from producing five units to producing six units and then we plot this marginal cost as if it is for the fifth and a half unit. Notice the marginal cost curves in your text. Although it is not discussed explicitly in your text, each marginal cost curve is plotted in this manner. In like manner, if we were plotting the marginal cost of production as we move from producing 50 units to producing 60 units, we would plot the marginal cost of that change in production as if it were for the 55th unit.

3. The long run is usually defined as the period of time necessary for all inputs to become variable. That is, the long run is the period of time necessary for the firm to be able to change the size of the production facility or factory. Note that this period of time differs across industries. For example, it may take many years for all of the inputs of a railway to become variable because the rail tracks are quite permanent. However, a small independent retail shop could add on to its production facility in just a matter of months. Thus, its takes longer for a railroad to reach the long run than it does for an ice-cream shop.

TERMS AND DEFINITIONS

Choose a definition for each key term.

Key terms:

_____ Total revenue

_____ Total cost

_____ Profit

_____ Explicit costs

_____ Implicit costs

_____ Economic profit

_____ Accounting profit

_____ Production function

_____ Marginal product

_____ Diminishing marginal product

_____ Fixed costs

_____ Variable costs

_____ Average total cost

_____ Average fixed cost

_____ Average variable cost

_____ Marginal cost

_____ Efficient scale

_____ Economies of scale

_____ Diseconomies of scale

_____ Constant returns to scale

Definitions:

1. Costs that do not vary with the level of output produced

2. Total revenue minus total cost

3. The increase in total cost that arises from an extra unit of production

4. The property whereby long run average total cost falls as the level of output increases

5. The property whereby long run average total cost stays the same as the level of output changes

6. Input costs that do not require an outlay of money by the firm

7. The increase in output that arises from an additional unit of input

8. The market value of the inputs a firm uses in production

9. The property whereby long run average total cost rises as the level of output increases

10. Fixed costs divided by the level of output

11. Costs that vary with the level of output produced

12. The level of output that minimizes average total cost

13. The amount a firm receives for the sale of its output

14. The relationship between quantity of inputs used to make a good and the level of output of that good

15. Variable costs divided by the level of output

16. Total cost divided by the level of output

17. The property whereby the marginal product of an input declines as the quantity of the input increases

18. Total revenue minus total cost, including both explicit and implicit costs

19. Total revenue minus total explicit cost

20. Input costs that require an outlay of money by the firm

PROBLEMS AND SHORT-ANSWER QUESTIONS

Practice Problems

1. Paul runs a small boat factory. He can make ten boats per year and sell them for €25,000 each. It costs Paul €150,000 for the raw materials (fibreglass, wood, paint, and so on) to build the ten boats. Paul has invested €400,000 in the factory and equipment needed to produce the boats: €200,000 from his own savings and €200,000 borrowed at 10 per cent interest (assume that Paul could

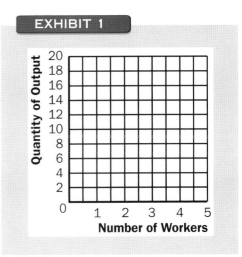

EXHIBIT 1

have loaned his money out at 10 per cent, too). Paul can work at a competing boat factory for €70,000 per year.

a. What is the total revenue Paul can earn in a year?
b. What are the explicit costs Paul incurs while producing ten boats?
c. What are the total opportunity costs of producing ten boats (explicit and implicit)?
d. What is the value of Paul's accounting profit?
e. What is the value of Paul's economic profit?
f. Is it truly profitable for Paul to operate his boat factory? Explain.

Number of Workers	Output	Product of Labour	Cost of Factory (€)	Cost of Workers (€)	Total Cost
0	0	_____	25	0	_____
1	6	_____	25	5	_____
2	11	_____	25	10	_____
3	15	_____	25	15	_____
4	18	_____	25	20	_____
5	20	_____	25	25	_____

2. a. Complete the following table. It describes the production and cost of hamburgers at a roadside stand. All figures are measured per hour.
   b. Plot the production function in Exhibit 1.
   c. What happens to the marginal product of labour as more workers are added to the production facility? Why? Use this information about the marginal product of labour to explain the slope of the production function you plotted above.
   d. Plot the total-cost curve in Exhibit 2.
   e. Explain the shape of the total-cost curve.

Quantity	FC (€)	VC (€)	TC (€)	AFC (€)	AVC (€)	ATC (€)	MC
0	16	0	_____	_____	_____	_____	_____
1	16	18	_____	_____	_____	_____	_____
2	16	31	_____	_____	_____	_____	_____
3	16	41	_____	_____	_____	_____	_____
4	16	49	_____	_____	_____	_____	_____
5	16	59	_____	_____	_____	_____	_____
6	16	72	_____	_____	_____	_____	_____
7	16	90	_____	_____	_____	_____	_____
8	16	114	_____	_____	_____	_____	_____
9	16	145	_____	_____	_____	_____	_____
10	16	184	_____	_____	_____	_____	_____

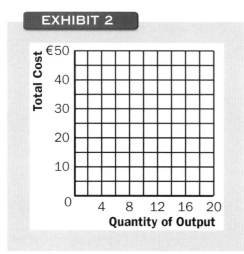

EXHIBIT 2

Total Cost (€) / Quantity of Output

3. a. The information below is for Kathryn's blue jeans manufacturing plant. All data is per hour. Complete the table. Note the following abbreviations: FC (fixed cost), VC (variable cost), TC (total cost), AFC (average fixed cost), AVC (average variable cost), ATC (average total cost), MC (marginal cost).

   b. Plot AFC, AVC, ATC, and MC in Exhibit 3. (Note: read Helpful Hint 2 above before plotting MC).
   c. Explain the shape of each of the curves you plotted in part (b) above.
   d. Explain the relationship between ATC and MC.
   e. Explain the relationship between ATC, AFC, and AVC.
   f. What is Kathryn's efficient scale? How do you find the efficient scale? Explain.

EXHIBIT 3

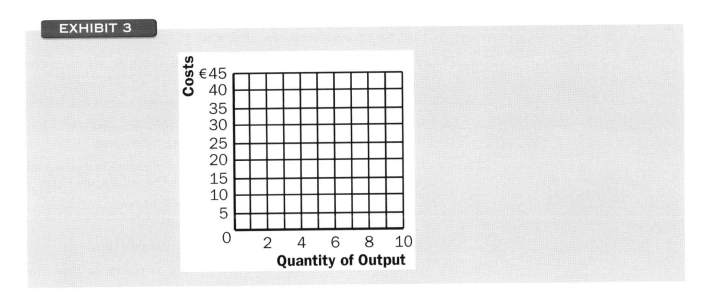

SHORT-ANSWER QUESTIONS

1. What is profit?

2. How does economic profit differ from accounting profit?

3. Suppose you own and operate your own business. Further, suppose that interest rates rise and another firm offers you a job paying twice what you thought you were worth in the labour market. What has happened to your accounting profit? What has happened to your economic profit? Are you more or less likely to continue to operate your own firm?

4. Explain the relationship between the production function and the total-cost curve.

5. Is the salary of management in a firm a fixed cost or a variable cost? Why?

6. What is the efficient scale of a firm?

7. Explain the relationship between marginal cost and average total cost.

8. What is the shape of the marginal-cost curve in the typical firm? Why is it shaped this way?

9. If a firm is operating in the area of constant returns to scale, what will happen to average total costs in the short run if the firm expands production? Why? What will happen to average total costs in the long run? Why?

10. When a small firm expands the scale of its operation, why does it usually first experience increasing returns to scale? When the same firm grows to a relatively large scale of operations, why might a further expansion of the scale of operation generate decreasing returns to scale?

SELF-TEST

True/False Questions

_____ 1. Total revenue equals the level of output the firm produces times the price at which it sells its output.

_____ 2. Wages and salaries paid to workers are an example of implicit costs of production.

_____ 3. If total revenue is €100, explicit costs are €50, and implicit costs are €30, then accounting profit equals €50.

_____ 4. If there are implicit costs of production, accounting profits will exceed economic profits.

_____ 5. When a production function gets flatter, the marginal product is increasing.

_____ 6. If a firm continues to employ more workers within the same size factory, it will eventually experience diminishing marginal product.

_____ 7. If the production function for a firm exhibits diminishing marginal product, the corresponding total-cost curve for the firm will become flatter as the level of output expands.

_____ 8. Fixed costs plus variable costs equal total costs.

_____ 9. Average total costs are total costs divided by marginal costs.

_____ 10. When marginal costs are below average total costs, average total costs must be falling.

_____ 11. If, as the quantity produced increases, a production function first exhibits increasing marginal product and later diminishing marginal product, the corresponding marginal-cost curve will be U-shaped.

_____ 12. The average total-cost curve crosses the marginal-cost curve at the minimum of the marginal-cost curve.

_____ 13. The average total-cost curve in the long run is flatter than the average total-cost curve in the short run.

_____ 14. The efficient scale for a firm is the level of output that minimizes marginal cost.

_____ 15. In the long run, as a firm expands its production facilities, it generally first experiences diseconomies of scale, then constant returns to scale, and finally economies of scale.

Multiple-Choice Questions

1. Economic profit is equal to total revenue minus
   a. implicit costs.
   b. explicit costs.
   c. the sum of implicit and explicit costs.
   d. marginal costs.
   e. variable costs.

Use the following information for the next two questions. Madelyn owns a small pottery factory. She can make 1,000 pieces of pottery per year and sell them for €100 each. It costs Madelyn €20,000 for the raw materials to produce the 1,000 pieces of pottery. She has invested €100,000 in her factory and equipment: €50,000 from her savings and €50,000 borrowed at 10 per cent (assume that she could have loaned her money out at 10 per cent, too). Madelyn can work at a competing pottery factory for €40,000 per year.

2. The accounting profit at Madelyn's pottery factory is
   a. €30,000.
   b. €35,000.
   c. €70,000.
   d. €75,000.
   e. €80,000.

3. The economic profit at Madelyn's pottery factory is
   a. €30,000.
   b. €35,000.
   c. €70,000.
   d. €75,000.
   e. €80,000.

4. The marginal product of a factor of production is the
   a. change in output divided by the change in the input of one unit of the factor of production.
   b. output divided by the total input of the factor of production.
   c. change in output divided by the change in the input of all factors of production.
   d. total output divided by the average product per unit of input.

   The following matrix shows the output produced by a firm when different combinations of capital and labour are employed. (The input of each factor used is shown in bold.)

Units of labour	4	40	80	120	160
	3	36	72	108	144
	2	30	60	90	120
		20	40	60	80
		Units of capital			

5. This firm experiences
   a. increasing marginal returns to labour.
   b. increasing marginal returns to capital.
   c. increasing returns to labour and diminishing returns to capital
   d. economies of scale.
   e. diseconomies of scale.

6. Which of the following is a variable cost in the short run?
   a. wages paid to factory labour.
   b. payment on the lease for factory equipment.
   c. rent on the factory.
   d. interest payments on borrowed financial capital.
   e. salaries paid to upper management.

7. When marginal costs are below average total costs,
   a. average fixed costs are rising.
   b. average total costs are falling.
   c. average total costs are rising.
   d. average total costs are minimized.

8. If marginal costs equal average total costs,
   a. average total costs are rising.
   b. average total costs are falling.
   c. average total costs are minimized.
   d. average total costs are maximized.

9. If, as the quantity produced increases, a production function first exhibits increasing marginal product and later diminishing marginal product, the corresponding marginal-cost curve will
   a. slope upward.
   b. be U-shaped.
   c. slope downward.
   d. be flat (horizontal).

10. If output is increasing and the short run average variable cost is rising, it must be true that the
    a. average total cost is rising.
    b. marginal cost is rising.
    c. average variable cost lies above the average fixed cost.
    d. marginal cost lies above the average fixed cost

11. The efficient scale of production is the level of output that minimizes
    a. average total cost.
    b. marginal cost.
    c. average fixed cost.
    d. average variable cost.

12. Which of the following statements is true?
    a. All costs are fixed in the long run.
    b. All costs are variable in the long run.
    c. All costs are fixed in the short run.
    d. All costs are variable in the short run.

ADVANCED CRITICAL THINKING

Your friend has a large garden and grows fresh fruit and vegetables to be sold at a local 'farmer's market'. Your friend comments, 'I hired a college student who was on summer vacation to help me this summer and my production more than doubled. Next summer, I think I'll hire two or maybe three helpers and my output should go up more than three or fourfold.'

1. If all production processes eventually exhibit diminishing marginal product of the variable inputs, could it be true that your friend hired a helper (doubled the labour) and more than doubled his production? Why?

2. Is it likely that he could hire more workers and continue to reap greater than proportional increases in production? Why?

3. In the long run, what must your friend do to the scale of his operation if he wants to continue to hire workers and have those workers generate proportional increases in production? Explain. Even in the long run, could your friend expand his scale of operation forever and continue to keep average total costs at a minimum? Explain.

SOLUTIONS

Terms and Definitions

__1__ Fixed costs

__2__ Profit

__3__ Marginal cost

__4__ Economies of scale

__5__ Constant returns to scale

__6__ Implicit costs

__7__ Marginal product

__8__ Total cost

__9__ Diseconomies of scale

__10__ Average fixed cost

__11__ Variable costs

__12__ Efficient scale

__13__ Total revenue

__14__ Production function

__15__ Average variable cost

__16__ Average total cost

__17__ Diminishing marginal product

__18__ Economic profit

__19__ Accounting profit

__20__ Explicit costs

Practice Problems

1. a. $10 \times €25{,}000 = €250{,}000$.
   b. $€150{,}000 + (€200{,}000 \times 0.10) = €170{,}000$.
   c. $€150{,}000 + (€400{,}000 \times 0.10) + €70{,}000 = €260{,}000$.
   d. $€250{,}000 - €170{,}000 = €80{,}000$.
   e. $€250{,}000 - €260{,}000 = -€10{,}000$.
   f. No. Paul could make €70,000 plus 10 per cent interest on his €200,000 financial capital for a total of €90,000 if he worked for the competitor instead of running his own factory. His factory makes an accounting profit of only €80,000 per year so it costs him €10,000 to run his own factory (the size of the economic loss).

2. a.

Number of Workers	Output (€)	Marginal Product of Labour (€)	Cost of Factory (€)	Cost of Workers	Total Cost
0	0		25	0	25
		6			
1	6		25	5	30
		5			
2	11		25	10	35
		4			
3	15		25	15	40
		3			
4	18		25	20	45
		2			
5	20		25	25	50

   b. See Exhibit 4.
   c. It diminishes because additional workers have to share the production equipment and the work area becomes more crowded. The slope of the production function is the change in output from a change in a unit of input, which is the marginal product of labour. Since it is diminishing, the slope of the production function gets flatter as a greater number of inputs are used.
   d. See Exhibit 5.
   e. The total-cost curve gets steeper as the quantity produced rises due to the diminishing marginal product of labour. That is, in order to produce additional equal increments of output the firm must employ ever greater amounts of inputs and costs rise at an increasing rate.

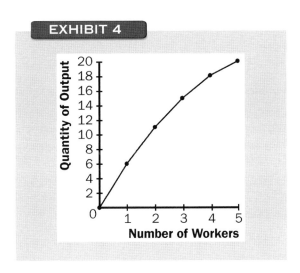

EXHIBIT 4

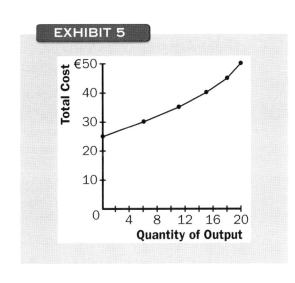

EXHIBIT 5

3. a.

Quantity	FC (€)	VC (€)	TC (€)	AFC (€)	AVC (€)	ATC (€)	MC (€)
0	16	0	16	—	—	—	
							18
1	16	18	34	16.00	18.00	34.00	
							13
2	16	31	47	8.00	15.50	23.50	
							10
3	16	41	57	5.33	13.67	19.00	
							8
4	16	49	65	4.00	12.25	16.25	
							10
5	16	59	75	3.20	11.80	15.00	
							13
6	16	72	88	2.67	12.00	14.67	
							18
7	16	90	106	2.29	12.86	15.14	
							24
8	16	114	130	2.00	14.25	16.25	
							31
9	16	145	161	1.78	16.11	17.88	
							39
10	16	184	200	1.60	18.40	20.00	

EXHIBIT 6

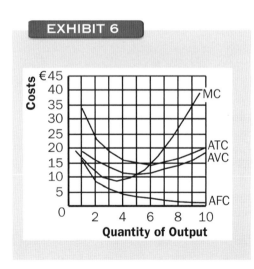

b. See Exhibit 6.

c. *AFC* declines as the quantity goes up because a fixed cost is spread across a greater number of units. *MC* declines for the first four units due to an increasing marginal product of the variable input. *MC* rises thereafter due to decreasing marginal product. *AVC* is U-shaped for the same reason as *MC*. *ATC* declines due to falling *AFC* and increasing marginal product. *ATC* rises at higher levels of production due to decreasing marginal product.

d. When *MC* is below *ATC*, *ATC* must be declining. When *MC* is above *ATC*, *ATC* must be rising. Therefore, *MC* crosses *ATC* at the minimum of *ATC*.

e. *AFC* plus *AVC* equals *ATC*.

f. Six pairs of blue jeans. Efficient scale is the output that minimizes *ATC*. It is also the place where *MC* crosses the average total cost curve.

Short-Answer Questions

1. Profit = total revenue − total cost.

2. Economic profit is total revenue minus explicit costs and *implicit costs*. Accounting profit is total revenue minus explicit costs.

3. Accounting profit is unchanged. Economic profit is reduced because implicit costs have risen—the opportunity cost of your invested money and of your time both went up. You are less likely to continue to operate your own firm because it is less profitable.

4. The total-cost curve reflects the production function. When an input exhibits diminishing marginal product, the production function gets flatter because additional increments of inputs increase output by ever smaller amounts. Correspondingly, the total-cost curve gets steeper as the amount produced rises.

5. It is a fixed cost because the salary paid to management doesn't vary with the quantity produced.

6. It is the quantity of production that minimizes average total cost.

7. When marginal cost is below average total cost, the average total-cost curve must be falling. When marginal cost is above average total cost, the average total-cost curve must be rising. Thus, the marginal-cost curve crosses the average total-cost curve at the minimum of average total cost.

8. Typically, the marginal-cost curve is U-shaped. The firm often experiences increasing marginal product at very small levels of output as workers are allowed to specialize in their activities. Thus, marginal cost falls. At some point, the firm will experience diminishing marginal product and the marginal-cost curve will begin to rise.

9. In the short run, the size of the production facility is fixed so the firm will experience diminishing returns and increasing average total costs when adding additional workers. In the long run, the firm will expand the size of the factory and the number of workers together and, if the firm experiences constant returns to scale, average total costs will remain fixed at the minimum.

10. As a small firm expands the scale of operation, the higher production level allows for greater specialization of the workers and long run average total costs fall. As an enormous firm continues to expand, it will likely develop coordination problems and long run average total costs begin to increase.

True/False Questions

1. T

2. F; wages and salaries are explicit costs of production because euros flow out of the firm.

3. T

4. T

5. F; marginal product is the slope of the production function so marginal product is decreasing when the production function gets flatter.

6. T

7. F; diminishing marginal product means that it requires ever greater amounts of an input to produce equal increments of output so total costs rise at an increasing rate.

8. T

9. F; average total costs are total costs divided by the level of output.

10. T

11. T

12. F; the marginal-cost curve crosses the average total-cost curve at the minimum of the average total cost curve.

13. T

14. F; efficient scale minimizes average total costs.

15. F; a firm generally experiences economies of scale, constant returns to scale, and diseconomies of scale as the scale of production expands.

Multiple-Choice Questions

1. c	5. d	9. b
2. d	6. a	10. b
3. a	7. b	11. a
4. a	8. c	12. b

Advanced Critical Thinking

1. Yes. Many production processes first exhibit increasing marginal product of the variable inputs (in this case, workers). This result may occur due to specialization of labour. After the second worker is hired, one worker specializes in weeding while the other specializes in watering.

2. No. At some point, if any input is fixed (say the size of the garden) the firm will experience diminishing marginal product of the variable inputs. That is, at some point, the garden will become crowded and additional workers will add smaller and smaller amounts to output.

3. It is likely that the garden is small enough that the firm would experience economies of scale if it increased its scale of operation by expanding the size of the garden and hiring more workers. No, your friend cannot expand his scale of operation forever because, at some point, the firm becomes so large that it develops coordination problems and the firm experiences diseconomies of scale.

⌐In this chapter you will

Learn what characteristics make a market competitive

Examine how competitive firms decide how much output to produce

Examine how competitive firms decide when to shut down production temporarily

Examine how competitive firms decide whether to exit or enter a market

See how firm behaviour determines a market's short run and long run supply curves

OUTCOMES

⌐You should be able to

List up to three conditions that characterize a competitive market

Locate the supply curve for a competitive firm on a graph of its cost curves

Demonstrate why firms shut down if the price they receive for their output is less than average variable cost

Demonstrate why firms exit a market permanently if the price they receive for their output is less than average total cost

Show why the long run supply curve in a competitive market is more elastic than the short run supply curve

FIRMS IN COMPETITIVE MARKETS

CHAPTER OVERVIEW

Context and Purpose

Chapter 14 is the second chapter in a five-chapter sequence dealing with firm behaviour and the organization of industry. Chapter 13 developed the cost curves on which firm behaviour is based. These cost curves are employed in Chapter 14 to show how a competitive firm responds to changes in market conditions. Chapters 15 through 17 will employ these cost curves to see how firms with market power (monopolistic, oligopolistic, and monopolistically competitive firms) respond to changes in market conditions.

The purpose of Chapter 14 is to examine the behaviour of competitive firms—firms that do not have market power. The cost curves developed in the previous chapter shed light on the decisions that lie behind the supply curve in a competitive market.

CHAPTER REVIEW

Introduction

In this chapter, we examine the behaviour of competitive firms—firms that do not have *market power*. Firms that have market power can influence the market price of the goods they sell. The cost curves developed in the previous chapter shed light on the decisions that lie behind the supply curve in a competitive market.

What is a Competitive Market?

A **competitive market** has two main characteristics:

- There are many buyers and sellers in the market.

- The goods offered for sale are very good substitutes for each other.

The result of these two conditions is that each buyer and seller is a *price taker*. A third condition sometimes thought to characterize competitive markets is:

- Firms can freely enter or exit the market.

Firms in competitive markets try to maximize profits, which equals total revenue minus total cost. Total revenue (TR) is $P \times Q$. Since a competitive firm is small compared to the market, it takes the price as given. Thus, total revenue is proportional to the amount of output sold—doubling output sold doubles total revenue.

Average revenue (AR) equals total revenue (TR) divided by the quantity of output (Q) or $AR = TR/Q$. Since $TR = P \times Q$, then $AR = (P \times Q)/Q = P$. That is, for all firms, *average revenue equals the price of the good.*

Marginal revenue (MR) equals the change in total revenue from the sale of an additional unit of output or $MR = \Delta TR/\Delta Q$. When Q rises by one unit, total revenue rises by P euros. Therefore, for competitive firms, *marginal revenue equals the price of the good.*

Profit Maximization and the Competitive Firm's Supply Curve

Firms maximize profit by comparing marginal revenue and marginal cost. For the competitive firm, marginal revenue is fixed at the price of the good and marginal cost is increasing as output rises. As long as marginal revenue exceeds marginal cost, increasing the quantity produced raises profit. *Profit is maximized when firms produce output up to the point where marginal cost equals marginal revenue.*

Assume that we have a firm with typical cost curves. Graphically, marginal cost (MC) is upward sloping, average total cost (ATC) is U-shaped, and MC crosses ATC at the minimum of ATC. If we draw $P = AR = MR$ on this graph, we can see that the firm will choose to produce a quantity that will maximize profit based on the intersection of MR and MC. That is, the firm will choose to produce the quantity where $MR = MC$. At any quantity lower than the optimal quantity, $MR > MC$ and profit is increased if output is increased. At any quantity above the optimal quantity, $MC > MR$ and profit is increased if output is reduced.

If the price were to increase, the firm would respond by increasing production to the point where the new higher $P = AR = MR$ is equal to MC. That is, the firm moves upwards along its MC curve until $MR = MC$ again. Therefore, with one proviso discussed in the following paragraph, *because the firm's marginal-cost curve determines how much the firm is willing to supply at any price, it is the competitive firm's supply curve.*

A firm will *shut down* (produce nothing) *if the revenue that it would get from producing is less than the variable costs (VC) of production.* Sometimes, shutting down might only be temporary. Examples of temporary shut downs are farmers leaving land idle for a season and restaurants closing for lunch. For the temporary shutdown decision, the firm ignores fixed costs because these are considered to be **sunk costs** or costs that are not recoverable because the firm must pay them whether they produce output or not. Mathematically, the firm should temporarily shut down if $TR < VC$. Divide by Q to obtain $TR/Q < VC/Q$ which is $AR = MR = P < AVC$. That is, the firm should shut down if $P < AVC$. Therefore, *the competitive firm's short run supply curve is the portion of its marginal-cost curve that lies above the average variable cost curve.*

In general, beyond the example of a competitive firm, all rational decision-makers think at the margin and ignore sunk costs when making economic decisions. Rational decision-makers undertake activities where the marginal benefit exceeds the marginal cost.

In the long run, a firm will *exit the market* (permanently cease operations) *if the revenue it would receive from producing is less than its total costs.* If the firm exits the industry, it saves on both the fixed and variable costs, that is, total costs. Mathematically, the firm should exit if $TR < VC$. Divide by Q to obtain $TR/Q = TC/Q$ which is $AR = MR = P < ATC$. That is, the firm should exit if $P < ATC$. Therefore, *the competitive firm's long run supply curve is the portion of its marginal-cost curve that lies above the average total-cost curve.*

A competitive firm's profit $= TR - TC$. Divide and multiply by Q to obtain Profit $= (TR/Q - TC/Q) \times Q$ or Profit $= (P - ATC) \times Q$. If price is above ATC, the firm is profitable. If price is below ATC, the firm generates losses and would eventually choose to exit the market.

The Supply Curve in a Competitive Market

In the short run, the number of firms in the market is fixed because firms cannot quickly enter or exit the market. Therefore, in the short run, the market supply curve is the horizontal sum of the portion of the individual firm's marginal cost curves that lie above their average variable cost curves. That is, the market supply curve is simply the sum of the quantities supplied by each firm in the market at each price. Since the individual marginal cost curves are upward sloping, *the short run market supply curve is also upward sloping*.

In the long run, firms are able to enter and exit the market. Suppose all firms have the same cost curves. If firms in the market are making profits, new firms will enter the market increasing the quantity supplied and causing the price to fall until economic profits are zero. If firms in the market are making losses, some existing firms will exit the market decreasing the quantity supplied and causing the price to rise until economic profits are zero. In the long run, *firms that remain in the market must be making zero economic profit*. Since profit $= (P - ATC) \times Q$, *profit equals zero only when $P = ATC$*. Since for the competitive firm, $P = MC$ and MC intersects ATC at the minimum of ATC, *the long run equilibrium of a competitive market with free entry and exit must have firms operating at their efficient scale*. Also, since firms enter or exit the market if the price is above or below minimum ATC, the price always returns to the minimum ATC for each firm, but the total quantity supplied in the market rises and falls with the number of firms. Thus, there is only one price consistent with zero profits and *the long run market supply curve must be horizontal* (perfectly elastic) at that price.

Competitive firms stay in business even though they are making zero economic profits in the long run. Recall that economists define total costs to include all the opportunity costs of the firm, so the zero-profit equilibrium is compensating the owners of the firm for their time and their money invested.

In the short run, an increase in demand increases the price of a good and existing firms make economic profits. In the long run, this attracts new firms to enter the market causing a corresponding increase in the market supply. This increase in supply reduces the price to its original level consistent with zero profits, but the quantity sold in the market is now higher. Thus, if at present firms are earning relatively high profits in a competitive industry, they can expect new firms to enter the market and prices and profits to fall in the future.

While the standard case is one where the long run market supply curve is perfectly elastic, the long run market supply curve might, in reality, be upward sloping for two reasons:

- If an input necessary for production is in limited supply, an expansion of firms in that industry will raise the costs for all existing firms and increase the price as output supplied increases.

- If firms have different costs (some are more efficient than others) in order to induce new less-efficient firms to enter the market, the price must increase to cover these less efficient firms' costs. In this case, only the *marginal firm* earns zero economic profits, while more efficient firms earn economic profits in the long run.

Regardless of this, because firms can enter and exit more easily in the long run than in the short run, *the long run market supply curve is more elastic than the short run market supply curve*.

Conclusion: Behind the Supply Curve

The supply decision is based on marginal analysis. In competitive markets, firms produce where marginal cost equals price equals minimum average total cost.

HELPFUL HINTS

1. We have determined that, in the short run, the firm will produce the quantity of output where $P = MC$ as long as the price equals or exceeds average variable cost. An additional way to see the logic of this behaviour is to recognize that since fixed costs must be paid regardless of the level of production, any time the firm can at least cover its variable costs, any additional revenue beyond its variable costs can be applied to its fixed costs. Therefore, in the short run, the firm loses less money than it would if it shut down whenever the price exceeds its average variable costs. As a result, the short run supply curve for the firm is the portion of marginal cost curve that is above the average variable cost curve.

2. Recall that rational decision makers think at the margin. The decision rule for any action is that we should undertake activities for which the marginal benefit exceeds the marginal cost and continue until the marginal benefit equals the marginal cost. This decision rule translates directly to the firm's production decision in that the firm should continue to produce additional output until marginal revenue (the marginal benefit to the firm) equals marginal cost.

3. In this chapter, we derived the equation for profit as Profit $= (P-ATC) \times Q$. It helps to remember that, in words, this formula says that profit simply equals the average profit per unit times the number of units sold. This holds true even in the case of losses. If the price is less than average total cost, then we have the average loss per unit times the number of units sold.

TERMS AND DEFINITIONS

Choose a definition for each key term.

Key terms:

_____ Price takers

_____ Competitive market

_____ Average revenue

_____ Marginal revenue

_____ Shut down

_____ Exit

_____ Sunk cost

Definitions:

1. A short run decision to cease production due to current market conditions

2. A market with many buyers and sellers trading identical products so that each buyer and seller is a price taker

3. Total revenue divided by the quantity sold

4. A cost to which one is already committed and which is not recoverable

5. The change in total revenue from an additional unit sold

6. Buyers and sellers in a competitive market that must accept the price that the market determines

7. A long run decision to permanently cease production and leave the market

PROBLEMS AND SHORT-ANSWER QUESTIONS

Practice Problems

1. In which of the following markets are firms likely to be price takers. Explain.
   a. The market for flowers.
   b. The market for blue jeans.
   c. The market for agricultural products such as wheat and potatoes.
   d. The market for electricity.
   e. The market for cable television.

2. a. The following table contains information about the revenues and costs for Zina's golf ball manufacturing firm. All data are per hour. Complete the first group of columns which correspond to the firm's production if $P = €3$. (TR = total revenue, TC = total cost, MR = marginal revenue, MC = marginal cost)

Q	TR, P = €3	TC (€)	Profit	MR	MC	TR, P = €2	Profit	MR
0	____	1	____			____	____	
1	____	2	____	____	____	____	____	____
2	____	4	____	____	____	____	____	____
3	____	7	____	____	____	____	____	____
4	____	11	____	____	____	____	____	____
5	____	16	____	____	____	____	____	____

   b. If the price is €3 per golf ball, what is Zina's optimal level of production? What criteria did you use to determine the optimal level of production?
   c. Is €3 per golf ball a long run equilibrium price in the market for golf balls? Explain. What adjustment will take place in the market for golf balls and what will happen to the price in the long run?
   d. Suppose the price of golf balls falls to €2. Fill out the remaining three columns of the table above. What is the profit-maximizing level of output when the price is €2 per golf ball? How much profit does the firm earn when the price of golf balls is €2?
   e. Is €2 per golf ball a long run equilibrium price in the market for golf balls? Explain. Why would Zina continue to produce at this level of profit?
   f. Describe the slope of the short run supply curve for the market for golf balls. Describe the slope of the long run supply curve in the market for golf balls.

3. a. In Exhibit 1, show the cost curves of a representative firm in long run equilibrium along side the corresponding market equilibrium.
   b. Suppose there is a *decrease* in demand for this product. In Exhibit 2, show the shift in demand in the market for this product and the corresponding profit or loss on the cost curves of the representative firm.
   c. In Exhibit 3, show the adjustment that takes place in order to return the market and firm to long run equilibrium.
   d. After the market has returned to long run equilibrium, is the price higher, lower, or the same as the initial price? Are there more, fewer, or the same number of firms producing in the market?

EXHIBIT 1

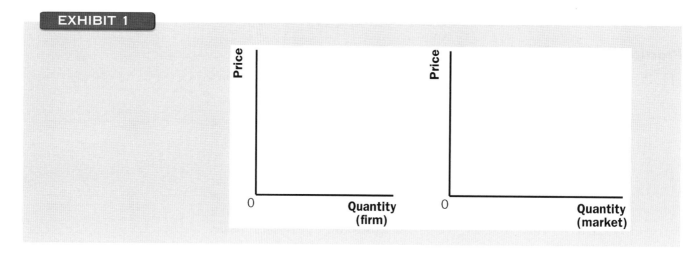

EXHIBIT 2

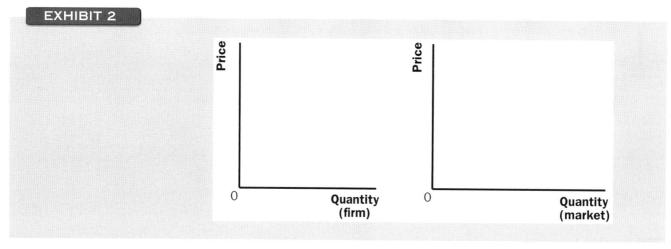

EXHIBIT 3

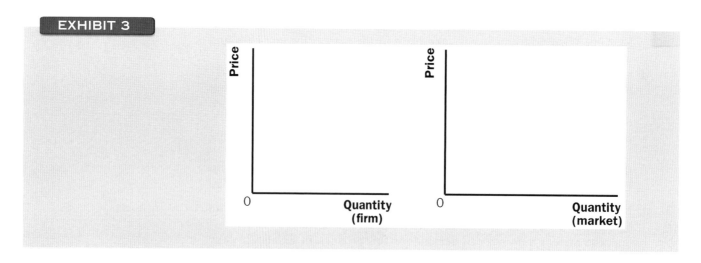

Short-Answer Questions

1. What are the three conditions that characterize a competitive market?

2. If a firm is in a competitive market, what happens to its total revenue if it doubles its output? Why?

3. If a firm is producing a level of output where marginal revenue exceeds marginal cost, would it improve profits by increasing output, decreasing output, or keeping output unchanged? Why?

4. What constitutes a competitive firm's short run supply curve? Explain.

5. What constitutes a competitive firm's long run supply curve? Explain.

6. You go to your campus bookstore and see a coffee mug emblazoned with your university's shield. It costs €5 and you value it at €8, so you buy it. On the way to your car, you drop it and it breaks into pieces. Should you buy another one or should you go home because the total expenditure of €10 now exceeds the €8 value that you place on it? Why?

7. Suppose the price for a firm's output is above the average variable cost of production but below the average total cost of production. Will the firm shut down in the short run? Explain. Will the firm exit the market in the long run? Explain.

8. Why must the long run equilibrium in a competitive market (with free entry and exit) have all firms operating at their efficient scale?

9. Why is the short run market supply curve upward sloping while the standard long run market supply curve is perfectly elastic?

10. Under what conditions would the long run market supply curve be upward sloping?

SELF-TEST

True/False Questions

_____ 1. For a competitive firm, marginal revenue equals the price of the good it sells.

_____ 2. A firm always maximizes profit when it produces where the average total cost is minimized.

_____ 3. If marginal cost exceeds marginal revenue at a firm's current level of output, the firm can increase profit if it increases its level of output.

_____ 4. In the short run, if the price a firm receives for a good is above its average variable costs but below its average total costs of production, the firm will shut down.

_____ 5. In a competitive market, both buyers and sellers are price takers.

_____ 6. In the long run, if the price firms receive for their output is below their average total costs of production, some firms will exit the market.

_____ 7. In the short run, the market supply curve for a good is the sum of the quantities supplied by each firm at each price.

_____ 8. The short run market supply curve is more elastic than the long run market supply curve.

_____ 9. In the long run, perfectly competitive firms with the same cost curves can earn small but positive economic profits.

_____ 10. In the long run, if firms are identical and there is free entry and exit in the market, all firms in the market operate at their efficient scale.

Multiple-Choice Questions

1. Which of the following is *not* a characteristic of a competitive market?
   a. There are many buyers and sellers in the market.
   b. The goods offered for sale are largely the same.
   c. Firms can freely enter or exit the market.
   d. Firms generate small but positive economic profits in the long run.
   e. All of the above are characteristics of a competitive market.

2. For a competitive firm, marginal revenue is
   a. equal to the price of the good sold.
   b. average revenue divided by the quantity sold.
   c. total revenue divided by the quantity sold.
   d. equal to the quantity of the good sold.

EXHIBIT 4

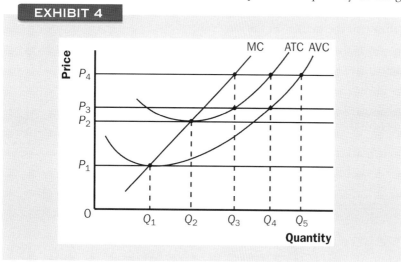

Use Exhibit 4 for problems 3 through 7.

3. If the price is P_4, a competitive firm will maximize profits if it produces
   a. Q_1.
   b. Q_2.
   c. Q_3.
   d. Q_4.
   e. Q_5.

4. If the price is P_4, the firm will earn profits equal to the area
   a. $(P_2-P_1) \times Q_2$.
   b. $(P_3-P_2) \times Q_3$.
   c. $(P_4-P_2) \times Q_4$.
   d. $(P_4-P_3) \times Q_3$.
   e. none of the above.

5. In the short run, competitive firms will temporarily shut down production if the price falls below
   a. P_1.
   b. P_2.
   c. P_3.
   d. P_4.

6. In the long run, some competitive firms will exit the market if the price is below
   a. P_1.
   b. P_2.
   c. P_3.
   d. P_4.

7. In the long run, the competitive equilibrium is
   a. P_1, Q_1.
   b. P_2, Q_2.
   c. P_4, Q_3.
   d. P_4, Q_4.
   e. P_4, Q_5.

8. In the long run, some firms will exit the market if the price of the good offered for sale is less than
   a. marginal revenue.
   b. marginal cost.

c. average revenue.

d. average total cost.

9. If all firms in a market have identical cost structures and if inputs used in the production of the good in that market are readily available, then the long run market supply curve for that good should be

a. perfectly elastic.

b. downward sloping.

c. upward sloping.

d. perfectly inelastic.

10. If an input necessary for production is in limited supply so that an expansion of the industry raises costs for all existing firms in the market, then the long run market supply curve for a good could be

a. perfectly elastic.

b. downward sloping.

c. upward sloping.

d. perfectly inelastic.

11. If the long run market supply curve for a good is perfectly elastic, an increase in the demand for that good will, in the long run, cause

a. an increase the price of the good and an increase in the number of firms in the market.

b. an increase the price of the good but no increase in the number of firms in the market.

c. an increase in the number of firms in the market but no increase in the price of the good.

d. no impact on either the price of the good or the number of firms in the market.

12. In long run equilibrium in a competitive market, firms are operating at

a. the minimum of their average total-cost curves.

b. the intersection of marginal cost and marginal revenue.

c. their efficient scale.

d. zero economic profit.

e. all of the above.

ADVANCED CRITICAL THINKING

In some regions of the country it is common for Tesco stores and other large supermarkets to stay open 24 hours a day, 365 days a year.

1. You walk into a Tesco store at 2:00 a.m. with a friend to buy some VCR tapes. Your friend says, 'I can't believe that these stores stay open all night. Only 1 out of 15 checkout lines is open. There can't be more than ten shoppers in this store. It just doesn't make any sense for this store to be open all night.' Explain to your friend what conditions must be true for it to be to the advantage of Tesco to stay open all night.

2. Are the costs of rent, equipment, fixtures, salaries of management, and so on, relevant when Tesco makes the decision whether to stay open at night? Why?

3. If Tesco had the same number of customers during its day-time hours as you observed during its night-time hours, do you think it would continue to operate? Explain.

SOLUTIONS

Terms and Definitions

__1__ Shut down

__2__ Competitive market

__3__ Average revenue

__4__ Sunk cost

__5__ Marginal revenue

__6__ Price takers

__7__ Exit

Practice Problems

1. a. Yes, many buyers and sellers each of which is likely to be very small and the product of different sellers is identical.
    b. Probably not, many buyers and sellers but the product is not identical (Levi, Lee, Ralph Lauren...) so each seller is not a price taker.
    c. Yes, many buyers and sellers and the product of different sellers is identical.
    d. Yes. Although there are few sellers, the product is identical and it is easy to switch suppliers. There are exceptions and in some countries there is only a single supplier. In this case the firm is certainly not a price taker.
    e. No, few sellers (often only one). If there were multiple sellers, the product would be nearly identical.

2. a.

Q	TR, P = €3	TC	Profit	MR	MC	TR, P =€2	Profit	MR
0	€0	€1	−€1			€0	−€1	
				€3	€1			€2
1	3	2	1			2	0	
				3	2			2
2	6	4	2			4	0	
				3	3			2
3	9	7	2			6	−1	
				3	4			2
4	12	11	1			8	−3	
				3	5			2
5	15	16	−1			10	−6	

  b. Optimal production is either two or three golf balls per hour. This level of production maximizes profit (at €2) and it is the level of output where $MC = MR$ (at €3).
  c. No, because Zina is earning positive economic profits of €2. These profits will attract new firms to enter the market for golf balls, the market supply will increase, and the price will fall until economic profits are zero.
  d. See answers for the table in part (a) above. Optimal production is either one or two golf balls per hour. Zero economic profit is earned by Zina.
  e. Yes. Economic profits are zero and firms neither enter nor exit the industry. Zero economic profits means that Zina doesn't earn anything beyond her opportunity costs of production, but her revenues do cover the cost of her inputs and the value of her time and money.
  f. The slope of the short run supply curve is positive because when $P = €2$, quantity supplied is one or two units per firm and when $P = €3$, quantity supplied is two or three units per firm. In the long run, supply is horizontal (perfectly elastic) at $P = €2$ because any price above €2 causes firms to enter and drives the price back to €2.

EXHIBIT 5

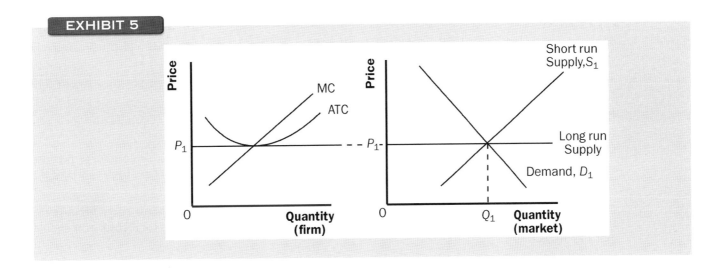

EXHIBIT 6

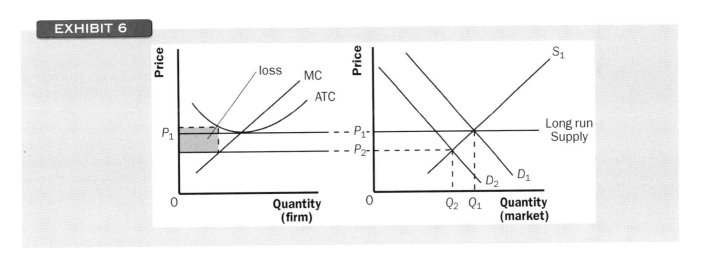

EXHIBIT 7

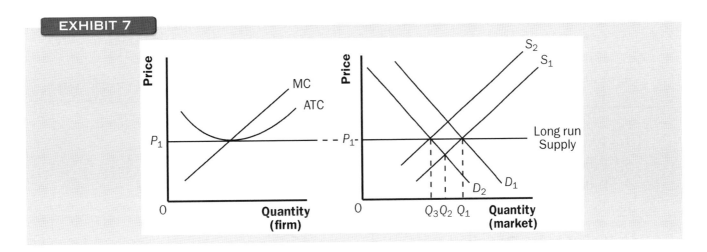

3. a. See Exhibit 5.
    b. See Exhibit 6.
    c. See Exhibit 7.
    d. The price has returned to its initial level. There are fewer firms producing in this market.

Short-Answer Questions

1. There are many buyers and sellers, the goods offered for sale are largely the same, and firms can freely enter or exit the market.

2. Total revenue doubles. This is because, in a competitive market, the price is unaffected by the amount sold by any individual firm.

3. If $MR > MC$, increasing output will increase profits because an additional unit of production increases revenue more than it increases costs.

4. It is the portion of the firm's marginal cost curve that lies above its average variable cost curve because the firm maximizes profit where $P = MC$ and, in the short run, fixed or sunk costs are irrelevant and the firm must only cover its variable costs to remain in the industry.

5. It is the portion of the firm's marginal cost curve that lies above its average total cost curve because the firm maximizes profit where $P = MC$ and, in the long run, the firm must cover its total costs or it should exit the market.

6. You should buy another mug because the marginal benefit (€8) still exceeds the marginal cost (€5). The broken mug is a sunk cost and is not recoverable. Therefore, it is irrelevant.

7. No. In the short run, the firm's fixed costs are sunk costs so the firm will not shut down because it only needs to cover its variable costs. Yes. In the long run, the firm must cover total costs and if $P < ATC$ the firm generates losses in the long run and it will exit the market.

8. In long run equilibrium, firms must be making zero economic profits so that firms are not entering or exiting the industry. Zero profits occur when $P = ATC$ and for the competitive firm $P = MC$ determines the production level. $P = ATC = MC$ only at the minimum of ATC.

9. In the short run, firms cannot exit or enter the market so the market supply curve is the horizontal sum of the upward-sloping MC curves of the existing firms. However, in the long run, if the price is above or below minimum ATC, firms will enter or exit the market causing the price to always return to minimum ATC for each firm, but the total quantity supplied in the market rises and falls with the number of firms. Thus, the market supply curve is horizontal.

10. If an input necessary for production is in limited supply or if firms have different costs.

True/False Questions

1. T

2. F; firms aim to maximize profit and produce where MC = MR. In competitive markets the equality between MC and MR also coincides with minimum ATC—but firms do not AIM to minimize ATC!

3. F; the firm increases profits if it reduces output.

4. F; the firm will continue to operate in the short run as long as price exceeds average variable costs.

5. T

6. T

7. T

8. F; the long run market supply curve is more elastic than the short run market supply curve.

9. F; they earn zero economic profits in the long run.

10. T

Multiple-Choice Questions

1. d	5. a	9. a
2. a	6. b	10. c
3. c	7. b	11. c
4. d	8. d	12. e

Advanced Critical Thinking

1. For Tesco to stay open all night (and not undertake a temporary shut down) it must be true that its total revenue at night must equal or exceed its *variable costs* incurred from staying open the additional hours (electricity, wages of night shift workers, etc.).

2. No. These costs are fixed costs or sunk costs—costs that cannot be recovered even if Tesco chooses not to operate at night.

3. It is unlikely. This is because the temporary shut-down decision (staying open additional hours at night) depends on whether total revenue equals or exceeds *variable costs*, but the decision to remain in the market in the long run depends on whether total revenue equals or exceeds *total costs*. It is unlikely that the revenue earned at night covers total costs (both fixed and variable costs).

15

GOALS

⌐In this chapter you will

Learn why some markets have only one seller

Analyse how a monopoly determines the quantity to produce and the price to charge

See how the monopoly's decisions affect economic welfare

Consider the various public policies aimed at solving the problem of monopoly

See why monopolies try to charge different prices to different customers

OUTCOMES

⌐You should be able to

List three reasons why a monopoly can remain the sole seller of a product in a market

Use a monopolist's cost curves and the demand curve it faces to show the profit earned by a monopolist

Show the deadweight loss from a monopolist's production decision

Show why forcing a natural monopoly to charge its marginal cost of production creates losses for the monopolist

Demonstrate the surprising result that price discrimination by a monopolist can raise economic welfare above that generated by standard monopoly pricing

MONOPOLY

CHAPTER OVERVIEW

Context and Purpose

Chapter 15 is the third chapter in a five-chapter sequence dealing with firm behaviour and the organization of industry. Chapter 13 developed the cost curves on which firm behaviour is based. These cost curves were employed in Chapter 14 to show how a competitive firm responds to changes in market conditions. In Chapter 15, these cost curves are again employed, this time to show how a monopolistic firm chooses the quantity to produce and the price to charge. Chapters 16 and 17 will address the decisions made by oligopolistic and monopolistically competitive firms.

A monopolist is the sole seller of a product without close substitutes. As such, it has market power because it can influence the price of its output. That is, a monopolist is a price maker as opposed to a price taker. The purpose of Chapter 15 is to examine the production and pricing decisions of monopolists, the social implications of their market power, and the ways in which governments might respond to the problems caused by monopolists.

CHAPTER REVIEW

Introduction

Monopolists have market power because they can influence the price of their output. That is, monopolists are *price makers* as opposed to *price takers*. While competitive firms choose to produce a quantity of output such that the given market price equals the marginal cost of production, monopolists charge prices that exceed marginal cost. In this chapter we examine the production and pricing decisions of monopolists, the social implications of their market power, and the ways in which governments might respond to the problems caused by monopolists.

Why Monopolies Arise

A **monopoly** is a firm that is the sole seller of a product without close substitutes. A monopoly is able to remain the only seller in a market only if there are *barriers to* *entry*. That is, other firms are unable to enter the market and compete with it. There are three sources of barriers to entry:

- *A key resource is owned by a single firm*. For example, if a firm owns the only well in town, it has a monopoly for the sale of water. DeBeers essentially has a monopoly in the market for diamonds because it controls 80 per cent of the world's production of diamonds. This source of monopoly is somewhat rare.

- *The government gives a single firm the exclusive right to produce some good*. When the government grants patents (which last for 20 years) to inventors and copyrights to authors, it is giving someone the right to be the sole producer of that good. The benefit is that it increases incentives for creative activity. The costs will be discussed later in the chapter.

- *The costs of production make a single producer more efficient than a large number of producers*. A **natural monopoly** arises when a single firm can supply a good to an entire market at a smaller cost than could two or more firms. This happens when there are economies of scale over the relevant range of output. That is, the average-total-cost curve for an individual firm continually declines at least to the quantity that could supply the entire market. This cost advantage is a natural barrier to entry because firms with higher costs find it undesirable to enter the market. Common examples are utilities such as water and electricity distribution.

How Monopolies Make Production and Pricing Decisions

A competitive firm is small relative to the market so it takes the price of the good it produces as given. Since it can sell as much as it chooses at the given market price, the competitive firm faces a demand curve that is perfectly elastic at the market price. A monopoly is the sole producer in its market so it faces the entire downward-sloping market demand curve. The monopolist can choose any price/quantity combination on the demand curve by choosing the quantity and seeing what price buyers will pay. As with competitive firms, monopolies choose a quantity of output that maximizes profit (total revenue minus total cost).

Since the monopolist faces a downward-sloping demand curve, it must lower the price of the good if it wishes to sell a greater quantity. Therefore, when it sells an additional unit, the sale of the additional unit has two effects on total revenue ($P \times Q$):

- *The output effect*: Q is higher.

- *The price effect*: P is lower (on the marginal unit *and on the units it was already selling*).

Since the monopolist must reduce the price on every unit it sells when it expands output by one unit, marginal revenue ($\Delta TR/\Delta Q$) for the monopolist declines as Q increases and *marginal revenue is always less than the price of the good*.

As with a competitive firm, the monopolist maximizes profit at the level of output where marginal revenue (MR) equals marginal cost (MC). As Q increases, MR decreases and MC increases. Therefore, at low levels of output, $MR > MC$ and an increase in Q increases profit. At high levels of output, $MC > MR$ and a decrease in output increases profit. The monopolist, therefore, should produce up to the point where $MR = MC$. That is, the profit maximising level of output is determined by the intersection of the marginal revenue and marginal cost curves. Since the MR curve lies below the demand curve, the price the monopolist charges is found by reading up to the demand curve from the $MR = MC$ intersection.

Recall that for the competitive firm, since the demand curve facing the firm is perfectly elastic so that $P = MR$, the profit maximizing equilibrium requires that

$P = MR = MC$. However, for the monopoly firm, $MR < P$ so the profit maximizing equilibrium requires that $P > MR = MC$. As a result, *in competitive markets, price equals marginal cost while in monopolized markets, price exceeds marginal cost.*

Evidence from the pharmaceutical drug market is consistent with our theory. While the patent is enforced, the price of a drug is relatively high. When the patent expires and generic drugs become available, the price falls substantially.

As with the competitive firm, Profit = $(P - ATC) \times Q$, or profit equals the average profit per unit times the number of units sold.

The Welfare Cost of Monopoly

Does a monopoly market maximize economic welfare as measured by total surplus? Recall that total surplus is the sum of consumer surplus and producer surplus. Equilibrium of supply and demand in a competitive market naturally maximizes total surplus because all units are produced where the value to buyers are greater than or equal to the cost of production to the sellers.

For a monopolist to produce the socially efficient quantity (maximize total surplus by producing all units where the value to buyers exceeds or equals the cost of production) it would have to produce the level of output where the marginal cost curve intersects the demand curve. However, the monopolist chooses to produce the level of output where the marginal revenue curve intersects the marginal cost curve. Since for the monopolist the marginal revenue curve is always below the demand curve, *the monopolist produces less than the socially efficient quantity of output.*

The small quantity produced by the monopolist allows the monopolist to charge a price that exceeds the marginal cost of production. Therefore, the monopolist generates a *deadweight loss* because, at the high monopoly price, consumers fail to buy units of output where the value to them exceeds the cost to the monopolist.

The deadweight loss from a monopoly is similar to the deadweight loss from a tax and the monopolist's profit is similar to tax revenue except that the revenue is received by a private firm. Since the profit earned by a monopolist is simply a transfer of consumer surplus to producer surplus, a monopoly's profit is not a social cost. The social cost of a monopoly is the deadweight loss generated when the monopolist produces a quantity of output below that which is efficient.

Public Policy towards Monopolies

Monopolies fail to allocate resources efficiently because they produce less than the socially optimal quantity of output and charge prices that exceed marginal cost. Policy-makers can respond to the problem of monopoly in one of four ways:

- *By trying to make monopolised industries more competitive.* In the UK, the Director-General of Fair Trading can use anti-competitive laws (statutes aimed at reducing monopoly power) to prevent mergers that reduce competition, break up extremely large companies to increase competition, and prevent companies from colluding. However, some mergers result in synergies that reduce costs and raise efficiency. Therefore, it is difficult for government to know which mergers to block and which ones to allow.

- *By regulating the behaviour of the monopolies.* The prices charged by natural monopolies such as utilities are often regulated by government. If a natural monopoly is required to set its price equal to its marginal cost, the efficient quantity will be consumed, but the monopoly will lose money because marginal cost must be below average variable cost if average variable cost is declining. Thus, the monopolist will exit the industry. In response, regulators can subsidize a natural monopoly with tax revenue (which creates its own deadweight loss) or allow average total cost pricing which is an improvement over monopoly pricing but it is not as socially efficient as marginal cost pricing. Another problem with regulating prices is that monopolists have no incentive to reduce costs because their prices are reduced when their costs are reduced.

- *By turning some private monopolies into public enterprises.* Instead of regulating the prices charged by a natural monopoly, the government can run the monopoly itself. In many countries the postal service and the railways are examples. Economists generally prefer private ownership to public ownership because private owners have a greater incentive to minimize costs.

- *By doing nothing at all.* Since each of the solutions above has its own shortcomings, some economists urge that monopolies be left alone. They believe that the 'political failure' in the real world is more costly than the 'market failure' caused by monopoly pricing.

Price Discrimination

Price discrimination is the business practice of selling the same good at different prices to different customers. Price discrimination can only be practiced by a firm with market power such as a monopolist. There are three lessons to note about price discrimination:

- Price discrimination is a rational strategy for a profit maximizing monopolist because a monopolist's profits are increased when it charges each customer a price closer to his or her individual willingness to pay.

- Price discrimination is only possible if the monopolist is able to separate customers according to their willingness to pay—by age, income, location, and so on. If there is *arbitrage*—the process of buying a good in one market at a lower price and selling it in another market at a higher price—price discrimination is not possible.

- Price discrimination can raise economic welfare because output increases beyond that which would result under monopoly pricing. However, the additional surplus (reduced deadweight loss) is received by the producer, not the consumer.

Perfect price discrimination occurs when a monopolist charges each customer his or her exact willingness to pay. In this case, the efficient quantity is produced and consumed and there is no deadweight loss. However, total surplus goes to the monopolist in the form of profit. In reality, perfect price discrimination cannot be accomplished. Imperfect price discrimination may raise, lower, or leave unchanged total surplus in a market.

Examples of price discrimination include movie tickets, airline tickets, discount coupons, financial aid for college tuition, and quantity discounts. Prescription drug manufacturers sometimes charge different prices for the same drug when selling for use by people than they do when selling for use with animals, and when selling to people from different countries. Sometimes price discrimination allows a manufacturer to sell drugs to the residents of poor countries at a discounted price so that more people receive the drug than would under a single price policy. Sometimes differential pricing just raises prices.

Conclusion: The Prevalence of Monopoly

In one sense, monopolies are common because most firms have some control over the prices they charge. On the other hand, firms with substantial monopoly power are rare. Monopoly power is a matter of degree.

HELPFUL HINTS

1. A monopolist can choose the quantity and see what price buyers will pay or a monopolist can choose the price and see what quantity buyers will purchase.

That is, a monopolist is still subject to the demand curve for its product. The monopolist cannot choose both a high price and a large quantity if that combination does not lie on the demand curve facing the monopolist.

2. A monopolist is not guaranteed to earn profits. Any one of us can be the monopolist in the production of gold-plated textbook covers (since there is currently no producer of such a product) but the demand for such a product is likely to be too low to cover the costs of production. In like manner, gaining a patent on a product does not guarantee the holder of the patent future profits.

TERMS AND DEFINITIONS

Choose a definition for each key term.

Key terms:

_____ Monopoly

_____ Natural monopoly

_____ Price discrimination

_____ Arbitrage

_____ Perfect price discrimination

Definitions:

1. A monopoly that arises because a single firm can supply a good or service to an entire market at a smaller cost than could two or more firms

2. A firm that is the sole seller of a product without close substitutes

3. A situation in which the monopolist is able to charge each customer precisely his or her willingness to pay

4. The business practice of selling the same good at different prices to different customers

5. The process of buying a good in one market at a lower price and selling it in another market at a higher price

PROBLEMS AND SHORT-ANSWER QUESTIONS

Practice Problems

1. a. What are the three sources of the barriers to entry that allow a monopoly to remain the sole seller of a product?
   b. What is the entry barrier that is the source of the monopoly power for the following products or producers? List some competitors that keep these products or producers from having absolute monopoly power.
      1. Postal services in most countries.
      2. Perrier Spring Water.
      3. Prozac (a brand-name drug).
      4. DeBeers Diamonds.
      5. *Principles of Economics*, by N. Gregory Mankiw and Mark P. Taylor (your textbook).

2. Suppose a firm has a patent on a special process to make a unique smoked salmon. The following table provides information about the demand facing this firm for this unique product.
   a. Complete the table on page 169.
   b. Plot the demand curve and the marginal revenue curve in Exhibit 1. (Read Helpful Hint 2 in Chapter 13 of this study guide for a reminder on how to plot marginal values.)
   c. Suppose that there are no fixed costs and that the marginal cost of production of smoked salmon is constant at €6 per pound.

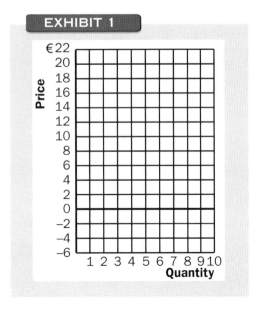

EXHIBIT 1

Pounds of Salmon	Price (€)	(P × Q) Total Revenue	(ΔTR/ΔQ) Marginal Revenue
0	20	_____	
			_____
1	18	_____	
			_____
2	16	_____	
			_____
3	14	_____	
			_____
4	12	_____	
			_____
5	10	_____	
			_____
6	8	_____	
			_____
7	6	_____	

(Thus, the average total cost is also constant at €6 per pound.) What is the quantity and price chosen by the monopolist? What is the profit earned by the monopolist? Show your solution on the graph you created in part (b) above.

d. What is the price and quantity that maximizes total surplus?

e. Compare the monopoly solution and the socially efficient solution. Is the monopolist's price too high or too low for economic efficiency? Why? Is the monopolist's quantity too high or too low? Why?

f. Is there a deadweight loss in this market if the monopolist charges the monopoly price? Explain.

g. If the monopolist is able to costlessly and perfectly price discriminate, is the outcome efficient? Explain. What is the value of consumer surplus, producer surplus, and total surplus? Explain.

3. a. What type of market is represented in Exhibit 2: perfect competition, monopoly, or natural monopoly? Explain.

b. Show the profit or loss generated by this firm in Exhibit 2 assuming that the firm maximizes profit.

c. Suppose government regulators force this firm to set the price equal to its marginal cost in order to improve efficiency in this market. In Exhibit 3 show the profit or loss generated by this firm.

d. In the long run, will forcing this firm to charge a price equal to its marginal cost improve efficiency? Explain.

Short-Answer Questions

1. Does a profit maximizing monopolist always produce where demand is elastic or inelastic? Explain.

2. What are possible public policies in response to the problem of monopoly? Which one(s) might be the most suitable in case of monopoly?

3. Does a monopolist charge the highest possible price for its output? Why? How does a monopolist choose the price it will charge for its product?

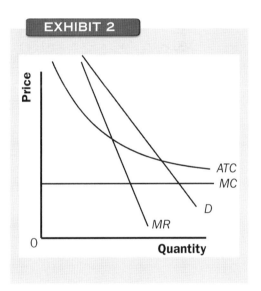

EXHIBIT 2

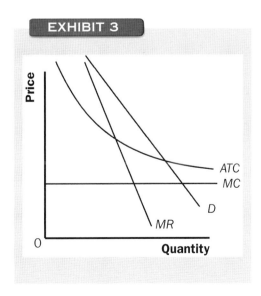

EXHIBIT 3

4. Why does a monopolist produce less than the socially efficient quantity of output?

5. Are the monopolist's profits part of the social cost of monopoly? Explain.

6. Why can a monopolist not simultaneously set the price of the product and the quantity produced?

7. Should anti-competitive laws be utilized to stop all mergers? Why?

8. What are some of the problems associated with regulating the price charged by a natural monopoly?

9. Is perfect price discrimination efficient? Explain. Who receives the surplus?

10. What is the necessary condition for a monopolist to be able to price discriminate?

SELF-TEST

True/False Questions

_____ 1. Monopolists are price takers.

_____ 2. A natural monopoly is a monopoly that uses its ownership of natural resources as a barrier to entry into its market.

_____ 3. The demand curve facing a monopolist is the market demand curve for its product.

_____ 4. For the monopolist, marginal revenue is always less than the price of the good.

_____ 5. The monopolist chooses the quantity of output at which marginal revenue equals marginal cost and then uses the demand curve to find the price that will induce consumers to buy that quantity.

_____ 6. The supply curve for a monopolist is derived from its marginal cost curve.

_____ 7. A monopolist produces an efficient quantity of output, but it is still inefficient because it charges a price that exceeds marginal cost and the resulting profit is a social cost.

_____ 8. Price discrimination is only possible if there is no arbitrage.

_____ 9. Perfect price discrimination is efficient, but all of the surplus is received by the consumer.

_____10. Universities are engaging in price discrimination when they charge different levels of tuition to poor and wealthy students.

Multiple-Choice Questions

1. A monopolist can always be distinguished from a firm in perfect competition because a monopolist
   a. always charges a higher price than a firm in perfect competition.
   b. has complete control over supply and demand for the product.
   c. produces where average revenue is greater than average cost in the short run.
   d. faces a downward-sloping demand curve whereas the firm in perfect competition does not.

2. When a monopolist produces an additional unit, the marginal revenue generated by that unit must be
   a. above the price because the output effect outweighs the price effect.
   b. above the price because the price effect outweighs the output effect.
   c. below the price because the output effect outweighs the price effect.
   d. below the price because the price effect outweighs the output effect.

3. Which of the following statements about price and marginal cost in competitive and monopolized markets is true?
   a. In competitive markets, price equals marginal cost; in monopolized markets, price equals marginal cost.
   b. In competitive markets, price exceeds marginal cost; in monopolized markets, price exceeds marginal cost.
   c. In competitive markets, price equals marginal cost; in monopolized markets, price exceeds marginal cost.
   d. In competitive markets, price exceeds marginal cost; in monopolized markets, price equals marginal cost.

   Use Exhibit 4 to answer questions 4 through 7.

EXHIBIT 4

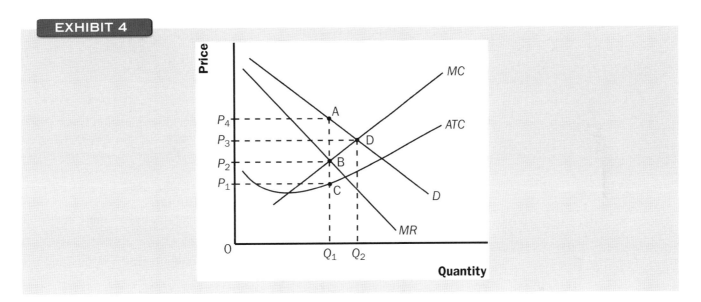

4. The profit maximizing monopolist will choose the price and quantity represented by point
   a. A.
   b. B.
   c. C.
   d. D.

5. The profit earned by the profit maximizing monopolist is represented by the area
   a. P_4ABP_2.
   b. P_4ACP_1.
   c. P_4AQ_10.
   d. P_3DQ_20.

6. The deadweight loss associated with monopoly pricing is represented by the area
   a. P_4ABP_2.
   b. P_4ACP_1.
   c. ABD.
   d. P_2BCP_1.

7. The efficient price and quantity are represented by point
   a. A.
   b. B.
   c. C.
   d. D.

8. The inefficiency associated with monopoly is due to
   a. the monopoly's profits.
   b. the monopoly's losses.
   c. overproduction of the good.
   d. underproduction of the good.

9. Compared to a perfectly competitive market, a monopoly market will usually generate
   a. higher prices and higher output.
   b. higher prices and lower output.
   c. lower prices and lower output.
   d. lower prices and higher output.

10. Using government regulations to force a natural monopoly to charge a price equal to its marginal cost will
    a. reduce output and profit.
    b. raise the price of good.
    c. attract additional firms to enter the market.
    d. cause the monopolist to exit the market.

11. Which of the follow statements about perfect price discrimination is *not* true?
    a. Price discrimination can raise economic welfare.
    b. Price discrimination requires that the seller be able to separate buyers according to their willingness to pay.
    c. Perfect price discrimination generates a deadweight loss.
    d. Price discrimination increases a monopolist's profits.
    e. For a monopolist to engage in price discrimination, buyers must be unable to engage in arbitrage.

12. A monopoly is able to continue to generate economic profits in the long run because
    a. potential competitors sometimes don't notice the profits.
    b. there is some barrier to entry to that market.
    c. the monopolist is financially powerful.
    d. anti-competitive laws eliminate competitors for a specified number of years.

ADVANCED CRITICAL THINKING

You are watching a television news show. A consumer advocate is discussing the airline industry. He says, 'There are so many rates offered by airlines that it is technically possible for a 747 to be carrying a full load of passengers where no two of them paid the same price for their tickets. This is clearly unfair and inefficient.' He continues, 'In addition, the profits of the airlines have doubled in the last few years since they began this practice and these additional profits are clearly a social burden. We need legislation that requires airlines to charge all passengers on an aeroplane the same price for their travel.'

1. List some of the ways airlines divide their customers according to their willingness to pay.

2. Is it necessarily inefficient for airlines to charge different prices to different customers? Why?

3. Is the increase in profits generated by this type of price discrimination a social cost? Explain.

SOLUTIONS

Terms and Definitions

__1__ Natural monopoly

__4__ Price discrimination

__2__ Monopoly

__5__ Arbitrage

__3__ Perfect price discrimination

Practice Problems

1. a. A key resource is owned by a single firm (monopoly resource), the government gives a single firm the exclusive right to produce a good (government created monopoly), the costs of production make a single producer more efficient (natural monopoly).

    b. 1. Natural monopoly. E-mail, Fax machines, telephone, private delivery such as DHL.

       2. Monopoly resource. Other bottled water, soft drinks.

       3. Government created monopoly due to a patent. Other drugs for depression, generic drugs when the patent expires.

       4. Monopoly resource. Other gems such as emeralds, rubies, sapphires.

       5. Government created monopoly due to copyright. Other principles of economics texts.

2. a.

Pounds of Salmon	Price (€)	(P × Q) Total Revenue	(ΔTR/ΔQ) Marginal Revenue
0	20	0	
1	18	18	18
2	16	32	14
3	14	42	10
4	12	48	6
5	10	50	2
6	8	48	−2
7	6	42	−6

b. See Exhibit 5.

c. Q = between 3 and 4 units (say 3.5), P = between €12 and €14, (say €13). Profit = $TR - TC$ or profit = $(3.5 \times €13) - (3.5 \times €6) = €45.50 - €21.00 = €24.50$. (Or profit = $(P - ATC) \times Q = (€13 - €6) \times 3.5 = €24.50$.) See Exhibit 6.

d. 7 units at €6 each. (The efficient solution is where the market produces all units where benefits exceed or equal costs of production which is where demand intersects MC.)

e. The monopolist's price is too high and quantity produced too low because the monopolist faces a downward-sloping demand curve that makes $MR < P$. Therefore, when the profit maximising monopolist sets $MR = MC$ and the MR curve is below the demand curve, the quantity is less than optimal and the price charged exceeds the MC of production.

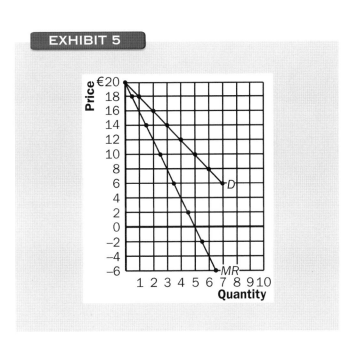

EXHIBIT 5

EXHIBIT 6

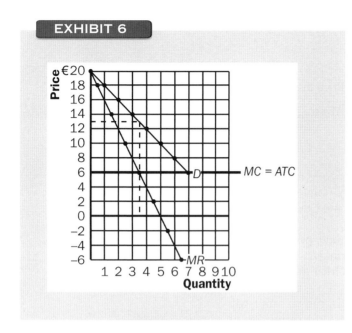

f. Yes. Units from 3.5 to 7, or an additional 3.5 pounds of salmon are valued by the consumer at values in excess of the €6 per pound *MC* of production and these units are not produced and consumed when the price is €13. (Deadweight loss = the deadweight loss triangle = 1/2 (7–3.5) × (€13 − €6) = €12.25.)

g. Yes, all units are produced where the value to buyers is greater than or is equal to the cost of production (7 units). Total surplus is now producer surplus and there is no consumer surplus. Total surplus and producer surplus is the area under the demand curve and above the price or 1/2(€20 − €6) × 7 = €49. Consumer surplus = €0.

3. a. Natural monopoly because *ATC* is still declining at the quantity that could satisfy the entire market.
   b. See Exhibit 7.
   c. See Exhibit 8.
   d. No. Since marginal cost must be below average total cost if average total cost is declining, this firm will generate losses if forced to charge a price equal to marginal cost. It will simply exit the market, which eliminates all surplus associated with this market.

Short-Answer Questions

1. A profit maximizing monopolist will always produce where demand is elastic. Remember from Chapter 5 that if demand is price inelastic, a reduction in price will lead to a reduction in total revenue. This implies that marginal revenue is negative. Since marginal cost can never be negative, it follows that a monopolist must always produce where demand is price elastic.

2. Government can try to make monopolized industries more competitive, to regulate the behaviour of the monopolies, to turn some private monopolies into public enterprises or to do nothing at all. To solve

EXHIBIT 7

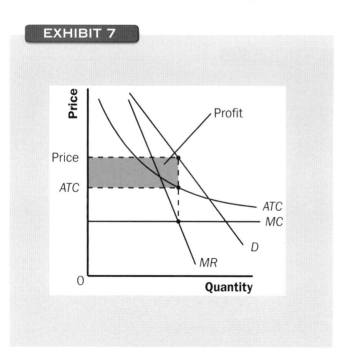

EXHIBIT 8

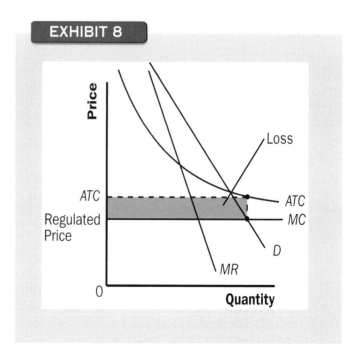

the problem of a resource monopoly the most suitable government policies can be regulation of the behaviour of the monopoly or turning the private monopoly into public enterprise.

3. No. Even a monopolist is subject to the law of demand for its product so a high price would cause buyers to buy very little of the good. The monopolist chooses its price by first choosing the optimal quantity based on the intersection of MR and MC and then charging the price consistent with that quantity.

4. For a monopolist, $P > MR$ because for a monopolist to sell another unit, it must reduce the price on the marginal unit *and all of its previous units*. Therefore, while a monopolist equates MR and MC, it charges a price that is greater than MC, which causes consumers to buy less than the efficient amount of the good.

5. No. The monopolist's profits are a redistribution of consumer surplus to producer surplus. The social cost of monopoly is the deadweight loss associated with the reduced production of output.

6. A monopolist can control market supply but not market demand. The monopolist can therefore either set price (up to the limit consumers will pay) and supply that level of output that will bring supply and demand into equilibrium at that price, or the monopolist can fix supply and allow demand to determine price.

7. No, many mergers capture synergies between the merging firms that reduce costs and increase efficiency.

8. If the monopolist is compelled to reduce price and is not simultaneously offered a subsidy, its profits will fall and it might exit the market. Subsidies to prevent this require taxes that also generate deadweight losses. Regulated monopolists have little incentive to reduce costs.

9. Yes, because every unit is produced where the value to buyers is greater than or equal to the cost to the producer. However, the entire total surplus is received by the producer (the monopolist).

10. The monopolist must be able to separate buyers according to their willingness to pay.

True/False Questions

1. F; monopolists are price makers.

2. F; a natural monopoly is a firm with an average total cost curve that continually declines at least to the quantity that satisfies the entire market.

3. T

4. T

5. T

6. F; monopolists have no supply curve.

7. F; the inefficiency generated by a monopoly results from the failure of the monopolist to produce units of output where the value to consumers equals or exceeds the cost of production. The monopolist's profits are not a cost to society, but are just a redistribution from consumer surplus to producer surplus.

8. T

9. F; all of the surplus is received by the producer.

10. T

Multiple-Choice Questions

1. d   5. b   9. b
2. d   6. c   10. d
3. c   7. d   11. c
4. a   8. d   12. b

Advanced Critical Thinking

1. Airlines segment people by age (young and old fly cheaper), by location (more competitive routes are cheaper), by length of time between leaving and returning (tourists fly cheaper than business travellers), by length of time of advance booking (later bookings can be more expensive until the very last minute when it may become cheaper again) and so on.

2. No. Price discrimination can improve efficiency. By charging buyers their willingness to pay, the monopolist increases production to the point where all units are produced where the value to buyers is greater than or equal to the cost of production.

3. No. Some of the additional profits are from the creation of additional surplus that accrues entirely to the producer and some of the profits are a redistribution of surplus from consumer surplus to producer surplus.

OLIGOPOLY

┌ In this chapter you will

See what market structures
lie between monopoly and
competition

Examine what outcomes are
possible when a market is
an oligopoly

Learn about the prisoners'
dilemma and how it applies to
oligopoly and other issues

Consider how the anti-competitive
laws try to foster competition in
oligopolistic markets

OUTCOMES

┌ You should be able to

Describe the characteristics of
oligopoly and monopolistic
competition

Describe the conditions under
which an oligopolistic market
generates the same outcome as a
monopolistic market

Show why the outcome of the
prisoners' dilemma may change if
the game is repeated

Show why some business practices
that appear to reduce competition
may have a legitimate business
purpose

CHAPTER OVERVIEW

Context and Purpose

Chapter 16 is the fourth chapter in a five-chapter sequence dealing with firm behaviour and the organization of industry. The previous two chapters discussed the two extreme forms of market structure—competition and monopoly. The market structure that lies between competition and monopoly is known as *imperfect competition*. There are two types of imperfect competition—oligopoly and monopolistic competition. Chapter 16 addresses oligopoly while the final chapter in this sequence, Chapter 17, addresses monopolistic competition.

The purpose of Chapter 16 is to discuss *oligopoly*—a market structure in which only a few sellers offer similar or identical products. Since there are only a few sellers in an oligopolistic market, oligopolistic firms are interdependent while competitive firms are not. That is, in a competitive market, the decisions of one firm have no impact on the other firms in the market while in an oligopolistic market, the decisions of any one firm may affect the pricing and production decisions of the other firms in the market.

CHAPTER REVIEW

Introduction

The market structure that lies between competition and monopoly is known as *imperfect competition*. One type of imperfectly competitive market is **oligopoly**—a market structure in which only a few sellers offer similar or identical products. Oligopoly differs from competition because in a competitive market the decisions of one firm have no impact on the other firms in the market while in an oligopolistic market, the decisions of any one firm may affect the pricing and production decisions of other firms in the market. Oligopolistic firms are interdependent.

Between Monopoly and Perfect Competition

Competitive firms charge a price equal to marginal cost. In the long run, this is equal to average total cost causing each firm to earn no economic profits. A monopolist charges a price that exceeds marginal cost. This reduces output and causes a deadweight loss. The market structure that lies between the extremes of competition and monopoly and contains elements of both is known as imperfect competition. There are two types of imperfect competition—oligopoly and monopolistic competition. *Oligopoly* is a market structure in which only a few sellers offer similar or identical products. **Monopolistic competition** is a market structure in which many firms sell products that are similar but not identical. To summarize the distinguishing characteristics of the various market structures:

- Monopoly has only one firm,

- Oligopoly has a few firms selling similar or identical products,

- Perfect competition has many firms selling identical products,

- Monopolistic competition has many firms selling differentiated products.

It is often difficult to decide which structure best describes a particular market.

Markets with Only a Few Sellers

A *duopoly* is an oligopoly with only two firms. If a market were perfectly competitive, the price of output would equal marginal cost. If a market were monopolistic, the profit maximizing price would exceed marginal cost and the result would be inefficient.

Collusion is an agreement among firms in a market about quantities to produce or prices to charge. A **cartel** is a group of firms acting in unison. If duopolists collude and form a cartel, the market solution is the same as if it were served by a monopolist and the two firms divide the monopoly profits in some agreed ratio.

Oligopolists may fail to cooperate because anti-competitive laws prohibit collusion or because self-interest makes it difficult to agree on how to divide the profits. Without a binding agreement, each oligopolist will maximize its profit given the production levels of the other firms. A **Nash equilibrium** is a situation in which economic agents interacting with one another each choose their best strategy given the strategies that all the other agents have chosen. A Nash equilibrium is a type of oligopolistic equilibrium. When oligopolists individually choose production levels to maximize individual profits they produce a quantity that is greater than the level produced by monopoly, but less than that produced by competition. Similarly they will charge a price that is less than the monopoly price, but greater than the competitive price.

The larger the oligopoly (more firms) the more difficult it is for them to form a cartel and behave as a monopolist. If they each choose their own level of production to maximize individual profits, they will make the marginal decision of whether to produce an additional unit based on the following:

- *The output effect*: Because price is above marginal cost, selling one more unit at the going price will raise profit.

- *The price effect*: Raising production one unit will increase the total sold, but it will lower the price and the profit on all of the other units sold.

If the output effect exceeds the price effect, the oligopolist will produce another unit and it will continue to expand output until these two effects balance. The greater the number of sellers in an oligopoly, the smaller the price effect because each individual firm's impact on the price is small. Thus, the level of output increases. As the number of sellers in an oligopoly grows larger, the price approaches marginal cost and the quantity approaches the socially efficient level. When there are a large number of firms, the price effect disappears altogether and the market becomes competitive.

Unrestricted international trade increases the number of firms in domestic oligopolies and moves the outcome of the market closer to the competitive solution where prices are equal to marginal cost.

Two examples of cartels are the Atlantic shipping cartels that set the prices for cargo shipping across the Atlantic and OPEC (Organisation of Petroleum Exporting Countries) which limits the production of oil. Oligopolies may become a larger portion of the economy because high tech industries have high fixed costs and small marginal costs, so mergers are particularly attractive. We observe this effect in cable television, publishing, and Web site providers.

Game Theory and the Economics of Cooperation

Game theory is the study of how people behave in strategic situations. Strategic situations are when decision-makers must consider how others might respond to their actions. The **prisoners' dilemma** is a particular 'game' between two captured prisoners that illustrates why cooperation is difficult to maintain even when it is mutually beneficial. The game applies to oligopoly because oligopolistic firms would always be better off to cooperate, yet they often do not.

An example of a prisoners' dilemma is the following: Two criminals are captured. If one confesses and the other does not, the confessor goes free while the other receives a long sentence. If both confess they each receive an intermediate term. If neither confess, they each receive a very short term. If the two could cooperate, the best strategy is for each to keep quiet. However, since they cannot guarantee cooperation after they are caught, the best strategy for each is to confess. That is, confessing is a **dominant strategy**—a strategy that is best for a player in a game regardless of the strategies chosen by the other players.

The prisoners' dilemma applies to oligopoly in the following manner: Two oligopolists are better off if they cooperate by keeping production low and sharing the monopoly profits. However, after the agreement is made, the dominant strategy for each is to cheat and produce more than they agreed to produce to enhance their individual profits. The result is that profits fall for both. Self-interest makes it difficult to maintain cooperation.

The prisoners' dilemma applies to:

- *Arms races*: Each country prefers to live in a safe world, but the dominant strategy is to increase armaments and the world is less safe.

- *Advertising*: Each firm prefers not to advertise and simply divide the market and the profits, but the dominant strategy is to advertise and joint profits fall.

- *Common resources*: Users of a common resource would find it more profitable to jointly limit their use of the resources, but the dominant strategy is to overuse the resource and joint profits fall.

Lack of cooperation in the cases above is harmful to society. However, lack of cooperation between oligopolists regarding the level of production may be bad for the oligopolists, but it is good from the standpoint of society as a whole.

While cooperation is difficult to maintain, it is not impossible. If the game is repeated, the prisoners' dilemma can be solved and agreements can be maintained. For example, oligopolies may include a penalty for violation of the agreement. If the penalty is that they all maintain high production forever if someone cheats, then all should maintain low production levels and share monopoly profits. If the game is played on a periodic basis (each week, month, or year new production levels are chosen) then a simple strategy of tit-for-tat generates the greatest likelihood of cooperation. *Tit-for-tat* is when a player in a game starts by cooperating and then does whatever the other player did last period. If the other player cooperated, then cooperate in the next period. If the other player defected (cheated), then cheat in the next period, and so on.

Public Policy towards Oligopolies

Since cooperating oligopolists reduce output and raise prices, policy-makers try to induce firms in an oligopoly market to compete rather than cooperate. Article 81 of the Treaty of Rome prohibits agreements among suppliers that restrict trade and Article 82 outlaws the abuse of market power by a dominant firm. Price fixing clearly reduces economic welfare and is illegal.

There is some disagreement over the use of anti-competitive laws against some business practices that appear to have similarities with price fixing. For example:

- *Resale price maintenance* or *fair trade* is when a manufacturer requires retailers to charge a certain price. This appears to prevent retailers from competing on price. However, some economists defend the practice as legitimate because (1) if the manufacturer has market power it is at wholesale not retail, and the manufacturer would not gain from eliminating competition at the retail level, and (2) resale price maintenance stops discount retailers from free riding on the services provided by full service retailers.

- *Predatory pricing* occurs when a firm cuts prices with the intention of driving competitors out of the market so that the firm can become a monopolist and later raise prices. Some economists think that this behaviour is unlikely because it hurts the firm that is engaged in predatory pricing the most.

- *Tying* occurs when a manufacturer bundles two products together and sells them for one price. Courts argue that tying gives the firm more market power by connecting a weak product with a strong product. Some economists disagree. They suggest that it allows the firm to price discriminate, which may actually increase efficiency. Tying remains controversial.

An anti-competitive case has been brought against Microsoft for tying its browser to its operating system. Some economists argue that future anti-competitive suits should take into account that the new high tech industries may be natural monopolies—firms whose costs continue to decline at least to the quantity that satisfies the entire market.

Conclusion

Oligopolies will look more like a competitive market if there are a large number of firms and more like a monopoly if there are a small number of firms. The prisoners' dilemma shows why cooperation is difficult to maintain even when it is in the best interest of the oligopolists. The use of anti-competitive laws against price fixing improves economic efficiency, but their use in other areas is more controversial.

HELPFUL HINTS

1. Oligopoly lies between monopoly and perfect competition. If oligopolists are able to collude and form a cartel, the market solution is the same as that for a monopoly. If oligopolists are unable to collude and form a cartel, the production and pricing in the market depends on the number of firms. The fewer the number of firms, the more the result appears like monopoly where the price exceeds marginal cost and the quantity is below the efficient level. The greater the number of firms, the more the result appears like competition where the price equals marginal cost and the quantity is efficient.

TERMS AND DEFINITIONS

Choose a definition for each key term.

Key terms:

_____ Imperfect competition

_____ Oligopoly

_____ Monopolistic competition

_____ Duopoly

_____ Collusion

_____ Cartel

_____ Nash equilibrium

_____ Game theory

_____ Prisoners' dilemma

_____ Dominant strategy

Definitions:

1. The study of how people behave in strategic situations

2. A market structure in which many firms sell products that are similar but not identical

3. An agreement among firms in a market about quantities to produce or prices to charge

4. A strategy that is best for a player in a game regardless of the strategies chosen by the other players

5. The market structure that lies between competition and monopoly

6. An oligopoly with only two firms

7. A market structure in which only a few sellers offer similar or identical products

8. A particular 'game' between two captured prisoners that illustrates why cooperation is difficult to maintain even when it is mutually beneficial

9. A situation in which economic agents interacting with one another each choose their best strategy given the strategies that all the other agents have chosen

10. A group of firms acting in unison

PROBLEMS AND SHORT-ANSWER QUESTIONS

Practice Problems

1. In which market structure would you place each of the following products—monopoly, oligopoly, monopolistic competition, or perfect competition? Why?
   a. Principles of economics textbooks.
   b. *Principles of Economics*, by N. Gregory Mankiw and Mark P Taylor.
   c. Photographic film.
   d. Restaurants in a large city.
   e. Car tyres.
   f. Garbage collection.
   g. Legal services in a large city.
   h. Gold bullion.
   i. Air travel from any one airport.

2. The following information describes the demand schedule for a unique type of apple. This type of apple can only be produced by two firms because they own the land on which these unique trees spontaneously grow. As a result, the marginal cost of production is zero for these duopolists, causing total revenue to equal profit.
   a. Complete the following table.
   b. If the market were perfectly competitive, what price and quantity would be generated by this market? Explain.

Price per bushel (€)	Quantity (in bushels)	Total revenue (profit)
12	0	_____
11	5	_____
10	10	_____
9	15	_____
8	20	_____
7	25	_____
6	30	_____
5	35	_____
4	40	_____
3	45	_____
2	50	_____
1	55	_____
0	60	_____

c. If these two firms colluded and formed a cartel, what price and quantity would be generated by this market, what is the level of profit generated by the market, and what is the level of profit generated by each firm?

d. If one firm cheats and produces one additional increment (five units) of production, what is the level of profit generated by each firm?

e. If both firms cheat and each produces one additional increment (five units) of production (compared to the cooperative solution), what is the level of profit generated by each firm?

f. If both firms are cheating and producing one additional increment of output (five additional units compared to the cooperative solution), will either firm choose to produce an additional increment (five more units)? Why? What is the value of the Nash equilibrium in this duopoly market?

g. Compare the competitive equilibrium to the Nash equilibrium. In which situation is society better off? Explain.

h. What would happen to the price and quantity in this market (qualitatively) if an additional firm were able to grow these unique apples?

i. Use the data from the duopoly example above to fill in the boxes of the prisoners' dilemma. Place the value of the profits earned by each duopolist in the appropriate box in Exhibit 1.

j. What is the solution to this prisoners' dilemma? Explain.

k. What might the solution be if the participants were able to repeat the 'game'? Why? What simple strategy might they use to maintain their cartel?

EXHIBIT 1

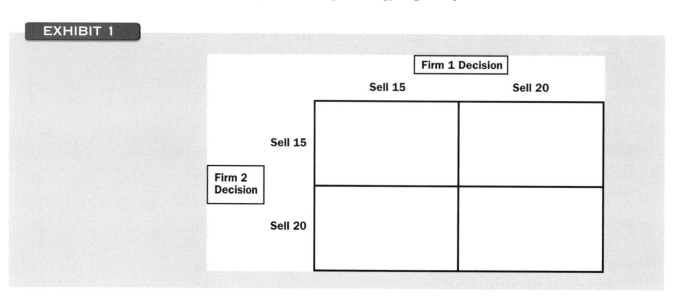

Short-Answer Questions

1. Why are oligoplistic markets without collusion characterized by interdependence among firms?

2. What is the outcome in an oligopolistic market if the oligopolists collude and form a cartel? Explain.

3. Why is the prisoners' dilemma relevant in analysing oligopolistic behaviour?

4. Suppose a group of oligopolists do not collude but instead reach a Nash equilibrium. What price and quantity will result in this oligopolist market when compared to the monopolistic or competitive result?

5. Referring to question 4 above, what would happen to the price and quantity in the Nash equilibrium if an additional firm were to join the oligopoly? Why?

6. If oligopolists would be better off if they collude, why do they so often fail to cooperate?

7. Is it better for society as a whole if oligopolists cooperate? Explain. What measures do we take to try to prevent cooperation between oligopolists?

8. Suppose High-Tech Software sells two products—a word processing package and a spreadsheet package. Suppose that the business community values the word processing package at €100 per unit and the spreadsheet package at €250 per unit while the university community values the word processing package at €125 and the spreadsheet at €200. (Assume that the marginal cost of each unit is zero.) What are the profit maximizing prices that High-Tech should charge if they sell each product separately and what is the total price of the two goods? If High-Tech is able to engage in tying, what is the profit maximizing price for the two products as a bundle? Should this be legal?

9. What is a dominant strategy equilibrium?

10. What is a Nash equilibrium?

SELF-TEST

True/False Questions

_____ 1. An oligopoly is a market structure in which many firms sell products that are similar but not identical.

_____ 2. When oligopolists collude and form a cartel, the outcome in the market is similar to that generated by a perfectly competitive market.

_____ 3. The price and quantity generated by a Nash equilibrium is closer to the competitive solution than the price and quantity generated by a cartel.

_____ 4. When applied to oligopoly markets, the net result of a prisoners' dilemma game involving two firms is that joint profits are maximized.

_____ 5. The prisoners' dilemma demonstrates why it is difficult to maintain cooperation even when cooperation is mutually beneficial.

_____ 6. There is a constant tension in an oligopoly between cooperation and self-interest because after an agreement to reduce production is reached, it is profitable for each individual firm to cheat and produce more.

_____ 7. The dominant strategy for an oligopolist is to cooperate with the group and maintain low production regardless of what the other oligopolists do.

_____ 8. A Nash equilibrium is always a dominant strategy equilibrium in monopolistic competition.

_____ 9. Predatory pricing occurs when a firm cuts prices with the intention of driving competitors out of the market so that the firm can become a monopolist and later raise prices.

_____ 10. If a prisoners' dilemma game is repeated, the participants are more likely to independently maximize their profits and reach a Nash equilibrium.

Multiple-Choice Questions

1. If oligopolists engage in collusion and successfully form a cartel, the market outcome is
   a. the same as if it were served by a monopoly.
   b. the same as if it were served by competitive firms.
   c. efficient because cooperation improves efficiency.
   d. known as a Nash equilibrium.

2. When an oligopolist individually chooses its level of production to maximize its profits, it produces an output that is
   a. more than the level produced by a monopoly and less than the level produced by a competitive market.
   b. less than the level produced by a monopoly and more than the level produced by a competitive market.
   c. more than the level produced by either monopoly or a competitive market.
   d. less than the level produced by either monopoly or a competitive market.

3. A situation in which oligopolists interacting with one another each choose their best strategy given the strategies that all the other oligopolists have chosen is known as a
   a. collusion solution.
   b. cartel.
   c. Nash equilibrium.
   d. dominant strategy.

Use the table below to answer questions 4 through 6. The table shows the demand schedule for tickets to watch amateur football games in a town. The city provides the football pitches and the players play for free, so the marginal cost of providing the games is zero. The city has authorized two companies to provide football games on two pitches and the public considers the games in each stadium to be equivalent.

Price (€)	Quantity
6	0
5	1,000
4	2,000
3	3,000
2	4,000
1	5,000
0	6,000

4. Under competition, the price and quantity in this market would be
   a. €4; 2,000.
   b. €3; 3,000.
   c. €2; 4,000.
   d. €1; 5,000.
   e. €0; 6,000.

5. If the duopolists in this football market collude and successfully form a cartel, what is the price that each should charge in order to maximize profits?
   a. €5.
   b. €4.

   c. €3.

   d. €2.

   e. €1.

6. If the duopolists are unable to collude, how much profit will *each* earn when the market reaches a Nash equilibrium?

   a. €2,500.

   b. €4,000.

   c. €4,500.

   d. €8,000.

   e. €9,000.

Use the prisoners' dilemma game in Exhibit 2 to answer questions 7 and 8. Exhibit 2 shows the possible profits for duopolists (Kathryn and Paul) that own the only two restaurants in town. Each restaurant can choose how many hours to be open for business.

EXHIBIT 2

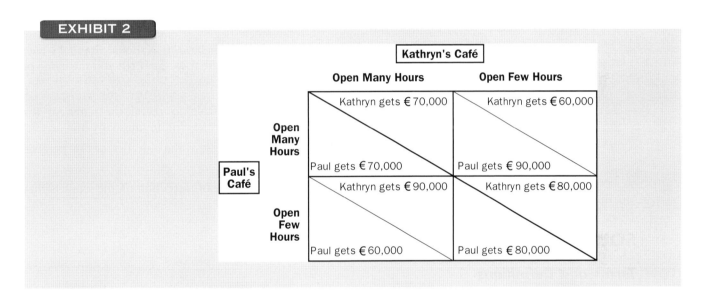

7. The dominant strategy for Kathryn and Paul is for

   a. both to be open for many hours.

   b. both to be open for few hours.

   c. Kathryn to be open for many hours while Paul is open for few hours.

   d. Kathryn to be open for few hours while Paul is open for many hours.

   e. There is no dominant strategy in this prisoners' dilemma game.

8. Suppose Kathryn and Paul agreed to collude and jointly maximize their profits. If Kathryn and Paul were to be able to repeatedly play the game shown above and they agreed on a penalty for defecting from their agreement, what is the likely outcome of the game?

   a. Both are open for many hours.

   b. Both are open for few hours.

   c. Kathryn is open for many hours while Paul is open for few hours.

   d. Kathryn is open for few hours while Paul is open for many hours.

Use the following information to answer questions 9 and 10. Suppose that ABC Publishing sells an economics textbook and accompanying study guide. Simon is willing to pay €75 for the text and €15 for the study guide. Becky is willing to spend €60 for the text and €25 for the study guide. Suppose both the book and study guide have a zero marginal cost of production.

9. If ABC Publishing charges separate prices for both products, its best strategy is to charge prices that, when combined, total
    a. €60.
    b. €75.
    c. €80.
    d. €85.
    e. €90.

10. If ABC Publishing engages in tying, its best strategy is to charge a combined price of
    a. €60.
    b. €75.
    c. €80.
    d. €85.
    e. €90.

ADVANCED CRITICAL THINKING

You are watching television. An advertisement begins, 'Come on down to Warehouse Electronics. We've got deals so great you won't believe it! National brand 13-inch colour television sets for €99. The price is so low that we can't tell you the name of the manufacturer!'

1. Why would Warehouse Electronics be unable to reveal the name of the manufacturer when it advertises its television sets for an unusually low price?

2. Although this activity appears like price fixing, is the objective of this practice to reduce competition? Why?

3. Why would the manufacturer place this type of restriction on the retailers that sell its products?

SOLUTIONS

Terms and Definitions

_1_	Game theory	_6_	Duopoly
_2_	Monopolistic competition	_7_	Oligopoly
_3_	Collusion	_8_	Prisoners' dilemma
_4_	Dominant strategy	_9_	Nash equilibrium
_5_	Imperfect competition	_10_	Cartel

Practice Problems

1. a. Monopolistic competition, many firms each selling differentiated products.
   b. Monopoly, only one firm can produce it due to copyright laws.
   c. Oligopoly, few firms (Fuji, Kodak) selling similar products.
   d. Monopolistic competition, many firms each selling differentiated products.
   e. Oligopoly, few firms (Goodyear, Firestone, Michelin) selling very similar products.
   f. Monopoly, only one firm from which to purchase.
   g. Monopolistic competition, many firms each selling differentiated products.
   h. Perfect competition, many firms selling identical products.
   i. Oligopoly, few airlines from which to choose at any one airport, similar product.

Note: While monopoly and competition are more easily distinguished, the line between oligopoly and monopolistic competition is not as sharp. For example, (b) might be considered to be an oligopoly since there are relatively few publishers and economic text books may be considered to be very similar, and (j) might be considered to be monopolistic competition if the products are considered to be differentiated, and so on.

2. a.

Price per bushel (€)	Quantity (in bushels)	Total revenue (profit)
12	0	0
11	5	55
10	10	100
9	15	135
8	20	160
7	25	175
6	30	180
5	35	175
4	40	160
3	45	135
2	50	100
1	55	55
0	60	0

b. In a competitive market, competition reduces the price until it equals marginal cost (which is zero in this case), therefore $P = €0$ and $Q = 60$.

c. These duopolists would behave as a monopolist, produce at the level that maximizes profit, and agree to divide the production levels and profit. Therefore, $P = €6$, $Q = 30$ for the market. Profit $= €6 × 30 = €180$. Each firm produces 15 units at €6 and receives profit of €90 (half of the €180).

d. Cheating firm: $20 × €5 = €100$, other firm: $15 × €5 = €75$.

e. Each firm: $20 × €4 = €80$.

f. No, because the profit would fall for the cheater to $25 × €3 = €75$ which is below €80 profit from part (e) above. Therefore, the Nash equilibrium is each firm producing 20 units (40 for the market) at a price of €4, creating €160 of profit for the market and each duopolist receives €80 profit.

g. The Nash equilibrium has a higher price (€4 compared to €0) and a smaller quantity (40 units compared to 60 units). Society is better off with competitive equilibrium.

h. The new Nash equilibrium would have a lower price and a larger quantity. It would move toward the competitive solution.

i. See Exhibit 3.

j. The dominant strategy for each is to cheat and sell 20 units because each firm's profit is greater when it sells 20 units regardless of whether the other firm sells 15 or 20 units.

EXHIBIT 3

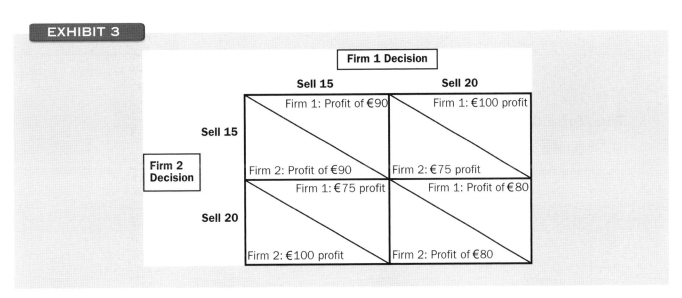

k. They might be able to maintain the cooperative (monopoly) production level of 30 units and each produce 15 units because if the game is repeated, the participants can devise a penalty for cheating. The simplest penalty is 'tit-for-tat'.

Short-Answer Questions

1. Oligopolistic markets are characterized by interdependence because there are few firms and each accounts for a substantial part of the market. Any action by one firm such as a change in price, will therefore impact on other firms. If the impact is adverse, these firms will almost certainly retaliate with an action of their own.

2. The outcome is the same as if the market were served by a monopolist. Monopoly profits are divided among the firms and production levels are limited by agreement to the level that a monopoly would produce.

3. The prisoners' dilemma is a game in which every player has a dominant strategy and this is the optimal strategy for each individual player given that they do not know the strategy chosen by the other player. If each knew the strategy of the other, they would each choose a different strategy from the dominant strategy. This is relevant to analysing oligopolistic behaviour because the optimal strategy for both players is to cooperate (form a cartel) and share monopoly profits. However, the dominant strategy for each individual firm is to produce more than the agreed quota of output (set a lower price). In other words, the dominant strategy then becomes to cheat on the cartel.

4. The price will be lower than monopoly but higher than competition. The quantity sold will be greater than monopoly but less than competition.

5. The price would fall and the quantity sold would rise. This is because with the addition of another firm, the individual firm's impact on the price is reduced, which causes the output effect to exceed the price effect and the profit maximizing output level of the group is increased. As members are added, the outcome approaches a competitive solution.

6. Once an agreement to reduce production is made, it is always profitable for the individual firm to cheat and produce in excess of the agreement regardless of whether the others cheat or maintain the agreement. Cheating is a dominant strategy. This is the prisoners' dilemma.

7. It is better if they do not cooperate because the Nash equilibrium is closer to the efficient competitive solution than the monopoly solution would have been. Anti-trust laws make it illegal for firms to make agreements not to compete.

8. Word processing price = €100, spreadsheet price = €200, total = €300. If tying the two together, price = €325. Maybe, because it may be just a method of price discrimination which, recall, increases total surplus (is more efficient) but it moves surplus from the consumer to the producer.

9. A dominant-strategy equilibrium is a set of strategies (one for each player) in which every player is playing a dominant strategy—that is, a strategy that is best regardless of what the other players do.

10. A Nash equilibrium is a set of strategies (one for each player) in which every player is playing a strategy that is a best response to the other players' equilibrium strategies.

True/False Questions

1. F; an oligopoly is where a few sellers offer similar or identical products.

2. F; it is the same as that generated by a monopoly.

3. T

4. F; prices are set below the level of joint profits maximization.

5. T

6. T

7. F; the dominant strategy is to increase production regardless of the choices of the other firms.

8. F; a dominant strategy *might* be a Nash equilibrium, but it is not *necessarily* a Nash equilibrium.

9. T

10. F; repeated games are more likely to generate cooperation because a penalty for cheating can be enforced.

Multiple-Choice Questions

1. a	5. c	9. b
2. a	6. b	10. d
3. c	7. a	
4. e	8. b	

Advanced Critical Thinking

1. The manufacturer may be engaging in 'resale price maintenance' or 'fair trade' practices with its retailers (including Warehouse Electronics). This may restrict the retailer's right to advertise a price below the suggested retail price for the product.

2. No, because any reduction in competition at the retail level generates market power for the retailer and fewer units will be sold. This is not in the interest of the manufacturer.

3. The purpose is to stop discount retailers from free riding on the services provided by full service retailers—retailers with a knowledgeable sales force, a repair shop, and so on.

17

MONOPOLISTIC COMPETITION

CHAPTER OVERVIEW

Context and Purpose

Chapter 17 is the final chapter in a five-chapter sequence dealing with firm behaviour and the organization of industry. Chapters 14 and 15 developed the two extreme forms of market structure—competition and monopoly. The market structure that lies between competition and monopoly is known as imperfect competition. There are two types of imperfect competition—oligopoly, which we addressed in the previous chapter, and monopolistic competition, which is the topic of the current chapter. The analysis in this chapter is again based on the cost curves developed in Chapter 13.

The purpose of Chapter 17 is to address *monopolistic competition*—a market structure in which many firms sell products that are similar but not identical. Recall, that oligopoly differs from perfect competition because there are only a few sellers in the market. Monopolistic competition differs from perfect competition because each of the many sellers offers a somewhat different product. As a result, monopolistically competitive firms face a downward sloping demand curve, while competitive firms face a horizontal demand curve at the market price. Monopolistic competition is a very common market form.

CHAPTER REVIEW

Introduction

Monopolistic competition shares some features of competition and monopoly:

- *Many sellers*: This is in common with competition.

- *Product differentiation*: This is in common with monopoly—each firm's product is slightly different so each firm is a price maker and faces a downward-sloping demand for its product.

- *Free entry*: This is in common with competition—firms can enter or exit without restriction so economic profits are driven to zero.

Examples of monopolistically competitive markets are the market for books, CDs, movies, restaurants, and so on. Monopolistically competitive markets are a common feature of modern economies.

Oligopoly differs from perfect competition because there are only a few sellers in the market. Monopolistic competition differs from perfect competition because each of the many sellers offers a somewhat different product. As a result, monopolistically competitive firms face a downward sloping demand curve while competitive firms face a horizontal demand curve at the market price.

Competition with Differentiated Products

Similar to a monopolist, a monopolistically competitive firm faces a downward sloping demand curve for its product. Therefore, it follows the same rule for profit maximization as a monopolist—it produces the quantity at which marginal cost equals marginal revenue and then uses the demand curve to determine the price consistent with this quantity. In the short run, if the price exceeds average total cost, the firm makes economic profits. If the price is below average total cost, the firm generates losses.

As in a competitive market, if the firm is making profits, new firms have incentive to enter the market. Entry reduces the demand faced by each firm already in the market (shifts their demand curves to the left) and reduces their profits in the long run. If the firm is generating losses, incumbent firms have an incentive to exit the market. Exit increases the demand faced by each firm that remains in the market (shifts their demand curves to the right) and reduces their losses. Entry and exit continues until the firms in the market are making zero economic profits. In long run equilibrium, the demand curve facing the firm must be tangent to the average total cost curve so that $P = ATC$ and profits are zero.

The long run equilibrium for a monopolistically competitive firm exhibits the following characteristic features:

- As in monopoly, price exceeds marginal cost because profit maximisation requires that $MR = MC$, and MR is always less than demand if demand is downward sloping.

- As in competition, price equals average total cost so economic profits equal zero because, unlike in monopoly, free entry drives profits to zero.

The long run equilibrium under monopolistic competition differs from the long run equilibrium under perfect competition in two ways:

- *Excess capacity*: Monopolistically competitive firms produce in the downward sloping portion of their average total cost curve. Therefore, they produce a quantity that is less than that which would be produced at the *efficient scale* (minimum *ATC*) of the firm. As a result, they are said to have *excess capacity*. Competitive firms produce at the efficient scale.

- *Markup over marginal cost*: A monopolistically competitive firm charges a price that exceeds its marginal cost. A competitive firm charges a price that equals its marginal cost. As a result, if a monopolistically competitive firm could attract another customer, it would increase its profits.

Monopolistic competition might be inefficient for two reasons:

- Since price exceeds marginal cost, some units that buyers value in excess of the cost of production are not produced and consumed. This is the standard deadweight loss associated with monopoly. Regulating a monopolistically competitive firm in order to reduce the deadweight loss is not easily accomplished—the task is similar to regulating a natural monopoly.

- The number of firms in the market might not be optimal because the entering firm only considers its own profits, but its entry generates two external effects:

    (1) *The product-variety externality*: Entry creates consumer surplus in the new market, which is a positive externality.
    (2) *The business-stealing externality*: Entry causes other firms to lose customers and profits and reduces existing surplus, which is a negative externality.

Therefore, the entry of new firms into a monopolistically competitive market can raise or lower social surplus.

Monopolistically competitive markets do not ensure the maximisation of total surplus. However, there is no easy way for public policy to improve the market outcome.

Advertising

Since monopolistically competitive firms sell differentiated products at prices above marginal cost, each firm has incentive to advertise to attract more buyers. Firms that sell highly differentiated consumer products spend considerably more on advertising than firms which sell industrial products, and firms that sell undifferentiated products spend nothing at all.

Economists debate the social value of advertising. Critics argue that advertising manipulates people's tastes to create a desire that otherwise would not exist and that advertising impedes competition by increasing the perception of product differentiation, which increases brand loyalty, causes demand to be more inelastic, and allows the firm to charge a greater markup over marginal cost. Defenders of advertising argue that advertising provides information to customers about prices, the existence of new products, and the location of retail outlets. This information increases competition because consumers are aware of price differentials and it provides new firms with the means to attract customers from existing firms.

Advertising that appears to contain little information might be useful because it provides a *signal* of product quality. Firms are likely to spend a great deal on advertising only if they think their product is of high quality. Therefore, consumers might be rational to try new products that are expensively advertised because it signals that the product is of high quality. The content of the advertisement is irrelevant. What is important is that the advertisement is expensive.

Advertising is related to *brand names*. Critics of brand names argue that brand names cause consumers to perceive differences between goods that do not exist. Defenders of brand names argue that brand names ensure that the product is of high quality because (1) brand names provide *information* about the quality of a product and (2) brand names give firms the *incentive* to maintain high quality.

Conclusion

Monopolistic competition contains characteristics of both monopoly and competition. Like monopoly, firms face downward sloping demand curves and charge prices above marginal cost. Like competition, entry and exit drives profits to zero in the long run. Many markets are monopolistically competitive. The allocation of resources under monopolistic competition is not perfect, but policy-makers might not be able to improve on it.

HELPFUL HINTS

1. A source of inefficiency in monopolistic competition is underproduction. That is, some units are not produced that buyers value in excess of the cost of production. The monopolistically competitive firm charges a price that exceeds marginal cost, while the competitive firm charges a price equal to marginal cost. However, the higher price charged by the monopolistically competitive firm is

not the source of inefficiency. As with monopoly, it is the lower quantity demanded that results from the higher price that is the source of inefficiency. By itself, the higher price simply redistributes surplus from the buyer to the seller, but it does not reduce total surplus.

TERMS AND DEFINITIONS

Choose a definition for each key term.

Key terms:

_____ Monopolistic competition

_____ Free entry

_____ Efficient scale

Definitions:

1. A situation where firms can enter the market without restriction

2. The quantity that minimizes average total cost

3. A market structure in which many firms sell products that are similar, but not identical

PROBLEMS AND SHORT-ANSWER QUESTIONS

Practice Problems

1. Categorize each of the following markets as either competitive, monopolistic, or monopolistically competitive. Explain.
   a. toothpaste.
   b. cable television.
   c. flowers at retail.
   d. local newspapers.
   e. magazines.
   f. wheat.
   g. video games.
   h. beer.

2. Suppose that there are many restaurants in the city and that each has a somewhat different menu.
   a. In Exhibit 1, draw the diagram of the cost curves (average total cost and marginal cost), demand curve, and marginal revenue curve for Mario's Pizza when it is in long-run equilibrium.
   b. Is Mario's Pizza profitable in the long run? Explain.
   c. Is Mario's Pizza producing at the efficient scale? Explain. Why doesn't Mario's expand its output if it has excess capacity?
   d. In Exhibit 1, show the deadweight loss associated with Mario's level of output. Does this deadweight loss occur because the price is higher than a competitive firm would charge or because the quantity is smaller than a competitive firm would produce? Explain.
   e. Suppose that Mario's engages in an advertising campaign that is a huge success. In Exhibit 2, draw the diagram of Mario's cost curves, demand curve, and marginal-revenue curve and show Mario's profit in the short run. Can this situation be maintained in the long run? Explain.

3. For each of the following pairs of firms, which firm would likely spend a higher proportion of its revenue on advertising? Explain.

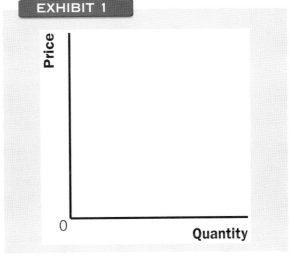

EXHIBIT 1

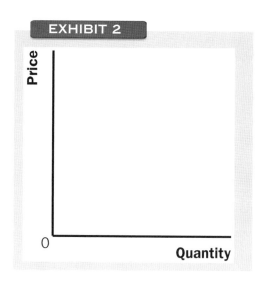

EXHIBIT 2

Price

0

Quantity

a. the maker of Bayer Aspirin or the maker of generic aspirin.
b. a firm introducing a low quality ice cream or a firm introducing a high quality ice cream that each cost about the same to make.
c. John Deere farm tractor division or John Deere lawnmower division.

Short-Answer Questions

1. What characteristics does monopolistic competition have in common with monopoly?

2. What characteristics does monopolistic competition have in common with perfect competition?

3. How does a monopolistically competitive firm choose the quantity and price that maximizes its profits?

4. Is it possible for a monopolistically competitive firm to generate economic profits in the long run? Why?

5. How does the long run equilibrium in monopolistic competition differ from the long run equilibrium in perfect competition?

6. Is the long run equilibrium in monopolistic competition efficient? Explain.

7. What do firms in monopolistic competition have a monopoly over and how is this useful in explaining their behaviour?

SELF-TEST

True/False Questions

_____ 1. Monopolistic competition is a market structure in which few firms sell similar products.

_____ 2. Advertising is the main instrument of competition in monopolistic competition.

_____ 3. In the long run, firms in monopolistically competitive markets produce at the minimum of their average total cost curves.

_____ 4. Collusion is likely to be a common feature of monopolistically competitive markets.

_____ 5. Both monopolists and monopolistically competitive firms produce the quantity at which marginal revenue equals marginal cost and then use the demand curve facing the firm to determine the price consistent with that quantity.

_____ 6. Since a monopolistically competitive firm charges a price that exceeds marginal cost, the firm fails to produce some units that the buyers value in excess of the cost of production and thus monopolistic competition is inefficient.

_____ 7. In the long run, a monopolistically competitive firm charges a price that exceeds average total cost.

_____ 8. Firms that sell highly differentiated consumer products are more likely to spend a large percentage of their revenue on advertising.

_____ 9. Even advertising that appears to contain little information about the product might be useful because it provides a signal about the quality of the product.

_____10. In the long run, a monopolistically competitive firm produces at the efficient scale while a competitive firm has excess capacity.

Multiple-Choice Questions

1. Which of the following is not a characteristic of a monopolistically competitive market?
   a. many sellers.
   b. differentiated products.
   c. long-run economic profits.
   d. free entry and exit.

2. Which of the following products is least likely to be sold in a monopolistically competitive market?
   a. video games.
   b. breakfast cereal.
   c. beer.
   d. cotton.

3. Which of the following is true regarding the similarities and differences in monopolistic competition and monopoly?
   a. The monopolist faces a downward sloping demand curve while the monopolistic competitor faces an elastic demand curve.
   b. The monopolist makes economic profits in the long run while the monopolistic competitor makes zero economic profits in the long run.
   c. Both the monopolist and the monopolistic competitor operate at the efficient scale.
   d. The monopolist charges a price above marginal cost while the monopolistic competitor charges a price equal to marginal cost.

4. Consider the following information about a firm in a monopolistically competitive market. Price = €10, MC = MR = €6, ATC = €8. This firm
   a. is maximizing profit and is in long run equilibrium.
   b. will experience a reduction in demand for its product in the long run.
   c. is operating at minimum average total cost.
   d. will be forced out of the industry in the long run.

5. Because of product differentiation, a firm in monopolistic competition
   a. faces little competition in the long run.
   b. does not produce where demand is elastic.
   c. is able to restrict the entry of new firms into the market.
   d. always has some market power.

6. Which one of the following is not correct? Advertising
   a. might facilitate lower costs of average total costs of production.
   b. might reduce elasticity of demand for a firm's product.
   c. might reduce competition in an industry.
   d. might encourage firms to create new brands for their products.

7. Which of the following is true with regard to monopolistically competitive firms' scale of production and pricing decisions? Monopolistically competitive firms produce
   a. at the efficient scale and charge a price equal to marginal cost.
   b. at the efficient scale and charge a price above marginal cost.

c. with excess capacity and charge a price equal to marginal cost.

d. with excess capacity and charge a price above marginal cost.

8. One source of inefficiency in monopolistic competition is that
   a. since price is above marginal cost, surplus is redistributed from buyers to sellers.
   b. since price is above marginal cost, some units are not produced that buyers value in excess of the cost of production and this causes a deadweight loss.
   c. monopolistically competitive firms produce beyond their efficient scale.
   d. monopolistically competitive firms earn economic profits in the long run.

9. When firms enter a monopolistically competitive market and the business-stealing externality is larger than the product-variety externality, then
   a. there are too many firms in the market and market efficiency could be increased if firms exited the market.
   b. there are too few firms in the market and market efficiency could be increased with additional entry.
   c. the number of firms in the market is optimal and the market is efficient.
   d. the only way to improve efficiency in this market is for the government to regulate it like a natural monopoly.

10. Which of the following firms has the least incentive to advertise?
    a. a manufacturer of home heating and air conditioning.
    b. a manufacturer of breakfast cereal.
    c. a wholesaler of crude oil.
    d. a restaurant.

ADVANCED CRITICAL THINKING

You are watching a sporting event on television. An advertisement featuring Tiger Woods (a famous golfer) is broadcast during a commercial break. In the advertisement, Tiger Woods does nothing but hit golf balls. He never speaks. There is no written copy. At the end of the advertisement, the Nike front man appears on the screen along with the words 'Nike Golf' A short time earlier, you read in a newspaper that Tiger Woods received €40 million to be the spokesperson for Nike golf equipment.

1. A friend watches the Nike advertisement with you and says, 'What a waste of society's resources. I didn't learn anything about Nike golf equipment from that advertisement. I think there should be government regulations requiring advertisements to be informative in some way.' Explain to your friend what you did learn from Tiger Wood's presence in this advertisement.

2. Did the use of the Nike name and Nike 'swoosh' provide any information? Explain.

3. In general, does advertising tend to decrease competition and raise prices to consumers or increase competition and reduce prices to consumers? Why?

SOLUTIONS

Terms and Definitions

__1__ Free entry

__2__ Efficient scale

__3__ Monopolistic competition

Practice Problems

1. a. monopolistically competitive—many firms, differentiated products, free entry.
   b. monopoly—one firm.
   c. competitive—many firms, identical products.
   d. monopoly—one firm (Could be a natural monopoly because one firm can satisfy the entire market on the downward sloping portion of its *ATC* curve.).
   e. monopolistically competitive—many firms, differentiated products, free entry.
   f. competitive—many firms, identical products.
   g. monopolistically competitive—many firms, differentiated products, free entry.
   h. monopolistically competitive—many firms, differentiated products, free entry.

2. a. See Exhibit 3.
   b. No. Since there is free entry, profit causes firms to enter the industry, which reduces the existing demand faced by profitable firms until *P* = *ATC* and profit is zero.
   c. No. Profits attract new firms, which reduces the demand for an incumbent firm's product to the point where its demand is tangent to its *ATC* curve causing *P* = *ATC* and profits equal zero. Since the tangency of demand and *ATC* is in the negatively sloping portion of *ATC*, the firm is operating at less than the efficient scale. If Mario's expanded output, *MC* would exceed *MR* and *P* < *ATC* so profits would be negative.
   d. See Exhibit 4. The deadweight loss occurs because firms fail to produce units that the buyer values in excess of the cost of production. That is, the loss is due to the reduced quantity in monopolistic competition.
   e. See Exhibit 5. No. Profits attract entry which reduces the demand faced by each firm to the point where it is again tangent to its *ATC* curve.

3. a. Bayer Aspirin because it is a branded or differentiated consumer good.
   b. Firm generating high quality ice cream because advertising is more profitable if there are repeat buyers.
   c. John Deere lawnmower division because lawnmowers are sold to consumers as opposed to industry.

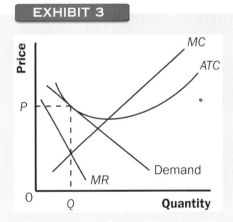

EXHIBIT 3

Short-Answer Questions

1. Both market structures involve a differentiated product so firms face downward sloping demand curves, equate *MC* and *MR*, and charge a price above *MC*.

2. Both market structures have many sellers and free entry and exit. Thus, profits are driven to zero in the long run.

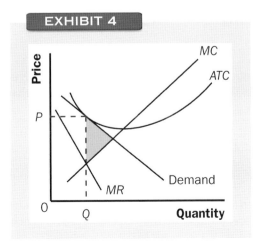

EXHIBIT 4

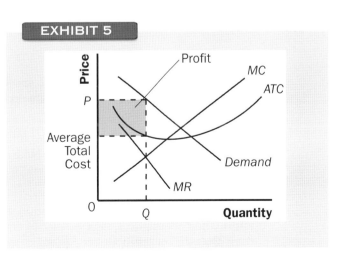

EXHIBIT 5

3. It chooses the quantity by equating *MC* and *MR* and then uses the demand curve to find the price that is consistent with this quantity (just like a monopolist).

4. No. Profits attract new firms to the market which reduces the demand faced by each of the incumbent firms until the demand faced by each firm is tangent to its *ATC* curve and profits are zero.

5. Monopolistic competition has excess capacity because monopolistically competitive firms produce at less than efficient scale and they charge prices in excess of marginal cost. Competitive firms produce at the efficient scale and charge prices equal to marginal cost.

6. No. Since price exceeds marginal cost, there is underproduction—some units that buyers value in excess of marginal cost are not produced. Also, the number of firms in the market might not be ideal because entry into the industry creates the positive product-variety externality and the negative business-stealing externality.

7. Firms in monopolistic competition have a monopoly over their own brand and this differentiates their product from other brands which compete in the same market. This explains why advertising to reinforce product differentiation is an important feature of monopolistically competitive markets.

True/False Questions

1. F; monopolistic competition is a market structure in which many firms sell differentiated products.

2. T

3. F; monopolistic competitors produce in the downward sloping portion of their *ATC* curve where the *ATC* curve is tangent to the demand curve faced by the firm.

4. F; there are far too many producers to make collusion a realistic possibility!

5. T

6. T

7. F; monopolistically competitive firms charge a price equal to *ATC*.

8. T

9. T

10. F; monopolistically competitive firms have excess capacity while competitive firms produce at the efficient scale.

Multiple-Choice Questions

1. c	3. b	5. d	7. d	9. a
2. d	4. b	6. c	8. b	10. c

Advanced Critical Thinking

1. Viewers learned that Nike was willing to spend an enormous amount of money to promote their new line of golf equipment. This signals that their market research suggests that they have a high quality product that will generate repeat sales.

2. Yes. The use of the brand name provides information that the product is of high quality and that the firm has incentive to maintain high quality. Nike is a multi-billion dollar company that would not want to risk losing existing sales of shoes and athletic ware by marketing poor quality golf equipment marked with the Nike brand name.

3. Advertising tends to increase competition and decrease prices to consumers because it often provides information about prices, the existence of new products, the location of retail outlets, and it provides new firms with the means to attract customers from existing firms.

⌈ In this chapter you will

Analyse the labour demand of competitive, profit maximizing firms

Consider the household decisions that lie behind labour supply

Learn why equilibrium wages equal the value of the marginal product of labour

Consider how the other factors of production—land and capital—are compensated

Examine how a change in the supply of one factor alters the earnings of all the factors

OUTCOMES

⌈ You should be able to

Explain why the labour demand curve is the value of the marginal product curve for labour

Explain why the labour supply curve is usually upward sloping

Explain why a competitive firm maximizes profit when it hires labour to the point where the wage equals the value of the marginal product of labour

Demonstrate the similarity between the labour market and the market for other factors of production

Explain why the change in the supply of one factor alters the value of the marginal product of the other factors

THE MARKETS FOR THE FACTORS OF PRODUCTION

CHAPTER OVERVIEW

Context and Purpose

Chapter 18 is the first chapter in a three-chapter sequence that addresses the economics of labour markets. Chapter 18 develops and analyses the markets for the factors of production—labour, land, and capital. Chapter 19 builds on Chapter 18 and explains in more detail why some workers earn more than others. Chapter 20 addresses the distribution of income and the role the government can play in altering the distribution of income.

The purpose of Chapter 18 is to provide the basic theory for the analysis of factor markets—the markets for labour, land, and capital. As you might expect, we find that the wages earned by the factors of production depend on the supply and demand for the factor. What is new in our analysis is that the demand for a factor is a *derived demand*. That is, a firm's demand for a factor is determined by its decision to supply a good in another market.

CHAPTER REVIEW

Introduction

The **factors of production** are the inputs used to produce goods and services. The most important inputs are labour, land, and capital. This chapter provides the basic theory for the analysis of factor markets. We will find that the supply and demand for a factor determines the wage earned by that factor. What is new in our analysis is that the demand for a factor is a *derived demand*. That is, a firm's demand for a factor is determined by its decision to supply a good in another market. In this chapter, we analyse the factor demand of competitive profit maximizing firms.

The Demand for Labour

The wage of labour is determined by the supply and demand for labour. The demand for labour is a derived demand in that it depends on the firm's decision to supply output in another market. Suppose that a firm is *competitive* in both its output market and in the market for labour. Also, suppose that the firm is *profit maximizing*. In order to derive the demand for labour, we first have to determine how the use of labour affects the amount of output the firm produces. A **production function** shows the relationship between the quantity of inputs used to make a good and the quantity of output of that good. Since rational decision makers think at the margin, we derive the **marginal product of labour**—the increase in the amount of output from an additional unit of labour holding all other inputs fixed—from the production function. Production functions exhibit **diminishing marginal product**, which is the property whereby the marginal product of an input declines as the quantity of the input increases.

The firm is concerned with the *value* of the output generated by each worker rather than the output itself. Thus, we calculate the **value of the marginal product**, which is the marginal product of an input times the price of the output. Another name for the value of the marginal product is *marginal revenue product*. Since the output is sold in a competitive market, the price is constant regardless of the amount produced and sold and therefore, the *value* of the marginal product declines in concert with the decline in the marginal product as the quantity of the input increases.

Since the firm is also a competitor in the market for labour, it takes the wage as given. It is profitable for the firm to hire a worker if the value of the marginal product of that worker is greater than the wage. This analysis implies that:

- a competitive, profit maximizing firm hires workers up to the point where the value of the marginal product of labour equals the wage, and

- the value-of-marginal-product curve *is* the labour demand curve for a competitive, profit maximizing firm.

Since the demand for labour is the value-of-marginal-product curve, the demand for labour shifts when the value of the marginal product of labour changes due to changes in the following:

- *The output price*: an increase in the price of output increases the value of the marginal product and shifts the labour demand curve rightwards.

- *Technological change*: an advance in technology raises the marginal product of labour and shifts the labour demand curve rightwards.

- *The supply of other factors*: an increase in the supply of a factor used with labour in production increases the marginal product of labour and shifts the labour demand curve rightwards.

For a competitive, profit maximizing firm, the demand for a factor is closely related to its supply of output because the production function links inputs and output. If W is the wage, MC is marginal cost, and MPL is the marginal product of labour, then $MC = W/MPL$. Thus, diminishing marginal product is associated with increasing marginal cost. In terms of inputs, a profit maximizing firm hires until the value of the marginal product of labour equals the wage or $P \times MPL = W$. Rearranging, we get $P = W/MPL$. Substituting MC for W/MPL from above we get, $P = MC$. Thus, when a competitive firm hires labour up to the point at which the value of the marginal product equals the wage, it also produces up to the point at which the price of the product equals marginal cost.

The Supply of Labour

The supply of labour arises from individuals' trade off between work and leisure. An upward-sloping labour supply curve means that people respond to an increase in the wage by enjoying less leisure and working more hours. While labour supply need not be upward sloping in all cases, for now we will assume that it is upward sloping.

The following events will cause the labour supply curve to shift:

- *Changes in tastes*: Changes in attitudes towards working such that women are more likely to work outside the home will shift the supply of labour curve to the right.

- *Changes in alternative opportunities*: If better opportunities arise in alternative labour markets, labour supply will decrease in the market under consideration and the labour supply curve will shift to the left.

- *Immigration*: When immigrants come to Europe, the European supply of labour curve shifts to the right.

Equilibrium in the Labour Market

In competitive labour markets:

- The wage adjusts to balance the supply and demand for labour and,

- The wage rate equals the value of the marginal product of labour.

As a result, any event that changes the supply or demand for labour must change the equilibrium wage and the value of the marginal product by the same amount because these must always be equal.

For example, suppose that immigration causes an increase in the supply of labour (supply of labour shifts right). This reduces the equilibrium wage, increases the quantity demanded of labour because it is profitable for firms to hire additional workers, and reduces the marginal product of labour (and the value of the marginal product of labour) as the number of workers employed rises. In the new equilibrium, both the wage and the value of the marginal product of labour have fallen.

Alternatively, suppose there is an increase in the demand for the output produced by firms in an industry. This causes an increase in the price of the good and increases the *value* of the marginal product of labour. This event increases the demand for labour (rightward shift in the labour demand curve), increases the equilibrium wage, and increases employment. Again, the value of the marginal product of labour and the wage move together (both increase in this case). When there is a change in the demand for a firm's output, the prosperity of firms and their workers move together.

Our analysis of labour demand shows that the wage rate equals the marginal product of labour. Therefore highly productive workers should earn more than less productive workers. In addition, real wages should increase in relation to the increase in productivity. When productivity grows quickly, real wages grow quickly.

A market with only a single buyer is called a *monopsony*. When a firm is a monopsonist in a labour market, the firm uses its market power to reduce the number of workers hired, reduce the wage it pays, and increase its profits. As in monopoly, the market is smaller than is socially optimal, which causes deadweight losses.

The Other Factors of Production: Land and Capital

A firm's factors of production fall into three categories—labour, land, and capital. **Capital** is the stock of equipment and structures used to produce goods and services. The *rental price* of a factor is the price one pays to use the factor for a limited period of time while the *purchase price* of a factor is the price one pays to own that factor indefinitely.

Since the wage is the rental price of labour, we can apply the theory of factor demand we used for the labour market to the markets for land and capital. For both land and capital, the firm increases the quantity hired until the value of the factor's marginal product equals the factor's price and thus the demand curve for each factor is the factor's value of marginal product curve. As a result, labour, land, and capital each earn the value of their marginal contribution to the production process because each factor's rental price is equal to the value of its marginal product.

Capital is often owned by firms as opposed to being owned directly by households. Therefore, capital income is often paid first to a firm. Capital income is later paid to those households that have lent money to the firm in the form of *interest* and to those households that own stock in the firm in the form of *dividends*. Alternatively, the firm retains some of its capital income to buy more capital. This portion of capital income is known as *retained earnings*. Regardless of how capital income is allocated, its total value equals the value of the marginal product of capital.

The purchase price of land and capital is based on the stream of rental income it generates. Thus, the purchase price of land or capital depends on both the current and expected future value of the marginal product of that factor.

Because of diminishing returns, a factor in abundant supply has a relatively low marginal product and a relatively low price, while a factor in scarce supply has a relatively high marginal product and a relatively high price. However, when the supply of a factor changes it has an effect on other factor markets because factors are used together in production. For example, the destruction of capital in an industry increases the rental price of the remaining capital. In the labour market the workers are now working with less capital, which reduces their marginal product. This reduces the demand for labour and reduces the wage of workers. In a real world example, the bubonic plague that ravaged Europe in the fourteenth century reduced the labour force by one-third and increased the wage of the remaining workers. This event decreased the rental price of land because the marginal product of land fell due to the reduction in workers available to farm the land.

Conclusion

The theory developed in this chapter of how labour, land, and capital are compensated is known as the *neo-classical theory of distribution*. It suggests that the amount earned by a factor depends on supply and demand and that the demand for a factor depends on its marginal productivity. In equilibrium, each factor earns the value of its marginal product. This theory is widely accepted.

HELPFUL HINTS

1. Your text provides examples of the impact of an increase in the supply of labour and an increase in the demand for labour on the marginal product of labour and the wage. The same logic used in those examples can be applied to the cases of a decrease in the supply of labour or a decrease in the demand for labour. For example, a decrease in the supply of labour (leftward shift in the labour supply curve) increases the equilibrium wage, decreases the quantity demanded of labour because it is profitable for firms to hire fewer workers, and increases the marginal product of labour (and the value of the marginal product of labour) as the number of workers employed decreases. In the new equilibrium, both the wage and the value of the marginal product of labour have risen. Alternatively, suppose there is a decrease in the demand for the output produced by firms in an industry. This causes a decrease in the price of the good and decreases the *value* of the marginal product of labour. This event decreases the demand for labour (leftward shift in the labour demand curve), decreases the equilibrium wage, and decreases employment.

2. The categories of the factors of production are labour, land, and capital. In this context, land is more than just the land on which one might grow crops. Land is generally considered to be 'nature's bounty' and is all forms of natural

resources that have not yet been altered by people. This would include rivers, oil reserves, minerals, and land itself.

3. To see the impact of a change in the quantity employed of one factor on the earnings of a second factor, always look at the impact on the marginal product of the second factor. For example, an increase in the available capital will reduce the marginal product of capital and its rental rate. However, the increase in capital will increase the marginal product of labour because workers have additional capital with which to work and their wages will rise accordingly.

TERMS AND DEFINITIONS

Choose a definition for each key term.

Key terms:

_____ Factors of production

_____ Derived demand

_____ Production function

_____ Marginal product of labour

_____ Diminishing marginal product

_____ Value of the marginal product

_____ Capital

_____ Rental price (of a factor)

Definitions:

1. The property whereby the marginal product of an input declines as the quantity of the input increases

2. The equipment and structures used to produce goods and services

3. The inputs used to produce goods and services

4. The increase in the amount of output from an additional unit of labour

5. The relationship between the quantity of inputs used to make a good and the quantity of output of that good

6. The price a person pays to use a factor for a limited period of time

7. The marginal product of an input times the price of the output

8. The demand for a factor of production which is derived from the firm's decision to supply another good

PROBLEMS AND SHORT-ANSWER QUESTIONS

Practice Problems

1. Suppose that labour is the only variable input in the production process for a competitive profit maximizing firm that produces coffee mugs. The firm's production function is shown below.

Labour (number of workers)	Output per Hour	Marginal Product of Labour	Value of MPL when P = €3	Value of MPL when P = €5
0	0	_____	_____	_____
1	9	_____	_____	_____
2	17	_____	_____	_____
3	24	_____	_____	_____
4	30	_____	_____	_____
5	35	_____	_____	_____
6	39	_____	_____	_____
7	42	_____	_____	_____
8	44			

EXHIBIT 1

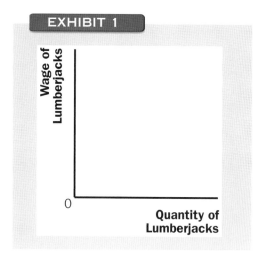

EXHIBIT 2

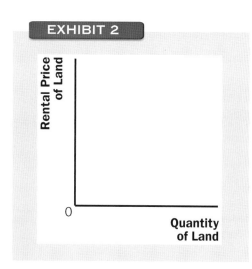

EXHIBIT 3

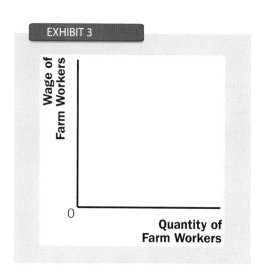

a. Fill out columns three and four of the table above (the marginal product of labour and the value of the marginal product of labour when the price of output equals €3 per mug).

b. Suppose that the competitive wage for workers who can make coffee mugs is €19 per hour. How many workers should this firm hire? Why?

c. Suppose that schools that teach pottery skills increase the supply of workers that can make coffee mugs and that this event lowers the competitive wage for coffee mug workers to €13 per hour. How many workers should this firm hire? Why? Does this represent a shift in the firm's demand for labour curve or a movement along the firm's demand for labour curve? Explain.

d. Suppose there is an increase in the demand for coffee mugs and that the price of coffee mugs rises to €5 per mug. Fill out the last column of the table above to show the value of the marginal product of labour when the price of mugs is €5 per mug.

e. Suppose that the competitive wage for coffee mug workers remains at €13 per hour and the price of mugs is €5 per mug. How many workers should this firm now hire? Why? Does this represent a shift in the firm's demand for labour curve or a movement along the firm's demand for labour curve? Explain.

2. Suppose there is an increase in the demand for lumber, which raises the price of lumber.

a. Show the impact of the increase in the price of lumber on the market for lumberjacks in Exhibit 1.

b. What effect does the increase in the price of lumber have on value of the marginal product of lumberjacks and the wage of lumberjacks? Explain.

c. What will happen to the value of the marginal product and the rental rate for timber land and for capital that is used for cutting and shipping timber? Explain.

d. How has this event affected the prosperity of the firm and the owners of the factors of production employed by the firm? Explain.

3. Suppose that a relatively large amount of forest land is cleared for agricultural use in Brazil.

a. Show the impact of this event on the market for agricultural land in Brazil in Exhibit 2. What will happen to the marginal product of land and the rental price of land in Brazil?

b. Show the impact of this event on the market for Brazilian farm workers in Exhibit 3. What will happen to the marginal product of farm labour and the wage of farm labour?

4. Explain how economic theory describes the impact of the following events on the market for car workers in Munich (where BMW cars are manufactured).

a. BMW extends its factory in Munich.

b. *Which?*, the consumer magazine suggests that BMW cars are best value cars in their class.

c. Immigrants with manufacturing skills from other countries relocate in Munich.

Short-Answer Questions

1. Why is the firm's demand curve for labour the value of the marginal product of labour?

2. Why does the firm's demand curve for labour slope downward with respect to the wage rate (that is, why is it sloped negatively)?

3. Prove that when a competitive firm hires up to the point at which the value of the marginal product equals the wage rate, it also produces up to the point at which price equals marginal cost.

4. Why must the equilibrium wage in the market for labour equal the value of the marginal product of labour for each firm?

5. What rationale underpins the assumption that the supply of labour curve for an industry (and an economy) slopes upward with respect to the wage rate (that is, why does it slope positively)?

6. Why does an increase in the amount of capital reduce the rental rate of capital? Why does this same event increase the wage of labour?

7. Explain the difference between the rental price of a factor and the purchase price of a factor. How are they related?

8. When households own capital directly, capital income is in the form of rental payments to households. In what form is capital income paid when businesses own capital?

9. What events will shift the demand for labour to the right?

10. What events will shift the supply of labour to the right?

SELF-TEST

True/False Questions

_____ 1. The demand for labour is considered to be a derived demand because it is derived from the supply of labour.

_____ 2. For a competitive profit maximizing firm, the marginal product of labour equals the average product of labour.

_____ 3. A factor exhibits diminishing marginal productivity if employing additional units of the factor reduces output.

_____ 4. If there is an increase in the equilibrium wage, there must have been an increase in the value of the marginal product of labour.

_____ 5. An increase in the demand for textbooks will increase the value of the marginal product of textbook writers.

_____ 6. A decrease in the supply of labour reduces the value of the marginal product of labour, decreases the wage, and decreases employment.

_____ 7. The demand for labour is downward sloping because the production function exhibits diminishing marginal productivity of labour.

_____ 8. In equilibrium, when a competitive firm hires labour up to the point at which the value of the marginal product of labour equals the wage, it also produces up to the point at which the price equals marginal cost.

_____ 9. An increase in the supply of capital will increase the marginal product of capital and the rental rate of capital.

_____ 10. As a factor of production, land is defined to include known but untapped mineral and ore deposits.

Multiple-Choice Questions

1. If a factor exhibits diminishing marginal product, hiring additional units of the factor will
   a. generate ever smaller amounts of output.
   b. cause a reduction in output.
   c. have no effect on output.
   d. increase the marginal product of the factor.

Use the following table to answer questions 2 through 4

Labour (number of workers)	Output per Hour	Marginal Product of Labour	Value of the MPL
0	0		
1	5		
2	9		
3	12		
4	14		
5	15		

2. What is the marginal product of labour as the firm moves from using three workers to using four workers?
   a. 0.
   b. 2.
   c. 12.
   d. 14.
   e. none of the above.

3. If the price of output is €4 per unit, what is the value of the marginal product of labour as the firm moves from using four workers to using five workers?
   a. €4.
   b. €8.
   c. €12.
   d. €56.
   e. €60.

4. If this profit maximizing firm sells its output in a competitive market for €3 per unit and hires labour in a competitive market for €8 per hour, then this firm should hire
   a. one worker.
   b. two workers.
   c. three workers.
   d. four workers.
   e. five workers.

5. For a competitive, profit maximizing firm, the value of the marginal product curve for capital is the firm's
   a. production function.
   b. marginal cost curve.
   c. supply curve of capital.
   d. demand curve for capital.

6. An increase in the supply of labour
   a. increases the value of the marginal product of labour and increases the wage.
   b. decreases the value of the marginal product of labour and increases the wage.
   c. increases the value of the marginal product of labour and decreases the wage.
   d. decreases the value of the marginal product of labour and decreases the wage.

7. What will a decrease in the supply of fishermen do to the market for capital employed in the fishing industry?
   a. increase the demand for fishing boats and increase rental rates on fishing boats.
   b. decrease the demand for fishing boats and decrease rental rates on fishing boats.
   c. increase the demand for fishing boats and decrease rental rates on fishing boats.
   d. decrease the demand for fishing boats and increase rental rates on fishing boats.

8. If both input and output markets are competitive and firms are profit maximizing, then in equilibrium each factor of production earns
   a. an equal share of output.
   b. the value of its marginal product.
   c. the amount allocated by the political process.
   d. an amount equal to the price of output times total output.

9. In a competitive market, an individual firm's demand for a factor of production
   a. slopes downward due to the factor's diminishing marginal product.
   b. slopes downward because an increase in the production of output reduces the price at which the output can be sold in a competitive market, thereby reducing the value of the marginal product as more of the factor is used.
   c. slopes upward due to the factor's increasing marginal product.
   d. is perfectly elastic (horizontal) if the factor market is perfectly competitive.

10. An increase in the demand for a firm's output
    a. increases the prosperity of the firm but decreases the prosperity of the factors hired by the firm.
    b. decreases the prosperity of the firm but increases the prosperity of the factors hired by the firm.
    c. increases the prosperity of both the firm and the factors hired by the firm.
    d. decreases the prosperity of both the firm and the factors hired by the firm.

ADVANCED CRITICAL THINKING

You are watching a debate about immigration on public television with a friend. The participants represent two camps—organized labour and corporate industry. Organized labour argues against open immigration while European industry argues in favour of more open immigration. Your friend says, 'I can't believe that these two groups can't get together on this issue. Both firms and workers join forces to produce our industrial output. I would think that their interests would be similar. Maybe a better arbitrator could help these groups find a position on immigration that would satisfy both groups.'

1. If there were open immigration, what would happen to the value of the marginal product of labour and the wage?

2. If there were open immigration, what would happen to the value of the marginal product of capital and land and their rental rates?

3. Are the positions that each group takes on immigration consistent with their interests? Explain. Is there likely to be a solution that satisfies both?

SOLUTIONS

Terms and Definitions

1	Diminishing marginal product	5	Production function
2	Capital	6	Rental price (of a factor)
3	Factors of production	7	Value of the marginal product
4	Marginal product of labour	8	Derived demand

Practice Problems

1. a.

Labour (number of workers)	Output per Hour	Marginal Product of Labour	Value of MPL when P = €3	Value of MPL when P = €5
0	0			
		9	€27	€45
1	9			
		8	24	40
2	17			
		8	21	35
3	24			
		6	18	30
4	30			
		5	15	25
5	35			
		4	12	20
6	39			
		3	9	15
7	42			
		2	6	10
8	44			

b. Three workers because the value of the marginal product of each of the first three workers exceeds the €19 wage so each worker adds to profits but the fourth worker only has a value of marginal product of €18 so hiring the fourth worker would reduce profits.

c. Five workers because the value of the marginal product of each of the first five workers now exceeds the €13 wage, but the sixth worker only has a value of marginal product of €12 so hiring the sixth worker would reduce profits. This is a movement along the firm's demand curve for labour because the value of the marginal product of labour for each worker is remaining the same, but the wage facing the firm has changed.

d. See the fifth column in the table in part (a) above.

e. Seven workers because the value of the marginal product of each of the first seven workers exceeds the €13 wage, but the eighth worker only has a value of marginal product of €10 so it would be unprofitable to hire that worker. This is a shift in the demand curve for labour because the value of the marginal product of labour has increased for each worker because the price of output rose. Thus, the firm demands more workers at the same €13 wage.

2. a. See Exhibit 4.

b. Increase the value of the marginal product of labour and the wage.

c. When the price of output rises, the value of the marginal product of all of the inputs increases accordingly. Thus, the value of the marginal product of both land and capital will rise and so will their rental rates.

d. When the price of output changes, the prosperity of the firm and the inputs move together. In this case, the prosperity of the firm and the inputs are increased.

3. a. See Exhibit 5. This event increases the supply of agricultural land and decreases the marginal product of land and the rental price of land.

b. See Exhibit 6. The increase in the supply of agricultural land increases the marginal product of labour and shifts the demand for farm labour to the right which increases the wage.

4. a. The increase in capital available for workers increases the marginal product of labour, shifts the demand for labour to the right, and increases the wage.

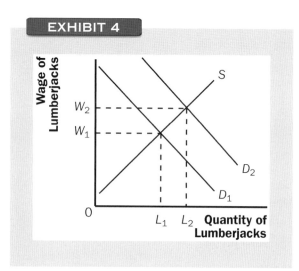

EXHIBIT 4

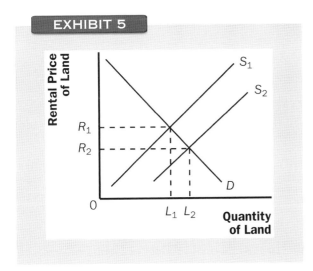

EXHIBIT 5

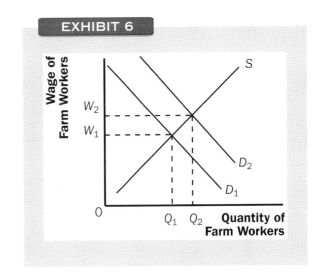

EXHIBIT 6

b. This event increases the demand for BMW cars and increases the price of BMW cars. The increase in the price of BMW cars increases the value of the marginal product of labour, shifts the demand for labour to the right, and increases the wage.

c. This event increases the supply of labour, decreases the marginal product of labour, and decreases the wage.

Short-Answer Questions

1. The profit maximizing firm will hire workers up to the point where the value of the marginal product of labour is equal to the wage. Beyond that point, additional workers cost more than the value of their marginal product and their employment would reduce profit. Since the value of the marginal product curve determines how many workers the firm will hire at each wage, it *is* the demand curve for labour.

2. The marginal product of labour is diminishing as more labour is added to the production process. Since the price of output is given in a competitive market, it follows that the *value* of the marginal product also declines as the quantity of labour is increased.

3. Given: $MC = W/MPL$. If the firm hires up to the point where the wage equals the value of the marginal product, then $P \times MPL = W$, or $P = W/MPL$. Substituting, MC for W/MPL we get $P = MC$.

4. The equilibrium wage is determined by supply and demand for labour in the market for labour. Each firm then hires workers up to the point where that wage equals the value of the marginal product of labour in each firm.

5. The price mechanism works in the labour market as well as the product market. If other things are equal, the supply of labour to an industry responds positively to a rise in nominal wages because the higher wage competes workers away from alternative employment.

6. Since there is a declining marginal product of capital as more capital is used, an increase in capital reduces the marginal product of capital and its rental rate. The increase in capital, however, increases the marginal product of labour and increases its wage.

7. The rental price is the price one pays to use the factor for a limited period of time, while the purchase price of a factor is the price one pays to own that factor indefinitely. The purchase price of a factor depends on the current and expected future value of the marginal product of the factor.

8. Interest, dividends, and retained earnings.

9. An increase in the price of output produced by labour, an advance in technology used in production, and an increase in the supply of factors used with labour in production.

10. A shift in tastes toward working outside the home, a reduction in alternative opportunities for employment, and immigration.

True/False Questions

1. F; the demand for labour is derived from the demand for the produce that labour produces.

2. F; the marginal product of labour equals the change in the total output that is produced when an additional worker is employed that is produced.

3. F; a factor exhibits diminishing marginal productivity if the increase in output generated from an additional unit of input diminishes as the quantity of the input increases.

4. T

5. T

6. F; a decrease in the supply of labour increases the value of the marginal product of labour, increases the wage, and decreases employment.

7. T

8. T

9. F; an increase in the supply of capital will decrease the value of the marginal product of capital and decrease the rental rate.

10. T

Multiple-Choice Questions

1. a   6. d
2. b   7. b
3. a   8. b
4. c   9. a
5. d   10. c

Advanced Critical Thinking

1. Labour would be less scarce so the value of the marginal product of labour would decrease and so would the wage.

2. Additional labour could be applied to capital and land, which would increase the value of the marginal product of capital and land and increase their rental rates.

3. Yes. Organized labour aims to keep the wage of labour relatively high so it would prefer to restrict immigration. Corporate interests wish to raise the return to capital and land so it would prefer to allow open immigration. No.

19

Examine how wages compensate
for differences in job characteristics

Learn and compare the human
capital and signalling theories of
education

Examine why in some occupations
a few superstars earn tremendous
incomes

Learn why wages rise above the
level that balances supply and
demand

Consider why it is difficult to
measure the impact of
discrimination on wages

See when market forces can and
cannot provide a natural remedy
for discrimination

OUTCOMES

⌈You should be able to
Explain why an economics
professor earns less than a
corporate economist of similar age,
background, and training

Explain the differing impact of
policies aimed at increasing the
educational attainment of all
workers under the signalling and
the human capital view of
education

List the characteristics of a market
where superstars can arise

List three reasons why a wage can
rise above the equilibrium wage

Explain why differences in wages
among groups do not by
themselves say anything about how
much discrimination there is in the
labour market

Explain why competitive
employers are unlikely to
discriminate against groups of
employees unless the customers or
the government demands it

EARNINGS AND DISCRIMINATION

CHAPTER OVERVIEW

Context and Purpose

Chapter 19 is the second chapter in a three-chapter sequence that addresses the economics of labour markets. Chapter 18 developed the markets for the factors of production. Chapter 19 goes beyond the supply and demand models developed in Chapter 18 to help explain the wide variation in wages we find in the economy. Chapter 20 addresses the distribution of income and the role the government can play in altering the distribution of income.

The purpose of Chapter 19 is to extend the basic neoclassical theory of the labour market that we developed in Chapter 18. Neoclassical theory argues that wages depend on the supply and demand for labour and that labour demand depends on the value of the marginal productivity of labour. To explain the wide variation in wages that we observe, we must examine more precisely what determines the supply and demand for various types of labour.

CHAPTER REVIEW

Introduction

Wage differentials between different workers are a readily observed feature of any developed economy. The explanation for these differentials is not always self-evident and the economist attempts to give some rationale for them.

Some Determinants of Equilibrium Wages

Workers differ from one another. Jobs also differ in terms of the wages they pay and their non-monetary characteristics. These differences affect labour supply, labour demand, and equilibrium wages.

Some jobs are easy, fun, and safe while others are hard, dull, and dangerous. If the wages were the same, most people would prefer to do easy, fun, and safe jobs. Therefore, workers require a higher wage in order to be induced to do a difficult, dull, and dangerous job. A **compensating differential** is the difference in wages that arises to offset the non-monetary characteristics of different jobs. For example, people who work in coal mines or on the night shift receive a compensating differential to compensate for the disagreeable nature of their work.

Capital is a factor of production that itself has been produced. Capital includes the economy's accumulation of equipment and structures and also includes a less tangible form of capital known as human capital. **Human capital** is the accumulation of investments in people, such as education and on-the-job training. Workers with more human capital earn more than those with less for the following reasons: with regard to labour demand, educated workers have a higher marginal product, and so firms are willing to pay more for them; with regard to labour supply, workers are only willing to educate themselves if they are rewarded for doing so. In effect, there is a compensating differential between educated and uneducated workers to compensate for the cost of becoming educated. In 1979, people with a university degree in the UK earned an average 38 per cent more than people without a university degree. By 2003, this differential had increased to more than 50 per cent. Economists offer two possible explanations for the differential. First, the growth in international trade has allowed the UK to import goods made by unskilled workers in foreign countries where unskilled workers are plentiful, and export goods produced by skilled labour. In the domestic economy, this increases the demand for skilled workers and decreases the demand for unskilled workers. Second, increases in technology have increased the demand for skilled workers and decreased the demand for unskilled workers.

Natural ability, effort, and chance help explain wages. Some people are smarter and stronger than others and they are paid for their natural ability. Some people work harder than others and are compensated for their effort. Chance plays a role in that someone's education and experience can be made valueless if there is a change in technology that eliminates that person's job.

The human capital view of education argues that workers with more education are paid more because the education made them more productive. As an alternative, the **signalling** view of education argues that firms use education as a method of sorting high-ability workers from low-ability workers. Educational attainment signals high ability because it is easier for high-ability people to earn a college degree than it is for low-ability people and firms are willing to pay more for high-ability people. Just as with the signalling theory of advertising where the advertisement itself contains no real information, the signalling theory of education suggests that schooling has no real productivity benefit. According to the human capital view of education, a policy of increasing educational attainment for all workers should raise all workers' wages. According to the signalling view of education, additional education would not affect productivity or wages. However, it does signal a person's potential advantages to an employer by their willingness to spend time being educated. The benefits of education are probably a combination of both human capital and signalling effects.

A few superstars earn salaries vastly in excess of the average. These superstars are often performers such as athletes, actors, writers, and so on. Superstars arise in markets that have two characteristics:

- Every customer in the market wants to enjoy the goods supplied by the best producer.

- The goods are produced with a technology that makes it possible for the best producer to supply every customer at low cost.

So far, we have addressed why workers might earn different *equilibrium* wages. However, some workers might earn higher wages because their wages are held above equilibrium due to the following:

- *Minimum wage laws.* This mostly affects less-experienced and less-skilled workers.

- *The market power of trade unions.* A **union** is a worker association that bargains with employers over wages and working conditions. The union can hold wages 10 to 20 per cent above equilibrium because they can threaten to **strike** or withhold labour from the firm.

● *Efficiency wages.* **Efficiency wages** occur when firms choose to hold wages above equilibrium to increase productivity because higher wages reduce worker turnover, increase worker effort, and raise the quality of workers that apply for jobs at the firm.

Whenever the wage is held above equilibrium, the result is unemployment.

The Economics of Discrimination

Wages can differ due to discrimination. **Discrimination** involves offering different opportunities to similar individuals who differ only by race, ethnic group, sex, age, or other personal characteristics. Discrimination is an emotional issue.

Wages differ across races and sexes for a number of reasons. Ethnic minorities might find it more difficult to gain employment simply on the grounds of ethnic or racial discrimination. To the extent that this happens, racial minorities might be employed at lower wages and are likely to be more highly concentrated in low-wage occupations. Men generally have more years of education and more job experience than women. Men may also receive a compensating differential for doing more unpleasant jobs than women choose to do. While some of the wage differentials are likely to be due to discrimination, there is no agreement with regard to how much. Economists would agree that *because the differences in average wages among groups in part reflect differences in human capital and job characteristics, they do not by themselves say anything about how much discrimination there is in the labour market.*

While it is difficult to measure discrimination, suppose that we have evidence that there is discrimination in the labour market. If some employers discriminate against certain groups of employees, then the demand for the services of those that are discriminated against will be lower and their wages will be lower while the demand for those workers not discriminated against will be higher and their wages will be higher. In a competitive market, employers that discriminate against certain groups of employees will be at a competitive disadvantage because their labour costs will be higher. Firms that care only about profits and do not discriminate will tend to replace those that do discriminate because they will be more profitable. The firms that do not discriminate will increase the demand for the labour services of the group that was discriminated against, decrease the demand for the group not discriminated against, and the wages will be equalized across groups. Thus, competitive markets can be a cure for employer discrimination.

However, if customers or governments demand discrimination, then competition and the profit motive of firms may not correct the wage differential. If bigoted customers are willing to pay extra to be served by a certain group in a restaurant and are not willing to be served by another group, then the wage differential can persist even in a competitive market. If the government mandates discriminatory practices, then competition will again fail to equalize a discriminatory wage differential. If a wage differential persists in a competitive market, this implies that either bigoted customers are willing to pay for discrimination or the government requires it.

Conclusion

In competitive markets, workers earn a wage equal to the value of their marginal product. The workers' value of marginal product is higher if they are more talented, diligent, experienced, and educated. Firms pay less to those workers against whom customers discriminate because they are less profitable to the firm.

HELPFUL HINTS

1. The wage rate is explained by supply and demand. Characteristics of both people and jobs affect supply, demand, and the wage rate for labour in each labour market. For example, education, experience, and hard work increase the value of the marginal productivity of workers, increase the demand for their services, and increase their wage. An increase in the disagreeable nature of the work, the expense of training, and the required ability to do the job reduces the pool of workers willing and able to do a particular job, reduces the supply of labour in that market, and increases the wage. Even the market for superstars can be explained with supply and demand. Since superstars can satisfy every customer at the same time through television, movies, music CDs, and so on, the value of their marginal product is enormous and so is the demand for their services.

2. Different pay for different groups of people is not, by itself, evidence of labour market discrimination because differences in pay among groups in part reflect differences in human capital and job characteristics. What seems to be discrimination might simply be a compensating differential that is paid for the disagreeable nature of a job. In addition, a wage differential could be due to a difference in the average productivity across groups of workers.

TERMS AND DEFINITIONS

Choose a definition for each key term.

Key terms:

_____ Compensating differential

_____ Human capital

_____ Union

_____ Strike

_____ Efficiency wages

_____ Discrimination

Definitions:

1. The offering of different opportunities to similar individuals who differ only by race, ethnic group, sex, age, or other personal characteristics

2. A difference in wages that arises to offset the non-monetary characteristics of different jobs

3. The organized withdrawal of labour from a firm by a union

4. The accumulation of investments in people, such as education and on-the-job training

5. Above-equilibrium wages paid by firms in order to increase worker productivity

6. A worker association that bargains with employers over wages and working conditions

PROBLEMS AND SHORT-ANSWER QUESTIONS

Practice Problems

1. Within each of the following pairs of workers, which worker is likely to earn more and why? (It may be obvious which one is paid more. The real issue is to explain why one is paid more than the other.)
    a. A carpenter working at the top of a 600 foot cooling tower of a nuclear power plant or a carpenter who frames houses?
    b. A clerk in a grocery store or a solicitor?
    c. A solicitor with one year of experience or a solicitor with six years of experience?
    d. A car worker in a factory who works the day shift or a car worker in a factory who works the night shift?

    e. An economics professor or a corporate economist?
    f. Your favourite local blues band that plays regularly at a nearby campus bar or David Bowie?
    g. The best joiner on the planet or the best writer on the planet?

2. a. Explain the human capital view of education and the signalling view of education.
   b. What are the implications for education policy under each view?
   c. Which of the above is true? Explain.

Short-Answer Questions

1. Why, on average, does someone with more human capital acquired though education earn more than someone with less human capital with no educational qualifications?

2. List some characteristics of a job that might require a positive compensating differential.

3. What has happened to the relative wages of skilled and unskilled workers in the UK over the last 20 years? Why?

4. What are the necessary conditions for a superstar to arise in a market? Explain.

5. Does a difference in average wages among groups by itself suggest that there is discrimination in the labour market? Explain.

6. If a discriminatory wage differential persists in a competitive market, is it due to discrimination on the part of the employer or must it be from some other source? Explain.

7. If firms pay efficiency wages does this imply that they are not maximizing profits?

8. List the occupations of most superstars. What do these professions have in common?

9. Why is a plumber's apprentice paid less than a master plumber?

10. Provide three reasons why wages might be set above the equilibrium wage. Explain.

SELF-TEST

True/False Questions

_____ 1. A compensating differential is the difference in wages paid to workers who are discriminated against and those who are not discriminated against.

_____ 2. Firms are willing to pay more for workers with greater human capital because workers with greater human capital have a greater value of marginal product.

_____ 3. Some superstars can earn incomes millions of times greater than the average because, in some markets, everyone wants the goods supplied by the best producer and technology has made it possible for the best producer to satisfy every customer at low cost.

_____ 4. If the signalling view of education is true, a policy of increasing the education of workers will increase the wages of all workers.

_____ 5. Ability, effort, and chance must play an important role in wage determination since less than half of the variation in wages can be explained by workers' education, experience, age, and job characteristics.

_____ 6. If a company in a competitive market persistently pays a discriminatory wage to a certain group, it must be because the employer perceives different groups as having different marginal revenue productivities.

_____ 7. If there is a difference in wages among groups, it is evidence that there is discrimination in the labour market.

_____ 8. If it were not for minimum wage laws, workers would always be paid the equilibrium wage.

_____ 9. When firms pay higher wages to their workers in order to increase workers' effort, they are said to pay efficiency wages.

_____10. Minimum wage laws always result in a wage higher than the free market equilibrium wage and unemployment.

Multiple-Choice Questions

1. If a person who works in a coal mine gets paid more than a person with a similar background and skills who works in a safer job, then
   a. we have evidence of discrimination against workers outside the coal mine.
   b. we have observed a compensating differential.
   c. coal miners must have greater human capital than others.
   d. coal miners must be more attractive than other workers.

2. According to the human capital view of education, education
   a. increases human capital and the wages of workers.
   b. only helps firms sort workers into high-ability and low-ability workers.
   c. ultimately results in a shortage of skilled manual workers.
   d. enables workers to gain efficiency wages.

3. According to the signalling view of education, education
   a. increases human capital and the wages of workers.
   b. only helps firms sort workers into high-ability and low-ability workers.
   c. reduces the wage gap between high-skill and low-skill workers.
   d. increases the marginal productivity of labour.

4. The ability of a trade union to secure an increase in wage rates for its members without decreasing the numbers employed is influenced by all of the following *except*
   a. the ease with which other factors can be substituted for labour.
   b. the elasticity of demand for the goods union members produce.
   c. the proportion of total cost represented by labour costs.
   d. the market price of the product that union members produce.

5. The relative wage of unskilled workers has fallen in the UK most likely as a result of a relative
   a. increase in the number of unskilled workers available because workers are more poorly educated.
   b. increase in the number of unskilled workers available due to immigration into the UK.
   c. decrease in the demand for unskilled workers because workers are more poorly educated.
   d. decrease in the demand for unskilled workers because of increases in technology and increases in international trade.

6. In order for a market to support superstars it must have which of the following characteristics?
   a. It must be involved in professional athletics.
   b. Every customer must be willing to pay an enormous amount for the product and the product must be a necessity.

   c. Every customer must want the goods supplied by the best producer and the technology must exist for the best producer to supply every customer at low cost.

   d. Every customer must be indifferent to the price they pay and the seller must be a competitor in the market for the product.

7. Which of the following statements regarding discrimination is true?
   a. Discrimination cannot exist in a competitive labour market.
   b. Discrimination can only persist in a competitive labour market if customers are willing to pay to maintain the discriminatory practice or the government requires discrimination.
   c. Bigoted employers are the main source of a persistent discriminatory wage differential in a competitive market.
   d. The existence of a wage differential among groups is strong evidence of discrimination in the labour market.

8. Which of the following is likely to generate a compensating differential?
   a. One employee is paid higher efficiency wages than another.
   b. One employee works harder than another.
   c. One employee is willing to work the nightshift while another is not.
   d. One employee is more educated than another.
   e. All of the above generate compensating differentials.

9. Which of the following could result in women being paid less than men?
   a. customers preferring to deal with men.
   b. women preferring to work in pleasant clean safe work places.
   c. women entering and leaving the labour force to care for children.
   d. women obtaining less human capital because they don't plan to work continuously to the age of retirement.
   e. all of the above.

10. Efficiency wages might be paid by firms in order to achieve all of the following except
   a. reduce unemployment.
   b. increase worker effort.
   c. raise quality of workers.
   d. increase productivity of workers.

ADVANCED CRITICAL THINKING

You are at a political rally with some friends. A candidate for parliament states that working women earn about 60 cents for each euro that working men earn. The candidate says, 'This is clearly evidence that employers discriminate against women. This gap between the earnings of men and women will never close because professions women tend to choose are traditionally low paying and the professions men choose are traditionally high paying. I will propose that the government create a panel to decide what jobs should pay so that people of similar skills and education earn the same amount.'

1. Suppose a secretary and a truck driver are judged to require the same level of education and skills, yet a secretary earns €30,000 while a truck driver earns €40,000. What would happen to the quantities supplied and demanded in the market for secretaries and truck drivers if the wage for these professions were set by law at €35,000?

2. What would happen to the level of effort and natural ability of the workers available in each market? What would happen to the quality of work generated in each market?

3. Suppose it is true that the skills and education required to do each job are, in fact, nearly identical. What explanation would an economist likely propose to explain why the equilibrium wage differs by €10,000 across these markets?

SOLUTIONS

Terms and Definitions

 1 Discrimination

 2 Compensating differential

 3 Strike

 4 Human capital

 5 Efficiency wages

 6 Union

Practice Problems

1. a. The carpenter working at the 600 foot height because he/she will likely require a compensating differential for the danger of the job.
   b. A solicitor because the solicitor has greater human capital from years of education and the solicitor requires a compensating differential to compensate for the cost and effort of becoming educated.
   c. A solicitor with six years of experience because work experience is part of human capital.
   d. The nightshift worker because the nightshift is disagreeable and the worker requires a compensating differential.
   e. The corporate economist because the corporate economist requires a compensating differential to compensate for the disagreeable nature of the work. Also, the corporate economist may have a greater value of marginal product.
   f. Superstar David Bowie—because, through technology, he is able to satisfy the entire market at the same time. (He is the first rock star to have a net worth in excess of one billion dollars).
   g. The best writer because the writer is in a market that can support a superstar while the carpenter is not.

2. a. Education increases human capital and raises the value of the marginal product of labour and, thus, the wage. Alternatively, education is only a signal of high ability.
   b. According to the human capital view, policies that increase educational attainment for all will increase all wages. According to the signalling view, an increase in educational attainment will not affect wages because education does not increase productivity.
   c. Probably both are true. It is unclear regarding the relative sizes of these two effects.

Short-Answer Questions

1. Because workers with greater human capital are more productive and firms are willing to pay more for workers with a greater value of marginal product. In addition, workers must be compensated for the cost of educating themselves.

2. A compensating differential is paid for the disagreeable, unpleasant nature of a job. Other things being equal, jobs will pay more if they are dirty, noisy, smelly, solitary, unsafe, hard, require travel, require working odd hours such as the nightshift or swing shift, require working with unpleasant people, and so on.

3. The gap between skilled and unskilled wages has risen, possibly because the growth in international trade has allowed the UK to import goods made by unskilled workers in countries where unskilled labour is plentiful,

and export goods made by skilled workers. This would increase the relative demand for skilled workers. Or it could be that increases in technology have increased the relative demand for skilled workers.

4. Every customer in the market wants to enjoy the good supplied by the best producer and the good is produced with a technology that makes it possible for the best producer to supply every customer at low cost.

5. No. Since average wages among groups are in part based on differences in human capital and job characteristics, a wage differential among groups alone tells us nothing about discrimination.

6. If customers are not bigoted and government does not require discrimination, competition will ensure that employers cannot continuously discriminate. If a wage differential persists, it must be because the customers are willing to pay for it (they are bigoted) or the government requires it. It cannot simply be due to a bigoted employer.

7. Efficiency wages imply that the wage rate is above the market clearing rate. Firms pay efficiency wages as an incentive to increase productivity (or 'efficiency'). To the extent that this happens, paying efficiency wages is entirely consistent with profit maximising behaviour.

8. Writers, athletes, television and movie actors, movie directors, musicians, artists, software creators, motivational speakers, and so on. Customers want only the best and technology allows the seller to satisfy all customers at low cost.

9. Because the apprentice's value of marginal product is less and because the apprentice is being paid, in part, with on-the-job training that increases the apprentice's human capital and future earnings.

10. Minimum-wage laws (government imposed wage floor), the market power of trade unions (threat of strike raises wage), and efficiency wages (firms pay above equilibrium wage to increase productivity because high wages reduce turnover, increase effort, and raise the quality of job applicants).

True/False Questions

1. F; it is the difference in wages that arises to offset the non-monetary characteristics of different jobs.

2. T

3. T

4. F; education would not increase productivity and would have no effect on wages.

5. T

6. F; it must be because the customer is willing to pay for the discrimination or because the government requires it.

7. F; the difference in wages may be due to differences in human capital or job characteristics.

8. F; unions may pressure firms to raise wages above equilibrium, and firms may choose to pay efficiency wages, which are above equilibrium.

9. T

10. F; this is not necessarily so, and happens only if the minimum wage is set by law at the level higher than the equilibrium wage.

Multiple-Choice Questions

1.	b	6.	c
2.	a	7.	b
3.	b	8.	c
4.	d	9.	e
5.	d	10.	a

Advanced Critical Thinking

1. There will be a surplus of secretaries and a shortage of truck drivers. That is, it will increase the quantity supplied of secretaries and decrease the quantity demanded while it will decrease the quantity supplied of truck drivers and increase the quantity demanded.

2. Hardworking, high-ability workers would avoid the truck driving market and the quality of truck driving would be reduced. Hardworking and high-ability workers would be attracted to the secretary market and the quality of secretarial services would be increased.

3. An economist would argue that €10,000 is the compensating differential necessary to get someone to undertake the disagreeable nature of truck driving—working alone, overnight travel away from children, less clean and less safe work environment, and so on.

20

Examine the degree of economic inequality in our society

Consider some problems that arise when measuring economic inequality

See how political philosophers view the government's role in redistributing income

Consider the various policies aimed at helping poor families escape poverty

OUTCOMES

┌You should be able to

Explain how greater labour market participation by females has affected income distribution of income in Europe

Name some factors that cause the measurement of income distribution to exaggerate the degree of income inequality

Compare and contrast utilitarianism, liberalism, and libertarianism

Explain the concept of a negative income tax

INCOME EQUALITY AND POVERTY

CHAPTER OVERVIEW

Context and Purpose

Chapter 20 is the third chapter in a three-chapter sequence that addresses the economics of labour markets. Chapter 18 developed the markets for the factors of production. Chapter 19 extended the basic supply and demand model to help explain the wide variation in wages we find in the economy. Chapter 20 addresses the measurement of the distribution of income and looks at the role the government plays in altering the distribution of income.

The purpose of Chapter 20 is to address income distribution. The discussion proceeds by answering three questions. First, how much inequality is there? Second, what do different political philosophies have to say about the proper role of government in altering the distribution of income? And third, what are the various government policies that are used to help the poor?

CHAPTER REVIEW

Introduction

This chapter addresses the distribution of income by answering three questions. First, how much inequality is there? Second, what do different political philosophies have to say about the proper role of government in altering the distribution of income? And third, what are the various government policies that are used to help the poor? We will find that governments may be able to improve on the distribution of income generated by the market but at the expense of a distortion in incentives and a reduction in efficiency.

The Measurement of Inequality

There are a variety of ways to describe the distribution of income. One way is to show what per cent of total before tax income that is earned by families in each quintile group of the income distribution. In the UK in 2002, the top fifth of income earners earned about 42 per cent of total before tax income while the bottom fifth earned about 7.5 per cent. That is, the top fifth earns about five and a half times what the bottom fifth earns. The distribution of income has changed little since 1990. However, more significant changes took place during the 1980s. In 1979, the bottom fifth of income earners earned 10 per cent of total before tax income and the top fifth earned 35 per cent of total before tax The increase in income inequality might be because increased international trade and increases in technology have reduced the demand for unskilled workers while raising the demand for skilled workers. This would cause a change in relative wages.

There are problems associated with measuring inequality. Although data on the income distribution and the poverty rate are useful in measuring inequality, these measures are not perfect measures of someone's ability to maintain a standard of living for the following reasons:

- **In kind transfers** are transfers to the poor given in the form of goods and services rather than cash. They are not accounted for in the standard measures of income inequality.

- The economic **life cycle** is the regular pattern of income variation over a person's life. Young and old may earn little income but the young can borrow and the old can live off past saving. Standard measures of income inequality exaggerate the variation in living standards because annual income has greater variation than living standards.

- *Transitory versus permanent income.* Incomes vary due to random and transitory forces. That is, events can cause income to be unusually high or low for any given year. Again, people can borrow and lend so that they can maintain stable living standards even when there is variation in income. A family's living standard depends largely on its permanent income. **Permanent income** is a person's normal, or average, income.

For each of the reasons listed above, standard measures of income distribution exaggerate the inequality of living standards.

The Political Philosophy of Redistributing Income

We saw in Chapter 1 that economics alone cannot tell us whether governments *should* do anything about economic inequality since this is a matter of normative judgement rather than positive economics. Nevertheless, various schools of political philosophy have addressed the issue and here we summarize their views.

- **Utilitarianism:** the political philosophy according to which the government should choose policies to maximize the total utility of everyone in society. **Utility** is a measure of happiness or satisfaction and it is assumed to be the ultimate objective of all actions. If there is diminishing marginal utility for each additional euro of income, then taking away a euro from a rich person and giving it to a poor person lowers the rich person's utility less than the gain in utility received by the poor person. Utilitarians reject complete equalisation of income because they realize that people respond to incentives and, thus, taxes create deadweight losses and there is less total income to be redistributed. The founders of this philosophy are the English philosophers Jeremy Bentham and John Stuart Mill.

- **Liberalism:** the political philosophy according to which the government should choose policies deemed to be just, as evaluated by an impartial observer behind a 'veil of ignorance'. This means that the only objective measure of economic justice is to set the rules for society as if every person were ignorant about the station in life each will end up filling—top, bottom, or middle. John Rawls, the originator of this theory of justice, argues that we would be concerned about being at the bottom of the income distribution so we would create a social rule known as the

maximin criterion—the notion that the government should aim to maximize the well being of the worst off person in society. As a result, redistribution of income is a type of social insurance. Although not equalizing income completely, it would require greater redistribution than utilitarianism. Critics argue that rational people behind a veil of ignorance would not necessarily be so risk averse as to follow the maximin criterion.

- **Libertarianism:** the political philosophy according to which the government should punish crimes and enforce voluntary agreements but not redistribute income. Libertarians, such as Robert Nozick, argue that society earns no income—only individuals earn income. Therefore, income is not a shared resource to be distributed by a social planner. To a libertarian, if the *process* is fair, the *outcome* is fair, no matter how unequal. Thus, the government should punish stealing and cheating to make a fair playing field, but should not be concerned with the final score if the rules were fair. Equality of opportunity is more important than equality of incomes.

Policies to Reduce Poverty

Regardless of political philosophy, most people think that the government should help the most needy because the poor are more likely to experience homelessness, drug dependency, domestic violence, health problems, teenage pregnancy, illiteracy, unemployment, low educational attainment, and they are more likely to commit crimes and be victims of crime. Here are some policy options:

- *Minimum-wage laws*: Advocates argue that minimum wage laws help the poor without any cost to government. Critics argue that they raise the wage above equilibrium for the lowest skill workers and cause unemployment among those workers. Those that keep their jobs gain while those that become unemployed lose. The more elastic the demand for labour, the greater the job loss from a given minimum wage above the market equilibrium.

- *Welfare*: **Welfare** is a broad term which encompasses various government schemes that supplement the incomes of the needy. These schemes are cash assistance for people who have relatively low incomes and have demonstrated a 'need' such as caring for a relative, or who have a disability. Critics argue that these programmes encourage the problems they hope to cure. For example, assistance is available for unmarried mothers so long as the father of the child is not resident in the household. The allegation is that this encourages fathers to abandon their families, causing broken homes, and may encourage unwed women to have illegitimate children. Evidence does not support the claim that welfare caused the decline in the two-parent family.

- *Negative income tax*: A **negative income tax** is a tax system that collects revenue from high-income households and gives transfers to low-income households. Under this tax system, a progressive income tax on the rich would be used to subsidize or provide a 'negative tax' to low-income families. Poor families would not have to demonstrate need beyond simply being poor. This would not subsidize the breakup of families or subsidize illegitimate births, but it would subsidize those that are just lazy.

- *In kind transfers*: In kind transfers occur when the poor are directly provided goods and services as opposed to being provided cash payments. In the UK, low income families might qualify for free school meals for their children and medical benefits such as free prescriptions for medicines, free eye tests and so on. Supporters argue that this method insures that the poor actually receive what they need as opposed to giving them money that they could spend on alcohol, drugs, and so on. (Alcohol and drug abuse is more common among lower income earners than among higher income earners.) Advocates of cash payments argue that in kind transfers are inefficient because the government doesn't know what the poor need most. In addition, they argue that it is insulting to the poor to be forced to accept in kind transfers.

Some anti-poverty programmes have the unintended effect of reducing the incentive for the poor to work. For example, suppose the government were to guarantee a fixed minimum level of income. If anyone below that income level were to work and earn a euro, then the government would simply reduce that person's benefits by one euro. As a result, the effective tax rate is 100 per cent on any new income and there is no incentive to work. In general, benefit entitlement falls when a recipient earns more income. This discourages work and might create a 'culture of poverty.' That is, welfare recipients lose their job skills, their children fail to see the benefits of work, and multiple generations of families become dependent on government. If benefits are reduced gradually as income rises, the incentive to work is not reduced as much. However, this increases the cost of fighting poverty because families above the poverty line will receive some benefits.

Work disincentives created by anti-poverty schemes can be reduced by restrictions which regulate the distribution of benefits in some way. In the UK, unemployed people qualify for job-seekers allowance, but the continued payment of this depends on the recipient demonstrating that he/she is available for and actively seeking work

Universal education should shrink the gap between rich and poor. However, universal education does not mean that it must be provided in government schools. Some economists argue that parents should be given school vouchers provided by the government to purchase the education of their choosing. This would be similar to food stamps—funding is provided by the government but it need not be spent in government food stores. Some economists argue that new private schools would be more efficient and provide improved education. This could help narrow the income distribution.

Conclusion

It is difficult to measure inequality and there is little agreement about what to do about it. If we choose to do something about inequality, we should remember there is a trade off between equity and efficiency. That is, the more equally the pie is divided, the smaller the pie becomes.

HELPFUL HINTS

1. People in poverty are more likely to experience homelessness, drug dependency, domestic violence, health problems, teenage pregnancy, illiteracy, unemployment, and low educational attainment. They are also more likely to commit crimes and be victims of crime. However, while it is clear that poverty is associated with these social ills, it is unclear whether poverty causes these social ills or whether these social ills cause poverty. That is, it may be that drug dependency, health problems, having children while young and out of wedlock, illiteracy, and so on are as much a cause of poverty as they are an effect of poverty.

2. There are a variety of reasons why an individual's current annual income can differ from his or her average lifetime income. The individual's income will depend on whether they are young, middle age, or old, and whether they have had an unusually productive or unproductive year. Since people can borrow and lend, standards of living are more stable than incomes and thus, standard measures of income distribution will exaggerate the degree of economic inequality.

3. An additional reason why some people prefer the government to provide for the poor using in kind transfers instead of cash payments is that in kind transfers

are thought to generate less fraud. This is because there is little incentive for an individual to file a fraudulent claim to receive medical benefits that the individual doesn't need, but there may be a great incentive to file a fraudulent welfare claim to receive cash.

TERMS AND DEFINITIONS

Choose a definition for each key term.

Key terms:

_____ In kind transfers

_____ Life cycle

_____ Permanent income

_____ Utilitarianism

_____ Utility

_____ Liberalism

_____ Maximin criterion

_____ Libertarianism

_____ Welfare

_____ Negative income tax

Definitions:

1. A measure of happiness or satisfaction

2. A person's normal income

3. Government programmes that supplement the incomes of the needy

4. Transfers to the poor given in the form of goods and services rather than cash

5. The political philosophy according to which the government should choose policies to maximize the total utility of everyone in society

6. A tax system that collects revenue from high-income households and gives transfers to low-income households

7. The political philosophy according to which the government should choose policies deemed to be just, as evaluated by an impartial observer behind a veil of ignorance

8. The political philosophy according to which the government should punish crimes and enforce voluntary agreements, but not redistribute income

9. The claim that the government should aim to maximize the well-being of the worst-off person in society

10. The regular pattern of income variation over a person's life

PROBLEMS AND SHORT-ANSWER QUESTIONS

Practice Problems

1. a. Describe three reasons why the measure of income distribution expressed in Table 2 in Chapter 20 may not truly measure someone's ability to maintain a certain standard of living. As a result, are the standard measures of income distribution likely to exaggerate or understate the true distribution of the standard of living? Explain.

 b. What is permanent income? Why might we wish to use permanent income when measuring the distribution of income? If we used permanent income instead of current annual income when measuring the distribution of income, would this tend to exaggerate or understate the true distribution of the standard of living? Explain. (Hint: If you are a full-time student, can you borrow as much as you want in order to perfectly smooth out your lifetime consumption?)

2. Susan earns five times as much as Joe.
    a. What would the political philosophy of utilitarianism, liberalism, and libertarianism likely suggest should be done in this situation? Explain.
    b. Compare the degree of redistribution each suggests.

3. Suppose the government has to choose between two anti-poverty programmes. Each programme guarantees that every family has at least €15,000 of income. One scheme establishes a negative income tax where: Taxes = (0.50 of income) − €15,000. The other scheme is for the government to guarantee every family at least €15,000 to spend and if a family falls short, the government will simply make up the difference.
    a. Using the negative income tax scheme described above, fill out the following table.

Earned Income (€)	Taxes Paid (€)	After-tax Income (€)
0	_____	_____
5,000	_____	_____
10,000	_____	_____
20,000	_____	_____
30,000	_____	_____
40,000	_____	_____

    b. What is the value of income for which this family neither receives a subsidy nor pays any tax? (That is, how high does income have to be for the family to stop receiving a subsidy?)
    c. Under the second scheme where the government simply guarantees at least €15,000 to every family, what is the level of income at which a family stops receiving a subsidy? Explain.
    d. Which plan is likely to be more expensive to the government? Explain
    e. Suppose a poor family that only earns €5,000 per year decides to plant a garden and sell the produce in a 'farmer's market' in the city. Suppose the family earns an additional €5,000 selling the produce. What is the family's final income under each scheme? What is the effective tax rate on the €5,000 earned by the family under each scheme? Which scheme promotes a work ethic among the poor and which one discourages work? Explain.

Short-Answer Questions

1. Does poverty affect all groups within the population the same? Explain.

2. Of the three political philosophies discussed in your text, which one differs the most from the other two and why? What does each school of thought suggest about income redistribution?

3. Why don't the political philosophies of utilitarianism and liberalism suggest that income be completely equalized across the population?

4. Suppose there is a minimum wage. Under which of the following conditions is employment of unskilled workers reduced by the greatest amount: When labour demand is relatively inelastic or when labour demand is relatively elastic? Why? Is labour demand likely to be more elastic or inelastic in the long run? Why?

5. How could welfare programmes exacerbate the problems they are supposed to cure?

6. What are some examples of in kind transfers? Why do some people prefer that the government provide cash payments to the needy instead of in kind transfers?

7. Is economic inequality and poverty the cause of social ills of the poor such as homelessness and illiteracy or the effect of these social ills?

8. What are the major policy options for poverty reduction?

SELF-TEST

True/False Questions

_____ 1. Economic analysis and argument supports the view that income should be distributed more equally.

_____ 2. Children are more likely than average and the elderly are less likely than average to live in poverty.

_____ 3. Because of in kind transfers to the poor and because people's incomes vary from year to year and across their lifetimes, standard measures of income distribution exaggerate the degree of inequality in standards of living.

_____ 4. The political philosophies of utilitarianism and liberalism both suggest that income should be equalized across the population.

_____ 5. Libertarians are more concerned with equal opportunity than with equal outcome.

_____ 6. Robert Nozick argues that economic justice would result if society chose a set of rules for the redistribution of income from behind a 'veil of ignorance' and he argues that the set of rules would be the maximin criterion.

_____ 7. If the demand for labour is relatively inelastic, an increase in the minimum wage will increase unemployment among unskilled workers by a relatively small amount.

_____ 8. When compared to other welfare programmes, a negative income tax would be more costly to the government but it would provide a greater incentive for the poor to work.

_____ 9. It is more efficient for the government to provide in kind transfers instead of cash payments.

_____10. If permanent income were utilized to measure the income distribution instead of current annual income, the income distribution would appear to be wider.

Multiple-Choice Questions

1. Because in kind transfers are not accounted for in standard measures of income distribution, the standard measures of income distribution
   a. exaggerate the inequality of living standards.
   b. understate the inequality of living standards.
   c. accurately represent the true inequality of living standards.
   d. could exaggerate or understate the inequality of living standards depending on whether the transfers are goods or services.

2. Permanent income is
   a. Social Security income of the elderly and disabled.
   b. equal to the minimum wage.
   c. a person's normal, or average, income.
   d. wages fixed by a union or other labour contract.

3. Because people's incomes vary over the life cycle and because there are transitory shocks to people's incomes, the standard measures of income distribution
   a. exaggerate the inequality of living standards.
   b. understate the inequality of living standards.
   c. accurately represent the true inequality of living standards.
   d. could exaggerate or understate the inequality of living standards depending on whether the transitory shocks are positive or negative.

4. If people can borrow and lend to perfectly smooth out their lifetime living standards, then
   a. current annual income is a good measure of the distribution of living standards.
   b. permanent income is a good measure of the distribution of living standards.
   c. transitory income is a good measure of the distribution of living standards.
   d. life-cycle income is a good measure of the distribution of living standards.
   e. none of the above.

5. Hazel earns more than Richard and she came by her income honestly. Which of the following political philosophies would argue against the redistribution of income from Hazel to Richard?
   a. utilitarianism.
   b. liberalism.
   c. libertarianism.
   d. all of the above.

6. Rank utilitarianism, liberalism, and libertarianism in sequence from the political philosophy that would redistribute income the greatest to the one that would redistribute income the least.
   a. utilitarianism, liberalism, libertarianism.
   b. libertarianism, liberalism, utilitarianism.
   c. liberalism, libertarianism, utilitarianism.
   d. liberalism, utilitarianism, libertarianism.
   e. All three political philosophies argue for similar degrees of income redistribution.

7. Utilitarianism suggests that the government should choose policies that maximize the total utility of everyone in society by
   a. allowing each individual to maximize their own utility without interference from the government.
   b. redistributing income from rich to poor because, due to the diminishing marginal utility of income, taking a euro from the rich reduces their utility by less than the gain in utility generated by giving a euro to the poor.
   c. redistributing income from rich to poor because this would maximize the well-being of the worst-off person in society.
   d. redistributing income from rich to poor because this is what the members of society would choose to do if they were behind a 'veil of ignorance.'

8. An increase in the minimum wage will cause a relatively large increase in unemployment among
   a. unskilled workers if the demand for labour is relatively elastic.
   b. unskilled workers if the demand for labour is relatively inelastic.
   c. skilled workers if the demand for labour is relatively elastic.
   d. skilled workers if the demand for labour is relatively inelastic.

9. Current anti-poverty programmes discourage work because
   a. they make recipients more comfortable than most middle-class Europeans.
   b. benefits are reduced at such a high rate when recipients earn more income that there is little or no incentive to work once one is receiving benefits.
   c. anti-poverty programmes attract naturally lazy people to begin with.
   d. in order to be eligible for benefits, a recipient cannot have a job.

10. The greatest advantage of a negative income tax is that it
    a. reduces the cost to the government of fighting poverty.
    b. generates a smaller disincentive to work than most alternative anti-poverty programmes.
    c. would not provide benefits to lazy people.
    d. ensures that the poor actually receive what the government thinks they need.
    e. does all of the above.

ADVANCED CRITICAL THINKING.

Suppose a friend comments to you, 'I think welfare recipients are simply lazy spendthrifts. I have a friend who receives Job Seekers Allowance and when she was offered a part-time job, she turned it down.'

1. What happens to a welfare recipient's benefits if they increase their earnings?

2. What is the effective tax rate on their additional income if they were to lose €1 in benefits for each euro of additional income?

3. How does this system affect a welfare recipient's incentive to work? Is a welfare recipient necessarily lazy if they turn down a part-time job?

SOLUTIONS

Terms and Definitions

_1_	Utility	_6_	Negative income tax
_2_	Permanent income	_7_	Liberalism
_3_	Welfare	_8_	Libertarianism
_4_	In kind transfers	_9_	Maximin criterion
_5_	Utilitarianism	_10_	Life cycle

Practice Problems

1. a. In kind transfers are not included, the economic life-cycle is not recognized, and transitory versus permanent income is not recognized. All three problems suggest that standard measures exaggerate economic inequality because the poor receive transfers in the form of goods and services and because the variation in income can be smoothed by borrowing and lending.
   b. Permanent income is a person's normal, or average, income. Using it removes the life-cycle effects and the transitory effects that cause any given year's income to be non-representative of the person's true standard of living. This would probably tend to understate the true distribution of the standard of living because, in reality, we cannot fully smooth our living standards by borrowing when young or when we have a bad year.

2. a. Utilitarianism: Since there is diminishing marginal utility of income as income grows large, it would harm Susan less than it would help Joe if we redistributed income from Susan to Joe. Thus, to maximize total utility, redistribute from Susan to Joe. Liberalism: Both Susan and Joe would agree that if they didn't know their station in life, they would choose to socially insure each other with a maximin system in case they were to be the one on the bottom end of the income distribution. So, redistribute from Susan to Joe. Libertarian: Since equal opportunity is more important than equal outcome, if each came by their income fairly and honestly, then no redistribution need take place.
   b. From least redistribution to most, libertarianism, utilitarianism, liberalism.

3. a.

Earned Income (€)	Taxes Paid (€)	After-tax Income (€)
0	−15,000	15,000
5,000	−12,500	17,500
10,000	−10,000	20,000
20,000	−5,000	25,000
30,000	0	30,000
40,000	5,000	35,000

b. €30,000

c. €15,000. The government simply guarantees that each family has €15,000 so once a family reaches that level, it fails to receive a subsidy.

d. The negative income tax because, under this tax scheme, the government will continue to subsidize families in the €15,000 to €30,000 range.

e. If negative income tax, final income = €10,000 earned income + €10,000 subsidy = €20,000. If €15,000 guarantee, final income = €10,000 + €5,000 subsidy = €15,000. If negative income tax, tax rate equals 0.50 because when income went up €5,000, take home pay went up €2,500 or €2,500/€5,000 = 0.50. If €15,000 guarantee, tax rate equals 100 per cent, because when income went up €5,000, final take home pay stayed the same at €15,000 because benefits were reduced by €5,000 or €5,000/€5,000 = 100 per cent. The €15,000 guarantee discourages work because there is no gain whatsoever from working when income is in the €0 to €15,000 range.

Short-Answer Questions

1. No. With regard to race, minorities are more likely to live in poverty. With regard to age, young are more likely than average and old are less likely than average to live in poverty. With regard to family composition, families headed by females are more likely to live in poverty.

2. Libertarianism differs from both utilitarianism and liberalism because libertarianism argues that income is earned only by individuals and not by society so no social planner has the right to alter the distribution of income if it was generated by a fair playing field. Utilitarianism redistributes income because of the diminishing marginal utility of income and liberalism redistributes income because of a maximin criterion for social insurance.

3. Because they recognize that taxes cause disincentives to work so that too much redistribution causes the pie to become so small that both rich and poor lose.

4. When labour demand is relatively elastic because an increase in the wage causes a large reduction in labour demand. More elastic in the long run because firms have time to adjust production in response to the rise in wages.

5. Welfare programmes could cause families to break up and unwed mothers to have children. They can cause a disincentive to work. Children fail to see the advantages of work and multiple generations become dependent on government.

6. Food stamps and Medicaid. Some argue that in kind transfers are inefficient because the government doesn't know what the poor need most and they argue that in kind transfers are insulting to the poor.

7. There is no answer to this at present and the jury is still out on this one! The question invites you to think about this issue and exercise your own judgement.

8. The major policy options to reduce poverty are minimum-wage laws, welfare, negative income tax, and in kind transfers.

True/False Questions

1. F; views on the desirability of a particular distribution of income are normative views.

2. T

3. T

4. F; both schools of thought recognize the disincentive to work and the reduction in total output caused by a tax system that would perfectly equalize income. Complete equality would cause both rich and poor to be worse off.

5. T

6. F; John Rawls has made this argument.

7. T

8. T

9. F; it is more efficient to provide cash payments, but recipients may spend it on things taxpayers don't appreciate.

10. F; income distribution would appear to be narrower.

Multiple-Choice Questions

1. a   6. d

2. c   7. b

3. a   8. a

4. b   9. b

5. c   10. b

Advanced Critical Thinking

1. They tend to lose benefits at a very high rate.

2. The tax rate would be 100 per cent on the additional income.

3. Once one is on welfare, there is little or no incentive to work. Once on welfare, one need not be lazy to remain on it. It may be rational to remain on welfare if every time a person makes a euro, the person loses a euro in benefits.

21

THE THEORY OF CONSUMER CHOICE

CHAPTER OVERVIEW

Context and Purpose

Chapter 21 is the first of two unrelated chapters that introduce you to some advanced topics in microeconomics. These two chapters are intended to whet your appetite for further study in economics. Chapter 21 is devoted to an advanced topic known as the theory of consumer choice.

CHAPTER REVIEW

Introduction

Chapter 21 develops the theory that describes how consumers make decisions about what to buy. So far, we have summarized these decisions with the demand curve. We now look at the theory of consumer choice which underlies the demand curve. After developing the theory, we apply the theory to the following questions:

- Do all demand curves slope downward?

- How do wages affect labour supply?

- How do interest rates affect household saving?

The Budget Constraint: What the Consumer Can Afford

A *budget constraint* is the limit on the consumption bundles that a consumer can afford (given the consumer's income and the prices of the goods the consumer wishes to buy). On a graph that measures the quantity of a consumption good on each axis, a budget constraint is a straight line connecting the maximum amounts that could be purchased of each commodity given the prices of each commodity and the consumer's income. For example, if a consumer has income of €1,000 and the price of Pepsi is €2 per pint, the maximum amount of Pepsi that could be purchased is €1,000/€2 = 500 pints. If the price of pizza is €10, the maximum amount of pizza that could be purchased is €1,000/€10 = 100 pizzas.

The slope of the budget constraint is the *relative price* of the two goods. In this case since a pizza costs five times what a pint of Pepsi costs, the consumer can trade one pizza for five pints of Pepsi. If the quantity of Pepsi is plotted on the vertical axis and the quantity of pizza on the horizontal axis, the slope of the budget constraint is 5/1 which equals the price of pizza divided by the price of Pepsi or €10/€2 = 5. Since the budget constraint always slopes downward or negatively, we often ignore the negative sign.

Preferences: What the Consumer Wants

A consumer's preferences can be represented with indifference curves. If two bundles of commodities suit a consumer's tastes equally well, the consumer is indifferent between them. Graphically, an *indifference curve* is a curve that shows consumption bundles that give the consumer the same level of satisfaction. When drawn on a graph that measures the quantity consumed of each good on each axis, an indifference curve must be downward sloping because if consumption of one good is reduced, the consumption of the other good must be increased for the consumer to be equally happy. The slope at any point on an indifference curve is known as the *marginal rate of substitution* or *MRS*. The *MRS* is the rate at which a consumer is willing to trade one good for another while maintaining a constant level of satisfaction.

There are four properties of indifference curves:

- Higher indifference curves (further from the origin) are preferred to lower ones because consumers prefer more of a good to less of it.

- Indifference curves are downward sloping because if consumption of one good is reduced, the consumption of the other good must be increased for the consumer to be equally happy.

- Indifference curves do not cross because it would suggest that a consumer's preferences are contradictory.

- Indifference curves are bowed inward (that is, convex to the origin) because a consumer is willing to trade a greater amount of a good for another good if they have an abundance of the good they are trading away. Conversely they are willing to trade a lesser amount of a good for another good if they have comparatively little of the good they are trading away.

When goods are easily substituted for each other, the degree to which the indifference curve is bowed is less than when there is very little substitutability between goods. In other words the marginal rate of substitution is lower. This is demonstrated by two extreme cases:

- *Perfect substitutes*: two goods with straight-line indifference curves. An example of perfect substitutes is different denominations of cash notes—two five euro notes for one ten euro note.

- *Perfect complements*: two goods with right-angle indifference curves. An example of perfect complements is right shoes and left shoes—additional shoes that don't come in pairs do not increase satisfaction.

Optimization: What the Consumer Chooses

When we combine the budget constraint and the consumer's indifference curves, we are able to determine the amount of each commodity that the consumer will buy. The consumer will try to reach the highest indifference curve subject to remaining on the budget constraint. The point where an indifference curve just touches the budget constraint determines the *optimum* amount of purchases of each good. At the optimum, the indifference curve is *tangent* to the budget constraint and the slope of the indifference curve and the budget constraint are the same. Thus, the consumer chooses consumption of the two goods so that the marginal rate of substitution (slope of the indifference curve) equals the relative price of the two goods (slope of the budget constraint). At the optimum, the tradeoff between the goods that the consumer is willing to make (slope of the indifference curve) is equal to the trade off between the goods that the market is willing to make (slope of the budget constraint).

An alternative way to describe preferences and optimization is with the concept of utility. Utility is an abstract measure of the happiness or satisfaction a consumer receives from consuming a bundle of goods. Therefore, an indifference curve is actually an 'equal-utility' curve. The *marginal utility* of a good is the increase in utility one gets from consuming an additional unit of that good. Goods exhibit *diminishing marginal utility* as more of any good is consumed. Since the marginal rate of substitution (the slope of the indifference curve) is the trade off between two goods that the consumer is willing to make, it must also equal the marginal utility of one good divided by the marginal utility of the other good. Therefore, for two goods X and Y, at the optimum:

$$MRS = P_x/P_y = MU_x/MU_y \text{ or,}$$
$$MU_x/P_x = MU_y/P_y$$

At the optimum, the marginal utility of a euro spent on X must be equal to the marginal utility of a euro spent on Y. Similarly, we can say that, at the optimum, the indifference curve is tangent to the budget constraint.

Suppose the income of the consumer were to increase. Because the consumer can now consume more of both goods and because the relative price of the two goods remains unchanged, an increase in income shifts the budget constraint outward in a parallel fashion. The consumer can now reach a new optimum on a higher indifference curve. It is most common that the consumer will choose to consume more of both goods. Thus, a *normal good* is a good for which an increase in income raises the quantity demanded. Alternatively, an *inferior good* is a good for which an increase in income reduces the quantity demanded. Bus rides are an inferior good.

Suppose the price of one of the goods were to fall. If the consumer allocates all of his income to the good whose price has fallen, the consumer can buy more of that good. If the consumer allocates all of his income to the good whose price is unchanged, the maximum amount he can purchase remains unchanged. This causes the budget constraint to rotate outward. That is, the budget constraint only shifts outward on the axis of the good whose price has fallen. The consumer can now reach a new optimum on a higher indifference curve.

The impact of a change in the price of a good can be decomposed into two effects: an income effect and a substitution effect. The *income effect* is the change in consumption that results when a price change moves the consumer to a higher or lower indifference curve. The *substitution effect* is the change in consumption that results when a price change moves the consumer along a given indifference curve to a point with a new marginal rate of substitution. Graphically, the substitution effect is the change in consumption that results from the change in relative prices which rotates the budget line along a given indifference curve. The income effect is the change in consumption that results from the parallel shift in the budget constraint to the new optimum on the new indifference curve.

A demand curve can be derived from the consumer's optimising decisions that result from the consumer's budget constraint and indifference curves. The combined income and substitution effect shows the total change in quantity demanded from a change in the price of a good. When these values are plotted on a price/quantity graph, the points form the consumer's demand curve.

Three Applications

- *Do all demand curves slope downward?* Theoretically, demand can sometimes slope upward. If an increase in the price of an inferior good has a larger income effect than substitution effect (the good is very strongly inferior) then an increase in the price of the good would cause the quantity demanded to rise. A *Giffen good* is a good for which an increase in the price raises the quantity demanded. Giffen goods are so rare that economists are not certain that one has ever existed!

- *How do wages affect labour supply?* The theory of consumer choice can be applied to the allocation decision between work and leisure. In this case, the two goods are consumption and leisure. The maximum amount of leisure is the number of hours available. The maximum amount of consumption is the number of hours available times the wage. The individual's indifference curves determine an optimum amount of leisure and consumption. Suppose the wage were to rise. The substitution effect induces more consumption and less leisure (more work). However, if both leisure and consumption are normal goods, the income effect suggests that the individual will wish to have both more consumption and more leisure (less work). If the substitution effect outweighs the income effect, an increase in wages will increase the quantity of labour supplied and labour supply is upward sloping. If the income effect outweighs the substitution effect, an increase in wages will decrease the quantity of labour supplied and labour supply slopes backward. Evidence that the length of the working week is decreasing suggests that the income effect is very strong and the labour supply curve bends backward when measured over long periods of time. Evidence on the behaviour of lottery winners and people who receive large bequests supports the view that at relatively high income levels, the labour-supply curve is backward sloping.

- *How do interest rates affect household saving?* The theory of consumer choice can be applied to the decision of how much income to consume today and how much to save for tomorrow. In this case, we measure consumption when younger on the horizontal axis and consumption when older on the vertical axis. A person can consume all of his earnings when relatively young and have nothing when older, or consume nothing when younger, save all of his income, earn interest on the saving, and consume a greater amount when older. A person's preferences determine the optimal amounts of consumption in each period. If the interest rate rises, the budget constraint becomes steeper because the maximum possible consumption when older increases. When the interest rate rises, the substitution effect suggests that the consumer should increase consumption when older and decrease consumption when younger (save more) because consumption when old has become relatively cheaper. However, if consumption in both periods is a normal good, the income effect suggests that the individual should consume more in both periods (save less). If the substitution effect outweighs the income effect, an increase in the interest rate will cause the individual to save more. If the income effect outweighs the substitution effect, an increase in the interest rate will cause the individual to save less. Evidence on this issue is mixed, so there is no clear recommendation for public policy toward the taxation of interest.

Conclusion: Do People Really Think This Way?

While consumers may not literally make decisions in the manner suggested by the theory of consumer choice, the model of consumer choice describes a process that permits economic analysis. The theory is useful in many applications.

HELPFUL HINTS

1. We have noted that the slope of the budget constraint is equal to the relative prices of the two goods represented on the graph. But which price should we

put in the numerator and which price should we put in the denominator of the slope? Place the price of the good represented on the horizontal axis in the numerator and the price of the good represented on the vertical axis in the denominator of the slope. For example, if the quantity of chocolate bars is measured on the horizontal axis and the quantity of soft drinks is measured on the vertical axis, and if the price of a bar of chocolate is €2 while the price of a soft drink is €1, then 2 soft drinks can be exchanged for one bar of chocolate. The slope of the budget constraint is €2/€1 or 2. (Again, the slope of the budget constraint is always negative so we often ignore the sign.)

2. A mapping of an individual's preferences generates an infinite set of indifference curves. Each indifference curve divides the commodity space into three areas—points preferred to those on the indifference curve (points outside the indifference curve or away from the origin), points inferior to the indifference curve (points inside the indifference curve or toward the origin), or points of equal satisfaction as those on the indifference curve (points on the indifference curve). While there are an infinite set of indifference curves it is customary to represent on a graph only those indifference curves that are tangent to a budget constraint and thus, only those indifference curves that determine an optimum.

3. The slope of the indifference curve is the marginal rate of substitution which is the marginal utility of one good compared to the marginal utility of the other good. The slope of the budget constraint is equal to the relative prices of the two goods. Since at the optimum the indifference curve is tangent to the budget constraint, it follows that at the optimum the relative prices of the two goods equals the relative marginal utilities of the two goods. Thus, at the optimum, the additional utility gained by the consumer from an additional euro's worth of one good is the same as the additional utility gained by the consumer from an additional euro's worth of the other good. That is, at the optimum, the consumer cannot increase his total satisfaction by moving expenditures from one good to the other good.

TERMS AND DEFINITIONS

Choose a definition for each key term.

Key terms:

_____ Budget constraint

_____ Indifference curve

_____ Marginal rate of substitution

_____ Perfect substitutes

_____ Perfect complements

_____ Normal good

_____ Inferior good

_____ Income effect

_____ Substitution effect

_____ Giffen good

Definitions:

1. The change in consumption that results when a price change moves the consumer to a higher or lower indifference curve

2. The rate at which a consumer is willing to trade one good for another

3. The limit on the consumption bundles that a consumer can afford

4. A good for which an increase in income raises the quantity demanded

5. A good for which an increase in the price raises the quantity demanded

6. Two goods with right-angle indifference curves

7. A curve that shows consumption bundles that give the consumer the same level of satisfaction

8. A good for which an increase in income reduces the quantity demanded

9. Two goods with straight-line indifference curves

10. The change in consumption that results when a price change moves the consumer along a given indifference curve to a point with a new marginal rate of substitution

PROBLEMS AND SHORT-ANSWER QUESTIONS

Practice Problems

1. Suppose a consumer only buys two goods—pepsi and pizzas. Suppose the price of pepsi is €1, the price of a pizza is €2, and the consumer's income is €20.
   a. Plot the consumer's budget constraint in Exhibit 1. Measure the quantity of pepsi on the vertical axis and the quantity of pizzas on the horizontal axis. Explicitly plot the points on the budget constraint associated with the even numbered quantities of pizza (0, 2, 4, 6...).
   b. Suppose the individual chooses to consume six pizzas. What is the maximum amount of pepsi that he can afford? Draw an indifference curve on the figure above that establishes this bundle of goods as the optimum.
   c. What is the slope of the budget constraint? What is the slope of the consumer's indifference curve at the optimum? What is the relationship between the slope of the budget constraint and the slope of the indifference curve at the optimum? What is the economic interpretation of this relationship?
   d. Explain why any other point on the budget constraint must be inferior to the optimum.

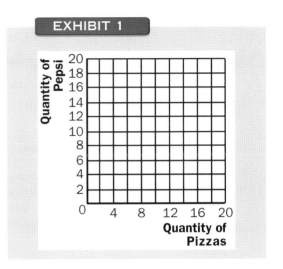

2. Use Exhibit 2 to answer the following questions.
   a. Suppose the price of a magazine is €2, the price of a book is €10, and the consumer's income is €100. Which point on the graph represents the consumer's optimum—X, Y, or Z? What are the optimal quantities of books and magazines this individual chooses to consume?
   b. Suppose the price of books falls to €5. What are the two optimum points on the graph that represent the substitution effect (in sequence)? What is the change in the consumption of books due to the substitution effect?
   c. Again, suppose the price of books falls to €5. What are the two optimum points on the graph that represent the income effect (in sequence)? What is the change in the consumption of books due to the income effect? Is a book a normal good or an inferior good for this consumer? Explain.
   d. For this consumer, what is the total change in the quantity of books purchased when the price of books fell from €10 to €5?
   e. Use the information in this problem to plot the consumer's demand curve for books in Exhibit 3.

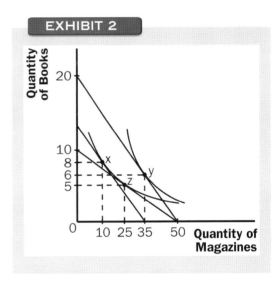

Short-Answer Questions

1. Suppose that there are two goods available to the consumer—pens and pencils. Suppose that the price of a pen is €2.00 while the price of a pencil is €0.50. If we measure the quantity of pens on the horizontal axis and the quantity of pencils on the vertical axis, what is the slope of the budget constraint? Do you need to know the income of the consumer to answer this question? Why?

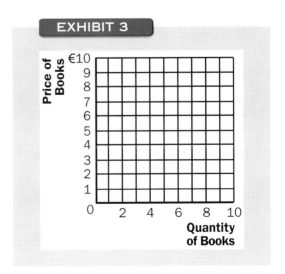

2. If we measure 'goods' on each axis, is an indifference curve positively (upward) sloped or negatively (downward) sloped? Why? If we measure a 'good' on one axis but a 'bad' (such as pollution) on the other axis, what type of slope do you think an indifference curve would have? Why?

3. Why are most indifference curves bowed inward, that is, convex to the origin?

4. Consider the following two pairs of goods:

   - Graduation caps and graduation gowns
   - Petrol at an BP station and petrol at a Shell station

   Which of the pairs of goods above is likely to be nearly perfect substitutes and which is likely to be nearly perfect complements? Explain.

5. Referring to question 4 above, what is the shape of the indifference curves that you would expect each pair of goods to generate, straight line or right angle? For which pair of goods would you observe the greatest substitution effect if the relative prices of the two goods were to change? Why?

6. Suppose there are two goods available to the consumer—coffee and tea. Suppose that the price of coffee decreases. What impact will the substitution effect and income effect have on the quantity demanded of coffee if coffee is a normal good? Explain. What impact will the substitution effect and income effect have on the quantity demanded of coffee if coffee is an inferior good? Explain.

7. Suppose there are only two goods available to you, apples and oranges. Suppose that the prices of apples and oranges double and that your income also doubles. What will happen to the amount of apples and oranges that you choose to consume? Explain. (Hint: What has happened to the slope of the budget constraint? What has happened to the maximum amount of apples or oranges that you could consume if you allocated all of your income to one good or the other?)

8. Some people argue that the tax rate should be reduced on interest earned from saving because it will increase the after-tax return to saving, increase the quantity of saving supplied, and increase economic growth. Are we certain that a decrease in the tax rate on interest earned from saving will increase the quantity of saving? Explain.

9. List the properties of the indifference curves.

SELF-TEST

True/False Questions

_____ 1. If we measure the quantity of French fries on the horizontal axis and the quantity of pizzas on the vertical axis, and if the price of French fries is €0.60 and the price of a pizza is €2.40, then the slope of the budget constraint is 1/4 (and it is negative).

_____ 2. A budget constraint is a set of commodity bundles that provide the consumer with the same level of satisfaction.

_____ 3. Indifference curves measure the consumer's willingness to trade one good for another good while maintaining a constant level of satisfaction.

_____ 4. When drawn on a graph that measures the quantity of a good on each axis, indifference curves are usually straight lines that slope downward (negatively).

_____ 5. At the consumer's optimum point, the marginal rate of substitution of apples for oranges is equal to the ratio of the price of oranges to the price of apples.

_____ 6. If the price of a good falls, the substitution effect always causes an increase in the quantity demanded of that good.

_____ 7. If the price of a good falls and the good is a normal good, the income effect causes a decrease in the quantity demanded of that good.

_____ 8. The income effect is measured as the change in consumption that results when a price change moves the consumer along a given indifference curve to a point with a new marginal rate of substitution.

_____ 9. An increase in the interest rate will always lead to a greater amount of saving.

_____10. The theory of consumer choice can be used to demonstrate that labour supply curves must be upward sloping.

Multiple-Choice Questions

1. Indifference curves for perfect substitutes are
   a. straight lines.
   b. bowed inward (concave to the origin).
   c. bowed outward (convex to the origin).
   d. right angles.
   e. nonexistent.

2. The consumer's optimal purchase of any two goods is the point where
   a. the consumer reaches the highest indifference curve subject to remaining on the budget constraint.
   b. the consumer has reached the highest indifference curve.
   c. the two highest indifference curves cross.
   d. the budget constraint crosses the indifference curve.

3. Which of the following is true about the consumer's optimum consumption bundle? At the optimum,
   a. the indifference curve is tangent to the budget constraint.
   b. the slope of the indifference curve equals the slope of the budget constraint.
   c. the relative prices of the two goods equals the marginal rate of substitution.
   d. all of the above are true.
   e. none of the above are true.

4. If an increase in a consumer's income causes the consumer to increase his quantity demanded of a good, then the good is
   a. an inferior good.
   b. a normal good.
   c. a substitute good.
   d. a complementary good.

Suppose that the consumer must choose between buying socks and belts. Also, suppose that the consumer's income is €100. Use Exhibit 4 to answer questions 5 through 8.

5. If the price of a belt is €10 and the price of a pair of socks is €5, the consumer will choose to buy the commodity bundle represented by point
   a. X.
   b. Y.

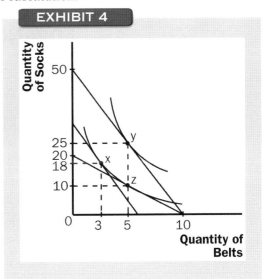

EXHIBIT 4

    c. Z.

    d. the optimal point cannot be determined from this graph.

6. Suppose that the price of a pair of socks falls from €5 to €2. The substitution effect is represented by the movement from point

    a. Y to point X.

    b. X to point Y.

    c. Z to point X.

    d. X to point Z.

7. Suppose that the price of a pair of socks has falls from €5 to €2. The income effect is represented by the movement from point

    a. Y to point X.

    b. X to point Y.

    c. Z to point X.

    d. X to point Z.

8. A pair of socks is

    a. an inferior good.

    b. a normal good.

    c. a Giffen good.

    d. none of the above.

9. If leisure is a normal good, an increase in the wage rate

    a. will always increase the quantity of labour supplied.

    b. will always decrease the amount of labour supplied.

    c. will increase the amount of labour supplied if the income effect outweighs the substitution effect.

    d. will increase the amount of labour supplied if the substitution effect outweighs the income effect.

10. Which of the following is <u>not</u> true regarding the outcome of a consumer's optimization process?

    a. The consumer has reached his highest indifference curve subject to his budget constraint.

    b. The marginal utility per euro spent on each good is the same.

    c. The consumer is indifferent between any two points on his budget constraint.

    d. The marginal rate of substitution between goods is equal to the ratio of the prices between goods.

    e. The consumer's indifference curve is tangent to his budget constraint.

ADVANCED CRITICAL THINKING

Suppose you have a wealthy aunt. Your aunt dies and leaves you a great deal of money (potentially). When you attend the reading of the will, you discover that she has bequeathed her millions to a 'family incentive trust' As the lawyer reads the will, you discover that you only get the money if you get married, have children, stay with your spouse and raise your children, don't become dependent on drugs or alcohol, and if you *continuously have a full-time job*. (Note: Family incentive trusts are real and becoming very common.)

1. Why might your aunt include the requirement that you continuously have a full-time job?

2. Does the evidence about how people behave after they receive an inheritance suggest that your aunt's concerns are well-founded? Explain.

3. What does this evidence suggest about the slope of the labour supply curve? Explain.

SOLUTIONS

Terms and Definitions

_1_	Income effect	_5_	Giffen good	_8_	Inferior good
_2_	Marginal rate of substitution	_6_	Perfect complements	_9_	Perfect substitutes
_3_	Budget constraint	_7_	Indifference curve	_10_	Substitution effect
_4_	Normal good				

Practice Problems

1. a. See Exhibit 5.
    b. Eight. For the indifference curve, see Exhibit 5.
    c. Slope = 2/1. This is also the price ratio of price of pizza to price of pepsi = €2/€1. The slope of the indifference curve is also 2/1. (Note: all of these slopes are negative.) At the optimum, the indifference curve is tangent to the budget constraint so their slopes are equal. Thus, the tradeoff between the goods that the individual is willing to undertake (*MRS*) is the same as the trade off that the market requires (slope of budget constraint).
    d. Since the highest indifference curve reachable is tangent to the budget constraint, any other point on the budget constraint must have an indifference curve running through it that is below the optimal indifference curve so that point must be inferior to the optimum.

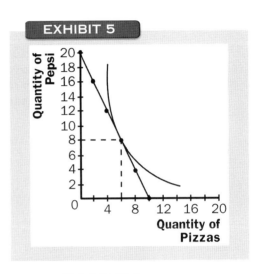

EXHIBIT 5

2. a. Point Z. Five books and twenty five magazines.
    b. From point Z to point X. From five books to eight books.
    c. From point X to point Y. From eight books to six books. Books are inferior because an increase in income decreases the quantity demanded of books.
    d. The quantity demanded increased from five books to six books.
    e. See Exhibit 6.

Short-Answer Questions

1. Slope = 4/1 or 4. It is also the ratio of the price of pens to the price of pencils or €2.00/€0.50 = 4. (All slopes are negative.) No. Income simply must be any positive amount. A change in income shifts the budget constraint in or out but does not change its slope.

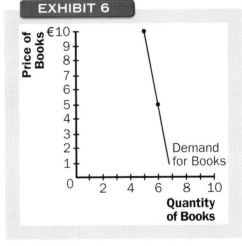

EXHIBIT 6

2. Negatively sloped because, for a consumer to be equally happy, if consumption of one good is reduced the consumption of the other good must be increased. Positively sloped because, for a consumer to be equally happy, if consumption of the bad item is increased the consumption of the good item must also be increased.

3. Because the marginal rate of substitution (MRS) is not constant along most indifference curves. A consumer is willing to trade a greater amount of a good for another if they have an abundance of the good they are trading away. They are willing to trade a lesser amount away if they have very little of the good they are trading away.

4. Petrol at BP and at Shell are nearly perfect substitutes because the marginal rate of substitution is fixed at about one—one gallon of Esso petrol for one gallon of Shell petrol. Graduation caps and gowns are nearly perfect complements because additional units of caps without gowns or additional units of gowns without caps provide little or no additional satisfaction.

5. BP petrol and Shell petrol would have nearly straight line indifference curves while graduation caps and gowns would have nearly right angle indifference curves. A change in the relative prices of petrol would cause a great substitution between petrol at each station while a change in the relative prices of caps and gowns would cause little or no substitution of caps for gowns or gowns for caps.

6. The substitution effect will cause an increase in the quantity demanded of coffee regardless of whether coffee is normal or inferior. If coffee is normal, the income effect will cause an increase in the quantity demanded of coffee. If coffee is inferior, the income effect will cause a decrease in the quantity demanded of coffee.

7. There will be no impact because the slope of the budget constraint is unaltered (relative prices are the same so the market tradeoff is the same) and the position of the budget constraint is unaltered (the maximum amount of each good that can be purchased is unaltered so the end points of the budget constraint are the same).

8. No. An increase in the return to saving should increase consumption when old (substitution effect increases saving) but an increase in the return to saving increases income and should increase consumption when young and old (income effect decreases saving). If the income effect outweighs the substitution effect, a greater after-tax return on saving would decrease saving.

9. Higher indifference curves are preferable to lower ones. Indifference curves are downward-sloping. Indifference curves do not intersect. Indifference curves are bowed inward (towards the origin).

True/False Questions

1. T

2. F; a budget constraint is the limit on the consumption bundles that a consumer can afford.

3. T

4. F; indifference curves are negatively sloped, but they are usually bowed inward, that is, convex to the origin.

5. T

6. T

7. F; the income effect would cause an increase in the quantity demanded.

8. F; the income effect is measured as the change in consumption that results when a change in price moves the consumer to a higher or lower indifference curve.

9. F; if the income effect from a change in interest rates outweighs the substitution effect the individual will save less.

10. F; labour supply curves can be backward sloping if the income effect from a change in the wage outweighs the substitution effect.

Multiple-Choice Questions

1. a   3. d   5. c   7. b   9. d
2. a   4. b   6. c   8. b   10. c

Advanced Critical Thinking

1. She is probably afraid that her gift of millions would tempt you to become lazy and cause you to lead a less useful life than you otherwise would.

2. Her concerns may be well-founded. People who win lotteries or receive large inheritances often quit work or reduce the hours they work.

3. This evidence suggests that the labour supply curve may be backward sloping. We generally assume that a higher wage increases the quantity supplied of labour (upward sloping labour supply) but, in fact, a higher wage may decrease the quantity of labour supplied (backward sloping labour supply) if leisure is a normal good and the income effect of an increase in the wage outweighs the substitution effect.

GOALS

⌈In this chapter you will

Examine the problems caused by asymmetric information

Learn about market solutions to asymmetric information

Consider why democratic voting systems might not represent the preferences of society

Consider why people might not always behave as rational maximizers

OUTCOMES

⌈You should be able to

Describe the information asymmetry in the labour market

Explain why insurance companies screen potential customers

Generate an example of the Condorcet voting paradox

Explain why people are willing to save a portion of their monthly salary to a retirement pension scheme

FRONTIERS OF MICROECONOMICS

CHAPTER OVERVIEW

Context and Purpose

Chapter 22 is the last chapter in the microeconomics portion of the text. It is the second of two unrelated chapters that introduce you to some advanced topics in microeconomics. These two chapters are intended to whet your appetite for further study in economics.

The purpose of Chapter 22 is to give you a taste of three topics on the frontier of microeconomic research. The first topic we address is *asymmetric information*, a situation when one person in an economic relationship has more relevant knowledge than the other person. The second topic is *political economy*, the application of economic tools to the understanding of the functioning of government. The third topic we address is *behavioural economics*, the introduction of psychology into the study of economic issues.

CHAPTER REVIEW

Introduction

The study of economics is always seeking to expand the understanding of human behaviour and society. This chapter addresses three areas on the frontier of economic study. The first topic we address is *asymmetric information*, a situation when one person in an economic relationship has more relevant knowledge than the other person. The second topic is *political economy*, the application of economic tools to the understanding of the functioning of government. The third topic we address is *behavioural economics*, the introduction of psychology into the study of economic issues.

Asymmetric Information

A difference in access to relevant knowledge is called an *information asymmetry*. We address two types of information asymmetries: *hidden actions* and *hidden characteristics*.

Hidden actions might occur. When a person (called the **agent**) performs some task on behalf of another person (called the **principal**). Generally, the agent knows more about his effort and performance than the principal. The problem of **moral hazard** arises if the principal cannot perfectly monitor the agent, so the agent tends to engage in dishonest or undesirable behaviour. In the employment relationship, the employer is the principal and the worker is the agent. Employers respond to the moral hazard problem with:

- *Better monitoring.* Employers use video cameras to catch irresponsible behaviour of workers.

- *High wages.* Firms pay efficiency wages (above equilibrium wages) to raise the cost to the worker of being fired and make the worker less likely to shirk.

- *Delayed payment.* Year-end bonuses and higher pay later in life reduce shirking today.

- *Piece rates.* Workers are paid an amount that is partly based on the amount they have produced or, in the case of sales personnel, the amount they have sold. In the latter case such payments are usually referred to as 'commission'.

Insurance can generate moral hazard because the insured might have less incentive to reduce the risk of an accident.

Hidden Characteristics are when a seller knows more than the buyer about the good being sold. *Hidden characteristics* might generate a problem known as **adverse selection**—the buyer risks selecting goods of low quality. Adverse selection might occur in the market for:

- *Used cars.* Buyers might choose not to buy even slightly used cars because they surmise that sellers know something bad about the cars. This is known as the 'lemons' problem.

- *Labour.* If a firm reduces the wage it pays, high productivity workers tend to quit and the firm is left with low productivity workers.

- *Insurance.* People with hidden health problems are more likely to want to buy health insurance than people with average or good health.

When markets suffer from adverse selection, people might continue to drive used cars they would rather sell, firms might pay wages above equilibrium and cause unemployment, and relatively healthy people might fail to purchase health insurance because it is too expensive. That is, markets might become inefficient.

Markets respond to asymmetric information in several ways.

Signalling is when an informed party takes actions to reveal information to an uninformed party. Recall from previous chapters that firms spend money on expensive advertising to signal that they sell high-quality products. Students attend high-quality schools to signal that they are high-ability people. For a signal to be effective, it must be costly, but less costly to the person with the higher-quality product. Signalling is rational for both the buyer and seller. A personal gift qualifies as a signal of love because it is costly (it takes time to purchase) and if someone loves another the most, they know what to buy (takes less time to buy than it would for a simple acquaintance).

Screening is when an uninformed party acts to induce an informed party to reveal information. Buyers of used cars might have a mechanic check out a used car. Car insurers might check a driver's driving history, or offer different policies that have different degrees of appeal to risky and safe drivers so the two kinds of drivers will reveal their driving characteristics.

Although markets might fail to allocate resources efficiently when there is asymmetric information, it is not clear that public policy actions can improve market outcomes because,

- Private markets can sometimes deal with the problem by using signalling and screening.

- The government rarely has more information than private parties so it cannot improve upon the current imperfect allocation of resources. Thus, the market is not first-best, but is second-best.

- The government itself is an imperfect institution.

Political Economy

Political economy, also known as *public choice*, applies the methods of economics to study how the government works. Before we choose to have the government attempt to improve market outcomes, we must recognise that government is also imperfect.

The Condorcet voting paradox. The failure of majority rule to produce transitive preferences for society. *Transitivity* is the property that if A is preferred to B, and B is preferred to C, then A must be preferred to C. When society has to choose between more than two outcomes, majority rule democracy might not tell us what alternative society really wants because pairwise voting across three or more alternatives does not guarantee transitivity, a phenomena known as the **Condorcet paradox**. That is, it is possible under pairwise voting that A is preferred to B, and B is preferred to C, yet C is preferred to A. Because the property of transitivity is required for majority-rule democracy to accurately aggregate preferences, two conclusions can be drawn: (1) majority-rule voting does not necessarily tell us what society wants and, (2) setting the order in which items are voted can affect the outcome.

Arrow's impossibility theorem. Arrow's impossibility theorem is a mathematical result showing that, under certain assumed conditions, there is no scheme for aggregating individual preferences into a valid set of social preferences. Due to the Condorcet paradox, alternative voting systems have been proposed. A *Borda count* allows voters to rank and give points to possible outcomes when there are more than two outcomes—like sports team rankings. However, Arrow has shown that *no voting system* can satisfy the following properties required of a perfect voting scheme:

- *Unanimity*: If everyone prefers A to B, then A should beat B.

- *Transitivity*: If A beats B, and B beats C, then A should beat C.

- *Independence of irrelevant alternatives*: The rankings between any two outcomes should not depend on whether some third outcome is available.

- *No dictators*: There is no person that always gets his way.

For example, majority rule does not always satisfy transitivity and the Borda count does not always satisfy the independence of irrelevant alternatives. While democracy should not be abandoned, all voting schemes are flawed mechanisms for social choice.

The median voter is king. The median-voter theorem is a mathematical result showing that if voters are choosing a point along a line and each voter wants the point closest to his most preferred point, then majority rule will pick the most preferred point of the median voter. The median voter is the voter exactly in the middle of the distribution. Majority rule voting will always generate an outcome that is preferred by the median voter if each voter votes for the outcome that is closest to his most preferred outcome. This outcome will not necessarily be the average preferred outcome or the modal outcome. In addition, minority views are not given much weight.

Politicians are self-interested. Self-interest might cause politicians to maximise their own well-being as opposed to maximising the well-being of society. Some politicians might act out of greed and others might sacrifice the national interest to improve their local popularity. Therefore, actual economic policy often fails to resemble the ideal policy derived in economics textbooks.

Behavioural Economics

In *behavioural economics*, economists make use of basic psychological insights.

People aren't always rational. Economists generally assume that people and firms behave rationally. But people might not act as rational maximizers but instead as *satisficers*. Or people might exhibit 'near rationality' or 'bounded rationality'. People make the following systematic errors:

- People are over confident
- People give too much weight to a small number of vivid observations
- People are reluctant to change their minds

Regardless of these issues, economic models based on rationality might be good approximations of reality.

People care about fairness. The *ultimatum game* is a game where one player decides what portion of €100 to give to another player. The second player must either accept the split or both get nothing. Rational wealth maximizers would choose €99 and offer €1. The second player would accept because €1 is better than nothing. However, in experiments the first player tends to give much more than €1 (but less than €50) to the second player and the second player usually rejects small offerings. People might be driven by a sense of fairness as opposed to their normal self-interest. As a result, firms might pay above equilibrium wages during profitable years to be fair or to avoid retaliation on the part of workers.

People are inconsistent over time. People tend to desire instant gratification as opposed to delayed gratification. Therefore, they fail to follow through on plans to do things that are dreary, take effort, or cause discomfort. For example, people often save less than they plan. To help follow through on a plan, people might restrict their future behaviour: Smokers throw away their cigarettes, dieters put a lock on the refrigerator, and workers sign up for a retirement plan.

Conclusion

This chapter introduced areas of continuing economic research. Asymmetric information should make us more wary of market outcomes. Political economy should make us more wary of government solutions. Behavioural economics should make us more wary of human decision-making.

HELPFUL HINTS

1. The market for insurance demonstrates many of the problems and market solutions generated by asymmetric information. For car insurance, firms first screen prospective customers to reduce *adverse selection*—the problem of

selling insurance to worse than average drivers. After the sale of the insurance, car insurance companies sometimes require a deductible or co-payment on collision insurance, that is, the insured pays a part of the cost of damage repair on any claim. This reduces *moral hazard*—the problem of insured drivers driving more recklessly once they are insured.

2. No method of economic decision-making is always perfect. Markets might not maximise total surplus due to externalities, public goods, imperfect competition, and asymmetric information. In addition, people and firms might not always rationally maximise their own well-being. But government might not be able to improve upon the situation because governments might not have any better information than markets, all voting schemes are imperfect, and politicians might choose to maximise their own well-being instead of the well-being of society.

TERMS AND DEFINITIONS

Choose a definition for each key term.

Key terms:

_____ Moral hazard

_____ Agent

_____ Principal

_____ Adverse selection

_____ Signalling

_____ Screening

_____ Condorcet paradox

_____ Arrow impossibility theorem

_____ Median voter theorem

3. A person for whom another person, called the agent, is performing some act

4. The tendency of a person who is imperfectly monitored to engage in dishonest or otherwise undesirable behaviour

5. A mathematical result showing that if voters are choosing a point along a line and each voter wants the point closest to his most preferred point, then majority rule will pick the most preferred point of the median voter

6. A mathematical result showing that, under certain assumed conditions, there is no scheme for aggregating individual preferences into a valid set of social preferences

7. The tendency for the mix of unobserved attributes to become undesirable from the standpoint of an uninformed party

8. A person who is performing an act for another person, called the principal

9. An action taken by a uninformed party to induce a informed party to reveal information

Definitions:

1. An action taken by an informed party to reveal private information to a uniformed party

2. The failure of majority rule to produce transitive preferences for society

PROBLEMS AND SHORT-ANSWER QUESTIONS

Practice Problems

1. For each of the following situations, identify the principal and the agent, describe the information asymmetry involved, and explain how moral hazard has been reduced.
   a. Dental insurance companies offer free annual check-ups.
   b. Firms compensate travelling sales persons with commissions (a percentage of the value of the sales).
   c. Agricultural seed companies pay migrant workers bonuses if they work the entire summer season.
   d. McDonald's pays twice the minimum wage to high school students.

2. For each of the following situations, describe the information asymmetry involved, name the type of action that has been taken to reduce adverse selection (signalling or screening), and explain how adverse selection has been reduced.
   a. McDonald's only hires high school students with good grades.
   b. Hyundai (a Korean car manufacturer) provides a 100,000-mile warranty on its new cars.
   c. A health insurance company requires prospective customers to take a physical examination.

3. In each of the following situations, describe the behaviour that suggests that people might not always behave as self-interested rational maximizers.
   a. Workers agree to a labour contract that gives them a 5 per cent raise for each of the next three years. After one year passes, they discover that the firm's profits have increased by 100 per cent. The workers go on strike and receive no income during the strike.
   b. A worker plans to start saving 20 per cent of his income starting three months from now because he has to first pay off some overdue bills. After three months pass, the worker saves nothing and instead spends all of his monthly income.
   c. After a famous rock star dies in a plane crash, many people decide to ride the train rather than fly.
   d. Richard wants to go on a fishing trip and his wife, Hazel, wishes to take a different type of trip. The newspaper reports that the size and number of fish being caught in the area where Richard intends to fish is greater than normal because the temperature has become unseasonally cool. Richard is more sure about his choice of the fishing trip and Hazel is more sure about her desire to go on a different type of trip.

Short-Answer Questions

1. What is *moral hazard*? What steps might a firm take to avoid moral hazard in the employment relationship?

2. What is *adverse selection*? Would you pay as much for a home that is only a year old (but has been lived in by people that have since built another home in the local area) as you would for a brand new home that has yet to be lived in? Why? What steps might you take to avoid adverse selection?

3. Would you expect the buyers of car insurance to have a higher or lower than average probability of having a car accident? Why? How does the insurance company address the problem of adverse selection in this market? How does it address the moral hazard problem in this market?

4. To reduce adverse selection, firms signal high quality with expensive advertising. What are the necessary characteristics of an effective signal? Why don't firms producing low-quality goods use expensive advertising to falsely signal high quality?

5. Is adverse selection more likely to be a feature of perfectly competitive markets or imperfectly competitive markets? Explain why.

6. Suppose that 30 per cent of the voters want to spend €10,000 on a new park, 30 per cent want to spend €11,000, and 40 per cent wish to spend €25,000. How much does the average voter want to spend? How much does the median voter want to spend? If each voter chooses the point closest to his most preferred choice, what will be the final choice between these three choices of a majority rule? Does the Condorcet paradox arise?

7. If people were rational wealth maximizers, what result would we expect from the 'ultimatum game'? What results do we actually find in experiments? What does this imply about wage determination?

8. The most popular major on campus is economics. Your best friend takes an introductory economics class and tells you that it was the worst class she has ever taken. You avoid taking any economics. Is this rational? Explain.

9. What are the properties of a perfect voting scheme in Arrow's impossibility theorem?

SELF-TEST

True/False Questions

_____ 1. Asymmetric information is a problem that occurs when one person in a transaction knows more about what is going on than the other.

_____ 2. In the principal–agent relationship, the principal performs a task on behalf of the agent.

_____ 3. Employers might pay higher than equilibrium wages to avoid moral hazard in the employment relationship by raising the cost of shirking.

_____ 4. To avoid the problem of adverse selection, insurance companies screen their prospective customers to discover hidden health problems.

_____ 5. Signals to convey high quality are most effective when they are costless to all firms in the industry.

_____ 6. If A is preferred to B, B preferred to C, and A is preferred to C, then these preferences exhibit the property of unanimity.

_____ 7. The Condorcet paradox shows that majority-rule voting always tells us the outcome that society really wants.

_____ 8. Arrow's impossibility theorem shows that no voting system can satisfy the properties required of a perfect voting system.

_____ 9. According to the median voter theorem, majority rule will produce the average preferred outcome.

_____ 10. Since people are reluctant to change their minds in the face of new information, we can conclude that people do not always behave as rational maximizers.

Multiple-Choice Questions

1. Matthew's car is in need of repair so he decides to sell it to avoid the repair bill. Unaware of the problem, Jo buys the car. This is an example of
   a. adverse selection.
   b. moral hazard.
   c. inapprporiate signalling.
   d. hidden actions.

2. Which of the following is an example of a signal that is used to reveal private information?
   a. Alan carefully chooses a special gift for Sharon.
   b. Jaguar advertises its cars during the FA Cup final.
   c. Madelyn earns her MBA from the London Business School.
   d. All of the above are correct.

3. Which of the following is *not* a method firms use to avoid the moral hazard problem in the employment relationship?

    a. pay above equilibrium wages

    b. put hidden video cameras in the workplace.

    c. buy life insurance on their workers.

    d. pay employees with delayed compensation such as a year-end bonus.

4. Which of the following best demonstrates the problem of moral hazard?

    a. Pete doesn't buy health insurance because it is too expensive and he is healthy.

    b. Julie chooses to attend a well-respected college.

    c. Alan drives more recklessly after he buys car insurance.

    d. Les is forced to take a physical examination before a company sells him private medical insurance.

Use the following set of voter preferences to answer questions 5 through 8.

	Voter type		
	Type 1	Type 2	Type 3
Per cent of Electorate	35	25	40
First Choice	C	A	B
Second Choice	A	B	C
Third Choice	B	C	A

5. What per cent of the population votes for A when the choice is between A and B?

    a. 25 per cent.

    b. 35 per cent.

    c. 40 per cent.

    d. 60 per cent.

    e. 75 per cent.

6. Under pairwise majority voting, which outcome wins?

    a. A.

    b. B.

    c. C.

    d. These preferences suffer from the Condorcet paradox, and so there is no clear winner.

7. If we first compare A to C, and then compare the winner to B, which outcome is the winner?

    a. A.

    b. B.

    c. C.

    d. These preferences suffer from the Condorcet paradox, and so there is no clear winner.

8. Using a Borda count, which outcome is preferred?

    a. A.

    b. B.

    c. C.

    d. These preferences do not exhibit transitivity, and so there is no clear winner.

9. Which of the following is *not* true about how people make decisions?

    a. People are sometimes too sure of their own abilities.

    b. People are reluctant to change their minds in the face of new information.

    c. People give too much weight to a small number of vivid observations.

    d. People are always rational maximizers.

    e. All of the above are actually true statements about how people make decisions.

10. Which of the following help explain why firms pay bonuses to workers during particularly profitable years to prevent workers from becoming disgruntled?
    a. People are rational maximizers.
    b. People are inconsistent over time.
    c. People care about fairness.
    d. People are reluctant to change their minds.

ADVANCED CRITICAL THINKING

You are watching a television news story about the AIDS crisis with a friend. Your friend says, 'I think it is terrible that people infected with AIDS often can't buy health insurance. People that are ill are the ones that really need health insurance. Even worse, once someone gets health insurance, they often have to pay a deductible equal to 20 per cent of the first €3,000 of their medical bills each year. Only then does the insurance company cover the remainder of the medical bills.'

1. What problem caused by asymmetric information are insurance companies trying to avoid when they deny coverage to someone who might already be ill? What would happen if the insurance companies did not deny coverage to people who are already ill?

2. What problem does charging a deductible help solve? What might happen if insurance companies didn't require a deductible?

3. How might public policy address the problems in the market for health insurance? What are some of the shortcomings of a public policy solution?

SOLUTIONS

Terms and Definitions

_1_ Signalling

_2_ Condorcet paradox

_3_ Principal

_4_ Moral hazard

_5_ Median voter theorem

_6_ Arrow impossibility theorem

_7_ Adverse selection

_8_ Agent

_9_ Screening

Practice Problems

1. a. The insurance company is the principal; the insured is the agent. Only the agent knows how well he takes care of his teeth. By checking the insured's teeth each year, the insurance company can better monitor the behaviour of the insured and reduce major future claims.
    b. The firm is the principal; the salesperson is the agent. The firm does not know how hard the salesperson works. By only paying the salesperson a commission, the firm is able to better monitor the sales person's work habits, and the worker is less likely to shirk.
    c. The firm is the principal; the worker is the agent. The firm does not know how hard the migrant worker works. By paying a large bonus for completing the season, the firm raises the cost of shirking and the cost of being fired. The worker is less likely to shirk.
    d. McDonald's is the principal; the student is the agent. McDonald's does not know how hard the student works. By paying above market wages, McDonald's increases the cost of shirking and the cost of being fired. The worker is less likely to shirk.

2. a. McDonald's doesn't know the abilities of the potential workers as well as do the workers. McDonald's *screens* potential workers using past educational performance and it is able to select high-ability workers.

    b. Buyers don't know the quality of Hyundai cars because they are relatively new to this market. Hyundai *signals* high quality with a long warranty and buyers are able to select high quality cars.

    c. The insurance company does not know as much about the health of the insurance buyer as does the buyer. The insurance company *screens* prospective customers with a physical exam to find hidden health problems so its insurance pool is not sicker than average.

3. a. People care about fairness and might be willing to accept nothing so that their adversary gets nothing if they think the split was unfair.

    b. People are inconsistent over time. From 3 months away, saving seems like a good idea but as that date approaches, the desire for immediate gratification takes over.

    c. People give too much weight to a small number of vivid observations. The probability of a plane crash has probably not changed, and yet people are more afraid to fly due to one highly publicized case.

    d. People are reluctant to change their minds. Both Richard and Hazel use the same information to defend their original opinion.

Short-Answer Questions

1. The tendency of a person who is imperfectly monitored to engage in immoral behaviour. Better monitoring, and paying higher wages or delaying some payment to raise the cost of shirking.

2. When unobserved attributes become undesirable from the standpoint of the uninformed party. No. Because you might assume that the sellers know something bad about the house—flooding, poor construction, bad neighbours or schools, and so on. Have the house inspected and check out the neighbourhood and schools.

3. Higher, because buyers of insurance know more about their probability of an accident and those with a high probability of having accidents will need insurance. Insurance companies check a driver's driving history and offer policies that appeal differently to risky and safe drivers, and then they charge higher premiums to risky drivers. They require a deductible to avoid moral hazard.

4. It must be costly, but less costly to the individual with the higher-quality product. Since low-quality firms will not generate repeat purchases from their advertising, it is not cost effective for them to engage in expensive advertising.

5. Adverse selection will be a more common feature of imperfectly competitive markets than perfectly competitive markets because in perfectly competitive markets, firms produce a homogenous product so that advertising by individual firms is impossible. In imperfectly competitive markets firms might advertise their product in a way that signals quality, when, in reality, their product is of inferior quality compared to that of rival producers.

6. $0.3(€10,000) + 0.3(€11,000) + 0.4(€25,000) = €16,300$. Median voter wants to spend €11,000. €11,000 wins. No. Take any pair, find the winner, and then compare it to the remaining choice and €11,000 always wins.

7. The first person would take €99 and give €1 to the other, and the other would accept. The first person usually offers more than €1 and the second person rejects small offers. Firms that are having particularly profitable years might pay above-equilibrium wages to be fair or to avoid retaliation.

8. No. People give too much weight to a small number of vivid observations. In this case, the friend is just one additional observation out of thousands.

9. Unanimity (if A is better than B for everyone, than A must be the voting outcome), transitivity (if A is better than B and B is better than C, than A should be better than C as a result of voting), independence of irrelevant alternatives (the ranking of pairs of alternatives has to be independent of any third alternative available), absence of dictator (there should be no person or a party always getting its way).

True/False Questions

1. T

2. F; the agent performs a task on behalf of the principal.

3. T

4. T

5. F; signals must be costly, yet less costly to the firm with the higher-quality product.

6. F; these preferences exhibit transitivity.

7. F; it shows that the order in which items are voted can determine the outcome, therefore majority-rule voting does not always tell us what society wants.

8. T

9. F; it will produce the outcome preferred by the median voter.

10. T

Multiple-Choice Questions

1.	a	6.	d
2.	d	7.	b
3.	c	8.	c
4.	c	9.	d
5.	d	10.	c

Advanced Critical Thinking

1. Adverse selection. People who are already ill would seek to buy insurance. Their medical bills would be far higher than average, causing premiums to rise. At the artificially high price for insurance, fewer healthy people would buy insurance because the cost would exceed their expected bills. When healthy people drop out of the market, the price rises even further for the remaining participants, further reducing the size of the insurance market.

2. Moral hazard. Without a deductible, people might go to the doctor even if they don't really need medical attention. They also have little incentive to take care of themselves to avoid illness because they bear no cost of the illness. As above, this raises the cost of insurance above the expected bills of healthy people and many will fail to buy insurance.

3. Some people advocate government-provided health insurance where everyone (sick and healthy) would be forced to participate. Majority-rule democratic institutions might not generate the amount of health care that people want. Self-interested politicians might choose to provide an amount of health care that is different than what people actually want.

MEASURING A NATION'S INCOME

CHAPTER OVERVIEW

Context and Purpose

Chapter 23 is the first chapter in the macroeconomic section of the text. It is the first of a two-chapter sequence that introduces you to two vital statistics that economists use to monitor the macroeconomy—GDP and the consumer price index. Chapter 23 develops knowledge of how economists measure production and income in the macroeconomy. Chapter 24 develops knowledge of how economists measure the level of prices in the macroeconomy. Taken together, Chapter 23 concentrates on the *quantity* of output in the macroeconomy while Chapter 24 concentrates on the *price* of output in the macroeconomy.

The purpose of this chapter is to provide you with an understanding of the measurement and use of gross domestic product (GDP). GDP is the single most important measure of the health of the macroeconomy. Indeed, it is the most widely reported statistic in every developed economy.

CHAPTER REVIEW

Introduction

Microeconomics is the study of individual markets and the decision-making of individual firms and households that transact business in those markets. **Macroeconomics** is the study of the economy as a whole. This chapter, and the remainder of this text, deal with macroeconomics.

The Economy's Income and Expenditure

In a nation's macroeconomy, income must equal expenditure. This is true because in every transaction, the income of the seller must be equal to the expenditure of the buyer. GDP is a measure of the total income or total output in the economy. Since income equals expenditure, GDP can be measured by adding up the income earned in the economy (wages, rent, and profit) or the expenditure on goods and services produced in the economy. That is, income equals expenditure equals GDP.

The Measurement of Gross Domestic Product

GDP is defined as the market value of all final goods and services produced within a country in a given period of time.

- 'Market value' means that production is valued at the price paid for the output. Hence, items sold at higher prices are more heavily weighted in GDP.

- 'Of all' means that GDP attempts to measure all production in the economy that is legally sold in markets. For example, GDP excludes the production and sale of illegal drugs and household production such as when home owners clean their own houses. However, in an attempt to be comprehensive, GDP does include the estimated rental value of owner-occupied housing as production of housing services.

- 'Final' means that GDP includes only goods and services that are sold to the end user. Thus, GDP counts the sale of a Ford Focus when it is sold at retail, but it excludes Ford's purchases of intermediate goods such as glass, steel, and tyres used up during the production of the car. *Intermediate goods* are goods that are produced by one firm to be further processed by another firm. Counting only final goods and services avoids double counting intermediate production.

- 'Goods and services' means that while GDP clearly includes tangible manufactured items such as cars and trucks, it also includes intangible items such as lawyers' and doctors' services.

- 'Produced' means that we exclude the sale of used items which were produced (and counted) in a previous period. Again, this avoids double counting.

- 'Within a country' means that GDP measures the value of production within the geographic borders of a country.

- 'In a given period of time' means that we measure GDP per year or per quarter.

GDP data is statistically seasonally adjusted to eliminate the systematic variations in the data which are caused by seasonal events such as Christmas.

Other measures of income besides GDP are listed below, from largest to smallest.

- *Gross National Product (GNP)*: GNP measures the income or production of a nation's permanent residents or 'nationals' (both people and their factories) no matter where they are located.

- *Net National Product (NNP)*: NNP is the total income of a nation's residents (GNP) minus depreciation. Depreciation is the value of the wear and tear on the economy's capital stock.

- *National income*: national income is the total income earned by a nation's residents. It is NNP-less indirect business taxes plus business subsidies.

- *Personal income*: personal income is the income of households and non-corporate businesses. It excludes retained earnings (corporate income not paid out as dividends) but includes interest income households receive from government debt and government transfer payments (social security).

- *Disposable personal income*: this is income of households and non-incorporated businesses after they pay their obligations to the government (primarily income tax).

The Components of GDP

GDP can be measured by adding up the value of the expenditures on final goods and services. Economists divide expenditures into four components: consumption (C), investment (I), government purchases (G), and net exports (NX).

- *Consumption* is spending by households on goods and services, with the exception of new housing.

- *Investment* is spending on capital equipment, additions to stocks, and structures such as new housing. Investment does not include spending on company equity (shares) and bonds.

- *Government purchases* is spending on goods and services by all levels of government (federal, state, and local). Government purchases do not include *transfer payments* such as government payments for social security, welfare, and unemployment benefits because the government does not receive any product or service in return.

- *Net exports* is the value of foreign purchases of UK domestic production (exports) minus UK domestic purchases of foreign production (imports). Imports must be subtracted because consumption, investment, and government purchases include expenditures on all goods, foreign and domestic, and the foreign component must be removed so that only spending on domestic production remains.

Denoting GDP as Y, we can say that $Y = C + I + G + NX$. The variables are defined in such a way that this equation is an identity.

Real Versus Nominal GDP

Nominal GDP is the value of output measured in the prices that existed during the year in which the output was produced (current prices). Real GDP is the volume of output produced in some year. If we observe that nominal GDP has risen from one year to the next, we are unable to determine whether the quantity of goods and services has risen or whether the prices of goods and services have risen. However, if we observe that GDP at constant prices has risen, we are certain that the quantity of goods and services has risen because the output from each year is valued in terms of the same base year prices. Thus, GDP at constant prices is the better measure of production in the economy.

The GDP deflator = (nominal GDP/real GDP) × 100. It is a measure of the level of prices in the current year relative to the level of prices in the base year.

In the UK, real GDP tends to grow at a rate of about two and half per cent per year. Occasional periods of decline in real GDP are known as *recessions*.

GDP and Economic Well-being

GDP at constant prices is a strong indicator of the economic well-being of a society because countries with a large real GDP per person tend to have better educational systems, better health care systems, more literate citizens, better housing, a better diet, a longer life expectancy, and so on. That is, a larger real GDP per person generally indicates a higher level of consumption per person. However, GDP is not a perfect measure of material well-being because it excludes leisure, the quality of the environment, and goods and services produced at home and not sold in markets such as child-rearing, housework, and voluntary work. In addition, GDP says nothing about the *distribution* of income. GDP also fails to capture the underground or shadow economy—the portion of the economy that does not report its economic activity. For example, GDP does not measure illegal drug sales or income that is unreported to avoid taxation.

HELPFUL HINTS

1. GDP measures production. When we set out to measure GDP, we must first remember that we are measuring *production* (and the income earned from

producing it) over a period of time. If we can remember that, we will generally account for unusual types of production correctly. Examples:

- How should we handle the measurement of the production of a cruise ship that takes three years to build and is sold at the end of the third year? Logically, we should count the portion of the ship that was completed during each year and apply it to that year's GDP. In fact, that is what economists do. If we had accounted for the entire ship in the year in which it was sold, we would have overestimated GDP in the third year and underestimated GDP in the previous two years.

- Similarly, if a new house were built during one year but sold for the first time during the next year, we should account for it during the first year because that is when it was produced. That is, the builder 'purchased' the finished home during the first year and added it to his or her stocks of unsold homes.

While in general we only wish to count final goods and services, we do count the production of intermediate goods that were not used during the period, but were added to a firm's stocks. Why? Because this production will not be captured by counting all of the final goods.

2. GDP does not include all expenditures. We have learned that we can measure GDP by adding the expenditures on final goods and services ($Y = C + I + G + NX$). However, once we have learned the expenditure approach, we must not forget the words 'on final goods and services' and mistakenly count all expenditures. When we include expenditures on used items, intermediate goods, stocks and bonds, or government transfer payments, we get a very large euro value, but it has nothing to do with GDP. The euro value of total transactions in the economy is many times that of GDP.

3. Intermediate goods and final goods are distinct. It should be helpful to clarify the distinction between intermediate goods and final goods with an example. Recall:

- Intermediate goods are goods that are produced by one firm to be further processed by another firm.

- Final goods are sold to the end user.

GDP only includes the value of the final goods and services because the value of the intermediate goods used in the production of a final good or service is fully captured in the price of the final good or service. If we include the value of intermediate production in GDP, we would double count the intermediate goods.

If we understand this distinction, can we list the *items* in the economy that are intermediate or final? For example, is a tyre an intermediate good or a final good? The answer is: it depends on who bought it. When General Motors buys a tyre from Goodyear, the tyre is an intermediate good because General Motors will attach it to a car and sell it. When you buy a tyre from your Goodyear dealer, it is a final good and should be counted in GDP. Thus, it is difficult to list items in the economy that are intermediate or final without knowledge of the buyer.

4. Comparisons of GDP across countries and time can be biased. We should be cautious when we compare GDP across nations of different levels of market development and when we compare GDP across long periods of time within a single nation. This is because GDP excludes most non-market activities. Clearly, a greater proportion of the output of lesser-developed nations is likely to be household production such as when someone does their own farming, cleaning, sewing, and maybe even home construction. Since these activities are not captured by a market transaction, they are not recorded in lesser-developed nations or in earlier periods of industrialized nations when market development was less extensive. This results in an even lower estimate of their GDP.

TERMS AND DEFINITIONS

Choose a definition for each key term.

Key terms:

_____ Inflation

_____ Macroeconomics

_____ Microeconomics

_____ Total income

_____ Total expenditure

_____ Gross Domestic Product

_____ Intermediate production

_____ Final production

_____ Gross National Product

_____ Depreciation

_____ Consumption

_____ Investment

_____ Government purchases

_____ Net exports

_____ Transfer payment

_____ Nominal GDP

_____ Base year

_____ GDP deflator

_____ Recession

Definitions:

1. The production of goods and services produced within a particular country and valued at current year prices

2. Spending by households on goods and services, excluding new housing

3. Spending on domestically produced goods by foreigners (exports) minus spending on foreign goods by domestic residents (imports)

4. Period of decline in GDP

5. Market value of all final goods and services produced within a country in a given period of time

6. Wages, rent, and profit

7. The rate at which prices are rising

8. Market value of all final goods and services produced by a nation's residents in a given period of time

9. Spending on capital equipment, inventories, and structures, including household purchases of new housing

10. Spending on goods and services by all levels of government

11. A measure of the price level calculated as the ratio of nominal GDP to real GDP, then multiplied by 100

12. Expenditures by government for which they receive no goods or services

13. The study of how households and firms make decisions and how they interact in markets

14. Goods that are produced by one firm to be further processed by another firm

15. The study of economy-wide phenomena

16. Finished products sold to the end user

17. Consumption, investment, government purchases, and net exports

18. The year from which prices are used to measure real GDP

19. Value of worn out equipment and structures

PROBLEMS AND SHORT-ANSWER QUESTIONS

Practice Problems

1. a. Complete the following table.

	Year 1	Year 2	Year 3
Gross Domestic Product	4,532	4,804	
Consumption		3,320	3,544
Investment	589	629	673
Government Purchases	861		977
Net Exports	−45	−58	−54

b. What is the largest expenditure component of GDP?

c. Does investment include the purchase of company equity and bonds? Why?

d. Do government purchases include government spending on social security? Why?

e. What does it mean to say that net exports are negative?

2. Suppose the base year in the following table is 2003.

Year	Production of X	Price per Unit of X (€)
2003	20 units	5
2004	20 units	10
2005	20 units	20

a. What is nominal GDP for 2003, 2004, and 2005?

b. What is GDP at constant 2003 prices for 2004, and 2005?

3. Suppose the following table records the total output and prices for an entire economy. Further, suppose the base year in the following table is 2004.

Year	Price of Potatoes (€)	Quantity of Potatoes	Price of Jeans (€)	Quantity of Jeans
2004	1.00	200	10.00	50
2005	1.00	220	11.00	50

a. What is the value of nominal GDP in 2004?

b. What is the value of GDP in 2004 at constant 2004 prices?

c. What is the value of nominal GDP in 2005?

d. What is the value of GDP in 2005 at constant 2004 prices?

e. What is the value of the GDP deflator in 2004?

f. What is the value of the GDP deflator in 2005?

g. From 2004 to 2005, prices rose to approximately what percentage?

h. Was the increase in nominal GDP from 2004 to 2005 mostly due to an increase in real output or due to an increase in prices?

4. Complete the following table.

Year	Nominal GDP (€)	Real GDP (€)	GDP deflator
1		100	100
2	120		120
3	150	125	

a. What year is the base year? How can you tell?

b. From year 1 to year 2, did real output rise or did prices rise? Explain?

c. From year 2 to year 3, did real output rise or did prices rise? Explain?

Short-Answer Questions

1. Why does income = expenditure = GDP?

2. Define GDP and explain the important terms in the definition.

3. What are the components of expenditure? Provide an example of each.

4. Provide an example of a transfer payment. Do we include it in GDP? Why?

5. What is the problem of double counting and why is it important?

6. Give some examples on non-market transactions and explain why such transactions are sometimes included and sometimes excluded from the national income accounts.

7. If you buy a €20,000 Toyota that was produced entirely in Japan, does this affect UK GDP? Show how this transaction would affect the appropriate expenditure categories that make up GDP.

8. Explain the difference between GDP and GNP. If the residents of the UK generate as much production in the rest of the world as the rest of the world produces in the UK, what should be true about UK GDP and GNP?

9. Which contributes more when measuring GDP, a new diamond necklace purchased by a wealthy person or a bottle of water purchased by a thirsty person? Why?

10. If your neighbour hires you to mow her lawn instead of doing it herself, what will happen to GDP? Why? Did output change?

SELF-TEST

True/False Questions

_____ 1. For an economy as a whole, income equals expenditure because the income of the seller must be equal to the expenditure of the buyer.

_____ 2. The profits of an insurance company are excluded from GDP statistics.

_____ 3. If a timber yard sells €1,000 of timber to a carpenter and the carpenter uses the timber to build a summer house which he sells for €5,000, the contribution to GDP is €5,000.

_____ 4. The value of output produced abroad is excluded from a country's GDP statistics but is included in its GNP statistics.

_____ 5. Wages are an example of a transfer payment because there is a transfer of payment from the firm to the worker.

_____ 6. In the UK, consumption is the largest component of GDP.

_____ 7. A new car produced in 2002, but first sold in 2003, should be counted in 2003 GDP because that is when it was first sold as a final good.

_____ 8. A recession occurs when real GDP declines.

_____ 9. Depreciation is the value of the wear and tear on the economy's equipment and structures.

_____ 10. Net National Product always exceeds a nation's total income because of depreciation and taxes.

Multiple-Choice Questions

1. Changes in real GDP will differ from changes in nominal GDP because of changes in
   a. prices.
   b. depreciation.
   c. exports and imports.
   d. output.

2. Gross Domestic Product can be measured as the sum of
   a. consumption, investment, government spending and exports.
   b. consumption, government spending, wages, and profits.

c. investment, wages, profits, and rent.

d. the value added at each stage of production.

3. If a cobbler buys leather for €100 and thread for €50 and uses them to produce and sell €500 worth of shoes to consumers, the contribution to GDP is

a. €50.

b. €100.

c. €500.

d. €600.

e. €650.

The following table contains information about an economy that produces only pens and books. The base year is 2003. Use this information for questions 4 through 8.

Year	Price of Pens (€)	Quantity of Pens	Price of Books (€)	Quantity of Books
2003	3	100	10	50
2004	3	120	12	70
2005	4	120	14	70

4. What is the value of nominal GDP for 2004?

a. €800.

b. €1,060.

c. €1,200.

d. €1,460.

e. none of the above.

5. What is the value of GDP for 2004 at constant 2003 prices?

a. €800.

b. €1,060.

c. €1,200.

d. €1,460.

e. none of the above.

6. What is the value of the GDP deflator in 2004?

a. 100.

b. 113.

c. 116.

d. 119.

e. 138.

7. What is the approximate percentage increase in prices from 2004 to 2005?

a. 0 per cent.

b. 13 per cent.

c. 16 per cent.

d. 22 per cent.

e. 38 per cent.

8. What is the percentage increase in real GDP from 2004 to 2005?

a. 0 per cent.

b. 7 per cent.

c. 22 per cent.

d. 27 per cent.

e. 32 per cent.

9. If UK GDP exceeds UK GNP, then

a. foreigners are producing more in the UK than UK citizens are producing in foreign countries.

b. UK citizens are producing more in foreign countries than foreigners are producing in the UK.

c. real GDP exceeds nominal GDP.

d. real GNP exceeds nominal GNP.

e. intermediate production exceeds final production.

10. How is your purchase of a €40,000 BMW automobile that was produced entirely in Germany recorded in the UK GDP accounts?

a. Investment increases by €40,000 and net exports increases by €40,000.

b. Consumption increases by €40,000 and net exports decreases by €40,000.

c. Net exports decreases by €40,000.

d. Net exports increases by €40,000.

e. There is no impact because this transaction does not involve domestic production.

Advanced Critical Thinking

You are watching a news report with your father. The news anchor points out that Nigeria generated a GDP per capita of only $1,000 per year. Since your father knows that UK GDP per capita is approximately $29,600 in 2004, he suggests that we are materially twenty nine and a half times better off in the UK than in Nigeria.

1. Is your father's statement accurate?

2. What general category of production is not captured by GDP in both the UK and Nigeria?

3. Provide some examples of this type of activity.

4. Why would the exclusion of this type of production affect the measurement of Nigerian output more than UK output?

5. Does this mean that residents of Nigeria are actually as well off materially as residents in the UK?

SOLUTIONS

Terms and Definitions

_1_	Nominal GDP	_8_	Gross National Product	_15_	Macroeconomics
_2_	Consumption	_9_	Investment	_16_	Final production
_3_	Net exports	_10_	Government purchases	_17_	Total expenditure
_4_	Recession	_11_	GDP Deflator	_18_	Base year
_5_	Gross Domestic Product	_12_	Transfer payment	_19_	Depreciation
_6_	Total income	_13_	Microeconomics		
_7_	Inflation	_14_	Intermediate production		

Practice Problems

1. a.

	Year 1	Year 2	Year 3
Gross Domestic Product	4,532	4,804	5,140
Consumption	3,127	3,320	3,544
Investment	589	629	673
Government Purchases	861	913	977
Net Exports	−45	−58	−54

b. consumption

c. No, because that transaction is a purchase of a financial asset, not a purchase of currently produced capital goods.

d. No, because unemployment benefits are expenditures for which the government receives no production in return.

e. It means that imports exceed exports.

2. a. €100, €200, €400.

   b. €100, €100.

3. a. €700.

   b. €700.

   c. €770.

   d. €720.

   e. 100.

   f. 107.

   g. $(107 - 100)/100 = 0.07 = 7\%$.

   h. Per cent increase in nominal = $(€770 - €700)/700 = 0.10 = 10\%$. Per cent increase in prices = 7%, therefore most of the increase was due to prices.

4. a. Year 1, because the deflator = 100.

   b. Prices rose 20 per cent and real output stayed the same.

   c. Prices stayed the same and real output rose 25 per cent.

Year	Nominal GDP (€)	Real GDP (€)	GDP deflator
1	100	100	100
2	120	100	120
3	150	125	120

Short-Answer Questions

1. Because the income of the seller equals the expenditure of the buyer and GDP can be measured with either one.

2. Market value of all final goods and services produced within a country in a given period of time. 'Market value' = price paid, 'of all' = all legal production, 'final' = to end users, 'goods and services' = includes services, 'produced' = no used items, 'within a country' = inside the country's borders, 'in a given period' = per quarter or year.

3. Consumption (food), investment (factory), government purchases (military equipment), net exports (sale of a Ford to France minus purchase of a Toyota from Japan).

4. Social Security payments. No, because the government received no good or service in return.

5. Double counting literally involves counting the value of some transactions twice. For example, electricity is used to produce goods and services, but if we count the output of the electricity industry and the final value of output produced by other industries who use electricity as an input, we would double count the value of electricity used in the production of other goods and services. This consequence would be that measured GDP statistics would overstate the actual value of GDP. The data would consequently be less useful.

6. Non-market transactions include public goods (street lighting, national defence, etc.) and merit goods (education, health care etc.) where they are provided through the state. However, non-market transactions also include self-provided commodities such as DIY activities, gardening, house work, and so on. Public goods and merit goods are included in GDP and are valued at resource cost (the cost of resources used to provide the activity) whereas self-provided commodities are excluded because it is impossible to estimate their aggregate value.

7. No. Consumption would increase by €20,000 and net exports would decrease by €20,000. As a result, UK GDP is unaffected.

8. GDP is the production within the borders of the UK GNP is the creation of UK incomes no matter where the production takes place. They should be equal.

9. A diamond necklace because GDP measures market value.

10. GDP will rise because the mowing of the lawn was a market transaction. However, output didn't really rise.

True/False Questions

1. T

2. F; profits are the return for risk taking and they are always included in GDP data.

3. T; the summer house is the final good, valued at €5,000.

4. F; only that part of output produced abroad using domestically owned assets is included in a nation's estimates of its GNP statistics.

5. F; transfer payments are expenditures for which no good or service is received in return.

6. T

7. F; goods are counted in the year they are produced.

8. T

9. T

10. F; total income—depreciation = NNP.

Multiple-Choice Questions

1. a	3. c	5. b	7. d	9. a
2. d	4. c	6. b	8. a	10. b

Advanced Critical Thinking

1. No.

2. Non-market activities such as household production.

3. Household production done by an individual without pay such as gardening, cleaning, sewing, home improvement or construction, child supervision, and so on.

4. A greater proportion of the output produced by less-developed nations is non-market output. That is, it is not sold and recorded as a market transaction.

5. No. It just means that quantitative comparisons between nations of greatly different levels of development are very difficult to do and are often inaccurate.

⌈**In this chapter you will**

Learn how the consumer price index (CPI) is constructed

Consider why the CPI is an imperfect measure of the cost of living

Compare the CPI, RPI and the GDP deflator as techniques for measuring changes in the overall price level

See how to use a price index to compare euro amounts from different times

Learn the distinction between real and nominal interest rates

⌈**You should be able to**

List the five steps necessary to calculate the inflation rate

Discuss three reasons why the CPI may be biased

Describe two differences between the CPI and GDP deflator

Convert a value measured in 1965 sterling to its value measured in 1990 sterling

Explain the relationship between the real interest rate, the nominal interest rate, and the inflation rate

MEASURING THE COST OF LIVING

CHAPTER OVERVIEW

Context and Purpose

Chapter 24 is the second chapter of a two-chapter sequence that deals with how economists measure output and prices in the macroeconomy. Chapter 23 addressed how economists measure output. Chapter 24 develops ideas about how economists measure changes in the overall price level in the macroeconomy.

The purpose of Chapter 24 is twofold: first, to show you how to generate a price index and, second, to teach you how to employ a price index to compare euro figures from different points in time and to adjust interest rates for inflation. In addition, you will learn some of the shortcomings of using the Retail Price Index as a measure of the cost of living and why the main measure of inflation in the UK is now the Consumer Price Index. (You will also learn the limitations of the CPI.)

CHAPTER REVIEW

Introduction

To compare the income of a worker in, say, 1930, to the income of a worker today, we must first convert the sterling amount of each of their incomes into a comparable measure of purchasing power because there has been inflation over this time period. This chapter explains how economists correct economic variables for the effects of inflation. Inflation is generally measured by the Consumer Price Index (CPI).

The Consumer Price Index

The **Consumer Price Index** is a measure of the overall cost of the goods and services bought by a typical consumer. It is calculated in the UK by the Office for National Statistics.

There are five steps to calculating a CPI:

- *Fix the basket*. Estimate the *quantities* of the products purchased by the typical consumer (i.e. the basket of goods and services).

- *Find the prices.* Locate the prices of each item in the basket for each point in time (each year for an annual CPI).

- *Compute the basket's cost.* Use the prices and quantities to calculate the cost of the basket for each year.

- *Choose a base year and compute the index.* Choose a year as the benchmark against which the other years can be compared (i.e. the base year). (This must be the same year you surveyed consumers and fixed the quantities in the consumption basket.) Make a ratio of the cost of the basket for each year to the cost in the base year. Multiply each ratio by 100. Each resulting number is the value of the index for that year.

- *Compute the rate of inflation.* Inflation is the percentage change in the price index from the preceding year. For example:

$$\text{Inflation rate in 2005} = \frac{(\text{CPI in year 2005} - \text{CPI in year 2004})}{\text{CPI in year 2004}} \times 100$$

The actual CPI is calculated both monthly and annually. In addition, in the UK the Office for National Statistics calculates a **producer price index** (PPI), which measures the cost of a basket of goods and services purchased by firms. Changes in the PPI usually precede changes in the CPI because firms often pass on higher costs in the form of higher consumer prices.

The major categories in the CPI basket in the UK are transport (about 15 per cent), recreation and culture (about 15 per cent), restaurants and hotels (about 14 per cent), food and non-alcoholic beverages (10 per cent), housing and fuels (10 per cent), furniture, household equipment, and maintenance (7.5 per cent), and clothing and footwear (6 per cent).

The *cost of living* is the amount by which incomes must rise in order to maintain a constant standard of living in conditions of inflation. There are three problems with using the CPI to measure changes in the cost of living:

- *Substitution bias:* Over time, some prices rise more than others. Consumers will substitute towards goods that have become relatively less expensive. However, the CPI is based on a fixed basket of purchases. Because the CPI fails to acknowledge the consumer's substitution of less expensive products for more expensive products, the CPI overstates the increase in the cost of living.

- *Introduction of new goods:* When new goods are introduced, a euro has increased in value because it can buy a greater variety of products. Because the CPI is based on a fixed consumer basket, it does not reflect this increase in the purchasing power of the euro (equivalent to a reduction in prices). Thus, again, the CPI overstates the increase in the cost of living.

- *Unmeasured quality change:* If the quality of a good rises from year to year, as with tyres and computers, then the value of a euro is rising even if actual prices are constant. This is equivalent to a reduction in prices. To the degree that an increase in quality is not accounted for by the Office for National Statistics, the CPI overstates the increase in the cost of living. The opposite is true for a deterioration of quality.

Research at the Bank of England estimates that these three factors have caused the CPI to overestimate inflation by about 0.6 of 1 per cent each year. This small overestimation of inflation might cause overpayment of Social Security benefits because Social Security benefits are tied to the CPI.

Until 2004, the main measure of inflation in the UK was the Retail Price Index (RPI) which is a broadly based measure of changes in prices paid by consumers. However, the CPI is considered a superior measure because it ignores many items especially related to housing which have no relevance to the underlying rate of inflation. For example, when interest rates change, this changes mortgage repayments which triggers a change in the RPI even though the underlying rate of inflation has not changed. It also has greater coverage. For example the RPI ignores pensioners who derive more than three-quarters of their income from state benefits, foreign visitors to the UK, and certain items such as university tuition fees.

Different countries sometimes measure inflation in slightly different ways. The basic technique (index numbers) is always the same, but they sometimes construct their price index differently in the same way that in the UK there are differences between the CPI and the RPI. To facilitate comparison of relative inflation rates across EU Members, a Harmonized Index of Consumer Prices (HICP) has been developed. While Member States might use a different index as their primary measure of inflation, they all compute a price index according to the principles underlying the HICP to facilitate cross-country comparisons of inflation within the EU.

Recall that the GDP deflator is the ratio of nominal GDP (current output valued at current prices) to real GDP (current output valued at base year prices). Thus, the GDP deflator is a price index, too. It differs from the CPI in two ways:

- First, the basket of goods is different. The GDP deflator utilizes the prices of all goods and services produced domestically. The CPI utilizes the prices of goods and services *bought by consumers* only, regardless of where the goods were produced. Therefore, a change in the price of foreign oil which raises the price of petrol is captured by the CPI but not by the GDP deflator, while a change in the price of a domestically produced missile is captured by the GDP deflator but not by the CPI.

- Second, the GDP deflator utilizes the quantities of goods and services in *current* output, so the 'basket' changes each year. The CPI utilizes the quantities in a *fixed* basket, so the basket changes only when the Office for National Statistics chooses. Although the CPI and GDP deflator should track each other very closely, the CPI might tend to rise slightly faster due to its inherent substitution bias and the bias associated with the introduction of new goods.

Correcting Economic Variables for the Effects of Inflation

Economists use the CPI to correct *income* and *interest rates* for the effects of inflation.

We correct income for inflation so that we can compare income from different years. The general formula for comparing euro values from different years is:

Value in year X euros = Value in year Y euros × (CPI in year X/CPI in year Y)

In words, to make the above conversion, multiply the sterling (or euro) value you wish to adjust by the ratio of the ending price level to the starting price level. Your value will now be measured in euros consistent with the ending price level.

For example, suppose your aunt earned €20,000 in 1999 and earned €20,500 in 2004. Over those 5 years, has her standard of living increased?

CPI in 1999 = 104.8

CPI in 2004 = 111.2

€20,000 × (111.2/104.8) = €21,221 > €20,500

A €20,000 salary in 1999 would buy as much as a €21,221 salary in 2004. Since your aunt only earned €20,500 in 2004, her real income fell and her standard of living actually decreased.

When a euro amount, for example a Social Security payment, is automatically adjusted for inflation, we say that it has been **indexed** for inflation. A contract with this provision is said to contain a *COLA* or cost-of-living-allowance.

We also correct interest rates for inflation. A correction is necessary because, if prices have risen during the term of a loan, the euros used for repayment will not buy as much as the euros originally borrowed.

The **nominal interest rate** is the interest rate uncorrected for the effects of inflation. The **real interest rate** is the interest rate corrected for the effects of inflation. The formula for correcting the nominal interest rate for inflation is:

$$\text{real interest rate} = \text{nominal interest rate} - \text{inflation rate}$$

For example, if the bank paid you a nominal interest rate of 4 per cent on your account, and the inflation rate were 3 per cent, the real interest rate on your account would be only 1 per cent: $4\% - 3\% = 1\%$.

HELPFUL HINTS

1. The year we choose to determine the typical consumption basket must also be chosen as the base year. When we construct the CPI, we choose a year to survey consumers and *fix the basket*. The year we choose to fix the basket must also be chosen as the base year. That is, we also use that year as the benchmark year against which other years are to be compared.

2. Your particular consumption basket may not be typical. Since the GDP deflator and the CPI are based on different baskets of goods and services, each will provide a slightly different measurement of the cost of living. Continuing in this same line of thinking, your particular consumption basket may differ from the typical consumption basket used by the Office for National Statistics when they calculate the CPI. For example, when you are a young adult, your basket may be more heavily weighted towards electronics and clothing. If clothing prices are rising faster than average, young people may have a greater increase in the cost of living than is suggested by the CPI. In like manner, when you become older, your consumption basket may be more heavily weighted towards medicine and travel. Exceptional increases in these prices may cause the cost of living for the elderly to rise more quickly than suggested by the CPI.

3. Sterling (or euro) values can be adjusted backwards in time as well as forwards. In the earlier section, there is a numerical example that converts €20,000 of income in 1999 into the amount of income that would be necessary in 2004 to generate the same purchasing power. We discovered that it would take €21,221 for your aunt to have the same standard of living in 2004 as she had in 1999. Because she only made €20,500 in 2004, we argued that her standard of living actually fell over the five-year period.

    Alternatively, we can convert her 2004 salary of €20,500 into its equivalent purchasing power measured in 1999 sterling and compare the resulting figure with her €20,000 income in 1999. We arrive at the same conclusion—she was better off in 1999.

    $$€20,500 \times (104.8/111.2) = €19.320 < €20,000$$

    Her €20,500 income in 2004 is equivalent to (or generates the same standard of living as) a €19,320 income in 1999. Since she actually made €20,000 in 1999, she had a higher standard of living in 1999.

4. When correcting interest rates for inflation, think like a lender. If you loan someone €100 for one year, and you charge them 7 per cent interest, you will receive €107 at the end of the year. Did you receive 7 additional euros of purchasing power? Suppose inflation was 4 per cent. You would need to receive €104 at the end of the year just to break even. That is, you would need €104 just to be able to buy the same set of goods and services that you could have

purchased for €100 at the time you granted the loan. In this sense, you received only 3 additional euros of purchasing power for having made the €100 loan, or a 3 per cent real return. Thus, the *real interest rate* on the loan is 3 per cent. Using your formula:

$$7\% - 4\% = 3\%$$

Although not explicitly stated, the interest rate example in your text is also approached from the lender's perspective. That is, when you deposit money in a bank and receive interest, the deposit is actually a loan from you to the bank.

TERMS AND DEFINITIONS

Choose a definition for each key term.

Key terms:

_____ Consumer price index

_____ Inflation rate

_____ GDP deflator

_____ Basket (of goods and services)

_____ Base year

_____ Office for National Statistics

_____ Producer price index

_____ Cost of living

_____ Standard of living

_____ Substitution bias

_____ Nominal GDP

_____ At constant prices GDP

_____ Indexed contract

_____ (COLA) cost of living allowance

_____ Nominal interest rate

_____ Real interest rate

Definitions:

1. The income necessary to maintain a constant standard of living

2. A contract that requires that a euro amount be automatically corrected for inflation

3. The ratio of the value of the fixed basket purchased by the typical consumer to the basket's value in the base year, multiplied by 100

4. The quantities of each item purchased by the typical consumer

5. The ratio of the value of a fixed basket of goods and services purchased by firms to the basket's value in the base year, multiplied by 100

6. The percentage change in a price index

7. The interest rate corrected for the effects of inflation

8. An automatic increase in income in order to maintain a constant standard of living

9. The inability of the CPI to account for consumers' substitution towards relatively cheaper goods and services

10. Material well-being

11. Output valued at base year prices

12. Output valued at current prices

13. The ratio of nominal GDP to GDP at constant prices, multiplied by 100

14. The interest rate uncorrected for the effects of inflation

15. The benchmark year against which other years are compared

16. The government agency responsible for tracking prices in the UK

PROBLEMS AND SHORT-ANSWER QUESTIONS

Practice Problems

1. The following table shows the prices and the quantities consumed in a particular country. Suppose the base year is 2003. *This is the year the typical consumption basket was determined so the quantities consumed during 2003 are the only quantities needed to calculate the CPI in every year.*

Year	Price of Books (€)	Quantity of Books	Price of Pencils (€)	Quantity of Pencils	Quantity of Pens (€)	Price of Pens (€)
2003	50	10	1	100	5	100
2004	50	12	1	200	10	50
2005	60	12	1.50	250	20	20

   a. What is the value of the CPI in 2003?
   b. What is the value of the CPI in 2004?
   c. What is the value of the CPI in 2005?
   d. What is the inflation rate in 2004?
   e. What is the inflation rate in 2005?
   f. What type of bias do you observe in the CPI and corresponding inflation rates you generated above? Explain.
   g. If you had a COLA clause in your wage contract based on the CPI calculated above, would your standard of living likely increase, decrease, or stay the same over the years 2003–2005? Why?
   h. Again, suppose you had a COLA clause in your wage contract based on the CPI calculated above. If you personally only consume pens (no paper or pencils), would your standard of living likely increase, decrease, or stay the same over the years 2003–2005? Why?

2. The following table contains the CPI and the average household gross disposable income for the UK for the period 1988 through 2004.

Year	CPI	Average household gross disposable income
1988	72.1	5,130
1989	75.8	5,686
1990	81.1	6,309
1991	87.2	6,917
1992	90.9	7,438
1993	93.2	7,893
1994	95.1	8,155
1995	97.6	8,602
1996	100.0	9,088
1997	101.8	9,625
1998	103.4	9,939
1999	104.8	10,390
2000	105.6	10,972
2001	106.9	11,643
2002	108.3	11,971
2003	109.8	12,500
2004	111.2	12,897

   a. Inflate the 1988 level of average household disposable income to its equivalent value measured in 2000 prices.
   b. What happened to the standard of living of the average household over this 12-year period?

    c. Deflate the 2000 level of household disposable income to its equivalent value measured in 1988 prices.

    d. Do these two methods give you consistent results with regard to the standard of living of average household over time?

3. Suppose that you lend your roommate €100 for one year at 6 per cent nominal interest.

    a. How many euros of interest will your roommate pay you at the end of the year?

    b. Suppose at the time you both agreed to the terms of the loan, you both expected the inflation rate to be 2.5 per cent during the year of the loan. What do you both expect the real interest rate to be on the loan?

    c. Suppose at the end of the year, you are surprised to discover that the actual inflation rate over the year was 1 per cent. What was the actual real interest rate generated by this loan?

    d. In the case described above, actual inflation turned out to be lower than expected. Which of the two of you had the unexpected gain or loss? Your roommate (the borrower), or you (the lender)? Why?

    e. What would the real interest rate on the loan have been if the actual inflation rate had turned out to be 7 per cent?

    f. Explain what it means to have a negative real interest rate.

Short-Answer Questions

1. What does the Consumer Price Index attempt to measure?

2. What are the steps that one must go through in order to construct a consumer price index?

3. Which would have a greater impact on the CPI: a 20 per cent increase in the price of Rolex watches or a 20 per cent increase in the price of food? Why?

4. Suppose there is an increase in the price of imported BMW cars (which are produced in Germany). Would this have a larger impact on the CPI or the GDP deflator? Why?

5. If the Office for National Statistics failed to recognize the increase in memory, power, and speed of newer model computers, in which direction would the CPI be biased? What do we call this type of bias?

6. Why does it matter that the CPI has an upward bias?

7. Why are items weighted in the CPI and what determines their weight?

8. Why is inflation in different EU Member States measured by a Harmonized Index of Consumer Prices?

9. What does the real interest rate measure?

10. If workers and firms negotiate a wage increase based on their expectation of inflation, who gains or loses (the workers or the firms) if actual inflation turns out to be higher than expected? Why?

SELF-TEST

True/False Questions

_____ 1. The CPI measures changes in the price level in an economy.

_____ 2. Because an increase in petrol prices causes consumers to ride their bikes more and drive their cars less, the CPI tends to overestimate the cost of living.

_____ 3.   An increase in the price of diamonds will have a greater impact on the CPI than an equal percentage increase in the price of food because diamonds are so much more expensive.

_____ 4.   The 'base year' in a price index is the benchmark year against which other years are compared.

_____ 5.   The CPI, RPI, and HICP use slightly different techniques to measure changes in the rate of inflation.

_____ 6.   The producer price index (PPI) is constructed to measure the change in price of total production.

_____ 7.   If the Office for National Statistics fails to recognize that recently produced cars can be driven for many more miles than older models, then the CPI tends to overestimate the cost of living.

_____ 8.   It is possible for real interest rates to be negative.

_____ 9.   If lenders demand a real rate of return of 4 per cent and they expect inflation to be 5 per cent, then they should charge 9 per cent interest when they extend loans.

_____10.   If borrowers and lenders agree on a nominal interest rate and inflation turns out to be greater than they had anticipated, lenders will gain at the expense of borrowers.

Multiple-Choice Questions

1.   The CPI of the UK will be most influenced by a 10 per cent increase in the price of which of the following consumption categories?
     a. housing and fuels.
     b. recreation and culture.
     c. clothing and footwear.
     d. food and non-alcoholic beverages.

2.   In 1990, the CPI was 81.1. In 2004, it was 111.2. What was the average rate of inflation over this period?
     a. 2.15 per cent.
     b. 2.65 per cent.
     c. 2.71 per cent.
     d. 3.71 per cent.

3.   Which of the following would likely cause the CPI in the UK to rise more than the GDP deflator?
     a. an increase in the price of Ford cars.
     b. an increase in the price of John Deere tractors.
     c. an increase in the price of tanks purchased by the military.
     d. an increase in the price of domestically produced fighter planes sold exclusively to Israel.
     e. an increase in the price of Hondas produced in Japan and sold in the US.

4.   The basket on which the CPI is based is composed of
     a. goods most frequently purchased by consumers.
     b. total purchases in the economy.
     c. the weighted average of purchases made by consumers.
     d. products purchased by the typical consumer.

Use the following table for questions 5 through 10. The table shows the prices and the quantities consumed in Carnivore Country. The base year is 2000.

This means that 2000 is the year the typical consumption basket was determined so the quantities consumed in 2000 are the only quantities needed to calculate the CPI in each year.

Year	Price of Beef (€)	Quantity of Beef	Price of Pork (€)	Quantity of Pork
2000	2.00	100	1.00	100
2001	2.50	90	0.90	120
2002	2.75	105	1.00	130

5. What is the value of the basket in the base year?
   a. €300.
   b. €333.
   c. €418.75.
   d. €459.25.

6. What are the values of the CPI in 2000, 2001, and 2002, respectively?
   a. 100, 111, 139.6.
   b. 100, 109.2, 116.
   c. 100, 113.3, 125.
   d. 83.5, 94.2, 100.

7. What is the inflation rate for 2001?
   a. 0 per cent.
   b. 9.2 per cent.
   c. 11 per cent.
   d. 13.3 per cent.

8. What is the inflation rate for 2002?
   a. 0 per cent.
   b. 10.3 per cent.
   c. 11 per cent.
   d. 13.3 per cent.

9. The table shows that the 2001 inflation rate is biased upwards because of
   a. bias due to the introduction of new goods.
   b. bias due to unmeasured quality change.
   c. substitution bias.
   d. base year bias.

10. Suppose the base year is changed in the table from 2000 to 2002 (now use the 2002 consumption basket). What is the new value of the CPI in 2001?
    a. 90.6.
    b. 100.0.
    c. 114.7.
    d. 134.3.

ADVANCED CRITICAL THINKING

Your grandfather quit smoking cigarettes in 1995. When you ask him why he quit, you get a surprising answer. Instead of reciting the health benefits of quitting smoking, he says, 'I quit because it was just getting too expensive. I started smoking in 1965 and cigarettes were only 45 cents a pack. The last pack I bought was €2.00 and I just couldn't justify spending more than four times as much on cigarettes as I used to.'

1. Assume that in 1965 the CPI was 31.5 and that in 1995 its value was 152.4. While it is commendable that your grandfather quit smoking, what is wrong with his explanation?

2. What is the equivalent cost of a 1965 pack of cigarettes measured in 1995 prices?

3. What is the equivalent cost of a 1995 pack of cigarettes measured in 1965 prices?

4. Do both methods give you the same result?

5. The preceding example demonstrates what economists refer to as 'money illusion'. Why do you think economists might choose the phrase 'money illusion' to describe this behaviour?

SOLUTIONS

Terms and Definitions

_1_	Cost of living	_9_	Substitution bias
_2_	Indexed contract	_10_	Standard of living
_3_	Consumer price index	_11_	GDP at constant prices
_4_	Basket (of goods and services)	_12_	Nominal GDP
_5_	Producer price index	_13_	GDP deflator
_6_	Inflation rate	_14_	Nominal interest rate
_7_	Real interest rate	_15_	Base year
_8_	Cost of living allowance (COLA)	_16_	Office for National Statistics

Practice Problems

1. a. (€1,100/€1,100) × 100 = 100.
    b. (€1,600/€1,100) × 100 = 145.5.
    c. (€2,750/€1,100) × 100 = 250.
    d. [(145.5 − 100)/100] × 100 = 45.5 per cent.
    e. [(250 − 145.5)/145.5] × 100 = 71.8 per cent.
    f. Substitution bias, because as the price of pens increased, the quantity consumed declined significantly.
    g. Increase, because this CPI overstates the increase in the cost of living.
    h. Decrease, because the price of pens has increased a greater percentage than the CPI.

2. a. €5,130 × (105.6/72.1) = €7,514.
    b. It went up because €10,972 > €7,514.
    c. €10,972 × (72.1/105.6) = €7,491.
    d. Yes, because €7,491 > €5,130. The higher real disposable income in 2000 implies that, on average, households were better off in 2000.

3. a. €100(1.06) − €100 = €6.
    b. 6 per cent − 2.5 per cent = 3.5 per cent.
    c. 6 per cent − 1 per cent = 5 per cent.
    d. Your roommate (the borrower) lost; you gain because the borrower repaid the loan with an amount of euros that gave greater purchasing power than the amount of euros borrowed.
    e. 6% − 7% = −1%
    f. Because of inflation, the interest payment is not large enough to allow the lender to break even (maintain constant purchasing power compared to the day the loan was made).

Short-Answer Questions

1. The rate of inflation or the fall in the value of money over some period of time. This is done by measuring the change in the amount of money required to purchase a given basket of goods.

2. Fix the basket, find the prices, compute the basket's cost, choose a base year and compute the index.

3. Food, because there is greater expenditure on food in the typical consumption basket.

4. The CPI, because BMWs are in the typical consumption basket, but BMWs are not included in UK GDP.

5. Upwards, unmeasured quality change.

6. The upwards bias in the CPI is important because some transfer incomes such as social security payments and certain pensions are linked to it. It is also a major statistic on which wage negotiations are based.

7. With a fixed basket of goods, price changes might exaggerate the importance of the resulting change in the cost of living. This problem is minimised by weighting each good in the basket according to its importance in the typical household budget. So, for example, if all other things are equal, a good that is bought more frequently will have a higher weight in the CPI than a good that is bought infrequently.

8. A Harmonized Index of Consumer Prices measures inflation in different EU Member States and potential EU entrants using the same procedures. This facilitates cross country comparisons of inflation among EU Members. Since relative rates of inflation are an important measure of EU convergence, it is important that relative rates of inflation are measured consistently.

9. The interest rate adjusted for the effects of inflation.

10. Firms gain, workers lose, because wages didn't rise as much as the cost of living.

True/False Questions

1. F; the CPI measures changes in the average price of the goods included in the basket of goods used to construct the CPI.

2. T; the CPI tends to overstate the cost of living because people substitute towards cheaper goods.

3. F; prices in the CPI are weighted according to how much of each good consumers buy and food is a larger portion of the consumption basket.

4. T

5. F; they are all based on the same fundamental techniques.

6. F; the PPI measures changes in the price of raw materials.

7. T

8. T; if inflation exceeds the nominal interest rate, the real interest rate is negative.

9. T

10. F; borrowers will gain at the expense of lenders.

Multiple-Choice Questions

1. b	5. a	9. c
2. a	6. c	10. a
3. e	7. d	
4. d	8. b	

Advanced Critical Thinking

1. He is only looking at the cost of cigarettes uncorrected for inflation. It is likely that the real cost has not risen as much as first appears or maybe even gone down.

2. €0.45 × (152.4/31.5) = €2.18 > €2.00.

3. €2.00 × (31.5/152.4) = €0.41 < €0.45.

4. Yes, each method suggests that, after correcting for inflation, cigarettes were actually more expensive in 1965.

5. When people base decisions on values uncorrected for inflation, there may be an illusion that the cost of living has risen.

GOALS

⌐In this chapter you will
See how much economic growth differs around the world

Consider why productivity is the key determinant of a country's standard of living

Analyse the factors that determine a country's productivity

Examine how a country's policies influence its productivity growth

OUTCOMES

⌐You should be able to
List the countries with the highest GDP per person and the countries whose GDP per person is growing the fastest

Explain why production limits consumption in the long run

List and explain the factors of production

Explain seven areas of policy action that might influence a country's productivity and growth

PRODUCTION AND GROWTH

CHAPTER OVERVIEW

Context and Purpose

Chapter 25 is the first chapter in a four-chapter sequence on the production of output in the long run. Chapter 25 addresses the determinants of the level and growth rate of output. We find that capital and labour are among the primary determinants of output. In Chapter 26, we see how saving and investment in capital goods affect the production of output, and in Chapter 27, we learn about some of the tools people and firms use when choosing capital projects in which to invest. In Chapter 28, we address the market for labour.

The purpose of Chapter 25 is to examine the long-run determinants of both the level and the growth rate of real GDP per person. Along the way, we will discover the factors that determine the productivity of workers and examine what governments might do to improve the productivity of their citizens.

CHAPTER REVIEW

Introduction

There is great variation in the standard of living across countries at any point in time and within a country across time—for example, between the UK and India today, and between the UK of today and the UK of 100 years ago. Growth rates also vary from country to country with East Asia growing relatively quickly and Africa growing relatively slowly. This chapter examines the long-run determinants of both the *level* and the *growth rate* of real GDP per person.

Economic Growth around the World

There is great variation across countries in both the *level* of real GDP per person and the *growth rate* of real GDP per person.

- At present, the *level* of real GDP per person in the UK is about 9 times that of India and 6 times that of China.

- However, since the *growth rate* of real GDP per person also varies across countries, the ranking of countries by real GDP per person changes over time. For example, over the past 100 years, the ranking of Japan and Brazil has risen relative to others because they have had an above average growth rate while the ranking of the UK has fallen due to its below average growth rate.

Due to economic growth, the average European today enjoys conveniences, such as television, air conditioning, cars, telephones, and medicines, that the richest European didn't have 150 years ago. Since our measures of inflation and output fail to fully capture the introduction of new goods, we overestimate inflation and underestimate economic growth.

Productivity: Its Role and Determinants

A country's standard of living depends directly on the productivity of its citizens because an economy's income is equal to an economy's output. **Productivity** refers to the quantity of goods and services that a worker can produce per hour. The productivity of a worker is determined by the available physical capital, human capital, natural resources, and technological knowledge. These inputs or *factors of production* are explained below:

- **Physical capital** (or just capital): the stock of equipment and structures that are used to produce goods and services. Note that these tools and machines are themselves the output from prior human production.

- **Human capital:** the knowledge and skills that workers acquire through education, training, and experience. Note that human capital, like physical capital, is a human-made or produced factor of production.

- **Natural resources:** inputs provided by nature's bounty, such as land, rivers, and mineral deposits. Natural resources come in two forms: renewable and non-renewable.

- **Technological knowledge:** understanding about the best ways to produce goods and services. Examples of advances in technology are the discovery and application of herbicides and pesticides in agriculture and of the assembly line in manufacturing.

Technological knowledge differs from human capital in that technological knowledge is society's understanding of the best production methods, while human capital is the amount of understanding of these methods that has been transmitted to the labour force.

A *production function* establishes the relationship between the quantity of inputs used in production and the quantity of output from production. If a production function has *constant returns to scale*, then doubling all of the inputs doubles output.

In summary, output per worker depends on physical capital per worker, human capital per worker, natural resources per worker, and the state of technology.

The only factor of production that is not a produced factor is natural resources. Since there is a fixed supply of non-renewable natural resources, many people have argued that there is a limit to how much the world's economies can grow. However, so far technological advances have found ways around these limits. Evidence of stable or falling prices of natural resources in the long run suggests that we are continuing to succeed at stretching our limited resources.

Economic Growth and Public Policy

Physical capital, human capital, natural resources, and technological knowledge determine productivity. Productivity determines living standards. If a government wishes to raise the productivity and standard of living of its citizens, it should pursue policies that:

- *encourage saving and investment.* If society consumes less and saves more, it has more resources available to invest in the production of capital. Additional capital increases productivity and living standards. This additional growth has an opportunity cost—society must give up current consumption in order to attain more growth. Investment in capital may be subject to **diminishing returns:** As the stock of capital rises, the extra output produced by an additional unit of capital declines. Thus, an additional increment of capital in a poor country increases growth more than the same increment in an already rich country. This is known as the **catch-up-effect** because it is easier for a relatively poor country to grow quickly. However, because of diminishing returns to capital, higher saving and investment in a poor country will lead to higher growth only for a period of time, with growth slowing down again as the economy accumulates a higher level of capital stock.

- *encourage investment from abroad*, by removing restrictions on the ownership of domestic capital and by providing a stable political environment. In addition to using domestic saving to invest in capital, countries can attract investment by foreigners. There are two categories of foreign investment. *Foreign direct investment* is capital investment that is owned and operated by a foreign entity. *Foreign portfolio investment* is capital investment that is financed with foreign money, but operated by domestic residents. Investment from abroad increases a country's GDP more than its GNP because the investing country earns the profits from the investment. The World Bank and the International Monetary Fund help channel foreign investment towards poor countries.

- *encourage education.* Education is investment in human capital. Education not only increases the productivity of the recipient, it may provide a positive *externality.* An externality occurs when the actions of one person affect the well-being of a third party. An educated individual might generate ideas that become useful to others. This is an argument for public education. Poor counties may suffer from *brain drain* when their educated workers emigrate to rich counties. Children in very poor countries might work instead of going to school because the opportunity cost of going to school is too great. Paying parents for sending their children to school might both reduce child labour and increase the education of very poor children.

- *protect property rights and establish political stability.* *Property rights* refer to the ability of people to exercise control over their resources. For individuals to be willing to work, save and invest, and trade with others by contract, they must be confident that their production and capital will not be stolen and that their agreements will be enforced. Even a remote possibility of political instability creates uncertainty with regard to property rights because a revolutionary government might confiscate property—particularly capital.

- *encourage free trade.* Free trade is like a technological advance. It allows a country to transform the output from its production into products that another country produces more efficiently. The *infant-industry argument* suggests that developing countries should pursue *inward-oriented policies* by restricting international trade to protect fledgling domestic industry from foreign competition. Most economists disagree with the infant industry argument and promote *outward-oriented policies* that reduce or eliminate trade barriers.

- *encourage research and development.* Most of the increase in the standard of living is due to an increase in technological knowledge that comes from research and development. After a time, knowledge is a *public good* in that we can all use it at the same time without diminishing another's benefits. Research and development might be encouraged with grants, tax breaks, and patents to establish temporary property rights to an invention. Alternatively, it might be encouraged by simply maintaining property rights and political stability.

- *address population growth.* Population growth might affect productivity in both positive and negative ways. Rapid population growth might *stretch natural resources* across more people. Thomas Malthus (1766–1834) argued that population growth will always rise to the limit imposed by the food supply, causing mankind to live forever in poverty. Any attempt to alleviate poverty will simply cause the poor to have more children, returning them to subsistence living. Malthus' predictions have not come true because he underestimated the ability of technological progress to expand the food supply. Rapid pop-ulation growth *dilutes the capital stock* (both physical and human capital) by spreading it across more workers. Educated women tend to have fewer children because the opportunity cost of having children increases as opportunities grow. However, a larger population might *promote technological progress.* Throughout history, most technological progress has come from larger population centres where there are more people able to discover things and exchange ideas.

The rate of productivity growth is not steady. Productivity grew quickly during the 1950s and 1960s, slowly from 1970–1995, and then quickly again from 1995 to the present. Many economists attribute the changes in productivity to changes in the growth of technology. Others argue that growth during the period 1950–1970 was unusually high and that we have just returned to normal.

HELPFUL HINTS

1. A simple example more clearly defines the factors of production. The simpler the production process, the easier it is to separate and analyse the factors of production. For example, suppose output is holes dug in the ground. In this case, the production function is:

$$Y = A \, F(L, K, H, N)$$

where Y is the number of holes dug, A is technological knowledge, L is labour, K is physical capital, H is human capital, and N is natural resources. If we have more workers, there is an increase in L and Y would increase. If we have more shovels, there is an increase in K and Y would increase. If workers are educated so that more of them dig with the spaded end of the shovel as opposed to digging with the handle, there is an increase in H and Y would increase (note, the number of workers and the number of shovels is unchanged). If our country has softer soil so that digging is easier here, N is larger and therefore Y is larger. Finally, if we discover that it is more productive to dig after it rains rather than during a drought, there is an increase in A and Y should increase.

TERMS AND DEFINITIONS

Choose a definition for each key term.

Key terms:

_____ Real GDP per person

_____ Growth rate

_____ Productivity

_____ Physical capital

_____ Factors of production

_____ Human capital

_____ Natural resources

_____ Renewable resource

_____ Non-renewable resource

_____ Technological knowledge

_____ Production function

_____ Constant returns to scale

_____ Diminishing returns

_____ Catch-up effect

_____ Foreign direct investment

_____ Foreign portfolio investment

_____ Externality

_____ Property rights

_____ Infant-industry argument

_____ Inward-oriented policies

_____ Outward-oriented policies

_____ Public good

Definitions:

1. The knowledge and skills that workers acquire through education, training, and experience

2. Capital investment owned and operated by foreigners

3. The relationship between inputs and output from production

4. A good that we may all use at the same time without diminishing another's benefits

5. The ability of people to exercise control over their resources

6. The quantity of goods and services available for the average individual in the economy

7. The stock of equipment and structures used to produce output

8. When the incremental increase in output declines as equal increments of an input are added to production

9. A production process where doubling all of the inputs doubles the output

10. Natural resource that can be reproduced

11. Restricting international trade to protect fledgling domestic industry from foreign competition

12. Policies that decrease international trade restrictions

13. The view that poorer countries tend to grow more rapidly than richer countries

14. The annual percentage change in output

15. Inputs used in production, such as labour, capital, and natural resources

16. Natural resource that is limited in supply

17. When the actions of one person affect the well-being of a third party

18. Policies that increase international trade restrictions

19. A society's understanding about the best ways to produce goods and services

20. The quantity of goods and services that a worker can produce per hour

21. Inputs into production provided by nature

22. Capital investment financed with foreign money, but operated by domestic residents

PROBLEMS AND SHORT-ANSWER QUESTIONS

Practice Problems

1.

Country	GDP per person at constant prices (€)	Current growth rate (%)
Northcountry	15,468	1.98
Southcountry	13,690	2.03
Eastcountry	6,343	3.12
Westcountry	1,098	0.61

a. Which country is richest? How do you know?

b. Which country is advancing most quickly? How do you know?

c. Which country would likely see the greatest benefit from an increase in capital investment? Why?

d. Referring to (c): Would this country continue to see the same degree of benefits from an increase in capital investment forever? Why?

e. Referring to (d): Why might investment in human capital and research and development fail to exhibit the same degree of diminishing returns as investment in physical capital?

f. Which country has the potential to grow most quickly? List some reasons why it may not be living up to potential.

g. If GDP per person at constant prices in Northcountry next year is €15,918, what is its annual growth rate?

2. Imagine a kitchen. It contains a cook, the cook's diploma, a recipe book, a stove and utensils, and some wild pig harvested from the forest.

a. Link each object in the kitchen to a general category within the factors of production.

b. While the different factors of production exhibit different levels of durability, which one is special in that it does not wear out?

3. a. List the policies governments might pursue to increase the productivity of their citizens.

b. Which two, at the very least, are fundamentally necessary as a background in which the other policies may operate? Why?

c. Does a growing population enhance or inhibit growth in productivity? Explain.

Short-Answer Questions

1. Economists measure both the level of GDP at constant prices per person and the growth rate of GDP at constant prices per person. What different concept does each statistic capture?

2. Must poor countries stay relatively poor forever and most rich countries stay relatively rich forever? Why?

3. What factors determine productivity? Which of these are produced by humans?

4. How does human capital differ from physical capital?

5. Explain the opportunity cost of investing in capital. Is there any difference in the opportunity cost of investing in human capital versus physical capital?

6. Why does an increase in the rate of saving and investment only increase the rate of growth temporarily?

7. If foreigners buy newly issued equity in British Oxygen Corporation (BOC), and BOC uses the proceeds to expand capacity by building new plants and equipment, which will rise more in the future: UK GDP or UK GNP? Why? What do we call this type of investment?

8. Some economists argue for lengthening patent protection while some economists argue for shortening it. Why might patents increase productivity? Why might they decrease productivity?

SELF-TEST

True/False Questions

_____ 1. Human capital refers to human-made capital such as tools and machinery.

_____ 2. If a production function exhibits constant returns to scale, then doubling all of the inputs doubles output.

_____ 3. In very poor countries, paying parents to send their children to school might increase the education of poor children and decrease the use of child labour.

_____ 4. An increase in capital should cause the growth rate of a relatively poor country to increase more than that of a rich country.

_____ 5. An increase in the rate of saving and investment permanently increases a country's rate of growth.

_____ 6. A country can only increase its level of investment by increasing its saving.

_____ 7. Investment in human capital and technology might be particularly productive because of positive spillover effects.

_____ 8. If Germans invest in the UK economy by building a new Mercedes factory, in the future, UK GDP will rise by more than UK GNP.

_____ 9. If productivity in a country rises, real GDP must rise.

_____10. The opportunity cost of additional growth is that someone must forgo current consumption.

Multiple-Choice Questions

Questions 1 through 3 are based on the following data which gives information on four different countries.

1. Which country had the highest standard of living in Year 1?

Year 1

	GNP at Factor cost €m	Population (millions)	Index of Prices
Country A	15,000	30	125
Country B	4,000	40	120
Country C	12,000	25	100
Country D	2,000	10	110

Year 2

	GNP at Factor cost €m	Population (millions)	Index of Prices
Country A	18,000	31	150
Country B	4,000	44	180
Country C	14,400	25	120
Country D	3,000	11	110

    a. Country A.
    b. Country B.
    c. Country C.
    d. Country D.

2. Which country had the same standard of living in Year 2 as in Year 1?
    a. Country A.
    b. Country B.
    c. Country C.
    d. Country D.

3. Which country is most likely to be a poor developing country?
    a. Country A.
    b. Country B.
    c. Country C.
    d. Country D.

4. The opportunity cost of growth is
    a. a reduction in current investment.
    b. a reduction in current saving.
    c. a reduction in current consumption.
    d. a reduction in taxes.

5. If a production function exhibits constant returns to scale,
    a. doubling all of the inputs has absolutely no impact on output because output is constant.
    b. doubling all of the inputs doubles output.
    c. doubling all of the inputs more than doubles output due to the catch-up effect.
    d. doubling all of the inputs less than doubles output due to diminishing returns.

6. Which of the following describes an increase in technological knowledge?
    a. A farmer discovers that it is better to plant in the spring rather than in the fall.
    b. A farmer buys another tractor.
    c. A farmer hires another day labourer.
    d. A farmer sends his child to agricultural college and the child returns to work on the farm.

7. Which of the following government policies is *least* likely to increase growth in Africa?
    a. increase expenditures on public education.
    b. increase restrictions on the importing of Japanese automobiles and electronics.
    c. eliminate civil war.
    d. reduce restrictions on foreign capital investment.
    e. All of the above would increase growth.

8. If BMW builds a new plant in the UK,
    a. in the future, UK GDP will rise more-than UK GNP.
    b. in the future, UK GDP will rise less than UK GNP.
    c. in the future, UK GDP and GNP will both fall because some income from this investment will accrue to foreigners.
    d. in the future, UK GDP and GNP will both rise because a greater level of output is produced.

9. Which of the following expenditures to enhance productivity is most likely to emit a positive externality?
    a. Megabank buys a new computer.
    b. Ross pays his college tuition fee.
    c. BP leases a new oil field.
    d. BMW buys a new drill press.

10. To increase growth, governments should do all of the following except
    a. promote free trade.
    b. encourage saving and investment.
    c. encourage foreigners to investment in your country.
    d. encourage research and development.
    e. impose additional taxes on imports.

ADVANCED CRITICAL THINKING

You are having a discussion with other Generation X-ers. The conversation turns to a supposed lack of growth and opportunity in the UK when compared to some Asian countries such as Japan, South Korea, Taiwan, and Singapore. Your roommate says, 'These Asian countries must have cheated somehow. That's the only way they could have possibly grown so quickly.'

1. Have you learned anything in this chapter that would make you question your roommate's assertion?

2. The phenomenal growth rate of Japan since the 1940s has often been referred to as the 'Japanese miracle'. Is it a miracle or is it explicable?

3. Are the high growth rates found in these Asian countries without cost?

SOLUTIONS

Terms and Definitions

_1_	Human capital	_9_	Constant returns to scale	_17_	Externality
_2_	Foreign direct investment	_10_	Renewable resource	_18_	Inward oriented policies
_3_	Production function	_11_	Infant industry argument	_19_	Technological knowledge
_4_	Public good	_12_	Outward oriented policies	_20_	Productivity
_5_	Property rights	_13_	Catch-up effect	_21_	Natural resources
_6_	Real GDP per person	_14_	Growth rate	_22_	Foreign portfolio investment
_7_	Physical capital	_15_	Factors of production		
_8_	Diminishing returns	_16_	Non-renewable resource		

Practice Problems

1. a. Northcountry, because it has the largest GDP at constant prices per person.
   b. Eastcountry, because it has the largest growth rate.
   c. Westcountry is the poorest and likely has the least capital. Since capital exhibits diminishing returns, it is most productive when it is relatively scarce.
   d. No. Because of diminishing returns to capital, the additional growth from increasing capital declines as a country has more capital.
   e. Human capital emits a positive externality. Research and development is a public good after dissemination.
   f. Westcountry, because it is currently the poorest and could easily benefit from additional capital. It may have trade restrictions (inward oriented policies), a corrupt or unstable government, few courts and a lack of established property rights, and so on.
   g. (€15,918 − €15,468)/€15,468 = 0.029 = 2.9%.

2. a. cook = labour, diploma = human capital, recipes = technological knowledge, stove and utensils = capital, pig = natural resource.
   b. Recipes (technological knowledge) never wear out. Labour and human capital die, the stove and utensils wear out slowly, and the pig is used up (although it is probably renewable).

3. a. Encourage saving and investment, investment from abroad, education, free trade, research and development, protect property rights and establish political stability.
   b. Property rights and political stability are necessary for there to be any incentive to save, invest, trade, or educate.
   c. The answer is uncertain. A rapidly growing population may reduce productivity by stretching natural resources across more people and by diluting the capital stock across more workers. However, there is evidence that more technological progress takes place in areas with large populations.

Short-Answer Questions

1. Level of GDP at constant prices per person measures standard of living. Growth rate measures rate of advance of the standard of living.

2. No. Since growth rates vary widely across countries, rich can become relatively poorer and poor can become relatively richer.

3. Physical capital per worker, human capital per worker, natural resources per worker, and technological knowledge. All except natural resources.

4. Human capital is the knowledge and skills of the worker. Physical capital is the stock of equipment and structures.

5. Someone must forgo current consumption. No, someone must save instead of consuming regardless of whether education or machines are purchased with the saving.

6. Because there are diminishing returns to physical capital.

7. GDP. GNP measures only the income of the UK while GDP measures income generated inside the UK. Therefore, GDP will rise more than GNP because some of the profits from the capital investment will accrue to foreigners in the form of dividends. Foreign portfolio investment.

8. Patents provide a property right to an idea; therefore people are willing to invest in research and development because it is more profitable. Research and development is a public good once the information is disseminated.

True/False Questions

1. F; human capital is the knowledge and skills of workers.
2. T
3. T
4. T
5. F; due to diminishing returns to capital, growth rises temporarily.
6. F; it can attract foreign investment.
7. T
8. T
9. F; an increase in productivity is consistent with a fall in total production, for example when unemployment rises.
10. T

Multiple-Choice Questions

1. a	5. b	9. b
2. c	6. a	10. e
3. b	7. b	
4. c	8. a	

Advanced Critical Thinking

1. Yes. There are many sources of growth and a country can influence all of them except natural resources.

2. Japan's growth is explicable. Indeed, all of the high-growth Asian countries have extremely high investment as a per cent of GDP.

3. No. The opportunity cost of investment is that someone must forgo current consumption in order to save and invest.

26

⌐In this chapter you will

Learn about some of the important financial institutions in the UK economy

Consider how the financial system is related to key macroeconomic variables

Develop a model of the supply and demand for loanable funds in financial markets

Use the loanable funds model to analyse various government policies

Consider how government budget deficits affect the UK economy

OUTCOMES

⌐You should be able to

List and describe four important types of financial institutions

Describe the relationship between national saving, government deficits, and investment

Explain the slope of the supply and demand for loanable funds

Shift supply and demand in the loanable funds market in response to a change in taxes on interest or investment

Shift supply and demand in the loanable funds market in response to a change in the government's budget deficit

SAVING, INVESTMENT, AND THE FINANCIAL SYSTEM

CHAPTER OVERVIEW

Context and Purpose

Chapter 26 is the second chapter in a four-chapter sequence on the production of output in the long run. In Chapter 25, we found that capital and labour are among the primary determinants of output. For this reason, Chapter 26 focuses on the market for saving and investment in capital, and Chapter 27 focuses on the tools people and firms use when choosing capital projects in which to invest. Chapter 28 will focus on the market for labour.

The purpose of Chapter 26 is to show how saving and investment are coordinated by the loanable funds market. Within the framework of the loanable funds market, we are able to see the effects of taxes and government deficits on saving, investment, the accumulation of capital, and ultimately, the growth rate of output.

CHAPTER REVIEW

Introduction

Some people save some of their income and have funds that are available to loan. Some people wish to invest in capital equipment and thus need to borrow. The **financial system** consists of those institutions that help match, or balance, the lending of savers to the borrowing of investors. This is important because investment in capital contributes to economic growth.

Financial Institutions in the UK Economy

The financial system is made up of financial institutions that match borrowers and lenders. Financial institutions can be grouped into two categories: financial markets and financial intermediaries.

Financial markets allow firms to borrow *directly* from those that wish to lend. The two most important financial markets are the bond market and the stock market.

- The *bond market* allows large borrowers to borrow directly from the public. The borrower sells a **bond** (a certificate of indebtedness or IOU) which specifies the *date* *of maturity* (the date the loan will be repaid), the amount of interest that will be paid periodically, and the *principal* (the amount borrowed and to be repaid at maturity). The buyer of the bond is the lender.

Bond issues differ in three main ways.

(1) Bonds are of different *terms* (time to maturity). Longer-term bonds are riskier and, thus, usually pay higher interest because the owner of the bond may need to sell it before maturity at a depressed price.

(2) Bonds have different *credit risks* (probability of default). Higher-risk bonds pay higher interest. *Junk bonds* are exceptionally risky bonds.

(3) Bonds have different *tax treatment*. The interest received from owning a *municipal bond* (bond issued by state or local government) is tax exempt. Thus, municipal bonds pay lower interest.

- The *stock market* allows large firms to raise funds for expansion by taking on additional 'partners' or owners of the firm. The sale of **stock** is called *equity finance* while the sale of bonds is called *debt finance*. Owners of stock share in the profits or losses of the firm while owners of bonds receive fixed interest payments as creditors. The stockholder accepts more risk than the bondholder, but has a higher potential return. Stocks don't mature or expire and are traded on stock exchanges such as the London Stock Exchange and Frankfurt Stock Exchange. Stock prices are determined by supply and demand and reflect expectations of the firm's future profitability. A *stock index*, such as the FTSE All Share Index, is an average of all equity prices quoted on the London Stock Exchange (LSE) or the DAX 30 which is an average 30 specific companies quoted on the Frankfurt Stock Exchange.

Financial intermediaries are financial institutions through which savers (lenders) can *indirectly* loan funds to borrowers. That is, financial intermediaries are middle institutions between borrowers and lenders. Two of the most important financial intermediaries are banks and investment trusts.

- **Banks** collect deposits from people and businesses (savers) and lend them to other people and businesses (borrowers). Banks pay interest on deposits and charge a slightly higher rate on their loans. Small businesses usually borrow from banks because they are too small to sell stock or bonds. Banks create a *medium of exchange* when they accept a deposit because individuals can write checks against the deposit to engage in transactions. Other intermediaries only offer savers a *store of value* because their saving is not as accessible.

- **Investment trusts** are institutions that sell shares to the public and use the proceeds to buy a group of stocks and/or bonds. This allows small savers to *diversify* their asset *portfolios* (own a variety of assets). It also allows small savers access to professional money managers. However, few money managers can beat *index funds*, which buy all of the stocks in a stock index without the aid of active management. There are two reasons why index funds outperform actively managed funds. First, it is hard to pick stocks whose prices will rise because the market price of a stock is already a good reflection of a company's true value. Second, index funds keep costs low by rarely buying and selling, and by not having to pay the salaries of professional money managers.

Although there are many differences among these financial institutions, the overriding similarity is that they all direct resources from lenders to borrowers. The importance of this can be seen in the case of China which has lacked free financial markets resulting in inefficient capital investment. China is moving slowly towards freer capital markets and this partly accounts for the improving growth achieved in recent years by China.

Saving and Investment in the National Income Accounts

In order to truly appreciate the role of the financial system in directing saving into investment, we must begin to understand saving and investment from a macroeconomic perspective. The national income accounts record the relationship between income, output, saving, investment, expenditures, taxes, and so on. There are a number of national income *identities* (equations that are true by definition) that expose relationships between these variables.

Recall, GDP is the value of output, the value of income earned from producing it, and *the value of expenditures* on it. Therefore,

$$Y = C + I + G + NX$$

where Y = GDP, C = consumption expenditures, I = investment expenditures, G = government purchases, and NX = net exports. To simplify, we assume there is no international sector which means that we have a *closed economy*. (An *open economy* includes a foreign sector.) Therefore, for our example

$$Y = C + I + G$$

National saving or just **saving** is the income left over after paying for consumption and government purchases. To find saving, subtract C and G from both sides.

$$Y - C - G = I \quad \text{or} \quad S = I$$

which says, saving = investment.

To appreciate the impact of the government's purchases and taxes on saving, we need to define saving as above:

$$S = Y - C - G$$

which says again that saving is income left over after consumption and government purchases. Now add and subtract T (taxes) from the right side:

$$S = (Y - T - C) + (T - G)$$

This says that saving is equal to **private saving** $(Y - T - C)$ which is income left over after paying taxes and consumption, and **public saving** $(T - G)$ which is the government's **budget surplus**. Often G is greater than T, and the government runs a negative surplus or a **budget deficit**.

In summary, $S = I$ for the economy as a whole and the amount of saving available for investment is the sum of private saving and public saving. Although $S = I$ for the entire economy, it is not true for each individual. That is, some people invest less than they save and have funds to lend while others invest more than they save and need to borrow funds. These groups interact in the **market for loanable funds.** Note that saving is the income that remains after paying for consumption and government purchases while investment is the purchase of new capital.

The Market for Loanable funds

For simplicity, imagine that there is one loanable funds market where all savers take their funds to be loaned and where all investors go to borrow funds.

- The *supply* of loanable funds comes from national saving. A higher real interest rate increases the incentive to save and increases the quantity supplied of loanable funds.

- The *demand* for loanable funds comes from households and firms that wish to borrow to invest. A higher real interest rate increases the cost of borrowing and reduces the quantity demanded of loanable funds.

The supply and demand for loanable funds combine to generate a market for loanable funds. This market determines the equilibrium real interest rate and the equilibrium quantity of funds loaned and borrowed. Since the funds that are loaned are national savings and the funds that are borrowed are used for investment, the loanable funds market also determines the equilibrium level of saving and investment.

The following three policies increase saving, investment, and capital accumulation and, hence, these policies increase economic growth.

Reduced taxation on interest and dividends increases the return to saving for any real interest rate and, thus, increases the desire to save and loan at each real interest rate. Graphically, this policy will shift the supply of loanable funds to the right, lower the real interest rate, and raise the quantity demanded of funds for investment. Real interest rates fall while saving and investment rise.

Reduced taxation if one invests, for example an investment tax credit, will increase the return to investment in capital for any real interest rate and, thus, increase the desire to borrow and invest at each real interest rate. Diagrammatically, this policy will shift the demand for loanable funds to the right, raise the real interest rate, and increase the quantity supplied of funds. Real interest rates, saving, and investment rises.

A reduction in government debt and deficits (or an increase in a budget surplus) increases public saving $(T - G)$ so more national saving is available at each real interest rate. Graphically, this policy will shift the supply of loanable funds to the right, decrease the real interest rate, and increase the quantity demanded of funds for investment. Real interest rates fall, and saving and investment rise.

Note that a *budget deficit* is an excess of government spending over tax revenue. The accumulation of past government borrowing is called the *national debt*. A *budget surplus* is an excess of tax revenue over government spending. When government spending equals tax revenue, there is a *balanced budget*. An increase in the deficit reduces national saving, shifts the supply of loanable funds to the left, raises the real interest rate, and reduces the quantity demanded of funds for investment. When private borrowing and investment are reduced due to government borrowing, we say that government is **crowding out** investment. Government surpluses do just the opposite of budget deficits.

HELPFUL HINTS

1. A financial intermediary is a middle institution. An intermediary is an economic agent whose role lies between two groups. For example, we have intermediaries in labour negotiations that sit between a firm and a union. In like manner, a bank is a financial intermediary in that it sits between the ultimate lender (the depositor) and the ultimate borrower (the firm or home builder) and 'negotiates' the terms of the loan contracts. Banks don't lend their own money. They lend their depositor's money.

2. Investment is not the purchase of stocks and bonds. In casual conversation, people use the word 'investment' to mean the purchase of stocks and bonds. For example, 'I just invested in ten shares of IBM.' (Even an economist might say this.) However, when speaking in economic terms, *investment* is the actual purchase of capital equipment and structures. In this technical framework, when I buy ten shares of newly issued ICI stock, there has been only an exchange of assets—ICI has my money and I have their stock certificates. If ICI takes my money and buys new equipment with it, their purchase of the equipment is economic *investment*.

3. Don't include consumption loans in the supply of loanable funds. In casual conversation, people use the word 'saving' to refer to their new deposit in a bank. For example, 'I just saved €100 this week.' (An economist might say this, too.) However, if that deposit were loaned out to a consumer who used the funds to purchase airline tickets for a vacation, there has been no increase in *national*

saving (or just *saving*) in a macroeconomic sense. This is because saving, in a macroeconomic sense, is income (GDP) that remains after *national* consumption expenditures and government purchases ($S = Y - C - G$). No national saving took place if your personal saving was loaned and used for consumption expenditures by another person. Since national saving is the source of the supply of loanable funds, consumption loans do not affect the supply of loanable funds.

4. Demand for loanable funds is private demand for investment funds. The demand for loanable funds only includes private (households and firms) demand for funds to invest in capital structures and equipment. When the government runs a deficit, it does absorb national saving but it does not buy capital equipment with the funds. Therefore, when the government runs a deficit, we consider it a reduction in the supply of loanable funds, not an increase in the demand for loanable funds.

TERMS AND DEFINITIONS

Choose a definition for each key term.

Key terms:

_____ Financial system

_____ Financial markets

_____ Financial intermediaries

_____ Bank

_____ Medium of exchange

_____ Bond

_____ Stock

_____ Investment trust

_____ Closed economy

_____ National saving (saving)

_____ Private saving

_____ Budget surplus

_____ Budget deficit

_____ Government debt

_____ Investment

_____ Demand for loanable funds

_____ Supply of loanable funds

_____ Crowding out

Definitions:

1. Spendable asset such as a checking deposit

2. A shortfall of tax revenue relative to government spending causing public saving to be negative

3. An economy with no international transactions

4. Financial institutions through which savers can indirectly lend to borrowers

5. The group of institutions in the economy that help match borrowers and lenders

6. The amount of borrowing for investment desired at each real interest rate

7. The income that remains after consumption expenditures and taxes

8. The accumulation of past budget deficits

9. The amount of saving made available for lending at each real interest rate

10. Institution that collects deposits and makes loans

11. Institution that sells shares and uses the proceeds to buy a diversified portfolio

12. Financial institutions through which savers can directly lend to borrowers

13. Certificate of ownership of a small portion of a large firm

14. An excess of tax revenue over government spending causing public saving to be positive

15. The income that remains after consumption expenditures and government purchases

16. A decrease in investment as a result of government borrowing

17. Expenditures on capital equipment and structures

18. Certificate of indebtedness or IOU

PROBLEMS AND SHORT-ANSWER QUESTIONS

Practice Problems

1. Fly-by-night Corporation is in need of capital funds to expand its production capacity. It is selling short-term and long-term bonds and is issuing stock. You are considering the prospect of helping finance their expansion.
   a. If you are to buy both short-term and long-term bonds from Fly-by-night, from which bond would you demand a higher rate of return: short term or long term? Why?
   b. If a reputable credit rating agency lowered the credit worthiness of Fly-by-night, would this affect the rate of return you would demand when buying their bonds? Why?
   c. If Fly-by-night has exactly the same credit worthiness as Deadbeat City and each is issuing the same term to maturity bonds, which issuer must pay the higher interest rate on its bonds? Why?
   d. If Fly-by-night is issuing both stocks and bonds, from which would you expect to earn the higher rate of return over the long run? Why?
   e. Which would be safer: putting all of your personal saving into Fly-by-night stock, or putting all of your personal saving into a mutual fund that has some Fly-by-night stock in its portfolio? Why?

2. Use the saving and investment identities from the National Income Accounts to answer the following questions. Suppose the following values are from the national income accounts of a country with a closed economy (all values are in billions).

$$Y = €6,000$$
$$T = €1,000$$
$$C = €4,000$$
$$G = €1,200$$

   a. What is the value of saving and investment in this country?
   b. What is the value of private saving?
   c. What is the value of public saving?
   d. Is the government's budget policy contributing to growth in this country or harming it? Why?

3. The following information describes a loanable funds market. Values are in billions.

Real Interest Rate (%)	Quantity of Loanable funds Supplied (€)	Quantity of Loanable funds Demanded (€)
6	1,300	700
5	1,200	800
4	1,000	1,000
3	800	1,200
2	600	1,500

   a. Plot the supply and demand for loanable funds in Exhibit 1. What is the equilibrium real interest rate and the equilibrium level of saving and investment?
   b. What 'market forces' will not allow 2 per cent to be the real interest rate?
   c. Suppose the government suddenly increases its budget deficit by €400 billion. What is the new equilibrium real interest rate and equilibrium level of saving and investment? (Show graphically in Exhibit 2.)
   d. Starting at the original equilibrium, suppose the government enacts an investment tax credit that stimulates the demand for loanable funds for

EXHIBIT 1

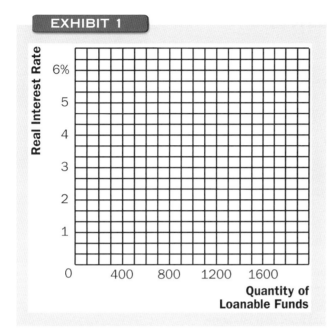

EXHIBIT 2

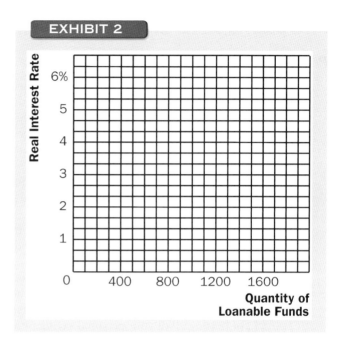

EXHIBIT 3

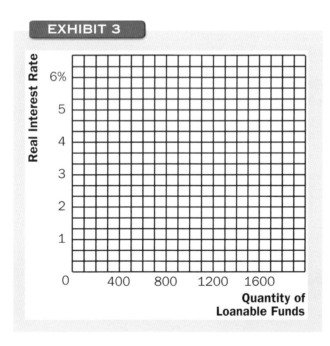

capital investment by €400 billion at any real interest rate. What is the new equilibrium real interest rate and equilibrium level of saving and investment? (Show graphically in Exhibit 3.)

e. With regard to (c) and (d), which policy is most likely to increase growth? Why?

Short-Answer Questions

1. Which is likely to give you a greater rate of return: a deposit at a bank or the purchase of a corporate bond? Why?

2. What is the difference between debt finance and equity finance? Provide an example of each.

3. What is meant by the terms 'saving' and 'investment' in the national income accounts and how does this definition differ from the casual use of the words?

4. In a closed economy, why can investment never exceed saving?

5. What is private saving? What is public saving?

6. Utilizing the national income identities, if government purchases were to rise, and if output, taxes, and consumption were to remain unchanged, what would happen to national saving, investment, and growth?

7. Suppose citizens of a particular economy become more frugal. That is, they consume a smaller per cent of their income and save a larger per cent. Describe the changes in the loanable funds market. What would likely happen to growth?

8. Suppose the government runs a smaller deficit. Describe the changes in the loanable funds market. What would likely happen to growth?

9. An increase in the government's budget deficit forces the government to borrow more. Why doesn't an increase in the deficit increase the demand for loanable funds in the loanable funds market?

10. What is the fundamental difference between financial markets and financial intermediaries?

SELF-TEST

True/False Questions

_____ 1. People who buy stock in a firm have loaned money to the firm.

_____ 2. In a closed economy, saving is what remains after consumption expenditures and government purchases.

_____ 3. Public saving is always positive.

_____ 4. In a closed economy, investment is always equal to saving regardless of where the saving came from—public or private sources.

_____ 5. Investment is the purchase of capital equipment and structures.

_____ 6. The quantity supplied of loanable funds is greater if real interest rates are higher.

_____ 7. If the real interest rate in the loanable funds market is temporarily held above the equilibrium rate, desired borrowing will exceed desired lending and the real interest rate will fall.

_____ 8. A reduction in the budget deficit should shift the supply of loanable funds to the right, lower the real interest rate, and increase the quantity demanded of loanable funds.

_____ 9. Public saving and the government's budget surplus are the same thing.

_____10. An increase in the budget deficit that causes the government to increase its borrowing shifts the demand for loanable funds to the right.

Multiple-Choice Questions

1. National saving (or just saving) is equal to
   a. private saving + public saving.
   b. investment + consumption expenditures.
   c. GDP − government purchases.
   d. GDP + consumption expenditures + government purchases.

2. If government spending exceeds tax collections,
   a. there is a budget surplus.
   b. there is a budget deficit.
   c. private saving is positive.
   d. public saving is positive.

3. If GDP = €1,000, consumption = €600, taxes = €100, and government purchases = €200, how much is saving and investment?
   a. saving = €200, investment = €200.
   b. saving = €300, investment = €300.
   c. saving = €100, investment = €200.
   d. saving = €200, investment = €100.
   e. saving = €0, investment = €0.

4. If the public consumes €100 billion less and the government purchases €100 billion more (other things unchanging), which of the following statements is true?
   a. There is an increase in saving and the economy should grow more quickly.
   b. There is a decrease in saving and the economy should grow more slowly.
   c. Saving is unchanged.
   d. There is not enough information to determine what will happen to saving.

5. Which of the following sets of government policies is the most growth oriented?
   a. lower taxes on the returns to saving, provide investment tax credits, and lower the deficit.
   b. lower taxes on the returns to saving, provide investment tax credits, and increase the deficit.
   c. increase taxes on the returns to saving, provide investment tax credits, and lower the deficit.
   d. increase taxes on the returns to saving, provide investment tax credits, and increase the deficit.

6. An increase in the budget deficit that causes the government to increase its borrowing
   a. shifts the demand for loanable funds to the right.
   b. shifts the demand for loanable funds to the left.
   c. shifts the supply of loanable funds to the left.
   d. shifts the supply of loanable funds to the right.

7. An increase in the budget deficit will
   a. raise the real interest rate and decrease the quantity of loanable funds demanded for investment.
   b. raise the real interest rate and increase the quantity of loanable funds demanded for investment.
   c. lower the real interest rate and increase the quantity of loanable funds demanded for investment.
   d. lower the real interest rate and decrease the quantity of loanable funds demanded for investment.

8. An increase in the budget deficit is
   a. an increase in public saving.
   b. a decrease in public saving.
   c. an increase in private saving.
   d. a decrease in private saving.

9. If the government increases investment tax credits and reduces taxes on the return to saving at the same time,
   a. the real interest rate should rise.
   b. the real interest rate should fall.
   c. the real interest rate should not change.
   d. the impact on the real interest rate is indeterminate.

10. An increase in the budget surplus
   a. shifts the demand for loanable funds to the right and increases the real interest rate.
   b. shifts the demand for loanable funds to the left and reduces the real interest rate.
   c. shifts the supply of loanable funds to the left and increases the real interest rate.
   d. shifts the supply of loanable funds to the right and reduces the real interest rate.

ADVANCED CRITICAL THINKING

You are watching a debate between two prospective parliamentary candidates. When a candidate is questioned about his position on economic growth, he says 'We need to get this country growing again. We need to use tax incentives to stimulate saving and investment, and we need to get that budget deficit down so that the government stops absorbing our nation's saving.'

1. If government spending remains unchanged, what inconsistency is implied by the candidate's statement?

2. If he truly wishes to decrease taxes and decrease the budget deficit, what has the candidate implied about his plans for government spending?

3. If policy-makers want to increase growth, and if policy-makers have to choose between tax incentives to stimulate saving and tax incentives to stimulate investment, what might they want to know about supply and demand in the loanable funds market before making their decision? Explain.

SOLUTIONS

Terms and Definitions

 1   Medium of exchange

 2   Budget deficit

 3   Closed economy

 4   Financial intermediaries

 5   Financial system

 6   Demand for loanable funds

 7   Private saving

 8   Government debt

 9   Supply of loanable funds

 10   Bank

 11   Investment trust

 12   Financial markets

 13   Stock

 14   Budget surplus

 15   National saving (saving)

 16   Crowding out

 17   Investment

 18   Bond

Practice Problems

1. a. Long term, because it is more likely that you may need to sell the long-term bond at a depressed price prior to maturity.
    b. Yes, the credit risk has increased and lenders would demand a higher rate of return.
    c. Fly-by-night. Unlike municipal bonds, interest receipts are taxable to the owners of corporate bonds.
    d. Owners of stock demand a higher rate of return because it is riskier.
    e. It is safer to put money in a mutual fund because it is diversified (not all of your eggs in one basket).

2. a. (€6,000 − €1,000 − €4,000) + (€1,000 − €1,200) = €800 billion.
    b. €6,000 − €1,000 − €4,000 = €1,000 billion.
    c. €1,000 − €1,200 = − €200 billion.
    d. It is harming growth because public saving is negative so less is available for investment.

3. a. Equilibrium real interest rate = 4%, equilibrium S and I = €1,000 billion. (See Exhibit 4.)
    b. At 2 per cent interest, the quantity demanded of loanable funds exceeds the quantity supplied by €900 billion. This excess demand for loans (borrowing) will drive interest rates up to 4 per cent.
    c. Equilibrium real interest rate = 5%, equilibrium S and I = €800 billion.
    d. Equilibrium real interest rate = 5%, equilibrium S and I = €1,200 billion. (See Exhibit 6.)

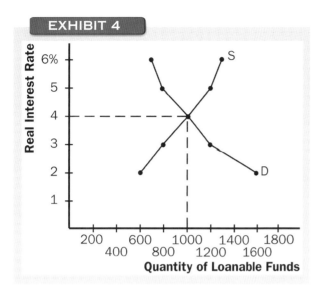

EXHIBIT 4

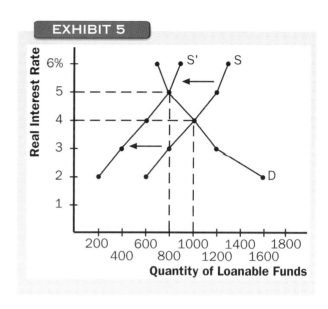

EXHIBIT 5

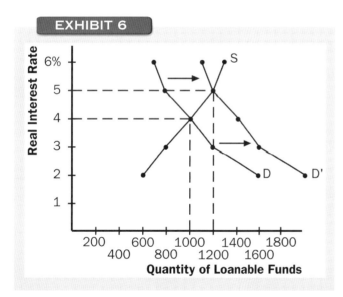

EXHIBIT 6

e. An investment tax credit, because it shifts the demand for loanable funds to invest in capital to the right, raising the level of investment in capital and stimulating growth.

Short-Answer Questions

1. A corporate bond, because the bond is riskier and because 'direct' lending through a financial market has fewer overhead costs than 'indirect' lending through an intermediary.

2. Debt finance is borrowing such as when a firm sells a bond. Equity finance is taking on additional partners such as when a firm sells stock.

3. Saving is what remains after consumption and government purchases. Investment is the purchase of equipment and structures. In casual conversation, saving is what remains out of our income (even if someone else borrows it for consumption) and investment is the purchase of stocks and bonds.

4. Because saving is the GDP left over after consumption expenditures and government purchases, and this is the limit of the output available to be used to purchase equipment and structures.

5. Private saving = $Y - T - C$, public saving = $T - G$.

6. Public saving would decrease and cause national saving and investment to decrease by the same amount, slowing growth.

7. The supply of loanable funds would shift right, the real interest rate would fall, and the quantity demanded of loanable funds to purchase capital would increase. Growth would increase.

8. The supply of loanable funds would shift right, the real interest rate would fall, and the quantity demanded of loanable funds to purchase capital would increase. Growth would increase.

9. The demand for loanable funds is defined as private demand for borrowing to purchase capital equipment and structures. An increase in the deficit absorbs saving and reduces the supply of loanable funds.

10. In a financial market, savers lend directly to borrowers. Through financial intermediaries, savers lend to an intermediary who then lends to the ultimate borrower.

True/False Questions

1. F; stockholders are owners.

2. T

3. F; public saving is negative when there is a government budget deficit.

4. T

5. T

6. T

7. F; desired lending exceeds desired borrowing.

8. T

9. T

10. F; it decreases the supply of loanable funds.

Multiple-Choice Questions

1. a   6. c

2. b   7. a

3. a   8. b

4. c   9. d

5. a   10. d

Advanced Critical Thinking

1. Tax incentives to stimulate saving and investment require a reduction in taxes. This would increase the deficit, which would reduce national saving and investment.

2. The candidate plans to reduce government spending.

3. Policymakers would want to know the elasticity (similar to the steepness) of the supply and demand curves. If loanable funds demand is inelastic, changes in loanable funds supply have little effect on saving and investment, so tax incentives to increase saving at each interest rate do little for growth. If loanable funds supply is inelastic, changes in loanable funds demand have little effect on saving and investment, so tax incentives to increase investment at each interest rate do little for growth.

THE BASIC TOOLS OF FINANCE

CHAPTER OVERVIEW

Context and Purpose

Chapter 27 is the third chapter in a four-chapter sequence on the level and growth of output in the long run. In Chapter 25, we learned that capital and labour are among the primary determinants of output and growth. In Chapter 26, we addressed how saving and investment in capital goods affect the production of output. In Chapter 27, we will learn about some of the tools people and firms use when choosing capital projects in which to invest. Since both capital and labour are among the primary determinants of output, Chapter 28 will address the market for labour.

The purpose of Chapter 27 is to introduce you to some tools that people use when they participate in financial markets. We will learn how people compare different sums of money at different points in time, how they manage risk, and how these concepts combine to help determine the value of a financial asset, such as a share of stock.

CHAPTER REVIEW

Introduction

Financial markets coordinate saving and investment. Financial decisions involve two elements—time and risk. For example, people and firms must make decisions today about saving and investment based on expectations of future earnings, but future returns are uncertain. The field of **finance** studies how people make decisions regarding the allocation of resources over time and the handling of risk. We will learn how people compare different sums of money at different points in time, how they manage risk, and how these concepts combine to help determine the value of a financial asset, such as a share of stock.

Present Value: Measuring the Time Value of Money

The **present value** of any future value is the amount today that would be needed, at current interest rates, to produce that future sum. The **future value** is the amount of money in the future that an amount of money today will yield, given prevailing interest rates. Suppose r = the interest rate expressed in decimal form, n = years to maturity (when the loan expires), PV = present value, and FV = future value. Further, suppose that interest is paid annually and that the interest is put in the account to earn more interest—a process called **compounding**. Then:

(1) $$PV(1 + r)^n = FV \quad \text{and}$$

(2) $$FV/(1 + r)^n = PV$$

For example, suppose a person deposited €100 into a bank account for 3 years earning 7 per cent interest. Using equation (1) where r = 0.07, PV = €100, and n = 3, we find that in three years the account will hold about €122.50. That is, the future value is €122.50.

Alternatively, suppose you were offered a bank deposit that would provide you with €122.50 three years from now. At an interest rate of 7 per cent, what would you pay for that account today? Using equation (2) where r = 0.07, FV = €122.50, and n = 3, we find that the present value of €122.50 three years from today is €100.

The relationship between present value and future value demonstrates the following:

- Receiving a given sum in the present is preferred to receiving the same sum in the future. The larger the interest rate, the more pronounced is this result.

- In order to choose between two sums, a value today or a larger value at some later date, find the present value of the larger future sum and compare it to the value today.

- Firms undertake investment projects if the present value of the future returns exceeds the cost. The larger the interest rate, the less likely the project will be undertaken because the present value of the project becomes smaller. Thus, investment declines as interest rates rise.

Small differences in growth rates can make enormous differences in a country's level of income after many years. This result is also true for an individual's income or for money deposited in a bank. The concept of *compound growth* shows why. Each year's growth is based on the previous year's accumulated growth or, in the case of interest, interest is earned on previously earned interest. The effects of compound growth are demonstrated by the *rule of 70*, which states that if some variable grows at a rate of x per cent per year, its value will double in approximately $70/x$ years. If your income grows at 1 per cent per year, it will about double in 70 years. However, if your income grows at 4 per cent, it will double in approximately $70/4 = 17.5$ years.

Managing Risk

Most people are **risk averse**, which means that they avoid risk and will only become exposed to it if the prospect of a reward is sufficient to persuade them to take on risk. This is because people's utility functions exhibit diminishing marginal utility of wealth. Thus, the utility lost from losing a €1,000 bet is greater than that gained from winning a €1,000 bet. People can reduce risk by buying insurance, diversifying their risk, and accepting a lower return on their assets.

- *People can reduce the risk they face by buying insurance.* Insurance allows the economy to spread the risk more efficiently because it is easier for 100 people to bear 1/100 of the group's risk of a house fire than for each to bear the entire risk of one house fire alone. There are two problems with insurance markets. *Adverse selection* occurs because a high-risk person is more likely to buy insurance than a low-risk person. *Moral hazard* occurs because after people buy insurance, they have less incentive to be careful. Some low-risk people don't buy insurance because these problems may cause the price of insurance to be too high for low-risk people.

- *People can reduce the risk they face through diversification.* **Diversification** is the reduction of risk achieved by replacing a single risk with a large number of smaller unrelated risks. This is summarized by the phrase, 'Don't put all of your eggs in one basket.' Risk is diversified through insurance because it is easier for 100 people to bear 1/100 of the group's risk of a house fire than for each to bear the entire risk of one house fire alone. The risk on a portfolio of stocks, as measured by the *standard deviation* (volatility) of the returns, is reduced by diversifying the portfolio—buying a small amount of a large number of stocks instead of a large amount of one stock. Diversification can eliminate **idiosyncratic risk**—the uncertainty associated with specific companies. It cannot eliminate **aggregate risk**—the uncertainty associated with the entire economy.

- *People can reduce the risk they face by accepting a lower rate of return on their investments.* People face a trade off between risk and return in their portfolio. In order to earn greater returns, people must accept more risk. In order to have less risk, people must accept lower returns. The optimal combination of risk and return for a person depends on that person's degree of risk aversion, which depends on that person's preferences.

Asset Valuation

The price of a share of stock is determined by supply and demand. People often try to buy stock that is *undervalued*—shares of a business whose value exceeds its price. If the price exceeds the value, the stock is considered *overvalued* and if the price and value are equal, the stock is *fairly valued*. The price of the stock is known. The value of a stock is uncertain because it is the present value of the future stream of dividends and the final sales price. The dividends and final sales price depend on the firm's future profitability. **Fundamental analysis** is a detailed analysis of a company's accounting statements and future prospects to determine its value. You can perform fundamental analysis yourself, rely on stock market analysts, or buy into an investment trust whose manager does fundamental analysis.

According to the **efficient markets hypothesis**, asset prices reflect all publicly available information about the value of an asset. This theory argues that professional money managers monitor news to determine a stock's value. The stock's price is set by supply and demand so at any point in time shares sold equal shares bought, implying that an equal number believe that the stock is overvalued as think it is undervalued. Thus, the average analyst thinks it is fairly valued all the time. According to this theory, the stock market is **informationally efficient**, which means that prices in the stock market reflect all available information in a rational way. If this is true, stock prices should follow a **random walk**, the path of which is impossible to predict from available information because all available information has already been incorporated into the price. As a result, no stock is a better buy than any other and the best you can do is to buy a diversified portfolio.

Index funds provide evidence in support of the efficient markets hypothesis. Index funds are investment trusts that buy all of the stocks in a particular stock index. Actively managed funds use research to try to buy only the best stocks. Actively managed funds fail to outperform index funds because they trade more frequently, incurring trading costs plus they charge fees for their alleged expertise.

Some people suggest that markets are irrational. That is, stock prices often move in ways that are hard to explain on the basis of rational analysis of news and so appear to be driven by psychological trends. However, if this were true, traders should be able to take advantage of this fact and buy better than average stocks. However, beating the market regularly and consistently is impossible.

Evidence from behavioural economics studies suggests that people sometimes suffer from 'self-serving attribution bias'. Many people think that their successes are the result of skill rather than luck. If people are overconfident in their investment choices, they can create speculative bubbles in the stock market (pushing overvalued stocks even higher) and they can fail to diversify their own portfolios. Thus, it may not be unreasonable to restrict people's choices for their retirement options through mandated saving plans such as defined-benefit pension plans and Social Security.

Conclusion

The concept of present value shows us that a euro today is worth more than a euro at a later date, and it allows us to compare sums at different points in time. Risk management shows us ways that risk-averse people can reduce their risk exposure. Asset valuation reflects a firm's future profitability. There is controversy regarding whether stock prices are a rational estimate of a company's true value.

HELPFUL HINTS

1. Compound growth is the same as compound interest. Compound interest is when you earn interest on your previously earned interest. Assuming annual compounding, when you deposit €100 in a bank at 10 per cent, you receive €110 at the end of the year. If you leave it in for two years, you receive compound interest in that you receive €121 at the end of two years—the €100 principal, €10 interest from the first year, €10 interest from the second year, *plus €1 interest on the first year's €10 interest payment.* Next year, interest would be earned not on €100, or €110, but on €121, and so on.

   In like manner, after a number of years, a faster growing economy is applying its percentage growth rate to a much larger base (size of economy) and total output accelerates away from economies that are growing less quickly. For example, applying the rule of 70, an economy that is growing at 1 per cent should double in size after about 70 years (70/1). An economy growing at 4 per cent should double in size every 17.5 years (70/4). After 70 years, the 4 per cent growth economy is 16 times its original size (2^4) while the 1 per cent growth economy is only twice its original size. If both economies started at the same size, the 4 per cent growth economy is now eight times the size of the 1 per cent growth economy because of compound growth.

2. Risk-averse people benefit from insurance because, due to their diminishing marginal utility of wealth, the reduction in utility from a single big expense exceeds the reduction in utility from a number of small payments into the insurance fund. For example, suppose there are 50 people in town. One house burns down each year so each person has a 1 in 50 chance of losing their entire home in any given year. People can pay 1/50 of the value of their home into the insurance fund each year and, thus, they will have paid premiums equal to the value of their home after 50 years. Alternatively, they can fail to buy insurance, but on average they will replace their home once every 50 years due to fire. Although the expected value of these two expenses are the same, risk-averse people choose to buy insurance because the reduction in utility from paying once for one entire home exceeds the reduction in utility from paying 50 times for 1/50 of a home.

3. The volatility of the return of a stock portfolio decreases as the number of stocks in the portfolio increases. When a portfolio is comprised of just one stock, the volatility of the portfolio is the same as the volatility of the single stock. When a portfolio is comprised of two stocks, it could be that when one stock is paying a return that is less than its average, the other may be paying more than its average and the two tend to cancel out. As a result, the portfolio

has less volatility than each of the stocks in the portfolio. This effect continues as the number of stocks in the portfolio increases. However, the majority of the risk reduction occurs by the time there are 20 or 30 stocks in the portfolio. Note that in order to achieve the projected risk reduction from diversification, the risks on the stocks must be unrelated. Therefore, randomly choosing stocks should generate more risk reduction than choosing stocks of firms that are, for example, all in the same industry or all located in the same geographic area.

4. The price of a stock depends on supply and demand. The demand for a stock depends on the present value of the stream of dividend payments and the final sales price. Therefore, an increase in either the expected dividends or the final sales price, or a decrease in the prevailing interest rate, will increase the demand for a stock and increase its price. The demand for a stock also depends on risk factors associated with the stock. Because people are risk averse, an increase in aggregate risk will reduce the demand for all stocks and all stock prices should decrease. Oddly, an increase in idiosyncratic risk (the portion of the standard deviation in the returns on a particular stock that are associated with the specific company) should not affect the demand for the stock because this type of risk can be eliminated through diversification.

TERMS AND DEFINITIONS

Choose a definition for each key term.

Key terms:

_____ Finance

_____ Present value

_____ Future value

_____ Compounding

_____ Diversification

_____ Idiosyncratic risk

_____ Aggregate risk

_____ Fundamental Analysis

_____ Efficient markets hypothesis

_____ Informationally efficient

_____ Random walk

Definitions:

1. Reflecting all available information in a rational way

2. The amount of money today that would be needed to produce, using prevailing interest rates, a given future amount of money

3. The study of a company's accounting statements and future prospects to determine its value

4. The field that studies how people make decisions regarding the allocation of resources over time and the handling of risk

5. The path of a variable whose changes are impossible to predict

6. Risk that affects only a single economic agent

7. The accumulation of a sum of money in an account where interest is earned on previously paid interest

8. The theory according to which asset prices reflect all publicly available information about the value of an asset

9. The amount of money in the future that an amount of money today will yield, given prevailing interest rates

10. The reduction of risk achieved by replacing a single risk with a large number of smaller unrelated risks

11. Risk that affects all economic agents at once

PROBLEMS AND SHORT-ANSWER QUESTIONS

Practice Problems

1. Whitewater Raft Tour Company can purchase rafts today for €100,000. They will earn a €40,000 return on the rafts at the end of each of the next three years.
   a. If the interest rate were 12 per cent, what is the present value of each of the future returns that Whitewater Raft expects to receive?
   b. If the interest rate were 12 per cent, should Whitewater Raft invest in the rafts? Explain.
   c. If the interest rate were 7 per cent, should Whitewater Raft invest in the rafts? Explain.
   d. Compare your answers to parts (b) and (c) above. What general principle about the relationship between investment and the interest rate is demonstrated?

2. Use the *rule of 70* to answer the following questions. Suppose that real GDP/person in Fastcountry grows at an annual rate of 2 per cent and that real GDP/person in Slowcountry grows at an annual rate of 1 per cent.
   a. How many years does it take for real GDP/person to double in Fastcountry?
   b. If real GDP/person in Fastcountry is €2,000 in 1930, how much will it be in the year 2000?
   c. How many years does it take for real GDP/person to double in Slowcountry?
   d. If real GDP/person in Slowcountry is €2,000 in 1930, how much will it be in the year 2000?
   e. Use the numbers you calculated above to help explain the concept of compound growth.
   f. If Fastcountry stopped growing in the year 2000, how many years would it take for the standard of living in Slowcountry to catch that of Fastcountry?

3. For each of the following, determine the type of problem from which the insurance market suffers (adverse selection or moral hazard) and explain.
   a. Susan buys health insurance at the non-smoker rate. After she obtains the rate, she begins smoking again.
   b. Bryce discovers that he has a liver condition that will shorten his life. He seeks life insurance to help pay for his children's college expenses.
   c. Fred gets a new job and will have to commute to London. Fearing that he will be involved in a car accident in the heavy traffic, he changes his car insurance policy from third party, fire and theft (the basic policy) to fully comprehensive.
   d. After Lisa gets fire insurance on her house, she burns fires in the fireplace without closing the fireplace doors.

Short-Answer Questions

1. Suppose that the interest rate is 6 per cent. Which would you prefer to receive: €100 today or €110 one year from today? Why?

2. Suppose you put €100 in your savings account at your bank. If your account earns 8 per cent interest and it is compounded annually, how much will be in your account after one year? After two years? How much more interest did you earn in the second year? Why?

3. You just won a lottery that pays you €100,000 at the end of each of the next three years. Alternatively, the lottery is willing to pay you a lesser amount in one lump sum today. What is the least you should accept in a lump sum payment today if the interest rate is 9 per cent? Explain.

4. According to the *rule of 70*, how long will it take for your income to double if you get a 5 per cent raise every year? If you start work at the age of 23 earning €40,000 per year and get a 5 per cent raise every year, how much will you be earning if you retire at 65?

5. What property of an individual's utility function is necessary for that individual to be risk averse? Explain.

6. Suppose that people wreck their cars once every ten years and the autos are a total loss. People can buy insurance with annual premiums of 1/10 of the value of a car. Would a risk-averse person buy collision insurance for his car? Why?

7. What are the two types of risk someone faces when they buy stock? Which type of risk can be reduced with diversification and which type cannot? Explain.

8. Which are riskier, stocks or government bonds? Why? How can people use this information to adjust the amount of risk they face? If people reduce risk in this way, what happens to their return? Explain.

9. What are three ways that people can reduce the risk they face in their investment portfolios?

10. What is fundamental analysis and what are three ways to perform fundamental analysis?

SELF-TEST

True/False Questions

_____ 1. If interest is compounded annually, €100 placed in a bank account earning 10 per cent interest should generate €30 interest after three years.

_____ 2. According to the *rule of 70*, if your income grows at 7 per cent per year, it will double in ten years.

_____ 3. The present value of a future sum is the amount of money today that would be needed, at prevailing interest rates, to produce that future sum.

_____ 4. If people are risk averse, the utility gained from winning €1,000 is equal to the utility lost from losing a €1,000 bet.

_____ 5. If someone's utility function exhibits diminishing marginal utility of wealth, this person is risk averse.

_____ 6. The insurance market demonstrates the problem of adverse selection when those that are sicker than average seek health insurance.

_____ 7. People can reduce what is known as *aggregate risk* by diversifying their portfolios.

_____ 8. Increasing the diversification of a portfolio from 1 stock to 10 stocks reduces the portfolio's risk by the same amount as increasing the diversification from 10 to 20 stocks.

_____ 9. The efficient markets hypothesis suggests that since markets are efficient, it is easy to engage in fundamental analysis to purchase undervalued stock and then earn greater than average market returns.

_____10. If the efficient markets hypothesis is true, stock prices follow a random walk. Therefore, buying a diversified portfolio, by purchasing an index fund or by throwing darts at the stock page, is probably the best that you can do.

Multiple-Choice Questions

1. BMW has the opportunity to purchase a new factory today that will provide them with a €50 million return four years from now. If prevailing interest rates are 6 per cent, what is the maximum that the project can cost for BMW to be willing to undertake the project?
   a. €34,583,902.
   b. €39,604,682.
   c. €43,456,838.
   d. €50,000,000.
   e. €53,406,002.

2. An increase in the prevailing interest rate
   a. decreases the present value of future returns from investment, and decreases investment.
   b. decreases the present value of future returns from investment, and increases investment.
   c. increases the present value of future returns from investment, and decreases investment.
   d. increases the present value of future returns from investment, and increases investment.

3. If people are risk averse, then
   a. they dislike bad things more than they like comparably good things.
   b. their utility functions exhibit the property of diminishing marginal utility of wealth.
   c. the utility they would lose from losing a €50 bet would exceed the utility they would gain from winning a €50 bet.
   d. all of the above are true.
   e. none of the above are true.

4. Idiosyncratic risk is the
   a. uncertainty associated with the entire economy.
   b. uncertainty associated with specific companies.
   c. risk associated with moral hazard.
   d. risk associated with adverse selection.

5. Compared to a portfolio composed entirely of stock, a portfolio that is 50 per cent government bonds and 50 per cent stock will have a
   a. higher return and a higher level of risk.
   b. higher return and a lower level of risk.
   c. lower return and a lower level of risk.
   d. lower return and a higher level of risk.

6. The study of a company's accounting statements and future prospects to determine its value is known as
   a. diversification.
   b. risk management.
   c. information analysis.
   d. fundamental analysis.

7. Which of the following reduces risk in a portfolio the greatest?
   a. increasing the number of stocks in the portfolio from 1 to 10.
   b. increasing the number of stocks from 10 to 20.
   c. increasing the number of stocks from 20 to 30.
   d. All of the above provide the same amount of risk reduction.

8. Which of the following should cause the price of a share of stock to rise?
   a. a reduction in aggregate risk.
   b. an increase in expected dividends.
   c. a reduction in the interest rate.
   d. all of the above.
   e. none of the above.

9. Speculative bubbles may occur in the stock market
   a. when stocks are fairly valued.
   b. only when people are irrational.
   c. because rational people may buy an overvalued stock if they think they can sell it to someone for even more at a later date.
   d. during periods of extreme pessimism because so many stocks become undervalued.

10. Stock prices will follow a random walk if
    a. people behave irrationally when choosing stock.
    b. markets reflect all available information in a rational way.
    c. stocks are undervalued.
    d. stocks are overvalued.

ADVANCED CRITICAL THINKING

You are a student in the business college at an exclusive private university. The tuition is extremely expensive. Near the end of your senior year, your parents come to visit you in your room. As they enter the room, they see you throwing darts at the stock pages on your bulletin board. You inform them that you received an enormous signing bonus from the company for which you agreed to work after graduation. You are now in the process of picking the stocks in which you plan to invest. Your parents are horrified and they want their money back for your expensive education. Your father says, 'There's got to be a better way to choose stocks. I can give you the phone number of my stock analyst or you could at least buy a well-known, well-managed investment trust.'

1. What is the stock valuation method to which your father is referring, and what is its goal?

2. Explain the efficient markets hypothesis to your parents. If the efficient markets hypothesis is true, can your father's method for picking stocks achieve its goal?

3. If the efficient markets hypothesis is true, what is the only goal of your dart throwing exercise? Explain.

4. If the efficient markets hypothesis is true, which will likely provide the greater return in the long run: your dart throwing exercise or an actively managed investment trust? Why?

SOLUTIONS

Terms and Definitions

_1_	Informationally efficient	_7_	Compounding
_2_	Present value	_8_	Efficient markets hypothesis
_3_	Fundamental analysis	_9_	Future value
_4_	Finance	_10_	Diversification
_5_	Random walk	_11_	Aggregate risk
_6_	Idiosyncratic risk		

Practice Problems

1. a. €40,000/1.12 = €35,714.29; €40,000/(1.12)^2 = €31,887.76; €40,000/(1.12)^3 = €28,471.21.
   b. No, the cost is €100,000 but the present value of the return is only €96,073.26.
   c. Yes. Although the cost is still €100,000, the present value of the returns is now the sum of €40,000/1.07; €40,000/(1.07)^2; €40,000/(1.07)^3 which is €104,972.65.
   d. Investment is inversely related to the interest rate—lower interest rates stimulate investment.

2. a. 70/2 = 35 years.
   b. €8,000.
   c. 70/1 = 70 years.
   d. €4,000.
   e. Fastcountry adds €2,000 to its GDP/person in the first 35 years. Growing at the same per cent, it adds €4,000 to its GDP over the next 35 years because the same growth rate is now applied to a larger base.
   f. Another 70 years.

3. a. Moral hazard, because after she obtained the insurance, she is less careful with her health.
   b. Adverse selection, because after he knows that his probability of death is higher than average, he seeks life insurance.
   c. Adverse selection, because after he knows that his probability of an accident is higher than average, he seeks more auto insurance.
   d. Moral hazard, because after she obtains the insurance, she becomes less careful with fire.

Short-Answer Questions

1. You should prefer €110 one year from today because the PV of €110 one year from today is €110/1.06 = €103.77 and this is greater than €100.

2. After one year: €100(1.08) = €108. After two years: €100(1.08)^2 = €100(1.1664) = €116.64. The account earned €0.64 more interest in the second year because the account earned interest on the first year's interest payment: 0.08(€8) = €0.64.

3. The least you should accept is the present value of the future stream of payments which is: €100,000/1.09 + €100,000/(1.09)^2 + €100,000/(1.09)^3 = €91,743.12 + €84,168.00 + €77,218.35 = €253,129.47.

4. 70/5 = 14 years. Your income would double three time in the 42-year period or €40,000(2)^3 = €320,000 per year.

5. Diminishing marginal utility of wealth. Therefore, the increase in utility from a €1 gain is less than the decrease in utility from a €1 loss.

6. Yes. Due to diminishing marginal utility of wealth, the reduction in utility from a lump sum payment to replace a car exceeds the reduction in utility from the payment of 10 premiums of 1/10 of the value of a car.

7. Idiosyncratic risk—the uncertainty associated with specific companies, and aggregate risk—the uncertainty associated with the entire economy. Idiosyncratic risk can be eliminated with diversification because when one firm does poorly another unrelated firm may do well reducing the volatility in returns. Aggregate risk cannot be reduced because when the entire economy does poorly, the market portfolio does poorly.

8. Stocks, because the standard deviation in the returns to government bonds is zero while the standard deviation in stock returns is significantly higher. People can vary the proportion they invest in stocks versus risk-free government bonds. Low-risk assets generate low returns, and so putting a larger portion of the portfolio in government bonds lowers the return of the portfolio.

9. Buy insurance, diversify a portfolio, and accept a lower return on the portfolio.

10. Determining a company's value by analysing its accounting statements and future prospects. You can do it yourself, rely on financial analysts, or buy an investment trust that is actively managed.

True/False Questions

1. F; €10 the first year, €11 the second year, €12.10 the third year for a total of €33.10.

2. T

3. T

4. F; the utility lost from losing €1,000 is greater.

5. T

6. T

7. F; diversification reduces idiosyncratic risk.

8. F; diversification of a portfolio from 1 stock to 10 stocks reduces the portfolio's risk to a greater degree.

9. F; if markets are efficient, stocks are always fairly valued.

10. T

Multiple-Choice Questions

1. b		5. c		9. c	
2. a		6. d		10. b	
3. d		7. a			
4. b		8. d			

Advanced Critical Thinking

1. Fundamental analysis is the detailed analysis of a firm's accounting statements and future prospects to determine its value. The goal is to choose stocks that are undervalued—those whose stock prices are less than their values.

2. The efficient markets hypothesis argues that the stock market is informationally efficient in that it reflects all available information about the value of the traded stocks. That is, market participants monitor news that affects the value of a stock. Since at any given time the number of buyers of a stock equals the number of sellers, an equal number of people think a stock is undervalued as overvalued. Thus, stock is fairly valued all the time and its price should follow a random walk. If true, it is not possible to consistently buy undervalued stock.

3. The only thing a person can do is diversify their portfolio to reduce idiosyncratic risk.

4. If you throw enough darts to remove most of the idiosyncratic risk (your portfolio starts to resemble the entire market like an index fund) and if you bought and held the stock (you didn't trade often), then it is likely that throwing darts would give you the greater return. This is because active managers of investment trusts incur trading costs and charge fees as compensation for their alleged expertise, yet they cannot reduce aggregate risk.

⌐In this chapter you will
Learn about the data used to
measure the level of unemployment

Consider how unemployment
arises from the process of job
search

Consider how unemployment can
result from minimum-wage laws

See how unemployment can arise
from bargaining between firms and
unions

Examine how unemployment
results when firms choose to pay
efficiency wages

⌐You should be able to
Use data on the number of
employed, unemployed, and not in
the labour force to calculate the
unemployment rate and the
labour-force participation rate

Explain why some job search
unemployment is inevitable

Show diagrammatically the impact
of the minimum wage on high
wage and low wage sectors

List the reasons why unions cause
unemployment and, alternatively,
why unions might increase
efficiency in some cases

Describe the four reasons why
firms may choose to pay wages in
excess of the competitive wage

UNEMPLOYMENT

CHAPTER OVERVIEW

Context and Purpose

Chapter 28 is the fourth chapter in a four-chapter sequence on the level and growth of output in the long run. In Chapter 25, we learned that capital and labour are among the primary determinants of output and growth. In Chapter 26, we addressed how saving and investment in capital goods affect the production of output. In Chapter 27, we learned about some of the tools people and firms use when choosing capital projects in which to invest. In Chapter 28, we see how full utilization of our labour resources improves the level of production and our standard of living.

The purpose of Chapter 28 is to introduce you to the labour market. We will see how economists measure the performance of the labour market using unemployment statistics. We will also address a number of sources of unemployment and some policies that the government might use to lower certain types of unemployment.

CHAPTER REVIEW

Introduction

If a country keeps its workers fully employed, it achieves a higher level of GDP than if it leaves many workers idle. In this chapter, we are concerned largely with the **natural rate of unemployment**, which is the amount of unemployment that the economy experiences in the long run. 'Natural' does not mean constant or impervious to economic policy. It means that it is the unemployment that doesn't go away on its own. This chapter discusses the measurement and interpretation of unemployment statistics, and some causes and cures for unemployment.

Identifying Unemployment

Government statisticians use the claimant count to measure the number of adults (16 and over) who are unemployed. They derive an estimate of the total labour force in employment from income tax returns. Adding to this the number of unemployment benefit claimants is a measure of the total labour force, and expressing the claimant count as a proportion of the labour force is a measure of the unemployment rate. The government also relies on labour force surveys based on procedures established by the International Labour Office (ILO). In the UK about 60,000 households are surveyed every quarter. According to the responses received, adults are classed at employed, unemployed or not in the labour force.

- employed: worked most of the previous week at a paid job

- unemployed: on temporary layoff, or looked for a job, or waiting to start a new job

- not in the labour force: not in previous two categories (student, homemaker, retired) Government statisticians then compute:

- labour force = number of employed + number of unemployed

- unemployment rate = (number of unemployed/labour force) × 100

- labour-force participation rate = (labour force/adult pop.) × 100.

The **labour force** includes all people who have made themselves available for work. The **unemployment rate** is the per cent of the labour force that is unemployed. The **labour force participation rate** is the per cent of the total adult population who are in the labour force. The unemployment rate and the labour force participation rate varies widely across demographic groups—men, women, ethnic minorities, young, old.

The long run equilibrium rate of unemployment around which the unemployment rate fluctuates is the *natural rate of unemployment*, The deviation in unemployment from the natural rate is known as **cyclical unemployment**.

Unemployment statistics might inaccurately measure the actual rate of unemployment because

- Some people are counted in the labour force but unemployed even though they are only pretending to look for work so that they can collect government assistance or because they are being paid 'cash in hand'. This behaviour biases the unemployment statistics upward.

- Some people have had an unsuccessful search for a job and have given up looking for work so they are not counted in the labour force. These individuals are called **discouraged workers**. This behaviour biases the unemployment statistics downward.

Knowledge about the duration of unemployment spells might help design corrective policies for unemployment. Evidence suggests that *most spells are short-term, but most unemployment at any given time is long-term*. This means that many people are unemployed for short periods, but a few people are unemployed for very long periods. Economists think short-term unemployment is much less of a social problem than long-term unemployment.

In most markets, prices adjust to balance supply and demand. In the ideal labour market, wages would adjust so that there would be no unemployment. However, even when the economy is buoyant, the unemployment rate never falls to zero. The following sections offer four reasons why the labour market falls short of the ideal market. The first source of unemployment we discuss is due to job search. **Frictional unemployment** is the unemployment that results from the time it takes for workers to search for the jobs that best suit their tastes and skills. The next three sources of unemployment fall within the category of structural unemployment. **Structural unemployment** is the unemployment that results because the number of jobs available in some labour markets is insufficient for everyone who wants a job to find one. Structural unemployment occurs because the wage is held above the equilibrium wage. Three possible sources to an excessive wage are minimum-wage laws, unions, and efficiency wages. Frictional unemployment tends to explain shorter spells of unemployment, while structural unemployment tends to explain longer spells of unemployment.

Job Search

Job search is the process of matching workers and jobs. Just as workers differ in their skills and tastes, jobs differ in their attributes. Moreover, information about jobs disseminates slowly. Therefore, it takes time for job candidates and job vacancies to match. *Frictional unemployment* is due to this search time.

Frictional unemployment is inevitable in a dynamic economy. As the demand for products changes, some industries and regions will experience growth while others will contract. These changes in the composition of demand among industries or regions are called *sectoral shifts*. Sectoral shifts cause temporary frictional unemployment as workers in contracting sectors lose their jobs and search for work in the growing sectors.

Frictional unemployment might be reduced by improved information about job openings provided by the Internet. Government might be able to lower frictional unemployment by engaging in activities that shorten the job search time. Two such programs are (1) government-run employment agencies (job centres) that give out information on employment vacancies to help match workers and jobs, and (2) public training schemes to retrain workers laid off from contracting sectors. Critics argue that government is ill-suited to do these things and that the market does a more efficient job at matching and retraining.

Unemployment insurance (referred to as National Insurance in the UK) pays laid off workers a certain sum for a period of time. Unemployment insurance increases frictional unemployment because unemployed workers are more likely to (1) devote less effort to their job search, (2) turn down unattractive job offers, and (3) be less concerned with job security. This does not mean unemployment insurance is bad. Unemployment insurance does provide the worker partial protection against job loss and it may improve the efficiency of the job market by allowing workers to search longer for the most suitable job match.

Minimum-Wage Laws

Structural unemployment results when the number of jobs is insufficient for the number of workers. Minimum-wage laws are one source of structural unemployment. Recall that minimum-wage laws usually force the wage to remain above the equilibrium wage. This causes the quantity of labour supplied to exceed the quantity of labour demanded and implies a surplus of labour or unemployment. Since the equilibrium wage for most workers exceeds the minimum wage, the minimum wage tends to cause unemployment only for the least skilled and least experienced, such as teenagers.

Although only a small portion of total unemployment is due to the minimum wage, an analysis of the minimum wage points out a general rule: *If a wage is held above the equilibrium level, the result is unemployment.* The next two sections develop two additional reasons why the wage may be held above the equilibrium level. That is, the next two sections provide two additional sources for structural unemployment.

Note that with frictional unemployment, workers are *searching* for the right job even if the wage is at the competitive equilibrium. In contrast, structural unemployment exists because the wage exceeds the competitive equilibrium wage and workers are *waiting* for jobs to open up.

Unions and Collective Bargaining

A **union** is a worker association that engages in **collective bargaining** with employers over wages and working conditions. A union is a cartel because it is a group of sellers organized to exert market power. If the union and firm fail to reach an agreement, the union can **strike**—that is, withdraw its labour services from the firm. Because of the threat of a strike, workers in unions are likely to be more successful in gaining wage increases than would otherwise be possible.

Unions benefit *insiders* (members) at the expense of *outsiders* (non members). When the union raises the wage above the equilibrium wage, unemployment results. Insiders earn higher wages and outsiders are either unemployed or must take jobs with non-union firms. This increases the supply of labour in the non-union sector and lowers the wage further for non-union workers.

Most cartels are illegal, but unions are exempt from competition laws because it is believed that workers need market power to bargain with their employer.

There is little agreement about whether unions are good or bad for the economy. Critics argue that unions are cartels that raise the price of labour above the competitive equilibrium. This is inefficient (causes unemployment) and inequitable (insiders gain at the expense of outsiders). Supporters of unions argue that firms have market power and are able to depress the wage, so unions are just a counterbalance to the firm's power. This is most likely to be true in a *company town* where one firm hires most of the workers in the region. Supporters also argue that unions are efficient because firms don't have to bargain with individual workers about salary and benefits. That is, unions may reduce transactions costs.

The Theory of Efficiency Wages

The theory of **efficiency wages** suggests that firms may intentionally hold wages above the competitive equilibrium because it is efficient for them to do so. Efficiency wages are similar in their effect to minimum-wage laws and unions, because, in all three cases, unemployment results from wages being held above the equilibrium wage. However, an efficiency wage is unusual in that it is paid voluntarily by the firm. Below, we consider four reasons why firms might find it efficient (or profitable) to pay a wage in excess of the competitive equilibrium:

- *Worker health* may be improved by paying a higher wage. Better paid workers eat a better diet and are more productive. This is more applicable to firms in developing nations and is probably not relevant for firms in the UK.

- *Worker turnover* may be reduced by paying a higher wage because workers will find it difficult to find alternative jobs at the higher wage. Firms might find it profitable to reduce worker turnover because there is a cost associated with hiring and training new workers and because new workers are not as experienced.

- *Worker effort* might be increased by paying a higher wage. When a worker's effort cannot be easily monitored, workers might shirk their responsibilities. If caught and fired, a worker earning the competitive equilibrium wage can easily find another job at the same wage. Higher wages make workers eager to keep their jobs and might encourage greater effort and initiative on their part.

- *Worker quality* can be improved by paying a higher wage. Firms cannot perfectly gauge the quality of their job applicants. Higher quality workers have a higher *reservation wage*—the minimum wage they are willing to accept. By paying a wage above the competitive equilibrium, firms have a higher probability of attracting high quality applicants for a job opening.

HELPFUL HINTS

1. Job search takes time even at the competitive equilibrium wage. Minimum-wage laws, unions, and efficiency wages all create an excess supply of labour

(unemployment) by holding the wage above the competitive equilibrium wage. However, frictional unemployment exists even at the competitive equilibrium wage because it is inevitable that it takes time for workers and firms to match regardless of the wage. For this reason, structural unemployment resulting from the wage being held above the equilibrium wage can often be thought of as additional unemployment beyond the inherent frictional unemployment.

2. The natural rate of unemployment is persistent, not constant. Changes in minimum-wage laws, unions, efficiency wages, and changes in the job search process due to the information revolution all have an impact on the natural rate of unemployment. Therefore, the natural rate will change as government policies, institutions, and behaviours change. But since policies, institutions, and behaviours change slowly, so does the natural rate of unemployment.

TERMS AND DEFINITIONS

Choose a definition for each key term.

Key terms:

____ Natural rate of unemployment

____ Cyclical unemployment

____ Labour force

____ Unemployment rate

____ Labour-force participation rate

____ Discouraged workers

____ Structural unemployment

____ Union

____ Collective bargaining

____ Strike

____ Insiders

____ Outsiders

____ Efficiency wages

____ Reservation wage

____ Frictional unemployment

____ Sectoral shifts

____ National insurance

Definitions:

1. Workers who stop looking for work due to an unsuccessful search

2. The deviation of the unemployment rate from its natural rate

3. Wages voluntarily paid in excess of the competitive equilibrium wage to increase worker productivity

4. Changes in the composition of demand across industries or regions

5. The lowest wage a worker will accept

6. Unemployment due to the time it takes for workers to search for the jobs that best suit their tastes and skills

7. Normal rate of unemployment about which the unemployment rate fluctuates

8. Percentage of the adult population in the labour force

9. An organized withdrawal of labour from the firm

10. Worker association that bargains with employers over wages and working conditions

11. Those employed in union jobs

12. A government programme that pays laid off workers benefit when they are unemployed

13. The total number of workers, which is the sum of the unemployed and the employed

14. Unemployment that results because the number of jobs available in some labour market is insufficient for everyone who wants a job to get one.

15. Percentage of the labour force that is unemployed

16. The process by which unions and firms agree on labour contracts

17. Those not employed in union jobs

PROBLEMS AND SHORT-ANSWER QUESTIONS

Practice Problems

1. Use the following information about Employment Country to answer question 1. Numbers are in millions.

	2004	2005
population	223.6	226.5
adult population	168.2	169.5
number of unemployed	7.4	8.1
number of employed	105.2	104.2

   a. What is the labour force in 2004 and 2005?
   b. What is the labour force participation rate in 2004 and 2005?
   c. What is the unemployment rate in 2004 and 2005?
   d. From 2004 to 2005, the adult population went up while the labour force went down. Provide a number of explanations why this might have occurred.
   e. If the natural rate of unemployment in Employment Country is 6.6 per cent, how much is cyclical unemployment in 2004 and 2005? Is Employment Country likely to be experiencing a recession in either of these years?

2. Suppose the labour market is segmented into two distinct markets: the market for low-skill workers and the market for high-skill workers. Further, suppose the competitive equilibrium wage in the low-skill market is €3.00/hour while the competitive equilibrium wage in the high-skill market is €15.00/hour.
   a. If the minimum wage is set at €5.00/hour, which market will exhibit the greatest amount of unemployment? Use Exhibit 1 to demonstrate this diagrammatically.
   b. Does the minimum wage have any impact on the high skill market? Why?
   c. Do your results seem consistent with labour market statistics? Explain.
   d. Suppose the high-skill market becomes unionized and the new negotiated wage is €18.00/hour. Will this have any affect on the low skill market? Explain.

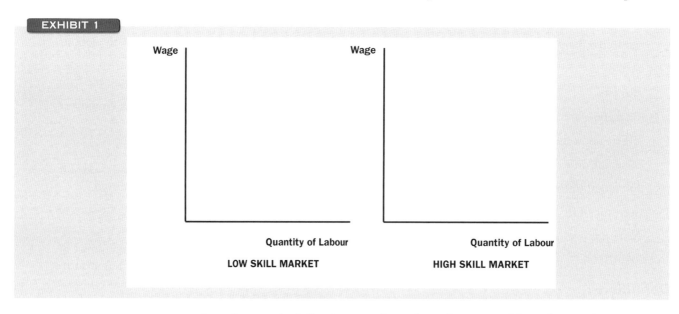

EXHIBIT 1

LOW SKILL MARKET   HIGH SKILL MARKET

3. Answer the following questions about the composition of unemployment.
   a. What are some of the sources of unemployment?
   b. Which type of unemployment is initiated by the firm?
   c. Why might a firm pay wages in excess of the competitive equilibrium?

d. Which type of efficiency wage is unlikely to be relevant in the UK? Why?

e. How does frictional unemployment differ from the other sources of unemployment?

Short-Answer Questions

1. Name two reasons why the unemployment rate is an imperfect measure of joblessness.

2. Explain the statement, 'Most spells of unemployment are short, and most unemployment observed at any given time is long term'.

3. Where would a labour union be more likely to increase efficiency rather than reduce it: a small remote town with one large employer or a major city with many employers? Why?

4. Name two ways that a union increases the disparity in wages between members and non-members.

5. If a union succeeds in raising the wages of its members above the existing equilibrium rate, does this always cause unemployment for union members? Explain.

6. Does the minimum wage cause much unemployment in the market for accountants? Why?

7. Which type of unemployment will occur even if the wage is at the competitive equilibrium? Why?

8. What is 'natural' about the natural rate of unemployment?

9. Does the existence of a natural rate of unemployment imply that the rate of unemployment does not change in the long run?

10. Which of the following individuals is most likely to be unemployed for the long term: a farrier who loses his job when hunting with hounds is banned, or a waitress who is laid off when a new cafe opens in town and her existing place of work closes? Why?

SELF-TEST

True/False Questions

_____ 1. The natural rate of unemployment can be reduced in the short run but not in the long run.

_____ 2. If the unemployment rate falls, we can be certain that more workers have jobs.

_____ 3. Since the mid 80s the labour-force participation rate in the UK has been rising for women and has been falling for men.

_____ 4. A minimum wage is likely to have a greater impact on the market for skilled workers than on the market for unskilled workers.

_____ 5. Paying efficiency wages tends to increase worker turnover because workers can get continually higher wages if they frequently change jobs.

_____ 6. Firms might voluntarily pay wages above the level that balances the supply and demand for workers because the higher wage improves the average quality of workers that apply for employment.

_____ 7. If wages were always at the competitive equilibrium, there would be absolutely no unemployment.

_____ 8. Due to the existence of 'discouraged workers', the official unemployment rate might overstate true unemployment.

_____ 9. The presence of unemployment insurance (national insurance in the UK) tends to decrease the unemployment rate because recipients of unemployment benefits are not counted in the labour force.

_____10. In general, paying efficiency wages will lead to job losses in firms paying efficiency wages.

Multiple-Choice Questions

1. According to the Office for National Statistics, a husband who chooses to stay home and take care of the household is
    a. unemployed.
    b. employed.
    c. not in the labour force.
    d. a discouraged worker.

Use the following table for questions 2 through 4. Numbers are in millions.

total population	58.8
adult population	47.3
number of unemployed	1.4
number of employed	28.4

2. The labour force is
    a. 28.4 million.
    b. 29.8 million.
    c. 45.9 million.
    d. 47.3 million.

3. The unemployment rate is
    a. 1.4 per cent.
    b. 3.0 per cent.
    c. 4.7 per cent.
    d. 4.9 per cent.

4. The labour-force participation rate is
    a. 48.3 per cent.
    b. 50.7 per cent.
    c. 60.0 per cent.
    d. 63.0 per cent.

5. Which one of the following types of unemployment results from the wage being held above the competitive equilibrium wage?
    a. structural unemployment.
    b. cyclical unemployment.
    c. frictional unemployment.
    d. sectoral unemployment.

6. If, for any reason, the wage is held above the competitive equilibrium wage,
    a. unions will likely strike and the wage will fall to equilibrium.
    b. the quality of workers in the applicant pool will tend to fall.
    c. the quantity of labour supplied will exceed the quantity of labour demanded and there will be unemployment.
    d. the quantity of labour demanded will exceed the quantity of labour supplied and there will be a labour shortage.

7. A 'reservation wage' is the
    a. maximum wage the firm is willing to pay.
    b. minimum wage the worker is willing to accept.
    c. efficiency wage.
    d. competitive equilibrium wage.

8. Which of the following government policies would fail to lower the unemployment rate?
   a. reduce unemployment benefits.
   b. establish employment agencies.
   c. establish worker training programs.
   d. raise the minimum wage.

9. Some frictional unemployment is inevitable because
   a. efficiency wages may hold the wage above the equilibrium wage.
   b. of minimum wage laws.
   c. there are changes in the demand for labour among different firms.
   d. of unions.
   e. all of the above.

10. Unions tend to increase the disparity in pay between insiders and outsiders by
    a. increasing the wage in the unionized sector which may create an increase in the supply of workers in the non-unionized sector.
    b. increasing the wage in the unionized sector which may create a decrease in the supply of workers in the non-unionized sector.
    c. decreasing the demand for workers in the unionized sector.
    d. increasing the demand for workers in the unionized sector.

ADVANCED CRITICAL THINKING

You are watching the national news with your roommate. The news reader says, 'Unemployment statistics released by the Department of Labour today show an increase in unemployment from 6.1 per cent to 6.2 per cent. This is the third month in a row where the unemployment rate has increased.' Your roommate says, 'Every month there are fewer and fewer people with jobs. I don't know how much longer the country can continue like this.'

1. Can your roommate's statement be deduced from the unemployment rate statistic? Why?

2. What information would you need to determine whether there are really fewer people with jobs?

SOLUTIONS

Terms and Definitions

1	Discouraged workers	7	Natural rate of unemployment	13	Labour force
2	Cyclical unemployment	8	Labour force participation rate	14	Structural unemployment
3	Efficiency wages	9	Strike	15	Unemployment rate
4	Sectoral shifts	10	Union	16	Collective bargaining
5	Reservation wage	11	Insiders	17	Outsiders
6	Frictional unemployment	12	National insurance		

Practice Problems

1. a. 2004: $7.4 + 105.2 = 112.6$ million.
      2005: $8.1 + 104.2 = 112.3$ million.
   b. 2004: $(112.6/168.2) \times 100 = 66.9\%$.
      2005: $(112.3/169.5) \times 100 = 66.3\%$.
   c. 2004: $(7.4/112.6) \times 100 = 6.6\%$.
      2005: $(8.1/112.3) \times 100 = 7.2\%$.

d. Earlier retirements, students staying in college longer, more parents staying at home with children, discouraged workers discontinuing their job search.

e. 2004: 6.6% − 6.6% = 0%
2005: 7.2% − 6.6% = 0.6%

In 2004, unemployment is 'normal' for Employment Country; therefore, there is no recession. However, in 2005, unemployment is above normal (positive cyclical unemployment), so Employment Country may be in a recession.

2. a. The low-skill market will experience unemployment because there will be an excess supply of labour. (See Exhibit 2.)

EXHIBIT 2

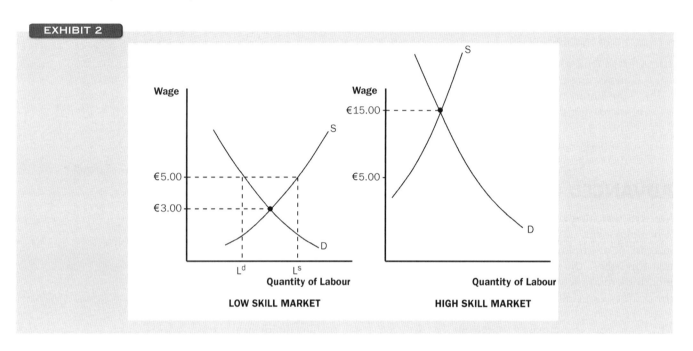

b. No, because the competitive equilibrium wage is above the wage floor.

c. Yes. We observe a greater amount of unemployment among low-skill workers who are often young and inexperienced.

d. Yes. The excess supply of skilled workers may cause some skilled workers to move to the unskilled market increasing the supply of labour in the unskilled market, further reducing the competitive equilibrium wage and causing even more unemployment there.

3. a. Job search, minimum wage, unions, efficiency wages.

b. Efficiency wages.

c. To improve worker health, lower worker turnover, increase worker effort, improve worker quality.

d. Worker health, because in the UK workers' wages are significantly above subsistence.

e. Frictional unemployment exists even when the wage is at a competitive equilibrium.

Short-Answer Questions

1. Some people claim to be looking for work just to collect unemployment benefits or they are being paid 'under the table'. Others are discouraged workers and have stopped looking for work due to an unsuccessful search.

2. Many people are unemployed for short periods. A few people are unemployed for very long periods.

3. In a small 'company' town where a single company has market power that may depress the wage below the competitive equilibrium. This may need to be offset by organized labour.

4. It raises the wage above the competitive equilibrium in the unionized sector. Some of those unemployed in the unionized sector move to the non-unionized sector increasing the supply of labour and lowering the wage in the non-union sector.

5. If all other things remain equal, raising wages above the existing equilibrium will certainly cause some union members to lose their jobs. However, productivity might increase, the firm might be able to increase the price of its product without significant loss of sales, the firm might accept a cut in profits and in all of these cases it does not necessarily follow that higher wages will lead to lost jobs for union members.

6. No, because the competitive equilibrium wage for accountants exceeds the minimum wage and, hence, the minimum wage is not a binding constraint for accountants.

7. Frictional unemployment, because job matching takes time even when the wage is at the competitive equilibrium. Also, continuous sectoral shifts and new entrants into the job market make some frictional unemployment inevitable.

8. The natural rate of unemployment is the rate of unemployment to which the economy tends in the long run. The natural rate of unemployment is natural in the sense that, left to itself and without changes in aggregate demand, the economy would settle at the natural rate of unemployment.

9. The natural rate hypothesis holds that changes in aggregate demand have no impact on the level of unemployment in the long run. This does not imply that the natural rate never changes. It will change as the factors that determine the natural rate (minimum wage legislation, the extent of unemployment insurance, whether firms pay efficiency wages and so on) change.

10. The farrier. He will have to retrain because the reduction in demand for shoeing horses is, to all intents and purposes, permanent. The waitress, on the other hand, might just have to relocate, possibly just down the street.

True/False Questions

1. F; the factors that determine the natural rate are structural and cannot be altered in the short run.

2. F; the unemployment rate also falls when unemployed workers leave the labour force.

3. T

4. F; a minimum wage has a greater impact on low wage workers.

5. F; efficiency wages reduce turnover.

6. T

7. F; there would still be frictional unemployment.

8. F; the official unemployment rate may understate true unemployment.

9. F; unemployment insurance increases the unemployment rate because it increases frictional unemployment.

10. T

Multiple-Choice Questions

1. c	5. a	9. c
2. b	6. c	10. a
3. c	7. b	
4. d	8. d	

Advanced Critical Thinking

1. No. The unemployment rate is the ratio of the number of unemployed to the labour force. If the labour force grows (new graduates, house wives and house husbands entering the labour force) and if few of the new members of the labour force find work, then the unemployment rate will rise but the number of employed could stay the same or even rise.

2. The number of employed is a component of the labour force and you can get information on that number directly.

GOALS

⌐In this chapter you will

Consider what money is and what functions money performs in the economy

Learn what a central bank (the Bank of England in the UK) does

Examine how the banking system helps determine the supply of money

See what tools the central bank uses to alter the supply of money

OUTCOMES

⌐You should be able to

Define money and list the three functions of money

Explain the role of the central bank in money creation

Explain the money multiplier in a fractional reserve banking system

List and explain the three tools the central bank uses to change the money supply

THE MONETARY SYSTEM

CHAPTER OVERVIEW

Context and Purpose

Chapter 29 is the first chapter in a two-chapter sequence dealing with money and prices in the long run. Chapter 29 describes what money is and analyses how the central bank controls the quantity of money. Since the quantity of money influences the rate of inflation in the long run, the following chapter concentrates on the causes and costs of inflation.

The purpose of Chapter 29 is to help you develop an understanding of what money is, what forms money takes, how the banking system helps create money, and how the central bank controls the quantity of money. An understanding of money is important because the quantity of money affects inflation and interest rates in the long run, and production and employment in the short run.

CHAPTER REVIEW

Introduction

If there were no such thing as money, people would have to rely on barter. Barter is when people trade goods and services directly for other goods and services. Barter requires that there be a double coincidence of wants. For a trade to take place, each trader has to have what the other one wants—an unlikely event. The existence of money facilitates production and trade, which allows people to specialize in what they do best and raise the standard of living.

The Meaning of Money

Money is the set of assets commonly used to buy goods and services. That is, money is the portion of someone's wealth that is directly spendable or exchangeable for goods and services.

There are three functions of money:

- Money serves as a **medium of exchange** because money is the most commonly accepted asset when a buyer purchases goods and services from a seller.

- Money serves as a **unit of account** because money is the yardstick with which people post prices and record debts.

- Money serves as a **store of value** because people can use money to transfer purchasing power from the present to the future. Other types of wealth—stocks, bonds, rare art—might be a better store of value, but they are not as good at providing liquidity. **Liquidity** is the ease with which an asset can be converted into a medium of exchange. Money is liquid, but loses value when prices rise. The value of rare art tends to rise with inflation, but it is much less liquid.

Money can be divided into two fundamental types—commodity money and fiat money.

- **Commodity money** is money that has 'intrinsic value'. That is, it has value independent of its use as money. Gold, silver, and cigarettes in a prisoner of war camp are all examples of commodity money. When a country uses gold as money, it is operating under a gold standard.

- **Fiat money** is money without intrinsic value. It is money by government fiat or declaration. Paper pounds sterling (£10 note) are an example of fiat money.

When we measure the quantity of money, sometimes called the money stock, we should clearly include **currency** (paper bills and coins in the hands of the public) and **demand deposits** (balances in bank accounts that can be accessed on demand by cheque) because these assets are a medium of exchange. However, savings balances can easily be transferred into chequeing; other more restrictive chequeing accounts, such as investment trusts, offer some degree of spendability. In an economy with a complex financial system, it is difficult to draw the line between assets that are money and assets that are not. For this reason, in the UK we calculate multiple measures of the money stock, three of which are shown below:

- M0: Sterling notes and coin in circulation outside the Bank of England (including those held in banks' and building societies' tills); and banks' operational deposits with the Bank of England

- M1: Monthly changes of monetary financial institutions' sterling and all foreign currency M1 liabilities to private and public sectors (in sterling millions)

- M4: Monthly amounts outstanding of monetary financial institutions' sterling M4 liabilities to private sector (in sterling millions)

The intricacies of these different definitions of money need not concern us here, but we should note that M0 is a narrow measure of money and reflects immediate spending potential in the economy. M1 is an intermediate measure of money and includes assets that are easily transformed into an immediate means of payment in the economy and M4 is a broad measure of money that includes assets (such as bonds) that can be converted into the means of payment, but whose value is uncertain from one day to the next. For our purposes, we consider money in the UK to be currency and spendable deposits.

Credit cards are not counted in the stock of money because they are not a means of payment but are instead a method of deferring payment. Debit cards are like an electronic cheque in that money from the buyer's account is directly transferred to the seller's account. Thus, the value is already captured by the account balance.

The Central Bank System

The **European Central Bank (ECB)** is the **central bank** of the EU. The ECB was created in 1998 with the primary objective of ensuring price stability throughout the EU.

This is defined as a percentage increase in harmonized index of consumer prices of 2 per cent per annum and ECB has responsibility for implementing a monetary policy designed to achieve this objective.

An important feature of the ECB is its independence from any interference from other central banks or politicians. To ensure this, monetary policy decisions are taken by the Governing Council of the ECB. This is composed of the President and Vice President of the ECB, four other people of high repute in the banking world and the governors of all the central banks from each of the Member States. Each of these has a fixed tenure on the Governing Council and none are politically motivated appointments. The Governing Council meets every two weeks in Frankfurt and decides on the level of the ECB's key interest rate, the refinancing rate.

The **Bank of England** is the **central bank** of the UK. It is designed to oversee the banking system and regulate the quantity of money in the economy.

The Bank of England was founded in 1694 and the most important event in its recent history is that it was granted independence in setting interest rates in 1997. Decisions about adjusting the refinancing (repo) rate are taken by the Monetary Policy Committee consisting of the Governor and two Deputy Governors of the Bank of England, two other members appointed by the Bank after consultation with the Chancellor of the Exchequer (the UK Finance Minister) and four other members appointed by the Chancellor. The Governor and the two Deputy Governors serve five-year renewable terms of office, while other MPC members serve three-year renewable terms. The MPC meets monthly and its interest-rate decision is announced immediately after the meeting.

The central bank has two main jobs:

- to regulate the banks and ensure the health of the banking system. The central bank monitors each bank's financial condition and helps clear cheques. In a crisis, when banks find themselves short of cash, the central bank may act as the *lender of last resort* to the banks.

- to control the quantity of money in the economy, called the **money supply**. The central bank's decisions about the money supply are called **monetary policy**.

The central bank primarily changes the money supply with **open-market operations,** which involves the purchase and sale of bonds from the banking sector in the open market for debt.

- To increase the money supply, the central bank creates currency and uses this to purchase bonds. After the transaction, additional currency is in the hands of the public, so the money supply is larger.

- To decrease the money supply, the central bank sells bonds to the public. After the transaction, less currency is the hands of the public, so the money supply is smaller.

Changing the money supply changes inflation in the long run and may change employment and output in the short run.

Banks and the Money Supply

Recall that the public can hold its money as currency or demand deposits. Since these deposits are in banks, the behaviour of banks affects the money supply. This complicates the central bank's task of controlling the money supply.

The impact that banks have on the money supply can be seen by going through the following three cases:

- Suppose there are *no banks*. Then currency is the only money. If there is €1,000 of currency, there is €1,000 of money.

- Suppose there is *100-per cent-reserve banking*. Deposits that are received by a bank but are not loaned out are called **reserves**. With 100 per cent reserve banking, banks are safe places to store money, but they are not lenders. If the public deposits all €1,000 of its currency in Bank 1, Bank 1's T-account, which records changes in the bank's assets and liabilities, would be the following:

Bank 1

Assets (€)		Liabilities (€)	
Reserves	1,000	Deposits	1,000

Bank 1 has liabilities of €1,000 because it owes the €1,000 deposit back to the depositor. It has assets of €1,000 because it has cash reserves of €1,000 in its vault. Since currency held by the public has gone down by €1,000 and deposits held by the public have increased by €1,000, the money supply is unaffected. *If banks hold all deposits on reserve, banks do not influence the money supply.*

- Suppose there is **fractional reserve banking**. Since few people request the return of their deposit on any given day, Bank 1 need not hold all €1,000 of the deposit as cash reserves. It could lend some of the €1,000 and keep only the remainder on reserve. This is called fractional reserve banking. The fraction of deposits held as reserves is the **reserve ratio**. The central bank sets the minimum reserve ratio with a reserve requirement. Suppose Bank 1 has a *reserve ratio* of 10 per cent which means that it keeps 10 per cent of its deposits on reserve and lends out the rest. Its T-account becomes:

Bank 1

Assets (€)		Liabilities (€)	
Reserves	100	Deposits	1,000
Loans	900		

Bank 1 has created money because it still holds a €1,000 deposit, but now a borrower has €900 in currency. *When banks hold only a fraction of deposits as reserves, banks create money.*

This story is not complete. Suppose the borrower of the €900 spends it and the receiver of the €900 deposits it in Bank 2. If Bank 2 also has a reserve ratio of 10 per cent, its T-account becomes:

Bank 2

Assets (€)		Liabilities (€)	
Reserves	90	Deposits	900
Loans	810		

Bank 2 has created another €810 by its lending activity. Each time money is deposited and a portion of it loaned, more money is created.

If this process continues indefinitely, the total amount of money created by the banking system from the original deposit of €1,000 is €1,000 + €900 + €810 + €729 + ⋯ = €10,000 (in this case, each loan is 90 per cent of the previous loan).

The amount of money the banking system creates from each euro of reserves is called the **money multiplier**. The money multiplier is the reciprocal of the reserve ratio. If R is the reserve ratio, then the money multiplier is $1/R$. In the case described above, the money multiplier is 1/.10 or 10. Thus, €1,000 of new reserves created from the original €1,000 deposit can create a total of €10,000 in deposits. The smaller the reserve ratio, the greater the amount of lending from the same amount of reserves and, hence, the larger the money multiplier. The larger the reserve ratio, the smaller the multiplier.

Fractional reserve banking does not create net wealth because when a bank loans reserves, which creates money (someone's asset), it also creates an equal value debt contract (someone's liability).

The central bank has three main tools it uses to alter the money supply:

- *Open-market operations:* Recall, when the central bank buys government bonds from the public, the euros it uses to pay for them increase the euros in circulation. Each new euro held as currency increases the money supply by one euro. Each euro deposited with banks increases bank reserves and thus increases the money supply by some multiple. When the central bank sells government securities, euros are removed from circulation and reserves are reduced at banks. This reduces lending, and further reduces the money supply. Open market operations can easily be used for small or large changes in the money supply. Hence, it is the day-to-day tool of the central bank.

- *Reserve requirements:* **Reserve requirements** set the minimum reserve ratio for a bank. An increase in the reserve requirement reduces the money multiplier and decreases the money supply. A decrease in the reserve requirement increases the money multiplier and increases the money supply. The central bank rarely changes reserve requirements because changes in reserve requirements disrupt the business of banking. For example, an increase in reserve requirements immediately restricts bank loans.

- *Refinancing rate:* The **refinancing rate** is the interest rate the central bank charges on loans to banks. When the central bank raises the refinancing rate, banks tend to borrow fewer reserves from the central bank and the money supply decreases. When the central bank decreases the discount rate, banks tend to borrow more reserves from the central bank and the money supply increases. The central bank also acts as a lender of last resort to banks during a crisis when depositors withdraw unusually large amounts of their deposits from banks.

Despite this, the central bank's control of the money supply is not precise because:

- The central bank does not control the amount of money people choose to hold as deposits versus currency. When the public deposits a greater amount of their currency, bank reserves increase and the money supply increases.

- The central bank does not control the amount of reserves that the banks lend. The reserve requirement sets the minimum reserve ratio, but banks can hold *excess reserves*—reserves in excess of those required. If banks increase their excess reserves, lending decreases and the money supply decreases.

At times in the past, depositors have sometimes lost confidence in their bank amid fear that, because the bank had made unsound loans, it might become bankrupt. In these circumstances depositors 'run' to withdraw their deposits. This is known as a 'bank run'. With fractional reserves, only a few depositors can immediately get their money back. This behaviour causes a decrease in the money supply for two reasons. First, people increase their holdings of currency by withdrawing deposits from banks. This reduces reserves, bank lending, and the money supply. Secondly, banks, fearing deposit withdrawal, hold excess reserves and further decrease lending and the money supply. This is no longer a problem since banks now take out some kind of deposit insurance against illiquidity up to certain limits. Additionally central banks now widely acknowledge their role as 'lender of last resort' to the banking system and undertake to relieve shortages of liquidity within the system.

HELPFUL HINTS

1. Fiat money maintains value due to artificial scarcity. Gold has value because people desire it for its intrinsic value and because it is naturally scarce (alchemists have never been able to create gold). However, fiat money is cheap and easy to produce. Therefore, fiat money maintains its value only because of self-restraint on the part of the supplier. If euros are a quality store of value, it is because the euro is difficult to counterfeit and the ECB shows self-restraint in the supply of euros.

2. Paper euros are considered 'currency' only when in the hands of the non-bank public. When economists use the word currency, we mean currency in the hands of the non-bank public. When you deposit currency in the bank, you now own a deposit and your paper euros are now the reserves of the bank. Currency in the hands of the non-bank public has decreased while deposits have increased by an equal amount. At this point, the money supply is unaltered because money is the sum of currency (in the hands of the non-bank public) and deposits.

3. The money multiplier is most easily understood in words. If we state the relationship between reserves, deposits, and the multiplier in words, it clarifies the relationship. Since a fractional reserve system implies that reserves are some per cent of deposits, it follows that deposits are some multiple of reserves. For example, if reserves are 1/5 (or 20 per cent) of deposits, then deposits are five times (or 1/.20) reserves. Since deposit expansion actually takes place due to banks' lending some of their reserves, it is most useful for us to think in terms of deposits as some multiple of reserves.

4. It is easy to remember the impact of open-market operations by asking yourself, 'Who pays?' When the central bank buys a bond from the public, the central bank pays with 'new' euros and the money supply expands. When the central bank sells bonds, the public pays with euros and the central bank retires the euros. That is, the euros cease to exist when the central bank receives payment.

TERMS AND DEFINITIONS

Choose a definition for each key term.

Key terms:

_____ Barter

_____ Double coincidence of wants

_____ Money

_____ Medium of exchange

_____ Unit of account

_____ Store of value

_____ Liquidity

_____ Commodity money

_____ Fiat money

_____ Currency

_____ Demand deposits

_____ Central bank

Definitions:

1. A banking system in which banks hold only a fraction of deposits as reserves

2. Paper bills and coins in the hands of the public

3. The function of money when used to transfer purchasing power to the future

4. The interest rate the central bank charges on loans to banks

5. Trading goods and services directly for goods and services

6. The function of money when used as a yardstick to post prices and record debts

7. Money in the form of a commodity with intrinsic value

8. The set of assets generally accepted in trade for goods and services

_____ Money supply

_____ Monetary policy

_____ Open-market operations

_____ Reserves

_____ Fractional-reserve banking

_____ Reserve ratio

_____ Money multiplier

_____ Refinancing rate

_____ Excess reserves

9. The fraction of deposits held as reserves

10. Reserves held beyond the minimum reserve requirement

11. The quantity of money in the economy

12. Money without intrinsic value

13. The function of money when used to purchase goods and services

14. The purchase and sale of bonds by the central bank

15. The accident that two people bartering have what the other wants

16. Decisions by the central bank concerning the money supply

17. Balances in bank accounts that can be accessed on demand by cheque

18. The amount of money the banking system generates from each euro of reserves

19. An institution designed to regulate the banking system and money supply

20. The ease with which an asset can be converted into the economy's medium of exchange

21. Deposits that banks have received but have not lent out

PROBLEMS AND SHORT-ANSWER QUESTIONS

Practice Problems

1. Suppose the central bank purchases a bond from you for €10,000.
   a. What is the name of the central bank's action?
   b. Suppose you deposit the €10,000 in First Student Bank. Show this transaction on First Student Bank's T-account.

First Student Bank
Assets	Liabilities

   c. Suppose the reserve requirement is 20 per cent. Show First Student Bank's T-account if they loan out as much as they can.

First Student Bank
Assets	Liabilities

   d. At this point, how much money has been created from the central bank's policy action?
   e. What is the value of the money multiplier?
   f. After infinite rounds of depositing and lending, how much money could be created from the central bank's policy action?

g. If during the rounds of depositing and lending some people keep extra currency and fail to deposit all of their receipts, will there be more or less money created from the central bank's policy action than you found in part (f)? Why?

h. If during the rounds of depositing and lending, some banks fail to loan the maximum amount of reserves allowed but instead keep excess reserves, will there be more or less money created from the central bank's policy action than you found in part (f)? Why?

2. Suppose the entire economy contains €1,000 worth of one euro bills.

a. If people fail to deposit any of the euros but instead hold all €1,000 as currency, how large is the money supply? Explain.

b. If people deposit the entire €1,000 worth of bills in banks that are required to observe a 100 per cent reserve requirement, how large is the money supply? Explain.

c. If people deposit the entire €1,000 worth of bills in banks that are required to observe a 20 per cent reserve requirement, how large could the money supply become? Explain.

d. In part (c), what portion of the money supply was created due to the banks? (Hint: €1,000 of bills already existed).

e. If people deposit the entire €1,000 worth of bills in banks that are required to observe a 10 per cent reserve requirement, how large could the money supply become?

f. Compare your answer in part (e) to part (c). Explain why they are different.

g. If people deposit the entire €1,000 worth of bills in banks that are required to observe a 10 per cent reserve requirement, but they choose to hold another 10 per cent as excess reserves, how large could the money supply become?

h. Compare your answer in part (c) to part (g). Are these answers the same? Why?

Short-Answer Questions

1. What is barter and why does it limit trade?

2. What are the three functions of money?

3. What are the two basic kinds of money?

4. What two main assets are clearly money in the EU and how do they differ from all other assets? (i.e. define money)

5. What are the two main jobs of the central bank?

6. What are the two main monetary policy instruments of the ECB?

7. If the central bank wished to expand the money supply, how should they adjust each of the two policy instruments described in question 6 above?

8. If the central bank buys €1,000 of bonds from you and you hold all of the payment as currency at home, by how much does the money supply rise?

9. If the central bank buys €1,000 of government bonds from you, you deposit the entire €1,000 in a demand deposit at your bank, and banks observe a 10 per cent reserve requirement, by how much could the money supply increase?

10. Suppose the reserve requirement is 20 per cent. If you write a cheque on your account at Bank 1 to buy a €1,000 government bond from your roommate, and your roommate deposits the €1,000 in her account at Bank 2, by how much will the money supply change?

SELF-TEST

True/False Questions

_____ 1. Money and wealth are the same thing.

_____ 2. Commodity money has value independent of its use as money.

_____ 3. Money has three functions: It acts as a medium of exchange, a unit of account, and a hedge against inflation.

_____ 4. Credit cards are part of the M2 money supply and are valued at the maximum credit limit of the card holder.

_____ 5. If there is 100 per cent reserve banking, the money supply is unaffected by the proportion of the euros that the public chooses to hold as currency versus deposits.

_____ 6. If the central bank purchases €100,000 of government bonds, and the reserve requirement is 10 per cent, the maximum increase in the money supply is €10,000.

_____ 7. If the central bank desires to contract the money supply, it could do either of the following: sell government bonds and raise the discount rate.

_____ 8. If the central bank sells €1,000 of government bonds, and the reserve requirement is 10 per cent, deposits could fall by as much as €10,000.

_____ 9. An increase in the reserve requirement increases the money multiplier and increases the money supply.

_____10. If banks choose to hold excess reserves, lending decreases and the money supply decreases.

Multiple-Choice Questions

1. An example of fiat money is
   a. gold.
   b. paper euros.
   c. coins.
   d. cigarettes in a prisoner-of-war camp.

2. Commodity money
   a. has no intrinsic value.
   b. has intrinsic value.
   c. is used exclusively in the UK.
   d. is used as reserves to back fiat money.

3. Where minimum reserve ratios are imposed on banks, they are a fixed percentage of their
   a. loans.
   b. assets.
   c. deposits.
   d. government bonds.

4. Which of the following policy actions by the central bank is likely to increase the money supply?
   a. reducing reserve requirements.
   b. selling government bonds.
   c. increasing the discount rate.
   d. All of these will increase the money supply.

5. Suppose Joe changes his €1,000 demand deposit from Bank A to Bank B. If the reserve requirement is 10 per cent, what is the potential change in demand deposits as a result of Joe's action?
   a. €1,000.
   b. €9,000.
   c. €10,000.
   d. €0.

6. Which of the following policy combinations would consistently work to increase the money supply?
   a. sell bonds, decrease reserve requirements, decrease the refinancing rate.
   b. sell bonds, increase reserve requirements, increase the refinancing rate.
   c. buy bonds, increase reserve requirements, decrease the refinancing rate.
   d. buy bonds, decrease reserve requirements, decrease the refinancing rate.

7. Suppose the central bank purchases a €1,000 bond from you. If you deposit the entire €1,000 in your bank, what is the total potential change in the money supply as a result of the central bank's action if reserve requirements are 20 per cent?
   a. €1,000.
   b. €4,000.
   c. €5,000.
   d. €0.

8. Suppose all banks maintain a 100 per cent reserve ratio. If an individual deposits €1,000 of currency in a bank,
   a. the money supply is unaffected.
   b. the money supply increases by more than €1,000.
   c. the money supply increases by less than €1,000.
   d. the money supply decreases by more than €1,000.
   e. the money supply decreases by less than €1,000.

9. If the central bank engages in an open market purchase and, at the same time, it raises reserve requirements,
   a. the money supply should rise.
   b. the money supply should fall.
   c. the money supply should remain unchanged.
   d. we cannot be certain what will happen to the money supply.

10. Suppose the central bank purchases a government bond from a person who deposits the entire amount from the sale in her bank. If the bank holds some of the deposit as excess reserves, the money supply will
    a. rise less than the money multiplier would suggest.
    b. rise more than the money multiplier would suggest.
    c. fall less than the money multiplier would suggest.
    d. fall more than the money multiplier would suggest.

ADVANCED CRITICAL THINKING

Suppose you are a personal friend of the President of the ECB. He comes over to your house for lunch and notices your couch. The President is so struck by the beauty of your couch that he simply must have it for his office. The President buys it from you for €1,000 and, since it is for his office, pays you with a cheque drawn on the ECB.

1. Are there more euros in the economy than before? Why?

2. Why do you suppose that the central bank doesn't buy and sell couches, real estate, and so on, instead of bonds when they desire to change the money supply?

3. If the central bank doesn't want the money supply to rise when it purchases new furniture, what might it do to offset the purchase?

SOLUTIONS

Terms and Definitions

_1_	Fractional reserve banking	_12_	Fiat money
_2_	Currency	_13_	Medium of exchange
_3_	Store of value	_14_	Open market operations
_4_	Refinancing rate	_15_	Double coincidence of wants
_5_	Barter	_16_	Monetary policy
_6_	Unit of account	_17_	Demand deposits
_7_	Commodity money	_18_	Money multiplier
_8_	Money	_19_	Central bank
_9_	Reserve ratio	_20_	Liquidity
_10_	Excess reserves	_21_	Reserves
_11_	Money supply		

Practice Problems

1. a. Open market operations
   b.

   First Student Bank

Assets (€)		Liabilities (€)	
Reserves	10,000	Deposits	10,000

   c.

   First Student Bank

Assets (€)		Liabilities (€)	
Reserves	2,000	Deposits	10,000
Loans	8,000		

   d. €10,000 + €8,000 = €18,000.
   e. 1/.20 = 5.
   f. €10,000 × 5 = €50,000.
   g. Less, because a smaller amount of each loan gets redeposited to be available to be loaned again.
   h. Less, because a smaller amount of each deposit gets loaned out to be available to be deposited again.

2. a. €1,000, because there is €1,000 of currency and €0 of deposits.
   b. €1,000, because there is now €0 of currency and €1,000 of deposits.
   c. €1,000 × (1/.20) = €5,000, because €1,000 of new reserves can support €5,000 worth of deposits.
   d. The total potential increase is €5,000, but €1,000 was currency already in the system. Thus, an additional €4,000 was created by the banks.
   e. €1,000 × (1/.10) = €10,000.
   f. Banks can create more money from the same amount of new reserves when reserve requirements are lower because they can lend a larger portion of each new deposit.
   g. €1,000 × 1/(.10+.10) = €5,000.
   h. Yes, they are the same. With regard to deposit creation, it doesn't matter why banks hold reserves. It only matters how much they hold.

Short-Answer Questions

1. Barter is trading goods and services directly for other goods and services. It requires a double coincidence of wants.

2. Medium of exchange, unit of account, store of value.

3. Commodity money, fiat money.

4. Currency and demand deposits. They are the assets that are directly spendable or are commonly accepted in trade for goods and services.

5. To regulate banks and insure the health of the banking system, and to control the quantity of money in the economy.

6. Open-market operations and the refinancing rate.

7. Buy bonds and lower the refinancing rate.

8. €1,000.

9. €1,000 × (1/.10) = €10,000.

10. The money supply will not change at all. In this case, reserves are only moved from one bank to another.

True/False Questions

1. F; money is the spendable portion of one's wealth.

2. T

3. F; store of value, not a hedge against inflation.

4. F; credit cards are not included in the money supply.

5. T

6. F; the maximum increase in the money supply is €100,000 × (1/0.10) = €1,000,000.

7. T

8. T

9. F; an increase in the reserve requirement decreases the money multiplier, which decreases the money supply.

10. T

Multiple-Choice Questions

1. b	3. c	5. d	7. c	9. d
2. b	4. a	6. d	8. a	10. a

Advanced Critical Thinking

1. Yes. When the central bank purchases anything, it pays with newly created euros and there are more euros in the economy.

2. The transactions costs and storage costs would be staggering. Also, the value of the inventory of 'items' would never be certain. The open market for bonds is much more efficient.

3. The central bank could sell government bonds of equal value to offset other purchases.

MONEY GROWTH AND INFLATION

CHAPTER OVERVIEW

Context and Purpose

Chapter 30 is the second chapter in a two-chapter sequence dealing with money and prices in the long run. Chapter 29 explained what money is and how the central bank controls the quantity of money. Chapter 30 establishes the relationship between the rate of growth of money and the inflation rate.

The purpose of this chapter is to acquaint you with the causes and costs of inflation. You will find that, in the long run, there is a strong relationship between the growth rate of money and inflation. You will also find that there are numerous costs to the economy from relatively high inflation, but that there is no consensus on the importance of these costs when inflation is moderate.

CHAPTER REVIEW

Introduction

Inflation is a continuous increase in the overall level of prices. Deflation is a continuous decrease in the overall level of prices. Hyperinflation is extraordinarily high inflation. There is great variation in inflation over time and across countries. In this chapter, we address two questions: what causes inflation and why is inflation a problem? The answer to the first question is that inflation is caused when the government prints too much money. The answer to the second question requires more thought and will be the focus of the second half of this chapter.

The Classical Theory of Inflation

This section develops and employs the **quantity theory of money** as an explanation of the price level and inflation.

When prices rise, it is rarely because products are more valuable, but rather because the money used to buy them is less valuable. Thus, *inflation is more about the value of money than about the value of goods.* An increase in the overall price level is equivalent to a proportionate fall in the value of money. If P is the price level (the value of goods and services measured in money) then 1/P is the value of money measured in terms of goods and services. If prices double, the value of money has fallen to 1/2 its prior value.

The value of money is determined by the supply and demand for money. If we ignore the banking system, the central bank controls the money supply. Money demand reflects how much wealth people want to hold in liquid form. While money demand has many determinants, in the long run one is dominant—the price level. People hold money because it is a medium of exchange. If prices are higher, more money is needed for the same transaction and the quantity of money demanded is higher.

Money supply and money demand need to balance for there to be monetary equilibrium. Monetary equilibrium is shown in Exhibit 1 for money supply MS_1 at point A. Recall that the value of money measured in goods and services is 1/P. When the value of money is high, the price level is low and the quantity of money demanded is low. Therefore, the money demand curve slopes negatively in the graph. Since the central bank fixes the quantity of money, the money supply curve is vertical with respect to its value. In the long run, the overall level of prices adjusts to equate the quantity of money demanded to the quantity of money supplied.

Suppose the central bank doubles the quantity of money in the economy from MS_1 to MS_2. There is now an excess supply of money at the original price level. Since people are now holding more money than they desire at the existing price level, they will rid themselves of the excess supply of money by buying things—goods and services or bonds. Even if people buy bonds (lend money), the bond issuer (borrower) will take the money and buy goods and services. Either way, an injection of money increases the demand for goods and services. Since the ability of the economy to produce goods and services has not changed, an increase in the demand for goods and services raises the price level. The price level will continue to rise (and the value of money will continue to fall) until the quantity of money demanded is raised to the level of the quantity of money supplied (point B). That is, the price level adjusts to equate money supply and money demand. Thus, the conclusions of the *quantity theory of money* are: (1) the quantity of money in the economy determines the price level (and the value of money) and (2) an increase in the money supply increases the price level which implies that growth in the money supply causes inflation.

The **classical dichotomy** suggests that economic variables can be divided into two groups—**nominal variables** (those measured in monetary units) and **real variables**

EXHIBIT 1

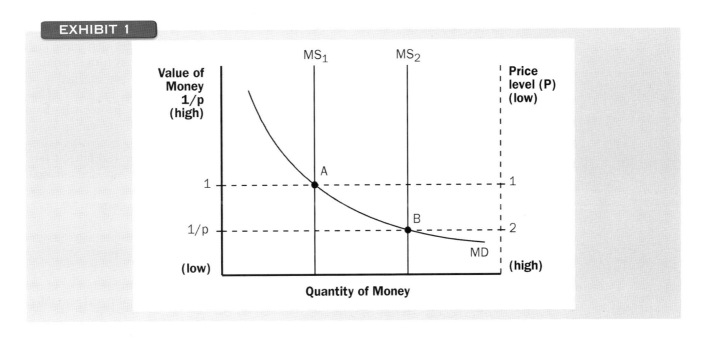

(those measured in physical units). Although prices are nominal variables, relative prices are real variables. For example, the ratio of your earnings per hour to the price of chocolate bars is a real variable measured in chocolate bars per hour. Changes in the money supply affect nominal variables, but not real variables. Real output is determined by productivity and factor supplies, and not by the quantity of money. However, the value of nominal variables is determined by, and is *proportional* to, the quantity of money. For example, if the money supply doubles, prices double, wages double, and all euro values double, but real output, employment, real interest rates, and real wages remain unchanged. This result is known as **monetary neutrality**. Money is unlikely to be neutral in the short run, but it is likely to be neutral in the long run.

The classical dichotomy and monetary neutrality can be demonstrated with the **quantity equation**. To begin, we define velocity as the speed of circulation of money. Then $V = (P \times Y)/M$ where V is the **velocity of money**, P is the price of output, and Y is the amount of real output (and $P \times Y$ = nominal GDP), and M is the quantity of money. If nominal output is €500 (500 items at €1 each) and M is €100, then $V = 5$. That is, in order for €100 to accommodate €500 of purchases and sales, each euro must be spent, on average, 5 times.

Rearranged, we get the **quantity equation**: $M \times V = P \times Y$. If the quantity of money increases, P or Y must rise, or V must fall. Our theory of inflation takes five steps:

- V is relatively stable in the long run.

- Therefore, changes in M cause proportional changes in nominal output ($P \times Y$).

- Real output (Y) is determined by productivity and factor supplies in the long run and is not affected by changes in M.

- Because Y is fixed, an increase in M causes *proportional* changes in P.

- Thus, inflation results from rapid growth in the money supply.

There is no precise definition of hyperinflation, but it exists at rates that are so high that money can no longer adequately perform its functions. For example, a rate of inflation of 50 per cent per month would clearly be hyperinflation. When countries experience hyperinflation, the data show that there is a close link between money growth and inflation. This supports the conclusions of the quantity theory.

Why do countries print too much money if they know it causes inflation? Governments do it to pay for expenditures. When governments spend, they get the money by taxing, borrowing, or printing more money. Countries that have high spending, inadequate tax revenue, and limited ability to borrow, may turn to printing money. When a government raises revenue by printing money, it has engaged in an **inflation tax**. When the government prints money and prices rise, the value of the existing money held by people falls. An inflation tax is a tax on people who hold money balances and an example of this mechanism of funding government spending occurred in Russia in the early 1990s.

If money is neutral, changes in money will have no effect on the real interest rate. Recall the relationship between the real interest rate, nominal interest rate, and inflation:

real interest rate = nominal interest rate − inflation rate

Solving for the nominal interest rate:

nominal interest rate = real interest rate + inflation rate

The real interest rate depends on the supply and demand for loanable funds. In the long run, money is neutral and only affects nominal variables, not real variables.

Thus, when the central bank increases the growth rate of money, there is an increase in the inflation rate and a one for one increase in the nominal interest rate, while the real interest rate remains unchanged. The one for one adjustment of the nominal interest rate to inflation is called the **Fisher effect**. Note that the nominal interest rate is set when the loan is first made and thus, the Fisher effect actually says that the nominal interest rate adjusts one for one with *expected inflation*.

The Costs of Inflation

People often argue that inflation is a serious economic problem because when prices rise, their incomes can't buy as many goods and services. Thus, they believe that inflation directly lowers their standard of living. However, this argument has a fallacy. Since people earn incomes by selling factor services, such as labour, inflation in nominal incomes goes hand in hand with inflation in prices. Therefore, inflation, on average, does not directly affect people's real purchasing power.

However, there are a number of more subtle costs of inflation:

- *Shoeleather costs*: Recall, inflation is a tax on people who hold money balances. To avoid the tax, people hold less money and keep more invested in interest bearing assets when inflation is higher than they do when inflation is lower. As a result, people have to go to the bank and withdraw money more often than they would if there were no inflation. These costs are sometimes metaphorically called **shoeleather costs** (since your shoes are worn out from all those trips to the bank). The actual cost of holding less cash is wasted time and inconvenience. At higher rates of inflation, this cost is more than just trivial.

- *Menu costs*: There are numerous costs associated with changing prices—cost of printing new menus, price lists, and catalogues, mailing costs to distribute them, the cost of advertising new prices, and the cost of deciding the new prices themselves.

- *Relative-price variability and the misallocation of resources*: Since it is costly to change prices, firms change prices as rarely as possible. When there is inflation, the relative price of goods whose price is held constant for a period of time is falling with respect to the average price level. This misallocates resources because economic decisions are based on relative prices. A good whose price is changed only once per year is artificially expensive at the beginning of the year and artificially inexpensive by the end of the year.

- *Inflation-induced tax distortions*: Inflation raises the tax burden on income earned from saving and thus, discourages saving and growth. Inflation affects two types of taxes on saving:

  (1) *Capital gains* are the profits made from selling an asset for more than its purchase price. Nominal capital gains are subject to taxation. Suppose you buy a unit of stock for €20 and sell it for €50. Also suppose the price level doubles while you owned the stock. You only have a €10 real gain (because you would need to sell the stock for €40 just to break even) yet you must pay taxes on the €30 nominal capital gain because the tax code does not account for inflation.

  (2) *Nominal interest* is taxed even though part of the nominal interest rate is to compensate for inflation. When government takes a fixed per cent of the nominal interest rate as taxes, the after-tax real return grows smaller as inflation increases. This is because the nominal interest rate rises one for one with inflation and taxes increase with the nominal interest rate, yet the

pre tax real return is unaffected by inflation. Therefore, the after tax real return falls.

Because there are taxes on nominal capital gains and nominal interest, inflation lowers the after tax real return on saving and thus, inflation discourages saving and growth. This problem can be solved by eliminating inflation or by indexing the tax system so that taxes are assessed only on real gains.

- *Confusion and inconvenience*: Money serves as the unit of account, which means that the euro is the yardstick by which we measure economic values. When the central bank increases the money supply and causes inflation, it decreases the value of money and shrinks the size of the economic measuring stick. This makes accounting for firms' profits more difficult and thus, makes choosing investments more complicated. It also makes daily transactions more confusing.

- *A special cost of unexpected inflation—arbitrary redistribution of wealth*: The costs of inflation described above exist even if inflation is stable and predictable. However, inflation has an additional cost to the economy if it is unexpected because it arbitrarily redistributes wealth. For example, the terms of a loan are generally expressed in nominal values based on a certain amount of expected inflation (see the Fisher effect equation above). Despite this, if inflation becomes higher than expected, borrowers are allowed to repay the loan with euros that purchase less than expected. Borrowers gain at the expense of lenders. The opposite is true when inflation is less than expected. If inflation were perfectly predictable, regardless of its size, this redistribution would not take place. However, higher rates of inflation are never stable. Therefore, lower rates of inflation are preferred because they are more stable and predictable.

HELPFUL HINTS

1. The price of money is $1/P$. Since we measure the price of goods and services in terms of money, we measure the price of money in terms of the quantity of goods and services for which money can be exchanged. For example, if a basket of goods and services costs €5, then $P = €5$. The price of a euro is then $1/P$ or 1/5 of the basket of goods. That is, one euro exchanges for 1/5 of the basket of goods. If the price of the basket of goods doubles so that it now sells for €10, the price of money has fallen to one half its original value. Numerically, since the price of the basket is now €10, or $P = €10$, the price of money has fallen to $1/P$ or 1/10 of the basket of goods. To summarize, when the price of a basket of goods and services double from €5 to €10, the price of money falls by half from 1/5 to 1/10 of the basket of goods.

2. When dealing with the quantity theory, imagine you are at an auction. At the end of the auction, we can calculate the number of items sold and the average price of each item sold. Suppose we repeat the auction, only now the doorman doubles the money each buyer takes into the auction—if you had €20, you now have €40, and so on. If all participants spend the same per cent of their money as at the prior auction (equivalent to a constant velocity) and if the items available to buy are unchanged (equivalent to a constant real output), what must happen to the average price of goods sold at the auction? Prices at the auction will precisely double, showing that prices are proportional to the quantity of money.

3. Unexpected inflation works like a tax on future receipts. We know that unexpected inflation redistributes wealth. Although it can be difficult to remember who wins and who loses on nominal contracts through time, you can always

keep things straight if you remember that *unexpected inflation works like a tax on future receipts and a subsidy to future payments*. Therefore, when inflation turns out to be higher than we thought it would be when a loan contract was written, the recipient of the future payments is worse off because they receive euros with less purchasing power than they had bargained for. The person who borrowed is better off because they were able to use the money when it had greater value, yet they were allowed to repay the loan with money of lower value. Therefore, when inflation is higher than expected, wealth is redistributed from lenders to borrowers. Alternatively, when inflation is less than expected, winners and losers are reversed.

This concept can be applied to any contract that extends through time. Consider a labour contract. Recall, when inflation is greater than expected, those who receive money in the future are harmed and those who pay are helped. Therefore, firms gain at the expense of workers when inflation is greater than anticipated. When inflation is less than expected, winners and losers are reversed.

TERMS AND DEFINITIONS

Choose a definition for each key term.

Key terms:

_____ Inflation

_____ Deflation

_____ Hyperinflation

_____ Quantity theory of money

_____ Nominal variables

_____ Real variables

_____ Classical dichotomy

_____ Money neutrality

_____ Velocity of money

_____ Quantity equation

_____ Inflation tax

_____ Nominal interest rate

_____ Real interest rate

_____ Fisher effect

_____ Shoeleather cost

_____ Menu cost

_____ Capital gains

Definitions:

1. Resources wasted when inflation causes people to economize on money holdings

2. The practice of a government raising revenue by printing money

3. The theory that the quantity of money determines prices and the growth rate of money determines inflation

4. Variables measured in physical units

5. The costs associated with changing prices

6. Interest rate uncorrected for inflation

7. Profits made from selling an asset for greater than the purchase price

8. The one to one adjustment of the nominal interest rate to inflation

9. An increase in the overall level of prices

10. Extraordinarily high inflation

11. $M \times V = P \times Y$

12. The theoretical separation of nominal and real variables

13. Interest rate corrected for inflation

14. Variables measured in monetary units

15. Rate at which money circulates

16. A decrease in the overall level of prices

17. The property that changes in the money supply affect nominal variables, but not real variables

PROBLEMS AND SHORT-ANSWER QUESTIONS

Practice Problems

1. Use the quantity equation for this problem. Suppose the money supply is €200, real output is 1,000 units, and the price per unit of output is €1.
   a. What is the value of velocity?
   b. If velocity is fixed at the value you solved for in part (a), what does the quantity theory of money suggest will happen if the money supply is increased to €400?
   c. Is your answer in part (b) consistent with the classical dichotomy? Explain.
   d. Suppose that when the money supply is doubled from €200 to €400, real output grows a small amount (say 2 per cent). Now what will happen to prices? Do prices more than double, less than double, or exactly double? Why?
   e. When inflation reaches relatively high rates, people do not like to hold money because it loses its value quickly. Therefore, they spend it faster. If when the money supply is doubled, people spend money more quickly, what happens to prices? Do prices more than double, less than double, or exactly double? Why?
   f. Suppose the money supply at the beginning of this problem refers to M1. That is, the M1 money supply is €200. What would the M4 quantity equation look like if the M4 money supply were €500 (and all other values were as stated at the beginning of the problem)?

2. The following questions are related to the Fisher effect.
   a. To demonstrate your understanding of the Fisher effect, complete the following table.

Real interest rate (%)	Nominal interest rate (%)	Inflation rate (%)
3	10	—
—	6	2
5	—	3

   The following questions about the Fisher effect are unrelated to the table above.
   b. Suppose people expect inflation to be 3 per cent and suppose the desired real interest rate is 4 per cent. What is the nominal rate?
   c. Suppose inflation turns out to be 6 per cent. What is the actual real interest rate on loans that were signed based on the expectations in part (b)?
   d. Was wealth redistributed to the lender from the borrower or to the borrower from the lender when inflation was expected to be 3 per cent, but in fact, turned out to be 6 per cent?
   e. What would have happened to the distribution of wealth had inflation turned out to be only 1 per cent?

3. Income taxes treat nominal interest earned on savings as income even though much of the nominal interest is simply to compensate for inflation.
   a. To see what this does to the incentive to save, complete the following table for both the low inflation and high inflation country.

	Low inflation country (%)	High inflation country (%)
Real interest rate	5	5
Inflation rate	3	11
Nominal interest rate		
Reduced interest rate due to a 25% tax		
After-tax nominal interest rate		
After-tax real interest rate		

b. In which country is there a greater incentive to save? Why?

c. What could the government do to eliminate this problem?

Short-Answer Questions

1. Why is it possible for the real interest rate to be negative, but the nominal interest rate must always be positive?

2. Within the framework of the classical dichotomy, which type of variables are affected by changes in money and which type are not? What phrase do we use to capture this effect?

3. Is money more likely to be neutral in the long run or the short run? Why?

4. Suppose the money supply were to increase by 10 per cent. Explain what would happen to each variable in the quantity equation.

5. What are the three sources of revenue a government can use to support its expenditures? Which method causes inflation and who bears the burden of this method of raising revenue?

6. In the long run, what does an increase in the growth rate of the money supply do to real and nominal interest rates?

7. What are the costs of inflation when inflation is perfectly anticipated?

8. Suppose inflation turns out to be lower than we had expected. Who is likely to gain: borrowers or lenders? union workers or firms? Why?

9. What is the inconsistency in the following statement? 'When inflation is high but stable and predictable, inflation does not redistribute wealth.'

10. Does inflation (if correctly anticipated) make borrowers worse off and lenders better off when it raises nominal interest rates? Why?

SELF-TEST

True/False Questions

_____ 1. An increase in the price level is the same as a decrease in the value of money.

_____ 2. The quantity theory of money suggests that an increase in the money supply increases real output proportionately.

_____ 3. If the price level were to double, the quantity of money demanded would double because people would need twice as much money to cover the same transactions.

_____ 4. In the long run, an increase in the money supply tends to have an effect on real variables but no effect on nominal variables.

_____ 5. If the money supply is €500, real output is 2,500 units, and the average price of a unit of real output is €2, the velocity of money is 10.

_____ 6. An inflation tax is 'paid' by those that hold money because inflation reduces the value of their money holdings.

_____ 7. Money neutrality implies that a change in the money supply doesn't cause a change in anything at all.

_____ 8. Inflation reduces the relative price of goods whose prices have been temporarily held constant to avoid the costs associated with changing prices.

_____ 9. The shoeleather costs of inflation should be approximately the same for a medical doctor and for an unemployed worker.

_____10. Inflation tends to stimulate saving because it raises the after tax real return to saving.

Multiple-Choice Questions

1. Which one of the following is least likely to be affected by inflation?
   a. A salesman paid on commission.
   b. A property owner.
   c. A person receiving a fixed income.
   d. A capital gains tax payer.

2. If the price level doubles,
   a. the quantity demanded of money falls by half.
   b. the money supply has been cut by half.
   c. nominal income is unaffected.
   d. the value of money has been cut by half.

3. In the long run, the demand for money is most dependent upon
   a. the level of prices.
   b. the availability of credit cards.
   c. the availability of banking outlets.
   d. the interest rate.

4. The quantity theory of money implies that an increase in the money supply causes
   a. a proportional increase in velocity.
   b. a proportional increase in real output.
   c. a proportional increase in prices.
   d. a proportional decrease in velocity.
   e. a proportional decrease in prices.

5. If money is neutral,
   a. an increase in the money supply does nothing.
   b. the money supply cannot be changed because it is tied to a commodity such as gold.
   c. a change in the money supply only affects real variables such as real output.
   d. a change in the money supply only affects nominal variables such as prices and euro wages.
   e. a change in the money supply reduces velocity proportionately; therefore there is no effect on either prices or real output.

6. An inflation tax
   a. is a tax on the value of expenditures.
   b. is a tax on people who hold money.
   c. is a tax on people who hold interest bearing savings accounts.
   d. is usually employed by governments with balanced budgets.

7. A major effect of unanticipated inflation is
   a. a transfer of wealth from borrowers to lenders.
   b. a fall in nominal money balances.
   c. a rise in the real profits of business.
   d. a greater risk of accelerating inflation.

8. Suppose that, because of inflation, a business in Brazil must calculate, print, and mail a new price list to its customers each month. This is an example of
   a. shoeleather costs.
   b. menu costs.

    c. costs due to inflation induced tax distortions.

    d. arbitrary redistributions of wealth.

    e. costs due to confusion and inconvenience.

9. If the real interest rate is 4 per cent, the inflation rate is 6 per cent, and the tax rate on interest is 20 per cent, what is the after tax real interest rate?

    a. 1 per cent.

    b. 2 per cent.

    c. 3 per cent.

    d. 4 per cent.

    e. 5 per cent.

10. Which one of the following is not consistent with the predictions of the quantity theory of money?

    a. If the money supply doubles prices will double in the long run.

    b. Velocity of money is constant.

    c. The price level cannot change unless there has been a prior increase in the money supply.

    d. A rise in prices will cause an increase in money growth.

ADVANCED CRITICAL THINKING

Suppose you explain the concept of an 'inflation tax' to a friend. You correctly tell them, 'When a government prints money to cover its expenditures instead of taxing or borrowing, it causes inflation. An inflation tax is simply the erosion of the value of money from this inflation. Therefore, the burden of the tax lands on those who hold money.' Your friend responds, 'What's so bad about that? Rich people have much more money than poor people so an inflation tax seems fair to me. Maybe the government should finance all of its expenditures by printing money.'

1. Is it true that rich people hold more money than poor people?

2. Do rich people hold a higher percentage of their income as money than poor people?

3. Compared to an income tax, does an inflation tax place a greater or lesser burden on the poor?

4. Are there any other reasons why engaging in an inflation tax is not good policy?

SOLUTIONS

Terms and Definitions

_1_	Shoeleather costs	_10_	Hyperinflation
_2_	Inflation tax	_11_	Quantity equation
_3_	Quantity theory of money	_12_	Classical dichotomy
_4_	Real variables	_13_	Real interest rate
_5_	Menu costs	_14_	Nominal variables
_6_	Nominal interest rate	_15_	Velocity of money
_7_	Capital gains	_16_	Deflation
_8_	Fisher effect	_17_	Money neutrality
_9_	Inflation		

Practice Problems

1. a. $(1,000 \times €1)/€200 = 5$.
   b. $€400 \times 5 = €2 \times 1,000$, prices will double from €1 to €2.
   c. Yes. The classical dichotomy divides economic variables into real and nominal. Money affects nominal variables proportionately and has no impact on real variables. In part (b), prices double, but real output remains constant.
   d. The quantity equation says that nominal output must change in proportion to money. Prices will still rise, but since real output is larger, prices will less than double.
   e. Money has a proportional impact on nominal output if V is constant. If V grows, a doubling of M will cause P to more than double.
   f. $€500 \times 2 = €1 \times 1,000$, M4 velocity is 2.

2. a.

Real interest rate (%)	Nominal interest rate (%)	Inflation rate (%)
3	10	7
4	6	2
5	8	3

   b. $3\% + 4\% = 7\%$.
   c. People would have signed loan contracts for 7 per cent nominal interest. Therefore, $7\% - 6\% = 1\%$.
   d. People expected a real interest rate of 4 per cent, but the actual real interest rate turned out to be 1 per cent. Wealth was redistributed to the borrower from the lender.
   e. The original loan contract would be the same. Thus $7\% - 1\% = 6\%$. The actual real rate is 6 per cent instead of 4 per cent so wealth is redistributed to lenders from borrowers.

3. a.

	Low inflation country (%)	High inflation country (%)
Real interest rate	5	5
Inflation rate	3	11
Nominal interest rate	8	16
Tax on nominal interest rate at 25%	2	4
After-tax nominal interest rate	6	12
After-tax real interest rate	3	1

   b. In the low inflation country because the after tax real interest rate is larger.
   c. They could eliminate inflation or tax only real interest income.

Short-Answer Questions

1. The real interest rate will always be negative when nominal rates are less than the rate of inflation. However, nominal interest rates can never be negative since no one would ever deposit money if it were certain that the nominal value of the amount deposited would fall. In other words, depositors would withdraw a smaller sum than the original amount deposited. In such circumstances people would prefer to hold money balances.

2. Nominal are affected. Real are not. Monetary neutrality.

3. In the long run, because it takes time for people and markets to adjust prices in response to a change in the money supply. In the short run, mistakes are likely to be made.

4. V remains constant. Y remains constant. M rises by 10 per cent and P rises by 10 per cent.

5. Taxes, borrowing, and printing money. Printing money. Those that hold money because its value decreases.

6. No impact on the real interest rate. Raises the nominal interest rate one to one with the increase in the growth rate of money and prices.

7. Shoeleather costs, menu costs, costs due to relative price variability which misallocates resources, tax distortions, confusion and inconvenience.

8. Lenders and workers. Those that receive euros in the future on contract receive euros of greater value that they bargained for.

9. When inflation is relatively high, it is always unstable and difficult to predict.

10. No. The nominal interest rate adjusts one to one with the rise in inflation so that the real rate is unaffected. Neither the borrower nor lender gain.

True/False Questions

1. T
2. F; it increases price proportionately.
3. T
4. F; the money supply tends to have an effect on nominal variables but not real variables.
5. T
6. T
7. F; it doesn't cause a change in real variables.
8. T
9. F; the opportunity costs of trips to the bank are greater for a medical doctor.
10. F; inflation tends to reduce the after-tax return to saving.

Multiple-Choice Questions

1. a	5. d	9. b
2. d	6. b	10. d
3. a	7. c	
4. c	8. b	

Advanced Critical Thinking

1. Yes, rich people probably hold more euros than poor people.

2. No, by a wide margin, poor hold a larger per cent of their income as money. In fact, the poor may have no other financial asset at all.

3. An inflation tax places a far greater burden on the poor than on the rich. The rich are able to keep most of their assets in inflation-adjusted, interest-bearing assets.

4. Inflation imposes many other costs on the economy besides the inflation tax: shoeleather costs, menu costs, tax distortions, confusion, etc.

OPEN ECONOMY MACROECONOMICS: BASIC CONCEPTS

CHAPTER OVERVIEW

Context and Purpose

Chapter 31 is the first chapter in a two-chapter sequence dealing with open economy macroeconomics. Chapter 31 develops the basic concepts and vocabulary associated with macroeconomics in an international setting: net exports, net capital outflow, real and nominal exchange rates, and purchasing power parity. The next chapter, Chapter 32, builds an open economy macroeconomic model that shows how these variables are determined simultaneously.

The purpose of Chapter 31 is to develop the basic concepts macroeconomists use to study open economies. We examine why a nation's net exports must equal its net capital outflow. We also address the concepts of the real and nominal exchange rate and develop a theory of exchange rate determination known as purchasing power parity.

CHAPTER REVIEW

Introduction

Earlier in the text, we learned that people gain from trade because they can specialize in the production of goods for which they have a comparative advantage and trade for other people's production. However, until now most of our study of macroeconomics has been based on a **closed economy**: one which does not interact with other countries. We now begin the study of macroeconomics in an **open economy**: an economy that interacts with other economies.

The International Flows of Goods and Capital

An open economy interacts with other economies in two ways: It buys and sells goods and services in world product markets, and it buys and sells capital assets in world financial markets.

The flow of goods and services: exports, imports, and net exports.
Exports are domestically produced goods and services sold abroad while **imports** are foreign-produced goods and services sold domestically. **Net exports** are the value of

a country's exports minus the value of its imports. Net exports are also called the **trade balance**. If exports exceed imports, net exports are positive and the country is said to have a **trade surplus**. If imports exceed exports, net exports are negative and the country is said to have a **trade deficit**. If imports equal exports, net exports are zero and there is **balanced trade**.

Net exports are influenced by the tastes of consumers for domestic versus foreign goods, the relative prices of foreign and domestic goods, exchange rates, foreign and domestic incomes, international transportation costs, and government policies towards trade. These factors will be addressed in the following chapter.

The UK economy has engaged in an increasing amount of international trade during the last four decades for the following reasons: (1) improved transportation such as larger cargo ships, (2) advances in telecommunications which allow for better overseas communication, (3) technologically advanced goods are more valuable per kilo and easier to transport, and (4) governments look more favourably on trade as evidenced by their support of the single market of the EU and the World Trade Organisation (WTO).

The flow of financial resources: net capital outflow. Net capital outflow is the purchase of foreign assets by domestic residents minus the purchase of domestic assets by foreigners. When a domestic resident buys and controls capital in a foreign country, it is known as *foreign direct investment*. When a domestic resident buys stock in a foreign corporation but has no direct control of the company, it is known as *foreign portfolio investment*.

Net capital outflow is influenced by the relative real interest rates paid on foreign versus domestic assets, the relative economic and political risks, and government policies that affect ownership of foreign assets. These factors will be considered in the following chapter.

The equality of net exports and net capital outflow. Net exports measure the imbalance of a country's imports and exports. Net capital outflow is the imbalance of a country's purchase and sale of assets. These two imbalances offset each other. That is, net capital outflow (NCO) equals net exports (NX):

$$NCO = NX$$

This is an identity because every international transaction is an exchange. When BMW sells a car to a UK resident, BMW receives sterling. NX has increased and NCO has increased because BMW is now holding additional foreign assets (sterling). If BMW chooses not to hold the sterling, any subsequent transaction undertaken by BMW preserves the equality of NX and NCO. For example, BMW could use the sterling to purchase UK goods of equal value, reversing the transaction so that NX and NCO return to their original values. Alternatively, BMW could use the sterling to buy other UK assets (stocks, etc.), maintaining the increase in NX and NCO. Finally, BMW could exchange the sterling for euros. The new owners of the euros could buy European assets, maintaining the increase in NX and NCO, or they could buy European goods, reducing NX and NCO to their original levels. Simply put, when someone exports goods and receives foreign currency, the foreign currency will either be held, used to buy goods from the importing country, or used to buy assets from the importing country. In each case, $NX = NCO$ is maintained.

Saving and investment in an open economy. Saving and investment are important for growth. Saving is the income of a nation that is left over after paying for consumption and government purchases. Recall, gross domestic product (Y) is the sum of consumption (C), investment (I), government purchases (G), and net exports (NX). Therefore,

$$Y = C + I + G + NX$$

and saving is,

$$Y - C - G = I + NX$$

or,

$$S = I + NX$$

Since $NX = NCO$ we can write,

$$S = I + NCO$$

Thus, in an open economy, when the UK economy saves a pound sterling, it can invest in domestic capital (I) or foreign capital (NCO). It does not have to invest only in domestic capital (I).

In summary, if a country runs a trade surplus, net exports (NX) are positive, domestic saving is greater than domestic investment, and net capital outflow (NCO) is positive. If a country runs a trade deficit, net exports (NX) are negative, domestic saving is less than domestic investment, and net capital outflow (NCO) is negative. If a country has balanced trade, net exports (NX) are zero, domestic saving is equal to domestic investment, and net capital outflow (NCO) is zero.

The Prices for International Transactions: Real and Nominal Exchange Rates

The **nominal exchange rate** is the rate at which people can trade one currency for another currency. An exchange rate between euros and any foreign currency can be expressed in two ways: foreign currency per euro or euros per unit of foreign currency. For example, if 140 yen are equal to 1 euro, the nominal exchange rate is 140 yen per euro or .007 (which is 1/40) euros per yen. We will always express exchange rates as foreign currency per euro. When the euro buys more foreign currency, there has been an **appreciation** of the euro. When the euro buys less foreign currency, there has been a **depreciation** of the euro. Because there are so many currencies in the world, the euro exchange rate is often expressed by an exchange rate index that compares a group of currencies to the euro.

The **real exchange rate** is the rate at which people can trade the goods and services of one country for the goods and services of another. Two things are considered when we directly compare the value of goods in one country to those in another: the relative values of the currencies (nominal exchange rate) and the relative prices of the goods to be traded. The real exchange rate is defined as:

$$\text{real exchange rate} = \frac{\text{nominal exchange rate} \times \text{domestic price}}{\text{foreign price}}$$

Just as the nominal exchange rate is expressed as units of foreign currency per unit of domestic currency, the real exchange rate is expressed as units of foreign goods per unit of domestic goods. For example: Suppose that a case of Russian vodka is 20 roubles while a case of German vodka is €10 and that the nominal exchange rate is 4 roubles per euro. The real exchange rate of Russian vodka to German vodka is

$$\text{real exchange rate} = \frac{(4 \text{ roubles}/1 \text{ euro}) \times (\$10/\text{case German vodka})}{20 \text{ roubles}/\text{case Russian vodka}}$$

$$= \frac{40 \text{ roubles}/\text{case German vodka}}{20 \text{ roubles}/\text{case Russian vodka}}$$

$$= \frac{40 \text{ roubles}}{\text{case German vodka}} \times \frac{\text{case Russian vodka}}{20 \text{ roubles}}$$

$$= \frac{2 \text{ case Russian vodka}}{1 \text{ case German vodka}}$$

The real exchange rate is the true relative cost of goods across borders. Since macroeconomists are concerned with the economy as a whole, they are concerned with overall prices rather than individual prices. Therefore, instead of using the price of vodka to compute the real exchange rate, macroeconomists use each country's price index:

$$\text{real exchange rate} = (e \times P)/P^*$$

where e is the nominal exchange rate, P is a domestic price index, and P^* is a foreign price index.

When this measure of the real exchange rate rises, European goods are more expensive relative to foreign goods and net exports fall. When this measure of the real exchange rate falls, European goods are cheaper relative to foreign goods and net exports rise.

A First Theory of Exchange-Rate Determination: Purchasing-Power Parity

The simplest explanation of why an exchange rate takes on a particular value is called **purchasing-power parity**. This theory says that a unit of any given currency should buy the same quantity of goods in all countries. The logic of this theory is based on the *law of one price*. The law of one price says that a good must sell for the same price in all locations because, if there were different prices for the same good, people would buy the good where it is cheap and sell it where it is expensive. This behaviour will continue to drive up the price where it was low and drive down the price where it was high until the prices are equalized. This process is called *arbitrage*. Thus, a euro should buy the same amount of vodka in Russia as it buys in Germany. If it did not, there would be opportunities for profit and traders would buy where it is cheap and sell where it is expensive.

If purchasing-power parity is true, the nominal exchange rate between two countries' currencies depends on the price levels in those two countries. For example, if vodka in Russia is 20 roubles per case while vodka in Germany is €10 per case, then the exchange rate should be 20 roubles per €10, or 2 roubles/euro so that one euro buys the same amount of vodka in both countries. Notice, *the nominal exchange rate of 2 roubles/euro is simply the ratio of the prices in the two countries.*

To put this concept into a formula, suppose P is the German price level, P^* is the foreign price level, and e is the exchange rate in terms of foreign currency per euro. A euro can buy $1/P$ units in Germany and e/P^* units in the foreign country. Purchasing-power parity suggests that a euro should buy the same amount in each country.

$$1/P = e^*/P$$

Solving for e,

$$e = P^*/P$$

Thus, if purchasing-power parity holds, the nominal exchange rate is the ratio of the foreign price level to the domestic price level.

Recall, a country's price level depends on how much money its central bank creates. If a central bank creates more money, its currency will buy fewer goods and services and fewer units of other currencies. That is, its currency will depreciate.

Purchasing-power parity is most likely to hold in the long run. However, even in the long run, the theory of purchasing-power parity is not completely accurate because (1) some goods are not easily traded (such as many services) and (2) even tradable goods are not always perfect substitutes.

HELPFUL HINTS

1. Negative net capital outflow augments domestic investment. National saving is used to support domestic investment and net capital outflow:

$$S = I + NCO$$

If *NCO* is negative, as it is for the UK, it means that foreigners invest more in the UK than UK citizens invest abroad. This allows domestic investment to remain adequate in spite of very small saving on the part of UK citizens. For example, suppose saving is €700 billion and net capital outflow is − €200 billion. Domestic investment is I = €700 + €200 or €900 billion.

2. Always express nominal and real exchange rates in terms of foreign units to domestic units. Expressing exchange rates in terms of foreign units relative to domestic units helps avoid confusion because a rise in this exchange rate is associated with a rise in the value of the domestic unit. For example, suppose the nominal exchange rate between the yen and the euro is expressed as 200 yen/euro. If the exchange rate rises to 210 yen/euro, the value of the euro has risen.

3. When generating nominal or real exchange rates, always identify the units of measurement. A common mistake committed by students when calculating exchange rates (particularly real exchange rates) is to fail to identify the units of measurement throughout the problem and to try to attach the units of measurement at the end of the problem after a numerical solution has been found. This leaves much room for error and confusion. Notice in the real exchange rate example about Russian vodka and German vodka that the units are attached to the numbers throughout. This is not just for your convenience. It is necessary to avoid making mistakes even if you have done it numerous times.

4. Purchasing-power parity should hold for goods of high value and low transportation costs. The law of one price applies to goods for which arbitrage is most likely. Hence, we might expect the euro price of diamonds to be the same in all countries because small deviations in the price of diamonds create substantial profit opportunities. However, large deviations in prices of hair cuts or bread between London and Paris are unlikely to create profit opportunities and a movement of goods or services. While many goods and services are not currently traded across borders, growth in the production and trade of light, high-technology, high-value commodities should increase the applicability of the purchasing-power parity theory.

TERMS AND DEFINITIONS

Choose a definition for each key term.

Key terms:

_____ Closed economy

_____ Open economy

_____ Exports

_____ Imports

_____ Net exports

_____ Trade surplus

_____ Trade deficit

_____ Net capital outflow

Definitions:

1. The amount by which exports exceed imports

2. Goods and services produced domestically and sold abroad

3. The rate at which people can trade the goods and services of one country for those of another country

4. Taking advantage of two prices for the same commodity by buying where it is cheap and selling where it is expensive

5. The rate at which people can trade one currency for another currency

_____ Nominal exchange rate

_____ Appreciation

_____ Depreciation

_____ Real exchange rate

_____ Purchasing-power parity

_____ Arbitrage

6. A decrease in the value of a currency measured in terms of other currencies

7. An economy that does not interact with other economies

8. The value of exports minus the value of imports or the trade balance

9. The theory that a unit of a country's currency should buy the same quantity of goods in all countries.

10. An increase in the value of a currency measured in terms of other currencies

11. An economy that interacts with other economies

12. The amount by which imports exceed exports

13. Goods and services produced in foreign countries and sold domestically

14. The purchase of foreign assets by domestic residents minus the purchase of domestic assets by foreigners

PROBLEMS AND SHORT-ANSWER QUESTIONS

Practice Problems

1. How would each of the following transactions affect UK NCO? Does the transaction affect direct investment or portfolio investment?
   a. Rover buys stock in Honda.
   b. Rover buys steel from a Japanese manufacturer to use in the production of its cars.
   c. Honda expands its plant in Derbyshire.
   d. A Japanese mutual fund buys shares of stock in Rover.
   e. Imperial Chemical Industries (ICI) builds a plant in Germany.

2. Suppose a resident of Great Britain buys a computer from a US manufacturer using British pounds.
   a. If the US manufacturer holds on to the British pounds, does $NX = NCO$ in this case? Explain.
   b. Suppose the US manufacturer uses the pounds to help build a factory in Great Britain. Does $NX = NCO$ in this case? Explain. What kind of foreign investment is this?
   c. Suppose the US manufacturer uses the pounds to buy stock in a British corporation. Does $NX = NCO$ in this case? Explain. What kind of foreign investment is this?
   d. Suppose the US manufacturer uses the pounds to buy computer chips manufactured in Great Britain. Does $NX = NCO$ in this case? Explain.

3. Suppose the price of a pair of Lee jeans is €40 in the Netherlands and 400 roubles in Russia.
   a. What is the nominal rouble/euro exchange rate if purchasing-power parity holds?
   b. Suppose Russia's central bank doubles its money supply, which doubles its price level. If purchasing-power parity holds, what is the new rouble/euro exchange rate? Did the rouble appreciate or depreciate?

c. Suppose the ECB now doubles the European money supply, which doubles the Euro zone price level. If purchasing-power parity holds, what is the value of the rouble/euro exchange rate? Did the euro appreciate or depreciate?

d. Compare your answer to part (a) and part (c). What has happened to the exchange rate? Why?

Short-Answer Questions

1. Identify four reasons why the UK economy has engaged in an increasing amount of trade over the last 40 years.

2. Define net capital outflow. When foreigners invest in the UK, what happens to the value of UK NCO?

3. What are the two mutually exclusive locations where national saving can be invested?

4. If national saving is held constant, what happens to domestic investment if NCO decreases? Why?

5. In terms of the real exchange rate, what three variables could change to make the pound sterling more competitive internationally?

6. Suppose a Ford Escort sells for 10,000 euros in Spain and 12,000 Canadian dollars in Canada. If purchasing-power parity holds, what is the Canadian dollar/euro exchange rate? How many euros will a Canadian dollar buy?

7. Suppose trade increases between countries. Would this increase or decrease the predictive accuracy of the purchasing-power parity theory of exchange rate determination?

8. Why might purchasing-power parity fail to be completely accurate?

SELF-TEST

True/False Questions

_____ 1. For any country, net exports are always equal to net capital outflow because every international transaction involves an exchange of an equal value of some combination of goods and assets.

_____ 2. For a given amount of UK national saving, an increase in UK net capital outflow decreases UK domestic investment.

_____ 3. If the yen/euro exchange rate rises, the euro has appreciated.

_____ 4. If a case of Pepsi costs €8 in the Netherlands and 720 yen in Japan, then according to the purchasing-power parity theory of exchange rates, the yen/euro exchange rate should be 5,760 yen/euro.

_____ 5. If purchasing-power parity holds, the real exchange rate is always equal to 1.

_____ 6. If the nominal exchange rate is 2 euros to one British pound and the price of a Big Mac is €3 in Germany and £1 in Great Britain, then the real exchange rate is 1/3 of a British Big Mac per German Big Mac.

_____ 7. In order to increase domestic investment, a country must either increase its saving or decrease its net foreign investment.

_____ 8. Arbitrage is the process of taking advantage of differences in prices of the same good by buying where the good is cheap and selling where it is expensive.

_____ 9. Arbitrage tends to cause prices for the same good to diverge from one another.

_____10. If a company based in the US prefers a strong euro (a euro with a high exchange value), then the company likely exports more than it imports.

Multiple-Choice Questions

1. Which of the following statements is true about a country with a trade deficit?
   a. Net capital outflow must be positive.
   b. Net exports are negative.
   c. Net exports are positive.
   d. Exports exceed imports.

2. If Japan exports more than it imports,
   a. Japan's net exports are negative.
   b. Japan's net capital outflow must be negative.
   c. Japan's net capital outflow must be positive.
   d. Japan is running a trade deficit.

3. If the UK saves £1,000 billion and UK net capital outflow is − £200 billion, UK domestic investment is
   a. −£200 billion.
   b. £200 billion.
   c. £800 billion.
   d. £1,000 billion.
   e. £1,200 billion.

4. Which of the following people or firms would be pleased by a depreciation of the euro?
   a. a US tourist travelling in Europe.
   b. a US importer of Russian vodka.
   c. an Italian importer of US steel.
   d. a French exporter of wine to the US.

5. Suppose a cup of coffee is 1.5 euros in Germany and $0.50 in the US. If purchasing-power parity holds, what is the nominal exchange rate between euros and euros?
   a. 1/3 euro per dollar.
   b. 3 euros per dollar.
   c. 1.5 euros per dollar.
   d. 0.75 euro per dollar.

6. Which of the following products would likely be the least accurate if used to calculate purchasing-power parity?
   a. gold.
   b. automobiles.
   c. diamonds.
   d. dental services.

7. When people take advantage of differences in prices for the same good by buying it where it is cheap and selling it where it is expensive, it is known as
   a. arbitrage.
   b. net capital outflow.

      c. purchasing power parity.
      d. net exports.
      e. currency appreciation.

8. Suppose a German resident buys a Jaguar car from Great Britain and the British exporter uses the receipts to buy stock in Bosch. Which of the following statements is true from the perspective of Germany?
    a. Net exports fall, and net capital outflow falls.
    b. Net exports rise, and net capital outflow rises.
    c. Net exports fall, and net capital outflow rises.
    d. Net exports rise, and net capital outflow falls.

9. Which of the following statements is *not* true about the relationship between national saving, investment, and net capital outflow?
    a. Saving is the sum of investment and net capital outflow.
    b. For a given amount of saving, an increase in net capital outflow must decrease domestic investment.
    c. For a given amount of saving, a decrease in net capital outflow must decrease domestic investment.
    d. An increase in saving associated with an equal increase in net capital outflow leaves domestic investment unchanged.

10. Suppose the inflation rate over the last 20 years has been 10 per cent in Great Britain, 7 per cent in Japan, and 3 per cent in Europe. If purchasing power parity holds, which of the following statements is true? Over this period,
    a. the value of the euro should have fallen compared to the value of the pound and the yen.
    b. the yen should have risen in value compared to the pound and fallen compared to the euro.
    c. the yen should have fallen in value compared to the pound and risen compared to the euro.
    d. the value of the pound should have risen compared to the value of the yen and the euro.

ADVANCED CRITICAL THINKING

You are watching a national news broadcast with your parents. The newscaster explains that the exchange rate for the euro just hit its lowest value in a decade. The on the spot report shifts to a spokesman for Phillips, the Dutch manufacturer of electrical goods. The spokesman reports that sales of their electrical goods has hit an all time high and so has the value of their stock. Your parents are shocked by the report's positive view of the low value of the euro. They just cancelled their Canadian vacation because of the euro's low value.

1. Why do Phillips and your parents have different opinions about the value of the euro?

2. Phillips imports many parts and raw materials for their manufacturing processes and they sell many finished products abroad. Since they are happy about a low euro, what must be true about the proportions of Phillips' imports and exports?

3. If someone argues that a strong euro is 'good for Europe' because Europeans are able to exchange some of their GDP for a greater amount of foreign GDP, is it true that a strong euro is good for *every* European citizen? Why?

SOLUTIONS

Terms and Definitions

_1_ Trade surplus

_2_ Exports

_3_ Real exchange rate

_4_ Arbitrage

_5_ Nominal exchange rate

_6_ Depreciation

_7_ Closed economy

_8_ Net exports

_9_ Purchasing power parity

_10_ Appreciation

_11_ Open economy

_12_ Trade deficit

_13_ Imports

_14_ Net capital outflow

Practice Problems

1. a. NCO rises. Foreign portfolio investment.
    b. UK NX falls and a Japanese manufacturer is holding UK pounds sterling, therefore, NCO falls. Foreign portfolio investment.
    c. NCO falls. Foreign direct investment.
    d. NCO falls. Foreign portfolio investment.
    e. NCO rises. Foreign direct investment.

2. a. Yes, NX has risen by the size of the sale and NCO has risen an equal amount and is the size of the company's holdings of foreign currency.
    b. Yes, NX has risen by the size of the sale and NCO has risen an equal amount and is the size of the company's purchase of foreign capital. Foreign direct investment.
    c. Yes, NX has risen by the size of the sale and NCO has risen an equal amount and is the size of the company's purchase of foreign capital. Foreign portfolio investment.
    d. Yes, NX and NCO are both unchanged because exports rise by the same amount as imports, leaving NX unchanged. NCO was not involved.

3. a. 400 roubles/40 euros = 10 roubles/euro.
    b. 800 roubles/40 euros = 20 roubles/euro, depreciate.
    c. 800 roubles/80 euros = 10 roubles/euro, depreciate.
    d. It is unchanged. When prices rise symmetrically, it has no effect on the nominal exchange rate if purchasing-power parity holds.

Short-Answer Questions

1. Improved transportation, advances in telecommunications, more valuable technologically advanced products, favourable government policies.

2. Purchase of foreign assets by domestic residents minus purchase of domestic assets by foreigners. NCO decreases or becomes negative.

3. Domestically (I) or foreign countries (NCO) because S = I + NCO.

4. Domestic investment grows because less national saving is allocated abroad, and/or more foreign saving is allocated here.

5. If UK prices fall, the foreign currency/sterling exchange rate falls, or the foreign price level rises, UK goods are less expensive to foreigners.

6. 1.2 Canadian dollars/euro. 1 euro/1.2 Canadian dollars = 0.83 or 83 (European) cents.

7. Increase the accuracy because the greater the number of traded goods, the more accurate is purchasing-power parity.

8. Some goods are not easily traded, and traded goods are not always perfect substitutes.

True/False Questions

1. T

2. T

3. T

4. F; the exchange rate should be 90 yen/euro.

5. T

6. F; the real exchange rate is 2/3 British Big Mac per German Big Mac.

7. T

8. T

9. F; arbitrage causes prices to converge.

10. F; companies preferring a strong euro import more than they export.

Multiple-Choice Questions

1. b	6. d
2. c	7. a
3. e	8. a
4. d	9. b
5. b	10. b

Advanced Critical Thinking

1. Phillips sells much of its output to foreigners and the low value of the euro makes its products inexpensive to foreigners. Your parents were going to buy foreign goods and services and the euro cost became higher.

2. Phillips must sell a greater amount of products abroad than they purchase. That is, they are a net exporter.

3. No. A strong euro benefits those European citizens who are net importers and harms those European citizens who are net exporters.

Build a model to explain an open economy's trade balance and exchange rate

Use the model to analyse the effects of government budget deficits

Use the model to analyse the macroeconomic effects of trade policies

Use the model to analyse political instability and capital flight

Explain the slope of supply and demand in the market for foreign currency exchange

Show why a budget deficit tends to cause a trade deficit

Demonstrate that a quota on imports fails to have an effect on net exports

Show why capital flight causes a currency to depreciate

A MACROECONOMIC THEORY OF THE OPEN ECONOMY

CHAPTER OVERVIEW

Context and Purpose

Chapter 32 is the second chapter in a two-chapter sequence on open economy macroeconomics. Chapter 31 explained the basic concepts and vocabulary associated with an open economy. Chapter 32 ties these concepts together into a theory of the open economy.

The purpose of Chapter 32 is to establish the interdependence of a number of economic variables in an open economy. In particular, Chapter 32 demonstrates the relationships between the prices and quantities in the market for loanable funds and the prices and quantities in the market for foreign currency exchange. Using these markets, we can analyse the impact of a variety of government policies on an economy's exchange rate and trade balance.

CHAPTER REVIEW

Introduction

This chapter constructs a model of the open economy that allows us to analyse the impact of government policies on net exports, net capital outflow, and exchange rates. This model is based on our previous long run analysis in two ways: (1) we assume that output is determined by technology and factor supplies so output is fixed or given, and (2) prices are determined by the quantity of money so prices are fixed or given. The model constructed in this chapter is composed of two markets—the market for loanable funds and the market for foreign currency exchange. These markets simultaneously determine the interest rate and the exchange rate (and also the level of overall investment and the trade balance).

Supply and Demand for Loanable Funds and for Foreign Currency Exchange

In this section, we address two markets the market for loanable funds and the market for foreign currency exchange.

The market for loanable funds in an open economy is just an extension of the domestic loanable funds market. We assume that there is one financial market where savers lend and investors borrow. However, in an open economy, $S = I + NCO$. Therefore, as before, the supply of loanable funds comes from national saving (S). The supply of loanable funds (desire to lend) is positively related to the real interest rate. However, the demand for loanable funds now comes from two sources—domestic investment (I) and net capital outflow (NCO). The demand for capital assets, both domestic and foreign, is negatively related to the real interest rate. That is, a higher real interest rate reduces the desire of domestic residents to borrow to buy UK capital assets, and a higher domestic real interest rate reduces the desire of UK residents to buy foreign assets (and increases foreigners desire to buy UK assets) thus reducing NCO. If NCO is positive, it adds to the demand for funds. If NCO is negative, it subtracts from it. Both the supply and demand for loanable funds are shown in panel (a) of Exhibit 1. At equilibrium, the amount people save is balanced by the amount people want to invest in domestic and foreign assets.

The second market in our model is the market for foreign currency exchange. Recall, net capital outflow = net exports or $NCO = NX$ because if NX are positive, UK citizens must be using the sterling earned from net exports to increase their holdings of foreign assets which makes NCO positive by the same amount. In the market for foreign currency exchange, NCO represents the quantity of sterling supplied to buy net foreign assets. NX represents the quantity of sterling demanded for the purpose of buying UK net exports. The demand for sterling is negatively related to the real exchange rate because a rise in the real exchange rate means that UK goods are relatively more expensive and less attractive to foreign and domestic buyers causing NX to fall. The supply of sterling on the foreign exchange market is vertical because NCO (the source of the supply of sterling) does not depend on the real exchange rate, but instead depends on the real interest rate. Here we assume that the real interest rate is given and focus on the foreign exchange market. The supply and demand for sterling in the foreign exchange market is shown in panel (c) of Exhibit 1. The supply and demand for sterling in this market determine the exchange rate. At equilibrium, the quantity of sterling demanded to buy net exports is balanced by the quantity of sterling supplied to buy net foreign assets.

Equilibrium in the Open Economy

The market for loanable funds is linked to the market for foreign currency exchange by net capital outflow (NCO). In the market for loanable funds, NCO is a portion of demand along with private investment. In the market for foreign currency exchange, NCO is the source of supply. The quantity of net capital outflow is negatively related to the real interest rate because when the UK real interest rate is relatively high, UK assets are more attractive and UK NCO is relatively low. This is shown in panel (b) of the previous graph.

Rather than viewing each panel in Exhibit 1 individually, we can view them as a group and see how these two markets determine simultaneously the equilibrium values of the real interest rate, the real exchange rate, NCO, NX (the trade balance), saving, and domestic investment.

The supply and demand for loanable funds in panel (a) determine the real interest rate. The real interest rate from panel (a) determines the quantity of NCO in panel (b). The quantity of NCO is the supply of sterling in the foreign currency exchange market in panel (c). This supply curve in conjunction with the demand for sterling (determined by NX) in the foreign currency exchange market determines the real exchange rate in panel (c).

EXHIBIT 1

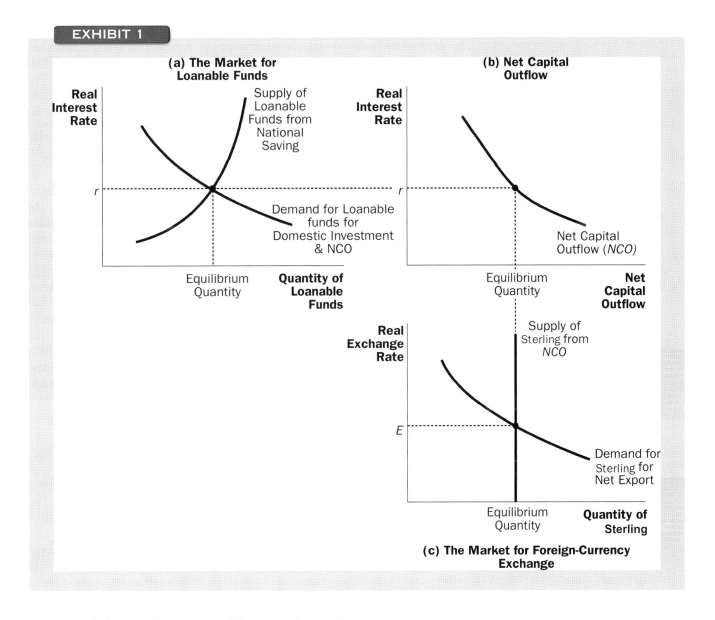

(a) The Market for Loanable Funds

Real Interest Rate

Supply of Loanable Funds from National Saving

r

Demand for Loanable funds for Domestic Investment & NCO

Equilibrium Quantity

Quantity of Loanable Funds

(b) Net Capital Outflow

Real Interest Rate

r

Net Capital Outflow (*NCO*)

Equilibrium Quantity

Net Capital Outflow

Real Exchange Rate

Supply of Sterling from *NCO*

E

Demand for Sterling for Net Export

Equilibrium Quantity

Quantity of Sterling

(c) The Market for Foreign-Currency Exchange

How Policies and Events Affect an Open Economy

We can use this model to see how various government policies and other events affect the equilibrium values of the variables in the model.

• *Government Budget Deficits*: An increase in the government's budget deficit reduces national saving and, thus, shifts the supply of loanable funds to the left in panel (a) of Exhibit 1. The decrease in the supply of loanable funds increases the domestic real interest rate and crowds out domestic investment. This is no different from the closed economy case. However, in an open economy, the rise in the domestic real interest rate makes foreign investments less attractive (and domestic investments more attractive to foreigners) so the quantity of net capital outflow decreases in panel (b). This reduces the supply of sterling in the foreign currency exchange market in panel (c) because fewer people are supplying sterling to buy foreign assets. This raises the real exchange rate of sterling and reduces net exports (to equal the reduction in *NCO*). Hence, an increase in the budget deficit reduces national saving, raises the real interest rate, crowds out investment, reduces *NCO*, raises the real exchange rate, and moves the trade balance toward deficit.

Note that our model suggests that government budget deficits cause trade deficits. Thus, budget and trade deficits are often referred to as the 'twin deficits' because they are closely related. In a famously documented series of events, the US budget deficit in the 1980s failed to crowd out domestic investment to the degree predicted by closed economy models because the increase in the trade deficit and the reduction in US *NCO* (increased foreign investment in the US) helped fund US investment needs.

- *Trade policy*: A **trade policy** is a government policy that directly affects the quantity of a country's imports or exports. A *tariff* is a tax on imported goods. An *import quota* is a limit on the quantity of a good which is produced abroad that can be sold domestically.

Suppose the government places an import quota on cars produced in Japan for the purpose of moving the UK trade balance toward surplus. The import restriction reduces imports at each exchange rate and, thus, increases net exports at each exchange rate. It follows that foreigners need more sterling at each exchange rate so the demand for sterling in the foreign currency exchange market shifts to the right in panel (c) of Exhibit 1 and raises the real exchange rate for sterling. Since there has been no change in the loanable funds market in panel (a) and no change in *NCO* in panel (b), the final net exports must remain unchanged because $S-I = NCO = NX$. Thus, the import quota reduces imports but the rise in the exchange value of sterling offsets this effect by reducing exports, *leaving the trade balance unchanged*. As a result, the UK imports fewer cars (which benefits UK car manufacturers) but sells less of other goods and services abroad (which harms UK producers), but there are no significant macroeconomic effects beyond the increase in the exchange rate. The impact of trade policy is more microeconomic than macroeconomic.

- *Political instability and capital flight*: **Capital flight** is a sudden reduction in the demand for domestic assets coupled with a sudden increase in the demand for foreign assets. It might occur due to domestic political instability.

Suppose the UK becomes politically unstable. Investors might decide to sell UK assets and buy foreign assets. This act increases net capital outflow and shifts the demand for loanable funds to be used for foreign investment at each real interest rate to the right in panel (a) of Exhibit 1. It simultaneously shifts the *NCO* curve to the right in panel (b). The increase in net capital outflow increases the supply of sterling in the foreign currency exchange market in panel (c), reducing the real exchange rate. Thus, capital flight increases the domestic real interest rate, increases net capital outflow and net exports, and reduces the value of sterling in the foreign currency exchange market. Note that the increase in the interest rate reduces domestic investment which slows capital accumulation and growth. It has the opposite effect on the country to which the capital is flowing.

HELPFUL HINTS

1. A change in national saving generates the same result regardless of whether the change was from private saving or public saving. In your text there is a demonstration of the impact of an increase in a government budget deficit on an open economy. It is shown that a budget deficit causes a reduction in the public saving component of national saving and shifts the supply of loanable funds to the left. Note that a reduction in the private saving component of national savings also shifts the supply of loanable funds to the left. Thus, the example given in your text can be utilized for cases when there is a change in private saving. (The source of the change in saving will generate differences in the amount of output purchased by consumers versus government, but it will not alter any of the international analysis.)

2. To find the change in NX (net exports), remember that $NX = NCO$ (net capital outflow). When we use our model to discover the impact of a government policy or an economic event on the economic variables in an open economy, there is no way to directly read net exports (the trade balance) from any of the diagrams. However, the quantity of NCO is always directly measurable from panel (b) of Exhibit 1. Since $NCO = NX$, whenever there is an increase in NCO, there is an equivalent increase in NX (which is an improvement in the trade balance). Whenever NCO declines, there is an equivalent decline in NX.

3. Capital flight reduces domestic investment. The discussion of capital flight in the text and in the chapter review above notes that capital flight increases net capital outflow and the supply of the domestic currency on the foreign currency exchange market, which lowers the exchange value of the domestic currency. Since these activities raise net exports (improve the trade balance), why is capital flight considered bad for the economy rather than good? Look at panel (a) of Figure 7 of your text. The increase in net capital outflow within the demand for loanable funds absorbs a greater amount of national saving than the tiny increase in national saving induced by the rise in the real interest rate. Thus, domestic investment is reduced by an amount similar to the increase in net exports. As a result, the prospect for long-term growth in a country exhibiting capital flight is reduced due to the reduction in domestic investment.

4. Work the examples in the text backward. The three policy problems demonstrated in your text require a significant degree of concentration to understand. Once you have mastered them, you should feel comfortable that you can follow someone else's demonstration. The next step is to work those same problems backward, alone. That is, address the effect of a reduction in the budget deficit, the lowering of a trade restriction, and the effect of capital inflow. So that you may check your work, the first practice problem below is composed of the chapter examples where the source of the change has been reversed.

TERMS AND DEFINITIONS

Choose a definition for each key term.

Key terms:

_____ Twin deficits

_____ Trade policy

_____ Tariff

_____ Import quota

_____ Capital flight

Definitions:

1. A limit on the quantity of a good which is produced abroad that can be sold domestically

2. A government policy that directly affects the quantity of country's imports or exports

3. A sudden reduction in the demand for domestic assets coupled with a sudden increase in the demand for foreign assets

4. The government budget deficit and the trade deficit

5. A tax on imported goods

PROBLEMS AND SHORT-ANSWER QUESTIONS

Practice Problems

1. This problem is composed of the examples in the chapter except the source of the change has been reversed. Use the model described by Exhibit 1 to answer the following questions.

a. Suppose the government reduces its budget deficit. Describe the sequence of events in the model by describing the shifts in the curves in Exhibit 1 and discuss the movements in the relevant macroeconomic variables.

b. Suppose the government reduces a quota on the importing of Japanese cars. Describe the sequence of events in the model by describing the shifts in the curves in Exhibit 1 and discuss the movements in the relevant macroeconomic variables.

c. Suppose there is a sudden inflow of capital into the UK because we are believed to be more politically stable than the rest of the world. Describe the sequence of events in the model by describing the shifts in the curves in Exhibit 1 and discuss the movements in the relevant macroeconomic variables.

2. a. Suppose private saving increased at each real interest rate. What would happen to the important macroeconomic variables in our model of an open economy?

b. Is there any difference between your answer above and the answer you would write if the government had reduced its deficit? Why?

c. Suppose the government passes an investment tax credit that increases domestic investment at each real interest rate. How would this change the important economic variables in the model?

d. Compare your answer in part (a) (an increase in saving at each real interest rate) to your answer in part (c) (an increase in domestic investment at each real interest rate). Are there any differences?

3. Suppose the European taste for Japanese cars increases. (Answer this question using the open economy model from the Japanese perspective.)

a. What happens to the demand for yen in the foreign currency exchange market?

b. What happens to the value of yen in the foreign currency exchange market?

c. What happens to Japanese net exports? Why?

d. If the Japanese are selling more cars, what must be true about Japanese imports and exports of other items?

e. Keeping in mind your answers to (a) through (c), do you think Japan runs an overall trade surplus with the rest of the world because its cars are better built or because of its domestic saving and *NCO?* Explain.

4. Suppose Canada is perceived to be politically unstable, which induces capital flight to the US.

a. Describe what happens in the foreign-currency exchange market from the perspective of Canada.

b. Describe what happens in the foreign-currency exchange market from the perspective of the US.

c. Are your answers to part (a) and (b) above consistent with one another? Why?

d. If the economy of Canada is small when compared to the economy of the US, what should this event do to each country's balance of trade?

e. Which country will tend to grow faster in the future? Why?

Short-Answer Questions

1. Explain the slope of the demand for loanable funds in an open economy.

2. Does net capital outflow add to, or subtract from, domestic investment when we create the demand for loanable funds? Explain.

3. Explain the source of the supply of euros in the market for foreign currency exchange.

4. Explain the source of the demand for euros in the market for foreign currency exchange.

5. Why might certain companies and unions support tariffs and import quotas even if they know that these restrictions cannot alter the trade balance?

6. Suppose the quality of UK goods and services falls and, as a result, foreigners choose to buy fewer UK goods. Does this affect the UK balance of trade? Why?

7. What happens to the value of a country's currency if there is capital flight from that country? Explain.

8. What would an increase in the saving of UK residents do to the UK trade balance and the sterling exchange rate? Explain.

9. Why are the budget and trade deficits referred to as the 'twin deficits'?

10. Do trade restrictions (such as tariffs and import quotas) alter *NX?*

SELF-TEST

True/False Questions

_____ 1. Net capital outflow is the purchase of domestic assets by foreigners minus the purchase of foreign assets by domestic residents.

_____ 2. A country's net capital outflow (*NCO*) is always equal to its net exports (*NX*).

_____ 3. Other things being the same, an increase in a country's real interest rate reduces net capital outflow.

_____ 4. An increase in UK net capital outflow increases the supply of sterling in the market for foreign currency exchange and decreases the real exchange rate of sterling.

_____ 5. If a government sponsored advertising campaign convinces UK residents to 'buy British', it will improve (move toward surplus) the UK trade balance.

_____ 6. If a country's net capital outflow (*NCO*) is positive, it is an addition to its demand for loanable funds.

_____ 7. An increase in the government's budget deficit shifts the supply of loanable funds to the right.

_____ 8. An increase in the government's budget deficit tends to cause the real exchange rate of sterling to depreciate.

_____ 9. The term 'twin deficits' refers to a country's trade deficit and its government budget deficit.

_____10. If UK residents increase their saving, sterling will appreciate in the market for foreign currency exchange.

Multiple-Choice Questions

1. An increase in the government budget deficit
    a. increases the real interest rate and crowds out investment.
    b. decreases the real interest rate and crowds out investment.
    c. has no impact on the real interest rate and fails to crowd out investment because foreigners buy assets in the deficit country.
    d. none of the above.

2. Which one of the following statements regarding the loanable funds market is true?
    a. An increase in private saving shifts the supply of loanable funds to the left.
    b. A decrease in the government budget deficit increases the real interest rate.

c. An increase in the government budget deficit shifts the supply of loanable funds to the right.

d. An increase in the government budget deficit shifts the supply of loanable funds to the left.

3. An increase in Europe's taste for US produced Fords would cause the dollar to
   a. depreciate and would increase US net exports.
   b. depreciate and would decrease US net exports.
   c. appreciate and would increase US net exports.
   d. appreciate and would decrease US net exports.
   e. appreciate, but the total value of US net export stays the same.

4. An increase in the UK government budget deficit
   a. increases UK net exports and decreases UK net capital outflow.
   b. decreases UK net exports and increases UK net capital outflow.
   c. decreases UK net exports and UK net capital outflow the same amount.
   d. increases UK net exports and UK net capital outflow the same amount.

5. Which of the following statements regarding the market for foreign currency exchange is true?
   a. An increase in UK net exports increases the supply of sterling and sterling depreciates.
   b. An increase in UK net exports decreases the supply of sterling and sterling depreciates.
   c. An increase in UK net exports decreases the demand for sterling and sterling appreciates.
   d. An increase in UK net exports increases the demand for sterling and sterling appreciates.

6. Which of the following statements regarding the market for foreign currency exchange is true?
   a. An increase in UK net capital outflow increases the supply of sterling and sterling appreciates.
   b. An increase in UK net capital outflow increases the supply of sterling and sterling depreciates.
   c. An increase in UK net capital outflow increases the demand for sterling and sterling appreciates.
   d. An increase in UK net capital outflow increases the demand for sterling and sterling depreciates.

7. If the EU reduces its a quota on imports of clothing from China, which of the following is true regarding the market for foreign currency exchange?
   a. The demand for euros increases and the euro appreciates.
   b. The demand for euros decreases and the euro depreciates.
   c. The supply of euros increases and the euro depreciates.
   d. The supply of euros decreases and the euro appreciates.

8. An increase in UK private saving
   a. increases UK net exports and decreases UK net capital outflow.
   b. decreases UK net exports and increases UK net capital outflow.
   c. decreases UK net exports and UK net capital outflow the same amount.
   d. increases UK net exports and UK net capital outflow the same amount.

9. An export subsidy should have the opposite effect of
   a. a tariff.
   b. capital flight.
   c. a government budget deficit.
   d. an increase in private saving.

10. Capital flight
    a. decreases a country's net exports and increases its long-run growth path.
    b. decreases a country's net exports and decreases its long-run growth path.
    c. increases a country's net exports and decreases its long-run growth path.
    d. increases a country's net exports and increases its long-run growth path.

ADVANCED CRITICAL THINKING

Hong Kong has a capitalist economic system. It was leased from China by Great Britain for 100 years. In 1997, it was returned to China, a socialist republic.

1. What do you think this event should do to the net capital outflow of Hong Kong? Why?

2. If the residents of Hong Kong chose Canada as a place to move some of their business activity, what impact do you suppose this will have on the value of the Canadian interest rate and exchange rate? Why?

3. Which Canadian industries, those engaged in importing or exporting, are likely to be pleased with Hong Kong's investment in Canada? Why?

4. What impact will Hong Kong's return to China have on the growth rate of Canada?

SOLUTIONS

Terms and Definitions

__1__ Import quota

__2__ Trade policy

__3__ Capital flight

__4__ Twin deficits

__5__ Tariff

Practice Problems

1. a. Panel (a), supply of loanable funds shifts right, real interest rate decreases. *NCO* increases, increasing the supply of sterling in the foreign currency exchange market and causing the real exchange rate to depreciate. Saving and domestic investment have increased and the trade balance has moved toward surplus.
    b. Panel (c), *NX* fall at each exchange rate as imports increase causing the demand for sterling in the foreign currency exchange market to shift left; the real exchange rate falls increasing *NX* to their original level. No change in trade balance, but a higher volume of trade (more imports and more exports).
    c. *NCO* falls as US residents and foreigners buy UK assets. In panel (a), demand for loanable funds shifts left. Panel (b), *NCO* shifts left because of a decrease in *NCO* at each interest rate causing the supply of sterling in the foreign currency exchange market to shift left and the exchange rate to rise. Result, real interest rate down, *NCO* and *NX* down, value of sterling up, increase in domestic investment.

2. a. Panel (a), supply of loanable funds shifts right, real interest rate decreases. *NCO* increases, increasing the supply of sterling in the foreign currency exchange market and causes the real exchange rate to depreciate. Saving and domestic investment have increased and the trade balance has moved toward surplus.
    b. No, because it doesn't matter why national saving increased. Either one will shift the supply of loanable funds to the right.
    c. Increase in the demand for loanable funds, raises real interest rate, lowers *NCO* and *NX*, decreases the supply of sterling in the foreign currency exchange market which raises the value of sterling. Domestic saving and investment have increased.

d. Both increase domestic saving and investment, but an increase in saving moves the trade balance toward surplus while an increase in investment demand moves it toward deficit.

3. a. Shifts right.
   b. Real exchange rate rises so value of yen rises.
   c. NCO is unchanged therefore NX as a total is unchanged.
   d. If NX are constant, they must be importing more or exporting less of other items.
   e. NX as a total are determined by NCO so Japan's overall level of trade surplus is based on its saving behaviour. However, the composition of its exports may be based on its relative quality of production.

4. a. The supply of Canadian dollars shifts right and the value of the Canadian dollar falls.
   b. The supply of US dollars shifts left and the value of the US dollar rises.
   c. Yes. A rise in the value of the US dollar relative to the Canadian dollar should correspond to the fall in the value of the Canadian dollar relative to the US dollar.
   d. The fall in the value of the Canadian dollar should improve its NX by a greater per centage than the fall in NX by the US.
   e. Canada is increasing its NCO in the US and the US is decreasing its NCO in Canada, so the United States will likely grow faster.

Short-Answer Questions

1. It is negatively sloped because a higher real interest rate reduces the desire to borrow funds to purchase capital domestically, and it discourages UK residents from buying foreign assets and encourages foreign residents to buy UK assets.

2. If NCO is positive, it adds to the demand for loanable funds. If NCO is negative, it subtracts.

3. It comes from euros euro zone residents used for NCO.

4. It comes from the need for euros from outsiders purchasing euro zone. NX.

5. Because trade restrictions can improve the sales of some domestic companies facing competition from imports, but largely at the expense of other domestic companies producing for export.

6. No, it reduces the demand for sterling in the market for foreign currency exchange and lowers the value of sterling to keep NX unchanged.

7. It increases the supply of their currency in the market for foreign-currency exchange and lowers the exchange rate.

8. It decreases the UK real interest rate, increases NCO and NX, increases the supply of sterling on the foreign currency exchange market, and lowers the sterling exchange rate.

9. Because a budget deficit tends to cause a trade deficit when it raises the domestic real interest rate, reducing NCO and NX.

10. Trade restrictions don't alter the total value of NX because NX = NCO. An increase in trade restrictions reduces both imports and exports by the same amount.

True/False Questions

1. F; NCO is the purchase of foreign assets by domestic residents minus the purchase of domestic assets by foreigners.

2. T

3. T

4. T

5. F; net exports are unchanged because NCO is unchanged.

6. T

7. F; an increase in the government's budget deficit shifts the supply of loanable funds to the left.

8. F; an increase in the government's budget deficit raises the real exchange rate.

9. T

10. F; sterling will depreciate.

Multiple-Choice Questions

1. a   6. b
2. d   7. b
3. e   8. d
4. c   9. a
5. d   10. c

Advanced Critical Thinking

1. It should increase the *NCO* of Hong Kong because foreigners are not buying assets in Hong Kong and Hong Kong residents are buying assets abroad—capital flight. Investors fear that China may nationalize much of Hong Kong's industry.

2. This will decrease Canada's *NCO*. This shifts the demand for loanable funds left and lowers the real interest rate. The reduced *NCO* reduces the supply of Canadian dollars in the foreign-currency exchange market, raises the exchange rate, and moves *NX* toward deficit.

3. The increase in the value of the Canadian dollar will make Canadian producers less competitive abroad, but will make imports cheaper.

4. The reduction in Canada's *NCO* (due to Hong Kong's increased *NCO*) increases the capital stock of Canada, causing it to grow.

In this chapter you will

Learn three key facts about short run fluctuations

Consider how the economy in the short run differs from the economy in the long run

Use the model of aggregate demand and aggregate supply to explain economic fluctuations

See how shifts in either aggregate demand or aggregate supply can cause booms and recessions

OUTCOMES

You should be able to

Explain why the term 'business cycle' is misleading

Explain why money is unlikely to be neutral in the short run

List three reasons why the aggregate demand curve is downward sloping

Demonstrate the short run and long run effects of an oil price shock on the economy

AGGREGATE DEMAND AND AGGREGATE SUPPLY

CHAPTER OVERVIEW

Context and Purpose

To this point, our study of macroeconomic theory has concentrated on the behaviour of the economy in the long run. Chapters 33 through 35 now focus on short run fluctuations in the economy around its long term trend. Chapter 33 introduces aggregate demand and aggregate supply and shows how shifts in these curves can cause recessions. Chapter 34 focuses on how policy makers use the tools of money and fiscal policy to influence aggregate demand. Chapter 35 analyses the relationship between inflation and unemployment.

The purpose of Chapter 33 is to develop the model economists use to analyse the economy's short run fluctuations—the model of aggregate demand and aggregate supply. We will learn about some of the sources for shifts in the aggregate demand curve and the aggregate supply curve and how these shifts can cause recessions. We will also introduce actions policy makers might undertake to offset recessions.

CHAPTER REVIEW

Introduction

Over the last 50 years, UK real GDP has grown at an average rate of about 2 per cent per year. However, in some years GDP has not grown at this average rate. A period when output and incomes fall, and unemployment rises, is known as a **recession** when it is mild and a **depression** when it is severe. This chapter focuses on the economy's short run fluctuations around its long term trend. To do this, we employ the model of aggregate demand and aggregate supply.

Three Key Facts About Economic Fluctuations

- *Economic fluctuations are irregular and unpredictable*: Although economic fluctuations are often termed *the business cycle*, the term 'business cycle' is misleading because it suggests that economic fluctuations follow a regular, predictable pattern. In reality, economic fluctuations are irregular and unpredictable.

- *Most macroeconomic quantities fluctuate together*: Although real GDP is usually used to monitor short run changes in the economy, it really doesn't matter which measure of economic activity is used because most macroeconomic variables that measure income, spending, or production move in the same direction, though by different amounts. Investment is one type of expenditure that is particularly volatile across the business cycle.

- *As output falls, unemployment rises*: When real GDP declines, the rate of unemployment rises because when firms produce fewer goods and services, they lay off workers.

Explaining Short Run Economic Fluctuations

Classical theory is based on the classical dichotomy and money neutrality. Recall, the classical dichotomy is the separation of economic variables into real and nominal, while money neutrality is the property that changes in the money supply only affect nominal variables, not real variables. Most economists believe these classical assumptions are an accurate description of the economy in the long run, but not in the short run. That is, over a period of a number of years, changes in the money supply should affect prices, but should have no impact on real variables such as real GDP, unemployment, real wages, and so on. However, in the short run, from year to year, changes in nominal variables such as money and prices are likely to have an impact on real variables. That is, in the short run, nominal and real variables are not independent.

We use the **model of aggregate supply and aggregate demand** to explain economic fluctuations. This model can be graphed with the price level, measured by the CPI or the GDP deflator on the vertical axis and real GDP on the horizontal axis. The **aggregate demand curve** shows the quantity of goods and services households, firms, and government wish to buy at each price level. It slopes negatively. The **aggregate supply curve** shows the quantity of goods and services that firms produce and sell at each price level. It slopes positively (in the short run). The price level and output adjust to balance aggregate supply and demand. This model looks like an ordinary microeconomic supply and demand model. However, the reasons for the slopes and the sources of the shifts in the aggregate supply and demand curves differ from those for the microeconomic model.

The Aggregate Demand Curve

Exhibit 1 illustrates the model of aggregate supply and aggregate demand.

EXHIBIT 1

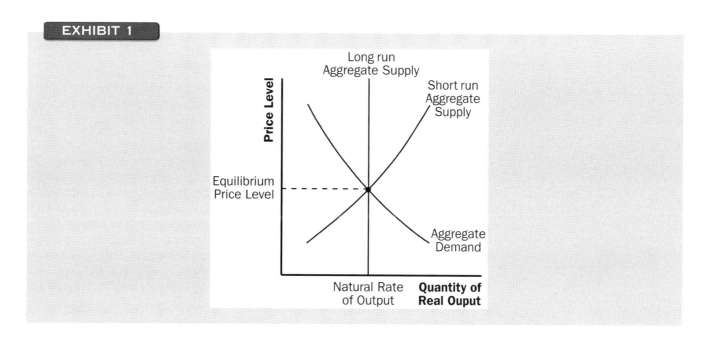

The aggregate demand curve shows the quantity of goods and services demanded at each price level. Recall, GDP = C + I + G + NX. To explain why aggregate demand slopes downward with respect to price, we analyse the impact of the price level on consumption (C), investment (I), and net exports (NX). (We ignore government spending (G) because it is a fixed policy variable.) A decrease in the price level increases consumption, investment, and net exports for the following reasons:

- The price level and consumption: *the wealth effect*. At a lower price level, the fixed amount of nominal money in consumer's pockets increases in value. Consumers feel wealthier and spend more, increasing the consumption component of aggregate demand.

- The price level and investment: *the interest rate effect*. At a lower price level, households need to hold less money to buy the same products. They lend some money by buying bonds or depositing in banks, either of which lowers interest rates and stimulates the investment component of aggregate demand.

- The price level and net exports: *the exchange rate effect*. Since, as described above, a lower price level causes lower interest rates, some U.S. investors will invest abroad, increasing the supply of dollars in the foreign currency exchange market. This act causes the real exchange rate of the dollar to depreciate, reduces the relative price of domestic goods compared to foreign goods, and increases the net exports component of aggregate demand.

All three explanations of the downward slope of the aggregate demand curve assume that the money supply is fixed.

When something causes a change in the quantity of output demanded at each price level, it causes a shift in the aggregate demand curve. The following events and policies cause shifts in aggregate demand:

- *Shifts arising from changes in consumption*: If consumers save more, if stock prices fall so that consumers feel poorer, or if taxes are increased, consumers spend less and aggregate demand shifts left.

- *Shifts arising from changes in investment*: If firms become optimistic about the future and decide to buy new equipment, if an investment tax allowance increases investment, if the central bank increases the money supply which reduces interest rates and increases investment, aggregate demand shifts right.

- *Shifts arising from changes in government purchases*: If central or local governments increase purchases, aggregate demand shifts right.

- *Shifts arising from changes in net exports*: If foreign countries have a recession and buy fewer goods from the UK or if the value of sterling rises on foreign exchange markets, net exports are reduced and aggregate demand shifts left.

The Aggregate Supply Curve

The aggregate supply curve shows the quantity of goods and services firms produce and sell at each price level. In the long run, the aggregate supply curve is vertical while in the short run it is upward (positively) sloping. Both can be seen in Exhibit 1.

The *long run aggregate supply curve* is vertical because, in the long run, the supply of goods and services depends on the supply of capital, labour, and natural resources, and on production technology. In the long run, the supply of goods and services is independent of the level of prices. It is the embodiment of the classical dichotomy and money neutrality. That is, if the price level rises and all prices rise together, there should be no impact on output or any other real variable.

The long run aggregate supply curve shows the level of production that is sometimes called *potential output* or *full employment output*. Since in the short run output can be temporarily above or below this level, a better name is the *natural rate of output* because it is the amount of output produced when unemployment is at its natural, or normal, rate. Anything that alters the natural rate of output shifts the long run aggregate supply curve to the right or left. Since in the long run, output depends on labour, capital, natural resources, and technological knowledge, we group the sources of the shifts in long run aggregate supply into these categories:

- *Shifts arising from labour*: If there is immigration from abroad or a reduction in the natural rate of unemployment from a reduction in the minimum wage, long run aggregate supply shifts right.

- *Shifts arising from capital*: If there is an increase in physical or human capital, productivity rises and long run aggregate supply shifts right.

- *Shifts arising from natural resources*: If there is a discovery of new resources, or a favourable change in weather patterns, long run aggregate supply shifts right.

- *Shifts arising from technical knowledge*: If new inventions are employed, or international trade opens up, long run aggregate supply shifts right.

Long run growth and inflation may be depicted as a rightward shift in the long run aggregate supply curve (from the events described above) and an even larger rightward shift in the aggregate demand curve due to increases in the money supply. Thus, over time, output grows and prices rise.

The short run aggregate supply curve slopes upward (positively) because a change in the price level causes output to deviate from its long run level for a short period of time, say, a year or two. There are three theories that explain why the short run aggregate supply curve slopes upward and they all share a common theme: output rises above the natural rate when the actual price level exceeds the expected price level. The three theories are:

- *The sticky wage theory*: Suppose firms and workers agree on a nominal wage contract based on what they expect the price level to be. If the price level falls below what was expected, the real wage W/P rises, raising the cost of production and lowering profits, causing the firm to hire less labour and reduce the quantity of goods and services supplied.

- *The sticky price theory*: Because there is a cost to firms for changing prices, termed *menu costs*, some firms will resist reducing their prices when the price level unexpectedly falls. Thus, their prices are 'too high' and their sales decline, causing the quantity of goods and services supplied to fall.

- *The misperceptions theory*: When the price level unexpectedly falls, suppliers only notice that the price of their particular product has fallen. Hence, they mistakenly believe that there has been a fall in the *relative price* of their product, causing them to reduce the quantity of goods and services supplied.

Note two features of the explanations above: (1) in each case, the quantity of output supplied changed because actual prices deviated from expected prices and (2) the effect will be temporary because people will adjust their expectations over time. We can express aggregate supply mathematically with the following equation:

$$\text{Quantity of Output Supplied} = \text{Natural Rate of Output} + a\left(\text{Actual Price Level} - \text{Expected Price level}\right)$$

where *a* is a number that determines how much output responds to unexpected changes in the price level.

Events that shift the long run aggregate supply curve also tend to shift the short run aggregate supply curve in the same direction. However, the short run aggregate supply curve can shift while the long run aggregate supply curve remains stationary. In the short run, the quantity of goods and services supplied depends on perceptions, wages, and prices, all of which were set based on the expected price level. For example, if people and firms expect higher prices, they set wages higher, reducing the profitability of production and reducing the quantity supplied of goods and service at each price level. Thus, the short run aggregate supply curve shifts left. A lower expected price level shifts the short run aggregate supply curve to the right. In general, things that cause an increase in the cost of production (an increase in wages or oil prices) cause the short run aggregate supply curve to shift left while a decrease in the cost of production causes the short run aggregate supply curve to shift right.

Two Causes of Economic Fluctuations

Exhibit 1 shows the model of aggregate supply and aggregate demand in long run equilibrium. That is, the level of output is at the long run natural rate where aggregate demand and long run aggregate supply intersect, and perceptions, wages, and prices have fully adjusted to the actual price level as demonstrated by short run aggregate supply intersecting at the same point.

There are two basic causes of a recession: a leftward shift in aggregate demand and a leftward shift in aggregate supply.

A leftward shift in aggregate demand. Suppose households cut back on their spending because they are pessimistic or nervous about the future. Consumers spend less at each price level so aggregate demand shifts left in Exhibit 2. In the short run, the economy moves to point B because the drop in the price level was unexpected so some wages and some prices are too high. We can see that the economy is in a recession at P_2, Y_2 because output is below the natural rate. Policy makers could try to eliminate the recession by increasing aggregate demand with an increase in government spending or an increase in the money supply. If judged correctly, the government moves the economy back to point A. If the government does nothing, the recession will remedy itself (self-correct) over time. Since actual prices are below prior expectations, price expectations will be reduced over time and wages and prices will fall to levels commensurate

EXHIBIT 2

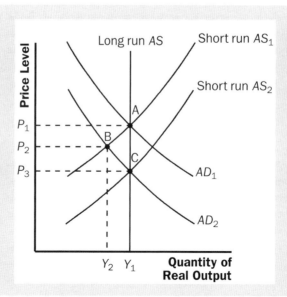

EXHIBIT 3

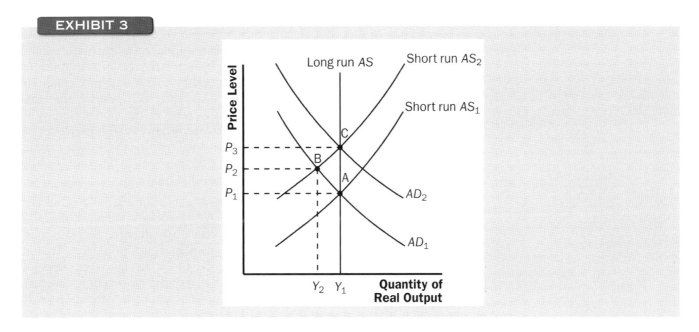

with P_3. The short run aggregate supply curve shifts right and the economy arrives at point C. To summarize, in the short run, shifts in aggregate demand cause fluctuations in output. In the long run, shifts in aggregate demand only cause changes in prices.

A leftward shift in aggregate supply. Suppose OPEC raises the price of oil which, through its effect on energy prices and distribution costs, raises the costs of production for most firms. This reduces profitability, firms produce less at each price level, and short run aggregate supply shifts to the left in Exhibit 3. Prices rise, reducing the quantity demanded along the aggregate demand curve and the economy arrives at point B. Since output has fallen (stagnation) and the price level has risen (inflation), the economy has experienced **stagflation**. If policy makers do nothing, the unemployment at Y_2 will, in time, put downward pressure on workers' wages, increase profitability, and shift aggregate supply back to its original position and the economy returns to point A. Alternatively, policy makers could increase aggregate demand and move the economy to point C, avoiding point B altogether. Here, policy makers *accommodate* the shift in aggregate supply by allowing the increase in costs to raise prices permanently. Output is returned to long run equilibrium, but prices are higher. To summarize, a reduction in short run aggregate supply causes stagflation. Policy makers cannot shift aggregate demand in a manner to offset both the increase in price and the decrease in output simultaneously.

HELPFUL HINTS

1. There are no changes in real variables along the long run aggregate supply curve. When all prices change equally, no real variables have changed. A vertical long run aggregate supply curve simply demonstrates this classical lesson. Pick any point on the long run aggregate supply curve. Now double the price level and all nominal values such as wages. Although the price level has doubled, relative prices have remained constant including the real wage, W/P. There has been no change in anyone's incentive to produce and, thus, no change in output. It follows that if the economy is temporarily producing a level of output other than the long run natural rate, then at least some wages or prices have failed to adjust to the long run equilibrium price level. This causes at least some relative prices to change, which stimulates or discourages production. This is, in fact, what is happening along a short run aggregate supply curve.

2. Output can fluctuate to levels both above and below the natural rate of output. The examples of economic fluctuations in the text tend to focus on recessions. That is, the examples deal with periods when output is less than the natural level. However, note that output can be above the natural rate temporarily because unemployment can be below its natural rate. This economic condition is known as a boom. A boom will occur when there is a positive aggregate demand shock—for example, if there is an increase in the money supply, an increase in domestic investment, or an increase in government purchases. A boom will also occur if there is a positive aggregate supply shock—for example, if the price of oil were to fall or union wage demands were to decrease. To help you, these cases are addressed in the problems that follow.

3. You might shift the short run aggregate supply curve left and right or up and down. Suppose there is an increase in the wage of workers. We have suggested that the rise in the wage will increase the cost of production, decrease profitability at each price level and decrease production at each price level. That is, it will shift the short run aggregate supply curve to the left. However, we could have suggested that the increase in the wage will increase the cost of production, requiring firms to charge a higher price in order to continue the same level of production. That is, it shifts the short run aggregate supply curve upward on the graph. In the first case, we lowered the quantity supplied at each price. In the second case, we raised the price at each quantity supplied. The resulting shift is the same.

TERMS AND DEFINITIONS

Choose a definition for each key term.

Key terms:

_____ Recession

_____ Depression

_____ The business cycle

_____ Model of aggregate demand and aggregate supply

_____ Aggregate demand curve

_____ Aggregate supply curve

_____ Natural rate of output

_____ Menu costs

_____ Stagflation

_____ Accommodative policy

Definitions:

1. Costs associated with changing prices

2. Short run economic fluctuations

3. A policy of increasing aggregate demand in response to a decrease in short run aggregate supply

4. A period of mildly falling incomes and rising unemployment

5. The quantity of goods and services that households, firms, and the government want to buy at each price level

6. The amount of output produced when unemployment is at its natural rate, sometimes called potential output or full employment output

7. A period of falling output and rising prices

8. A period of unusually severe falling incomes and rising unemployment

9. The quantity of goods and services that firms are willing to produce at each price level

10. The model most economists use to explain short run fluctuations in the economy around its long run trend

PROBLEMS AND SHORT-ANSWER QUESTIONS

When it will be helpful for you, draw a graph of the model of aggregate demand and aggregate supply on scrap paper to help you answer the following problems and questions.

Practice Problems

1. For the following four cases, trace the impact of each shock in the aggregate demand and aggregate supply model by answering the following three questions for each: What happens to prices and output in the short run? What happens to prices and output in the long run if the economy is allowed to adjust to long run equilibrium on its own? If policy makers had intervened to move output back to the natural rate instead of allowing the economy to self-correct, in which direction should they have moved aggregate demand?
   a. aggregate demand shifts left.
   b. aggregate demand shifts right.
   c. short run aggregate supply shifts left.
   d. short run aggregate supply shifts right.

2. The following events have their *initial impact* on which of the following: aggregate demand, short run aggregate supply, long run aggregate supply, or both short run and long run aggregate supply? Do the curves shift to the right or left?
   a. The government repairs aging roads and bridges.
   b. OPEC raises oil prices.
   c. The government raises unemployment benefits which raises the natural rate of unemployment.
   d. Europeans feel more secure in their jobs and become more optimistic.
   e. A technological advance takes place in the application of computers to the manufacture of steel.
   f. The government increases the minimum wage.
   g. Because price expectations are reduced, wage demands of new college graduates fall.
   h. The central bank decreases the money supply.
   i. Flooding destroys much of the agricultural crop.

3. Suppose the economy is in long run equilibrium. Then, suppose the central bank suddenly increases the money supply.
   a. Describe the initial impact of this event in the model of aggregate demand and aggregate supply by explaining which curve shifts which way.
   b. What happens to the price level and real output in the short run?
   c. If the economy is allowed to adjust to the increase in the money supply, what happens to the price level and real output in the long run? (compared to their original levels)
   d. Does an increase in the money supply move output above the natural rate indefinitely? Why?

4. Suppose the economy is in long run equilibrium. Then, suppose workers and firms suddenly expect higher prices in the future and agree to an increase in wages.
   a. Describe the initial impact of this event in the model of aggregate demand and aggregate supply by explaining which curve shifts which way.
   b. What happens to the price level and real output in the short run?
   c. What name do we have for this combination of movements in output and prices?
   d. If policy makers wanted to move output back to the natural rate of output, what should they do?

e. If policy makers were able to move output back to the natural rate of output, what would the policy do to prices?

f. If policy makers had done nothing at all, what would have happened to the wage rate as the economy self-corrected or adjusted back to the natural rate of output on its own?

g. Is it likely that an increase in price expectations and wages *alone* can cause a permanent increase in the price level? Why?

5. Suppose the economy is at a point such as point B in Exhibit 2. That is, aggregate demand has decreased and the economy is in a recession. Describe the adjustment process necessary for the economy to adjust on its own to point C for each of the three theoretical short run aggregate supply curves.

a. the sticky wage theory:

b. the sticky price theory:

c. the misperceptions theory:

d. Do you think the type of adjustments described above would take place more quickly from a recession or from a period when output was above the long run natural rate? Why?

Short-Answer Questions

1. Name the three key facts about economic fluctuations.

2. What are the three reasons the aggregate demand curve slopes downward? Explain them.

3. Suppose the economy is in long run equilibrium. If we employ the sticky wage theory of the short run aggregate supply curve, what initially happens to the real wage if there is a decrease in aggregate demand?

4. Referring to the previous question, if the economy is to adjust on its own back to the long run equilibrium level of output, what must happen to the real wage?

5. If the economy is in a recession, why might policy makers choose to adjust aggregate demand to eliminate the recession rather then let the economy adjust, or self-correct, on its own?

6. Does a shift in aggregate demand alter output in the long run? Why?

7. Which component of aggregate demand is most volatile over the business cycle?

8. Why is money unlikely to be neutral in the short run?

9. Suppose OPEC breaks apart and oil prices fall substantially. Initially, which curve shifts in the aggregate supply and aggregate demand model? In what direction does it shift? What happens to the price level and real output?

10. What causes both short run and long run aggregate supply to shift together. What causes only the short run aggregate supply to shift while the long run aggregate supply remains stationary?

SELF-TEST

True/False Questions

_____ 1. Investment is a particularly volatile component of spending across the business cycle.

_____ 2. An increase in price expectations shifts the long run aggregate supply curve to the left.

_____ 3. If the classical dichotomy and money neutrality hold in the long run, then the long run aggregate supply curve should be vertical.

_____ 4. Economists refer to fluctuations in output as the 'business cycle' because movements in output are regular and predictable.

_____ 5. The misperceptions theory explains why the long run aggregate supply curve is downward sloping.

_____ 6. A rise in price expectations that causes wages to rise causes the short run aggregate supply curve to shift left.

_____ 7. If the economy is in a recession, the economy will adjust to long run equilibrium on its own as wages and price expectations rise.

_____ 8. In the short run, if the government cuts back spending to balance its budget, it will likely cause a recession.

_____ 9. The short run effect of an increase in aggregate demand is an increase in output and an increase in the price level.

_____10. In the long run, changes in aggregate demand have no effect on the price level or the level of output in an economy.

Multiple-Choice Questions

1. According to the interest rate effect, aggregate demand slopes downward (negatively) with respect to price because
   a. lower prices increase the value of money holdings and consumer spending increases.
   b. lower prices decrease the value of money holdings and consumer spending decreases.
   c. lower prices reduce money holdings, increase lending, interest rates fall, and investment spending increases.
   d. lower prices increase money holdings, decrease lending, interest rates rise, and investment spending falls.

2. Suppose the price level falls but because of fixed nominal wage contracts, the real wage rises and firms cut back on production. This is a demonstration of the
   a. sticky wage theory of the short run aggregate supply curve.
   b. sticky price theory of the short run aggregate supply curve.
   c. misperceptions theory of the short run aggregate supply curve.
   d. classical dichotomy theory of the short run aggregate supply curve.

3. Suppose the economy is initially in long run equilibrium. Then suppose there is a reduction in military spending due to the end of the Cold War. According to the model of aggregate demand and aggregate supply, what happens to prices and output in the _short run?_
   a. Prices rise; output rises.
   b. Prices rise; output falls.
   c. Prices fall; output falls.
   d. Prices fall; output rises.

4. Suppose the economy is initially in long run equilibrium. Then suppose there is a reduction in military spending due to the end of the Cold War. According to the model of aggregate demand and aggregate supply, what happens to prices and output in the _long run?_
   a. Prices rise; output is unchanged from its initial value.
   b. Prices fall; output is unchanged from its initial value.
   c. Output rises; prices are unchanged from the initial value.
   d. Output falls; prices are unchanged from the initial value.
   e. Output and the price level are unchanged from their initial values.

5. Suppose the economy is initially in long run equilibrium. Then suppose there is a drought that destroys much of the wheat crop. According to the model of aggregate demand and aggregate supply, what happens to prices and output in the *short run?*
    a. Prices rise; output rises.
    b. Prices rise; output falls.
    c. Prices fall; output falls.
    d. Prices fall; output rises.

6. Suppose the economy is initially in long run equilibrium. Then suppose there is a drought that destroys much of the wheat crop. If policy makers allow the economy to adjust to long run equilibrium on its own, according to the model of aggregate demand and aggregate supply, what happens to prices and output in the *long run?*
    a. Prices rise; output is unchanged from its initial value.
    b. Prices fall; output is unchanged from its initial value.
    c. Output rises; prices are unchanged from the initial value.
    d. Output falls; prices are unchanged from the initial value.
    e. Output and the price level are unchanged from their initial values.

7. Which of the following events shifts the short run aggregate supply curve to the right?
    a. an increase in government spending on military equipment.
    b. an increase in price expectations.
    c. a drop in oil prices.
    d. a decrease in the money supply.
    e. none of the above.

Use Exhibit 4 to answer questions 8 and 9.

8. Suppose the economy is operating in a recession such as point B in Exhibit 4. If policy makers wished to move output to its long run natural rate, they should attempt to
    a. shift aggregate demand to the right.
    b. shift aggregate demand to the left.
    c. shift short run aggregate supply to the right.
    d. shift short run aggregate supply to the left.

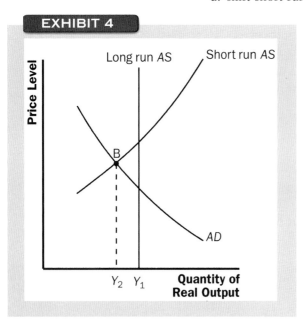

EXHIBIT 4

9. Suppose the economy is operating in a recession such as point B in Exhibit 4. If policy-makers allow the economy to adjust to the long run natural rate on its own,
    a. people will raise their price expectations and the short run aggregate supply will shift left.
    b. people will reduce their price expectations and the short run aggregate supply will shift right.
    c. people will raise their price expectations and aggregate demand will shift left.
    d. people will reduce their price expectations and aggregate demand will shift right.

10. According to the model of aggregate supply and aggregate demand, in the long run, an increase in the money supply should cause
    a. prices to rise and output to rise.
    b. prices to fall and output to fall.
    c. prices to rise and output to remain unchanged.
    d. prices to fall and output to remain unchanged.

ADVANCED CRITICAL THINKING

You are watching the evening news on television. The news reader reports that union wage demands are much higher this year because the workers anticipate an increase in the rate of inflation. Your roommate says, 'Inflation is a self-fulfilling prophecy. If workers think there are going to be higher prices, they demand higher wages. This increases the cost of production and firms raise their prices. Expecting higher prices simply causes higher prices.'

1. Is this true in the short run? Explain.

2. If policy makers do nothing and allow the economy to adjust to the natural rate of output on its own, does expecting higher prices cause higher prices in the long run? Explain.

3. If policy makers accommodate the adverse supply shock, does the expectation of higher prices cause higher prices in the long run? Explain.

SOLUTIONS

Terms and Definitions

_1_	Menu costs	_6_	Natural rate of output
_2_	The business cycle	_7_	Stagflation
_3_	Accommodative policy	_8_	Depression
_4_	Recession	_9_	Aggregate supply curve
_5_	Aggregate demand curve	_10_	Model of aggregate supply and demand

Practice Problems

1. a. Prices fall, output falls. Prices fall, output returns to the natural rate. Shift aggregate demand to the right.
   b. Prices rise, output rises. Prices rise, output returns to the natural rate. Shift aggregate demand to the left.
   c. Prices rise, output falls. Price level returns to original value, output returns to the natural rate. Shift aggregate demand to the right.
   d. Prices fall, output rises. Price level returns to original value, output returns to the natural rate. Shift aggregate demand to the left.

2. a. aggregate demand, right.
   b. short run aggregate supply, left.
   c. both short run and long run aggregate supply, left.
   d. aggregate demand, right.
   e. both short run and long run aggregate supply, right.
   f. both short run and long run aggregate supply, left.
   g. short run aggregate supply, right.
   h. aggregate demand, left.
   i. short run aggregate supply, left.

3. a. Aggregate demand shifts to the right.
   b. Price level rises and real output rises.
   c. Price level rises and real output stays the same.
   d. No. Over time, people and firms adjust to the new higher amount of spending by raising their prices and wages.

4. a. Short run aggregate supply shifts left.
   b. Prices rise and output falls.

    c. Stagflation.

    d. Shift aggregate demand to the right.

    e. Prices would rise more and remain there.

    f. The high unemployment at the low level of output would put pressure on the wage to fall back to its original value shifting short run aggregate supply back to its original position.

    g. No. Increases in the cost of production need to be 'accommodated' by government policy to permanently raise prices.

5.   a. At point B, nominal wage contracts are based on the expectation of a higher price level so the real wage has risen and workers were laid off. As workers and firms recognise the fall in the price level (learn to expect P_3), new contracts will have a lower nominal wage, the real wage falls, and firms increase production at each price level shifting the short run aggregate supply to the right.

    b. At point B, some firms have not reduced their prices because of menu costs. Their products are relatively more expensive and sales fall. When they realize the lower price level is permanent (learn to expect P_3), they lower their prices and output rises at each price level, shifting the short run aggregate supply to the right.

    c. At point B, some firms mistakenly believe that only the price of their product has fallen and they have cut back on production. As they realize that all prices are falling (learn to expect P_3), they will increase production at each price, which will shift short run aggregate supply to the right.

    d. More slowly from a recession because it requires prices to be reduced, and prices are usually more sticky downward. The adjustment when output is above normal requires prices and wages to rise.

Short-Answer Questions

1. Economic fluctuations are irregular and unpredictable, most macroeconomic quantities fluctuate together, and when output falls, unemployment rises.

2. Wealth effect: lower prices increase the value of money holdings and consumer spending increases. Interest rate effect: Lower prices reduce the quantity of money held, some is loaned, interest rates fall, and investment spending increases. Exchange rate effect: lower prices decrease interest rates, the dollar depreciates, and net exports increase.

3. Since the nominal wage is fixed for a period, the fall in the price level raises the real wage, W/P.

4. The nominal wage must fall so that the real wage can return to its initial level.

5. Because they think they can get the economy back to the long run natural rate of output more quickly or, in the case of a negative supply shock, because they are more concerned with output than inflation.

6. No. In the long run, output is determined by factor supplies and technology (long run aggregate supply). Changes in aggregate demand only affect output in the short run because it temporarily alters relative prices.

7. Investment.

8. Because a shift in aggregate demand from a change in the money supply may change the price level unexpectedly. Some prices and wages adjust to the change more quickly than others causing changes in relative prices in the short run.

9. Short run aggregate supply shifts right. Prices fall and output rises.

10. Changes in the available factors (labour, capital, natural resources) and technology shift both long run and short run aggregate supply. Changes in price expectations that may be associated with wage demands and oil prices only shift short run aggregate supply.

True/False Questions

1. T

2. F; changes in price expectations shift the short run aggregate supply curve.

3. T

4. F; fluctuations in output are irregular.

5. F; it explains why the short run aggregate supply curve is upward sloping.

6. T

7. F; in a recession, the economy adjusts to long run equilibrium as wages and prices fall.

8. T

9. T

10. F; changes in aggregate demand have no affect on output, but they certainly have an effect on the price level.

Multiple-Choice Questions

1. c   6. e

2. a   7. c

3. c   8. a

4. b   9. b

5. b   10. c

Advanced Critical Thinking

1. Yes. An increase in price expectations shifts the short run aggregate supply curve to the left and prices rise.

2. No. In the long run, the increase in unemployment will cause wages and price expectations to fall back to their prior levels.

3. Yes. If policy makers accommodate the adverse supply shock with an increase in aggregate demand, the price level will rise permanently.

THE INFLUENCE OF MONETARY AND FISCAL POLICY ON AGGREGATE DEMAND

CHAPTER OVERVIEW

Context and Purpose

Chapter 34 is the second chapter in a three-chapter sequence that concentrates on short run fluctuations in the economy around its long term trend. In Chapter 33, we introduced the model of aggregate supply and aggregate demand. In Chapter 34, we see how the government's monetary and fiscal policies affect aggregate demand. In Chapter 35, we will see some of the trade offs between short run and long run objectives when we analyse the relationship between inflation and unemployment.

The purpose of Chapter 34 is to analyse the short run effects of monetary and fiscal policies. In Chapter 33, we found that when aggregate demand or short run aggregate supply shifts, it causes fluctuations in output. As a result, policy makers sometimes try to offset these shifts by shifting aggregate demand with monetary and fiscal policy. Chapter 34 examines the theory behind these policies and some of the shortcomings of stabilization policy.

CHAPTER REVIEW

Introduction

Chapters 25 through 30 demonstrated the impact of fiscal and monetary policy on saving, investment, and long term growth. Chapter 33 demonstrated that shifts in aggregate demand and short run aggregate supply cause short run fluctuations in the economy around its long term trend and how monetary and fiscal policy makers might shift aggregate demand to stabilize the economy. In this chapter, we analyse the theory behind stabilization policies and some of the shortcomings of stabilization policy.

How Monetary Policy Influences Aggregate Demand

The aggregate demand curve shows the quantity of goods and services demanded at each price level. Recall from Chapter 33, aggregate demand slopes downward due to the wealth effect, the interest rate effect, and the exchange rate effect. Since money is a small part of total wealth, the interest rate effect and the exchange rate effect exert a much more powerful influence on the slope of the aggregate demand curve. Of the two, the interest rate is likely to be more powerful because a change in interest rates impacts on the whole economy whereas the exchange rate effect only impacts upon the traded goods sector.

The interest rate is a key determinant of aggregate demand. To see how monetary policy affects aggregate demand, we develop the Keynesian theory of interest rate determination called the **theory of liquidity preference.** This theory suggests that the rate of interest is determined by the supply and demand for money. Note that the interest rate being determined is both the nominal and the real interest rate because, in the short run, expected inflation is unchanged so changes in the nominal rate equal changes in the real rate.

Recall, the money supply is determined by the central bank and can be fixed at whatever level the central bank chooses. Therefore, the money supply is unaffected by the interest rate and is a vertical line in Exhibit 1. People have a demand for money because money, as the economy's most liquid asset, is a medium of exchange. Hence, people have a demand for it even though it has no rate of return because it can be used to buy things. The interest rate is the opportunity cost of holding money. When the interest rate is high, people hold more wealth in interest-bearing bonds and economize on their money holdings. Thus, the quantity of money demanded is reduced. This is shown in Exhibit 1. The equilibrium interest rate is determined by the intersection of money supply and money demand.

Note that, in the long run, the interest rate is determined by the supply and demand for loanable funds. In the short run, the interest rate is determined by the supply and demand for money. This poses no conflict.

- In the long run, output is fixed by factor supplies and technology, the interest rate adjusts to balance the supply and demand for loanable funds, and the price level adjusts to balance the supply and demand for money.

- In the short run, the price level is sticky and cannot adjust. For any given price level, the interest rate adjusts to balance the supply and demand for money, and output responds to changes in aggregate demand and short run aggregate supply.

Each theory highlights the behaviour of interest rates over a different time horizon. We can use the theory of liquidity preference to add precision to our explanation of the negative slope of the aggregate demand curve. Recall from previous chapters, the

EXHIBIT 1

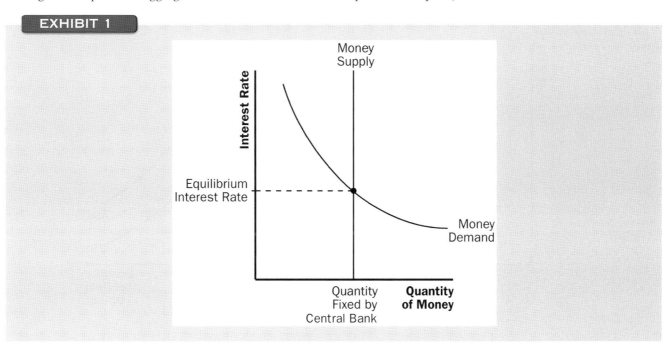

demand for money is positively related to the price level because at higher prices, people need more money to buy the same quantity of goods. Thus, a higher price level shifts money demand to the right, as shown in Exhibit 2, panel (a). With a fixed money supply, a larger money demand raises the interest rate. A higher interest rate reduces investment expenditures and causes the quantity demanded of goods and services to fall in Exhibit 2, panel (b).

Returning to the point of this section: How does monetary policy influence aggregate demand? Suppose the central bank buys government bonds shifting the money supply to the right, as in Exhibit 3, panel (a). The interest rate falls, reducing the cost of

EXHIBIT 2

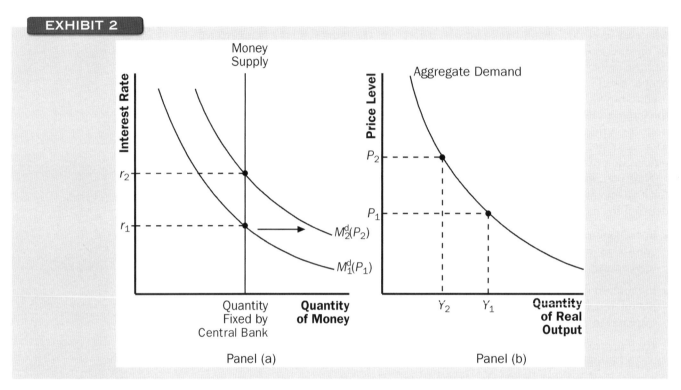

EXHIBIT 3

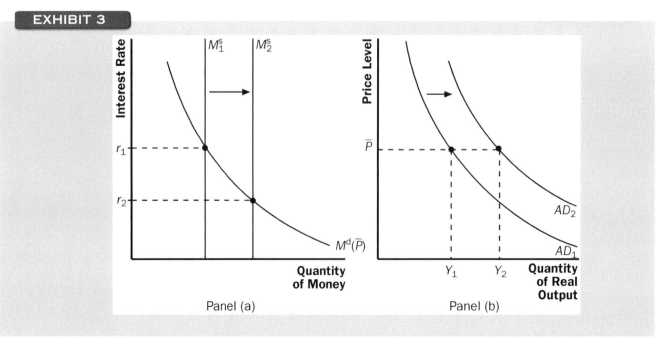

borrowing for investment. Hence, the quantity of goods and services demanded at each price level increases, shifting aggregate demand to the right in Exhibit 3, panel (b).

The central bank can implement monetary policy by targeting the money supply or interest rates. In recent years, the central bank has targeted the interest rate because the money supply is hard to measure. In particular, the ECB has targeted the *refinancing rate*—the interest rate at which the ECB will lend to the banking sector for short-term loans. Whether the central bank targets the money supply or interest rates has little effect on our analysis because every monetary policy can be described in terms of the money supply or the interest rate. For example, the monetary policy expansion used to increase aggregate demand in the example above could be described as an increase in the targeted money supply or a decrease in the targeted interest rate.

How Fiscal Policy Influences Aggregate Demand

Fiscal policy refers to the government's choices of the levels of government purchases and taxes. While fiscal policy can influence growth in the long run, its primary impact in the short run is on aggregate demand.

An increase in government purchases of €20 billion to build new roads is reflected in a rightward shift in the aggregate demand curve. There are two reasons why the actual rightward shift may be greater than or less than €20 billion:

- *The multiplier effect*: When the government spends €20 billion on road building, incomes rise in the form of wages and profits of the construction industry. The recipients of the new income raise their spending on consumer goods, which raises the incomes of people in other firms, which raises their consumption spending, and so on for many rounds. Since aggregate demand may rise by much more than the increase in government purchases, government purchases are said to have a **multiplier effect** on aggregate demand. There is a formula for the size of the multiplier effect. It says that for every euro the government spends, aggregate demand shifts to the right by $1/(1 - MPC)$, where *MPC* stands for the marginal propensity to consume—the fraction of extra income that a household spends on consumption. For example, if the *MPC* is 0.75, the multiplier is $1/(1 - 0.75) = 1/.25 = 4$ which means that €1 of government spending shifts aggregate demand to the right by a total of €4. An increase in the *MPC* increases the multiplier.

In addition to the multiplier, the increase in purchases may cause firms to increase their investment expenditures on new equipment, further increasing the response of aggregate demand to the initial increase in government purchases. This is known as the *investment accelerator*.

Thus, the aggregate demand curve might shift by more than the change in government purchases.

The logic of the multiplier effect applies to other changes in spending besides government purchases. For example, shocks to consumption, investment, and net exports might have a multiple effect on aggregate demand.

- *The crowding-out effect*: The **crowding-out effect** works in the opposite direction to the multiplier. An increase in government purchases (as in the case above) raises incomes, which shifts the demand for money to the right. This raises the interest rate, which lowers investment. Thus, an increase in government purchases increases the interest rate and reduces, or crowds out, private investment. Due to crowding out, the aggregate demand curve might shift right by less that the increase in government purchases.

Whether the final shift in the aggregate demand curve is greater than or less than the original change in government spending depends on which is larger: the multiplier effect or the crowding-out effect.

The other half of fiscal policy is taxation. A reduction in taxes increases households' take-home pay and, hence, increases their consumption. Thus, a decrease in taxes shifts aggregate demand to the right while an increase shifts aggregate demand to the left. The size of the shift in aggregate demand depends on the relative size of the multiplier and crowding-out effects described above. In addition, a reduction in taxes that is perceived by households to be permanent improves the financial condition of the household and generates a larger increase in aggregate demand than a reduction in taxes that is perceived to be only temporary.

Finally, fiscal policy might have an effect on aggregate supply for two reasons. First, a reduction in taxes might increase the incentive to work and cause aggregate supply to shift right. Supply-siders believe this effect is large. Secondly, government purchases of capital such as roads and bridges might increase the amount of goods supplied at each price level and shift the aggregate supply curve to the right. This effect is more likely to be important in the long run.

Using Policy to Stabilize the Economy

Keynes (and his followers) argued that the government should actively use monetary and fiscal policies to stabilize aggregate demand and, as a result, output and employment.

In the UK, the 1944 Employment Act holds the central government responsible for promoting full employment and production. The act has two implications: (1) The government should not be the cause of fluctuations, so it should avoid sudden changes in fiscal and monetary policy, and (2) the government should respond to changes in the private economy in order to stabilize it. For example, if consumer pessimism reduces aggregate demand, the proper amount of expansionary monetary or fiscal policy could stimulate aggregate demand to its original level, thereby avoiding a recession. Alternatively, if excessive optimism increases aggregate demand, contractionary monetary or fiscal policy could dampen aggregate demand to its original level, thereby avoiding inflationary pressures. Failure to actively stabilize the economy may allow for unnecessary fluctuations in output and employment.

Some economists argue that the government should not use monetary and fiscal policy to try to stabilize short run fluctuations in the economy. While they agree that, in theory, activist policy can stabilize the economy, they feel that, in practice, monetary and fiscal policy affect the economy with a substantial lag. The lag for monetary policy is at least six months so it may be hard for the central bank to 'fine tune' the economy. There are also lags associated with fiscal policy. For example, in the UK the Government has often tended to undershoot on its planned spending, partly because of problems in attracting sufficient extra staff into key public services such as transport, education, and health. These lags mean that activist policy could be destabilizing because expansionary policy could accidentally increase aggregate demand during periods of excessive private aggregate demand, and contractionary policy could accidentally decrease aggregate demand during periods of deficient private aggregate demand.

Automatic stabilizers are changes in fiscal policy that automatically stimulate aggregate demand in a recession so that policy makers do not have to take deliberate action. The tax system automatically lowers tax collections during a recession when incomes and profits fall. Government spending automatically rises during a recession because unemployment benefits and welfare payments rise. Hence, both the tax and government spending systems increase aggregate demand during a recession. A strict balanced budget rule would eliminate automatic stabilizers because the government would have to raise taxes or lower expenditures during a recession.

If there is to be activist monetary policy, most economists believe that the central bank will make better decisions if it continues to be politically independent. This is because it is politically difficult to increase interest rates and reduce aggregate demand when the economy is overheating (temporarily operating above the natural rate) but it may be necessary in order to avoid future inflation.

HELPFUL HINTS

1. The multiplier can be derived in a variety of different ways. Your text shows you that the value of the multiplier is $1/(1 - MPC)$. However, it doesn't show you how this number is generated. Below, you will find one of the many different ways that the value of the multiplier can be derived for the case of an increase in government spending:

$$\Delta \text{output demanded} = \Delta \text{spending on output,}$$

which says that the change in output demanded equals the change in spending on output. Denoting Y as output demanded, G as government spending, and noting that output equals income, then

$$\Delta Y = \Delta G + [(MPC) \times \Delta Y],$$

which says that the change in output demanded is equal to the change in total spending where total spending is composed of the change in government spending plus the change in consumption spending induced by the increase in income (say 0.75 of the change in income).

Solving for ΔY, we get

$$\Delta Y - [(MPC) \times \Delta Y] = \Delta G$$

$$\Delta Y \times (1 - MPC) = \Delta G$$

$$\Delta Y = 1/(1 - MPC) \times \Delta G,$$

which says that a €1 increase in government spending causes an increase in aggregate demand of $1/(1 - MPC) \times €1$. If the MPC equals 0.75, then $1/(1 - 0.75) = 4$ and a €1 increase in government spending shifts aggregate demand to the right by €4.

2. An increase in the MPC increases the multiplier. If the MPC were 0.80, suggesting that people spend 80 per cent of an increase in income on consumption goods, the multiplier would become $1/(1 - 0.80) = 5$. This is larger than the multiplier generated above from an MPC of 0.75. There is an intuitive appeal to this result. If people spend a higher percentage of an increase in income on consumption goods, any new government purchase will have an even larger multiplier effect and shift the aggregate demand curve further to the right.

3. The multiplier works in both directions. If the government reduces purchases, the multiplier effect suggests that the aggregate demand curve will shift to the left by a greater amount than the initial reduction in government purchases. When the government reduces purchases, wages, and profits of people are reduced and they reduce their consumption expenditures, and so on, creating a multiple contraction in aggregate demand.

4. Activist stabilization policy has many descriptive names. Activist stabilization policy is the use of discretionary monetary and fiscal policies to manage aggregate demand in such a way as to minimize the fluctuations in output and to maintain output at the long run natural rate. As such, activist stabilization policy is sometimes called *discretionary policy* to distinguish it from automatic stabilizers. It is also called *aggregate demand management* because monetary and fiscal policies are used to adjust or manage total spending in the economy. Finally, since policy makers attempt to counter the business cycle by reducing aggregate demand when it is too high and by increasing aggregate demand when it is too low, stabilization policy is sometimes referred to as *countercyclical policy*.

5. Activist stabilization policy can be used to move output towards the long run natural rate from levels of output that are either above or below the natural rate of output. As in the previous chapter, most of the examples of stabilization policy in the text assume the economy is in a recession—a period when output is below the long run natural rate. However, activist stabilization policy can be used to reduce aggregate demand and output in periods when output exceeds the long run natural rate. When output exceeds the natural rate, we sometimes say that the economy is in a boom, an expansion, or that the economy is overheating. When the economy's output is above the natural rate, the economy is said to be overheating because, left alone, the economy will adjust to a higher level of expected prices and wages and output will fall to the natural rate (short run aggregate supply shifts left). Most economists believe that the central bank needs political independence to combat an overheating economy. This is because the activist policy prescription for an overheating economy is a reduction in aggregate demand, which usually faces political opposition. That is, 'taking away the punch bowl just as the party gets going' is not likely to be politically popular.

TERMS AND DEFINITIONS

Choose a definition for each key term.

Key terms:

_____ Theory of liquidity preference

_____ Liquidity

_____ Refinancing rate

_____ Multiplier effect

_____ Investment accelerator

_____ Marginal propensity to consume, or *MPC*

_____ Crowding-out effect

_____ Stabilization policy

_____ Automatic stabilizers

Definitions:

1. The dampening of the shift in aggregate demand from expansionary fiscal policy which raises the interest rate and reduces investment spending

2. The interest rate the ECB charges for loans to the banking system

3. The amplification of the shift in aggregate demand from expansionary fiscal policy which raises investment expenditures

4. Keynes's theory that the interest rate is determined by the supply and demand for money in the short run

5. Changes in fiscal policy that do not require deliberate action on the part of policy-makers

6. The use of fiscal and monetary policies to reduce fluctuations in the economy

7. The amplification of the shift in aggregate demand from expansionary fiscal policy which raises incomes and further increases consumption expenditures

8. The ease with which an asset is converted into a medium of exchange

9. The fraction of extra income that a household spends on consumption

PROBLEMS AND SHORT-ANSWER QUESTIONS

Practice Problems

1. If the central bank were to engage in activist stabilization policy, in which direction should it move the *money supply* in response to the following events?
   a. A wave of optimism boosts business investment and household consumption.
   b. To balance its budget, the central government raises taxes and reduces expenditures.

    c. OPEC raises the price of crude oil.

    d. Foreigners experience a reduction in their taste for domestically produced cars.

    e. The stock market falls.

2. If the central bank were to engage in activist stabilization policy, in which direction should they move *interest rates* in response to the same events listed in the previous question?

    a. A wave of optimism boosts business investment and household consumption.

    b. To balance its budget, the central government raises taxes and reduces expenditures.

    c. OPEC raises the price of crude oil.

    d. Foreigners experience a reduction in their taste for domestically produced cars.

    e. The stock market falls.

    f. Explain the relationship between central bank policy in terms of the money supply and policy in terms of the interest rate.

3. If policy makers were to use fiscal policy to actively stabilize the economy, in which direction should they move government spending and taxes?

    a. A wave of pessimism reduces business investment and household consumption.

    b. An increase in price expectations causes unions to demand higher wages.

    c. Foreigners increase their taste for domestically produced cars.

    d. OPEC raises the price of crude oil.

4. Suppose the economy is in a recession. Policy makers estimate that aggregate demand is €100 billion short of the amount necessary to generate the long run natural rate of output. That is, if aggregate demand were shifted to the right by €100 billion, the economy would be in long run equilibrium.

    a. If the central government chooses to use fiscal policy to stabilize the economy, by how much should they increase government spending if the marginal propensity to consume (*MPC*) is 0.75 and there is no crowding out?

    b. If the central government chooses to use fiscal policy to stabilize the economy, by how much should they increase government spending if the marginal propensity to consume (*MPC*) is 0.80 and there is no crowding out?

    c. If there is crowding out, will the government need to spend more or less than the amounts you found in (a) and (b) above? Why?

    d. If investment is very sensitive to changes in the interest rate, is crowding out more of a problem or less of a problem? Why?

    e. If policy makers discover that the lag for fiscal policy is two years, should that make them more likely to employ fiscal policy as a stabilization tool or more likely to allow the economy to adjust on its own? Why?

5. a. What does an increase in the money supply do to interest rates in the short run? Explain.

    b. What does an increase in the money supply do to interest rates in the long run? Explain.

    c. Are these results inconsistent? Explain.

Short-Answer Questions

1. Why is the money supply curve vertical when it is drawn on a graph with the interest rate on the vertical axis and the quantity of money on the horizontal axis?

2. Why does the money demand curve slope negatively when it is drawn on a graph with the interest rate on the vertical axis and the quantity of money on the horizontal axis?

3. Why does an increase in the price level reduce the quantity demanded of real output? (Use the interest rate effect to explain the slope of the aggregate demand curve.)

4. Explain how an increase in the money supply shifts the aggregate demand curve.

5. Explain the intuition of the multiplier effect resulting from an increase in government spending. Why should a bigger *MPC* make the multiplier effect larger?

6. Explain how an increase in government spending might lead to crowding out.

7. Suppose the government spends €10 billion on a public works program, which is intended to stimulate aggregate demand. If the crowding-out effect exceeds the multiplier effect, will the aggregate demand curve shift to the right by more or less than €10 billion? Why?

8. How does a cut in taxes affect aggregate supply?

9. Which is likely to have a greater impact on aggregate demand: A temporary reduction in taxes or a permanent reduction in taxes? Why?

10. Explain why taxes and government spending might act as automatic stabilizers. What would a strict balanced-budget rule cause policy makers to do during a recession? Would this make the recession more or less severe?

SELF-TEST

True/False Questions

_____ 1. An increase in the interest rate increases the quantity demanded of money because it increases the rate of return on money.

_____ 2. Suppose investors and consumers become pessimistic about the future and cut back on expenditures. If the central bank engages in activist stabilization policy, the policy response should be to decrease the money supply.

_____ 3. In the short run, a decision by the central bank to increase the targeted money supply is essentially the same as a decision to decrease the targeted interest rate.

_____ 4. Because of the multiplier effect, an increase in government spending of €40 billion will shift the aggregate demand curve to the right by more than €40 billion (assuming there is no crowding out).

_____ 5. If the *MPC* (marginal propensity to consume) is 0.80, then the value of the multiplier is 8.

_____ 6. Crowding out occurs when an increase in government spending increases incomes, shifts money demand to the right, raises the interest rate, and reduces private investment.

_____ 7. Suppose the government increases its expenditure by €10 billion. If the crowding-out effect exceeds the multiplier effect, then the aggregate demand curve shifts to the right by more than €10 billion.

_____ 8. Many economists prefer automatic stabilizers because they affect the economy with a shorter lag than activist stabilization policies.

_____ 9. In the short run, the interest rate is determined by the loanable funds market, while in the long run, the interest rate is determined by money demand and money supply.

_____ 10. Unemployment benefits are an example of an automatic stabilizer because when incomes fall, unemployment benefits rise.

Multiple-Choice Questions

1. When the supply and demand for money are expressed in a graph with the interest rate on the vertical axis and the quantity of money on the horizontal axis, an increase in the price level
   a. shifts money demand to the right and increases the interest rate.
   b. shifts money demand to the left and increases the interest rate.
   c. shifts money demand to the right and decreases the interest rate.
   d. shifts money demand to the left and decreases the interest rate.

2. For the EU, the most important source of the downward slope of the aggregate demand curve is
   a. the exchange rate effect.
   b. the wealth effect.
   c. the fiscal effect.
   d. the interest rate effect.

3. In the market for real output, the initial effect of an increase in the money supply is to
   a. shift aggregate demand to the right.
   b. shift aggregate demand to the left.
   c. shift aggregate supply to the right.
   d. shift aggregate supply to the right.

4. The long run effect of an increase in the money supply is to
   a. increase the price level.
   b. decrease the price level.
   c. increase the interest rate.
   d. decrease the interest rate.

5. Suppose a wave of investor and consumer optimism has increased spending so that the current level of output exceeds the long run natural rate. If policy makers choose to engage in activist stabilization policy, they should
   a. decrease taxes, which shifts aggregate demand to the right.
   b. decrease taxes, which shifts aggregate demand to the left.
   c. decrease government spending, which shifts aggregate demand to the right.
   d. decrease government spending, which shifts aggregate demand to the left.

6. When an increase in government purchases raises incomes, shifts money demand to the right, raises the interest rate, and lowers investment, we have seen a demonstration of
   a. the multiplier effect.
   b. the investment accelerator.
   c. the crowding-out effect.
   d. supply-side economics.

7. Which of the following statements regarding taxes is correct?
   a. Most economists believe that, in the short run, the greatest impact of a change in taxes is on aggregate supply, not aggregate demand.
   b. A permanent change in taxes has a greater effect on aggregate demand than a temporary change in taxes.
   c. An increase in taxes shifts the aggregate demand curve to the right.
   d. A decrease in taxes shifts the aggregate supply curve to the left.

8. Suppose the government increases its purchases by €16 billion. If the multiplier effect exceeds the crowding-out effect, then
   a. the aggregate supply curve shifts to the right by more than €16 billion.
   b. the aggregate supply curve shifts to the left by more than €16 billion.
   c. the aggregate demand curve shifts to the right by more than €16 billion.
   d. the aggregate demand curve shifts to the left by more than €16 billion.

9. When an increase in government purchases causes firms to purchase additional plant and equipment, we have seen a demonstration of
   a. the multiplier effect.
   b. the investment accelerator.
   c. the crowding-out effect.
   d. supply-side economics.

10. Which of the following best describes how an increase in the money supply shifts aggregate demand?
    a. The money supply shifts right, the interest rate rises, investment decreases, and aggregate demand shifts left.
    b. The money supply shifts right, the interest rate falls, investment increases, and aggregate demand shifts right.
    c. The money supply shifts right, prices rise, spending falls, and aggregate demand shifts left.
    d. The money supply shifts right, prices fall, spending increases, and aggregate demand shifts right.

ADVANCED CRITICAL THINKING

You are watching a nightly network news broadcast. The opening report is a story about today's meeting of the ECB's Governing Council which sets monetary policy. The business correspondent reports that the central bank raised interest rates by a quarter of a per cent today to head off future inflation. The report then moves to interviews with prominent people from the business community. The response of one person to the central bank's move is negative. She says, 'The Consumer Price Index has not increased, yet the central bank is restricting growth in the economy, supposedly to fight inflation. My customers will want to know why they are going to have to pay more when they take out a loan, and I don't have a good answer. I think this is an outrage and I think the central bank's policy making powers should be placed in the hands of elected politicians who are accountable for their actions.'

1. What interest rate did the central bank raise?

2. State the central bank's policy in terms of the money supply.

3. Why might the central bank raise interest rates before the CPI starts to rise?

4. Use the businesswoman's statement to explain why most economists believe that the central bank needs to be independent of politics?

SOLUTIONS

Terms and Definitions

1	Crowding out	6	Stabilization policy
2	Refinancing rate	7	Multiplier effect
3	Investment accelerator	8	Liquidity
4	Theory of liquidity preference	9	Marginal propensity to consume or *MPC*
5	Automatic stabilizers		

Practice Problems

1. a. Decrease the money supply.
   b. Increase the money supply.

    c. Increase the money supply.

    d. Increase the money supply.

    e. Increase the money supply.

2. a. Increase interest rates.

    b. Decrease interest rates.

    c. Decrease interest rates.

    d. Decrease interest rates.

    e. Decrease interest rates.

    f. In the short run, with prices sticky or fixed, an increase in the money supply implies a reduction in interest rates and a decrease in the money supply implies an increase in interest rates.

3. a. Increase spending, decrease taxes.

    b. Increase spending, decrease taxes.

    c. Decrease spending, increase taxes.

    d. Increase spending, decrease taxes.

4. a. Multiplier $= 1/(1 - 0.75) = 4$; $100/4 = €25$ billion.

    b. Multiplier $= 1/(1 = 0.80) = 5$; $100/5 = €20$ billion.

    c. More, because as the government spends more, investors spend less so aggregate demand won't increase by as much as the multiplier suggests.

    d. More of a problem. Government spending raises interest rates. The more sensitive investment is to the interest rate—the more it is reduced or crowded out by government spending.

    e. More likely to allow the economy to adjust on its own because if the economy adjusts before the impact of the fiscal policy is felt, the fiscal policy will be destabilizing.

5. a. It lowers interest rates because, in the short run, with prices sticky or fixed, money demand is unchanging. Thus, an increase in the money supply requires a decrease in interest rates to induce people to hold the additional money.

    b. It has no effect because, in the long run, the increase in spending causes a proportional increase in prices, output is fixed at the natural rate, money is neutral, and interest rates are determined by the supply and demand for loanable funds which have not changed.

    c. No. Prices are likely to be sticky in the short run and flexible in the long run.

Short-Answer Questions

1. Because the quantity of money is fixed at whatever value the central bank chooses and this quantity is not dependent on the interest rate.

2. The interest rate is the opportunity cost of money since money earns no rate of return. Thus, an increase in the interest rate causes people to economize on cash balances and hold more wealth in interest bearing bonds.

3. An increase in the price level shifts money demand to the right, increases the interest rate, and decreases investment.

4. The money supply shifts right, the interest rate decreases, investment increases at each price level, which is a rightward shift in the aggregate demand curve.

5. When the government purchases goods, it causes an increase in the incomes of the sellers. They spend some per cent of their new higher income on goods and services, raising other's incomes, and so on. The higher the *MPC*, the greater the per cent of new income spent in each round.

6. An increase in government spending raises incomes, shifts money demand right, raises the interest rate, and reduces investment.

7. By less than €10 billion because the crowding-out effect, which reduces the shift in aggregate demand, more than offsets the multiplier effect, which amplifies the shift.

8. It causes an increase in aggregate supply by increasing the incentive to work.

9. Permanent, because it improves the financial condition of the household more and, thus, they spend more.

10. Income tax collections fall during a recession and government spending on welfare and unemployment benefits rises. It would cause the government to raise other taxes and lower other spending. More severe.

True/False Questions

1. F; an increase in the interest rate decreases the quantity demanded of money because it raises the opportunity cost of holding money.

2. F; the central bank should increase the money supply.

3. T

4. T

5. F; the value of the multiplier is 5.

6. T

7. F; the aggregate demand curve shifts to the right by less than €10 billion.

8. T

9. F; in the short run, the interest rate is determined by money demand and money supply, while in the long run, it is determined by the loanable funds market.

10. T

Multiple-Choice Questions

1.	a	6.	c
2.	d	7.	b
3.	a	8.	c
4.	a	9.	b
5.	d	10.	b

Advanced Critical Thinking

1. The central bank funds rate.

2. They decreased the money supply (or lowered its growth rate).

3. Because monetary policy acts on the economy with a lag. If the central bank waits until inflation has arrived, the effect of its policy will arrive too late. Thus, the central bank may wish to respond to its forecast of inflation.

4. Politicians must be responsive to the short-term needs of voters. Monetary policy must take a long term view and make politically painful decisions when the economy is overheating (when output is above the long run natural rate) because the proper policy response is to contract aggregate demand.

GOALS

⌐ **In this chapter you will**

Learn why policy makers face a short run tradeoff between inflation and unemployment

Consider why the inflation-unemployment tradeoff disappears in the long run

See how supply shocks can shift the inflation-unemployment tradeoff

Consider the short run cost of reducing the rate of inflation

See how policy makers' credibility affects the cost of reducing inflation

OUTCOMES

⌐ **You should be able to**

Draw a graph of a short run Phillips curve

Draw a graph of a long run Phillips curve

Show the relationship between a shift in the short run aggregate supply curve and a shift in the short run Phillips curve

Explain the sacrifice ratio

Explain why more than rational expectations are needed to reduce inflation costlessly

THE SHORT-RUN TRADEOFF BETWEEN INFLATION AND UNEMPLOYMENT

CHAPTER OVERVIEW

Context and Purpose

Chapter 35 is the final chapter in a three-chapter sequence on the economy's short run fluctuations around its long term trend. Chapter 33 introduced aggregate supply and aggregate demand. Chapter 34 developed how monetary and fiscal policy affect aggregate demand. Both Chapters 33 and 34 analysed the relationship between the price level and output. Chapter 35 will concentrate on a similar relationship between inflation and unemployment.

The purpose of Chapter 35 is to trace the history of economists' thinking about the relationship between inflation and unemployment. You will see why there is a temporary tradeoff between inflation and unemployment, and why there is no permanent tradeoff. This result is an extension of the results produced by the model of aggregate supply and aggregate demand where a change in the price level induced by a change in aggregate demand temporarily alters output, but has no permanent impact on output.

CHAPTER REVIEW

Introduction

Since both inflation and unemployment are undesirable, the sum of inflation and unemployment has been termed the *misery index*. Inflation and unemployment are independent in the long run because unemployment is determined by features of the labour market while inflation is determined by money growth. However, in the short run, inflation and unemployment are related because an increase in aggregate demand temporarily increases inflation and output while it lowers unemployment. In this chapter, we trace the history of our understanding of the relationship between unemployment and inflation.

The Phillips Curve

In 1958, a New Zealand economist named A.W. Phillips found a negative relationship between inflation and unemployment. That is, years of high inflation are associated with low unemployment. This negative relationship has been found for many other countries and has been termed the **Phillips curve**. The Phillips curve appears to offer policy makers a menu of inflation and unemployment choices. To have lower unemployment, one need only choose a higher rate of inflation.

The model of aggregate supply and aggregate demand can explain the relationship described by the Phillips curve. The Phillips curve shows the combinations of inflation and unemployment that arise in the short run as shifts in the aggregate demand curve move along a short run aggregate supply curve. For example, an increase in aggregate demand moves the economy along a short run aggregate supply curve to a higher price level, a higher level of output, and a lower level of unemployment. Since prices in the previous period are now fixed, a higher price level in the current period implies a higher rate of inflation, which is now associated with a lower rate of unemployment. This can be seen in Exhibit 1. An increase in aggregate demand, which moves the economy from point A to point B in panel (a), is associated with a movement along the short run Phillips curve from point A to point B.

Shifts in the Phillips Curve: The Role of Expectations

In 1968, US economists Friedman and Phelps argued that the Phillips curve is not a menu policy makers can exploit. This is because, in the long run, money is neutral and has no real effects. Money growth just causes proportional changes in prices and nominal incomes, and should have no impact on unemployment. Therefore, the long run Phillips curve should be vertical at the natural rate of unemployment—the rate of unemployment to which the economy naturally gravitates.

A vertical long run Phillips curve corresponds to a vertical long run aggregate supply curve. As Exhibit 1 illustrates, in the long run, an increase in the money supply shifts aggregate demand to the right and moves the economy from point A to point C in panel (a). The corresponding Phillips curve is found in panel (b) where an increase in money growth increases inflation but, because money is neutral in the long run, prices and incomes move together and inflation fails to affect unemployment. Thus, the economy moves from point A to point C in panel (b) and traces out the long run Phillips curve.

EXHIBIT 1

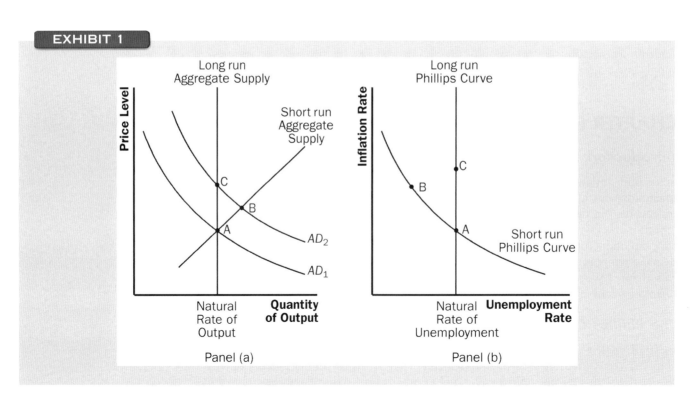

Panel (a)

Panel (b)

Friedman and Phelps used the phrase 'natural' rate of unemployment, not because it is either desirable or constant, but because it is beyond the influence of monetary policy. Changes in labour market policies such as changes in minimum wage laws and unemployment insurance that lower the natural rate of unemployment shift the long run Phillips curve to the left and the long run aggregate supply curve to the right.

Even though Friedman and Phelps argued that the long run Phillips curve is vertical, they argued that in the short run inflation could have a substantial impact on unemployment. Their reasoning is similar to that surrounding the short run aggregate supply curve in that they assume that in the short run, *price expectations* are fixed. Just as with short run aggregate supply, if price expectations are fixed in the short run, an increase in inflation could temporarily increase output and lower unemployment below the natural rate. In Exhibit 2, this is a movement from point A to point B. However, *in the long run, people adjust to the higher rate of inflation by raising their expectations of inflation and the short run Phillips curve shifts upward.* The economy moves from point B to point C with higher inflation but no change in unemployment. Thus policy makers face a short-run tradeoff between inflation and unemployment. However, if they attempt to exploit this relationship, it disappears and they arrive back on the vertical long run Phillips curve.

The analysis of Friedman and Phelps can be summarized by the following equation: Unemployment Rate = Natural Rate of Unemployment − a(Actual Inflation − Expected Inflation) This says that for any given expected inflation rate, if actual inflation exceeds expected inflation, unemployment will fall below the natural rate by an amount that depends on the parameter *a*. However, in the long run people learn to expect the inflation that actually exists and the unemployment rate will equal the natural rate.

Friedman and Phelps proposed the **natural rate hypothesis**, which states that unemployment eventually returns to its natural rate, regardless of inflation. While controversial, it seemed to fit the facts quite well. In the UK and many other countries during the 1960s, expansionary monetary and fiscal policies steadily increased the rate of inflation and unemployment fell. However, in the early 1970s, people raised their expectations of inflation and the unemployment rate returned to the natural rate—about five or six per cent.

EXHIBIT 2

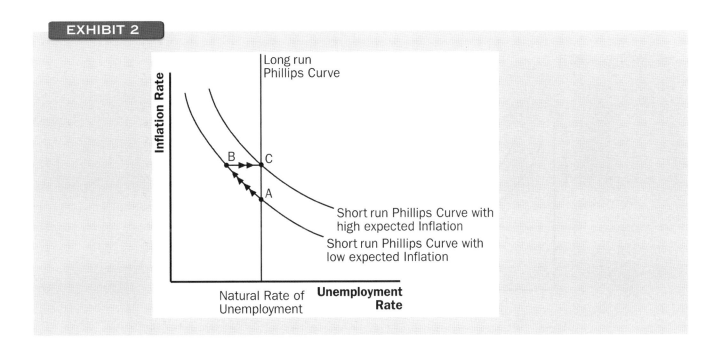

Shifts in the Phillips Curve: The Role of Supply Shocks

The short run Phillips curve can also shift due to a supply shock. A **supply shock** is an event that directly alters firms' costs and prices, shifting the economy's aggregate supply curve and Phillips curve. A supply shock occurred in 1974 when OPEC quadrupled oil prices. This act raised the cost of production and, for many countries, shifted the short run aggregate supply curve to the left, causing prices to rise and output to fall, or *stagflation*. Since inflation has increased and unemployment has increased, this corresponds to a rightward (upward) shift in the short run Phillips curve. Policy makers now face a less favourable tradeoff between inflation and unemployment. That is, policy makers must accept a higher inflation rate for each unemployment rate, or a higher unemployment rate for each inflation rate. Also, policy makers now have a difficult choice because if they reduce aggregate demand to fight inflation, they will further increase unemployment. If they increase aggregate demand to reduce unemployment, they further increase inflation.

If the supply shock raises expected inflation, the Phillips curve shift is 'permanent'. If it does not raise expected inflation, the shift is temporary. For many countries during the 1970s, their central banks accommodated two adverse aggregate supply shocks by increasing aggregate demand. This caused expected inflation to rise and the rightward (upward) shift in the Phillips curve was 'permanent'. By 1980, inflation was approaching 20 per cent and unemployment was over 6 per cent.

The Cost of Reducing Inflation

A reduction in the money supply reduces aggregate demand, reduces production and increases unemployment. This is shown in Exhibit 3 as a movement from point A to point B. Over time, expected inflation falls and the short run Phillips curve shifts downward and the economy moves from point B to point C.

The cost of reducing inflation is a period of unemployment and lost output. The **sacrifice ratio** is the number of percentage points of annual output that is lost to reduce inflation one percentage point. The amount of output lost depends on the slope of the Phillips curve and how fast people lower their expectations of inflation.

Some economists believe the sacrifice ratio is relatively large, perhaps as high as five. On the other hand, supporters of the **rational expectations** hypothesis suggest that the cost of disinflation could be much smaller and maybe zero. Rational expectations suggests that people optimally use all available information, including information

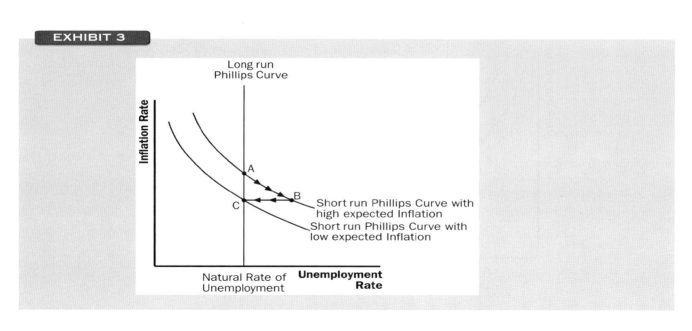

EXHIBIT 3

about government policies, when forecasting the future. Thus, an announced policy of disinflation *that is credible* could move the economy from point A to point C without travelling through point B.

In the UK in 1980, the Conservative Government under Margaret Thatcher announced its medium Term Financial Strategy which involved setting declining target rates of growth for the money supply. As monetary policy tightened, unemployment rose to around 11 per cent in 1982 and 1983. However, this does not invalidate the theory of rational expectations because unemployment, even at 11 per cent, was well below estimates predicted by the sacrifice ratio.

Since the latter part of the 1990s, the UK has experienced low unemployment and low inflation whereas many countries in Europe have experienced low inflation, but relatively high rates of unemployment. Several reasons account for the relatively low rates of inflation now experienced throughout Europe. These are:

- Tight monetary policy has reduced inflation expectations.

- Independent central banks adopt credible monetary policies.

- Commodity prices declined (including oil prices).

However, this does not explain why unemployment is lower in the UK than in the EU. A powerful explanation of this is that EU labour markets are more highly regulated than the UK labour market and are therefore less flexible in adapting to change.

Monetary policy cannot impact on real variables in the long run and it is targeted at achieving some particular rate of inflation. A money growth target is therefore an intermediate target aimed at achieving some rate of inflation. Present policy by-passes intermediate targets and many central banks now directly target the rate of inflation. In simple terms, interest rates are adjusted whenever the inflation target is threatened. There are two main problems with this approach:

- Interest rate changes impact on aggregate demand and therefore inflation only after a lag.

- Inflation can be affected by future events.

Central banks that target inflation therefore adjust policy in response to changes in the forecast rate of inflation.

HELPFUL HINTS

1. Short run and long run Phillips curves are almost a mirror image of short run and long run aggregate supply curves. Look at the supply curves that appear in Exhibit 1. Notice the aggregate supply curves in panel (a). Compare them to the Phillips curves in panel (b). They appear to be mirror images of each other. The long run aggregate supply curve is vertical because, in the long run, an increase in the price level is met by a proportionate increase in all prices and incomes so there is no incentive to alter production. Since an increase in prices has no effect on output in the long run, it has no effect on unemployment, and the long run Phillips curve is vertical in panel (b). In the short run with price expectations fixed, an increase in the price level provides an incentive for firms to increase production, causing the short run aggregate supply curve to be positively sloped in panel (a). When output rises, unemployment tends to fall, so the short run Phillips curve is negatively sloped in panel (b). In summary, since both diagrams employ some measure of prices on the vertical axis, and since each graph uses real measures of economic activity that are negatively correlated on their respective horizontal axes (an increase in output is associated with a decrease in unemployment) then aggregate supply curves and Phillips curves should 'mirror' each other.

2. To understand the short run Phillips curve, review short run aggregate supply. To gain confidence deriving and shifting short run Phillips curves, review the sources to the positive slope of the short run aggregate supply curve in Chapter 33.

There you will be reminded that there are a number of reasons why a short run aggregate supply-curve slopes positively—misperceptions about relative price, sticky wages, and sticky prices. Since short run aggregate supply curves and Phillips curves are mirror images of each other, the very same reasons that produce a positive slope in aggregate supply produce a negative slope in the Phillips curve. Also, recall that all three theories of the short run aggregate supply curve are based on the assumption of fixed price expectations. When price expectations rise, the short run aggregate supply curve shifts left. Correspondingly, since the short run aggregate supply curve and the Phillips curve are mirror images, a rise in price expectations shifts the Phillips curve to the right.

3. The Phillips curve establishes a relationship between inflation and unemployment, but it does not establish causation. Reading the Phillips curve from the unemployment axis to the inflation axis suggests that when unemployment is unusually low, the labour market is tight and wages and prices start to rise more quickly.

4. Estimates of the natural rate of unemployment vary widely, causing policy makers to disagree on the appropriate monetary and fiscal policies. When looking at a Phillips curve diagram or the model of aggregate supply and aggregate demand, it appears as if policy makers should always know whether to expand or contract aggregate demand or whether to leave aggregate demand alone. This is because we can see whether the economy is operating above or below the long run natural rate that we have chosen on the diagram. However, in reality the natural rate is very difficult to measure and policy makers are uncertain whether the economy is actually operating above or below the natural rate. For example, if the economy is currently operating at 6 per cent unemployment, the economy is operating below capacity if the natural rate of unemployment is 5 per cent, at capacity if the natural rate is 6 per cent, and above capacity of the natural rate is 7 per cent. Each situation might suggest a different stabilization policy, even though the actual rate of unemployment is unchanged at 6 per cent.

TERMS AND DEFINITIONS

Choose a definition for each key term.

Key terms:

_____ Misery index

_____ Phillips curve

_____ Natural rate of unemployment

_____ Natural rate hypothesis

_____ Disinflation

_____ Supply shock

_____ Sacrifice ratio

_____ Rational expectations

Definitions:

1. A reduction in the rate of inflation

2. The normal rate of unemployment toward which the economy gravitates

3. The theory that suggests that people optimally use all available information, including information about the outcome of government policies, when forecasting the future

4. The sum of inflation and unemployment

5. The theory that unemployment returns to its natural rate, regardless of inflation

6. The short-run tradeoff between inflation and unemployment

7. The number of percentage points of annual output lost in order to reduce inflation one percentage point

8. An event that directly alters firms' costs and prices, shifting the economy's aggregate supply curve and thus the Phillips curve

PROBLEMS AND SHORT-ANSWER QUESTIONS

Practice Problems

1. Describe the initial effect of the following events on the short run and long run Phillips curve. That is, describe the movements along a given curve or the direction of the shift in the curve.
   a. An increase in expected inflation.
   b. An increase in the price of imported oil.
   c. An increase in the money supply.
   d. A decrease in government spending.
   e. A decrease in the minimum wage which lowers the natural rate.

2. Use the Phillips curves in Exhibit 4 to answer the following questions.
   a. At what point is the economy located if people expect 10 per cent inflation and actual inflation is 10 per cent?
   b. Referring to (a) above, is unemployment above, below, or equal to the natural rate?
   c. At what point is the economy located if people expect 10 per cent inflation and the actual rate of inflation is 15 per cent?
   d. Suppose the economy is operating at point D. Over time, in which direction will people revise their expectations of inflation—up or down?
   e. Suppose the economy is operating at point D. As people revise their expectations of inflation, in which direction will the short run Phillips curve shift—right or left?
   f. Suppose the economy is operating at point E. In the short run, a sudden decrease in aggregate demand will move the economy toward which point?
   g. Suppose the economy is operating at point E. In the long run, a decrease in government spending will tend to move the economy toward which point?
   h. Suppose people expect 5 per cent inflation. If inflation actually ends up being 10 per cent, in which direction will unemployment move—above or below the natural rate?

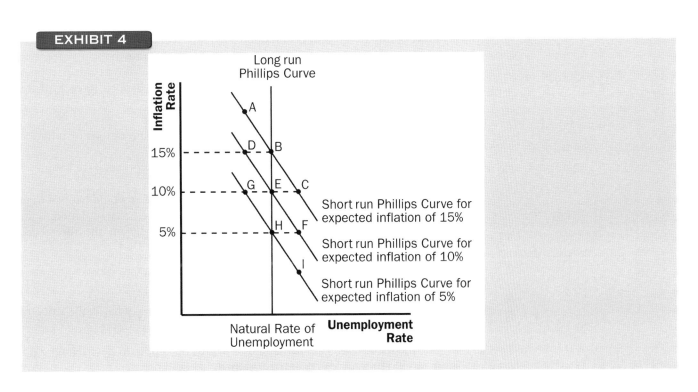

EXHIBIT 4

EXHIBIT 5

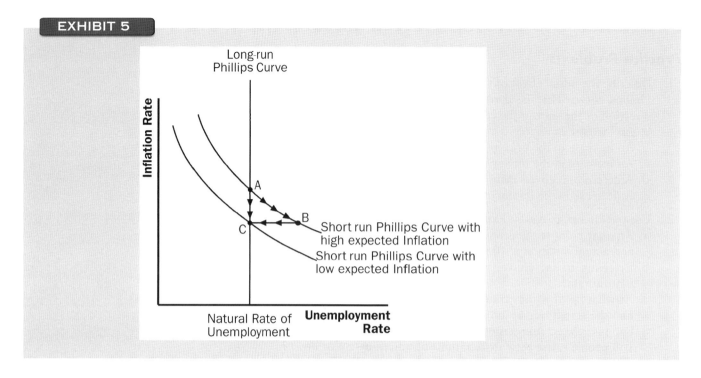

3. Use a Phillips curve graph to answer the following questions. Assume the economy is initially in long run equilibrium.
   a. What happens to unemployment and inflation in the short run if the central bank increases the growth rate of the money supply?
   b. What happens to unemployment and inflation in the long run if the central bank increases the growth rate of the money supply?
   c. Can printing money keep unemployment below the natural rate? Explain.
   d. What is the end result of a central bank repeatedly attempting to hold unemployment below the natural rate with expansionary monetary policy? Explain.

4. Suppose the economy is operating at the natural rate of unemployment with a high rate of inflation (point A in Exhibit 5). Suppose the central bank announces a sudden monetary contraction to reduce inflation. Shown below are two possible paths the economy might take to adjust to the new lower rate of money growth. Choose the path that best depicts what might happen in each of the following cases and explain your reasoning.
   a. The central bank's announcement is not believed.
   b. The central bank's announcement is believed and expectations of inflation are adjusted quickly.
   c. The central bank's announcement is believed but all workers have long term wage contracts that cannot be renegotiated.
   d. Which of the above cases (a, b, or c) best describes what would happen if, in the past, the central bank had repeatedly announced that inflation is its number one priority, but it failed to actually engage in the threatened monetary contraction? Why?

Short-Answer Questions

1. If unemployment is 6 per cent and inflation is 5 per cent, what is the value of the so-called misery index?

2. Use the model of aggregate demand and aggregate supply to describe why the short run Phillips curve is negatively sloped.

3. Use the model of aggregate demand and aggregate supply to describe why the long run Phillips curve is vertical.

4. Is the short run Phillips curve actually a menu of inflation and unemployment combinations permanently available to the policy maker? Why or why not?

5. What is the natural rate hypothesis?

6. If actual inflation exceeds expected inflation, is the unemployment rate above or below the natural rate? Why?

7. Which way does the short run Phillips curve shift when there is an adverse aggregate supply shock such as an increase in the price of imported oil? Why?

8. Referring to question 7 above, are the trade offs between unemployment and inflation that the economy now faces more favourable or less favourable than before the adverse supply shock? Explain.

9. Referring to question 8 above, if the central bank accommodates the adverse supply shock, what have they revealed about the weights they attach to the goals of low inflation and low unemployment?

10. If the sacrifice ratio is five, how much will output be reduced in order for inflation to be reduced four percentage points? If people have rational expectations, is the sacrifice ratio likely to be larger or smaller than five? Why?

SELF-TEST

True/False Questions

_____ 1. When unemployment is below the natural rate, the labour market is unusually tight putting pressure on wages and prices to rise.

_____ 2. A reduction in price expectations shifts the Phillips curve upwards and makes the inflation unemployment trade off less favourable.

_____ 3. When actual inflation exceeds expected inflation, unemployment exceeds the natural rate.

_____ 4. The natural rate hypothesis suggests that in the long run, unemployment returns to its natural rate regardless of inflation.

_____ 5. An adverse supply shock, such as an increase in the price of imported oil, shifts the Phillips curve upward and makes the inflation unemployment trade off less favourable.

_____ 6. A decrease in unemployment benefits reduces the natural rate of unemployment and shifts the long run Phillips curve to the right.

_____ 7. An increase in aggregate demand temporarily reduces unemployment, but after people raise their expectations of inflation, unemployment returns to the natural rate.

_____ 8. A sudden monetary contraction moves the economy up a short run Phillips curve, reducing unemployment and increasing inflation.

_____ 9. If people form expectations rationally, an announced monetary contraction by the central bank that is credible could reduce inflation with little or no increase in unemployment.

_____ 10. If the sacrifice ratio is four, a reduction of inflation from 9 per cent to 5 per cent requires a reduction in output of 8 per cent.

Multiple-Choice Questions

1. The Phillips curve is an extension of the model of aggregate supply and aggregate demand because, in the short run, an increase in aggregate demand increases prices and
   a. decreases growth.
   b. decreases inflation.
   c. increases unemployment.
   d. decreases unemployment.

2. Along a short run Phillips curve,
   a. a higher rate of growth in output is associated with a lower unemployment rate.
   b. a higher rate of growth in output is associated with a higher unemployment rate.
   c. a higher rate of inflation is associated with a lower unemployment rate.
   d. a higher rate of inflation is associated with a higher unemployment rate.

3. According to the Phillips curve, in the short run, if policy makers choose an expansionary policy to lower the rate of unemployment,
   a. the economy will experience a decrease in inflation.
   b. the economy will experience an increase in inflation.
   c. inflation will be unaffected if price expectations are unchanging.
   d. none of the above.

4. An increase in expected inflation
   a. shifts the short run Phillips curve upward and the unemployment inflation tradeoff is less favourable.
   b. shifts the short run Phillips curve downward and the unemployment inflation tradeoff is more favourable.
   c. shifts the short run Phillips curve upward and the unemployment inflation tradeoff is more favourable.
   d. shifts the short run Phillips curve downward and the unemployment inflation tradeoff is less favourable.

5. Which of the following would shift the long run Phillips curve to the right?
   a. an increase in the rate of VAT.
   b. an increase in expected inflation.
   c. an increase in aggregate demand.
   d. an increase in the minimum wage.

6. If price expectations are zero and unemployment is above the natural rate, which one of the following statements must be true?
   a. There is no inflation in the economy.
   b. The natural rate of unemployment will increase.
   c. Inflation can be reduced without increasing unemployment.
   d. Unemployment will fall in the long run.

7. A decrease the price of foreign oil
   a. shifts the short run Phillips curve upward, and the unemployment inflation tradeoff is more favourable.
   b. shifts the short run Phillips curve upward, and the unemployment inflation tradeoff is less favourable.
   c. shifts the short run Phillips curve downward, and the unemployment inflation tradeoff is more favourable.
   d. shifts the short run Phillips curve downward, and the unemployment inflation tradeoff is less favourable.

8. If people have rational expectations, a monetary policy contraction that is announced and is credible could
   a. reduce inflation but it would increase unemployment by an unusually large amount.
   b. reduce inflation with little or no increase in unemployment.
   c. increase inflation but it would decrease unemployment by an unusually large amount.
   d. increase inflation with little or no decrease in unemployment.

9. If the sacrifice ratio is five, a reduction in inflation from 7 per cent to 3 per cent would require
   a. a reduction in output of 5 per cent.
   b. a reduction in output of 15 per cent.
   c. a reduction in output of 20 per cent.
   d. a reduction in output of 35 per cent.

10. If the central bank were to continuously use expansionary monetary policy in an attempt to hold unemployment below the natural rate, the long run result would be
   a. an increase in the level of output.
   b. a decrease in the unemployment rate.
   c. an increase in the rate of inflation.
   d. all of the above.

ADVANCED CRITICAL THINKING

A worldwide drought has reduced food production. Inflation has increased, unemployment has risen above the natural rate. Citizens are frustrated with their government. Your room mate says, 'The perpetuation of this economic mess has got to be the government's fault. A year ago, both inflation and unemployment were lower. We desperately need policy makers that know how to get rid of this inflation and unemployment.'

1. Whose fault is the stagflation that is present in the economy?

2. Are the current inflation and unemployment choices facing the economy better or worse than before the supply shock? What has happened to the short run Phillips curve?

3. If policy makers *increase* aggregate demand in response to the supply shock, in what direction will the economy move along the new short run Phillips curve? What will happen to inflation and unemployment?

4. If policy makers *decrease* aggregate demand in response to the supply shock, in what direction will the economy move along the new short run Phillips curve? What will happen to inflation and unemployment?

5. Is there a policy that can immediately reduce both inflation and unemployment? Explain.

SOLUTIONS

Terms and Definitions

__1__ Disinflation

__2__ Natural rate of unemploymen

  3   Rational expectations

  4   Misery index

  5   Natural rate hypothesis

  6   Phillips curve

  7   Sacrifice ratio

  8   Supply shock

Practice Problems

1. a. Shifts short run Phillips curve to the right (upward).
     b. Shifts short run Phillips curve to the right (upward).
     c. Move up the short run Phillips curve.
     d. Move down the short run Phillips curve.
     e. Long run and short run Phillips curves shift left (downward).

2. a. E.
     b. Equal to the natural rate.
     c. D.
     d. Up.
     e. Right.
     f. F.
     g. H.
     h. Below the natural rate.

3. a. Inflation increases, unemployment decreases.
     b. Inflation increases, unemployment stays at the natural rate.
     c. No. Unemployment temporarily decreases, but as people grow to expect the higher inflation, unemployment returns to the natural rate.
     d. Continued attempts to move unemployment below the natural rate simply causes inflation.

4. a. Economy moves from A to B because people fail to reduce their price expectations and wage demands, so unemployment rises as inflation falls.
     b. Economy moves from A to C because people reduce their prices and wages proportionately.
     c. Economy moves from A to B because people are unable to actually reduce some of their wages and prices, so unemployment rises as inflation falls.
     d. Case (a), because people are rational to distrust a policy maker that has previously been untruthful.

Short-Answer Questions

1. 11 per cent.

2. An increase in aggregate demand increases prices and output along the short run aggregate supply curve, which reduces unemployment. Prices have increased and unemployment has decreased.

3. An increase in aggregate demand increases prices, but output remains at the natural rate due to a vertical long run aggregate supply curve. Prices have increased but unemployment remains at the natural rate.

4. No. When inflation increases above expected inflation, unemployment temporarily decreases. However, after people revise their price expectations upward, the Phillips curve shifts upward (to the right).

5. Unemployment returns to the natural rate in the long run, regardless of inflation.

6. Below, because if prices are higher than expected additional output is produced and additional people are employed, reducing unemployment.

7. Aggregate supply shifts left showing lower production at each price level. Thus, the Phillips curve shifts right (upward) showing more unemployment at each rate of inflation.

8. Less favourable. Now, at each level of unemployment, inflation is higher, or at each rate of inflation, unemployment is higher.

9. The central bank is more concerned with low unemployment.

10. 20 per cent. Smaller because they will reduce their price expectations more quickly, shifting the Phillips curve to the left.

True/False Questions

1. T

2. F; a reduction in price expectations shifts the Phillips curve downwards and makes the inflation unemployment tradeoff *more* favourable.

3. F; when actual inflation exceeds expected inflation, unemployment is below the natural rate.

4. T

5. T

6. F; it shifts the long run Phillips curve to the left.

7. T

8. F; a sudden monetary contraction moves the economy down a short run Phillips curve increasing unemployment and reducing inflation.

9. T

10. F; output must be reduced by $4 \times 4\% = 16\%$.

Multiple-Choice Questions

1.	d	6.	d
2.	c	7.	c
3.	b	8.	b
4.	a	9.	c
5.	d	10.	c

Advanced Critical Thinking

1. No one's. It was an act of nature.

2. Worse because the short run Phillips curve has shifted upward.

3. The economy moves upward along the new short run Phillips curve. Unemployment will be reduced but inflation will be increased.

4. The economy moves downward along the new short run Phillips curve. Inflation will be reduced, but unemployment will be increased.

5. No, the economy faces trade offs in the short run. A policy that reduces inflation increases unemployment. A policy that reduces unemployment increases inflation.

COMMON CURRENCY AREAS AND THE EUROPEAN MONETARY UNION

CHAPTER OVERVIEW

Context and Purpose

Chapter 36 is the penultimate chapter of the book. It focuses on the single currency in particular, and optimum currency areas in general. It extends some of the issues explored in Chapters 31 and 32.

The purpose of Chapter 36 is to provide both sides of the debate about the single currency. Ideas about joining a common currency are bound up with ideas of optimum currency areas and the creation of the euro has re-ignited the debate about optimum currency areas. This chapter helps you understand the issues on which the debate about joining the common currency focuses and the arguments used by supporters and opponents to further their case.

CHAPTER REVIEW

Introduction

For most of the last 200 years, the pound sterling was the major international currency. However, for the last sixty years the US dollar has been the world's most important currency and many of the commodities traded on the world's exchanges are now priced in dollars. Despite its current dominance, many observers think the supremacy of the dollar as an international currency will soon be challenged by the euro, the world's newest currency.

The Euro

On January 1st 1999, a new currency, the euro, was created and a number of European nations abandoned their own currencies and adopted the euro by joining the European Economic and Monetary Union. The creation of the euro was the culmination of a long process of integration begun in the 1950s. However, it was not until 1992 that the criteria for entry into the euro were established in the Maastricht Treaty. Among other things, this Treaty established convergence criteria against which a currency's suitability for entry into the euro is judged. The criteria are,

> A central government budget deficit of no more than three per cent of GDP.

> A debt to GDP ratio of no more than 60 per cent.

> Participation in the ERM (Exchange Rate Mechanism) II. This basically involves a fixed exchange rate against the euro that does not deviate by more than 15 per cent (up or down) against its par value, and is not devalued against its central parity with any other applicant country's bilateral exchange rate against the euro over the two years preceding entry.

> A rate of inflation that does not exceed the inflation rate in the 3 Member States with the lowest inflation by more than 1.5 percentage points.

> A long term rate of interest that does not exceed the inflation rate in the three Member States with the lowest inflation by more than 2 percentage points.

The original aim of the EU was to increase trade among members and through this to promote prosperity. Trade is promoted through the creation of the single European market and in 1992 the EU issued Directives to Member States charging them with achieving four goals:

- The free movement of goods, services, labour and capital between EU Member States.

- The approximation of relevant laws, regulations and administrative provisions between Member States.

- A common, EU-wide competition policy, administered by the European Commission.

- A system of common external tariffs implemented against countries who are not Members of the EU.

The benefits of the single market are undoubted. Resources are free to move to where they are most efficiently used within the EU. Firms are exposed to greater competition and the inefficient are forced to close. As the size of the market increases, firms will gain economies of scale and all of these effects will combine to generate lower prices for the consumer. It has been estimated that in the ten years since 1993, the single market has helped create 2.5 million new jobs and has generated €800 billion in additional wealth.

The Benefits and Costs of a Common Currency

Benefits

- *Transactions costs* are eliminated for intra EU because trade is conducted in a common currency.

- *Price discrimination* within the EU is more difficult because price transparency makes it impossible to disguise price differentials behind different currencies.

- *The elimination of exchange rate variability* and the implied uncertainty that this brings will benefit firms and consumers within the EU. Exchange rate fluctuations increase the variability of returns from international transactions and make it more difficult for firms to plan future sales. Because of this, it is also difficult for firms to plan future investment in plant, equipment and people.

Costs. The major disadvantage of adopting a common currency is that a country loses policy sovereignty. The common currency implies loss of the exchange rate as a policy instrument and the adoption of a common monetary policy. Why is this a problem? Suppose consumer preferences change so that demand for one country's goods, say Germany, falls and demand for another country's goods, say France, increases. The result is that aggregate demand in Germany falls and aggregate demand in France rises. Under flexible exchange rates, these changes in aggregate demand could be offset to some extent by a depreciation of the German currency (appreciation of the French currency) against the French currency (against the German currency). Without this flexibility, adjustment will be a long and drawn out process involving wage and price adjustments in both countries and the consequent fluctuations in output and employment.

Neither is it possible to accommodate the changes in aggregate demand by changes in monetary policy. The scenario we have hypothesized would imply a loosening of monetary policy in Germany to bolster aggregate demand, and a tightening of monetary policy in France to constrain aggregate demand. Within the eurozone, monetary policy is set by the ECB which takes a community wide perspective leaving each country with a 'one size fits all' monetary policy. The result is that policy cannot be adjusted to suit the individual needs of each individual country and countries might find themselves locked into a recession or locked into inflation. Adjustment through market forces will involve a higher 'misery index' than if economic policy could be adjusted individually by different countries.

The Theory of Optimum Currency Areas

Optimum currency area theory attempts to identify those criteria that make it optimal for a group of countries to adopt the same currency. A currency area is optimal when each country is able to limit the costs of the union and gain increased benefits by participating in the union.

Characteristics that Reduce the Costs of a Single Currency

Since the major costs of joining a monetary union involve the absence of adjustment mechanisms following an asymmetric shock, it follows that the costs of joining a union will be limited if countries follow the same economic cycle and are subject to the same economic shocks. That is, if all countries experience simultaneous and symmetric changes in aggregate demand.

However, if shocks are asymmetric, this does not necessarily pose a serious problem since areas which possess certain characteristics will adjust with relatively little impact on output and employment. There characteristics are,

- *Real wage flexibility* implies that long run equilibrium is restored relatively quickly following a shock with relatively small changes in output and employment.

- *Labour mobility* can also smooth the adjustment process. If aggregate demand in one country rises and labour is sufficiently mobile between countries, unemployed workers in one country will simply migrate to the country where demand is rising. In our example above, German workers would migrate to France.

- *Capital mobility* might also provide an adjustment mechanism when countries experience asymmetric shocks. Physical capital (plant and equipment) might be important when regional disparities are persistent, but it is the mobility of financial assets that is the main focus of attention here. When a country experiences a recession, residents of that country might wish to borrow to finance expenditures. However, savings will fall as incomes fall and so a capital inflow from countries which are booming might provide an adjustment mechanism.

Characteristics that Increase the Benefits of a Single Currency

The greater the amount of trade between a group of countries, the more they will benefit from adopting a common currency. One obvious reason is that trade between countries with different currencies involves transactions costs as one currency is exchanged for another currency. The greater the level of trade between countries, the greater the savings from adopting a common currency.

Is Europe an Optimum Currency Area?

In reality, it is difficult to establish categorically whether any area is an optimum currency area. However, we can certainly review whether the criteria outlined above apply to the EU.

Trade Integration is the sum of intra-union imports and exports. For the countries that have adopted the euro, the degree of intra-union trade is variable. For example, in 2004, intra-union exports and imports for Belgium were about 105 per cent of its GDP, while for Italy the corresponding figure was around 22 per cent. However, for all countries in the eurozone with the exception of Greece, intra-union trade is growing. This supports the view that the eurozone is an optimum currency area. However, it cannot be taken as proof! It is possible that being part of a common currency area might increase the volume of trade between members because of the elimination of transactions costs involved in converting currencies.

Real Wage Flexibility is not regarded as a feature of European labour markets which are among the most rigid in the world. One reason for this is that all EU countries have minimum wage laws, but a more important factor is the nature of collective bargaining arrangements. Typically wage agreements cover large numbers of workers and bargaining is highly centralized. For example, in France employers are legally obliged to bargain with worker representatives. In addition, the nature and level of payroll taxes in continental Europe make it relatively expensive to recruit or dismiss workers compared with the UK. All of these combine to make labour markets relatively inflexible in Europe and inhibit real wage adjustment to an asymmetric shock.

Labour market mobility is quite low within the EU compared to the US. Even within countries there seems to be a reluctance to move to new areas so this adjustment mechanism cannot be relied upon to alleviate asymmetric shocks within the EU!

Financial Capital Mobility is a well developed feature of European financial markets and following the introduction of the euro, a liquid euro money market with single interbank market interest rates was established. This means it is possible for a bank in Italy to borrow euros from another bank anywhere in the eurozone at the same rate of interest that it could borrow at from another bank in Italy. However, non-bank customers of banks still pay different rates of interest in different countries, so this mechanism of adjustment to asymmetric shocks still has scope for development.

Symmetric Demand Shocks Evidence seems to suggest that the Euro Area as a whole is subject to the same shocks and that business cycles, by and large, move together. To the extent that this is true, the 'one size fits all' monetary policy will be less of a problem for the Euro Area.

Fiscal Policy and Common Currency Areas

Much of the discussion about common currency areas focuses on monetary policy. However, there are also issues concerning fiscal policy that need to be addressed.

Fiscal Federalism

One approach to fiscal policy is for all countries to accept a fiscal policy set at the centre in the same way that a common monetary policy is set. The advantage of this is that fiscal policy within a union would function in the same way that fiscal policy operates within a particular country. Recall from Chapter 35 that there are automatic stabilizers built into which fiscal policy automatically bolster aggregate when output is falling and constrain aggregate demand when output is rising. In our case, it is especially important to note that if aggregate demand is falling in one region of the country, tax payments from that region will fall and transfers to the region will increase as social security payments, in response to rising unemployment, increase. In the same way, fiscal transfers would take place within a union if countries are subject to asymmetric shocks.

National Fiscal Policies in a Currency Union: The Free-Rider Problem

In reality, it might be politically impossible for the government of one country to subside the unemployed in another country. In these circumstances, the alternative to setting fiscal policy from the centre is for each country to independently implement its own fiscal policy. But this poses problems inside a union. Suppose one country experiences an asymmetric shock and offsets a fall in aggregate demand with an expansionist fiscal policy. As a result, central government debt rises and, if this rises far enough, the possibility of default will increase. Consequently, the market will demand higher returns from holding government debt and, because of linkages between markets, interest rates *throughout the union* will rise. The implication is that the deficit spending country experiences a lower rise in interest rates than would otherwise be the case if it were not part of the union. This, you might recognize, as another application of the free rider problem!

The Stability and Growth Pact

To constrain government spending, countries participating in the single currency have signed up to the Stability and Growth Pact (SGP). This imposes constraints on the conduct of national fiscal policies. The main components of the SGP are,

- Members should aim to achieve balanced budgets.

- Members with a budget deficit of more than 3 per cent of GDP will be subject to fines that may reach as high 0.5 per cent of GDP unless the country experiences exceptional circumstances (such as a natural disaster) or a very sharp recession in which GDP declines by 2 per cent or more in a single year.

Adhering to the SGP will avoid any free rider problem associated with excessive deficit spending by one country, but the crucial question is whether the budget deficit rule would allow sufficient scope for a country's automatic stabilizers to function effectively when the economy is in recession.

HELPFUL HINTS

1. The Maastricht Treaty establishes criteria for entry into the euro, but these criteria are not conditions that create an optimum currency area. They are conditions necessary to make a currency union sustainable.

2. The single market creates scope for economies of scale and allows resources to move to where they can be used most efficiently. The single currency, enhances the gains of the single market by increasing the degree of competition in markets. Since prices are quoted in the same currency, it is more difficult for suppliers to price discriminate by concealing price differences behind different currencies. There are other gains from the single currency since transactions costs involved in exchanging currencies are eliminated. The major disadvantage with the common currency is the loss of policy sovereignty.

3. The theory of optimum currency areas focuses on the factors that reduce the adjustment costs to asymmetric shocks. The greater the degree of real wage flexibility between regions, the smaller the adjustment cost following an asymmetric shock. Similarly adjustment costs will be reduced the greater the

degree of labour and capital mobility between regions. Note that any one of these mechanisms can reduce the costs of adjustment to an asymmetric shock. It is not necessary for them all to be in place simultaneously.

4. In a common currency area it is not necessary to adopt a common fiscal policy. However, doing so will facilitate fiscal transfers between countries in response to asymmetric shocks. In reality, the political fallout from this makes the adoption of a common fiscal policy unlikely. To avoid the possibility that markets will not punish high deficit spending countries, the Euro Area has signed up to the Stability and Growth Pact which places limits on deficit spending by individual countries.

TERMS AND DEFINITIONS

Choose a definition for each key term.

Key terms:

_____ Optimum currency area

_____ Stability and Growth Pact

_____ Trade integration

_____ Single market

_____ Adjustment mechanism

_____ Asymmetric demand shock

_____ Monetary sovereignty

_____ Real wage flexibility

_____ Maastricht Criteria

_____ Fiscal federalism

Definitions:

1. Within a currency union, the sum of intra-union imports and exports

2. A group of countries which would reap net benefits if exchange rates between them were rigidly fixed or a common currency adopted

3. A reduction in aggregate demand that only affects some members of a group of trading countries

4. A system involving taxes and transfer payments across countries

5. The ability to implement an independent monetary policy

6. A set of tests that countries wishing to join the Euro Area must pass before entry is allowed

7. An agreement between members of the Euro Area to limit each member's scope for independent fiscal actions

8. The way in which equilibrium is restored to an economy following a shock

9. The ease with which prices and wages move up or down

10. An arrangement between countries whereby restrictions on trade and the movement of factors of production are abolished

PROBLEMS AND SHORT-ANSWER QUESTIONS

Practice Problems

1. The Treaty of Maastricht establishes specific convergence criteria for countries wishing to join the euro. These are summarized below. Explain the importance of each of these criteria if a country is to adopt the euro as its currency.
   a. *Membership of ERM II* This basically implies that an applicant country pegs its exchange rate to the euro at some agreed value and maintains this peg without severe tensions for at least two years prior to entry into the Euro Area. A further condition is that it has not devalued its own bi-lateral central rate against any other applicant country's exchange rate.

b. *Price stability* The requirement here is that a country has a sustainable rate of inflation in the most recent twelve months and which is not more than one and a half percentage points above the best three performing Member States with the lowest rates of inflation over the same period.

c. *Long-term nominal interest rates* The Maastricht Treaty specifies that nominal long-term interest rates in the latest twelve months shall not exceed nominal long-term interest rates in the three Member States with the lowest rate of interest by more than two percentage points over the same period.

d. *Budget deficit* Convergence requires that the planned or actual central government budget deficit shall not exceed three per cent of an applicant country's GDP.

e. *Government debt* Convergence requires that the sum total of outstanding government debt shall not exceed sixty per cent of the applicant country's GDP.

2. Consider two countries A and B which have trading links, but which are not part of the same currency union. Now imagine that country A is subject to a negative demand side shock and country B is subject to a positive demand side shock. Explain how adjustment to the shock takes place under each of the following adjustment mechanisms.
a. Wages are flexible.
b. Labour is highly mobile between both countries.

Short-Answer Questions

1. Why might asymmetric shocks pose problems for a common currency area?

2. How does greater trade integration reduce the possibility of asymmetric shocks?

3. Why is it important to establish limits on fiscal freedom in a currency area?

4. In the absence of real wage flexibility, a high degree of labour and capital mobility and activist stabilization policy, how does an economy adjust following an aggregate demand shock.

5. Why has the EU adopted a Community wide competition policy?

6. Will countries gain from creating a single market even if they do not introduce a common currency?

7. Can a country gain by loss of policy sovereignty when it enters a common currency area?

SELF-TEST

True/False Questions

_____ 1. EMU stands for European Monetary Union.

_____ 2. As one of its convergence criteria, the Maastricht Treaty includes convergent business cycles.

_____ 3. Among other things, a single market requires a common competition policy.

_____ 4. Restrictions on capital flows between members of a currency union are impossible to apply.

_____ 5. There is no optimum number of countries that can form an optimum currency area.

_____ 6. Under fiscal federalism all countries set common tax policies.

_____ 7. If a group of countries is not an optimum currency area, introducing a common currency is unlikely to increase trade among them.

_____ 8. Price discrimination is still possible inside a single market.

_____ 9. The Stability and Growth Pact limits the actual amount individual governments can spend within the Euro Area.

_____10. Even if countries maintain a bi-lateral fixed exchange rate, they are not necessarily an optimum currency area.

Multiple-Choice Questions

1. Which one of the following was an aim of the architects of the Single European Market?
   a. Increasing the degree of competition between countries within the EU.
   b. Removal of risk due to exchange rate uncertainty among EU Members.
   c. Preventing any individual member of the community from exploiting a comparative advantage over other members.
   d. Ensuring that resources are allocated fairly between Members of the EU.

2. When a single market is created between countries, the benefits will be greater when
   a. markets are characterized by imperfect competition.
   b. countries retain their individual employment laws.
   c. funds saved in one country can be borrowed in another.
   d. countries have the same rate of population growth.

3. Which one of the following features of an economy would be desirable for a country entering a monetary union?
   a. Flexible real wages.
   b. A highly unionized labour force.
   c. A relatively closed economy.
   d. Flexible exchange rates.

4. When a country enters a monetary union, it might gain all of the following advantages _except_
   a. Lower costs of production from economies of scale.
   b. Increased control over monetary policy.
   c. Increased trade.
   d. Lower prices for consumers.

5. The main economic advantage of monetary union is that it
   a. makes it easier for the government to control the business cycle.
   b. reduces the divergence between inflation rates within the union.
   c. lowers transactions costs and risk.
   d. increases aggregate demand and employment.

6. In the European Single Market there is
   a. free trade between members with each member imposing its own individual trade restrictions against non members.
   b. free trade between members and a common tariff against non members.
   c. free trade among member countries and non member countries.
   d. free trade among non member countries and a common tariff among member countries.

7. Which one of the following in unlikely to be a consequence of creating a common currency area?
   a. Increased trade between members of the currency area.
   b. Lower transactions costs between members of the currency area.

    c. Increased factor mobility between members of the currency area.

    d. Lower real wages for members of the currency area.

8. For any country, the degree of trade integration with another country is best measured by:

    a. The value of that country's exports as a percentage of the other country's GDP.

    b. The combined value of exports and imports for both countries.

    c. The combined value of exports as a percentage of the combined value of imports.

    d. The sum of that country's exports and imports as a percentage of its GDP.

9. Under a single currency

    a. Members cannot pursue an independent fiscal policy to deal with asymmetric shocks.

    b. The costs of adjustment to an asymmetric shock are lower when prices are flexible.

    c. Monetary policy cannot be used to deal with symmetric shocks.

    d. The increased trade integration reduces the probability of symmetric shocks to members.

10. When a country joins the euro, which one of the following statements is correct?

    a. Balance of payments problems can no longer exist.

    b. The rate of inflation will be the same rate as in all other countries in the Euro Area.

    c. Banks will charge all customers in the Euro Area the same rate of interest.

    d. There is a limit of the growth of the budget deficit.

ADVANCED CRITICAL THINKING

You are watching a documentary about the evolution of the euro. The presenter says 'The architects of the euro hoped that it would rival the dollar as an international currency. There is no sign of this happening yet and many factors will determine whether it happens in the future. However, if the euro does eventually rival the dollar as an international currency, this will pose problems for the US.' Later you discuss the programme with your friend who has no training in economics. Your friend is very dismissive and argues that there is no chance that the euro will ever rival the dollar. She says 'In any case, the US gains nothing from being the major international currency'.

1. What factors determine whether a currency emerges as a major international currency?

2. Using your knowledge as an economist, explain whether you agree or disagree with the following statements made by your friend.

    a. 'The euro will never rival the dollar as an international currency.'

    b. 'The US gains nothing from being the major international currency.'

3. What problems would the US experience if the euro did emerge as a rival for the dollar on the world's foreign exchanges?

SOLUTIONS

Terms and Definitions

_1_	Trade integration	_6_	Maastricht Criteria
_2_	Optimum currency area	_7_	Stability and Growth Pact
_3_	Asymmetric demand shock	_8_	Adjustment mechanism
_4_	Fiscal federalism	_9_	Real wage flexibility
_5_	Monetary sovereignty	_10_	Single market

Practice Problems

1. a. The exchange rate criterion is important because if a country succeeds in maintaining the value of its currency against the euro within the bands of fluctuation for two years, it is reasonable to assume that the country would be able to deal with the binding constraints, such as loss of policy sovereignty, of a common currency.

    b. In a common currency area it is impossible to offset a competitive disadvantage between countries by adjusting the exchange rate. It is therefore important that countries at least have convergent rates of inflation otherwise high inflation countries will become increasingly uncompetitive. If real wages are inflexible and resources are not sufficiently mobile between regions, adjustment will involve falling output and rising unemployment in the high inflation countries.

    c. Divergent rates of interest are impossible when an area has a single currency and so a convergent rate of interest is important in ensuring a nation's prosperity inside the Euro Area. If a particular rate of interest is appropriate for some countries inside the Union but not others, this will hamper growth and prosperity in those countries where the common interest rate is higher than economic conditions would otherwise dictate. Because of the relationship between budget deficits and interest rates, an ability to meet the interest rate criterion also has implications for a country's ability to meet the budget deficit criterion.

    d. Convergence over the size of budget deficits is important because under a single currency regime, excessive borrowing by one country would drive up interest rates for all countries. That is, those countries that restrict their borrowing would be penalized by the actions of more profligate borrowers and the latter would go unpenalized by the market driving up their individual rate of interest.

    e. The ratio of public debt to GDP is important because as the size of the ratio of public debt to GDP rises, interest rates will again be driven upwards and will 'crowd out' private sector investment. More fundamentally, the market will eventually come to doubt the sustainability of rising levels of public debt and interest rates will be driven up as the market imposes a risk premium.

2. a. Wages will fall in country A as rising unemployment eases pressure in the labour market. As wages fall, prices fall and country A's products become more competitive and aggregate demand rises and unemployment falls. The opposite happens in country B. Rising aggregate demand pulls up prices and wages as the labour market tightens. Country B's products become less competitive. Aggregate demand falls and unemployment increases. This process continues until equilibrium is restored in both countries.

    b. This is easy! Unemployed workers in country A move to country B. As a result, excess labour supply falls in country A relieving unemployment without any downward pressure on wages and prices. Simultaneously the labour shortage is relieved in country B without any upward pressure on wages and prices.

Short-Answer Questions

1. In the absence of appropriate adjustment mechanisms, an asymmetric shock inside a currency union poses problems because the loss of policy sovereignty reduces the mechanisms available for activist stabilization policy.

2. As countries become more highly integrated, business cycles tend to become more symmetric. As the extent of economic activities becomes more highly correlated, shocks will tend to be symmetric rather than asymmetric.

3. Because inside a currency union high borrowers are not punished by the market by having to pay higher rates of interest. Instead, because a common interest rate exists within the union, all members face higher interest rates because of any excess borrowing by one member.

4. In these circumstances, adjustment falls on the real economy and will take the form of a fall in output and a rise in unemployment. This will continue until real wages are forced downwards.

5. The benefits of the single market will not be fully realized in the absence of a common approach to competition policy. Different approaches to competition policy will give firms in one country an unfair advantage over firms in another country and will prevent the full gains from specialization and trade from materialising.

6. Yes! Gains will come from freeing up trade allowing greater exploitation of respective comparative advantage, from economies of scale, from increased ability of resources to move to where rewards are greatest and so on.

7. The main gains come from the increased credibility that being part of a currency union generates. Credibility comes from the inability to use devaluation as an adjustment mechanism in response to an asymmetric shock, but it is *possible* that the central bank in a currency union is more credible in the conduct of monetary policy than a member country's national central bank.

8. Competition in product markets, regulation of markets (factor and product), the extent of trade union power over wages, whether minimum wage laws are in place and so on.

True/False Questions

1. F; it stands for Economic and Monetary Union.

2. F; No! This might be a desirable criteria, but it is not stipulated under the Maastricht Criteria which focuses only on convergence of nominal variables.

3. T

4. T

5. T

6. T

7. F; a common currency will still encourage greater trade because of an absence of exchange rate risk, elimination of transactions costs and greater price transparency.

8. T

9. F; No! It imposes limits on the size of the budget deficit.

10. T

Multiple-Choice Questions

1. a   3. a   5. c   7. d   9. b
2. c   4. b   6. b   8. d   10. d

Advanced Critical Thinking

1. The size of the country's economy determines the potential for its currency to become a major international currency. Other factors are the convertibility of the currency, the importance of the currency in international trade and the openness of the country's financial markets. Stability is also important—macroeconomic and political!

2. a) The euro has the potential to rival the dollar as an international currency. It satisfies all of the criteria outlined in 1 above and performs the functions of money that any international currency must perform. That is, it is a unit of account, a medium of exchange and a store of value. Despite all of this, whether the euro will rival the dollar is a matter of conjecture—but if this does happen, it certainly won't happen soon!

   b) The US gains a great deal by being the world's major international currency! One gain is, of course, the seignorage revenue that accrues to the issuer of money. However, another major benefit is that so long as the rest of world is prepared to hold dollars as an asset, the US is able to run a persistent current account deficit. This enables US citizens to consume more imports from abroad without having to pay for these with additional exports.

3. Seignorage revenue would be lost. Of more significance is that the demand for dollars would fall and supply would increase. This implies a depreciation of the dollar on the world's foreign exchanges. As this happened, dollars would be exchanged for goods and services from the US. Since a large proportion of the total number of dollars in existence circulate outside the US, the consequences for the US economy could be very serious indeed possibly involving higher interest rates to protect the dollar and recession as consumption and investment spending fell in response to higher rates if interest.

37

┌ In this chapter you will

Consider whether policy makers should try to stabilize the economy

Consider whether monetary policy should be made by rule rather than by discretion

Consider whether the central bank should aim for zero inflation

Consider whether the government should balance its budget

Consider whether the tax laws should be reformed to encourage saving

OUTCOMES

┌ You should be able to

Give an example of a macroeconomic policy response that 'leans against the wind'

Explain what is meant by the 'time inconsistency of policy'

List the costs of inflation

Explain the benefits of reducing the budget deficit

Explain why a consumption tax encourages saving but increases economic inequality

FIVE DEBATES OVER MACROECONOMIC POLICY

CHAPTER OVERVIEW

Context and Purpose

Chapter 37 is the final chapter in the text. It addresses five unresolved issues in macroeconomics, each of which is central to current political debates. The chapter can be studied all at once, or portions of the chapter can be studied in conjunction with prior chapters that deal with the related material.

The purpose of Chapter 37 is to provide both sides of five leading debates over macroeconomic policy. It employs information and tools that you have accumulated in your study of this text. This chapter might help you take a position on the issues addressed or, at least, it might help you understand the reasoning of others who have taken a position.

CHAPTER REVIEW

Introduction

This chapter presents both sides of five leading debates over macroeconomic policy. These issues are central to current political debates.

Should Monetary and Fiscal Policy Makers Try to Stabilize the Economy?

Pro: Policy makers should try to stabilize the economy. Pessimism on the part of households and firms reduces aggregate demand and causes a recession. The resulting reduction in output and the increase in unemployment is a waste of resources. This waste of resources is unnecessary because the government and the central bank have the power to 'lean against the wind' and stabilize aggregate demand by, in this case, increasing government spending, reducing taxes, and increasing the money supply. If aggregate demand is excessive, these policies can be reversed.

Con: Policy-makers should not try to stabilize the economy. Monetary and fiscal policy affect the economy with a substantial lag. Monetary policy involves adjusting interest rates and changes in these can influence residential and business investment spending over many months—perhaps as long as three years in the UK. A change in fiscal policy involves a long political process. Because forecasting is difficult and because many shocks are unpredictable, stabilization policy must be based on educated guesses about future economic conditions. Mistakes can make activist policy destabilizing. The first rule of policy should be to 'do no harm' so policy makers should refrain from intervening often in the economy.

Should Monetary Policy Be Made by Rule Rather than by Discretion?

Recall, every month the Monetary Policy Committee of the Bank of England meets and decides whether to change the repo rate, and every two weeks the Governing Council of the ECB meets to consider adjusting the refinancing rate. At present, the Monetary Policy Committee of the Bank of England and the Governing Council of the ECB set monetary policy with complete discretion.

Pro: Monetary policy should be made by rule. There are two problems with discretionary policy.

- First, discretionary policy does not limit incompetence and abuse of power. A central bank abuses its power when it manipulates monetary policy to favour a particular political candidate. It can increase the money supply prior to an election to benefit the incumbent government and the resulting inflation doesn't show up until after the election. This creates what is known as the *political business cycle*.

- Second, discretionary policy might lead to more inflation than is desirable due to the *time inconsistency of policy*. This occurs because policy makers are tempted to announce a low inflation target but, once people have formed their inflation expectations, policy makers can raise inflation to lower unemployment by exploiting the short run trade off between inflation and unemployment. As a result, people expect more inflation than policy makers say they are targeting, which shifts the Phillips curve upward to a less favourable position.

These problems can be avoided by committing the central bank to a policy rule. The government could remove some of the independence granted to the Bank of England in 1997 and require it to increase the money supply by a certain per cent each year, say two and a half per cent, which is just enough to accommodate growth in real output. Alternatively, the government could require a more active rule whereby the Bank of England would respond with a specific increase in the money supply if unemployment rose a certain per cent above the natural rate. Some argue that the policy rule should be implemented by a computer.

Con: Monetary policy should not be made by rule. Discretionary monetary policy is needed because monetary policy must be flexible enough to respond to unforeseen events such as a significant reduction in aggregate demand or a negative supply shock. Further, political business cycles might not exist and time inconsistency problems might be avoided if a central bank's announcements are credible. Finally, if monetary policy were to be guided by a rule, it is unclear what type of rule government should impose.

Should the Central Bank Aim for Zero Inflation?

Pro: The central bank should aim for zero inflation. Inflation imposes the following costs on society:

- shoeleather costs associated with reduced money holdings,

- menu costs associated with frequent adjustment of prices,

- increased variability of relative prices,
- unintended changes in tax liabilities due to non-indexation of the tax code,
- confusion and inconvenience resulting from a changing unit of account,
- arbitrary redistributions of wealth associated with euro-denominated debts.

The costs associated with reducing inflation to zero are temporary, while the benefits of zero inflation are permanent. The costs can be reduced further if an announced policy of zero inflation is credible. The policy would be more credible if the central bank is granted independence from government and price stability is defined as its major goal. Finally, zero inflation is the only non-arbitrary target for inflation. All other target levels can be incrementally revised upward.

Con: The central bank should not aim for zero inflation. There are a number of reasons why the central bank should not aim for zero inflation:

- The benefits of zero inflation are small and uncertain, while the costs of achieving it are large.
- The unemployment and social costs associated with the reduction in inflation are borne by the unskilled and inexperienced—those least able to afford it.
- People tend to dislike inflation because they mistakenly think it erodes their living standards, but incomes tend to rise with inflation.
- Many of the costs of inflation can be eliminated without reducing inflation by indexing the tax system and issuing inflation-indexed bonds.
- Reducing inflation costlessly is unlikely to be possible.
- Disinflation leaves permanent scars on the economy because the capital stock is smaller and the unemployed workers have diminished skills.

Should the Government Balance Its Budget?

Pro: The government should balance its budget. Government debt places a burden on future generations of taxpayers who must choose to pay higher taxes, cut government spending, or both. Current taxpayers pass the bill for current spending to future taxpayers. Moreover, the macroeconomic effect of a deficit is to reduce national saving by making public saving negative. This increases interest rates, reduces capital investment, reduces productivity and real wages and thus, reduces future output and income. As a result, deficits raise future taxes and lower future incomes.

Con: The government should not balance its budget. The problem of government debt cannot be analysed as a simple bookkeeping problem. For example, some government spending is on education and reducing the budget deficit by reducing spending on education might not improve the welfare of the next generation. Other government policies redistribute income across generations such as social security benefits. If people wish to reverse the intergenerational redistribution of income caused by budget deficits, they need only save more during their lifetime and leave bequests to their children so they can pay the higher taxes. Finally, government debt can continue to grow forever, yet not grow as a per cent of GDP as long as the debt fails to grow more quickly than the nation's nominal income. Suppose the output of the economy grows on average about 3 per cent per year. If the inflation rate averages around 2 per cent per year, then nominal income grows at a rate of 5 per cent per year. Government debt can therefore rise by 5 per cent per year without increasing the ratio of debt to income.

Current policy in the UK is based on two rules: 'the golden rule' and the 'sustainable investment rule'. The golden rule is that, over the economic cycle, the government will borrow only to invest and not to fund current spending. The 'sustainable investment rule' is that, over the economic cycle, the ratio of government debt to GDP will be set at a 'stable and prudent' level, defined by the Chancellor (the UK Minister of Finance) as not more than 40 per cent of GDP.

Should the Tax Laws Be Reformed to Encourage Saving?

Pro: The tax laws should be reformed to encourage saving. A nation's standard of living depends on its productive capability which in turn depends on how much it saves and invests. Since people respond to incentives, the government could encourage saving (or stop discouraging saving) by:

- Reducing taxes on the return to saving (interest income).

- Removing the double taxation of capital income from stocks. At present, corporations pay a corporate income tax, and then profits paid to stockholders in the form of dividends are subject to personal income tax.

- Reducing inheritance taxes so people will save and create bequests to the next generation.

- Reducing means tested government benefits such as housing allowance. These benefits are currently reduced for those that have been prudent enough to save which creates a disincentive to save.

- Increasing the availability of tax-advantaged savings accounts such as Individual Savings Account (ISA) which can consist of various combinations of bonds, equity and cash in a savings account. In these accounts, interest income and dividends are exempt from taxation. Similarly, money paid into a personal pension plan is exempt from income tax.

- Replacing the income tax with a consumption tax. The centrepiece of most tax systems is personal income tax. Many people advocate replacing this with a consumption tax so that income which is not spent is not taxed. In other words, saving would attract a complete tax exemption.

Con: The tax laws should not be reformed to encourage saving. One goal of taxation is to distribute the tax burden fairly. All of the proposals above will increase the incentive to save by reducing taxes on saving. Since high-income people save more than low-income people, this will increase the tax burden on the poor. Also, saving might not be sensitive to changes in the return to saving, so reducing taxes on saving will just enrich the wealthy. This is because a higher return to saving has both a *substitution effect* and an *income effect*. An increase in the return to saving will increase saving as people substitute saving for current consumption. However, the income effect suggests that an increase in the return to saving lowers the amount of saving needed to achieve any targeted level of future consumption.

A reduction in the deficit increases public saving and thus national saving. This could be accomplished by raising taxes on the wealthy. Indeed, reductions in taxes on saving might backfire by increasing the deficit and reducing national saving.

HELPFUL HINTS

1. A policy that destabilizes the economy moves the economy away from the natural rate of output. Stabilization policy is the use of monetary and fiscal policy to help move the economy toward the natural rate of output. However,

if policy lags are long and unpredictable, the economy might have adjusted back to the natural rate (from an aggregate demand or aggregate supply shock) before the impact of the stabilization policy is felt. In this case, the stabilization policy would then move the economy away from the long run natural rate and we would consider the policy to be destabilizing.

2. A political business cycle tends to involve both a monetary expansion prior to an election and a monetary contraction after an election. Political business cycles are discussed in the text with regard to the policy maker's behaviour prior to elections. That is, prior to an election, a monetary expansion could increase output and decrease unemployment, enhancing the probability of the incumbent party's re-election. However, since this will tend to cause inflation after the election, this type of abuse of power usually involves a monetary contraction after the election to reduce inflationary pressures. Thus, the economy would tend to fluctuate between good economic performance prior to an election, and poor economic performance after an election.

3. Zero money growth does not cause zero inflation if real output is growing. Recall from Chapter 30, the quantity theory equation states that $M \times V = P \times Y$, which says that money times velocity equals the price level times real output. If velocity is fixed, and if real output grows at about 3 per cent per year, then the money supply would have to grow at 3 per cent for prices to remain constant. Therefore, a monetary policy rule requiring the central bank to increase the money supply at 3 per cent should generate zero inflation. If output is growing at 3 per cent, money growth of 0 per cent would actually create deflation.

TERMS AND DEFINITIONS

Choose a definition for each key term.

Key terms:

_____ Leaning against the wind

_____ Destabilizing policy

_____ Discretionary policy

_____ Political business cycle

_____ Time inconsistency of policy

Definitions:

1. Economic fluctuations caused by policy makers allying themselves with elected politicians

2. Policy which moves output away from the long run natural rate

3. Engaging in a policy that stabilizes aggregate demand

4. The discrepancy between policy announcements and policy actions

5. A policy chosen by policy makers who have few guidelines

PROBLEMS AND SHORT-ANSWER QUESTIONS

Practice Problems

1. Suppose a wave of pessimism engulfs consumers and firms causing them to reduce their expenditures.
   a. Demonstrate this event in Exhibit 1 using the model of aggregate demand and aggregate supply and assuming that the economy was originally in long run equilibrium.
   b. What is the appropriate activist policy response for monetary and fiscal policy? In which direction would the activist policy shift aggregate demand?
   c. Suppose the economy can adjust on its own in two years from the recession described in part (a). Suppose policy makers choose to use fiscal policy to stabilize the economy, but the political battle over taxes and spending takes more than two years. Demonstrate these events in Exhibit 2 using the model of aggregate demand and aggregate supply.

EXHIBIT 1

Price Level

Quantity of
Real Ouput

EXHIBIT 2

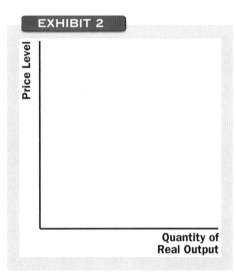

Price Level

Quantity of
Real Output

d. Describe the sequence of events shown in the graph you created in part (c) above.

e. Did the activist fiscal policy stabilize or destabilize the economy? Explain.

2. Suppose the central bank repeatedly announces that it desires price stability and that it is aiming for zero inflation. However, it consistently generates 3 per cent inflation.

a. Will this type of behaviour on the part of the central bank reduce unemployment below the natural rate in the long run? Why?

b. Once people have formed expectations of 3 per cent inflation, what would happen in the short run if the central bank actually did target zero inflation?

c. Would it help if the government passed a law requiring the central bank to target zero inflation?

Short-Answer Questions

1. Why would an improvement in our ability to forecast shocks to the macroeconomy improve our use of activist stabilization policy?

2. What three reasons are given in support of a monetary policy rule?

3. Why are the costs of inflation permanent, but the costs of reducing inflation temporary?

4. What could the government do to reduce the cost of continuous inflation?

5. In what two ways does a government budget deficit harm future generations?

6. Does a balanced government budget guarantee the elimination of all redistributions of wealth across generations? Explain.

7. For an increase in the after-tax return to saving to cause an increase in saving, which effect must outweigh the other—the substitution effect or the income effect? Why?

8. Why will reforming our tax laws to encourage saving tend to increase the tax burden on the poor?

SELF-TEST

True/False Questions

_____ 1. Monetary policy affects the economy with a lag, but fiscal policy has no lag.

_____ 2. Discretionary monetary policy suffers from time inconsistency because policy makers have an incentive to engage in a policy that differs from their policy announcements.

_____ 3. The political business cycle refers to a situation where corporate executives also hold political office.

_____ 4. Opponents of a monetary policy rule argue that a rule would make it more difficult for the central bank to respond to an unusual crisis.

_____ 5. Supporters of a zero inflation target for monetary policy argue that the cost of reducing inflation is temporary, while the benefits of reducing inflation are permanent.

_____ 6. Those opposed to a zero inflation target for monetary policy argue that many of the costs of inflation can be eliminated by inflation-indexed taxes and bonds.

_____ 7. Government budget deficits tend to redistribute wealth from the current generation to future generations.

_____ 8. If economic policy is decided by rules, aggregate demand will always grow by a predetermined amount.

_____ 9. Replacing the income tax with a consumption tax might increase saving, but it will tend to benefit the rich more than the poor.

_____10. A reduction in taxes on interest income will increase saving if the substitution effect from the increase in after-tax interest outweighs the income effect.

Multiple-Choice Questions

1. Suppose that the economy is suffering from pessimism on the part of consumers and firms. Which of the following is an activist stabilization policy that 'leans against the wind'?
   a. Policy makers should decrease the money supply.
   b. Policy makers should increase taxes.
   c. Policy makers should decrease government spending.
   d. Policy makers should decrease interest rates.

2. Economists who argue that policy makers should *not* try to stabilize the economy make all of the following arguments *except*
   a. Since stabilization policy affects the economy with a lag, well-intended policy could be destabilizing.
   b. Since forecasting shocks to the economy is difficult, well-intended policy could be destabilizing.
   c. Stabilization policy has no effect on the economy in the short run or the long run.
   d. The first rule of policy-making should be 'do no harm.'

3. Economists who argue that monetary policy should be made by a rule make all of the following arguments *except*
   a. A policy rule limits the incompetence of policy makers.
   b. A policy rule limits the abuse of power of policy makers.
   c. A policy rule is more flexible than discretionary policy.
   d. A policy rule eliminates the time inconsistency problem.

4. Which of the following is an example of a discretionary policy action that further destabilizes the economy?
   a. Investors become pessimistic, and the central bank responds with a reduction in interest rates.
   b. Consumers become pessimistic, and fiscal policy makers respond with a reduction in taxes.
   c. Investors become excessively optimistic, and the central bank responds with a reduction in the money supply.
   d. Consumers become pessimistic, and fiscal policy makers respond with a reduction in government spending.

5. Economists who support a zero inflation target for monetary policy make all of the following arguments *except*
   a. Even small levels of inflation impose permanent costs on the economy such as shoe leather costs and menu costs.
   b. Inflation erodes peoples' incomes and zero inflation eliminates this problem.
   c. The cost of reducing inflation to zero is temporary while the benefits are permanent.
   d. The cost of reducing inflation to zero could be nearly eliminated if a zero inflation policy were credible.

6. Which of the following is *not* true with regard to government budget deficits?
   a. Budget deficits place the burden of current spending on future taxpayers.
   b. Budget deficits reduce national saving.
   c. Budget deficits should be scrutinized because they are the only way to transfer wealth across generations of taxpayers.
   d. Budget deficits reduce capital investment, future productivity and, therefore, future incomes.

7. Economists who argue that the government need not balance its budget make all of the following arguments *except*
   a. The national debt per person is actually quite small compared to a person's lifetime earnings.
   b. The effects of budget deficits can be somewhat offset if the current generation saves more and leaves bequests to the next generation.
   c. Budget deficits will not become an increasing burden as long as they do not grow more quickly than a nation's nominal income.
   d. Budget deficits increase future growth because they transfer wealth from the present generation to future generations.

8. A reduction in taxes that increases the after-tax return to saving will increase the quantity of saving in the economy if the
   a. substitution effect from the increase in after-tax return to saving exceeds the income effect.
   b. income effect from the increase in after-tax return to saving exceeds the substitution effect.
   c. income effect from the increase in after-tax return to saving equals the substitution effect.
   d. policy is time inconsistent.

9. Tax reform that encourages saving tends to
   a. shift the tax burden toward high-income people away from low-income people.
   b. shift the tax burden toward low-income people away from high-income people.
   c. reduce the rate of growth of output.
   d. reduce the deficit.

10. If discretionary monetary policy is time inconsistent,
    a. the long run Phillips curve shifts to the right.
    b. the long run Phillips curve shifts to the left.
    c. the short run Phillips curve shifts upward.
    d. the short run Phillips curve shifts downward.

ADVANCED CRITICAL THINKING

Those opposed to government budget deficits argue, among other things, that budget deficits redistribute wealth across generations by allowing the current generation to enjoy the benefits of government spending while future generations must pay for it.

1. Under which of the following cases would you argue that there is a greater intergenerational transfer of wealth? Why?
   a. The government increases spending on social programs by buying apples and oranges for the poor but refuses to raise taxes and instead increases the budget deficit.
   b. The government increases spending on bridges, roads, and buildings but refuses to raise taxes and instead increases the budget deficit.

2. Does the preceding example provide a method by which we might judge when a government budget deficit is fair to each generation and when it is not? Explain.

3. Why might this method be difficult to enforce in practice?

SOLUTIONS

Terms and Definitions

__1__ Political business cycle

__2__ Destabilizing policy

__3__ Leaning against the wind

__4__ Time inconsistency of policy

__5__ Discretionary policy

Practice Problems

1. a. See Exhibit 3.
    b. Increase the money supply, increase government spending, decrease taxes. Shift aggregate demand to the right.
    c. See Exhibit 4.
    d. As short run aggregate supply shifts downward, the economy adjusts to the intersection of short run AS_2 and AD_2. Then the expansionary aggregate demand policy shifts aggregate demand to AD_3 and the economy moves to the intersection of short run AS_2 and AD_3.
    e. Destabilize, because the economy had already adjusted back to the long run natural rate so the increase in aggregate demand caused output to rise above the natural rate.

2. a. No. In the long run, people will grow to expect 3 per cent inflation and wages and prices will rise accordingly.
    b. We would move down a short run Phillips curve and inflation would fall, while unemployment would rise above the natural rate.
    c. Yes. The central bank's announcement of a zero inflation target would be more credible and the movement toward zero inflation would create a smaller increase in unemployment.

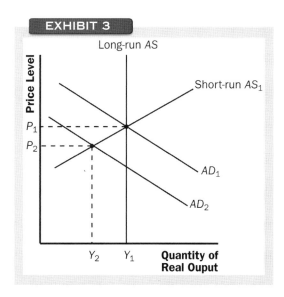

EXHIBIT 3

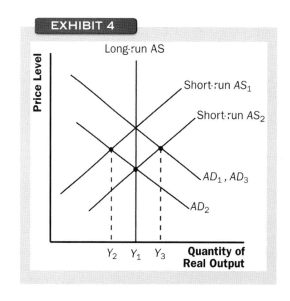

EXHIBIT 4

Short-Answer Questions

1. Macroeconomic shocks need to be forecast months or years into the future because there are lags in the implementation of activist stabilization policy.

2. A rule limits incompetence, abuse of power, and time inconsistency.

3. Inflation imposes continuous costs on the economy such as shoeleather costs and menu costs. Reducing inflation to zero will increase unemployment only temporarily, but it will eliminate the continuous costs of inflation.

4. Index the tax system and issue inflation-indexed bonds.

5. It increases future taxes and lowers future incomes because it reduces the capital stock.

6. No. An increase in social security benefits paid for by an increase in the payroll tax moves income from working people to retired people, yet the budget deficit is unaffected.

7. The substitution effect must outweigh the income effect. An increase in after-tax interest causes people to save more as people substitute saving for current consumption. However, the income effect of an increase in after-tax interest causes people to reduce the amount of saving necessary to reach a targeted amount of saving.

8. High-income people save more than low-income people so the tax relief would go disproportionately to the rich. Also, to maintain tax revenue, consumption taxes might have to be raised causing an additional burden on the poor.

True/False Questions

1. F; fiscal policy has a long decision lag due to the political process.

2. T

3. F; a political business cycle results when policy makers manipulate the economy to improve the incumbent's chance of re-election.

4. T

5. T

6. T

7. F; government budget deficits redistribute wealth to the current generation from future generations.

8. F; aggregate demand is determined by many factors other than just economic policy

9. T

10. T

Multiple-Choice Questions

1. d   6. c
2. c   7. d
3. c   8. a
4. d   9. b
5. b   10. c

Advanced Critical Thinking

1. Case (a), because the government purchased consumption goods that cannot be enjoyed by later generations, while in case (b) the government purchased capital which is durable and can be enjoyed by later generations.

2. It is more reasonable for the government to run a budget deficit and force future generations to pay for current expenditures if the expenditures are for capital goods.

3. Nearly every interest group can defend their spending as if it has a positive impact on future generations—military, education, etc.